OSTIA FROM THE AIR (1943)

See description of Pl. II

ROMAN OSTIA

BY

RUSSELL MEIGGS

SECOND EDITION

CLARENDON PRESS · OXFORD

Oxford University Press, Walton Street, Oxford OX2 6DP

OXFORD   LONDON   GLASGOW   NEW YORK
TORONTO   MELBOURNE   WELLINGTON   CAPE TOWN
IBADAN   NAIROBI   DAR ES SALAAM   LUSAKA   ADDIS ABABA
KUALA LUMPUR   SINGAPORE   JAKARTA   HONG KONG   TOKYO
DELHI   BOMBAY   CALCUTTA   MADRAS   KARACHI

ISBN 0 19 814810 0

© *Oxford University Press 1973*

First edition 1960
Second edition 1973
Reprinted 1977

PRINTED AND BOUND BY
WEATHERBY WOOLNOUGH,
WELLINGBOROUGH, NORTHANTS.

SODALIBVS OSTIENSIBVS

PREFACE TO THE FIRST EDITION

My first visit to Ostia was in 1925. I had set out to collect material for a thesis on 'Roman guilds in the light of recent excavations at Ostia'. In two long days among the ruins I found no evidence whatsoever—there was none: it was not until much later that the subject came alive. But from the first I was fascinated by the site, and it has retained its hold; Ostia is my second *patria*. By 1939 a short book was almost completed. It was stifled by the outbreak of war—mercifully, because by 1945 the subject had been transformed. The campaign of 1938–42 had doubled the excavated area. The evidence now required a different kind of book.

The foundation of the present study was laid during the summer of 1951 at the British School of Rome. I have returned for short visits whenever a busy teaching life and a tolerant wife have allowed; but my last visit was in September 1957. Had I waited longer a better book could have been written, for important problems concerning the course of the Tiber and the form of the Claudian harbour were then in sight of solution, and several hundred inscriptions still remained unpublished. Friends wisely warned me of the dangers of a receding horizon; since 1957, though minor additions have been made, I have concentrated on revision.

With some misgivings I have included the imperial harbours in my study. Their history is so closely linked with Ostia that they clearly form part of a common story, but I have not been able to study them in adequate detail. Many days have been spent in puzzling over the problems of the Claudian harbour on the site, but Trajan's harbour I know considerably less well. I was able to make two visits in 1926 and 1927, but during the critical stages of my work the site was inaccessible to scholars. An unorthodox entry ended, before I had reached my first objective, in humiliation.

In a short preface it is impossible to acknowledge all the kindnesses and help I have received. A wide range of benefactors, from ambassadors to schoolboys, must go unrecorded though I remain grateful to them; but certain debts must be mentioned. The most important part of my work was done in Italy among Italians and with their help. Dr. Guido Calza I remember with particular affection and respect. Even when I was a very immature student he gave me every facility I required; I owe much to his advice and encouragement. His colleague, Dr. Italo Gismondi, has helped me even more. No man knows, or ever will know, more of the unwritten history of Ostian buildings, and I have gained more from his shrewd wisdom than individual acknowledgements in text and notes can suggest. Successive directors have also been unfailingly kind to me, from Professor Romanelli to Professor Pietrogrande. But my closest associations have been with Professor Giovanni Becatti and Signora Raissa Calza. Their continuing hospitality and friendship have provided an ideal background for my work; many of my own views have been developed through discussion with them. Professor Barbieri's sharp eye in reading inscriptions has helped me to sharpen my own and he has generously given me access to a wide range of unpublished material. Similar kindness in her own fields has been shown by Dr. Maria Squarciapino. To these Ostian friends, *sodales Ostienses*, this book is offered. Nor shall I readily forget the warm welcome and practical assistance which 'professore capelli lunghi' has always received from the *custodi*.

I have been fortunate in having Mr. John Ward Perkins as Director of the British School in these last years. Archaeological argument has many pitfalls for the untrained; he has saved me from many crude mistakes, has made valuable suggestions at many points, and has helped me considerably with his camera. Mr. Richard Goodchild, while he was librarian of the School, was also more than once a stimulating critic in the field. Air photographs would have been less valuable to me without the co-operation of Mr. John Bradford in the library and on the ground.

When the British School was closed the American Academy hospitably adopted me. I owe much more to Professor Bloch than the precision and imagination of his own Ostian studies; discussion with him has always been fruitful. Miss Marion Blake has also given me valuable help in problems of construction, and the list of Americans who, directly or indirectly, have helped me would be a long one. Among friends of long standing in Rome Professor Boethius has been particularly stimulating. His enthusiasm for Ostia has added considerably to the pleasure and profit of my talks with him.

In England my main debt is to Professor A. H. M. Jones, who read my manuscript, and improved it by constructive criticism: I wish I could have been able to answer all his pertinent questions. In Oxford my Balliol colleagues, Mr. Gordon Williams and Mr. Robert Ogilvie, have helped me in form and substance, particularly on points of Latinity. Of past and present pupils who have helped me at various stages, Mr. Martin Frederiksen, Mr. Alan Hall, Mr. Glen Bowersock, and Mr. Graham Clarke deserve my special thanks. The chapter on religion has gained from Dr. Weinstock's learning and sympathy. My use of coins would have been even more amateurish without the guidance of Dr. C. H. V. Sutherland and Dr. C. Kraay. Mr. Frank Lepper and Mr. Eric Gray generously checked several points for me on the site.

It will be clear from text and notes how much I owe to previous writers, but my detailed criticisms of Professor Carcopino require a corrective. I have come to disagree with all the main hypotheses of his *Virgile et les origines d'Ostie*, and almost all my many references are critical. But few books have excited me more, and this would have been a more prosaic and superficial study if Carcopino had not stimulated me to ask difficult questions and to risk bold answers.

It is a great pleasure to offer my thanks here to those whose financial assistance helped me in my work. My first college, Keble, made it possible for me to serve my research apprenticeship in Italy by awarding me a post-graduate scholarship to supplement the University's Pelham Studentship. In the latter stages generous grants from the Leverhulme Trustees and the Craven Committee enabled me to attempt a scale that would otherwise have been beyond my means.

I cannot adequately thank the staff of the Clarendon Press. They have handled me with a friendly patience and understanding that has comfortably survived any possible strain.

The formal record of my wife's part in this production is easily made. She has typed an almost illegible manuscript; she has released me from domestic duties in times of crisis; she has allowed me to lead a very selfish life. It is more important to confess that without her encouragement and threats I should still be making detailed notes on crucial problems or writing further appendixes.

In the design of this book the opening chapters trace the history of Ostia in outline; they are followed by more detailed studies of various aspects of the town's life. Some repetition is necessary, but the number of forward references has been limited. The table of contents will show where what is treated cursorily in the general history is more fully developed.

I have deliberately not reproduced a detailed town plan. If the scale is sufficiently large for clarity the size becomes unmanageable. If a single-folding map is used the detail becomes unintelligible. An air photograph perhaps provides the most practical compromise. I have therefore used as a frontispiece an air photograph of Ostia in its setting, and have reproduced the area of the town, slightly enlarged, as the second of my plates. The modern division into regions, the numeration of blocks, and the most important street names are shown in a separate plan on p. 137.

The house plans were drawn by Mrs. Selina Ballance. They are based on the official Italian publications, but minor modifications have been made in the light of our joint surveys. The plans of other buildings have been taken by Miss Helen Gibson from Gismondi's large-scale plan in the first volume of *Scavi di Ostia*. The remaining illustrations in the text have been adapted by the Clarendon Press from my own rough sketches. Any merit that accrues is theirs; mistakes may be safely attributed to me. For my photographs I am indebted to the Italian authorities and to many friends at many times.

Concessions have been made to convenience. *Castrum* has become the accepted term for the fourth-century settlement; I have resisted the pleas of purists. It is virtually certain that the Romans did not call the main streets of their colonies Decumanus Maximus and Cardo Maximus, but the names are too traditional and convenient to be dropped; for the other streets the Italian names have been retained. It would have been more consistent to retain also the Italian names of houses, but the memory of travellers returning from their first visit to Italy with glowing accounts of their experiences in *Milano* and *Firenze* deterred me.

The third volume of *Scavi di Ostia* became available to me only when my text was in proof. I have added a long note on one of the problems discussed; otherwise I have had to be content with a few references in footnotes. Similar problems arise from other recent publications. I have commented briefly on the most relevant in four pages of Addenda.   R. M.

Holywell Manor, Oxford
August 1959

PREFACE TO THE SECOND EDITION

THE original edition of *Roman Ostia* went out of print in 1966 and the increasing interest in Ostian studies has now encouraged the publishers to reissue the book. Economic considerations rule out a complete resetting of the type, but the text has been substantially revised. Corrections required by misprints or careless slips have been made in the text: passages which, in the light of new evidence or new argument, need more radical change have been marked with an asterisk and notes will be found on pp. 594 ff. A supplementary Bibliography covers the years 1960–72, and in a separate chapter I have tried to summarize the striking advances that have been made in our understanding of Ostia during this period. Critics whose judgement I value have persuaded me to add a detailed town plan and I am very grateful to the American Academy in Rome for allowing me to adapt the plan used in J. E. Packer's *The Insulae of Imperial Ostia*, which is based on Gismondi's splendid master plan. Since references to the town plan are not normally given in the text a topographical index is now included.

Reviews and particularly the very constructive criticisms of Professor Becatti and Professor Bloch provided a starting-point for this revision, but any merit that it may have is mainly due to the help I received on the site. After more than ten years in which my main concentration had been on Athenian history and Ostia could only be a brief stop on the way back from Greece I returned like a prodigal son in the late summer of 1972. No prodigal son could have been more generously welcomed and for this I am most grateful to Professor Maria Squarciapino, the present director, and those who work with her and continue to make Ostia such a congenial site to study. My Bibliography would have been considerably leaner if I had not enjoyed free access to the library of the Soprintendenza, and the opportunity to discuss problems with those who are working with the material evidence was invaluable. I am particularly indebted to Dr. Fausto Zevi from whom I learnt much that I should otherwise have missed, and whose acute judgement saved me at more than one point from serious error.

The main work for this new edition was done at Ostia in September 1972, and for most of that month I lived with Giovani

Becatti and his family in their delightful house outside the Porta Romana designed by Ostia's 'grand master', Italo Gismondi. In May a cable brought news of Becatti's death. I had discussed with him the work that was to occupy his next five years, and realize what a serious loss his death means to his University and to Roman studies: the personal loss bites deeper. I owe more to his friendship and stimulating encouragement than I can express. This second edition is now dedicated to his memory: I wish it were better.

Garsington   R. M.
June 1973

CONTENTS

LIST OF FIGURES

LIST OF PLATES

ABBREVIATIONS

BOOKS

Carcopino	J. Carcopino, *Virgile et les origines d'Ostie*, Paris, 1919.
Ostia	G. Calza, G. Becatti, *Ostia*³ (Itinerari dei musei e monumenti d'Italia), Rome, 1954.
Paschetto	*Ostia colonia romana, storia e monumenti*, Rome, 1912.
RE	Pauly–Wissowa, *Real-Encyclopädie der classischen Altertumswissenschaft*.
Topografia	*Scavi, di Ostia, I, Topografia Generale*, Rome, 1954.

INSCRIPTIONS

I	*CIL* xiv. 1.
S I	*CIL* xiv, Supplement, 1.
I	Appendix XI, 1.
Bloch, 1	H. Bloch, *Notizie degli Scavi di Antichità*, 1953, 239–306.
Thylander, A 1 (B 1)	H. Thylander, *Inscriptions du port d'Ostie*, Lund, 1952.

PERIODICALS

AE	*L'année épigraphique.*
AJA	*American Journal of Archaeology.*
AJP	*American Journal of Philology.*
Ann. Inst.	*Annali dell' Istituto di Corrispondenza Archeologica.*
Arch. class.	*Rivista dell' Istituto di Archeologia della Università di Roma.*
BC	*Bulletino della Commissione Archeologica Communale di Roma.*
BSR	*Papers of the British School at Rome.*
Bull. Inst.	*Bulletino dell' Istituto di Corrispondenza Archeologica.*
JHS	*Journal of the Hellenic Society.*
JRS	*Journal of the Roman Society.*
MA	*Monumenti Antichi pubblicati per cura della Reale Accademia dei Lincei.*
MAAR	*Memoirs of the American Academy in Rome.*
Mélanges	*Mélanges d'archéologie et d'histoire de l'École française de Rome.*
Mem. Pont.	*Atti della Pontifica Accademia Romana di Archeologia, Memorie.*
NS	*Notizie degli Scavi di Antichità.*
RM	*Mitteilungen des Deutschen Archäologischen Instituts, Römische Abteilung.*
Rend. Pont.	*Atti della Pontifica Accademia Romana di Archeologia, Rendiconti.*
TAPA	*Transactions of the American Philological Association.*

I

THE NATURE OF THE EVIDENCE

OSTIA takes her name from her position. She was built at the mouth of the Tiber, fifteen miles from Rome, and therein lies her importance. Inland Rome, growing in power and population, came to depend increasingly on imports from overseas; these imports passed through Ostia and so up river to Rome. Ostia, Rome's harbour town, grew with the growth of Rome.

No Roman history of Ostia survives; it is probable that none was ever written. The Greek City States clung stubbornly to their individuality, even when they were engulfed in large empires; local histories abounded. In Italy all roads led to Rome. The towns were proud of their past and present, but Rome was the focus of literature. Some Ostian families, who remained in the forefront of local government for 200 years and more, were in an admirable position to record the history of their town from family traditions and local records; but there were no precedents to encourage them.

Even so, the contribution of classical writers to the history of Ostia is of primary importance, though much of it is buried in strange places, and it is not all easy to interpret. Ostia's importance as an essential link in the maintenance of Rome by overseas supplies is, as we should expect, well documented. Roman historians were never concerned with details of economic organization, but the fundamental importance of feeding the population of Rome could not be ignored. The misdemeanours of a Saturninus, responsible for the passage of corn through Ostia to Rome, had political repercussions and were therefore recorded; the building of a new harbour at Ostia had an undisputed title to a place in a history of Rome.

For the rest we rely on a strange medley of incidental references, sometimes ambiguous, sometimes trivial. It is interesting to know from the elder Pliny that Fausta of Ostia gave birth, in the principate of Augustus, to quadruplets, thus portending a famine.[1] It was the right place for such a portent to occur, but the incident cannot be pressed

[1] Pliny, *NH* vii. 33.

into wider service. Pliny's equally casual remark that a theatre at Rome was roofed by the architect Valerius Ostiensis would be more interesting if we knew whether this Ostian had learnt his trade at Ostia or Rome.[1] We can at least infer that a branch of the Valerii was already under Augustus established in the town, and to a social historian this is not irrelevant.

Also from Pliny come two of the most important sources for our knowledge of the great harbour built by Claudius. It is typical of his book that the first is an excursus on spectacular trees,[2] the second a footnote on the subject of whales.[3] In both passages circumstantial detail is given, and since Pliny had seen the harbour himself his evidence should be decisive. Unfortunately the obscurity of the Latin robs his evidence of much of its value.[4] His statement in his survey of vegetables that Ostia's leeks were famous is unambiguous,[5] and adds to our understanding of Ostian agriculture, which is further increased by a biographer's comment on an emperor's gluttony. Clodius Albinus ate ten Ostian melons at a sitting.[6]

But there are more important passages than these, and they are widely distributed. Polybius' account of the escape from Rome of the Syrian prince Demetrius gives us a vivid glimpse of the river harbour in the second century B.C.[7] A discussion by Galen on dislocation of the shoulder is our most important evidence for the relation of Ostia to the imperial harbours in the second century A.D.[8] A bitter polemic by Hippolytus against Pope Callistus includes a dramatic glimpse of a harbour scene.[9] The record of a famine at Rome in the fourth century attests the importance of the cult of Castor and Pollux at Ostia.[10]

Excavation has shown a shift of emphasis away from the river towards the sea-shore in the late Empire; casual stories in Suetonius[11] and Aulus Gellius[12] and the dialogue of Minucius Felix give colour and background to the picture. The record of his biographer that the emperor Aurelian gave to Ostia a Forum by the sea, in which the *praetorium publicum* was later installed,[13] points the same way.

For the history of Christianity at Ostia the literary sources are even more important. From excavation alone we might assume that there were few Christians in Ostia before the fourth century. The *Acts of the*

[1] Pliny, *NH* xxxvi. 102.   [2] Ibid. xvi. 202.   [3] Ibid. ix. 14.   [4] p. 155.

[5] Ibid. xix. 110.   [6] SHA, *Clodius Albinus*, 11. 3.   [7] Pol. xxxi. 11–15.

[8] Galen (ed. Kuhn), xviii. 348.   [9] Hippolytos, *Elenchos*, 9. 12–14.

[10] Amm. Marc. xix. 10. 4.   [11] Suet. *De rhet*. 1.

[12] Aul. Gell. xviii. 1.   [13] SHA, *Aurelian*, 45. 2.

martyrs, unreliable as many of them may be in much of their detail, provide a corrective. Even where no specifically Ostian evidence is available Roman writers are indispensable guides to a reconstruction of the background. One of the most striking contributions of the recent excavations has been the revelation of the handsome houses of the late Empire; Ammianus Marcellinus in his diatribes against the extravagant living of the nobility in Rome illuminates the Ostian picture.[1] Inscriptions tell us very little of the town's administration in the fourth century; the Theodosian Code provides a basis for reasonable inference.

When a historian has to rely on a random assortment of incidental passages, he is tempted to squeeze too much out of too little. The temptation is more easily resisted at Ostia owing to the wealth and variety of the archaeological evidence of buildings and inscriptions. The shells of the buildings remain, and, from a study of the changes in building technique, we shall eventually be able to reconstruct the town's development. For the Republic and the early Empire, however, we shall never secure more than a tentative outline, since the city we now see is a city of the second century A.D. with comparatively minor subsequent modifications. Earlier history can only be recovered by excavation below this level and the opportunities for such investigation are restricted.

For the tracing of Ostia's history the original date and function of a building are of primary importance, but reconstructions and changes of use also need study. They may not, however, all be significant. It is tempting to draw social and economic inferences from such observations as the blocking of a door, the changes in the size of flats, the encroachment of houses on shops; but only when examples are numerous enough to suggest a general tendency are such changes valuable to the historian. It is also tempting to simplify the history of a building by classifying its alterations into a limited number of periods; modern parallels remind us that changes which might logically be connected are not necessarily contemporary.

The evidence of buildings is supplemented by a wide range of inscriptions. More than 4,000 inscriptions in whole or part survive. The abundant records of the trade guilds are our main evidence for the commercial and industrial life of the town; the religious pattern is derived largely from dedicatory inscriptions. The careers of public men, from statue bases and tombstones, and official records of public acts,

[1] e.g. Amm. Marc. xvi. 8. 11 ff.; xxix. 1. 19; xxxi. 5. 14.

enable us to reconstruct the history of the town's administration and invite an analysis of its changing social structure. This analysis, however, depends to a large extent on the study of names, and Roman names can be deceptive. Since the father normally passed all his names to his eldest son, identification is often precarious. At least three men were named Aulus Egrilius Rufus in the first century A.D. The danger of confusion in such a case is apparent, but the continued prominence in Ostia of such families as the Egrilii is an adequate warning. It is easier to forget that when a rare name occurs only twice in surviving Ostian inscriptions, identification remains possible rather than probable unless there is evidence that the two inscriptions are roughly contemporary. Nor is it always possible to distinguish a family of free descent from descendants of its freedmen. Slaves when freed took their first two names from their owner. They normally retained their slave name as a cognomen; but their sons and grandsons could adopt more respectable names. Similarly a Greek cognomen usually implies oriental descent, but not always. Western slaves could be given Greek names, oriental slaves could be given Latin names. In using cognomina as evidence we deal only with probabilities.

Inscriptions can also help to identify and date buildings; but most of such Ostian inscriptions have lost something of their original value. In the late Roman period and in the early Middle Ages, inscriptions were taken from their original settings to serve as building material, to line floors or walls, to serve as thresholds, even to provide the seats of a public latrine. Only rarely therefore can they provide the clue to the identification of a building.

Sculpture has suffered the same fate. The aesthetic value of a portrait or relief is not affected if it is found in a drain; but for the social historian the main interest of sculpture is the context in which it is found, and this at Ostia is rarely the original context. Heads of some quality were used in a late raising of the level of the main street;[1] statues were used to block house entrances against raiders.[2] Even when a large nest of sculpture is found in a building it may have been collected from the general neighbourhood in order to be converted into lime.[3]

The nature of the site also affects the method of excavation.[4] Standing walls are buried under a deep mass of earth and rubble. From the minute sifting of this mass some precarious inferences might be drawn

---

[1] *NS* 1910, 10.　　　　[2] *NS* 1913, 230.　　　　[3] *NS* 1922, 87.
[4] For the principles adopted in excavation and restoration, G. Calza, *Topografia*, 43–52.

concerning the history of the site after the Roman period, but such a procedure generally applied, unless supported by a bottomless purse, would reduce the progress of excavation to a snail's pace for results that might be negligible. This problem is not always appreciated by critics, especially those who are accustomed to British and German methods. In Britain and Germany Roman remains are comparatively rare, and, with few notable exceptions, very little is preserved. The recovery of even the broadest outline of the history of the site requires meticulous attention to the minutest detail. If the same methods were applied at Ostia as in the excavation of a fort on Hadrian's wall, the excavation campaign which was completed between 1938 and 1943 would have lasted considerably more than 100 years. It is difficult to feel so generous towards our successors.

The campaign which began in 1938 was, however, an extreme case. An extensive campaign was dictated to prepare the site for an international exhibition in 1942; the speed of the work, accentuated by the uncertainties of war, was a dangerous precedent. There is little doubt that valuable evidence has been lost, though the immediate gain of seeing an almost complete ancient city is for the present generation no mean compensation. It is, however, significant that, even before the exhibition campaign was launched, the study of the pottery found at Ostia had lagged far behind the study of buildings, inscriptions, and sculpture.

On British sites so little remains that the smallest sherd of the commonest ware claims attention; at Ostia, where lorry-loads of sherds are taken from most buildings, the detailed examination of every piece is impracticable. But imported wares could provide valuable chronological controls, and the early economic history of Ostia should become less obscure when pottery, hitherto described loosely as 'Etrusco-Campanian', is classified by fabric and form.

The ruins, as we see them now, are not as the excavators found them. When the covering earth and rubble is removed, walls still stand to heights ranging from a few centimetres to more than 10 metres, but often much of the brick facing has fallen away. In the accumulation above and around are found fallen vaults, drums of columns, fragments of balcony, and, in one instance, a considerable stretch of walling from an upper floor including two windows. Walls would suffer if they were left as they were found. Unfaced concrete gradually disintegrates under the pressure of rain and frost; to restore the facing is essential. And, to give the evidence its full value to others than specialists, as much of the building is restored as surviving elements justify. Vaults are more intelligible when they spring from walls than when they lie on the ground. The handsome entrance to the Horrea Epagathiana et Epaphroditiana is not entirely ancient, but even a casual glance shows that enough of the original is incorporated to place the restoration beyond doubt.

Visitors tend to take the restorations they see for granted. Having seen many buildings in process of excavation, immediately after excavation, and again after restoration, and having been allowed to see a complete photographic documentation, I remain continuously impressed. This work of restoration is due primarily to the intimate knowledge of and feeling for Roman construction acquired by Gismondi during forty years at Ostia and on many other Roman sites in Italy and Africa: it is carried out by the inherited skill of Italian craftsmen.

Sometimes the restoration is rather too Roman than not Roman enough. One instance in particular has left smarting memories. I had become interested in the so-called Schola del Traiano on the western Decumanus, and in particular in the shallow basin that ran the length of the open court. It was a unique feature that I had not seen before and the bricks were unique. They were small, triangular, yellow, hard, and were still in very good condition. I had never seen such bricks at Rome or Ostia before, but logic was ready to solve the problem. The walls of the basin were preserved to a roughly level height of only a few centimetres; therefore, I argued, at some point they had been destroyed to this height. The bricks were in very good condition; therefore the long basin had been dispensed with after a very short life. The type of brick could not be found elsewhere; therefore they were specially made for this special job, probably at Ostia. I had evolved a highly satisfactory account of the history of the building when I learnt that the bricks were modern, and that the whole facing had been restored. Returning shamefacedly to the site I found that a very few of the original bricks survived in the lowest course at one point.

This is an extreme case; the basin had been completely renovated as a special feature for the intended international exhibition. But, even where much of the original facing remains, it is often difficult to determine where Roman work ends and modern begins. I have many times seen students minutely examining a completely restored surface on the assumption that they were collecting evidence for the dating of Roman buildings. It is right that such sites as Ostia should never become the monopoly of the specialist and student, but perhaps their interests were not given due weight when the international exhibition of 1942 was the focus of concern. The earlier practice of showing restoration by recessing restored brickwork is unsightly, but the demarcation of Roman from modern by an incised line, such as has been occasionally used, would seem to be a satisfactory compromise.

Some mosaic and marble pavements survive almost intact; more often part of the surface has disintegrated. If the scattered elements were left as they were found all trace even of the basic design would soon be lost. Resetting and restoration are the essential complements to excavation. Normally the pavement is restored as it existed in its final phase; in special cases late disfigurements are ignored. When, for instance, the grand mosaic of the Baths of Neptune was uncovered it was found to have been patched in the late Empire by random pieces of marble which completely ruined the total effect. The marble has wisely been removed and the mosaic restored to its original condition. But the state of the mosaic on discovery, not unimportant for the understanding of the late Empire at Ostia, is recorded in the published report.[1] So long as the condition on finding is publicly recorded when such restorations are made we have the best of both worlds.

To the romantic at least Ostia is more attractive today than she would have been when at the height of her prosperity. The judicious planting of trees and shrubs, the apparently effortless landscaping of the site, are responsible. Some archaeologists may resent this intrusion of nature and they are justified in those very few cases where creepers threaten damage to walls or conceal important features, but having seen Ostia stark and naked thirty years ago I rejoice to see the Judas trees in bloom, without losing my appetite for measuring bricks or counting the number of tesserae in a square metre.

The value of a site to the historian and archaeologist depends not only on the quality of the excavation and restoration, but also on the arrangement of the museum. I know no site in or outside Italy where the interests of specialists and the general public are better combined. The taking from Ostia to private collections and public museums of so many statues and reliefs from the Renaissance to the present century has not been an unmixed evil. A large museum loses much of its attraction. Enough sculpture of quality and interest remains to give a fair indication

[1] *NS* 1910, 9.

of Ostian standards, and the admirable display of photographs of sculptures that have been taken from the site in the past fills out the picture. Central in the museum is the town plan to the large scale of 1:200, a precedent which other sites might well follow. Here the visitor, exhausted by the ruins, can find his bearings again and the specialist can study, in the right setting, the many problems of the town plan and its development.

The museum has wisely not been overcrowded. It contains only a limited selection of the finds, and is so arranged that every exhibit can be comfortably seen. The minor finds, including pottery, lamps, and terra-cottas, are separately stored, but accessible to students. They form a valuable supplement to the evidence concentrated in the museum. Ostia has also set a fine example in concentrating the inscriptions from the site where they can be studied together. When most of Ostia's inscriptions were scattered through museums in Rome and elsewhere their study was considerably hampered. The policy of retaining all inscriptions on the site and concentrating them in the basement of the Capitolium and in the Via Tecta makes a comparative study practicable and profitable. It should not be too much to hope that the example of the National Museum in Rome in returning all Ostian inscriptions to Ostia will encourage others to follow. The few Ostian inscriptions in the Naples museum have little importance in so large a collection; they would be much more valuable if they could stand near other inscriptions from the same workshops. The funerary altar recording the career of Cn. Sentius Felix, which has perhaps been quoted more than any other Ostian inscription and to which we shall many times refer, now stands in a small unlighted room, closed to the public, in the Uffizi Galleries.[1] For that reason it has rarely been seen, and so unnecessarily misdated. It was set up to Felix by Cn. Sentius Lucilius Gamala, his adopted son. The same man set up a much smaller altar to his natural father; this now stands in the Archaeological Museum at Florence in company which gives it no significance.[2] If the two altars could be brought together in Ostia, their natural home, their value would be considerably enhanced.

The literary sources, the buildings, the sculpture and lesser objects, and the inscriptions are the main sources for a history of Ostia. But, for the study of Ostian territory outside the walls of the city, there is a further indispensable guide. The use of air photography in archaeology

[1] 5.   [2] 377.

is a comparatively modern development, but its value is now securely established. During the war British aircraft covered the area of Ostia from a height of 22,000 feet. The purpose was not archaeological, but the study of these photographs, taken without reference to the problems that concern us, shows how much could be achieved by a planned cover of the area at the right height, at the right time of year, and at the right time of day. I have been considerably helped by these aerial photographs, inherited by the British School at Rome from the Air Ministry. They have led me to sites which I might never have discovered on the ground and sharpened my understanding of the geography of the district. A planned campaign from the air would be the best approach to the plotting of the Roman roads, paths, and buildings of Ostia's territory.[1]

Meanwhile we can see much more clearly from the air than on the ground the essential features of the geographical setting. When these photographs were taken the Germans had flooded the coastal area by destroying the pumping installations. A large area that had been growing good crops was once again covered by water, reproducing conditions that had persisted from the Roman period onwards. The area of flood land stretches in a large arc behind the coast from Trajan's harbour to Tor Paterno, interrupted by a belt of higher ground where the Tiber in flood has deposited alluvium. The lake that formed in 1943 south of the road from Rome to Ostia and east of the modern village recalls the *Stagno di Ostia*, which was recovered for agriculture only towards the end of the nineteenth century. The large plain between Ostia and Acilia was once probably a lagoon, gradually shrinking from the accumulated humus of the marshy vegetation.

The land to the west of the modern village shows no trace of flood; the explanation is seen in geological maps which show a long line of islands of pleistocene sands stretching to north and south of the Tiber. When the coastline ran along the base of the hills that form the eastern limit of the coastal plain, these pleistocene sands were off-shore sand bars. As the sea receded they emerged earlier than the area behind them and became firm compact land, very suitable for habitation. It was on this land that the Roman Ostia we see today was settled in the fourth

---

[1] In the use of air photographs I have been generously helped by John Bradford, who has illustrated their value for Ostian studies in *Ancient Landscapes* (1957) 237–56. In interpreting the physical features of the landscapes I owe much to Professor J. A. Speers and to Dr. K. S. Sandford: they well deserved a more intelligent pupil.

century B.C. Its character is in marked contrast with the land not only to the east, but also to the west. The shoreline has advanced more than two miles since the Roman period, but the new land is very different from that on which Roman Ostia was built. From the air and on the ground it is seen as a series of dunes built up by the wind from the sand that the coastal current deposits on the shore.

The geographical distinction between the firm pleistocene sands and the drifting sand that stretches to modern Ostia Marina must be taken into account in calculating the rate of advance of the shoreline. It is clear from the evidence of watch-towers that the rate of advance in the post-Roman period has been very uneven, and considerably faster in recent centuries. We shall see reason to believe that during the Roman period the advance of the shoreline was negligible. For a long time the pleistocene sands marked the shoreline. Once they were passed the accumulation became increasingly rapid.

Geologists and geographers may be able to add considerably to our understanding of the fundamental facts governing the development of Ostia. Other important problems may be solved by further excavation. Roughly two-thirds of the Roman town have already been uncovered, but the excavation of the remaining areas may modify the general picture. The shoreline and the western end of the town have barely been touched. It is possible that in the late Empire they were, apart from the Forum, the main focus of public and private life. Nor has excavation yet reached the Tiber bank. We may still hope to learn much more about the organization of shipping and dock facilities.

2

OSTIA AND POMPEII

SOME fifty years ago, when Roman Ostia was almost completely
covered with grass, bush, and crops, Gaston Boissier, historian
and archaeologist, ranked the site with Pompeii in importance.
'These two towns are the best-preserved relics of Roman
antiquity. As they have the advantage of illustrating it from different
angles and are complementary, it is well, when we wish to understand
Rome, not to separate them.'[1] But while the excavations of Pompeii
became increasingly familiar to visitors and their evidence widely influenced accounts of Roman life, Ostia was for long neglected. Until
the electric railway to the coast was opened in 1923 a visit from Rome to
Ostia meant two hours in a carriage jolting over a bad road, or four
hours' hard walking. The site was uninviting except to the eye of faith.
In summer the district was still malarial, at all times the country around
was bare and monotonous. The land was being slowly restored, but the
struggle was still hard.

Nor were the ruins spectacular. The area excavated was considerably
smaller than at Pompeii; little more than bare walls remained. The
important contributions that Ostia was clearly making to Roman
studies had a limited currency; Pompeii still dominated the handbooks.
Roman housing in the imperial period, as reflected in Martial, Juvenal,
and in the Digest, had little in common with what could be seen at
Pompeii; but the Pompeian house continued to be regarded as the
normal Roman house. And the error persisted long after buildings had
been excavated at Ostia which fully satisfied the Roman evidence.

Only those who experienced the adventure before the railway was
opened can fully appreciate the change. The journey from Rome now
takes only half an hour in a smooth-running train. From the station a
large nursery can be seen, growing blooms for the Roman market.
Vines, fruit-trees, and vegetables grow freely in the house gardens
outside the village. The land is restored to health. Trees line the roads

---

[1] Cited from 'Les dernières fouilles de Pompéi et d'Ostie', *Revue des deux Mondes*,
Oct. 1878, by Carcopino, *Mélanges*, 30 (1910) 397 n. 1.

and landscape the ruins; in spring and summer the excavations are
flecked with a rich variety of wild flowers. Some two-thirds of the
ancient town have been uncovered, and the policy of judicious restoration developed between the two world wars makes the ruins more
intelligible and more attractive.

Calza's detailed analysis of the city type of house has focused attention
on the apartment blocks of Ostia; inscriptions, and particularly the
fragments of the town's official records, have made important contributions to the central stream of Roman history; and the new excavations
have illustrated the literature of the fourth century by a vivid picture of
a local aristocracy in the late Empire; Boissier's bold claim for the
importance of Ostia needed imagination; it no longer calls for defence.

Ostia is not another Pompeii; the two towns differed radically in
history and character. Pompeii had already had a long life before she
felt the impact of Rome. She may briefly have fallen within the Etruscan
orbit in the sixth century when Etruscan power stretched down to
Campania, but Etruscan influence was neither deep nor lasting. Her
early fabric is woven mainly from Samnite and Greek threads. A
Samnite invasion of the fifth or early fourth century B.C. provided the
dominant element in her population; the Greek colonies that fringed
the coast from Cumae to Herculaneum influenced her cults and buildings. Roman influence was felt in Campania from the late fourth
century, but in southern Campania the influence was remote. As late as
the second century Oscan and not Latin was the language of Pompeii;
her political constitution was radically different from the Roman
model; her buildings were a compound of native Italian and Greek
elements. When the Italian allies attempted to break the power of
Rome in the Social War Pompeii joined the rebels and fought hard. It
was not until the collapse of this resistance that Pompeii was incorporated in the Roman state.

The penalty for the town's stubborn resistance to Sulla's army was
the settlement of a colony of Sullan veterans. The colonists brought
with them Roman ways of living and Roman building methods; fric-
tion between the natives and the new settlers gradually died down and
the two groups intermarried. The constitution was remodelled on
Roman lines; the Latin language replaced Oscan. But to the end
Pompeii was Romanized rather than Roman. Neither in her buildings
nor in her people was Pompeii a typical Roman town.

Her position dictated her means of livelihood and general character.

Situated south of Naples, on the less fashionable side of the Roman Riviera, with Vesuvius in the background and, to the south, the hills that sweep out to Sorrento, Pompeii was a busy provincial town of prosperous bourgeois making comfortable livings from agriculture, small-scale industry, and trade. Though a small river harbour supported a modest flow of trade with other parts, the land was the main basis of her prosperity. Villas devoted to leisure remained exceptional, for the soil enriched by Vesuvius was too fertile to be given over to parks and ornamental gardens. It was to Baiae, Herculaneum, Naples, or Sorrento that men retired for recreation; Pompeii remained a town where fortunes were made as well as spent. But Pompeii plays little part in the main course of Roman history. She produces no senators, no high equestrian officials, few recruits to the armed forces; her outlook is local. Political passions are concentrated on the annual municipal elections. The feud with the local enemy from Nuceria can still flare up dangerously at the shows in the amphitheatre.

Ostia presents a very different picture. There may, as Roman tradition maintains, have been an early Roman settlement for the production of salt in the neighbourhood, but the site on which Roman Ostia developed was first occupied in the fourth century B.C. The primary function of this settlement was to defend the coast, but her position dictated a change of emphasis when Roman power was fully established. Situated at the mouth of the Tiber, she became inevitably Rome's harbour town. In the late Republic her main function was to receive, store, and send upstream the increasing volume of corn and other goods that Rome brought in by sea. Her importance to Rome demanded the attention of the authorities at Rome. The emperors, who were particularly sensitive to the danger of famine, could not afford to neglect her. It is natural therefore that the influence of Rome should be paramount in Ostia. Herein lies the main contribution of Ostia to Roman studies.

If we wish to clothe the bones of the marble plan of Rome with the flesh of buildings a visit to Ostia is an essential complement to a visit to Rome. Temples, basilicas, theatres, amphitheatres, baths, can still be better seen at Rome itself, but of the more prosaic buildings little remains. From the scattered and fragmentary ruins of house blocks in Rome it is difficult to visualize living conditions; at Ostia such houses can be seen with their ground floors fully preserved and, in some cases, large parts of the first floor. The streets of Ostia as rebuilt in the second century are the best illustration we can find of the *nova urbs* created

c

by Nero after the great fire of A.D. 64. The houses, three and more stories high, radically different from the Pompeian house, reflect the Rome of Martial and Juvenal. Of the large series of warehouses at the foot of the Aventine only one conspicuous ruin survives; at Ostia we can see the ground plan and general disposition of buildings used for the storage of corn, oil, and other products. In the series of mosaics from the Piazzale delle Corporazioni behind the theatre we can see the most vivid illustration of Roman overseas trade that survives. The imperial harbours of Claudius and Trajan emphasize the effective organization deployed in sustaining a population of over a million people in Rome. For a reconstruction of the quarters of the *vigiles* and urban cohorts in Rome we have to turn to the Barracks of the Vigiles in Ostia where a well-preserved mosaic emphasizes the imperial cult and writings on the wall bring the colour of life to the men's rooms.

Ostia, however, is not to be regarded as a suburb absorbed by Rome. She developed her own individual character and had her own changing social pattern. The earliest cults of the colony are distinctive and retained a strong hold even when oriental cults spread with the growth of overseas trade. Nor was Ostia merely a harbour settlement. Warehouses and shops were balanced by temples, basilicas, baths, theatre, and other public buildings. Her citizens were proud to be Ostians as well as citizens of Rome.

The difference between the buildings of Ostia and Pompeii derives partly from their different origins and character; it is emphasized by the difference in date. Pompeii's history ended abruptly in A.D. 79, the Ostia that we see today is predominantly a town of the second century A.D. Test excavations at a lower level have shown that the contrast between the two towns was less striking in the late Republic and early Empire.

The study of Ostia suffers seriously in one respect in comparison with Pompeii. When Vesuvius burst into eruption the disaster to Pompeii was sudden and overwhelming. The town was covered by a thick layer of ashes and no trace of it was left. Most of the inhabitants managed to escape and made new homes in the neighbouring towns of Campania. Neither the Roman government nor individuals found it practicable to uncover the buried town, and Pompeii remained almost untouched, preserved under its ashes. Modern methods of excavation have become so meticulous that houses can be completely restored with their original material and even the fountains in the gardens made to play again. Wooden shutters, beds, chairs, even stumps of trees, have left their moulds in the ashes and most of the instruments of daily life can be recovered. From the painted notices on the walls of the houses we can enter into the rivalry of the elections and even the slaves come to life in the scribblings on their kitchen walls. Ostia, on the other hand, died a slow and lingering death and, after it had been deserted, it long remained a quarry for builders and treasure hunters. Sculptures, coins, pottery, and bronzes are still found in the ruins, but they are an insignificant fraction of what was once there: the vividness of every-day life has largely departed.

We shall never find at Ostia a house that is such a revealing character study of its owners as the House of the Vettii; nor can we ever know an Ostian as well as we know Caecilius Jucundus, the shrewd Pompeian auctioneer. But from literary sources, buildings, and inscriptions we can recover the main lines of the town's history from the late Republic to the early Middle Ages. The beginnings are much more difficult to unravel.

3

THE ORIGIN AND EARLY GROWTH OF OSTIA

THE SETTLEMENT OF ANCUS MARCIUS

IN the first half of the second century A.D. Ostia, then at the height of her prosperity, commemorated in a finely cut inscription on marble her foundation as the first Roman colony by Ancus Marcius, fourth king of Rome.[1] This inscription reflects a tradition established in the popular mind at least as early as the end of the third century B.C.; for Ennius, in the second book of his great national poem, refers to the foundation in his record of the main events of Ancus Marcius' reign:

> Ostia munita est; idem loca navibus celsis
> munda facit; nautisque mari quaesentibus vitam.[2]

Ennius is the first of a long line of writers who attribute the foundation of Ostia to the fourth king of Rome.[3] When he wrote, Ostia looked primarily to the sea and had established her main value to Rome as a naval base in the war against Hannibal; his account of the foundation may be coloured by later events. Such colouring is clear in Florus.[4] When Florus tells us that the king foresaw that the wealth and trade of the world would flow to Ostia he confused cause and effect: in the regal period Rome had no such ambitions.

Livy's account is less spectacular and more credible: 'The Maesian forest was taken from Veii: Roman rule was advanced to the sea, and at the mouth of the Tiber a city was founded, and salt-beds established

---

[1] S 4338: 'A[NCO] | MAR[CIO] | REG[I] | QUART[O A R[OMUL[O] | QUI A[B URBE C]ONDIT[A | PRI]MUM COLON[IAM | —] DEDUX[IT].'

[2] Ennius, *Ann.* ii, fr. 22 (Vahlen).

[3] e.g. Cic. *De Rep.* ii. 5 and 33; Livy i. 33. 9; Dion. Hal. iii. 44. 4; Isid. *Orig.* xv. 1. 56. Cf. Pliny, *NH* iii. 56 ('a Romano rege'), but xxxi. 89 ('Ancius Marcius rex . . . salinas primus instituit').

[4] Florus i. 1. 4: 'iam tum videlicet praesagiens animo futurum ut totius mundi opes et commeatus illo velut maritimo urbis hospitio reciperentur.'

near by.'[1] Livy's account of the foundation fits intelligibly within his survey of the regal period. The early kings had destroyed Alba and carried on war with the Etruscans. Ancus Marcius had driven the Veientines from the salt-beds to the north of the Tiber, and now completed his work by advancing Roman territory along the left bank. Ficana was first destroyed.[2] It is to be identified with Dragoncello, which lies at the northern edge of the last ridge of high land between Rome and the sea and dominates the Tiber like a Greek acropolis.[3] Ficana eliminated, the control of the low coastal plain by the Tiber passed to Rome. Ostia, Livy implies, was settled so that Rome could control directly the nearest source of salt. Salt was a prime necessity, and, until Veii was broken, access to the northern beds across the Tiber could not be secure.

The credibility of such an early foundation of Ostia depends in large part on the credibility of the traditional Roman account of the regal period; and it is not surprising that it should be rejected by historians who regard that account as a tissue of patriotic invention. Pais, for example, held that the attribution of the colony to Ancus Marcius was a projection of fourth-century history into the past.[4] During the fourth-century wars against Etruria, C. Marcius Rutilus, first plebeian dictator, played a distinguished part: the recorded operations of Ancus Marcius are, according to Pais, a mere echo of these campaigns, assigned to a royal ancestor to increase the prestige of his house. Such rationalism is most unconvincing. The operations of the two leaders, in spite of superficial resemblance, are substantially different. The field of action is the same, but the first are offensive, the second defensive. The first come in a period of expansion; the second when Rome, crippled by the Gallic invasion, is virtually beginning her struggles again.

The attack on tradition appears less compelling now than it did a generation ago, for the new archaeological evidence reflects wider contacts and greater wealth in seventh- and sixth-century Rome than earlier evidence had suggested.[5] But while excavation at Rome might

---

[1] Livy i. 33. 9: 'silva Maesia Veientibus adempta. usque ad mare imperium prolatum et in ore Tiberis Ostia urbs condita, salinae circa factae.'   [2] Livy i. 33. 2.

[3] Nibby, *Annalisi*, ii. 41; Carcopino, 456. The identification is not perhaps certain; see p. 474, n. 9.

[4] E. Pais, *Storia critica di Roma* i (1918) 470; cf. Carcopino, 34.

[5] I. Scott Ryberg, *An Archaeological Record of Rome from the Seventh to the Second Century B.C.* (1940). Various excavations, notably on the Palatine and in the Forum, have since added more early Greek pottery. A modern review of the value of the literary

be held to make the tradition of Ostia's regal foundation more acceptable, excavation at Ostia itself has by many been considered a final
refutation of the tradition. For at the heart of the town of the imperial
period can still be seen the outline of a rectangular fort, called for convenience the Castrum, from which the later town developed. The
maturity of the construction of the walls of this fort and the type of
stone used preclude a date earlier than the fourth century. The earliest
pottery associated with the fort cannot be earlier than the fourth century. Neither within nor without the fort has any evidence of earlier
occupation been found.

There is thus clear evidence of the establishment of a Roman settlement in the fourth century, which is not even mentioned by the literary
authorities. Does their apparent ignorance of a foundation which is
proved to exist condemn their account of an earlier settlement of which
no traces have been found? In spite of the absence of archaeological
evidence, a tradition firmly established as early as Ennius should not be
lightly dismissed. Nor should Roman interest in the sea routes be
ignored. Livy's references to the early import of corn are convincing,
and Dionysius of Halicarnassus adds circumstantial detail. In 508, when
it was essential to retain the common people's loyalty after the expulsion
of the kings, the Romans sent to the Volscians and to Cumae for corn.[1]
In 492, when Rome was faced with famine, partly as the result of the
neglect of the fields during the secession of the plebs, convoys were sent
to collect corn from the Etruscan coastal area, from the territory south
of the Tiber as far as Cumae, and even from Sicily.[2] The Roman record
did not give the precise origin of the Sicilian corn. Some of the early
annalists guessed that it came from Dionysius of Syracuse; the substi-
tution of Gelo was at least chronologically consistent.[3] But these were
mere guesses; it is more likely that the corn came from the western
Carthaginian sphere, where Rome could expect a welcome under her
treaty with Carthage.[4] Sicilian corn appears again in Livy's record of
486.[5]

When the crops of the Roman campagna failed, Rome had to look
farther afield. The coastal plains of Caere and Vulci to the north, and the
Pomptine plain to the south, were the nearest sources from which a

tradition, P. Fraccaro, 'La storia romana arcaica' (discorso inaugurale, Ist. Lomb. di
Scienze e Lettere; Milano, 1952).
  [1] Livy iii. 9. 6.   [2] Livy ii. 34. 2–5.   [3] Dion. Hal. vii. 1. 3–6.
  [4] For the date of Rome's first treaty with Carthage, p. 481.   [5] Livy i. 41. 8.

surplus could be expected. Cumae was approached to tap the rich resources of Campania. When these areas were hostile or their supply inadequate Sicily was called in to fill the gap. Corn from these areas came to Rome up the Tiber. Such trade is no proof of a Roman occupation of the river mouth, but it makes an early settlement at Ostia more plausible.[1]

Excavation has shown beyond reasonable doubt that there was no occupation before the fourth century within the area of imperial Ostia. This negative evidence, however, loses its sting if the natural site for an earlier settlement lies elsewhere. Livy's account suggests a close association with salt-beds. In later times, and probably from the outset, Ostia's salt-beds lay on the north side of the road from Rome, roughly half a mile to the east of Roman Ostia. Above the salt-beds the land rises gradually towards the Tiber. It is on this higher ground near the river that we should expect to find a settlement that was intended primarily to produce salt. The search for such a settlement has not yet begun.

The existence of such a site before the fourth-century settlement might help to explain the elusiveness of early tombs. In spite of systematic searching no tombs that can be associated with the early stages of the Castrum have yet been found, though we should expect the earliest tombs to be not far from the walls. The reason may be that the fourth-century colonists at first continued to use the burial ground of earlier settlers east of the later town. It was in this area that a large hoard of coins deposited not later than the middle of the second century B.C. was found in 1911.[2] There is more direct evidence of two settlements in a tradition preserved by Festus: 'Ostiam urbem ad exitum Tiberis . . . Ancus Marcius rex condidisse fertur; quod sive ad urbem sive ad coloniam quae postea condita est refertur.'[3]

The traditional account of Ostia's foundation should be provisionally accepted, at least until the area east of the town has been explored. We may imagine a small band of settlers living in primitive huts of clay or wattle and daub, such as shepherds still use in the Roman campagna, growing their own food and sending salt to Rome. Rome's dependence on Ostian salt, however, was comparatively short-lived. By the crushing of Veii, and the successful fighting against the Etruscans in the middle of the fourth century, Rome was able to control securely the

[1] See also Appendix I, p. 479.
[2] S. L. Cesano, *Riv. It. Num.* 24 (1911) 275.
[3] Festus (Lindsay), 214, quoted by Dessau, *CIL* xiv, p. 3, n. 7; cf. Carcopino, 37.

larger and richer salt-beds on the right bank of the river. These became the *salinae Romanae*.[1] They satisfied the needs of Rome and provided a surplus for trade. Salt was still probably produced on the left bank, but a settlement nearer the river mouth became increasingly necessary for defence and for the servicing of shipping. The decisive step was taken in the fourth century.

THE FOURTH-CENTURY COLONY

The building on a new site of a strongly fortified colony marks a new departure in Roman policy. When in the fourth century Rome had successfully concluded her war with the Etruscans, her energies were diverted to meet land and sea raids on Latium. Plundering bands of Gauls were still active on land and in 349 B.C. we hear that Greek fleets ravaged the coast from Antium to the Tiber's mouth.[2] The Roman consul, Camillus, was dispatched against the Gauls and L. Pinarius, praetor, was deputed to guard the coastline against the Greeks. The consul, after a successful campaign against the Gauls, was ordered to join forces with the praetor, but operations came to a standstill: 'nec illi terra nec Romanus mari bellator erat.'[3] While Caere in south Etruria had been powerful her fleet had policed these seas, but Caere's power had declined by the fourth century and when she took advantage of Rome's apparent weakness to attack Roman territory in 353 she could no longer be trusted. The shores of Latium needed new protection.

It was this concern for the protection of the coast lands and the ineffectiveness of normal military action that led to the establishment of maritime colonies. Colonists were sent to Antium in 338, to Anxur (Terracina) in 329, to Minturnae and Sinuessa in 296, and, at an unknown date, to Pyrgi. To defend a coastline a series of forts is the most adequate substitute for a standing fleet: Rome's maritime colonies postponed the need but paved the way for sea power.

At what precise date the foundation of Ostia should be placed is uncertain, for the archaeological evidence is not decisive. The walls are built of a tufa easily recognized by the quantity of black scoriae that it contains. It is quarried over a wide area from Fidenae to Prima Porta,

---

[1] Livy vii. 19. 8.

[2] Livy vii. 25. 4: 'mare infestum classibus Graecorum erat oraque litoris Antiatis Laurensque tractus et Tiberis ostia.'

[3] Livy vii. 26. 13.

but it does not seem to have been used by the Romans before the conquest of Fidenae and Veii in the early fourth century.[1] Its use was comparatively short-lived, because it was more friable and less durable than other tufas equally accessible to the Roman builders. But, since the dating of those parts of the Roman walls which employ this tufa is still highly controversial, the walls of Ostia cannot offer a firm criterion of date.[2]

More important is the evidence of pottery. When the area beneath the imperial Forum, which lies in the centre of the Castrum, was explored, imported painted ware was found in small quantities at the lowest level. For dating purposes the most significant pieces are fragments of red-figured Attic vases and a series of so-called 'Genucilia' plates. The Attic fragments come from vases which can be closely paralleled from Olynthus and, since Olynthus was destroyed in 348 B.C., the production date of these vases should be not later or very little later than the middle of the fourth century, and some were probably made earlier.[3]

The production of Genucilia plates, whose design is centred on a female head, is generally thought to have begun in the late fourth or early third century at Falerii or some unknown centre in Etruria or Latium.[4] But there is reason to believe that production was transferred to Caere in the first half of the fourth century and moved back to Falerii in the middle of the century; the eleven examples found at Ostia have been attributed to Caere.[5] The archaeological evidence suggests a date not earlier than 400 and hardly later than 340.

Carcopino has suggested narrower limits by reference to Rome's relations with Antium. The Volscians of Antium had followed the Greeks in their attacks on the coastline, and had raided the territory of Ardea and the land by the Tiber mouth.[6] In 338 Antium was crushed by Rome and her fleet was surrendered. Carcopino places the foundation of Ostia between the eclipse of Antium in 338 and 317 when, he thinks, Antium received a Roman colony.[7] This latter date is selected as a

[1] T. Frank, *Roman Buildings of the Republic*, 21.

[2] M. E. Blake, *Ancient Roman Construction in Italy*, 27.

[3] See *Note A*, p. 471.

[4] J. D. Beazley, *Etruscan Vase Painting*, 10, 175; Ryberg, op. cit. 101.

[5] M. A. del Chiaro, *The Genucilia Group* (Univ. of California publications in Class. Arch., vol. 3, no. 4, 243–372). Chronology, 308–12; Ostian examples, 255–68.

[6] Livy viii. 12. 2: 'Antiates in agrum Ostiensem Ardeatem Solonium incursiones fecerunt.'   [7] Carcopino, 17–35.

terminus ante quem in order to preserve Ostia's traditional position as the
first Roman colony. But this argument points to a date before 338, for
Livy explicitly dates the Roman colony at Antium to the year of conquest[1] and the confusion which Carcopino finds in his narrative does not
exist. Livy states that in 317 Antium complained that she lacked clearly
defined laws and magistrates; as a result 'dati ab senatu ad iura statuenda
ipsius coloniae patroni'.[2] How, asks Carcopino, is this reconcilable
with a colony established in 338? The answer lies in the existence of two
separate communities at Antium, native and Roman.[3] The account of
317 in fact confirms the earlier colony. Nor are the subsidiary arguments
used to support Carcopino's date of substantial weight.

Carcopino considers that the bringing of captured ships from Antium
to Rome shows that there was no Roman settlement at the river's
mouth, and that the omission of Ostia in the *Periplous* of the pseudo-
Scylax, composed about the middle of the century, is good evidence
that Ostia had not yet been founded. Neither inference is valid. The
surrendered ships from Antium were brought to Rome for display;
their beaks were used to adorn the speakers' platform in the Forum.
The account of the *Periplous* is not sufficiently detailed to argue from
silence.

Carcopino's date has been generally accepted, but the evidence of the
pottery has not been given due weight. The Attic fragments in particular point to a date before or near 350, and such a date better fits the
historical context. In the first half of the fourth century Rome was
preoccupied with inland fighting; in 349 her attention was turned to
the coast by Greek raiders. The building of the Castrum may have been
an immediate response to the ineffectiveness of Roman operations in
349. After the crushing of Antium in 338 we hear no more in Livy's
narrative of the coastal region.[4]

When the limits are so narrowly fixed, however, the precise date is
less important than the character of the settlement, and of that there
can be little doubt.[5] The area enclosed is a rectangle of some $5\frac{1}{2}$ acres
(194 × 125·70 metres). The walls are strongly built of large blocks of
tufa laid in alternate courses of headers and stretchers without mortar,
the foundations being formed by four courses of smaller stones. The
thickness of the walls is constant at 1·65 metres, the maximum height

[1] Livy viii. 14. 8.   [2] Livy ix. 20. 10.
[3] A. N. Sherwin-White, *Roman Citizenship*, 77.
[4] Livy viii. 14, 12.   [5] G. Calza, *Topografia*, 63.

preserved, on the east side, is 6·60 metres. In the centre of each side (for the north side there is no specific evidence) a gate was set, and the foundations of two of these gates can still be seen below the level of the imperial Decumanus. It has been suggested by Säflund that these stone walls date only from the period of the wars against Carthage in the third century and were preceded perhaps by vallum and ditch;[1] but such defences would have been anomalous and old-fashioned by the fourth century.[2]

The colony is thus seen as little more than a strongly fortified camp, built in the angle between coast and river, standing back from, but commanding both. The distance from the river was 225 metres; the sea coast, the precise line of which cannot be determined, was probably farther from the walls. Three hundred colonists were sent to the maritime colony of Anxur;[3] the size of Ostia suggest a similar strength. The colonists could grow their own food; their main function was to defend the coastline and the river mouth. The nearest surviving parallel to this early Ostia is at Pyrgi on the coast some fifty miles to the north, where substantial tracts of the original wall, particularly on the northern side, can still be seen.[4] The style of construction of the walls, 'cyclopean' like those of Cosa (possibly a near contemporary), is different, but the plan is similar and the area not much larger. Pyrgi, like Ostia, was intended as a strong fort to defend the coastline.

Ostia's function in the fourth century was not limited solely to defence; the river harbour was already important to Rome. The range of Roman overseas trade in the fourth century cannot be assessed with any degree of security, but it was not negligible. Whatever may be thought of the date and nature of Rome's first treaty with Carthage, there is no good reason for discrediting the treaty assigned by Livy and Diodorus to 348 B.C.[5] A treaty implies contact existing or anticipated, and the incentive may have been Rome's repulse of Greek coastal raiders in the previous year. The terms are probably those attributed by Polybius to his second treaty: they exclude the Romans from Spain and Africa, with the exception of Carthage, but free access is allowed to the Carthaginian sphere in Sicily; the Carthaginians are given reciprocal

---

[1] G. Säf lund, *Le Mura di Roma Repubblicana*, 239.

[2] I. A. Richmond, *JRS* 22 (1932) 236, reviewing Säf lund.

[3] Livy viii. 21. 11.

[4] Dennis, *Cities and Cemeteries of Etruria*[2], i. (London, 1883) 289; F. Castagnoli, *Ippodamo e l'urbanistica a pianta ortogonale*, 87; id. (with L. Cozza, 'Appunti sulla topografia di Pyrgi', *BSR* 25 (1957) 16.   [5] Livy vii. 27. 2; Diod. xvi. 69, 1.

rights in Latium and Rome. The continued interest of Carthage in the Roman sphere is shown by the sending of a golden crown to Roman Jupiter to commemorate Rome's victory over the Samnites in 343,[1] the renewal of the treaty in 306,[2] and the offer of help when Pyrrhus invaded Italy.[3]

There are further signs that Rome's horizon was not limited to the land. Theophrastus refers to a Roman attempt to settle in Corsica before the end of the fourth century:[4] Rome's relations with Massilia presuppose an interest in trade with Gaul. A Roman dedication sent to Delphi to commemorate the capture of Veii in the early fourth century was set up in the Massiliote treasury,[5] and tradition records relations with Phocaeans, the founders of Massilia, as early as the sixth century;[6] trade is the natural explanation of such links. Rome's food problem also forced Rome's attention seawards. In the early Republic corn had come to Rome from Sicily, and the coastal plains to the south and north of the Tiber; in time of shortage imported corn was still needed from these areas. The Genucilia plates found at Ostia, if rightly identified as of Caeretan origin, reflect Rome's connexion with the coastal district of Etruria; the Attic vases whose fragments survive at Ostia might have been carried direct by Greek traders, but they could have come through Caere.

There is little doubt that in the second half of the fourth century merchantmen were coming to the Tiber mouth and that Ostia served the needs of trade as well as of defence. By the end of the third century the emphasis had shifted to the navy. When Antium's fleet was surrendered in 338, some of her ships were destroyed; it is reasonable to infer that Rome had not yet decided to maintain a large navy. But when it became clear that Rome was committed to the defence of the Campanian coastal towns warships were essential; in 311 *duumviri navales* were appointed 'to equip and keep in repair a fleet'.[7] A more important stage in the building up of Rome's naval organization is the appointment of additional quaestors in 267.

The number and function of these new quaestors are both controversial, since there is a lacuna at this point in the text of Livy's epito-

---

[1] Livy vii. 38. 2.   [2] Livy ix. 43. 26.   [3] Livy, *Ep.* 13.

[4] Theophr. *Hist. Plant.* v. 8. 2; but see J. H. Thiel, *A History of Roman Sea-power before the Second Punic War,* 1954, 19, who suggests that this was an Etruscan expedition. Theophrastus dates the expedition considerably before his time (ποτε); we know too little of sixth-century Rome to assume confusion in his account. Cf. Pliny, *NH* iii. 57: 'Theophrastus, qui primus externorum aliqua de Romanis diligentius scripsit.'

[5] Diod. xiv. 93. 5.   [6] Justin xliii. 3. 4.   [7] Livy ix. 30. 4.

mator and the notices of our authorities disagree. But Lydus may be right in recording their title as *classici*, the motive for their creation as hostilities against the allies of Pyrrhus, and their function the collection of funds.[1] Rome's triumph over Pyrrhus had emphasized her predominance in Italy and led to the consolidation of her power both in north and south. The title *classici* suggests that she had also wider ambitions. The removal of all serious opposition in Italy meant that Rome was free to turn her attention to Carthage. The new quaestors' duty was probably to collect money and ships from Rome's dependents and allies for her fleet; later in the Republic we hear no mention of them in connexion with naval preparations and their duties seem to have become more general. From 267 Ostia was the base of one of these new quaestors, and it has been suggested that a mint may have been temporarily installed in the colony.[2]

Rome was not yet a strong naval power, but the struggle with Carthage for Sicily, begun in 264 B.C., could not be decided by land forces alone, and Rome was forced to take more seriously to the sea. With typical stubbornness she replaced the fleets that bad weather and bad seamanship lost, and the decisive engagement of the war was a naval battle. No mention of Ostia is made by Polybius in his detailed narrative of the first Punic War, but Ostia was the natural assembly base for new fleets sailing to Sicily. Polybius refers to the building of large fleets, but he does not tell us where the ships were made. We may suspect that shipbuilders, drawing on the coastal pine, were busy at Ostia. When peace was made Rome was left with a strong navy and the annexation of the greater part of Sicily, soon followed by the seizure of Sardinia and Corsica, made a standing fleet necessary. From this point onwards there was a detachment of ships stationed at Ostia, which played its part in the struggle with Hannibal.

In this war the decisive engagements were fought on land, but the Roman fleet had important if less spectacular work to do. The securing of provisions from Sicily and Sardinia was vital to the Roman legions in Italy, supplies of men and equipment had to be convoyed to the

---

[1] Lydus, *De mag.* i. 27; Mommsen, *Staatsrecht*, ii (1)[3], 570.

[2] H. Mattingly, 'The first age of Roman coinage', *JRS* 25 (1945) 65, associates the first issues of silver and bronze coinage in the Roman name at four distinct mints, approximately contemporary, with the establishment of the *quaestores classici*. The evidence for a mint at Ostia is a very large hoard of early asses found 'near Ostia' (p. 68). In his analysis, the Ostian mint closes at the beginning of the second Punic War. The coins from this mint seem to have circulated mainly in Etruria and Cisalpine Gaul.

army in Spain, Philip of Macedon had to be paralysed, and reinforce-
ments for Hannibal from Africa had to be barred from Italy. Ostia
seems to have been the chief naval base of the period, and her function
is allusively illustrated in Livy's record of the war. In 217 transports
carrying supplies from Ostia to the army in Spain were intercepted
ninety miles up the coast off Cosa by a Carthaginian fleet and captured.
'The consul was immediately instructed to proceed to Ostia to man the
ships lying at Rome and Ostia with Roman troops and naval allies, to
pursue the enemy fleet and to protect the coast of Italy.'[1] The protection
of Italy's western coastline was in fact the main function of the Ostian
fleet; throughout the war a battle strength of thirty ships was maintained, normally commanded by a Roman praetor. But in an emergency
the Ostian fleet could be used farther afield. When in 215 envoys from
Philip to Hannibal were intercepted, the Ostian fleet was sent to
Tarentum, with instructions to carry an army across the Adriatic if
Philip's movements seemed dangerous.[2]

The importance of Ostia in Rome's naval organization is best illustrated in the crisis of 207. When Hasdrubal succeeded in bringing re-
inforcements into Italy desperate efforts had to be made to raise new
troops. Crippling losses in the early battles of the war had severely
reduced military manpower in Italy; the maritime colonies were now
called on to supply recruits. By statute they had exemption from military
service, but when they appeared before the senate to state their case, the
senate ruled that, since the enemy was on Italian soil, the legal privilege
must be waived. Ostia and Antium alone were exempted from service
in the legions, but the men of military age in these two colonies were
required to take an oath that they would not sleep outside their walls for
more than thirty days.[3]

Ostia was treated in this privileged way, because her men were needed
not only for ships' crews but also for maintenance services and to
handle the supplies that came to and were distributed from the river
harbour. In 216 Hiero, king of Syracuse, sent to Ostia 300,000 modii
of wheat and 200,000 modii of barley.[4] In 212 we hear of corn that
had come from Sardinia and Etruria being sent from Ostia to two
newly established forts on the coast of Campania so that the army
should have supplies through the winter.[5] In this emergency handling

---

[1] Livy xxii. 11. 6.   [2] Livy xxiii. 38. 8.
[3] Livy xxvii. 38. 4.   [4] Livy xxii. 37. 1–6.
[5] Livy xxv. 20. 3.

of large supplies of corn we see a foreshadowing of Ostia's main role of the late Republic and early Empire.

The privilege given to Ostia in 207 was not repeated when Italy was freed from danger. In 191 the Romans raised a fleet to carry war against Antiochus, king of Syria, and it was proposed to recruit for the fleet from the maritime colonies. The colonies appealed to the tribunes, who referred the issue to the senate. The senate unanimously ruled that they were not by statute exempt from service with the navy—'vacationem rei navalis his coloniis non esse'. Ostia had joined in the protest, but was no longer given special treatment.[1]

With the crushing of Carthage began the decline of Rome's naval power. For her wars in the east she relied mainly on the ships of her allies, and now that her only serious rival in the western Mediterranean was crippled, a large fleet seemed unnecessary. The Ostian squadron only reappears in our literary record in the period of pirate terrorization at the close of the Republic when the ships, under the command of a consul, were destroyed and the colony sacked.[2] Augustus was wise enough to learn from the mistakes of senatorial government and organized standing fleets to control the waterways and safeguard Mediterranean trade; but in the imperial system Misenum became the headquarters of the western fleet. There were triremes at Ostia during the following period, and a number of tombstones have been found, both in the colony and near the imperial harbours that were laid out to the north of the town, of men who died on service or veterans who lived after retirement in the town where they had served;[3] but these ships were only a small detachment from the main fleets of Misenum or Ravenna, and their main function was to police the harbours.

SECOND-CENTURY EXPANSION

At the end of the second Punic War Ostia was still first and foremost a naval base. A century later her primary importance to Rome was as a commercial harbour, and the small fort of the fourth century was growing into a trading town. This development is the indirect result of the social and economic changes that followed the long struggle with Hannibal. During the second century the population of the city of Rome rapidly increased, partly as a result of the migration of peasants from the land, partly by the influx of foreign slaves, brought back in the wake of victorious armies or supplied by an active slave trade.

---

[1] Livy xxxvi. 3. 4–6.   [2] Cicero, *De imp. Cn. Pomp.* 33.   [3] p. 216.

Though the main demand for these slaves was on the land, considerable numbers served to maintain in Rome the higher living standards that an increasingly wealthy aristocracy demanded. For successful war brought wealth to the rich; and the large-scale investment in land, when the poor were ready to sell and the public control of public land was weak, brought large fortunes to the shrewd and enterprising.

While the population of Rome increased, the natural sources of her grain were yielding less. The great plain between the Volscian hills and the sea, which stretches south from Antium, could have supplied a large part of the Roman market if the water had been carried from the hills to the sea by an adequate drainage system; but the manpower needed for intensive farming had been cruelly reduced by the fighting against Hannibal, and the easy profits of grazing provided a more attractive alternative to the rich. What had once been a fertile plain was soon to become the Pomptine marshes.[1] The cultivated area of Etruria, which had been an important source of supply for Rome, was also shrinking. It was here that Tiberius Gracchus on his way to Spain was shocked by the growth of large estates and the desertion of the fields.[2] Rome therefore urgently needed the corn that was now available from her provinces of Sicily and Sardinia.

The new emphasis on overseas corn and the recurrent danger of acute shortage is clearly reflected in Livy's narrative of the early second century. Annual tithes had been imposed on Sicily and Sardinia, but these were not enough. In 196 the aediles were able to distribute one million modii of wheat, which the Sicilians had sent in honour of C. Flaminius.[3] In 191 a second tithe was demanded from Sicily for the Roman army in Greece, and a second tithe from Sardinia to be sent to Rome.[4] In the same year Carthage and the Numidian prince Masinissa sent 500,000 modii of wheat and 250,000 of barley to Rome.[5] In 190 and 181 a second tithe was again imposed on Sicily and Sardinia to be divided between the army in the field and the population of Rome.[6] The corn dealers had to be closely watched. In 188 they were heavily fined for hoarding supplies against a rise in prices.[7]

---

[1] Pliny, *NH* iii. 59: 'palus Pomptina, quem locum XXIIII urbium fuisse Mucianus ter consul prodidit.' Fourth-century proposals to allocate part of the land to new settlers, Livy vi. 6. 1; vi. 21. 4.

[2] Plut. *Gracchi*, 8. 9.   [3] Livy xxxiii. 42. 8.   [4] Livy xxxvi. 2. 12.

[5] Livy xxxvi. 4. 5.   [6] Livy xxxvii. 2. 12; 50. 9.

[7] Livy xxxviii. 35. 5, dedications by the aediles 'ex pecunia qua frumentarios ob annonam compressam damnarunt'.

For the first half of the century Sicily and Sardinia remained the main sources of Rome's supply. The position was considerably easier when Carthage was destroyed and Africa made a province in 146. The amount of corn contributed in taxation by Africa was at first small, but there were rich corn lands in the province which gave ample scope to the corn dealer buying for the Roman market, and it was not long before Romans were seizing the opportunity to develop African land. When Gaius Gracchus provided for the settlement of 6,000 men from Italy on the territory of Carthage he may have been thinking partly of the need for African corn in Rome.[1] The lots assigned were large—200 *iugera*—and encouraged large-scale production. Optimate propaganda led to the repeal of his law, but much of the land had already been assigned and the new owners remained.

Conquest in east and west also stimulated trade. Though the men who seized the new opportunities were for the most part not Roman, but Italians and Greeks from Campania and the south of Italy, they had an eye on the Roman market where there was a growing demand for the refined products of the Hellenistic world and the specialities that could be found in Spain and later in Gaul. Puteoli, with its well-sheltered harbour and long association with Greek traders, controlled the larger part of Rome's eastern trade, and became the main distributing centre for the luxuries that Italy drew from the Hellenistic world; but there is no evidence and little probability that Puteoli also monopolized the trade with Spain, Gaul, and Sardinia.

Strabo, after cataloguing the rich resources of Roman Baetica, emphasizes the volume of exports carried in large merchantmen 'to Puteoli and Ostia, Rome's harbour'; in number, he says, they almost matched the shipping from Africa.[2] Spanish and African goods carried to Puteoli were not intended for the Roman market, but for distribution in thickly populated Campania and the south of Italy. Western goods exported to Rome came through Ostia. The distribution of Sicilian exports in Italy is less clear but it is probable that Puteoli secured the greater part of the trade. Even goods intended for Rome seem to have been unloaded at Puteoli. The harbour was better, the Greek background more congenial, and the dominance of corn ships in the restricted river harbour at Ostia probably made it difficult for other ships to unload their cargoes quickly. Though transport by land was considerably more expensive than by water such products as papyrus,

---

[1] Appian, *Pun.* 136.   [2] Strabo, 145.

glass, and linen from Egypt, sculpture and jewellery from Sicily, were probably carried by the Via Appia to Rome. Bulk supplies of corn, however, were different. Unless secure evidence is found to the contrary we should assume that the corn from Sicily as well as from Africa and Sardinia came to Rome through Ostia.

This great expansion in imports from overseas to Rome through Ostia is reflected in the early second-century building activity recorded by Livy. In 193 two Aemilii, aediles for the year, built a *porticus* outside the Porta Trigemina, adding an *emporium* by the Tiber.[1] In 174 the censors paved this *emporium* and fenced it round; at the same time they carried through a restoration of the Porticus Aemilia and provided steps from the Tiber to the *emporium*.[2] Livy's bare words tell us little, for *porticus* covers a wide range of construction, though we might infer from the reputation made by this aedileship that the work was of some importance. The ingenious identification by Gatti of a fragment of the imperial marble plan of Rome, together with surviving walls, gives us a clearer idea of the scale and nature of the work.[3] It seems that it had a total length parallel to the river of 487 metres and a depth of 90 metres; it was divided into fifty bays by tufa piers supporting barrel vaults. Considerable stretches of its walls, faced with irregular blocks of tufa (*opus incertum*), still survive to show the strength of the building.

In 192 we hear of a 'porticus extra portam Trigeminam inter lignarios'[4] whose position in the dock area indicates that these *lignarii* were handling timber carried up river to Rome. This early evidence of timber imports should not surprise us. Early in her history Rome had been well supplied with easily accessible oak and beech; later, softwoods could be carried down the Tiber from forests near the upper river. But it is clear from Livy's annalistic account that there was a tremendous expansion of public building at Rome in the early second century, a natural reflection of Rome's growing self-consciousness as an imperial city. The Porticus Aemilia shows the scale to which Roman builders could already work. Concrete and tufa were the basic materials of construction, but for roofing, shuttering, doors, windows, and general furnishing, the demand for timber, and particularly for long and stout beams, expanded sharply. It is possible that part of the demand was met from the coastal forests of oak and pine between Ostia and Antium, which could be brought to Ostia and shipped up to Rome or carted by

---

[1] Livy xxxv. 10. 12.   [2] Livy xli. 27. 8.
[3] G. Gatti, *BC* 62 (1934) 124.   [4] Livy xxxv, 41. 10.

ox wagon. But the coastal pine was weak timber and for many purposes softwoods were preferable to oak. In the Augustan period the mountains above Pisa and along the Ligurian coast were an important source of supply for Rome's builders;[1] this timber trade with Liguria may have developed after the second Punic War. Corsica also had accessible forests of large conifers which the Romans had learned to appreciate before the close of the fourth century.[2]

In his account of 179 Livy reports the building by M. Fulvius, censor, of a *porticus* outside the Porta Trigemina, and another beyond the *navalia*;[3] and, since the buildings sponsored by M. Fulvius were distinguished from those of his colleague as being of greater utility, we may believe that he too was attending to the needs of trade. This building activity outside the Porta Trigemina, in the dock area between Aventine and Tiber, is dictated by the growth of imports, particularly but not solely corn, coming up river to Rome. All goods that were handled at these Roman docks had first passed through Ostia, and, as the swift current and winding course of the Tiber made it impossible for the larger merchantmen to come upstream, there was much unloading and reloading to be done at the river mouth.

We therefore expect to find in the second century B.C. a development at Ostia corresponding to the building activity at Rome outside the Porta Trigemina. The rate and extent of this growth, however, is difficult to determine, for during the second century A.D. Ostia was almost completely rebuilt; republican Ostia can only be traced by excavation below this later level. Trial pits to the level of the sand have been dug at many points and much valuable evidence has been accumulated; but until the excavators have had time to extend their tests more widely conclusions can only be tentative. Traces of second-century extension, however, outside the fourth-century walls can already be seen at many points.

The clearest evidence perhaps is seen in concrete walls faced with blocks of tufa of irregular shape and size, *opus incertum*. It was probably not until after the second Punic War that the use of concrete, which revolutionized building construction, was firmly established at Rome; but already in the Porticus Aemilia at Rome we see a mature handling of the new technique. Nor does there appear to be any striking change in treatment during the century. The second half of the second century

[1] Strabo, 223.
[2] Theophrastus, *Hist. Plant.* v. 8. 2. [3] Livy xl. 51. 4–6.

was not a congenial period for new developments. Rome was pre-occupied with domestic crisis; of new public buildings we hear very little, in striking contrast to the early decades of the century. It was not until the turn of the century, and particularly in the period of Sullan domination, that the architects came into their own again. By Sulla's time the facing of walls is becoming more regular. The blocks of tufa are roughly squared, more uniform in shape and size and smaller: *opus incertum* is giving way to *opus quasi-reticulatum*.

We may with some confidence then place walls faced with *opus incertum* at Ostia between the opening of the second century and Sulla's dictatorship. They can be seen at scattered points along the main roads extending beyond the walls at least 50 metres to east, west, and south. The distribution at the lowest level of fragments of black glazed ware, typical of the second century, also testifies to the expansion, but a more detailed discussion of the problems involved may be postponed until we consider more closely the physical aspect of the town.

The passing of Gaius Gracchus' law sanctioning the cheap distribution of corn led, we may assume, to an increase in the efficiency and volume of the corn trade, which affected Ostia no less than Rome; and it is probably in the Gracchan period or shortly afterwards that Rome found it necessary to prevent uncontrolled development on the Tiber bank at Ostia which would interfere with services essential to the state. Five travertine boundary stones have been discovered, aligned along the Decumanus on its north side, with identical inscriptions: 'C. Caninius C. f. pr(aetor) urb(anus) de sen(atus) sent(entia) poplic(um) ioudic(avit).'[1] They cover a length of some 600 metres westwards from a point a little outside the eastern Sullan gate. Immediately beside the westernmost stone another was later added which marks the end of the public zone: 'privatum ad Tiberim usque ad aquam.'[2] The praetor ruled that the area marked by boundary stones between the Decumanus and the river was the public property of the Roman people. It was probably mainly along this stretch of river bank that in the Republic merchantmen unloaded their cargoes.

The emphasis on trade is reflected in the changing character of the

---

[1] S 4702; phot. *NS* 1910, 233. The lettering suggests a date not later than Sulla (Dessau, *ILS* 9376), 150–80 B.C. are the approximate limits. Identification with C. Caninius Rebilus, praetor in 171, supported by Carcopino (14) and Calza (*Topografia*, 19) must be ruled out; for Rebilius was praetor in Sicily (Livy xlii. 31. 9), not *praetor urbanus*.

[2] See *Note B*, p. 471.

duties of the quaestor stationed at Ostia. Originally, as his title *classicus* implied, his main concern was with the needs of the fleet. By the end of the second century he is preoccupied with the import of corn. It was from this post that Saturninus, not yet a revolutionary, was removed by the senate in 104 when the corn situation at Rome became critical; and the importance of the post is shown by the transfer of its duties to no less a person than M. Aemilius Scaurus, *princeps senatus*.[1] Later at least, according to Cicero, the post was not popular. It meant hard work without any compensating social and political distinction.[2]

Only one passage in literature throws intimate light on the harbour at Ostia during the second century, but it is a good story, and revealing. Polybius describes the escape of the Syrian prince Demetrius from Rome in 162 B.C. in some detail.[3] When Seleucus Philopator, the elder son of Antiochus the Great, died, he was succeeded by his younger brother Antiochus Epiphanes, who had been held as a hostage in Rome. In his place the Romans kept as hostage Demetrius, son of the later king. Epiphanes died in 163 and Demetrius, who had long been restless, pressed the senate for his release. When this was refused he determined to escape. Arrangements were made through a certain Menyllus of Alabanda, who had come to Rome on a mission from the Egyptian king. He undertook to have a ship in readiness to take Demetrius back to Syria to make his bid for the throne.

At the mouth of the Tiber Menyllus found a Carthaginian vessel, 'one of those specially selected to carry, according to ancestral custom, the first fruits to the gods of Tyre (mother city of Carthage)'. Menyllus chartered a passage for himself and his retinue, procured provisions for the voyage, and at the last moment explained that he himself had to stay in Rome, but was sending on some of his men. Demetrius and his small party came down after dark and boarded ship at midnight. The captain sailed at dawn thinking that he was carrying some soldiers to Ptolemy. It was four days before the truth was out, and by then it was too late; the ship had already passed the straits of Messina.

This circumstantial story shows that one could expect to sail east as well as west from Ostia, and it seems likely that, though most of the eastern trade came to Puteoli, some cargoes bound for Rome came to

---

[1] Cic. *De har. resp.* 43; *Pro Sestio*, 39; Diod. xxxvi. 12.
[2] Cic. *Pro Murena* 18: 'Illam (quaesturam) cui, cum quaestores sortiuntur, etiam adclamari solet, Ostiensem, non tam gratiosam et inlustrem quam negotiosam et molestam.'   [3] Polyb. xxxi. 11–15.

the Tiber mouth. Second-century Rhodian amphorae discovered at a low level beneath the four republican temples west of the theatre point the same way.[1] But it was not an eastern ship that Menyllus chartered. The Carthaginian merchantman which was glad to sell a passage to Syria was presumably on its way with Carthaginian first-fruits to Tyre. Why had it gone out of its way to call at Ostia? No doubt it had brought goods, probably corn, which had a ready market at Ostia, but it cannot have been expected to complete the longer half of the journey without some replacement. Perhaps the ship's captain could rely on collecting passengers for some eastern Mediterranean port, men of substance who could pay a good price.

The Carthaginian merchantman seems to have stayed some time in harbour. It was probably rare for ships to unload, turn about, and sail away at once; when the volume of shipping increased substantially the river harbour would clearly become too restricted. While ships stayed in the harbour they had to replenish their stocks of food and water; Menyllus buys his own provisions for Demetrius' journey. From this trade Ostia derived increasing profit; it helps to account for the virtual monopoly of street fronts by shops.

The dependence of Rome on Ostia in the late Republic is clearly reflected in the strategy of the Civil War between Sullans and Marians. When Marius returned from Africa to join Cinna in Italy, Ostia was his first major objective. The Roman senate had installed a garrison, but they chose the wrong commander. Marius was allowed to enter; he occupied the town and plundered it.[2] Three years later Sulla, returning from the east, instructed the commanders of his advance forces to occupy Ostia if they could not enter Rome.[3] Both sides realized that if they held Ostia they could hope to starve Rome into submission.

NEW TOWN WALLS

The plundering of the city by Marius must have been a serious set-back to the prosperity of Ostia, but with the establishment of Sulla's domination came order and security. It is probably to this period that the walls which were to serve the colony throughout its subsequent history, enclosing an area nearly thirty times as large as that of the fourth-century settlement (*c.* 160 acres), should be dated.[4] For the

---

[1] R. Paribeni, *MA* 23 (1914) 446, 479.
[2] Livy, *Ep.* 79; Appian, *BC* i. 67. 5.   [3] Appian, *BC* i. 88. 7.
[4] G. Calza, *BC* 53 (1925) 232; *Topografia*, 79.

date of these walls, a cardinal point in the history of Ostia, there is no direct evidence, but different approaches converge to a common context.

The style of the construction should be the decisive criterion, but in the period between 150 and 60 B.C. there is not enough dated material in the neighbourhood of Rome to provide a firm guide. The new Ostian walls were built of concrete, faced on the outside with small roughly squared blocks of tufa; on the inside they were unfaced and probably backed with a ramp of beaten earth. The character of the face, however, is not uniform and varies according to the different work parties involved. In some places it approaches very closely to the net-like regularity of *opus reticulatum*; in others the blocks are considerably more irregular and barely distinguishable from *opus incertum*. By the early Augustan period, *opus reticulatum* is fully developed at Ostia; the town walls are substantially earlier than Augustus, but how much earlier we could not say from their style alone. Outside Ostia the nearest parallel that I have seen is in the basilica at Ardea, which has been dated to the beginning of the first century B.C.[1] More general arguments support a Sullan dating.

When the eastern gate by which the Via Ostiensis passed into the town was restored in the early Empire the inscription set up on the attic recorded that the senate and people of Rome gave her walls to the colony of Ostia.[2] Such a formula, incongruous with the dominance of the emperor in the imperial period, recalls the Republic, and the inscription has been interpreted as a copy on the new gate of what stood before on the old. If Ostia had expanded without new walls in the early second century it is unlikely that the Roman senate would have attended to the problem in the disturbed period between the Gracchan revolution and the Social War. Such argument from general probability is by no means compelling, but it receives some support from the account of Marius' seizure of Ostia. Marius owed his entry into the town to the treachery of the commander of the cavalry garrison.[3] If

[1] E. Holmberg, *Boll. med. stud.* ii (1931) June–July, 16, pl. 3, fig. 4.

[2] *S* 4707: 'se[natu]s [p]opulu[sque R.] | c[olon]ia[e O]s[tie]nsium m[u]ro[s] dedi[t].' Restoration discussed by Wickert, *Sitz. Berl. Ak. phil.-hist. Kl.* 1928, 46. The sense is inescapable, but the abbreviation R for Romanus is very unpalatable. The length of line is based on the assumption that the inscription was flanked on each side by a winged Minerva. This is most uncertain.

[3] Granius Licinianus (Teubner, 1904) p. 18, l. 4: 'Marius Ostia urbe potitur ⟨per⟩ Valerium, cuius equites praesidebant.'

Ostia had been walled it would have been more appropriate to send infantry to hold it. The use of cavalry suggests that Ostia had no walls.

We conclude that Ostia's walls were not built before Sulla's dominance; the Sullan settlement provides the best historical context. There is a dangerous tendency to attach to the Sullan name all buildings of the late second and early first centuries that are not precisely dated, but it is at least clear from the sources that Sulla was a great builder who left his mark on Rome.[1] The fighting against the Marians had revealed the importance and vulnerability of Ostia; Sulla himself may have turned his attention to the town's needs. More generally, the Social War and its repercussions had focused attention on the towns of Italy and their relation to Rome; against this background the new walls of Ostia have a natural place. It is difficult to find such an appropriate setting later.

The new walls of Ostia were provided by Rome and it was probably on Roman initiative that they were built. They set a limit to expansion, marked the transformation of a naval base to a trading town, and encouraged Ostia to develop a new urban personality. The physical recognition by the new walls of a developed town may have been accompanied by constitutional change. When the colony was established by Rome in the fourth century it was directly controlled from Rome. Minor administration no doubt was carried on by local officials, whatever their title; major decisions and jurisdiction rested with Roman magistrates. In the imperial period Ostia had a fully developed constitution and managed her own affairs. It is possible that the charter which provided the new pattern of government accompanied the building of the new walls and that, though the general control of overseas trade bound for Rome rested with the Roman quaestor, the development of Ostia now rested with the Ostians themselves. If this is so the town records may have been set up on a public building from this date. When we first meet them they record the consuls of the year, selected events from the Roman record of the year, the chief local magistrates and major events concerning the buildings and constitution of Ostia. The first surviving fragment records events of 49 B.C., but it is clear that this is not the starting-point.[2]

---

[1] Pliny, *NH* xxxiv. 26 (Curia); Tac. *Hist.* iii. 72 (restoration of Capitolium). Further contemporary construction, E. B. Van Deman, 'The Sullan Forum', *JRS* 12 (1922) 1–31; M. E. Blake, *Ancient Roman Construction*, 137–45.

[2] A. Degrassi, *Inscr. Italiae*, xiii (Fasti et Elogia), 173.

In the generation that followed the building of the new walls there was much new construction, and the city began to develop more monumental features. Most of this new building is now buried under the later imperial city, but temples preserve their site and form. Trading was the life-blood of Ostia but throughout her history religion retained a strong hold and in some of her cults Rome was directly concerned. At approximately the same time as her new walls were built, possibly a little earlier, a sacred area was reserved west of the Castrum in which a large temple of Hercules was the dominant feature.[1] Near by is a smaller contemporary tetrastyle temple, unidentified; a little later a third temple was added. Before the end of the Republic another sacred area was reserved, standing back from the Decumanus east of the Castrum. Here on a common podium four small temples were built and surrounded by a large open area limited on three sides by a portico, open to the south from the Decumanus.[2]

The local aristocracy meanwhile could afford spacious houses, spreading horizontally, with atrium and peristyle such as their contemporaries were building at Pompeii. Beneath the imperial level, along the Cardo south of the Forum and along the Decumanus west of the Forum, the remains of several such spreading houses can be seen. Most of these houses had to be destroyed when space grew increasingly valuable and it was necessary to provide accommodation for a largely increased population within the same area; but two survived from the first century B.C. into the late Empire on the west side of the Cardo, immediately south of the Forum. Though they were modified more than once to meet changing tastes, their original plan can be largely recovered.[3] The ground plan of much smaller houses, confined to atrium and surrounding rooms can also be seen under the so-called Basilica House immediately north of the Curia.[4] A Pompeian coming to Ostia in the late Republic might have been bewildered by the shipping but he would have felt quite at home in the houses.

The period immediately following the building of the new walls was probably prosperous; political differences at Rome did not at this stage affect the volume of trade. Within twenty years, however, came a severe and unexpected check. Piracy, which had always been a serious menace in the Mediterranean when no strong fleet controlled the seas, had revived as a result of Rome's increasing apathy. Mithradates had

[1] p. 347.
[2] R. Paribeni, *MA* 23 (1914) 441.
[3] Becatti, *Topografia*, 107.
[4] *NS* 1923, 180.

encouraged and used the pirates, who were now organized in regular fleets. While Verres was governor they had raided Sicily; shortly before 67 B.C. they actually sailed into the Tiber mouth, destroyed a Roman fleet commanded by a consul and plundered Ostia. Cicero, supporting the Lex Manilia in 66, tersely emphasized the humiliation: 'Ostiense incommodum atque ignominiam rei publicae.'[1]

Dio gives a fuller account.[2] The pirates 'even sailed into the Tiber mouth, burnt the ships and plundered everything. Finally, when they met with no opposition, they stayed in the territory as if they were in their own homes, and disposed of the spoils and the inhabitants who escaped the sword.' No traces of widespread destruction have been found to mark this disaster, nor should we expect to find them, for the pirates had nothing to gain by destroying buildings. Their motive in risking such a bold attack was not to provoke or intimidate Rome but to seize the goods and movable wealth of a rich trading centre. Having seized the cargoes by the Tiber bank they no doubt raided storehouses, shops, and the wealthier houses. But their stay must have been comparatively short; they could not have risked an encounter with an organized Roman military force. The set-back to Ostia was temporary only and the disgrace helped to awaken public opinion at Rome. In 67 the people forced the senate's hand and Pompey was entrusted by the Lex Gabinia with an extraordinary command. Within three months he had cleared the seas and trade once again flowed freely to the quays of Ostia.

Much more serious to Ostia was the long period of unsettlement between Caesar's march on Rome and the final victory of Octavian at Actium. Ostia was near enough to Rome to follow nervously the growing tension between Caesar and the nobility. When in 49 Caesar crossed the Rubicon, sympathies at Ostia may well have been divided. What Ostia needed above all was security on the seas and settled conditions at home. Who was more likely to provide them quickly? Pompey had swept the pirates from the sea and more recently, under the special authority of a *cura annonae*, had relieved a corn crisis at Rome and had reorganized the flow of corn ships. For these services Ostia had good reason to feel respect and gratitude. But a trading city having close associations with Gaul will have realized more sharply than the average Italian the calibre of Caesar's generalship. It is not surprising that no

[1] Cic. *De imp. Cn. Pompeii*, 33.
[2] Dio xxxvi. 22.

chief magistrates were elected in Ostia at the normal time for 49; an *interregnum* was needed.[1]

For Ostia the first phase of civil war was less damaging than might have been expected. Caesar won loyalty in Italy by his speed, generosity, and tact. Pompey withdrew across the Adriatic and was defeated at Pharsalus before he could exploit the potential resources of sea power. There was as yet no interruption of the trade from Africa, Spain, and Gaul. This, however, came later, during the struggle for dominance between Octavian and Antony.

Shortly after the insecure renewal of the triumvirate at Brundisium, where Antony, Octavian, and Lepidus had once again divided the Roman world between them, Pompey's son Sextus made his bid for power. Controlling Sicily and Sardinia, he raised a substantial fleet, attempted to blockade the western coast of Italy, and raided as far north as Ostia.[2] Octavian's political survival depended on the elimination of Sextus and the reopening of the seas; but the struggle was difficult and drawn-out, for a fleet had to be built, and the crews trained. These were lean years for Ostia, and it was not until 36 that the issue was settled at the battle of Naulochus. During the crisis Lepidus, who at Misenum had received control of Africa and Spain, played an equivocal hand. After the defeat of Sextus Pompeius his legions went over to Octavian, who now had secure control of the west.

In the struggle between Octavian and Antony, Ostia's sympathies probably lay throughout with Octavian, for Ostia looked west and can have had little sympathy for Antony's eastern ambitions. She will have needed no intimidation to take the oath of loyalty to Octavian before the final campaign. But the long period of disturbance from 49 to 31 must have raised many delicate problems and certainly demanded cool-headed leadership in the colony. This leadership probably came from the *auctoritas* of a small local aristocracy.

Perhaps it is not fanciful to see the dominant figure of these years in C. Cartilius Poplicola. When he died he was honoured with a public funerary monument by the sea-shore, outside the Porta Marina; the inscription commemorates his services:

By public authority. For C. Cartilius Poplicola, son of Caius, [—], and his children and his decendants, by decree of the council and by the unanimous will of the citizens of the colony, a man of leadership. To

[1] *Fasti*, 49 B.C.   [2] Florus ii. 18. 2.

commemorate his services this monument was set up and the gratitude which he deserved was recorded. He was eight times, absent and present, elected duovir, three times with censorial power, by the verdict of the colonists. . . .

The monument is a rectangular tomb of solid masonry with a monumental façade. Above the inscription runs a frieze cut in marble, fragments of which have survived; they show the beaks of triremes and scenes of fighting. The style of the reliefs, the form of the monument, and the mixture of tufa, travertine, and **marble** in the construction suggest a date in the thirties or twenties B.C.[1]

This remarkable career of C. Cartilius, eight times chief magistrate, may well have spanned the difficult years. His standing is further reflected in his dedication of a heroic statue in his own image in the temple of Hercules.[2] He was elected to chief office *absens et praesens*: his absence may be explained by military service which his monument recalls. Perhaps we should see in Poplicola a local partisan of Octavian who helped to steer his town's policies along judicious channels. Another leading Ostian of this period can be suggested, though his date is considerably more controversial; for the long inscription recording his career has for more than a century been lost and most of those who have concerned themselves with the problem have preferred a second century (A.D.) date.[3]

Eleven Ostian inscriptions preserve the name of P. Lucilius Gamala: they cover the first two centuries A.D. and reflect a succession of generations of the same family holding high office. The Publius Lucilius Gamala with whom we are now concerned held the duovirate in Ostia after passing through the normal preliminary posts and was also *pontifex Volcani*, the highest religious authority in the town. He made a large number of public bequests and was given a public funeral. One clause of the inscription seems decisive for an Augustan date: 'item ahenea (statua) . . . posita proxume tribunal quaes. propterea quod cum respublica praedia sua venderet ob pollicitationem belli navalis HS $\overline{XV}$CC reipublicae donavit.' This Publius Lucilius Gamala had given 15,200 sesterces to the city when the government was having to sell public properties on account of a promise given in connexion with a

---

[1] This monument has now been published in *Scavi di Ostia*, III. i. 169 ff. See *Note K*, p. 475.
[2] R. Calza, *Arch. Anz.* 1938, 657, fig. 17; *Museo*, 121; *Scavi di Ostia*, III. i. 221.
[3] I. Further discussed, Appendix V, p. 493.

'bellum navale': in recognition of this service his statue in bronze was set up near a tribunal. The tribunal in question was presumably that of the quaestor, for quaes(toris) is the natural supplement of what was inscribed. But the Ostian quaestorship first instituted in 267 B.C. lapsed in the principate of Claudius, when the quaestor's duties were transferred to an imperial procurator.

This indication of an early date is supported by the reference to a 'bellum navale'. The phrase has been interpreted as the equivalent of 'naumachia', and such a desperate remedy is needed if the inscription is to be dated to Trajan's principate, but there is no good parallel for such usage.[1] 'bellum navale' should mean a naval war and, as Mommsen first saw (he changed his view later), the natural context is the war against Sextus Pompeius with which, as we have seen, Ostia was vitally concerned. Dio tells us that Octavian collected money from the cities of Italy.[2] Ostia will surely have been among the most willing subscribers. Nor is it difficult to understand why in the lean thirties she should have to sell public properties to realize her promised contribution.

If we are right in our interpretation, Publius Lucilius Gamala was one of Ostia's leading citizens during the Civil War.

THE AUGUSTAN REVIVAL

Actium marks the end of an ugly phase. After a brief transition the new order was formally established in the Roman senate at the beginning of 27 B.C. Constitutional practices were restored; Octavian, now Augustus, ruled. By every means in his power Augustus attempted to revive what was useful in past tradition and prepare Rome to advance along new paths. The poets reflect the pride and confidence of the new age; the settlement was also accompanied by a carefully calculated building programme.

We should expect to find a corresponding building activity in Ostia, for she was always sensitive to the capital's mood. Augustan Ostia, however, lies buried for the most part beneath the city of the second century and only where earlier buildings have been restored and transformed or where excavation has been carried to the lower levels can we hope to see signs of Augustan construction. Nor is it easy to distinguish the work of the age of Augustus from that of his early Julio-Claudian successors.[3] By the end of the Civil War *opus reticulatum* was

[1] p. 498.
[2] Dio xlviii. 49. 1.
[3] For changes in building styles, Appendix IX, p. 535.

mature; the net-like pattern of the surface was elegant and regular. Such construction continued in use until the end of the Julio-Claudian period, though fire-baked bricks were increasingly used at Ostia either alone or in conjunction with reticulate as the century developed.

Three temples, revealed by excavation, can with some assurance be dated to the principate of Augustus: a small temple of Bona Dea, and two unidentified temples on the north side of the Decumanus in the Forum.[1] An Ostian calendar of Roman religious festivals resembles calendars from other Italian towns which can be dated to this period; they are a typical reflection of Augustan religious policy.[2] It is probable that Augustus' call for a revival of the traditional cults of the Roman people found a ready response in Ostia.

Reticulate walls that may be Augustan can be seen in all quarters of the city and there is little doubt that Ostian builders were busily employed on houses, shops, and other commercial premises, as well as temples. There are also signs that space was becoming more precious within the city. When the four republican temples on a common platform were built in the first half of the first century B.C. they were surrounded by a large open area limited on three sides by a portico. Under Augustus, or shortly afterwards, a new boundary wall was built, drastically reducing the area on the north, east, and west sides and running less than 2 feet from the temples themselves.[3] The area between the new limiting wall and the back wall of the original portico was probably used for shops and housing. A similar new boundary wall reduced the free area of the Temple of Hercules, and an Augustan building below the later 'Curia' immediately adjoins the western of two temples in the Forum that were destroyed when the Hadrianic Capitolium was built.[4]

The most impressive of the new secular buildings was the theatre.[5] Its present form represents a thorough rebuilding and enlargement at the end of the second century, but the reticulate walls of the original construction can still be seen at the lateral entrances. Their style is typical of Augustan work and a fragment of a monumental inscription recording the name of Agrippa was found below the ruins of the stage.[6] The theatre was probably built on the initiative of Augustus' closest

---

[1] p. 351 f.   [2] S 4547. Augustan parallels, CIL i², pp. 220–42.
[3] This wall, marked in the plan (MA 23 (1914) 468), is not described in the text. The dark-red bricks are almost certainly pre-Claudian.
[4] Becatti, Topografia, 105.   [5] G. Calza, Il Teatro romano di Ostia.   [6] 82.

colleague. It accommodated some 3,000 spectators and was one of the earliest permanent theatres in Italy; not until 55 B.C. had Rome herself enjoyed such a luxury.

But the most striking feature of Agrippa's work was less the theatre itself than the treatment of the area behind to the north. Here was laid out an impressive double-colonnaded portico, making with the theatre a single architectural complex.[1] The addition of a portico to a theatre was not unusual, for it had a sound practical function to fulfil, as Vitruvius tells us: 'behind the stage porticoes should be built to provide a refuge for the audience when sudden showers interrupt the spectacle, and space for the setting up of the stage machinery'.[2] What is remarkable about the theatre portico at Ostia is its scale and use. The original length was 125 metres, the width 80 metres. Surrounding the area on east, west, and north was a light reticulate wall of the same character as the walls of the theatre, pierced at the north end towards the river by eight entrances. Round the three sides ran a double colonnade, the Ionic columns of brick concealed under plaster. On the south side immediately behind the theatre stage was a monumental portico extending along two-thirds of the width and carried on tufa piers. In the area thus enclosed no traces of contemporary building have been found: we imagine public gardens here, in the centre of which a temple was later built. By the Severan period this large colonnade was occupied by traders, mainly from the provinces. Its original function is less certain, but it will be argued later that it was intended from the outset for the use of traders and that it was controlled by the local authority.[3]

Augustus boasted that he had found Rome a city of unbaked brick and left it a city of marble.[4] In the scale of her buildings and the quality of their decoration Ostia lagged far behind the capital. Tufa was still the dominant building material; travertine, which had to be transported from quarries beyond Rome, was something of a luxury; marble very rarely used. The public monument of C. Cartilius Poplicola well illustrates the economy in the use of materials. The face is of marble, the sides of travertine, and the back of the monument, least exposed to view, of tufa. Even the theatre employs tufa throughout, nor is travertine used for the monumental portico immediately behind the stage. But though economy was shown in the choice of building materials, Ostian architects were capable of seizing the opportunities offered them.

[1] G. Calza, *BC* 43 (1916) 178.   [2] Vitruvius v. 9. 1.   [3] p. 283.   [4] Suet. *Aug.* 28. 3.

Until the early Empire Ostia had no aqueduct, and depended on wells. In spite of the nearness of the sea the water was untainted[1] and adequate drinking water is still drawn from a well on the site. But the lack of a generous supply of running water set limits to amenities. There could be no fountains to relieve the summer heat in the streets and public baths were severely restricted. How far cisterns were used to supplement wells by supplies from rainfall we do not know, but one large cistern survives and, though it is in an excellent state of preservation and is one of the most impressive of the surviving monuments, it has attracted little attention. It lies underneath the Baths of Neptune on the north side of the Decumanus, half-way between the Porta Romana and the Forum. It is roughly 36 metres long and 26 metres wide and is divided longitudinally into six interconnected compartments. Floor, walls, and vaulted ceiling are protected by a thick coat of cement.[2]

When the baths above it were built under Hadrian this cistern had passed out of use, for drains of the late first century cut across it. Originally it was above ground, on the same level as other walls immediately to the north which were partially destroyed when the baths were built; its water came from rain collected from the roof. Though it has been called republican this cistern dates from the early Empire, for at various points where the cement has broken away, large red bricks which did not come into use before Augustus can be seen. No traces of similar cisterns have been found at other points and this large reserve may have been designed to meet a special problem. A lead pipe ran from near the north-west angle in a north-easterly direction towards the river.[3] Gismondi has suggested to me that it may have been intended primarily to provide fresh water for the ships that docked by the Tiber bank.

If this be the explanation the need was short-lived, for very soon an aqueduct was built to bring in water from the high land four miles to the east, overlooking the coastal plain. The earliest emperor's name to be preserved on any of the pipes is that of Gaius:[4] the building of the aqueduct will fall between the date of the cistern, not earlier than Augustus, and the end of Gaius' principate, possibly under Tiberius. Very soon a set of public baths, remains of which can still be seen under the Via dei Vigiles, was built to capitalize the new luxury.[5]

---

[1] Pliny, *Ep.* ii. 17. 25.
[2] NS 1911, 262, 407, 452; NS 1913, 395 (plan).
[3] NS 1911, 452.   [4] S 5309⁹.   [5] NS 1912, 204.

As the Julio-Claudian period advanced, further improvements could be seen at Ostia. In the principate of Tiberius or shortly afterwards a temple of Rome and Augustus was built at the south end of the Forum. Only the reticulate walls of the substructure of the temple still stand, but sufficient elements of the marble pediment, cornice, and columns have been found to show that Ostian architecture was approaching much nearer to the standard of imperial Rome.[1] In decorative effect there is a striking advance from the modest temples of the late Republic and what we can infer of Augustan work in Ostia. On the east side of the southern Cardo can still be seen three large travertine columns that supported a portico probably constructed towards the middle of the century; under Augustus such a colonnade would have been carried on tufa piers or columns. Travertine was also used for the columns at the four angles of the portico of the Horrea of Hortensius on the south side of the Decumanus opposite the theatre. These *horrea* for the storage of corn are probably the earliest of those that can now be seen, and were perhaps the largest that had yet been built. A central free space is surrounded by a portico off which open a series of thirty-eight narrow, deep rooms. The building is severely practical in design, but has the merits of effective simplicity and is impressive in scale. The walls are of reticulate with a subsidiary use of brick, suggesting a date in the first half of the century.

Many towns in Italy display in their buildings the confidence and prosperity of the early Empire, but none felt the benefits of the new régime more continuously than Ostia. Even the weakest emperors knew the fundamental importance of a regular and adequate flow of corn to Rome. In the Republic it was not easy to pin down responsibility for a corn shortage, nor was the system of administration adjusted to deal with such problems. The emperors knew that in the last resort they were responsible, and Augustus found that remote control was inadequate. When crisis threatened in 22 B.C., he himself took over the *cura annonae*[2] and it was to the Ostian quaestorship that his step-son Tiberius was sent as the first important stage in his public career.[3] A more permanent solution was found towards the end of his life, when a special department was established under a *praefectus annonae* to ensure continuously that supply met demand. Augustus laid the foundations of an efficient administration from which Ostia directly benefited.

---

[1] *Topografia*, tav. ix; below, Pl. xxxix *a*.
[2] *Res gestae*, 5.   [3] Vell. Pat. ii. 94. 3.

E

During the Republic Ostia had grown accustomed to seeing the departure and return of governors of western provinces and Cato, returning from Cyprus,[1] was probably not the only distinguished senator to sail back from the east up the Tiber. But it is doubtful whether Ostia had seen much of Roman consuls in the Republic; imperial visits in the Empire became a commonplace and inscriptions record a long series of honours paid to emperors and their families.

Augustus must have used the harbour more than once in his travels, and it is possibly for this reason that one of his praetorian cohorts was stationed in the town.[2] Three Ostian inscriptions and a stamped tile record the sixth praetorian cohort and one of its men was honoured with a public funeral for his service in fighting a fire.[3] Perhaps the principal function of the praetorians, apart from a display of discipline if trouble broke out in the docks, was to do the work later assigned to a detachment of the regular fire service, the *vigiles*. When the praetorians were concentrated in Rome soon after Augustus' death their absence was felt. Seneca records that 'under Tiberius when a light had appeared in the sky the cohorts rushed to the help of the colony of Ostia, thinking that it was on fire'.[4]

Carcopino has suggested that there is a more important reflection of Augustus' concern for Ostia in Virgil's *Aeneid*.[5] He believes that Virgil chose the mouth of the Tiber as the setting for Aeneas' new Troy, against the general current of tradition, in order to popularize Augustan policy. Caesar had contemplated a new harbour at Ostia; Carcopino believes that Augustus revived the project, began the work, but abandoned it on the death of Agrippa. It is possible, though unlikely, that Augustus influenced the form of the legend that Virgil adopted. It is not impossible that Augustus gave some thought to Caesar's plans; but it is virtually certain that he did not begin the work. If Virgil intended to glorify an imperial harbour, projected or begun, he has left his intentions singularly obscure.[6]

Tiberius had started his political apprenticeship by serving at Ostia as quaestor, and it was from Ostia that he left for Rhodes,[7] an occasion no doubt of much muttering and gossip in Ostian streets. A more

---

[1] Plut. *Cato minor* 39. 1–2.

[2] Suet. *Aug.* 82. 1: 'Si quo pervenire mari posset, potius navigabat.' But Ostia might have been chosen merely because of its nearness to Rome: Suet. *Aug.* 49. 2: 'reliquas (cohortes) in hiberna et aestiva circa finitima oppida dimittere assuerat'.

[3] 215. 223, S 4494, 4495.   [4] Seneca, *Nat. Quaest.* i. 15. 5.

[5] Carcopino, 725–54.   [6] See also Appendix II, p. 483.   [7] Suet. *Tib.* 10. 2.

solemn occasion was the reception of the body of Lucius Caesar, Augustus' younger grandson, who died at Massilia in A.D. 2. The buildings were dressed in mourning and the Ostian magistrates carried the body through the town[1]. Similar scenes were repeated when Gaius, immediately on Tiberius' death, brought back the ashes of his mother and brothers with great ceremony.[2] On one occasion, however, Ostia acted too soon. A slave of Agrippa Postumus had intended, when Augustus died, to rescue his master from his island prison and challenge the succession of Tiberius. Bad weather and the prompt murder of Agrippa forestalled him. Instead he lay low for some time until his beard and hair had grown appropriately and then began to impersonate Agrippa. 'The rumour that Agrippa had been preserved by the grace of the gods spread through Italy, and was believed at Rome.'[3] At Ostia a huge crowd greeted him when he arrived. The town council must have felt very embarrassed when the adventurer was quickly exposed at Rome.

They had perhaps been even more disturbed in 23 B.C. when Fannius Caepio and Varro Murena conspired against Augustus. Both men were condemned in the courts, but Fannius escaped from Rome. A slave carried him in a chest to the Tiber where a boat took him down river. From Ostia he made his way by night to his father's Laurentine villa. He attempted to escape by sea, but was wrecked, and finally put to death at Naples.[4] This was the most serious crisis that Augustus had had to face since the Civil Wars. Fannius was probably well known to Ostians; the events of 23 may well have puzzled them.

The close association of the emperors with Ostia may have led to the establishment of an imperial residence in the town. An Ostian palace is clearly attested later under Commodus and is perhaps to be identified with a large and richly furnished building in the west of the town by the river, which Visconti partly excavated in the middle of last century. This building dates only from the reign of Antoninus Pius and the earlier history of the site is unknown, but there were already imperial freedmen and slaves at Ostia in the Julio-Claudian period. Under Augustus, C. Iulius Pothus, freedman of Nymphodotus, probably an imperial freedman, joined with his patron in restoring the Macellum; he became an *Augustalis* at Ostia and set up a tablet in honour of

---

[1] *Fasti*, A.D. 2: 'hominu[m plus —] | inta millia can[delis ardentibus] | obviam processe[runt. magistratus] | Ostiensium pulla[ti corpus tulerunt,] oppidum fuit orn[atum—].'
[2] Suet. *Cal.* 15. 1.   [3] Tac. *Ann.* ii. 40. 1.
[4] Macrobius i. 11. 21. For the conspiracy, R. Syme, *The Roman Revolution*, 331.

Drusus, son of Tiberius.[1] The handsome tomb of one of his freedmen, C. Iulius Amethystus, survives outside the Porta Laurentina, and it was used by imperial freedmen and slaves. Four slaves born in the imperial service, *vernae Caesaris*, are recorded in the tomb;[2] they were probably born and brought up in Ostia.

By the early Empire Ostia had grown into a substantial town that had long outlived its primitive function of defence. Meanwhile changes even greater had come over the area to the south. The coastline from the Tiber mouth to Antium forms a natural unity. On and behind this coastline had once stood powerful cities. At the southern end Antium had for long challenged Rome. Some six miles to the north, standing back from the coast, stood Ardea, spreading below her natural acropolis over a large plateau, defended by ravines and, on the landward side, where natural defences failed, by a huge rampart of earth; a strong, populous, and thriving centre in the sixth and fifth centuries, importing Greek wares and farming a large territory. Some distance farther to the north on high ground overlooking the sea was Laurentum, commanding the coastal territory to the Tiber's mouth;[3] later, but before Rome had advanced to this coastline, Lavinium grew up, spreading from a restricted acropolis over an ample table-land. Beside these cities fourth-century Ostia was but a village.

By the end of the Republic Ostia had eclipsed them all. Antium had been reduced by Rome in the middle of the fourth century, and submitted to a Roman colony. At first the two communities existed side by side; later they amalgamated, but Antium steadily declined until she developed a new livelihood as a favourite seaside resort for the wealthy. The emperor Nero had a magnificent villa here, but the veterans whom he settled in the town could not or would not make a living from the land.[4] Ardea was shrinking back within her acropolis; the neighbourhood had become marshy and unhealthy:

> locus Ardea quondam
> dictus avis, et nunc magnum manet Ardea nomen,
> sed fortuna fuit.[5]

---

[1] Bloch, 67; S 5322.   [2] Paschetto, 472; inscriptions, 482–9; plan, p. 458, Fig. 32.
[3] The independent existence of Laurentum is controversial. I accept in general the arguments of G. Bendz, *Opuscula Archaeologica*, i (1934) 46–63, and of B. Tilly, *Virgil's Latium*, 83–102. Much of the evidence is ambiguous, but Strabo (229 and 232) seems to have no doubt. The arguments for identifying the city of the Laurentines with Lavinium are most fully developed by Carcopino, 171–274.
[4] Tac. *Ann.* xiv. 27. 3.   [5] Virg. *Aen.* vii. 411.

Laurentum was almost deserted; Lavinium, preserved primarily for her
religious associations, was much reduced in size and wealth, and her
cult of Venus, common to the Latins, was administered from Ardea.
'The Samnites', Strabo tells us, 'sacked these regions and there remain
only the remnants of cities; but they have won fame through the passage
of Aeneas and the cults which are said to have been handed down from
those days.'[1]

In the religious revival of the Augustan age these old centres received
new respect because of the antiquity of their cults, and Virgil in the
later books of his *Aeneid* recalled their greatness; but they belonged to
the past. Land that had once supported large populations was now given
over mainly to the villas of the wealthy and to grazing. It is probable
that villas began to develop in this coastal area after the second Punic
War; by the end of the Republic it was becoming increasingly popular,
for the combination of sea and woodland provided an attractive setting
for the nobility. Though the Romans were not at home on the sea, they
enjoyed looking at it, and the boars and deer among the oak and pine
provided good hunting. The bay of Naples was more notorious for the
refinements of living, but the Laurentine villa of Hortensius could
probably compare with the extravagances of Baiae. By his villa
Hortensius had enclosed some thirty acres of woodland in which he
built a high pavilion where he dined his friends. At the note of a
trumpet 'such a crowd of deer, boars and other animals came running
up that the sight was as attractive as a hunting display in the Circus
Maximus'.[2] The emperors followed the nobility and surpassed them.
Where the coastal fort of Tor Paterno was much later built, Augustus
had his Laurentine villa, which in due course passed to Claudius.
Hortensius had enclosed a reserve for deer and boar: Claudius kept
elephants in his grounds.[3]

The land north of the Tiber from Ostia had less romantic associations
and a more colourless later history. Caere near the coast, some twenty
miles to the north, and Veii farther inland had once controlled this
area. Both were broken early by Rome and were no longer important
settlements. The coastline was taken under Rome's direct control and,
in 247 and 245, colonies were settled at Alsium and Fregenae.[4] These

---

[1] Strabo, 232.   [2] Varro, *RR* iii. 13. 2.
[3] *CIL* vi. 8583, a Claudian freedman 'procurator(i) Laurento ad elephantos'; cf. Juv.
xii. 102–7. Did some of these elephants go to Britain (Dio lx. 21. 2)?
[4] Vell. Pat. i. 14. 8.

colonies remained important while the coast was vulnerable. When Carthage's power was destroyed they could expect to become little more than residential villages.

But all was not well with Ostia. When Egypt was annexed after the battle of Actium, the Alexandrian corn ships did not come to the Tiber.[1] Augustus knew the value of Egypt. He hoped that by expanding corn production in the Delta he could eliminate the recurring corn crises that had increased political instability at Rome when rival dynasts were competing for power. In the Republic Rome had relied primarily on Sicily and the western provinces; Egypt's contribution was probably unimportant.[2] Augustus set the army in Egypt to revitalize the long-neglected irrigation system. Before he died, if we can believe a late authority, 20 million modii, more than six times the tithe from Sicily, had been added to Rome's annual supply.[3]

But the Alexandrian corn fleet ended its journey at Puteoli and not at Ostia. The river harbour was probably already dangerously over-crowded. More important, large ships could not enter the river mouth without transferring part of their cargoes to tenders at sea. The Alexandrian corn transports were among the largest merchantmen afloat; the risk could not be taken, and they unloaded their cargoes at Puteoli, whose excellent harbour facilities were already well known to Alexandrian traders. New granaries must have been built to store the Egyptian corn until it could be moved to Rome. It is possible that some of this corn was carried by mules along the Via Appia. It is more likely that it was reloaded into smaller vessels to complete the journey by water.

[1] p. 56.   [2] See *Note C*, p. 472.   [3] Aurelius Victor, *Epit.* 1.

4

THE IMPERIAL HARBOURS AND PROSPERITY

THE RIVER HARBOUR

IN spite of the prosperity of Ostia in the late Republic and early Empire, the river harbour was no longer proving adequate to meet the needs of Rome. The increase in the size of merchantmen and in the volume of imports emphasized a problem which had been developing for a long time. The sand bar at the river mouth was becoming increasingly dangerous. Nor were the sea approaches satisfactory. To the south there was no good harbour between Gaieta and the Tiber; similarly the coast to the north was harbourless below Portus Herculis by Cosa.[1] Until these weaknesses were remedied Rome's shipping faced serious risks.

We have two descriptions of the harbour at the river's mouth. Dionysius of Halicarnassus, writing at the close of the first century B.C., gives the more favourable picture:[2]

The river widens considerably as it reaches the sea and forms large bays, like the best sea harbours. And, most surprising of all, it is not cut off from its mouth by a barrier of sea sand, which is the fate even of many large rivers. It does not wander into changing marshes and swamps, thereby exhausting itself before its stream reaches the sea, but it is always navigable and flows into the sea through a single natural mouth, driving back (with the force of its current) the waves of the sea, though the wind frequently blows from the west and can be dangerous. Ships with oars, however large, and merchantmen with sails of up to 3,000 (amphorae)[3] capacity enter the mouth itself

---

[1] Pliny, *Ep.* vi. 31. 17, emphasizing the value of Trajan's new harbour at Centumcellae: 'nam per longissimum spatium litus importuosum hoc receptaculo utetur'; Dio xlviii. 49. 5, referring to the west coast during Octavian's struggle against Sextus Pompeius: 'ἀλίμενα γὰρ καὶ ἔτι τότε τὰ πλείω τῆς ἠπείρου ταύτης ἦν', implying the contrast with his own day.

[2] Dion. Hal. iii. 44.

[3] μεχρὶ τρισχιλίων: the unit is not specified; cf. Dio lvi. 27. 3 (restrictions on exiles): 'μήτε πλοῖα πλείω φορτικοῦ τε ἑνὸς χιλιοφόρου.' Volume was normally expressed in amphorae. 3,000 amphorae = 3,000 talents = 9,000 modii = *c.* 78 tons (capacity).

and row or are towed up to Rome; but larger ships ride at anchor outside
the mouth and unload and reload with the help of river vessels.

His younger contemporary Strabo emphasizes the disadvantages:[1]

Ostia is harbourless on account of the silting up which is caused by the
Tiber, since the river is fed by numerous small streams. Now although it
means danger for the merchant ships to anchor far out in the surge, still the
prospect of gain prevails; and in fact the plentiful supply of tenders which
receive the cargoes and bring back others in exchange makes it possible for
the ships to sail away quickly before they touch the river, or else, after being
partly relieved of their cargoes, they sail into the Tiber and run inland as far
as Rome.

There is no real contradiction between these two accounts. The
river mouth was navigable for ordinary small trading vessels, but large
merchantmen and especially the big corn transports had to ride out at
sea. The swift-flowing Tiber sweeps down large quantities of silt as it
rushes to the coast, and the channel was becoming difficult for ships
with a deep draught. There is already a hint of trouble in Ovid's story
of the arrival of the Great Mother in the crisis of the struggle with
Hannibal. There had been a long drought and the ship which carried
the sacred image grounded on the river mud:

> sicca diu fuerat tellus, sitis usserat herbas:
>   sedit limoso pressa carina vado.
> quisquis adest operi, plus quam pro parte laborat,
>   adiuvat et fortis voce sonante manus.
> illa velut medio stabilis sedet insula ponto.[2]

Silting was not the only problem. The river was only some 100
metres wide as it flowed past Ostia. Small merchantmen had ample
space for manœuvre, but, when the volume of shipping increased in
the late Republic, it must have become increasingly difficult to handle
the larger vessels, especially when the corn harvest arrived from overseas. The river harbour was too restricted for the needs of imperial
Rome.

The growing inadequacy of Rome's natural port was, like many
similar problems of a pressing nature, ignored in the political struggles
of the late Republic. But when a strong personal government emerged
from the Civil Wars, public works again claimed the attention due to

---

[1] Strabo, 231–2.   [2] Ovid, *Fasti*, iv. 299.

them. Caesar had been the first to think seriously of building a new harbour, and his plans are described in some detail by Plutarch:

In the midst of the Parthian expedition he was preparing to cut through the isthmus of Corinth, and had put Anienus in charge of the work. He also proposed to divert the Tiber immediately below Rome by a deep canal which was to run round to the Circaean promontory and be led into the sea at Terracina. By this means he would provide a safe and easy passage for traders bound for Rome. In addition he proposed to drain the marshes by Pometia and Setia and so provide productive land for thousands of men. In the sea nearest Rome he intended to enclose the sea by building moles, and to dredge the hidden shoals off the coast of Ostia, which were dangerous. So he would provide harbours and anchorages to match the great volume of shipping. These schemes were being prepared.[1]

With the draining of the Pomptine marshes which would be facilitated by the new canal we are not concerned. The canal, an ambitious project, was to be revived in a different form by Nero. It would have cut out the dangers of part of the west coast passage and, had it been wide and deep enough, would have enabled the largest merchantmen to dock at Rome. The improvements proposed at Ostia are not an alternative but a complement. The canal was intended primarily for shipping from Sicily and the east, perhaps also from Africa; it would not have been used by traders coming from Gaul, Spain, and Sardinia. What exactly Caesar proposed to do at Ostia is not clear from Plutarch's words. Literally interpreted they should mean that Caesar intended to dredge the foreshore near the Tiber's mouth and to provide a series of harbours enclosed by moles. It is possible that Caesar's intention was to provide a series of sheltered anchorages along the coast near the river mouth where ships could lie until conditions were favourable for their entry into the river. But, though this seems to be the literal interpretation of Plutarch, it is not convincing. Suetonius allows a less complicated solution. He speaks of 'portum Ostiensem . . . a Divo Iulio saepius destinatum ac propter difficultatem omissum'.[2] The natural interpretation is a single new harbour, anticipating that of Claudius. Whatever the precise nature of his schemes Caesar had a shrewd insight into the nature of the problem and realized that radical measures and not mere

---

[1] Plut. *Caes.* 58. 10: τῇ δ' ἔγγιστα τῆς Ῥώμης θαλάσσῃ κλεῖθρα διὰ χωμάτων ἐπαγαγών, καὶ τὰ τυφλὰ καὶ δύσορμα τῆς Ὠστιανῆς ἠϊόνος ἀνακαθηράμενος, λιμένας ἐμποιήσασθαι καὶ ναύλοχα πρὸς τοσαύτην ἀξιόπιστα ναυτιλίαν.

[2] Suet. *Claud.* 20. 1.

palliatives were needed. As in so many of his social and economic conceptions he anticipated the work and plans of later emperors.

Augustus was by temperament more cautious and, unlike Caesar, he determined to build the new order securely before tackling public works that could wait. His large-scale building in Rome was essential to his social policy; for the corn supply he was content to provide the basis of a more effective administration. When his main tasks were done he was getting old, and his own financial resources and those of the state were strained. His successor Tiberius was not the man to initiate bold and expensive schemes; he concentrated on financial consolidation. It was left to Claudius to begin the work.

THE CLAUDIAN HARBOUR

The project of Caesar may have played a part in influencing Claudius,[1] but more compelling was the threat of famine when he succeeded Gaius. According to Seneca there was only eight days' corn in reserve;[2] Claudius realized that the satisfaction of the mob at Rome was essential to his security. The immediate crisis could perhaps have been met by emergency measures, but Claudius took a long-term view. It was dangerous for the corn transports to ride at sea off the river mouth even in the summer; in winter it was impossible. Dio emphasizes the need for maintaining imports through the winter if necessary and there is no reason to discredit his emphasis.[3] Winter sailing was not popular, but if summer shipments proved inadequate to meet Rome's needs it was essential that some corn ships at least should continue in service when the normal sailing season was closed. This was particularly important if the ships available were barely adequate to carry the quantities needed, and Claudius' further action shows that there was indeed a shortage of transport. He offered incentives to shipowners who maintained their ships in the service of the corn supply, and by guaranteeing state insurance against losses by storm he removed one of the main deterrents to winter sailing.[4]

The building of a new harbour at Ostia was a considerably more difficult undertaking than the draining of the Fucine lake or the building of an aqueduct; and the proposal seems to have met with opposition from experts and amateurs. Dio reports that the architects tried to dissuade the emperor by exaggerating the expenditure that would be

---

[1] Suet. *Claud.* 20. 1.   [2] Sen. *De brev. vit.* 18. 5; cf. Orosius vii. 6. 17.
[3] Dio lx. 11. 3.   [4] Suet. *Claud.* 18. 2; Gaius, *Inst.* i. 32 c.

necessary,[1] and the discussion found its way into the textbooks. Quintilian cites as a typical example of a *coniectura*: 'an portus fieri Ostiae possit';[2] and in his manual of oratory there seems to be a hint of amateur interference: 'when the building of a harbour at Ostia was debated it was not for the orator to give his opinion, it was the calculation of the architect that was needed'.[3]

Claudius overrode the opposition and in A.D. 42 work was begun on a completely new harbour some two miles north of the Tiber. Two curving moles were built out into the sea, and between them an island was formed by the sinking of the huge merchantman which Gaius had used to transport from Egypt the obelisk that was erected in the circus on the Vatican hill.[4] It had taken in ballast 120,000 bushels of lentils and was large enough to serve as the foundation of a four-storied lighthouse:

> tandem intrat positas inclusa per aequora moles
> Tyrrhenhamque pharon porrectaque bracchia rursum
> quae pelago occurrunt medio longeque relinquunt
> Italiam.[5]

The building of the harbour was accompanied by a closer centralization of the corn administration under imperial control. The senatorial quaestor was withdrawn from Ostia and replaced by a procurator responsible to the *praefectus annonae*.[6]

The cutting of an outlet to drain the Fucine lake required, according to Suetonius, the labour of 30,000 men for eleven years;[7] the work involved in completing the Ostian harbour and its ancillary services was more extensive and more difficult. Considerable progress had already been made by 46, for a monumental inscription of that year which can still be seen near the site of the Claudian harbour records the cutting by Claudius of canals from the Tiber to the sea, to connect his new harbour directly with Rome and, at the same time, by providing a secondary outlet for the river, to save Rome from flood.[8] By 62 at the latest, when Tacitus records the loss of 200 vessels within the moles, the harbour must have been in regular use.[9] But it was not until 64 that a commemorative coinage was issued from the mints of Rome and Lugdunum depicting the new harbour.[10] It is possible that these coins

[1] Dio ix. 11. 3.   [2] Quint. *De inst. or.* iii. 8. 16.   [3] Ibid. ii. 21. 18.
[4] The relation of the lighthouse to the left mole is disputed: p. 155.
[5] Juv. xii. 75–78.   [6] Suet. *Claud.* 24. 2; Dio lx. 24. 3 (A.D. 44).
[7] Suet. *Claud.* 20. 2.   [8] 85.   [9] Tac. *Ann.* xv. 18. 3.
[10] C. H. V. Sutherland, *Coinage in Roman Imperial Policy*, 168.

commemorated the important part played by the harbour in saving
Rome from famine after the great fire; it is much more likely that they
mark the formal completion of the work. We infer that the moles and
lighthouse were built and that the harbour was already in use before
Claudius died, but that work continued on the harbour buildings for
the first ten years of Nero's rule.[1] The coins give the official title of the
new harbour, 'portus Augusti Ostiensis';[2] *portus Claudius* would have
been a fairer name.

It is generally assumed that Claudius hoped, by providing a larger
and safer harbour at Ostia, to make Rome independent of Puteoli. If
this was his intention it was not realized. Seneca, in a letter written
between 63 and 65, describes the scene of general excitement on the
sea front at Puteoli when the Alexandrian corn fleet is signalled.[3] He
implies that this is the end of their voyage, and that it is a regular event
in the town's life. Similarly when Statius' friend, Maecius Celer, sets
out for his legionary command in the east he sails on an Alexandrian
corn ship from Puteoli and not from Ostia.[4] St. Paul, appealing as a
Roman citizen to the emperor, lands at Puteoli,[5] as does Titus returning
to his Jewish triumph.[6] Mucianus reported that he had seen elephants
walking backwards down the gangway from their ship at Puteoli
because they were terrified of the distance from the shore;[7] the elephants
were probably bound for Rome. The evidence of Pliny the elder,
writing under Vespasian, points the same way. In recording fast sailing
times he quotes voyages from Spain, Gaul, and Africa to Ostia; Alexandria is linked with Puteoli.[8]

The continued attention paid by emperors to Puteoli confirms the
impression drawn from these scattered sources. Claudius sent an urban
cohort to Puteoli as well as to Ostia to act as a fire service;[9] the reason is

---

[1] Since no bronze coinage was issued under Nero until 64, the harbour might
have been completed earlier in the reign. See Addenda.

[2] The harbour may not have been called *portus Augusti* until its completion under
Nero. A Claudian procurator, in an inscription which should give the official title, is
proc. portus Ostiesis, 163. On Neronian coins roughly contemporary with the harbour
issues attention is drawn to the corn supply with the legend *Annona Augusti Ceres
s.c.* (*BMC Emp.* Nero, 126–9).

[3] Sen. *Ep.* 77.   [4] Statius, *Silvae*, iii. 2. 21–24.   [5] Acts xxviii. 13.

[6] Suet. *Tit.* 5. 3. An interesting exception is the arrival at Ostia rather than Puteoli of
Alexandrian envoys bound for Rome in the early Julio-Claudian period, H. A. Musurillo,
The Acts of the Pagan Martyrs, iii, p. 13, l. 4 (*P. bibl. univ. Giss.* 46). This, however, is not
a contemporary record and may reflect later conditions.

[7] Pliny, *NH* viii. 6.   [8] Pliny, *NH* xix. 3–4.   [9] Suet. *Claud.* 25. 2.

surely that Roman corn from Egypt was stored in the town. Domitian's rebuilding of the branch road that left the Via Appia near Sinuessa and rejoined it at Puteoli, cutting out the detour through Capua, implies that speed of travel between Puteoli and Rome was still important.[1]

Claudius was not intending to divert shipping from Puteoli; his main concern was to provide security for the corn from Africa, Sicily, Sardinia, and the western provinces. There remained the problem of Egyptian supplies. The emperor Gaius is praised by Josephus for beginning the enlargement of the harbour at Rhegium for the benefit of the Alexandrian corn fleet;[2] Claudius presumably completed the work. It provided shelter at a dangerous point on the voyage. But safe arrival at Puteoli was not the end of the matter. The Egyptian corn stored in Puteolan granaries had to be moved to Rome either by road or by sea. The quantity involved would have made land transport, by mule or wagon, extremely uneconomic; the sea route along the west coast, poorly provided with harbours, was dangerous.[3]

This problem Nero hoped to solve when he revived a plan that Caesar had first formulated. Caesar had intended a canal from Rome to Terracina; Nero's engineers designed a route from Lake Avernus to Ostia, and it may be significant that work was begun in 64, the year in which the harbour commemorative coinage suggests that work on the Ostian harbour was completed. Tacitus hardly takes the project seriously.[4] The object of Nero's architects was 'to fool away the resources of an emperor'; to him it was a scheme as extravagant and egoistic as the building of the Golden House. Suetonius is no more favourable.[5] He links it with Nero's personal extravagance; like the Golden House and the pleasure pool stretching from Misenum to Avernus it is mad expenditure, 'impendiorum furor'.

But, even if the scheme had not been thoroughly and practically prepared, there was a serious purpose behind it.[6] Caesar had thought some such scheme worth while, and in such matters Caesar was neither a fool nor a dreamer. Nero's projected canal, like Caesar's, would cut out part of the stormy passage up the west coast of Italy and bring the

---

[1] Statius, *Silvae*, iv. 3. Domitian commemorated by Puteoli, *AE* 1941, 73.

[2] Jos. *Ant.* xix. 205.

[3] Tac. *Ann.* xv. 46. 3, describes the loss of a large part of the Misenum fleet in a storm on its way from Formiae to Campania.

[4] Tac. *Ann.* xv. 42.   [5] Suet. *Nero*, 31. 3.

[6] For a more serious estimate of Nero's canal, B. W. Henderson, *The Life and Principate of the Emperor Nero*, 247.

corn along a sheltered waterway to Ostia and so to Rome by river or by a further canal. At the same time it would contribute effectively to the draining of the coastal marshes, an important problem created by the neglect of the Republic.

Tacitus, ignoring the motive, has also exaggerated and misrepresented the difficulties. He pictures the canal passing through a waterless waste until it came to the Pomptine marshes; but there is little doubt that the engineers intended to make use of the numerous coastal lagoons, and the canal could also have been fed from the Volturnus, the Liris, and other small rivers that flowed into the sea along its route. In this respect it presented less difficulty than Caesar's project. Nor were the hills an impassable obstacle. Agrippa had shown that the crater of Avernus could be successfully pierced, and the only other high ground in the way was the promontory of Caieta and the hills above Terracina. Indeed work was begun at several points and traces of 'the scheme that came to nothing' could still be seen when Tacitus wrote: Pliny the elder even attributed to it the main responsibility for the decline in the famous Caecuban wine.[1] But before long it was abandoned. The work may have proved more difficult, especially near Terracina, than was expected. Nero may have become discouraged by the increasing difficulties of the political situation.

TRAJAN'S POLICY

The scheme for a southern inland waterway to the Tiber, envisaged by Caesar and Nero, was never revived; a different solution of the problem was found by Trajan. Though this emperor's interests and abilities were primarily those of a soldier, he showed also a keen and intelligent interest in the agricultural and commercial prosperity of Italy. At Ostia he excavated a large land-locked inner basin of hexagonal form behind the Claudian harbour:

> sed trunca puppe magister
> interiora petit Baianae pervia cumbae
> tuti stagna sinus, gaudent ibi vertice raso
> garrula securi narrare pericula nautae.[2]

The fierce storm of 62 which had wrecked 200 ships within the Claudian moles had emphasized the danger of anchoring in mid-harbour; shelter could always be secured in the lee of one of the moles, but a sudden gale

---

[1] Pliny, *NH* xiv. 61.   [2] Juv. xii. 79–82.

would quickly whip up the wide expanse of shallow water. In 62 the harbour was probably particularly crowded, and the ships were taken by surprise. The new basin offered complete security and even the largest corn transports could now anchor in safety.

Trajan's work at Ostia had wider consequences. The increased harbour area and the security of the inner basin made it possible to bring the large merchantmen of the Alexandrian corn fleet, which had hitherto docked at Puteoli, to Ostia. The earliest specific evidence that their Italian headquarters had been transferred comes from the end of the second century;[1] but it is probable that the change of policy followed directly the completion of the new basin and that it was in fact one of Trajan's main motives in undertaking the work. Henceforward Ostia becomes the main reception port for merchantmen from the east as well as from the west.

The new Ostian harbour should be seen as the central feature of a comprehensive plan to set the maintenance of Rome on a more secure and economic basis. The dangers of the west coast passage from the south required points of shelter on the route. Nero had already built an artificial harbour at Antium;[2] it was probably Trajan who added a new harbour at Terracina.[3] To the north of the Tiber there was no good harbour between Cosa and Ostia; Trajan built a new harbour at Centumcellae.[4] This new harbour followed the Ostian model on a much reduced scale, having an inner basin entered from the main harbour, which was protected by moles and an island which was deliberately built as a breakwater on the seaward side of the entrance.[5] The new harbour at Centumcellae had a double purpose. It provided safe shelter for ships bound for Ostia or returning from Ostia in bad weather and served as an auxiliary port for goods dispatched from Gaul and Spain to Rome. The increase in shipping during the early second

---

[1] *IG* xiv. 918, a statue base in honour of Commodus, set up by οἱ ναύκληροι τοῦ πορευτικοῦ Ἀλεξανδρείνου στόλου. Probable evidence under Antoninus Pius, Pl. XVIII *d*, description.　　　　　　　　　　　　　　　　　　　　[2] Suet. *Nero*, 9.

[3] Lugli, *Forma Italiae, Regio I*, i. 126. There is no specific evidence that Trajan was responsible for the harbour, but it was certainly Trajan's engineers who cut through Pesco Montano to lead the Via Appia from the harbour along the coast. Lugli also interprets (p. 128) a relief, now in the National Museum, as illustrating Trajan supervising the construction. The genuineness of the relief, however, is with good reason disputed, W. H. Gross, 'Römisches Relief aus Terracina', *Arch. Anz.* 53 (1938) 148.

[4] Pliny, *Ep.* vi. 31. 15–17.

[5] S. Bastianelli, *Centumcellae, Castrum Novum* (Italia romana; municipi e colonie, ser. 1, vol. 14, 1954).

century would have overcrowded even the enlarged Ostian harbour at peak periods; Centumcellae, only thirty-five miles distant by the Via Aurelia from Rome, gave useful relief. Meanwhile in Rome itself the river embankment of the docks below the Aventine was rebuilt; Trajan was almost certainly responsible.[1]

By attracting eastern shipping to Ostia the building of Trajan's harbour marked a decisive stage in the decline of Puteoli's importance and prosperity. A letter addressed to the senate of Tyre on 23 July A.D. 174 by the Tyrian traders at Puteoli gives a lively illustration of the change.

By the gods and by the fortune of our lord emperor. As almost all of you know, of all the trading stations at Puteoli, ours, in adornment and size, is superior to the others. In former days the Tyrians living at Puteoli were responsible for its maintenance; they were numerous and rich. But now we are reduced to a small number, and, owing to the expenses that we have to meet for the sacrifices and the worship of our national gods, who have temples here, we have not the necessary resources to pay for the rent of the station, a sum of 100,000 denarii a year; especially now that the expenses of the festival of the sacrifice of bulls has been laid on us. We therefore beg you to be responsible for the payment of the annual rent of 100,000 denarii . . . We also remind you that we receive no subscriptions from ship owners or traders, in contrast to what happens with the station of the sovereign city of Rome. We therefore appeal to you and beg you to take thought of our fate and of the affair.[2]

In the Republic Puteoli had been of first importance to the Tyrian trader, but his ships could now pass on to the imperial harbours, and the main station was transferred to Rome. Similarly in the second century an Egyptian recruit for the fleet bound for headquarters at Rome to report for duty and learn to what unit he was to be attached sails on to Trajan's harbour, where he finds a man to take a letter to his mother. 'I am now writing to you from Portus for I have not yet gone up to Rome and been assigned.' A second letter tells us that he arrived in Rome on the same day.[3]

But though the Alexandrian corn fleet no longer discharged at Puteoli, the storage capacity designed for Egyptian corn was still available and it was sound sense to use it. That Puteoli was still con-

---

[1] G. Gatti, *BC* 64 (1936) 55.
[2] *BGU* 27; Dittenberger, *OGIS* 595; Dubois, *Pouzzoles antique*, 83.
[3] *Michigan Papyri*, viii (Youtie and Winter, 1951) 490, 491.

cerned with Rome's corn supply is clear from inscriptions. The finding
of a dedication to the *genius* of the colony at Rusicade,[1] an important
export centre for African corn, is inconclusive, for the corn exports
implied could have been for local distribution from Puteoli; but
Puteoli's inscriptions include records of two junior officials in the
Roman corn department, a paymaster[2] and a clerk,[3] and the paymaster's
duties covered Ostia as well, *disp(ensator) a fruminto Puteolis et Ostis*;
these men were concerned with Rome's corn. The natural inference is
that Roman corn was still stored at Puteoli. There was a limit to the
storage capacity that could be provided at Ostia, and it was a wise
insurance against widespread fire to distribute Rome's reserves. But a
secondary role in the provisioning of Rome was poor compensation for
the loss of the greater part of Rome's eastern trade. When Ostia was at
the height of her prosperity in the middle of the second century Puteoli
was being supervised by curators imposed by the central government,[4]
a sure indication that the town's economy had lost its buoyancy.

Ostia was now not merely the harbour of the world's largest con-
suming centre, but an important link also in the great trade route from
east to west. During the Republic there was no real unity between the
two halves of Rome's empire. On land there was a large block of un-
conquered territory between Macedonia and Gaul, and when on the sea
Rome successively took over the heritage of Carthage in the west and
of the Hellenistic kingdoms in the east, she made no continuous attempt
to control the Mediterranean effectively. Piracy shadowed the waterways and, apart from Pompey's well-organized campaign, nothing was
done to bring east and west together. To Augustus belongs the credit
of seeing this need and satisfying it. By the incorporation of Noricum,
Rhaetia, and Pannonia as provinces he postponed the danger of a partition of the empire which the Civil War had threatened, and, by laying
down the basis of a permanent naval organization for the policing of
the seas, he increased the volume and widened the limits of trade. There
was now free movement from Syria and Egypt to Gaul and Spain.
Eastern traders settled in Arles and Bordeaux, and penetrated to the
Rhine; the harbour system of Claudius and Trajan, the largest and most
efficient on the west coast of Italy, became of primary importance as
a port of call and possibly of exchange.

---

[1] *CIL* viii. 7959. [2] *CIL* x. 1562.
[3] *CIL* x. 1729: 'Aug(usti) lib(ertus) prox(imus) comm(entariorum) ann(onae).'
[4] *CIL* x. 1814 (A.D. 161); x. 1791 (A.D. 181).

F

The new harbours were connected by canal with the Tiber and so with Rome. The Via Campana had from the early Republic led to the salt-beds. It may have been extended to reach the harbour; but at some time a new road, the Via Portuensis was added.[1] It might be thought that the logical sequel was to develop a new town, transferring the storage capacity of Ostia to the harbour area and providing adequate accommodation for the working population to live near their work. Such a transfer could not have been made immediately, but the deliberate rebuilding of Ostia in the first half of the second century suggests that it was not then contemplated. The council and magistrates of Ostia controlled the site, and the Claudian harbour was not yet *portus Romae*, but *portus Ostiensis*. Ostia remained the centre of the trading guilds and still for a long time housed the greater part of the working population. A number of ferry services provided easy transport across the river and a road must have been laid across the island between river and canal. Trajan's harbour was surrounded with *horrea* but the new storage capacity built in the old town was more than was needed for her own population. Ostian *horrea* still held a reserve for Rome.

OSTIA'S DEVELOPMENT UNDER CLAUDIUS AND NERO

The new harbours brought increasing prosperity to Ostia, but it is more than a generation before clear signs of a dramatic development are seen in the excavated area. That the town benefited, however, from Claudius is highly probable. Certainly none of the early emperors was a more familiar figure in the town. It was from Ostia that he sailed to take the honours of the conquest of Britain[2] and the stiff rebuke to the town for not giving him an adequate reception, which Suetonius records, may mark his return.[3]

Later the building of his harbour probably brought him frequently down the river. Pliny records a picturesque and typically Claudian incident on one of these visits. A whale had been attracted into the harbour by the wreck of a cargo of hides imported from Gaul, and had stuck fast in the shallows. Claudius embarked his praetorians in small boats and directed the attack. Nets were stretched across the harbour

---

[1] For the Via Campana and Via Portuensis, T. Ashby, *The Roman Campagna in Classical Times*, 219. The Via Portuensis, not recorded before the fourth century, cannot be dated. Another road on the right bank remains a mystery, the Via Vitellia, which ran 'from the Janiculum to the sea' (Suet. *Vit.* 1. 3), Ashby, op. cit. 226 f.

[2] Dio lx. 21. 3.   [3] Suet. *Claud.* 38. 1.

entrances to prevent escape and the men hurled their spears. 'We saw one of the boats go down,' says Pliny, 'waterlogged from the spouting of the monster.'[1] It was at Ostia also that Claudius heard of Messalina's dangerous excesses. He was paying a state visit accompanied by his corn-supply prefect, the commander of the praetorian guard, his secretary Narcissus, and his main counsellors. His advisers took the news seriously and Claudius was rushed back along the Via Ostiensis. Vettius Valens, climbing a tree at Rome, saw 'a fierce storm coming from Ostia'.[2]

Claudius stationed at Ostia an urban cohort from Rome to provide a fire service for the granaries and warehouses.[3] The Grandi Horrea probably date from his principate,[4] and the baths that can be seen under the Via dei Vigiles are roughly contemporary.[5] A handsome mosaic depicting winds and provinces from one of the pavements in these baths may reflect the benefits to trade which were to come from the new harbour.[6] But it is doubtful whether new building at Ostia under Claudius was extensive; Ostian labour was probably diverted largely to the construction of the harbour.

Suetonius speaks of Nero's trips down the Tiber as though they were not infrequent,[7] but his principate has left no recognizable mark. It might have been very different if his imaginative ambitions had been tolerated longer. Suetonius records that he had conceived the plan of extending Rome's walls to Ostia and of bringing the sea from Ostia by canal to the old city.[8] This note follows in Suetonius a summary description of Nero's innovations in the rebuilding of Rome after the great fire in 64, and the association is plausible. The scale on which a large part of central Rome was converted into parkland for the Golden House makes the proposal for the inclusion of Ostia within Rome's bounds less incredible. This would have been a very new type of imperial city; but Nero was a very new type of emperor. A canal from Ostia to Rome, however, was a serious project, for the Tiber between Rome and Ostia follows a very winding course and the current is strong. It would have considerably eased the shipment of cargoes from

[1] Pliny, *NH* ix. 14. Cf. Dio lxxii. 4. 6.   [2] Tac. *Ann.* xi. 26. 7 ff.
[3] Suet. *Claud.* 25. 2.   [4] *NS* 1921, 360 (for the date, p. 380).
[5] *NS* 1912, 204; brickstamps, Bloch, *Bolli laterizi*, 219.   [6] p. 448.
[7] Suet. *Nero*, 27. 3: 'quotiens Ostiam Tiberi deflueret aut Baianum sinum praeternavigaret.'
[8] Suet. *Nero*, 16. 1: 'destinarat etiam Ostia tenus moenia promovere atque inde fossa mare veteri urbi inducere.'

the coast, and had a precedent in the canal dug in Narbonese Gaul by Marius' army to avoid the difficulties of the lower Rhône.[1]

The Civil War which accompanied the death of Nero did little harm to Ostia. She was not on the path of invading armies and, though the corn of Africa might have been withheld if Clodius Macer's bid for power had not been quickly stifled, there is not likely to have been any serious interruption in trade. A hoard of coins in Ostia, which was sealed at the very outset of Vespasian's principate, includes rebel issues of 69 from Gaul and Africa which presumably came over in merchant-men.[2] If Vespasian had been able to control the strategy of his sup-porters there would have been a crisis in Ostia, for it was his intention to force surrender by blockade; and Vespasian was at Alexandria from which the Egyptian corn fleet sailed—a good base for the purpose. But Antonius Primus did not wait for instructions, and Italy was won before the double-edged weapon of starvation was tried.

THE REBUILDING OF OSTIA

How much was built at Ostia under the early Flavians we do not know, but Vespasian's financial policy and encouragement of trade and above all his restoration of stability after the quixotic hellenism of Nero and the upheavals of 69 must have profited Ostia; the cult of Vespasian and Titus was long maintained in the colony.[3] Domitian received no such posthumous honours, for his memory was publicly damned by the Roman senate; but Ostia probably had good reason to be grateful to him.

Ostia was so intimately bound up with Rome and so vital to her economy that it is reasonable to see imperial policy in major develop-ments in the city. It was probably under Domitian that the building level was sharply raised in all new construction. Hitherto there had been no drastic change, though, with successive rebuilding, the level had slowly risen. The new buildings were now raised by at least a metre above the old, involving enormous quantities of earth and rubble for the fills. The practice, in such clear contrast with earlier custom, is deliberate policy and is so uniformly applied that it may well have been controlled by statute.[4] The purpose was probably twofold:

---

[1] Strabo, 183; Plut. *Mar.* 15. 3–4.
[2] M. F. Squarciapino, *NS* 1948, 326.
[3] Later *flamines*, 400, S 4664.
[4] Suggested by F. H. Wilson, *BSR* 13 (1935), 53.

to raise the town above flood level, for the Tiber was a dangerous neighbour and the water level may have risen; and to provide adequate foundations for a new type of domestic architecture. To house within an area restricted by cemeteries a population which steadily increased with the increase of trade it was necessary to follow the new architecture of Rome and to expand vertically. The new tall buildings required stronger support and the maturely developed technique of concrete foundations could provide it if the level was raised sufficiently to keep the foundation trenches dry.

This revolution in Ostian architecture is most apparent in the great rebuilding of the first half of the second century, but the evidence suggests that it was under Domitian that the new policy originated. The evidence is not conclusive, for no buildings of the period can be securely dated by inscriptions and the only criterion available is the character of the brickwork. In the second century it becomes easier to date Ostian buildings, for from the last years of Trajan a proportion of bricks were stamped with the consular date. Even in the first century, however, brickstamps, though undated, can be of considerable help, for the development in their form and the dated buildings in which they occur provide a rough chronological sequence. But early brickstamps are rare and their evidence has to be supplemented by a study of the bricks themselves. Since Ostia drew mainly on the brickfields that supplied Rome, buildings at Ostia can be approximately dated by comparison with buildings at Rome, and on the Palatine and elsewhere there is abundance of Domitianic work.

The Domitianic phase in Ostian building is best attested in the area which includes the Baths of Neptune and the Barracks of the Vigiles behind them to the north. This area was completely rebuilt under Hadrian and two streets at least, the Via dei Vigiles and the Via della Palestra, covering buildings of the Julio-Claudian period, involved a change of plan. There are, however, clear traces below the Hadrianic level that drains were laid and new building begun here (but perhaps never completed) before the Hadrianic plan was executed. The brickstamps found in this intermediate phase have been attributed to the end of the first century.[1]

The same approximate date has been assigned to the stamps found by Lanciani in the temple of the Piazzale delle Corporazioni.[2] This temple

---

[1] Bloch, *Bolli laterizi*, 240. Many of the broken bricks used in the concrete of the Hadrianic buildings seem to be Flavian.   [2] *NS* 1881, 113.

was regarded by Calza as an integral part of a general reconstruction of the square contemporary with the rebuilding of the theatre, at the end of the second century.[1] But the brickwork of the temple is very different from that of the theatre, and the thick triangular bricks are very similar to Domitianic bricks from Rome.

The brickwork of this temple is closely paralleled in the 'Curia' where one of the same stamps has been found.[2] The 'Curia' replaces a building, probably of Augustan date, at a much lower level and has been shown to be earlier than the building adjoining it to the west, which has early Hadrianic stamps. Its brickwork is very different from Trajanic work at Ostia and is probably Domitianic.[3] Opposite the Curia is the Basilica, which, from the close similarity of its brickwork, is clearly contemporary. These two public buildings, adjoining the Forum, were richly decorated with marble and considerably enhanced the dignity of the town centre. At scattered points other traces of Domitianic brickwork can be seen. Ostian builders were busy at the end of the first century.

The *damnatio memoriae* by which the Roman senate took belated revenge on Domitian may account for the lack of inscriptions in his honour at Ostia, but a colossal head found in the recent excavations seems to be a portrait.[4] This head had been broken but not defaced and the place of its finding may be significant. It came from a drain near the temple of Hercules, and·had perhaps once been set up in or near the temple; on the Via Appia near Rome Domitian had built a temple to Hercules and the cult statue had carried his own portrait head.[5] There may also be a reflection of Domitian's predilection for Minerva at Ostia. Some 30 metres inside the city from the Porta Romana was discovered a monumental statue of a winged Minerva.[6] The block from which the statue was cut is square dressed at the back and did not therefore stand free. It has been suggested that it is one of a balancing pair of statues which were incorporated in the decoration of the gate. Since it was found some considerable distance away this must remain doubtful, but the fact that it was made from the same Greek marble as the gate suggests that, at the least, it comes from a contemporary monument.

[1] G. Calza, *BC* 43 (1915) 183.   [2] Bloch, *Topografia*, 221 (under ii. 7. 5).
[3] For the date of the 'Curia', see also p. 220.
[4] *Inv.* 446. My attention was drawn to this head by Signora Calza.
[5] Martial ix. 101: 'Appia, quam simili venerandus in Hercule Caesar | consecrat, Ausoniae maxima fama viae.'
[6] *NS* 1910, 229.

The statue, on grounds of style, has been assigned to the late first or early second century;[1] a closer date could not be pressed but the emphasis on the cult of Minerva under Domitian and the very similar Minerva from the Forum of Domitian at Rome which was completed by Nerva favour a Domitianic context.

If this hypothesis is valid the main gate of Ostia will have been restored at this time. The architectural decoration and the letters of the inscription on the attic are consistent with such a date, but both would be equally fitting under Trajan.[2] The rebuilding was carried out in travertine with the main decorative elements in Greek marble; in style it is severe and dignified. It was built at the new higher level. But even if we are right in assigning the beginning of Ostia's rebuilding at the higher level to Domitian's principate, the work of this period was eclipsed by what followed in the first half of the second century.

Under Trajan, Hadrian, and Antoninus Pius, and helped in part by their generosity, Ostia was transformed. The pattern for the new Ostia was provided by experience at Rome, where the great fire of 64 had given the opportunity for the replanning of large areas with wider streets and systematized apartment blocks. But when Rome was rebuilt houses were still normally faced with tufa blocks; second-century Ostia was primarily a city of brick.

Fire-baked brick had by now firmly established its reputation, and had become the standard material for facing walls. It had been tentatively used under Augustus, and a good example of early Tiberian brickwork can still be seen in the outer wall of the praetorian camp at Rome. But brick production was a new industry and developed slowly. For nearly a hundred years at Rome and Ostia after the introduction of the new material *opus reticulatum* was still freely used. At first, while production was limited to comparatively small-scale producers, bricks may have been more expensive; and that may be a reason why, until the middle of Hadrian's principate, reticulate was often used in conjunction with brick. But demand created supply. The big landowners realized the possibilities of the new trade, and developed production wherever they held or could secure suitable clays. By inheritance and confiscation the emperors gradually absorbed this rich source of wealth until brick production became virtually an imperial monopoly and broke down with the collapse of imperial continuity in the third

[1] L. Savignoni, *Ausonia* 5 (1910) 69; E. Strong, *La Scultura Romana*, 132.
[2] Becatti, *Topografia*, 128, prefers a Trajanic date.

century. Though there was a small output of bricks in Ostian territory, most of her soil was too sandy for the purpose and Ostia drew her main supplies from the brickfields that fed Rome.

It is not easy to form a picture of Ostian housing in the Julio-Claudian period, for though clear traces of the houses of the rich can be seen, with atrium and peristyle, there is much less evidence for the middle and lower classes.[1] But it seems likely that Pompeii provides valid material for comparison. The two towns as they are now seen present a sharp contrast; but that is less because they fulfilled different functions and had been subjected to different traditions, than because Pompeii was destroyed before the architectural revolution had transformed Ostia. The houses of the rich in plan and size are closely similar during the early Empire, though their standards of comfort and decoration can no longer be compared: the small atrium houses at Ostia show the same architectural principles employed for humbler homes. And there is little doubt that the more modern type of housing for the common people brought to Pompeii by the Sullan colonists was widespread in Ostia. But, while building was still on or very little above the level of the sand, high buildings were out of the question at Ostia, nor was there need for them until the population problem became acute.

The new brick blocks were three, four, or even five stories high. The street fronts were in most parts of the city reserved for shops, with small mezzanine quarters for the shopkeeper's family above his work. The rest of the block was either divided into self-contained flats or reserved for the letting of rooms singly or in groups; but while the general principles of construction were the same there was considerable variety in their application, which will be described later. These new blocks were not intended merely for the manual workers, but included substantial apartments expensively decorated. Some were restricted in space and provided few amenities; others were liberally laid out around gardens available to all the tenants of the block. The House of the Paintings, which combines shops, flats, and garden, and other similar blocks, brings to life the terms of an Ostian will inscribed on marble, probably towards the middle of the second century:

Iunia D. f. Libertas hortorum et aedificiorum et tabernarum Hilaronianorum Iunianorum ita uti macerie sua propria clusi sunt quae iuris eius in his sunt usum fructumqu(e) dedit concessit libertis libertabusque suis.[2]

[1] Housing is more fully discussed, Ch. 12, p. 235.
[2] G. Calza, *Epigraphica*, 1 (1939) 160.

Junia Libertas bequeathed to her freedmen and freedwomen the use of and income from the gardens, buildings, and shops enclosed by their own boundary wall. This block with shops on the street front and apartments with a common garden had been built as a single unit and should have been a profitable investment.

A few of the large republican atrium houses have survived, but most were destroyed and replaced by the new insulae. Outside the walls space was less restricted and the suburban villas of the period probably showed a considerable advance in size, display, and comfort. One such villa, some 200 yards to the south-west of the Porta Laurentina, has been partially excavated. Its original construction seems to date from the early second century though it was restored and modified in the late Empire. From its ruins came a statue of Perseus and a handsome large fourth-century mosaic in colour of the seasons; it had its own private set of baths.[1] The district stretching south from Ostia was already popular among men of substance in the late Republic; the number of residential villas along the coast probably increased during the second century.[2]

It was in this area, perhaps some five miles from Ostia, that Pliny the younger had his Laurentine villa built, overlooking the sea, with woods behind it. From Tor Paterno a path leads northwards towards Castel Fusano. To the right is woodland; to the left rises a line of bush-covered mounds, the sites of villas, among them Pliny's. Behind them stretch sand dunes, bush, and coarse grass where the sea-shore has receded. Pliny brings the Roman scene to life: 'The villa roofs, now in unbroken line, now scattered, resemble a number of towns and add colour to the coastline with their charming irregularity.'[3] He also speaks of a small village with a few shops and three sets of baths, 'a great convenience if by chance a sudden arrival or some slight delay discourages your own heating system'.[4] This village, which may be identified with the *vicus Augustanorum* known from inscriptions and with the site two miles

---

[1] A brief report in *Arch. Anz.* 49 (1934) 436 and 51 (1936) 460; but the site is only vaguely indicated.

[2] The sites of coastal villas between Ostia and Castel Fusano were raided in the eighteenth century, but no details were published. A brief account, Fea, *Viaggio*, 63.

[3] Pliny, *Ep.* ii. 17. 27. A villa in the Castel Fusano estate has at various times been identified with Pliny's villa, but it is of the wrong date and in the wrong place.

[4] Ibid. 26, but his main supplies came from Ostia: 'suggerunt adfatim ligna proximae silvae; ceteras copias Ostiensis colonia ministrat.' The requirements of the rich villa residents must have helped to keep Ostian shopkeepers and market gardeners cheerful.

north of Tor Paterno which was excavated in the late nineteenth century,[1] benefited from the patronage of wealthy Ostians. M. Cornelius Valerianus Epagathianus, a Roman knight, who was a member of the Ostian council and patron of a boatmen's guild, became one of its quattuorvirs;[2] L. Arrius Vitalianus, who filled the same office in the village, had his tomb built outside the walls of Ostia.[3] P. Aelius Liberalis, an imperial freedman, who was *procurator annonae* at Ostia, was among its patrons.[4]

Within the city the new architecture reflects the rise of a middle class growing rich on the profits of trade. In the early Empire Ostia had still been controlled by a limited aristocracy of comparatively old families that had lived for long in Ostia or come to Ostia from other parts of Italy. As the volume and distribution of trade increased Ostia became increasingly cosmopolitan. Men from all parts of the Mediterranean were attracted to Rome's harbours; even more important was the rapid growth of freedman stock. Slaves who had been given freedom could not themselves hold office, but they could amass the fortune necessary to launch their families on a public career. There is little sign in the governing classes of Ostia of this new stock before the close of the first century; in the second century wealth could open doors previously closed. Descendants of old families still play their part in local government, but the sons and descendants of freedmen are increasingly prominent.

With the rise of the middle class comes a development in the number, size, and wealth of the guilds. The movement began in the association of workers in a common trade, and most of the wealthiest guilds took their titles from the trades most important in the life of the city, the corn merchants, the corn measurers, the men who controlled the various categories of shipping, the builders. But the tendency to form associations developed widely in the second century and their scope was extended to include public slaves, veterans, and burial clubs. In the period of growing prosperity these guilds attracted the patronage of the wealthy, and built guild houses and even temples.

The foundation of Ostia's wealth was trade and the magistrates and, even more, the town council, were drawn increasingly from

---

[1] The excavations of *vicus Augustanorum* have not been published. A passing reference, G. Henzen, *Bull. Inst.* 47 (1875) 3; cf. Carcopino, 183. The site is identified by an inscription, 2045.

[2] 341.   [3] 301.   [4] 2045.

business men and traders of the middle class. But Ostia's sea-shore attracted visitors from Rome and they were normally of a different stamp. Today the electric railway brings Ostia Marina within the reach of all classes. Before the railway was built, the fifteen miles from Rome required a carriage. This the poor could not afford. Young men of quality and distinguished philosophers figure in the only two actual sea-shore scenes that are preserved in literature;[1] they are probably typical. It was not incongruous when Minucius Felix made the setting of his dialogue between Christian and pagan a stroll along the water-front at Ostia.[2]

The new building of the prosperity period provided not only better accommodation for more people, but improved public amenities. Within little more than two generations at least eight new sets of public baths were built, three of them on an impressive scale—the Baths of Neptune, the Forum Baths, which have both been excavated, and a third set south-east of the Porta Marina which has only been partially uncovered. The Forum was enlarged and enhanced by the Basilica and 'Curia' on its western side and the great new Capitolium at its northern end. The sculptors kept pace with the builders and provided statues for public squares as well as for temples and other public buildings.

The growing infusion of foreign stock throughout this period led to the spreading of oriental cults in Ostia. Few traces of them survive from the Republic or early Empire in buildings, inscriptions, or other evidence; in the second century their growth is well attested. Cybele, Isis, and Serapis led the invasion. Mithraism, which eventually eclipsed them all in the number of shrines and devotees, developed strongly only after the middle of the century. But there is little evidence that these new cults exercised any strong influence on the governing class, and architecturally, apart from Cybele, they were comparatively insignificant. The temples that caught the visitor's eye as he wandered through the streets housed the traditional cults that had grown up with the Roman people.

The persistence of these traditional cults is proved beyond question by buildings, inscriptions, and dedications. The most impressive new monument of the age was the early Hadrianic temple dedicated to the Capitoline triad at the north end of the Forum.[3] The temple of Vulcan,

---

[1] Suet. *De rhet.* 1; Aulus Gellius xviii. 1.
[2] Minucius Felix, *Octavius.*   [3] p. 380.

whose cult was at the heart of early Ostian history, was impressively restored under Trajan;[1] and restorations of the second century can be seen in nearly all the temples surviving from the Republic. The Roman praetor still came down to Ostia every year to celebrate the games in honour of Castor and Pollux. It was more than a vague superstition that kept these cults alive.

The new Ostia that was virtually completed by the death of Antoninus Pius was a handsome city. Predominantly it was a city of brick freely declared, for the walls of the insulae were not faced with stucco. Surfaces were relieved by a generous supply of windows, and balconies of varying types; entrances were framed by brick columns or pilasters mounted by pediments that have an attractive Georgian flavour. Though some blocks were developed piecemeal, in most of the rebuilding large areas were planned as units giving an impressive regularity. Long porticoes carried on brick piers lined the most important streets and conferred coherence of design.

In contrast with the severity of the brickwork were the marble façades of temples and the rich decoration of public buildings. For the new prosperity is clearly emphasized in the choice of building materials. Travertine, which seems to have been a luxury under Augustus and was still handled with economy under the Julio-Claudians, is now freely used. Its great strength and durability made it the natural material to be used at points of stress where large tufa blocks had once been used; that is why odd blocks are often found in brick buildings where corners might be worn by passing traffic. But it is also now used in company with brick for purely decorative purposes. The freedom with which it is used is best illustrated by the treatment of thresholds. In the Horrea of Hortensius of the Julio-Claudian period there are at the threshold of every room two blocks of travertine, one at each side of the doorway. The gap between them is filled by brick, a cheaper material; and this was an adequate compromise because it was the sides only that had to carry the weight of the doors. In the second century travertine is normally used throughout, though a few instances of the old economy survive. Similarly travertine is commonly used for the first flight of stairs in the large house blocks. But, apart from the new dominance of brick, the greatest change lies in the widespread use of marble. Under Augustus marble was used in Ostia on a limited scale, and then only Italian marble from the quarries above Luna. Temple walls were still

---

[1] *Fasti*, A.D. 112.

stuccoed, columns were, normally at least, of tufa or brick. The temple of Rome and Augustus, built early in the Julio-Claudian period, marks a considerable advance in its freer use of marble, but it was probably not until the Flavian period that Ostian architects regarded marble as the natural dress of public buildings.

Though Italian marble was still normally used when large surfaces had to be covered, a rich variety from overseas was also now available. We find columns of Porta Santa in the Baths of Neptune, of Cipollino from Euboea in the Forum Baths, grey granite from Egypt and Elba at scattered points. But the Hadrianic Capitolium at the north end of the Forum was richest in the variety of marbles it used. The walls were lined with Luna, large fluted columns of Pavonazetto were used for the porch, the threshold was a solid block of Africano. The floor of the cella was paved with a geometric pattern of variegated marbles, with Giallo Antico from Numidia predominant.[1]

While architects and builders were carrying out their programmes, the craftsmen of the decorative arts were busier than ever before. The painters were the least impressive. Perhaps their best work has disappeared, but enough wall-paintings remain in the apartments of the middle class to judge the general level. It is only rarely that we see an artist at work as in the Insula of the Charioteers. The sculptors did better. Many of the copies and adaptations of Greek originals that were set up in public and private buildings were no doubt bought in Rome or imported from the Greek world, but the portraits of Ostian men and women, most of the sculpture of the cemeteries, and perhaps much else besides came from local workshops. In the series of portrait heads in the Ostian Museum we can feel respect for Ostian sculptors of this period. Nor should the cutters of inscriptions be forgotten. They produced their best work in the Flavian period and in the first half of the second century. They had learnt how to organize the spacing of long texts and in important commissions their letters were neither sophisticated nor careless.

No less impressive in their own field are the mosaic designers. In the apartments of the well-to-do most of the rooms had mosaics on their floors, usually of a geometric pattern: in public buildings, and especially in the baths, there was more scope for figured scenes. The art of the mosaic at Ostia reached its peak during this period, in the ingenious variety of its geometric designs and in the fine vigour of its more

[1] Guattani, *Monumenti inediti per l'anno 1805*, pp. cv–cxi.

ambitious compositions. It is seen at its best in the Frigidarium of the Baths of Neptune, where Neptune rides through his watery kingdom surrounded by Nereids and fanciful creatures in a well-ordered composition that conveys a fine sense of movement.[1]

The growing impressiveness of Ostia is reflected also in the patronage that she attracted. Trajan or Titus (the restoration is uncertain),[2] Hadrian,[3] and probably Lucius Aelius,[4] his adopted son, accepted the title of duovir and the imperial chest contributed handsomely to the rebuilding of the town. The patrons of the town included Roman senators and knights of high rank, and senators and knights became patrons of Ostian guilds. Meanwhile the number of Roman knights from Ostia increased and two families that had long played a leading part in local government, the Fabii and the Egrilii, rose to consular status.[5]

The phase that we have been considering covers three principates. Under Trajan the Ostian builders had first probably concentrated mainly on the new harbour; Trajanic work at Ostia falls largely towards the end of the reign, and is primarily concentrated in the north-west quarter of the city. It is the principate of Hadrian that has left the most abiding mark on Ostia. In 133 he was honoured by the city for having preserved and enhanced it with all indulgence and generosity: 'colonia Ostia conservata et aucta omni indulgentia et liberalitate eius.'[6] Hadrian deserved the tribute.

From this inscription alone it would be dangerous to infer too much, for Hadrian is honoured in somewhat similar terms by a wide range of communities. But Ostian excavation gives a substantial background to the words. At the beginning of his reign a large area between the Forum and the Tiber, comprising mainly warehouses and shops, was completely rebuilt at the new higher level.[7] This area is crowned by the new Capitolium, also built early in the reign, and the building of the Capitolium in turn leads to a transformation of the Forum into a more monumental and coherent public centre. The Capitolium appropriately balanced the temple of Rome and Augustus. The one symbolized the continuity of tradition; the other the benefits of imperial rule. The area between Capitolium and Decumanus was reserved as temple precinct, flanked by its own portico: the Forum to the south of

---

[1] p. 449.   [2] S 4674.   [3] *Fasti*, A.D. 126.
[4] p. 201.   [5] pp. 196–9.   [6] 95.
[7] Carcopino, *Mélanges* 30 (1910) 397; Bloch, *Bolli laterizi*, 87.

the Decumanus was framed on east and west by new porticoes. It is probable though not certain that the large-scale replanning derived from imperial initiative, for this central dock area was no less important to Rome than to Ostia.

There is less doubt about a second large area farther east, which was rebuilt towards the end of the reign.[1] The central buildings here are the Baths of Neptune, and the Barracks of the Vigiles which lay behind them to the north. But the blocks to east and west are an integral part of the same plan. The Barracks of the Vigiles must have been built by imperial authority: Hadrian was also responsible for the Baths of Neptune, promising two million sesterces for the purpose.[2] Amenity and utility were nicely balanced in these two adjacent buildings. The baths were probably the most luxurious that the city had yet enjoyed; the permanent establishment of a detachment of the Roman fire service met an urgent need.

In Augustus' principate the sixth praetorian cohort had been quartered in the town, and the public funeral given to one of the soldiers who died while fighting a fire suggests that they could be used as a fire brigade.[3] When the praetorians were concentrated in Rome by Sejanus in A.D. 23 no attempt was made to replace the Ostian force until Claudius sent down one of his two newly raised urban cohorts 'ad arcendos incendiorum casus'.[4] This cohort moved to Rome in the disturbances of A.D. 69,[5] and it is uncertain what provision if any was made for Ostia under the Flavians. The stamp on a Domitianic pipe which refers in an uncertain context to 'castra' suggests, however, that a contingent from Rome's urban troops had returned to Ostia.[6] Perhaps the significance of the building of the new barracks is Hadrian's decision to send *vigiles*, trained fire-fighters, to replace them.

Hadrian's personal interest in Ostia can also be inferred from the record of the Fasti for 126. This shows that in that year Hadrian held the title of duovir, chief magistrate of the colony, for the second time. To have accepted the title once would have indicated little, for Hadrian, we are told, accepted office in a wide range of towns in Italy; a second year of office is striking confirmation of his concern for Ostia.

---

[1] Ibid. 222.　　　　　　　　　　　　　　　　[2] 98. For the identification, p. 409.

[3] *S* 4494: 'Ostienses locum sepult(urae) dederunt publicoq(ue) funere efferun(dum) decrerunt, quod in incendio restinguendo interit.'

[4] Suet. *Claud.* 25. 2.　　　　　　　　　　　　　[5] Tac. *Hist.* 1. 80.

[6] G. Barbieri, 'Fistoule inedite', *NS* 1953, 153 (n. 4): '[i]mperatoris Domitiani Caesaris Aug. | [—] quae ducunt in castris.'

While the emperor may have been responsible for the two most impressive planning projects of the reign, private building was scarcely less active. In every quarter of the town Hadrianic work can be seen in large blocks of houses, shops, and markets. From this period date the Garden Houses, an ambitious composition of shops, apartments, and gardens, a garden city in miniature, which was probably a private investment.[1]

Under Antoninus Pius the expansion of Ostia continued. The pace was less intensive, but the new buildings include some of the most interesting that have survived. The Horrea Epagathiana et Epaphroditiana anticipate in essentials the Renaissance palace.[2] The Forum Baths, with the curving lines of their southern elevation, strike a new note in Ostian architecture; the 'Imperial Palace' eclipsed all other buildings known to us at Ostia in the quality of its decoration.[3] The title of 'Imperial Palace' was given by Visconti in the middle of last century. When he opened ground on the site he thought he was excavating another set of public baths, for the first rooms to be uncovered included a handsome Frigidarium. As excavation proceeded it became clear that the baths were an integral part of a much larger complex, with two further series of rooms based on spacious courts.

Excavators are notoriously romantic in their attributions and Visconti's title has rarely been taken seriously. But it does not lack evidence and Carcopino was not uncritical in accepting it.[4] The direct evidence is the name of the imperial princess Matidia stamped on a long stretch of water-pipe.[5] This could be either the daughter of Trajan's sister Marciana or her daughter who was given the same name; the latter is more probable since brickstamps suggest that the building dates from Antoninus Pius.[6] The indirect evidence is not negligible. From an inscription it is known that a 'crypta in palatio' was used as a Mithraic shrine.[7] The existence of an imperial establishment at Ostia in the second century is further confirmed by inscriptions which record an imperial slave who was 'vilicus a bybliotheca'[8] and another who was door-keeper, 'ostiarius'.[9]

A further reason for identifying Visconti's building with this establishment is the quality of its mosaics and sculptures and the remarkably

[1] p. 139.
[2] Becatti, *NS* 1940, 32; Calza, *Palladio*, 5 (1941) 19.   [3] Paschetto, 407.
[4] Carcopino, *Mélanges*, 31 (1911) 219.   [5] *CIL* xv. 7737.
[6] Bloch, *Topografia*, 225 f.; cf. Thylander, A 261, a slave of the younger Matidia living in Ostia.   [7] 66.   [8] 196.   [9] 201.

fine workmanship of its walls. The building was maintained in good repair until the late Empire and in every period the rebuilding, whether in brick, block and brick, or tufa blocks, is carefully done and superior to contemporary work in other parts of the town. Judgement should at least be suspended until the site has been cleared again and restudied, and the excavation completed to reveal the full plan of the building.

His biographer records that Pius gave a *lavacrum* to Ostia.[1] This gift may be less impressive than it sounds, for it is probably to be identified with the Baths of Neptune, which were nearly completed when Hadrian died. An inscription, the association of which with these baths is again probable rather than certain, tells us that Pius provided the money needed to complete the work: 'adiecta pecunia quantum amplius desiderabatur item marmoribus ad omnem o[rnatum perfecit]'.[2] The Forum Baths, built in the last years of the reign, may have been the gift to the town of Gavius Maximus, who served Pius for twenty years as praetorian prefect.[3]

In tracing the remarkable expansion of Ostia in the first half of the second century it is easy to give a misleading impression of her size and wealth. In spite of the transformation she was no rival to Alexandria, Carthage, or the great cities of the East. Her area was still little larger than that of Pompeii, considerably smaller than that of the leading towns of Africa, Spain, and Gaul, less than half the size of Lugdunum; though few towns can have been so densely populated. Her temples had grown in number and magnificence, but her baths, Forum, and other public places lacked the monumental spaciousness of a Cyrene or a Lepcis. Ostia still provided very few Roman senators and, though a large number of knights are recorded, none are known to have reached the highest ranks of the service.[4]

Ostia lacked the basic wealth of towns with large and fertile territories such as those of Cisalpine Gaul. Her industries seem to have catered primarily for her own population, and it is doubtful whether her shippers and merchants played any significant part in buying for the Roman market. Wealth was widely spread, but there were probably few spectacular fortunes. Ostia was essentially a middle-class town. Though she retained an individual character and was no mere suburb, her primary function was to provide the harbour services needed to maintain Rome's supplies. Her prosperity was therefore bound to

[1] SHA, *Pius*, 8, 3.   [2] 98; Bloch, *Bolli laterizi*, 245.   [3] p. 415.
[4] One possible exception, pp. 206 f.

depend on the fortunes of Rome herself; it is not surprising that under the late Antonines Ostia, like Rome, should appear less buoyant.

THE CHECK TO EXPANSION

Shortly after the middle of the century Ostia had reached her peak in prosperity and population. The new apartment blocks provided considerably more accommodation than the buildings they replaced, but we can only approximately guess the increase in the population. It may have risen from less than 20,000 at the close of the Republic to some 50,000 by the death of Antoninus Pius.[1]

In the second half of the century the tempo of building slackens and disturbing signs begin to appear. Nothing striking seems to have survived from the architecture of this period. Street fronts of shops, with accommodation over them, are continued on the newly established model but they do not form parts of large-scale plans: no new large blocks of apartments are to be seen in the excavated area. If the increase in prosperity had continued, a further growth of population would have dictated a raising of the level throughout the town except where temples stood. But the rebuilding of Ostia was not completed. Immediately within the Porta Romana, on the north side of the Decumanus, a large area has been left at the late republican level, the so-called Magazzini Repubblicani.[2] Traces can still be seen of the tufa piers and reticulate walls which were the framework of the original shops and business premises. At least three further phases of building in the area can be seen, but they represent readaptation only. If the value of land had continued to rise the old buildings would have been destroyed, the level raised, and new and taller buildings substituted. Similar areas which have retained their old-fashioned character can be seen behind the north side of the Via degli Aurighi and behind the Baths of the Six Columns on the Decumanus west of the Forum.

The guilds, however, still led a vigorous life, if we may judge from the number of commemorative tablets and statues that they set up. Political responsibility had long since passed from the popular assembly; the guild provided a more intimate *res publica* in which office was within the reach of all, freedman and free citizen alike. The further growth of the oriental cults, especially Mithraism, provided colourful relief to the working classes. But the capacity to sustain the standard of living

[1] See Appendix VIII, p. 532.
[2] Wilson, 'The so-called magazzini repubblicani', *BSR* 13 (1935) 77.

established by the middle of the century was being undermined by the
general weakening of the imperial economy. The late second century
in Ostia, as in many other parts of the Empire, was a period of decline.

In this transitional period the reign of Commodus may have profited
Ostia more than that of Marcus Aurelius, for the Ostian evidence
suggests that the organization of an African corn fleet on the model of
the Alexandrian[1] was not an isolated gesture. It was probably in his
reign that the Grandi Horrea, originally built under Claudius, were
completely reconstructed to provide a second floor,[2] and new *horrea*
for corn, not yet excavated, immediately to the west of the Magazzini
Repubblicani may also date from Commodus.[3] It was perhaps because
of Commodus' concern for the corn supply, and therefore for Ostia, that
the colony for a brief period took the title *colonia felix Commodiana*.[4]
The explanation for the title, however, might be more personal.
Commodus was particularly attached to the imperial Laurentine villa.
When plague raged at Rome, the laurel of the district, it was thought,
kept the air free from infection. Commodus was a frequent visitor,[5]
and Ostia was near by.

The institution of *sodales Herculani* may also be a tribute to Commodus, who, towards the end of his life, fancied himself as Hercules,
invictus Romanus Hercules.[6] Only two surviving inscriptions record the
priesthood at Ostia and neither is earlier than the late second century.[7]
The only other two examples known come from Rome and both
almost certainly date from the reign of Commodus.[8] A dedication
by Trajan's harbour to Liber Pater Commodianus[9] reflects something

---

[1] SHA, *Comm.* 17. 7: 'classem Africanam instituit, quae subsidio esset, si forte Alexandrina frumenta cessassent.'

[2] *NS* 1921, 381.   [3] p. 549.

[4] The title was reported from a lead pipe by the excavator, P. E. Visconti, in the
Giornale di Roma, 10 June 1856 (Paschetto, 77). Dessau, *RM* 28 (1913) 194, rejects this
evidence on the grounds that it was not mentioned in the published report by C. L.
Visconti and that the pipe is not in the Lateran with the main collection from these
excavations, and has not since been reported. Wickert (*S* 5309) follows Dessau. The
text, however, is plausible and invention unlikely. Cf. SHA, *Comm.* 17. 8: 'ridicule etiam
Carthaginem Alexandriam Commodianam togatam appellavit'; 8. 6–9, his proposal to
call Rome 'colonia Commodiana'. For Commodus and the corn supply, see also
Pl. xviii *d*, with description.   [5] Herodian 1, 12. 2.

[6] *ILS* 400; cf. Dio lxxiii. 15. 2 and 5: SHA, *Comm.* 8. 5.

[7] Bloch, 49. 54. ? Severan or a little later.

[8] *ILS* 1120, M. Atilius T. f. Severus, cos. *c.* 183 (*PIR*², A 684); *ILS* 1121, L. Annius
Ravus, cos. 186? (*PIR*², A 684).

[9] 30. For a possible reflection of this cult at Ostia, pp. 423 f.

of the same spirit, and it is a nice coincidence that the only non-literary evidence for the month Commodus is a graffito on an Ostian wall.[1]

Commodus may have been responsible for adding to the capacity of the theatre. In 196 the reconstructed theatre was dedicated.[2] The Augustan structure in tufa had been in large part destroyed, and the theatre rebuilt in brick to accommodate a larger audience. The dedicatory inscription is in the name of Septimius Severus and Caracalla, but the brickstamps that have been recorded are from Commodus' reign.[3] It is probable that the rebuilding was begun and nearly completed before Commodus died, and that Septimius Severus at the outset of his reign stole the credit.

Few emperors can have been more popular at Ostia than Septimius Severus if we are to judge by the number of inscriptions that have survived in his honour. In itself this is a criterion that should not be pressed, partly owing to the accidents of survival, partly because such tributes have to be weighed rather than counted. There are better general reasons for believing that Ostia would have appreciated his rule. After a period of confusion in the empire, when disintegration threatened, he gave at least the appearance of strength. Like Vespasian he set himself to restore stability, discipline, and trade, and his African origin may have given him a natural sympathy for a harbour town which had long and close trading associations with his native province. But, for an emperor who knew his business, attention to Ostia was a matter of common-sense policy which needed no personal prejudice to stimulate it.

The excavations confirm to a certain degree what historical probability would lead us to expect. The Grandi Horrea, which had already been reconstructed to provide greater capacity for the storage of corn, seem to have been further enlarged on their northern side at this time;[4] and the Piccolo Mercato was extensively repaired.[5] More important was a large semicircular 'emporium' by the Tiber, west of the excavated area. It was partly uncovered towards the end of the eighteenth century and is marked on maps of the early nineteenth century. The brickwork can no longer be seen, but the fact that statue bases of the Severan dynasty were found here makes it probable that this utilitarian

---

[1] *MA* 26 (1920) 369.   [2] 114.
[3] Bloch, *Topografia*, 221 (ii. 7. 2).
[4] *NS* 1921, 381.   [5] p. 549.

building, whatever its precise function, was Severan.[1] The detachment of *vigiles* was reorganized and their barracks enlarged by the incorporation of a row of shops on the west side into the main building; on a statue base Septimius is described as 'restitutor castrorum Ostiensium'.[2]

These restorations in the utilitarian premises of Ostia were accompanied by an extension of amenities. The monumental inscription which records the dedication at the very outset of the reign of the enlarged theatre by Septimius Severus and his son Caracalla is misleading if the main work was begun and nearly completed under Commodus; but a new set of baths was added in the Severan period on the line of the town walls west of the Porta Marina.[3] The accessibility of the sea coast south of Ostia was improved by the building of the new Via Severiana from the mouth of the Tiber to Terracina.

It is perhaps significant that the builders of Ostia should set up a statue in their guild house to Septimius Severus and inscribe on the base the roll of all their members.[4] If the area of the imperial harbours were systematically excavated we should perhaps see more clearly the impact of Septimius Severus, though the most conspicuous *horrea* which had long been regarded as Severan are now shown by their brickstamps to date from Marcus Aurelius.[5] Septimius Severus paid special attention to the corn supply and is said to have left a seven years' reserve at his death.[6]

The Severan successors of Septimius have left little recognizable mark on Ostia, but one striking new building may date from this period. The round temple which adjoins the Basilica to the west is the latest of the great buildings of Ostia within the excavated area. It is built on a monumental scale, and was preceded by a handsome court fronting on the Decumanus. It was richly decorated with marble, and strikes a completely new note in Ostian temple construction. The scale of the building in a period when prosperity was receding suggests imperial subsidy and influence. The date is controversial but the brickwork shows it to be later than Septimius Severus and the base of a statue of the wife of Gordian III found within the temple suggests that it is earlier than 244.[7] The reign of Alexander Severus (222–35), to

---

[1] Paschetto, 355; L. Canina, 'Sulla stazione delle navi di Ostia', *Diss. pont. acc. Rom. di arch.* 8 (1838) 273, was probably right in inferring the shape of the building from the lie of the ground, but he had no detailed evidence for his schematic plan.

[2] S 4387.

[3] Bloch, *Bolli Laterizi*, 277.

[4] S 4569.

[5] Bloch, op. cit. 279.

[6] SHA, *Sep. Sev.* 8. 5.

[7] S 4399.

which the temple has been most recently dated,[1] would be an appropriate context for he has left his mark on the building history of Rome; but Gordian himself, whose father may have lived in Ostia, is perhaps the more probable benefactor.[2]

The Severan improvements at Ostia pale into insignificance when compared with the rebuilding under Trajan and Hadrian, and there are other signs of growing strain. The financial office of quaestor seems to assume increased importance in the second half of the second century, suggesting that finance needed closer attention. No Severan example survives of a man holding the duovirate more than once, though this had been a marked feature of government in the first century; the expenses of office were outweighing the social advantages. Ostia still provides a large number of Roman knights, but the senatorial advance of old Ostian families such as the Fabii and Egrilii does not seem to be repeated. The Ostian guilds attract fewer Roman senators as patrons. The confidence created by the strong rule of Septimius Severus was short-lived.

[1] Becatti, *Mitrei*, 21. C. C. Briggs, 'The Pantheon of Ostia', *MAAR* 8 (1930) 168, suggested a date not earlier than Constantine on the strength of resemblances to Diocletian's palace at Split. Brickwork and architectural decoration are inconsistent with such a late date.

[2] R. Bianchi Bandinelli, *Boll. d'Arte*, 39 (1954) 200, argues persuasively that a very handsome sarcophagus found recently at Acilia, in Ostian territory, was designed for the father of Gordian III and illustrates his son's designation as Caesar, or more probably as Augustus. It may be significant that no less than three bases have been found at Ostia which carried statues of Gordian's wife: *S* 4399 (in the Round Temple), *S* 4398 (in the Barracks of the Vigiles, set up not by the local detachment but in the name of all seven cohorts), Bloch, 21 (reused to line a pavement). Gordian himself is commemorated on a statue base in the Barracks of the Vigiles (*S* 4397), and a colossal head survives from a bust (B. M. Felletti Maj, *Museo Nazionale Romano, i Ritratti* (1953) n. 281).

5

THE DECLINE OF OSTIA

THIRD-CENTURY DISINTEGRATION

THE period that followed the Severan dynasty was nearly fatal to the Empire. Revolt or assassination became normal means to power, and emperors succeeded with bewildering rapidity. There was little continuity in policy, central authority was inadequate to check centrifugal forces; the resources of empire were frittered away. This half-century of imperial disintegration brought acute distress to Ostia.

To trace the third-century history of Ostia in its buildings is peculiarly difficult, for with the breakdown of centralized power the brick industry collapsed. By the Severan period the emperors had secured a virtual monopoly of production, and the emperors also by their building programmes had for long created the main demand. Emperors whose position was precarious were too preoccupied to be great builders in Rome, and the complex organization of the brick industry needed a skill and continuity in administration which was now lacking. With the drying up in the supply of new bricks we lose the criterion of the dated brickstamp which established the chronology of the buildings of the second century, and it is doubtful whether a closer study of later walls will ever provide a certain typological sequence. The facing that normally replaced brick in this period is perhaps best described as brick and block; it combines bricks, which are often taken from older buildings, with tufa blocks. Normally rows of brick and of tufa blocks alternate: sometimes there are two rows or more of tufa to one of brick: occasionally, and perhaps this is an early sign, tufa courses appear in a predominantly brick surface. This style can be seen occasionally in subsidiary walls in the second century, perhaps even in the first. It is only in the third century that it is generally employed; but it lasts on into the fourth century, interrupted by a short phase of brick revival. We can distinguish good and bad work of this type, but not yet with confidence early and late.[1] In reviewing this phase of Ostia's development it is wiser to begin with other evidence.

[1] See Appendix IX, p. 544.

A comparison between the epigraphic evidence of the second and third centuries is revealing. There is a striking contrast between the rich harvest of public inscriptions from the second century and the lean crop from the third. Since in general the chances of survival increase with the lateness of the inscription the contrast is a fair indication of a decline in prosperity. This inference is strengthened by the increasing use of old material. Even a commemorative tablet set up by the whole town, 'universi cives Ostienses', in honour of the emperor Gallienus in 262 was inscribed on the back of a similar inscription set up officially, 'decreto colonorum', to Septimius Severus.[1]

The deterioration in the health of local government which probably began towards the end of the second century is sharply accentuated in the third. Ostia had in the early Empire received special attention from the imperial government, but the city had been controlled by her own magistrates and council, and local office was highly prized. In the third century imperial control becomes more direct and explicit. Honorary dedications had been set up earlier to the *praefectus annonae*, the official at Rome who controlled the corn supply and to the procurator who served at Ostia under him. It is not until after the middle of the third century that we find a *praefectus annonae* who is *curator* of the town, appointed by the central government to regulate the town's management directly.[2] In the late Empire this official's authority is paramount and permanent. Most of the old families that had served Ostia well for two centuries and perhaps more cannot be traced beyond the Severan period. We have no evidence in the late Empire of private bequests that benefited the city.

This change in the character and spirit of local government is not confined to Ostia; it is a reflection of wider and deeper tendencies that are seen throughout the Empire. *Curatores* had been appointed by the imperial government to manage the affairs of other Italian cities even before the end of the first century; centralized control of local government had increased throughout the second century, and was accompanied by a growing reluctance to undertake the financial responsibilities of local office. Such symptoms are not apparent in the

---

[1] *S* 5334, 5330. A dedication to Salonina, wife of the emperor Gallienus (*S* 5335) reuses a dedication to an imperial freedman of the late second century (*S* 5375). The base of a statue of P. Flavius Priscus, duovir and town patron, set up near the middle of the third century, was reused before the death of Constantine to provide an altar to Hercules and the original inscription was only partly erased (Bloch, 29).

[2] p. 186.

first half of the second century at Ostia, because the city had never been more prosperous. They emerge when the local profits of trade decline.

The decline in prosperity was almost certainly accompanied by a decline in population. When the large bakery east of the House of Diana, which had ample housing accommodation above its working premises, was destroyed by fire soon after the middle of the third century, it was not rebuilt. The ruins were left where they had fallen and a path was built over them.[1] The House of the Paintings also seems to have been abandoned shortly afterwards,[2] and another large block, which can no longer be identified, was reported by Visconti in the nineteenth century to have been similarly abandoned after a fire.[3] The explanation must surely be that there was now too much accommodation in Ostia. It was no longer possible to fill the big blocks that had been built against a much more prosperous background. The profits of trade had swollen Ostia's population: when trade declined Ostia was not a good place to make money though, as we shall see later, it could still be congenially spent there. The decline in prosperity is due primarily to the general shrinkage of trade, partly to special causes that deepened the crisis.

That Rome imported much less from overseas in the third century than the second is certain though the decline cannot be even approximately measured. The loss of life through the plague, brought back from the east by the army of Lucius Verus and recurring under Commodus, may be exaggerated in our sources, but it was heavy enough to reduce for some time the population and therefore the demand for corn, imported oil, wine, and other goods substantially. The marble trade which had grown to extravagant proportions in the second century must virtually have collapsed, because the main demand had come from the lavish building programmes of the emperors, and the post-Severan emperors of the third century built very little indeed. Ostia's difficulties were sharpened by a shift of emphasis to the imperial harbours.

THE GROWTH OF PORTUS

There is no reason to believe that the old Tiber harbour had been abandoned when Trajan's new basin gave complete security to shipping.

---

[1] *NS* 1915, 249.   [2] *MA* 26 (1920) 338.

[3] *Bull. arch. crist.* 1870, 77. Similarly when the House of the Sun was burnt down, probably in the fourth century, the ruins were not cleared away, but concealed by a new wall along the street front: Becatti, *Topografia*, 162.

The larger merchantmen would naturally go to the new harbour, but while smaller trading vessels could negotiate the sand-bar at the river mouth without difficulty, as they could when Dionysius of Halicarnassus wrote, many of them will have preferred to avoid the congestion of the crowded imperial harbours and to berth at the river bank. But the cutting of a canal to link the new harbours with the Tiber, by providing two outlets for the river, slowed down the current. The sanding-up at the river mouth is likely as a result to have been accentuated.

More serious was the development of the harbour area. How much living accommodation was provided near the Claudian harbour we cannot know, but it is clear that at least a small nucleus must have lived on the spot to guard the warehouses and attend to emergency needs in the harbour. Traces of them survive in a small group of tombs that was discovered near the south-east corner of Trajan's basin.[1] Most of these tombs were destroyed to give place later to a large granary, but one was deliberately preserved and incorporated in the new building; it had been built for the freedman of a Flavian emperor, a *tabularius*, engaged on checking cargoes.[2] It has been suggested above that the majority of the harbour workers continued to live in Ostia and walk each day to their work. The centre of gravity, however, gradually shifted.

The best evidence for the growth of population by the harbours during the second century comes from the cemetery that developed southwards towards Ostia from Trajan's canal. From the seventeenth to the nineteenth centuries individual tombs and their inscriptions were recovered from the neighbourhood of the church of S. Ippolito. In 1925 agricultural operations revealed that these tombs were part of a large cemetery stretching for some 400 metres southwards from the canal.[3] More than a hundred tombs were excavated, some of them in excellent state of preservation, and a much larger number still lie buried. Most of the excavated tombs date from the first half of the second century.

In one case we can trace a transfer from the old centre to the new. C. Torquatius C. f. Quir(ina) Novellus built a tomb for his wife

---

[1] NS 1925, 72.   [2] S 4483.
[3] G. Calza, *La Necropoli del porto di Roma nell' isola sacra* (Rome, 1940). Inscriptions collected, H. Thylander, *Inscriptions du port d'Ostia* (Lund, 1952). Their chronology and the development of the cemetery discussed, Thylander, *Étude sur l'épigraphie latine* (Lund, 1952), ch. 1.

Valeria Chelido at Ostia.[1] After her death he seems to have moved to the harbour, for, when he died at the age of seventy-six, his ashes and those of his son were laid to rest in the harbour cemetery.[2] Similar movement may be inferred from other names on inscriptions from these tombs. The majority of them are common in Ostia and probably represent younger generations of Ostian families or their freedmen. It is also significant that local trades are represented in this cemetery before the death of Antoninus Pius. Terra-cotta reliefs on the face of tombs include a maker and seller of tools, a water-seller, marble-workers, a doctor and midwife.[3] Those who lived by the harbours did not have to go to the old town for essential services.

That the harbour settlement was fast becoming a self-contained community is confirmed by other evidence. Most revealing is an incidental reference in Galen's discussion of the limits of Hippocrates' medical experience. He is discussing dislocated shoulders. Hippocrates only saw the commonest form; abnormal forms of dislocation are very rare. He himself has seen five cases, one as a student in Smyrna, four only at Rome, though all Roman doctors bring him their special cases. He adds that no cases in his time have been known at 'the harbour or the city near the harbour which they call Ostia'. He can vouch for this, for 'all the doctors in those places are my friends, and both are populous centres'.[4] Already, in the second half of the second century, a man at Rome can think of the harbour before Ostia and regard them as independent centres.

When the Claudian harbour was built its official title was 'portus Augusti Ostiensis', but Pliny the elder called it 'portus Ostiensis'[5] and this usage is confirmed by the title of a Claudian freedman, 'proc(urator) portus Ostiesis'.[6] No trace of this usage is found after the building of Trajan's harbour. The standard description thereafter on inscriptions is *portus uterque*,[7] occasionally set out more explicitly, *portus Augusti et Traiani felicis*.[8] But by the end of the second century men already spoke simply of 'Portus', and they meant not only the harbour itself but the settlement around it. A similar mark of growing independence is the adoption of the cognomen Portuensis, balancing Ostiensis, which remains common in the old town.

[1] Thylander, A 249.
[2] Ibid., A 249, 250.
[3] Calza, op. cit. 249–57.
[4] Galen (Kuhn), xviii. 348.
[5] Pliny, *NH* ix. 14; xvi. 202.
[6] 163. It is possible, as suggested above (p. 56), that this was the original title under Claudius.
[7] 125, 170.
[8] 408.

The harbour settlement had also its own temples, many of them dating from the second century; by the Severan period the Serapeum, reflecting the close association with the Egyptian corn fleet, was attracting handsome benefactions.[1] Harbour guilds were also established. In some trades the two centres combined. The bakers were *pistores coloniae Ostiensium et portus utriusque*,[2] the tanners were *pelliones Ostienses et Portuenses*.[3] But already before the end of the second century the shipbuilders were divided. There were *fabri navales Portuenses*[4] as well as *fabri navales Ostienses*.

In the early fourth century the mature status of the settlement was publicly recognized. Between 337 and 341 a statue was set up near the harbours to a *praefectus annonae* by the council and people of Portus, 'ordo et populus (civitatis) Fl(aviae) Constantinianae Portuenses'.[5] Constantine had made the harbour settlement an independent community. A more precise date has been inferred from ecclesiastical evidence. At a Council held in Rome in 313 the bishop of Ostia was present, but there was no representative from Portus.[6] The Council of Arles in the following year was attended by the bishop of Portus as well as by priests from Ostia.[7] The conclusion that Portus received its charter between these two dates is, however, not compelling. The Council at Rome was not a large gathering and the bishops of Centumcellae, Aquileia, and Arpi, who were present at Arles, were not included. It cannot therefore be safely inferred that Portus had no bishop in 313. And, even if the bishopric of Portus was first instituted at this time, it would not necessarily date the granting of a charter. Civil and ecclesiastical administration did not always coincide.

It is better to leave the date of the change open but, whenever it occurred, it marked the end rather than the beginning of a process. In economic importance Ostia had already been eclipsed by Portus. As the total volume of overseas trade declined it was natural that the Ostian warehouses which had been only a supplementary reserve should be increasingly neglected. No new *horrea* from the third century have yet been found, and there are no traces of large-scale repairs in the old. Probably the third century saw a sharper drift of workers from the old town to the imperial harbours. Business was still transacted by wholesale merchants and shippers in the Piazzale delle Corporazioni

[1] For the cults of Portus, p. 384. [2] 101, **15**.
[3] S 4549². [4] 169. [5] **13**.
[6] Duchesne, *Histoire ancienne de l'église*, ii⁴ (1910) 110. [7] Ibid. 213.

where some of the latest mosaics are certainly not earlier than the third century, and perhaps in the Forum Vinarium, but the goods unloaded by the river bank were probably confined to Ostia's own reduced needs. When men wrote or spoke of 'Portus' or 'Portus Romae' they no longer thought of Ostia.

LATE EMPIRE FASHIONS

There is no important new building or reconstruction at Ostia in areas once vital to her trade, east of the Forum between the Decumanus and river and west of the Forum between the river and the Via della Foce; but that it was not a period of complete stagnation is shown by two passages in the imperial biographies. The emperor Tacitus presented to the colony 100 twenty-foot marble columns of Giallo Antico from Numidia;[1] Aurelian had a new Forum built to take his name.[2] Aurelian's Forum was by the sea coast; it is probable that Tacitus' columns were also used on this side of the town; no traces of them have been found in the excavated area. These chance references provide an important clue. They suggest that tendencies which were fully developed in the fourth century go back to the third. The centre of gravity was shifting away from the river to the sea coast.

Minucius Felix, in the Severan period, referred to Ostia as a most attractive town, 'amoenissima civitas'.[3] The epithet is not one that Cicero would have applied to the Ostia of his day. Republican Ostia had looked to the river and its trade and had expanded first on this side. When the Sullan walls were built they stood well back from the sea. It was probably not until the early Empire that the seaward side of the town claimed serious attention and perhaps not until the prosperity period that it was fully developed. It was in this area that an impressive set of baths was built near the Porta Marina in the early second century and a smaller set was added later farther to the west.[4] It was from buildings near the old coastline that excavators exploiting the ruins for the art collections of the nobility in the late eighteenth century reaped their richest rewards in sculpture and inscriptions, the greater part of them going back to the second century.

Minucius Felix gives an attractive picture of the sea-front in his day. In his dialogue a group of friends come down from Rome to Ostia in September. Early in the morning they make their way through the

[1] SHA, *Tacitus*, 10. 5. [2] SHA, *Aurelian*, 45. 2.
[3] Minucius Felix, *Octavius*, 2. [4] p. 417.

town to the shore and then stroll at leisure along the sand southwards. Returning to the point from which they started they sit down on a breakwater and settle to a serious discussion of Christianity. Small boats are drawn up on the sand near by, and children play ducks and drakes in the sea.[1]

There were two sides to Ostia's life. With the busy trading of a harbour town was combined the more leisurely life of a seaside resort. For that reason the sharp decline of trade though serious was not fatal. Provided that amenities were maintained Ostia with a reduced population could still be an attractive town to live in. From the third century onwards the theatre and the baths are more important than the warehouses.

This new Ostia is fully developed in the fourth century, but we can see the transition in the third. In contrast with the lack of utilitarian building in the areas devoted mainly to trade we find, during the late period, a positive mania for public fountains or nymphaea; many of them probably date from the third century. Changing tastes are also seen in architecture. Until the middle of the second century curving lines were extremely rare in Ostian buildings except where they were functionally required, as in the theatre. Houses, shops, and warehouses were built in straightforward rectangular form. The Forum Baths, from the end of Antoninus Pius' reign, are the first known large building to break with the rectangular tradition in the curving ends of their southward-facing hot rooms. There followed the semicircular Severan 'emporium' at the west end of the town, and the round temple west of the Basilica. This change of taste is reflected also in private buildings. It becomes the fashion to reconstruct the most important room of the private house with an apsidal end as in the House of Fortuna Annonaria. The freedmen *Augustales*, as we might expect, are among the first to follow the new fashion. In most cases the building of these apses involves encroachment on other buildings, which would have been difficult when land values were high. But in the third century shopkeepers were having a lean time and the large house-blocks were not fully occupied. Only the men who are still rich enough to have independent houses can afford to expand.

INTERNAL STRAINS

The third century was a period of transition. As trade declined, the adjustment must have been painful to the workers at the Tiber docks

---

[1] See also Appendix iv, p. 490.

who no longer had sufficient employment, to shopkeepers competing for a much reduced demand, and to builders who had more labour available than was needed. Against this depressing background two new religions competed for men's allegiance. The rise of Christianity in Ostia is still very obscure. Ostian Christians there surely must have been during the Antonine period, but the absence of surviving evidence before the end of the century suggests that the Christian community was small and weak. In the third century Ostia has her Christian bishop and later tradition recalls an Ostian martyrdom shortly after the middle of the century. But to the literary tradition archaeology adds little. A considerable number of Christian lamps earlier than the fourth century have been found at scattered points and a small number of Christian tombs. Two small buildings on the north side of the Decumanus east of the Forum have been identified as Christian meeting places, but the evidence is slight, and late. So far as our evidence goes at present Christianity had not made a strong impression on Ostia before the middle of the third century.[1]

The evidence for Mithraism on the other hand is widespread and unmistakable. The earliest dated Mithraic inscription is from 162; the main development of the cult comes in the late second and in the third century. No less than fifteen Mithraea have been found at Ostia, and, though the shrines are small, the total number of adherents implied and their distribution throughout the town shows that Mithraism was in the third century a vital element in the town's religious life. But the worshippers seem mainly to have come from the lower classes and from freedman stock; there is no sign of the patronage of the local governing class. It was not on behalf of Mithraism that the aristocracy was to resist when the challenge of Christianity was more clearly and officially formulated.

When the imperial harbours became 'civitas Flavia Constantiniana' the main shift of population from Ostia had probably been completed and the most painful phase of adjustment was over. Moreover, the strong rule of Diocletian at the end of the third century, and later of Constantine, restored a measure of imperial stability and of public confidence. For Ostia, it is true, the general benefits of Constantine's rule were probably less appreciated than in other towns of Italy. For it was Constantine who had given independence to the harbour settlement and it was probably this newly recognized town that received the

[1] p. 388.

main benefit of imperial subsidies, though there is no reason to discredit the record that Constantine endowed a Christian basilica at Ostia.[1] Moreover, Ostian sympathies before the decisive battle at the Milvian bridge may have rested with Constantine's rival Maxentius; for in 312 Maxentius, when Aquileia was threatened, had transferred its mint to Ostia.[2] Ostia was probably selected for the purpose not only because it was near Rome but because with the town's decline there were ample premises available, and suitable labour to supplement the skilled craftsmen who would be transferred to the new site.[3] The imperial mint, besides giving much-needed employment, added to the town's prestige. Early in the reign of Constantine it was closed.

If we confined our attention to a selection of private houses and to inscriptions we might imagine that a real prosperity had returned to Ostia in the fourth century. At various points in the large area most recently excavated can be seen houses that show a striking display of apparent wealth. They include old houses that have survived from the late Republic and been readapted to new tastes, second-century houses, such as the house of Fortuna Annonaria, and houses adapted later from shops and commercial premises, such as the House of Psyche and Eros. These houses, though differing widely in origin and plan, have clearly marked common features. They make lavish use of marble to pave floors and to line walls; they have elaborate fountains or nymphaea; unlike the insulae, they have their own heating systems for selected rooms.[4]

These signs of wealth seem at first sight from the inscriptions to be accompanied by a revival in public prosperity; for, in contrast with the dearth of public inscriptions from the third century, the number of Ostian inscriptions recording the emperors of the fourth century is strikingly large, and many of them are associated with building work. We should not, however, take the fulsome language of these inscriptions too seriously. Trajan, who had added Dacia to the Roman Empire, was commemorated by his official titles alone: Valentinianus, Theodosius, and Arcadius, ruling in uneasy partnership while the frontiers weakened and Germans and Goths broke into the provinces, are 'victores ac triumphatores semper Augusti'.[7] They are honoured

[1] p. 395.
[2] Maurice, *Numismatique Constantinienne*, 263.
[3] Wilson, *BSR* 14 (1938) 161.
[4] Becatti, *Case Ostiensi del tardo impero* (Rome, 1949). Below, p. 258.
[5] S 4410.

'[pro felicita]te ac beatitudine clement[iaque tempo]rum', though the economy of the Empire was breaking down. This is the official language of the day, and such honours are dictated by imperial officials. The initiative for expressing the town's wishes no longer comes from the council, but from the *praefectus annonae*. The contrast of the times is seen not only in the empty vanity of the language, but in the deterioration of the craftsman's work. He was not attempting to express the spirit of a new age in a new style but doing his best to turn out a good piece of work. The irregularity of his lines, the crowding and lack of form of his letters, are a measure of the decline in standards from the days of Trajan and Hadrian.

Ostian sculpture of the day wins more respect. The life-size portrait statue of a fourth-century dignitary has a striking individuality and dignity;[1] and the late imperial portraits have an impressive strength. But if we wish to obtain a more balanced view of the fourth century at Ostia we must return to the excavations. From them it is clear that the sense of planning which informed the rebuilding or most of the rebuilding in the first half of the second century has been lost. Architects and builders no longer care to harmonize their new buildings with their surroundings.

At the west end of the excavated area on the north side of the Via della Foce can be seen a small set of baths built throughout in brick.[2] A Hadrianic stamp was found in the construction but that should deceive no one. These baths replace shops which formed the southern end of a line built not earlier than the third century and probably under Diocletian. The predominance of short lengths of brick in the baths shows without doubt that this is late work, reusing old material. These baths back on to the Via della Foce, but no attempt is made to conform to the line of the street. Similarly on the west side of the Cardo to the south of the Forum a handsome nymphaeum was built, probably in the fourth century.[3] Its walls and floor are lined with marble and three niches are reserved for sculpture; but it projects in front of the buildings on either side and destroys what had been a graceful curve. At the northern end of the Semita dei Cippi a large semicircular exedra of inferior and late workmanship was built; it crossed the street and blocked its outlet on the Decumanus.

[1] R. Calza, *BC* 69 (1941) 113; *Museo*, 55.
[2] Becatti, *Topografia*, 155; brickstamps, Bloch, *Topografia*, 219 (i. 19.5).
[3] Becatti, *Topografia*, 158. Below, Pl. XIII b.

Several inscriptions speak of restorations to public baths during the fourth century and it is clear from what remains that efforts were made to maintain the amenities of the town; but the character of the restorations shows only too clearly the poverty of the times. When marble paving has to be restored gaps are filled by inscriptions from cemeteries or public places.[1] Where mosaics have been worn away no attempt is made to preserve the design; odd pieces of marble are reused for the purpose.[2] When, towards the end of the century, the central entrance to the theatre from the Decumanus was remodelled, statue bases were dragged from the public gardens to the north and clamped together as a substitute for new walling.[3] Indeed, the reuse of old material is one of the chief characteristics of the fourth century. Statue bases are cut down to provide thresholds; walls are even repaired with fragments of reliefs. Many of the fragments of the town Fasti have been found lining the pavements of private homes: a new latrine, built probably in the fourth or early fifth century, at the south end of the Forum, uses for its marble seats inscribed stones rifled from cemeteries. Heavy penalties had been imposed for the violation of tombs. These sanctions no longer held.

A late-fourth-century inscription records the transfer of a statue to the Forum from a site that was no longer fit for it, 'ex sordentibus locis';[4] parts of the town were apparently falling into decay. Already in the third century, as we have seen, the ruins of large blocks had been left where they fell. The active rebuilding in the houses of the rich is not matched in the large insulae. In this contrast we can see the collapse of the middle class. It had grown rich on the profits of trade; there was no longer an active trade to sustain it. The colours, however, should not be made too sombre. Rich men still found it sufficiently attractive to live in Ostia.

Some of the well-furnished houses of this period were probably occupied by imperial officials. The *praefectus annonae*, who exercised direct control over the town, perhaps lived in Ostia for part of the year, and some of the rich traders and travellers whose main business was at Portus may well have preferred to stay in Ostia away from the noise

---

[1] Good examples can still be seen in the west wing of the Baths of Mithras. Many inscriptions were also recovered from the pavement of the main hall of the Forum Baths, Wickert, S (2), p. 845.

[2] e.g. The Neptune mosaic in the Baths of Neptune, NS 1910, 9.

[3] pp. 424 f.

[4] S 4721. The approximate date is inferred from the script.

and bustle of the harbour. That is perhaps why Augustine with his mother Monica lodged at an Ostian home while waiting to return to his native Africa.[1] But the majority of these houses will have belonged to the local aristocracy or to rich men who chose to live, perhaps not for the whole year, at Ostia. Ownership stamps on water-pipes show that Roman senators were among them, or at least owned properties in Ostia.[2] The collapse of the middle class had produced a gap between rich and poor as wide as in the late Republic and early Empire, when the government of the town was controlled by comparatively few families and the spreading houses of the rich contrasted so strongly with the cramped quarters of the poor. But in that earlier period the rich had the responsibility of office and the feeling that the future of Ostia lay largely in their hands; the honours of office were repaid by public benefaction. In the fourth century this feeling of responsibility had long been sapped; it was the imperial officials in whose hands the maintenance of the city lay.

The total absence of fourth-century inscriptions recording the public careers of local magistrates and the activities of the guilds is a sign of the times. From the Theodosian Code we can see that throughout the Empire the duties of office outweigh the privileges; *munera* loom larger than *honores*. A long series of imperial enactments is needed to prevent town councillors escaping from their responsibilities. Men no longer boast publicly of the number of offices they have held; their main anxiety is to hold as few as possible. 'Decurio splendidissimae coloniae Ostiensium' is the language of the second century not of the fourth. The guilds were no longer free institutions; men were tied to their work and essential trades became hereditary.

The earlier growth of prosperity in Ostia had strengthened a common loyalty and pride; disintegration produced cleavages. There was certainly tension between Christians and pagans, and we shall find reason to believe that the local aristocracy was dominantly pagan, perhaps until the end of the fourth century. Religious differences may have widened the gulf between the rich and the poor.

The nature of the evidence and, in particular, the difficulty of dating late building work has compelled us to speak of the general character of the fourth century. In a sense this is misleading. The shortage of

---

[1] Augustine, *Confessiones*, ix. 10. 23: 'illuc apud Ostia Tiberina, ubi remoti a turbis, post longi itineris laborem instaurabamus nos navigationi'.

[2] p. 212.

evidence does not reduce the length of time and in no period of a hundred years can we expect a steady rhythm of development or decay. If we were better informed we should see a more complex picture. In religion at least there were special periods of stress. The pagan reaction of Julian must have led to more open conflict at Ostia between pagan and Christian, and we hear in fact, in a Christian source that may be of some value, of the persecution of Ostian Christians. Later, when official policy became less tolerant towards pagan cults, the Christians doubtless had their revenge.

In what from a distance seems a period of steady economic decline there may have been temporary revivals. Already in 1910 Vaglieri drew attention to what seemed to be one such revival towards the end of the fourth century;[1] subsequent study has confirmed his judgement. No fourth-century official has left a more conspicuous mark on Ostia and Portus than Vincentius Ragonius Celsus, though he was *praefectus annonae* for less than four years. The measurers of Portus set up a statue in his honour in August 389 when he had laid down his office, and on the base they paid a handsome tribute to his qualities, particularly his fairness as a judge.[2] A similar tribute was paid on a second base, which commemorated his adoption as patron by Ostia or Portus: 'hinc denique factum est ut ordo noster consensu totius civitatis, ut meruit, patronum sibi perpetuum libenter optaret'.[3]

An inscription from Portus records new building or rebuilding under his authority;[4] further records survive from Ostia. He set up on behalf of Ostia a statue to the city of Rome.[5] He supervised restorations of the Forum Baths[6] and, probably, of the theatre.[7] A further building inscription refers to his immediate predecessor in office:[8] a little earlier, under Valens, Gratianus, and Valentinianus (375–8), the Maritime Baths were restored.[9] The survival of so many records from such a short period, contrasted with the small number preserved from the previous fifty years, is significant. But the building activity of this revival does not mark a return to old standards.

The statue of Roma was set up at the south-east corner of the theatre, on the Decumanus. The base had once carried a statue of a second-

---

[1] Vaglieri, *NS* 1910, 106.   [2] *CIL* vi. 1759.   [3] 173.
[4] 138.   [5] S 4716.   [6] 139, S 4717, 4718.
[7] For the restoration, p. 424. A clue to the date may be seen in the base reused for the statue of Roma set up by Celsus outside the theatre. It was probably taken from the Piazzale delle Corporazioni at the same time as other bases used in the theatre reconstruction.   [8] S 4410.   [9] 137.

century Ostian magistrate, and his inscription was not even erased.[1]
Probably the base was taken from the Piazzale delle Corporazioni
when other statues in the series were used to remodel the central
corridor of the theatre. The restoration of the Forum Baths was less
shoddy, but the tall arches that emphasize the newly created north
entrance almost completely block what had once been two shops; they
were probably no longer in use. The architectural decoration on the
block of marble which carries a building inscription of Celsus' predecessor is of fair quality, but it is not contemporary. The formless and
thinly cut inscription does not conceal a series of holes, which show
where the bronze letters of the original inscription were once fixed.[2]
This, like so much in the late Empire, is reused material.

During the fourth century Ostia was an attractive residential town
for those who could afford the amenities of a comfortable life. From the
beginning of the fifth century conditions became increasingly insecure,
for, when invasion threatened, there was little hope of protection. The
Sullan walls had been built for defence; the gates were flanked by strong
towers. But the security of the early Empire seemed to make fortifications redundant. Before Augustus died a large building, possibly a
tomb, had been constructed against the wall immediately to the south
of the Porta Romana, destroying its defensive function. Later, at various
points, other buildings abutted on the wall. The Sullan tower on the
west side of the Porta Laurentina was converted for religious use in the
first or early second century;[3] in the second century a Mithraeum was
built against the Sullan tower which, on the east side of the town, was
intended to guard the Tiber.[4] In the trial pits that were sunk to trace the
line of the walls some later work could be seen, but it is virtually certain
that in the fifth century when the crisis came the walls could offer no
serious defence.

In 410 Alaric with his Goths, Huns, and Alans sacked Rome. He had
first captured Portus, but Ostia he could afford to ignore, and her life
was not seriously disturbed. Restorations of two public buildings are
recorded in the early fifth century[5] and some of the restorations in the
larger houses of the wealthy are probably roughly contemporary. But
fifth-century Ostia was a decaying city.

[1] S. 4621.   [2] NS 1913, 175; S 4410.
[3] Calza, *Mem. pont.* 6 (1943) 197.
[4] Calza, NS 1924, 69; Becatti, *Mitrei*, 39.
[5] S 4719 (Macellum); 4720 (? Curia).

In the temporary lull that followed Alaric's death Rutilius, writing of his return from Rome to his native Gaul, dismisses Ostia briefly:

> tum demum ad naves gradior qua fronte bicorni
> dividuus Tiberis dexteriora secat.
> laevus inaccessis fluvius vitatur arenis.
> hospitis Aeneae gloria sola manet.[1]

Little remained but the barren pride of having once welcomed the legendary Aeneas. The silting up of the Tiber mouth had now become acute. Ostia was no longer of consequence to Rome.

Coastal raids decisively quickened the process of disintegration. In 455 the Vandals under Gaeseric attacked Italy. They sacked Portus and a record of their passage survived on the island between the two branches of the Tiber:

> Vandalica rabies hanc ussit martyris aulam
> quam Petrus antistes cultu meliore novata(m).[2]

The Vandals had crossed Trajan's canal and burnt the church of St. Hippolytus; it is unlikely that they ignored Ostia, an easy prey. Conditions in the impoverished community rapidly grew worse, but for 400 more years Roman Ostia was still inhabited. It was probably in the late fifth century that the public water supply broke down. It is unlikely that the aqueduct was cut by invaders; the will and organization were no longer adequate to maintain it. Once again the population relied on wells; old wells were reopened, new ones sunk. In a very late well in the Semita dei Cippi the well-head is formed of wine jars; another, in the middle of the Decumanus opposite the theatre, reuses old brick; in both the workmanship is crude. No less crude is the work where old buildings are readapted to provide living quarters for the much reduced population. Probably many of the buildings that they occupied had already partially collapsed. Doorways were blocked up, corridors partitioned to make homes in the ruins.[3] And when they died many of these Ostians were buried at scattered points within the town.[4] It was an impoverished society, left to its own resources, growing enough food to sustain itself and no more.

While Ostia relapsed, Portus maintained a vigorous life; for Portus remained vital to Rome so long as Rome depended on imports.

---

[1] Rutilius, *De reditu*, i. 179. [2] Cantarelli, *BC* 24 (1896) 67.
[3] *MA* 26 (1920) 335–8; Paschetto, 90, fig. 18. [4] e.g. *NS* 1909, 199 and 201.

Though it was occupied and sacked by Goths and Vandals it recovered. Towards the end of the fifth century or early in the sixth Cassiodorus recorded that the harbour was full of shipping: 'illic enim copiosus navium prospectatur adventus: illic veligerum mare peregrinos populos cum divina provinciarum merce transmittit.'[1] The picture drawn by Cassiodorus of the duties of the *comes portus*, who had replaced the pro-curator in charge of the harbours during the fourth century, is too rosy. He implies a steady flow of supplies and abundant shipping. Sidonius Apollinaris in a letter of 488, when he was *praefectus urbis*, suggests that the position was often precarious.[2] A friend had recommended to him the *praefectus annonae*. Sidonius is more concerned that the corn-supply prefect, his subordinate, should help him out of a crisis. 'I am afraid that the theatre crowd will raise the cry of famine and blame me for the shortage. In fact I am preparing to send him down at once to the harbour, because I have just heard that five ships from Brundisium with cargoes of wheat and honey have reached the Tiber mouth.'[3]

In his account of the war against the Goths, Procopius provides material for comparison between the two centres. In 573 the Gothic leader Vitigis found that he could not reduce Rome so long as Belisarius was able to introduce food by land and river. Like Marius before him he realized that to blockade Rome successfully he must possess Rome's harbour. But it is not against Ostia that he marches: his objective is Portus. There the harbour is full of river craft and the town strongly fortified. Ostia is little more than a memory, 'once of great account, but now completely defenceless'.[4]

Portus had strong walls, and it is clear from what remains of them today that they were long kept in repair; Procopius even believes that Belisarius could have held the town with 300 men. Ostia's walls had long since passed out of use. But when Portus was occupied by an enemy, entry by the river's natural mouth was the only hope of vessels bound for Rome. That Belisarius made an effort to hold and use Ostia shows that the river was not yet completely unnegotiable. But the town's newly rewon importance was short-lived; the war over, she was again neglected and relapsed into decay.

---

[1] Cassiodorus, *Variar.* vii. 9.   [2] Sid. Apoll., *Ep.* i. 10.

[3] 'ostia Tiberina tetigisse'. The phrase, normally applied to the natural mouth of the river, is used of Trajan's canal in the late Empire. Cf. Prudentius, *Contra Symmachum*, ii. 937, referring to corn supplies from Africa: 'respice, num Libyci desistat ruris arator | frumentis onerare rates et ad Ostia Thybris | mittere triticeos in pastum plebis acervos', Symmachus (Seeck), x. 9. 7.   [4] Procopius, *De bello Goth.* i. 26. 7–13.

The rise of the Saracens in Africa hastened the end. Sweeping down
on the western coast in the ninth century they found Ostia an easy
prey. It is probable that in this last phase the surviving population withdrew from the coast and made some attempt to defend itself at the
eastern end of the town. In his excavations near the Porta Romana in
the nineteenth century Visconti was struck by the widespread evidence
of insubstantial building that seemed to be very late.[1] Between the
Decumanus and the Tiber in this area he noted at several points a late
wall of very poor workmanship designed for defence.[2] Perhaps a wall
that still survives immediately to the south of the tombs of the Via dei
Sepolcri was part of this system; its level is significantly high. A massive
sarcophagus was found on the Via dei Sepolcri with a hole in the back
through which the cover had been levered off by a raider hoping for
treasure.[3]

An attempt was now made by the Pope to give protection. Gregory
IV (827–44), 'fearing that the people entrusted to him by God and the
blessed apostle Peter who lived in the towns of Portus and Ostia might
suffer tribulation and depradation from the impious Saracens, sighed
deeply in his heart and began to think wisely how he might help Ostia
and be able to free her'. Roman Ostia was in ruins; Gregory built a new
town with high walls and deep ditch and strengthened it with artillery.[4]
The long dispute whether Gregoriopolis, as the new town was first
called, was to be found within or without the old city is now of
academic interest only, for recent excavations have shown conclusively
that the fifteenth-century walls that can now be seen in the centre of
modern Ostia follow the line of and use as foundations the original walls
of the ninth century. This site was probably chosen because it was here
that a church had been built to commemorate Aurea, who was
martyred for her Christian faith in the third century. The size of the
new settlement shows the level to which the population of Ostia had
sunk. Gregory's walls enclose an area not quite as large as the settlement
of the fourth century B.C.; both were little more than a stronghold of
defence.

But without continuous support from Rome the settlement could
not defend itself. When in the middle of the ninth century the Saracens

---

[1] *Ann. Inst.* 29 (1857) 309.

[2] Ibid. 312. Visconti attributed these defences to Gregoriopolis, now known to have
been built outside the Roman town.

[3] Ibid. 298. The sarcophagus was found at a much higher level than the street paving.

[4] *Lib. Pont.* ii. 81.

came again, the inhabitants shut the gates and fled. The Saracens occupied the site and made it a base for plundering expeditions as far as Portus. And by now not even Portus resisted; the Saracens found it deserted. Under Nicholas I (858–67) the fortifications of Ostia were restored, and new gates and towers built,[1] but there can have been little vitality in the town. By the later Middle Ages Ostia's story has gone full circle, and we are reminded of the settlement of Ancus Marcius. The imperial harbour has in its turn become silted up and is no longer used: such ships as come upstream to Rome enter precariously by the Tiber mouth. The old salt-beds are being exploited, now by the Pope;[2] agriculture and salt are again the main basis of Ostian life. But even for these occupations conditions are much worse. The plain to the east, which at its lowest point is below sea-level, was always in danger of flood. Even in the early Empire it was marshland; by the Middle Ages a large lake had developed, and there were fish in it. The effective working of the salt-beds depended on the canal that brought the sea-water in and helped to drain the marsh; fishing interests required the maintenance of the lake and the blocking of the canal. Litigation was continuous and ineffectual, for authority was not sufficiently strong to control. The breakdown of effective drainage added malaria to the hardships of the population and further reduced its number.

By the twelfth century there was only a handful of people living in Ostia. A revival can be seen in the fifteenth century when the present walls and church were built and Baccio Pontelli designed for Cardinal Giuliano della Rovere the imposing castle that dominates the modern village. This castle was intended to guard the Tiber passage to Rome against raiders, but the change of the Tiber's bed in the great flood of 1557 left the river fort nearly half a mile from the river, and robbed it of its most important function. But even had the river continued to flow along its old channel there could be no real security at Ostia until the causes of malaria were eliminated. It was not until the second half of the nineteenth century that systematic steps were taken, at first by the Pope, and later by the new Italian government, to drain the *stagno di Ostia* and restore the land to agriculture; and then only after a protracted debate by experts. It is strange, now that the origin of malaria is known, to read the protests of serious men who opposed all drainage plans on the ground that the disease came from the land and would become more active if the water were carried away.

[1] *Lib. Pont.* ii. 164.   [2] C. Fea, *Storia delle saline* (Roma, 1823).

6

EXPLOITATION AND EXCAVATION

THE Roman town, abandoned as a living-centre in the ninth century, had already suffered heavily. Vandals and Saracens began the looting: it passed later into more respectable, but no less destructive, hands. A Papal Bull of 1191 records a place which is called 'the lime kilns' not far from Ostia—'non longe ab eadem Hostiensi civitate . . . in loco, qui vocatur calcaria';[1] the marble of Ostia was being converted into lime. Many traces of medieval lime-kilns can be seen among the ruins, where the marble lining of walls and floors and marble statues were reduced by fire to provide lime for the builder. The best-preserved of them all has led the excavators to name from it the street on which it stands, the Via della Calcara, on the east side of the Insula of Serapis. The brickwork of this large kiln is still intact and shows the marks of the intense heat to which it was submitted and traces of the lime which it produced. The collection of marble for the kilns must at the time have been attractively easy, for the ruins were not yet completely covered by earth. When Richard Cœur de Lion landed at the Tiber mouth he found 'immense ruins of ancient walls' and proceeding southward along the coast he could still follow the track of the Via Severiana for twenty-four miles through woods still full of deer and boars.[2]

But the marble and travertine of Ostia could also serve a more constructive use. The site was a happy hunting ground for the fleets of Pisa in the eleventh and twelfth centuries, and near the south-west angle of the transept of Pisa's cathedral, built towards the end of the eleventh century, can still be seen a dedication to the *genius* of the colony of Ostia brought back with other building material on one of these raids.[3] If one climbs up into the gallery of the Baptistery at Florence, one can still read opposite the main entrance an inscription on a statue base set up by the *fabri tignuarii* of Ostia in honour of the emperor Lucius Verus.[4] The inscribed surface faces inwards; the back

---

[1] *Bullar. Vatic.* i, col. 75.　　[2] *MGH* 27 (1885) 114.　　[3] 9.
[4] 105. The normal form, *tignarii*, is rarely found at Ostia.

of the base was cut off to provide a flat surface which was used as a bed for the mosaic decoration: it was probably through Pisa that the stone reached Florence. Ostia may also have provided material for the cathedral of Amalfi, for the Amalfi fleet helped to defeat the Saracens near the Tiber mouth, and an Ostian inscription can still be seen in the font of a near-by church.[1] In the early fourteenth century Ostian marble was used in the building of the cathedral of Orvieto.[2] From the fifteenth century the site was more systematically exploited for the buildings of Rome.

The Renaissance brought a further change. The newly awakened interest in classical art and civilization made Ostia an invaluable hunting ground for the connoisseur and with the fifteenth century begins the collecting and preserving of inscriptions by men of wealth and learning. Ligorio copied inscriptions at Ostia and Portus, and added to the number from his own fertile imagination. Poggio Bracciolini, in a brief account of a visit to the ruins with Cosimo di Medici, describes his disappointment at finding no inscriptions in the Capitolium,[3] and the catalogue of Lorenzo the Magnificent's famous collection of antiques included objects from Ostia.[4] Statues were especially eagerly sought out, and by the eighteenth century the demand had spread over Europe. The treasures of Ostia penetrated to England, France, Portugal, Spain, and Russia, to find a place in the private collections of the nobility, from which most of them have passed to national museums. The historian must regret these random raids on ancient sites, which concerned themselves only with movable treasures, and broke their way through walls without leaving any records of the buildings they unearthed; but men like the Scottish painter Gavin Hamilton are picturesque figures, and the excitement with which they worked and their genuine appreciation of what they found almost atone for the harm which they have done. One of Hamilton's letters to Lord Townsend, written in 1774, gives us the best impression of this phase of Ostian history:[5]

Being desirous of trying my fortune somewhere near the sea, I agreed with Cardinal Serbelloni, then Bishop of that place, who granted me liberty to make some trials in that immense field of antiquity. I got as near the Sea as possible, judging it the most probable place to find objects of taste. We

---

[1] 430. [2] L. Fumi, *Il Duomo di Orvieto* (1851), 46 n. xliv.
[3] Poggio Bracciolini, *Lettere* (ed. Thom. de Tonellis), i. 207.
[4] E. Müntz, *Les Collections des Médicis au XVᵉ siècle* (Paris, 1888), 57, 70, 76.
[5] *JHS* 21 (1901) 314.

opened ground on a spot now called Porta Marina. From the figure of the ruins they proved to be the remains of publick Thermae Maritimae, and from the inscriptions which were found of an unusual size, it seems those Baths had been restored by different Emperors down to Constantin. I gave a very elegant one of the time of Trajan to Carlo Albagine, but what gave me greatest hopes was to find some marks of my friend Hadrian, the great protectour of fine arts and in particular that of Sculptour. I did not remain long in suspense, for the first Statue that was brought to light was the fine Antinous in the character of Abundance, perhaps the finest of that subject in the world. Mr. Bary tells me it is arrived safe at his house in England, and where I hope by this time you have had the pleasure to consider it. Near this Statue was found a very indifferent one of an Esculapius, and a large Statue of his daughter Hygea, very entire, and of a great deal of merit; this Statue was sold with some other pieces of good sculptour to the Langrave of Hesse Cassel. We found next a most excellent Torso under the knees, of which there is a duplicate at the Capitol. . . . Little more of consequence was found at Porta Marina, as I found that others had been there before me, so we proceeded to another Ruin on the sea shore, which from some fragments found above ground gave great hopes. A Bath was first discovered with the pavement of Verd antique and a fine Torso of a young man of which most of the other parts were found much broke, excepting the Head. . . . Your small Venus holding a mirror is another of the precious ornaments of this Bath; four of the Labours of Hercules were found at some little distance from this place, which being very entire, and with their proper emblems, now add to the lustre of the Pope's Museum, to which I may add that tasty Tripod of Apollo, found near where we discovered your Mother of Venus and Muse, which, as they are in every respect two of my happiest discoveries, I am very happy that they should fall into so good hands as your own, especially as they make part of those select pieces of art which I hope will in time establish a good taste in England.

The profits from excavation must have been considerable to tempt such men as Hamilton to Ostia, for there was a serious risk of malaria in the summer and little that was attractive in the village or landscape. An English lady's account of her travels in the Roman Campagna, published in 1805, presents a gloomy picture.[1] 'The air is particularly unhealthy and the town is chiefly inhabited by galley slaves who work in the salt mines', for 'the salt mines are a constant source of advantage to the apostolic chamber.' She comments on the excellent water melons and other fruits, which alone recall the reputation of Roman Ostia, and in her description of Isola Sacra we find a quaint distorted echo of

[1] Charlotte Hanbury, *Description of Latium* (London, 1805), 100.

Claudius' whale hunt in the harbour. 'A ferry boat, directed by a chain, crosses over an arm of the Tiber to the Isola Sagra, an island formed by the mud, sand, and other casual ingredients, deposited by the stream. Some authors pretend that it originated from an immense whale, intercepted there in the time of Claudius.' But the island which had once been described as 'a garden of Venus' was now a dreary waste of marsh and coarse grass, providing pasture for buffaloes, 'extremely savage when at liberty'.

The striking contrast with the present day and the fine period flavour of the sentiments justify the quotation of her passing reflections.

All is now changed, and from this truly distressing scene the British traveller will naturally turn his thoughts with exultation to his native country, which at the time when Ostia flourished in wealth and activity, could boast of as little naval glory as that of modern Rome. Yet let him remember that triumphant fleets and victorious armies were often hailed by the once numerous inhabitants of this celebrated coast, who, while they welcomed their returning defenders, never perhaps anticipated the reverse of fortune, of which it now affords so striking an example. Let him therefore, while reflecting on the revolution of Empire and vicissitudes of human affairs, forebear to despise a people once our master, but unite his prayers and efforts for the continuation of that energy and those advantages which distinguish the island of Great Britain and secure her independence, while they render her the mistress of the seas.

Had this traveller been more inquisitive she might have found more to remind her of Roman Ostia than the melons, for the opening of the nineteenth century had seen a new approach to the ruins. Further private exploitation had been forbidden, largely as a result of the influence of Carlo Fea, director general of antiquities, and official excavations were inaugurated by Petrini under the Pope's authority. The intention was to uncover as much as possible of the city, to publish plans and accounts of the buildings recovered, and to enrich the Papal Collections with statues and other works of art. Petrini dug at scattered points in Ostia from 1802 to 1804. He selected the most prominent mounds which had not already been ransacked and reaped a rich harvest.

Fea has left a good account of the site at this time,[1] but his proposals for publication were very inadequately carried out. Plans of the Capitolium and of the Round Temple and descriptions of some sculptures

---

[1] C. Fea, *Relazione di un viaggio ad Ostia* (Roma, 1802).

were included in a serial publication of the time,[1] but of two important buildings which were at least partially excavated by Petrini no account was given. It seems clear that he explored the Forum Baths and the Basilica. It was probably in the Basilica that the imperial portrait heads that can now be seen in the Sala a Croce Greca of the Vatican Galleries were discovered.[2]

The various excavations carried out between 1824 and 1834 marked a return to the attitude of the eighteenth century.[3] They were designed to secure inscriptions and sculptures, and paid little attention to buildings: no systematic account was published, though Canina's contemporary description of Ostia is accompanied by a plan which preserves some useful information.[4]

The areas selected for exploitation were those that seemed likely to be the most rewarding, along the ancient coastline and among the tombs to the south of the town. Some of the inscriptions were left at Ostia, but the more important finds became the private property of Cardinal Pacca, who had financed the excavations. This collection has now been widely dispersed and some of the finer pieces have already passed through several hands. A magnificent sarcophagus found in 1825, depicting in high relief the story of Endymion, was sold at auction in London in 1913 and bought in 1947 by the Metropolitan Museum of Art in New York.[5] It is not always so easy to trace the sculpture found in these years.

A great advance was marked by the excavations within the town area begun by Visconti in 1855 under the authority of Pope Pius IX.[6] Visconti was anxious to trace the history of Ostia, and fuller accounts and better plans were published. But he worked under great difficulties. Paintings, sculpture, and mosaics were required for the Papal Collections, and he realized that the continuation of his work depended on results. In a report of July 1857, after giving a catalogue of recent finds,

---

[1] *Monumenti inediti per l'anno 1805*; Paschetto, 499–524.

[2] G. Lippold, *Die Skulpturen des Vaticanischen Museums*, iii. 1 (1936): n. 575 (Hadrian), 581 (Trajan), 583 (Marcus Aurelius), 595 (Antoninus Pius), all in the Sala a Croce Greca.

[3] Paschetto, 525–35.

[4] L. Canina, *Sulla stazione delle navi di Ostia* (Roma, 1838).

[5] F. Matz, *Metropolitan Museum of Art Bulletin*, Jan. 1957, 123.

[6] Paschetto, 537–59. The excavations were carried out by P. E. Visconti; reports were published by his nephew, C. L. Visconti, the first in *Ann. Inst.* 29 (1857) 281. Paschetto has also drawn on contemporary reports in the *Giornale di Roma*. The excavators' library at Ostia includes copies of Visconti's letters to the minister, which add a little further detail (cited as Visconti, *Letters*).

he was careful to point out that 'these objects, valued at the lowest price, must be worth not less than 5,000 *scudi Romani*, acquired this year at a cost of less than 700 *scudi*, without counting the buildings'.[1] He was also expected to supply material for building in Rome; in April 1864 he reported with special pleasure 'four granite blocks, two of them more than six palms long, useful for the new work to be carried out by the authority of his Holiness in the Piazza di S. Pietro'.[2] To maintain regular supplies he too dug at scattered points and rarely completed the excavation of the buildings he found. The systematic exploration of the area near the Porta Romana was abandoned for richer prizes in the west. The 'Imperial Palace' was only partly uncovered. In the area of Cybele, one of his richest discoveries, much remained for later excavators.

Sometimes the collector in him suppressed the historian. In digging at the eastern end of the town he found a large number of very late walls, and, according to his published account, he proposed, in opening an area to the west, to test whether such late occupation was general or limited to the east. But in his western dig he came almost at once on the 'Imperial Palace', rich in sculpture and mosaics. These were enthusiastically described; of the historical problem which he had set out to investigate nothing more was said in print.

Visconti also had continuous trouble with the local inhabitants.

It is an excellent idea to leave on the site the marble and decoration that are found beside the traces of walls. But this noble purpose that would allow us to see the customs and monuments of peoples who lived so many centuries ago is frustrated by the stupidity and ignorance of the peasants and shepherds in the district. One is moved to anger when one sees the destruction by such worthless people of records which will never again throw light on history and instruct posterity.[3]

Statues and architectural fragments were wantonly damaged; thefts were common. Two fine composite capitals disappeared soon after discovery; they were found later two miles away. Orders had to be given to stop all loaded carts leaving the site; the local boatman was sharply warned.

But Visconti did at least succeed in forming an Ostian museum and the published accounts of inscriptions and buildings laid the foundation for a serious study of the town. Ostia was also included in the grand

---

[1] Visconti, *Letters*, 14.   [2] Ibid. 85.   [3] Ibid. 23.

tour and kings, generals, and nobles were among the distinguished foreigners who came to see the excavations; once again carriages became a common sight on the road from Rome to Ostia.

An English lady's account makes a genial contrast with the social background and the effortless journey of the modern tourist in electric train or car.

Seven years ago there was much talk in Rome of the recent excavations at Ostia, the ancient port of the Eternal City, situated at the mouth of the Tiber; and a large merry party agreed to go and explore in a carriage and pair, just as a family of freedmen in the days of old may have packed up their little luxuries before moving from Rome to the seaside. This modern party was composed of elements well known to the Anglo-Saxons of the Piazza di Spagna. There was the white-haired American clergyman, and his only son, travelling that the youth might receive that European culture so highly esteemed by the Bostonians. There was the artist, twenty years of whose life had been passed in the sunny studio overlooking the long lines of the Quirinal gardens; he whose groups of gay children from the mountains, driving their goats, and playing on their slender flutes, commanded a sure market among wealthy lovers of Italy. . . .

Then there was that singular woman, the daughter of an English squire, the pale severe lines of whose face must have been so beautiful in youth, she who now lived up three storeys in a shabby house near the Tarpeian Rock, devoted to the copying in miniature of ancient frescoes and mosaics. To these were to be added in that large roomy carriage two English ladies, living at Frascati, who were to be in town by eight o'clock to join the excursion.[1]

The writer missed this trip, but made the journey later 'starting from Rome at nine o'clock of an April morning, in a small one-horse carriage, with only one companion, taking with us a cold leg of kid, six hard-boiled eggs, a great piece of plain cake, and a bottle of wine'. In her naïve account of the ruins there is an interesting reference to the destruction of tombs on Isola Sacra.[2] 'It is greatly to be deplored that valuable relics of bygone times, which ought to have proved a clue to important discoveries were, about ten years since, reinterred by the short-sighted cupidity of the owners of the land, who relentlessly destroyed these invaluable monuments and filled up the excavations with a view to converting it to pasture land.' It was part of this cemetery that was excavated, with spectacular results, between the two world wars.

The Papal excavations, which enriched the Vatican and Lateran galleries, came to an end in 1870 when the new Italian government was

[1] Bessie R. Parkes, *The Gentleman's Magazine*, Oct. 1866, 441.　　[2] Ibid. 454.

established and Ostia came under its control. Excavation was continued intermittently and important new areas were uncovered including the Hadrianic rebuilding north of the Forum, the theatre, and the Barracks of the Vigiles; but the published reports were tantalizingly brief. The long-established practice of digging at scattered points was not yet abandoned. There was no long-term plan to co-ordinate successive campaigns.

A completely new policy lay behind the digging which was begun in 1907. The work was now to be continuous, with the intention of uncovering the whole town systematically. Lower levels were to be examined to trace the early stages of the town's development; more attention was to be paid to the preservation of the ruins, which had been badly neglected. This policy was inaugurated by Dante Vaglieri and impressive results had already been won when he died in 1912. The tombs outside the Porta Romana, which Visconti had explored, were cleared again and re-examined more thoroughly to the lowest level. The buildings along the north side of the Decumanus from the Porta Romana were uncovered to link up with the Barracks of the Vigiles. To the barracks were added the Baths of Neptune and the block of shops and apartments on the Via della Fontana. A more balanced picture of the town was emerging.

Ostian studies were given a new impetus by the publication, in the year of Vaglieri's death, of the first comprehensive study of the town and its history. Fea, Nibby, Canina, and Fisch had paved the way in the nineteenth century by short accounts of the ruins, flavoured with references to the literary sources. In 1887 Dessau had edited in the fourteenth volume of the Corpus all the Ostian inscriptions then known. Individual problems had been discussed in learned journals. Paschetto was the first to combine literary, epigraphic, and archaeological records in a detailed historical survey. He had followed Vaglieri's work closely and filled many gaps left by contemporary reports. He had also carefully sifted such scattered evidence as remained of the sites and results of early excavations. Though much can now be added and some changes have to be made, Paschetto's book was a remarkable achievement and remains invaluable.

But Ostia as we see it today will, for the present generation at least, always be most closely associated with the name of Guido Calza. Calza came to Ostia as a young man in 1912. Later, for twenty years, he directed the course of excavation. Until 1938 the work proceeded at a steady but slow pace, restricted by a lean budget. The excavation of the north side of the eastern Decumanus was extended westwards from the theatre to the Forum and a little beyond. The Forum and some of the buildings in its neighbourhood were cleared. Sufficient new inscriptions had been found to justify a supplementary volume of the Corpus in 1930, and the unexpected discovery of the walls of the fourth-century Castrum in the centre of the town had compelled rethinking on the origin of Ostia. Roughly a third of the town could now be seen, but, though the line of the southern walls had been established, the southern and western areas were still covered with earth and grass.

In 1938 a more drastic change in policy was made when it was decided to clear the greater part of the site in preparation for an international exhibition to be held at Rome in 1942. The area to be excavated was defined, and, in spite of the war, the objectives were reached. Excavation was extended southwards to the Porta Laurentina and to the Porta Marina, westwards along both sides of the Via della Foce, and along the southern side of the eastern Decumanus. Within five years the excavated area had been more than doubled. The new campaign filled out the main lines of the town plan. The picture of Ostia in the middle Empire became more diversified and vivid; and an unexpected display of private wealth in houses of the late Empire was seen to accompany the general economic decline. New buildings, inscriptions, and sculptures widened our understanding of Ostia's social, religious, and economic life.

The pressure of this intensified campaign, the anxieties of the war, and the uncertainties that followed, imposed too great a strain: Calza died in 1946. But his main work had been completed. It remained for his successors to explore the lower levels of the excavated area in search of Ostia's history during the Republic and early Empire.

Before he died Calza had begun his record for publication, and his chapters are included in the first of a series of volumes designed to present a full picture of Ostia in the light of the new excavations. The first volume lays the essential foundation. It contains a history of the site, a detailed analysis of the town's development, and a chronological survey of construction styles. The various categories of building and objects—including temples, baths, houses, mosaics—will be more fully described in succeeding volumes. Not until these volumes and the rich crop of new inscriptions have been published can the detailed evidence of the 1938–42 excavations be fully assimilated.

7

TOWN PLAN AND TOWN DEVELOPMENT

THE SETTING

THE Via Ostiensis, the main highway to Ostia, left the republican walls of Rome at the Porta Trigemina, wound round the foot of the Aventine and passed through the Aurelian wall close to the pyramid tomb of Caius Cestius by the gate now known as Porta San Paolo. From that point it followed with little variation the straight line of the modern slow road to Ostia Marina, its direction contrasting with the winding course of the Tiber, close on its right. Having passed through the cemetery which flanked it on both sides after it had left the Aurelian wall, the road came in the fourth century to the Basilica of St. Paul: a little beyond on the right was Vicus Alexandrinus, a small river port with docks. This was the last settlement to be met, but the land on either side of the road was not deserted. There were olive groves and gardens where the buildings of the 1942 exhibition now dominate the skyline[1] and villas near the road whose lands were farmed for profit. M. Stlaccius Coranus, who in the course of a long public career commanded a cavalry squadron in Britain, was once one of the landowners on the route; his funerary stone still stands by the roadside.[2]

At frequent intervals the road passed over watercourses flowing into the Tiber, and remains of several of the bridges can still be seen under their modern successors.[3] Of the milestones one only has survived. It is preserved in the courtyard of the Lateran Museum and its inscription can still in part be read.[4] The archaic style and lettering indicate an early date, perhaps in the third century B.C. It is the earliest known monument from the road.

---

[1] NS 1887, 115.   [2] ILS 2730.

[3] The best examples surviving are at Magliana (M. E. Blake, *Ancient Construction in Italy*, 212 with pl. xxi, fig. 2) and just east of Acilia (Ponte della Refolta). A bridge near Risaro, on which the Roman road could still be seen, was destroyed in 1942, Pl. VI c. A brief account of the Via Ostiensis, with select bibliography, M. F. Squarciapino, *Il Museo della Via Ostiensis* (*Itinerari dei musei e monumenti d'Italia*, 1955). A fuller account, G. Tomassetti, *Archivio della Soc. Rom. di Storia Patria*, 1894–7.   [4] CIL I². 22.

This stone marked the eleventh mile on the road. It was hereabouts that the younger Pliny left the Via Ostiensis if he chose this route rather than the Via Laurentina to go to his villa by the coast.[1] Pliny's road probably started where now stand the farm buildings of Malafede, and

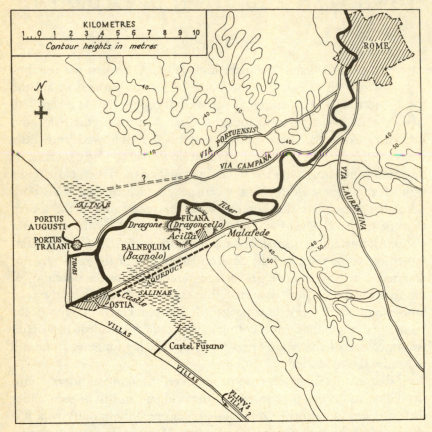

FIG. 1. From Rome to Ostia.

followed the line of the modern Via di Malafede; the remains of Roman villas can still be seen as it approaches the wooded estate of Castel Porziano. In Pliny's day the road passed through woods and open fields, where sheep, horses, and oxen were brought down from the hills for winter and spring grazing.[2]

Up to this point the Via Ostiensis could avoid hills and follow a level course. Shortly afterwards it climbed a small slope, dipped again, and

[1] Pliny, *Ep.* ii. 17. 2.   [2] Ibid. 17. 3.

then climbed to the highest point on its route to pass over a ridge of hills that stretches from the Tiber some three miles to the south. On this high land, known as Monti San Paolo, the little town of Acilia has now been built, the name given by Vaglieri to commemorate the distinguished senatorial family of the Acilii who were closely associated with Ostia and who are recorded in an inscription found near by.[1] Acilia commands good views. To the east Rome can be clearly seen; to the west the sea, though more than two miles farther distant than in Roman days, still shimmers in the distance.

Near Acilia clear traces of the Roman road can be seen. On the Rome-ward side, at the foot of the hill which leads up to the town it passes over a small watercourse running between high banks. Beneath the modern Ponte della Refolta the solid tufa structure of the Roman single-arched bridge remains substantially as it was built in the Republic. Originally it was incorporated in a viaduct carried on eleven[2] arches to maintain the level of the road, but only the bridge now remains. Towards the top of the hill, on the left of the modern road, is another small Roman bridge, almost perfectly preserved. Between the two bridges a stretch of the old road, grass-covered but clearly recognizable, can be followed. Beyond the second bridge, substantial remains of a retaining wall of well-coursed tufa blocks marks the line of the road along the shoulder of the hill.[3]

This high ground was also the source of Ostia's water supply in the Empire. The only trace of the aqueduct that can now be seen is a series of brick piers which meet the Sullan city wall south of Porta Romana, but in the sixteenth century its line could be followed over the plain beside the Via Ostiensis.[4] Its early course was cut through the hills and was discovered in 1912 when the road was being remodelled.[5]

[1] 74: 'Thiasus Acili Glabrion(is) inperatu aram fecit dominae.'

[2] Nibby, *Viaggio antiquario ad Ostia* (1829), 22.

[3] For the second bridge, Pl. vi *b*. On my last visit (1957) the scene had considerably changed. This bridge had been converted into a cellar; the traces of the Roman road were less recognizable.

[4] *Topografia*, 32, fig. 5. Remains of aqueduct piers, *BC* 20 (1892) 293.

[5] Two 'wells' (0·90 m. wide, 15 m. deep) were found, 71 m. apart: they were covered with slabs of travertine and had footholds in the side. These were inspection shafts and the interval between them corresponds with the standard of 240 Roman feet prescribed by Vitruvius (viii. 6. 3). At its lowest point the aqueduct channel (*specus*) was 20 m. below the surface. The 'wells' are misunderstood in *NS* 1913, 9; a better description in *BC* 40 (1912) 261. The fullest account I have seen (with a cross-section of the *specus*) in *La Tribuna*, 13 Dec. 1912. On the evidence of this report the Ostian aqueduct started near Km. 14.

After climbing the Acilia ridge the road gently descended into the coastal plain and it is probable that the slopes were thickly wooded on both sides.[1] The plain itself was very low-lying, liable to flood in winter and probably at its lowest points still marshy in summer. Livy in his record of 209 B.C. speaks of a 'lacus Ostiae';[2] and, after the great fire of A.D. 64, Nero proposed to send burnt rubble from Rome to fill up 'the Ostian marshes'.[3] These may also have been the marshes in which the *haruspices* advised that the remains of Rome's Capitoline Temple, burnt down in the civil war of A.D. 69, should be buried.[4] As it approached Ostia therefore the road had to be raised on a low causeway; some of the oak piles which supported it have been discovered and preserved.[5]

The most conspicuous silhouette for the traveller crossing the Ostian plain in imperial days was the Hadrianic Capitolium at the north end of the Forum. Today the eye naturally focuses on the fifteenth-century castle which dominates the modern village. The castle roof provides a good view of the setting of Roman Ostia. A group of pines on the horizon to the north-west marks the site of Trajan's harbour, two miles distant. To the south the view is closed by a straight line of woodland extending to the sea. These woods of pine, interspersed with oak and ilex, were planted in the early eighteenth century, but the view was probably not very different in Roman days, for the coastal district was wooded.[6] A little beyond the present northern edge of woodland ran the canal which fed sea-water to the salt-beds. Farther south was Laurentine territory.

To the west from the castle roof one sees the excavated area of Ostia, and hillocks covering ruins still buried. A mile away, at the extreme end of the ruins, on the Tiber bank can be seen Tor Boacciana, a ruined tower that reflects much of Ostia's history. At its core is a Roman building. It derives its name from the Bovazzani, who owned the surrounding land in the thirteenth century and converted the building with Roman material; later, in 1420, it was completely reconstructed by order of the Pope to defend the river. It marks the western end of Roman Ostia.[7]

---

[1] Woods are shown here on the earliest maps.

[2] Livy xxvii. 11. 2: 'Tacta de caelo . . . et Ostiae lacus': *lacus*, the more difficult reading, is to be preferred to the variants *locus* and *lucus*.

[3] Tac. *Ann.* xv. 43. 4.

[4] Tac. *Hist.* iv. 53: 'haruspices monuere ut reliquiae prioris delubri in paludes aveherentur.'   [5] Calza, *Topografia*, 65 and fig. 18.

[6] Pliny, *Ep.* ii. 17. 26; Varro, *RR* iii. 13. 2.   [7] Paschetto, 104.

But two factors in particular have radically altered the prospect. Fourth-century Ostia was built in the angle between the Tiber and the sea: today the sea is more than two miles distant, for the silt piled up at the river mouth and sand driven ashore by current and wind have advanced the coastline. It is, however, still possible to trace roughly from the line of the ruins how the ancient coast ran, at least in the late Empire. From Tor Boacciana it followed the line of the modern road from Fiumicino. Shortly beyond the Baths of Porta Marina it curved southwards and a series of low mounds, stretching to Castel Fusano, still mark the sites of coastal villas.

The river also has changed its course. In early sixteenth-century maps it is shown as a straight line from Tor Boacciana, parallel to the line of the Decumanus. A little to the east of the Porta Romana it makes a large bend crossing the line of the Via Ostiensis and returning in front of the castle which was built to dominate it. But, after a particularly heavy flood in 1557, the river abandoned its bed. The meander moved downstream to the centre of Ostia's river front and the old bed became a marshy depression, *fiume morto*, until it was filled with earth and rubble in the nineteenth century. Its line can still be traced on air photographs and can in part be followed on the ground.

Boundary stones set up on the right bank by the river commissioners in the Julio-Claudian period show that the line of the river within the town area was at least approximately the same in the Roman period as later,[1] but its course to the east of the Porta Romana is not yet resolved. In the Middle Ages the river curve crossed the line of the Via Ostiensis. Calza inferred that in the Roman period the curve was much less pronounced and that the river then flowed to the north without crossing the line of the road. He assumed that in the neglect of the post-Roman period the left bank of the curve was continuously eroded until it moved some 40 metres southwards.[2] Chance discoveries in 1957 showed that some modification is needed. What was assumed to be the Roman river bed east of the Porta Romana was found to be occupied by buildings and a further boundary stone was found in a position which implies, superficially at least, that the Roman course of the river was much closer to the medieval than had been expected. Until the new evidence has been sifted and wider soundings made, the precise course of the Tiber in this area during the Roman period must remain uncertain. ★

---

[1] S 4704 (*NS* 1921, 259); two further *cippi* found more recently, G. Barbieri, *Topografia*, 62 n. 2.   [2] *NS* 1921, 262; cf. Paschetto, 9–17.

THE CASTRUM

The Ostia that we see today is the enlarged city of the Empire. We can, however, trace the outline of its development from the fourth-century settlement. The original walls of the Castrum were largely destroyed when the town had outgrown them, but parts were incorporated in later buildings and their line can be traced. On the east side a considerable length can still be seen on the Via dei Molini, used as the back wall for shops:[1] some courses are incorporated in the south wall of the Piccolo Mercato; similar blocks can be seen on the west side, and on the south a small stretch survives below the south-east corner of the Forum Baths. The reused remnants of the ancient walls were not preserved for their historical association, but because they were useful and saved material. Other blocks were broken up and used for concrete filling, as when the level of the Decumanus was raised by the eastern gate of the Castrum and new buildings were erected on the north side.

In the centre of the eastern and western sides of the Castrum the foundation of gates can still be seen under the imperial Decumanus. Traces of a third gate of similar style were found at the central point of the southern wall under the temple of Rome and Augustus: a fourth gate probably lies under the Hadrianic Capitolium.[2] The basic structure of the colony was a rectangle divided into four parts by two main streets crossing at right angles. The east–west street, the Decumanus Maximus, was the continuation of the road from Rome; the street which crossed it in the centre, the Cardo Maximus, led from the Castrum northwards to the river, and southwards towards Laurentine territory.

For a settlement that was intended for defence, walls were vulnerable unless an open space was kept clear on both sides. The outer and inner limits of this *pomerium* were probably marked by later streets. The line of the outer *pomerium* is best seen in the Via dei Molini to the east, and in the Via del Tempio Rotondo to the south. Evidence for the inner *pomerium* is to be seen in the street behind and south of the Basilica, in the Via delle Domus Repubblicane and in the Via del Lario. These *pomerium* streets, as we may call them, survive now only in part, but in most cases one can see why their full lines were not preserved. The area within the inner *pomerium*, first divided by Decumanus and Cardo, will have been further subdivided into smaller blocks by subsidiary streets

---

[1] Pl. VII *a*.   [2] G. Calza, *Topografia*, 69.

running parallel to the main arteries; but how far the imperial streets within the Castrum followed the line of the original plan only further excavation can disclose.

It is doubtful whether fourth-century Ostia had a Forum. It would be most natural to look for it by the intersection of Decumanus and Cardo where the later Forum was subsequently developed. For in such matters societies are conservative. They enlarge or reduce their central squares but do not readily displace them. Calza's explorations, however, showed that what became the free area of the imperial Forum, south of the Decumanus, was once fully occupied by republican buildings.[1]

The land on which the colony was established was dangerously low-lying and may have been subject to serious flooding in the winter from the river. This danger was reduced as the building level was raised, but the earliest buildings are at the level of the sand. Drainage presented a more difficult problem than later when, from the higher level, a net-work of drains could be led to the river. The earliest drains significantly lead southward away from the river.[2]

PRE-SULLAN EXPANSION

In the early first century B.C., and probably in the period of Sulla's dominance, new walls were built round Ostia enclosing an area of roughly 160 acres, nearly thirty times as large as that of the Castrum.[3] The history of Ostian building between the establishment of the Castrum and the building of these new walls is extremely difficult to decipher and there is not yet sufficient evidence to provide more than a very general outline and to pose the main questions which it may one day be possible to answer.

The limitations of the evidence should first be stressed. Roughly two-thirds of the area enclosed by the Sullan walls have now been excavated, but the city uncovered is the city of the second century A.D. as modified in the late Empire and, to a much smaller degree, in the early Middle Ages. Some buildings of the mature Empire preserve and adapt earlier buildings, but in general the building history of the Republic and early Empire can only be retraced by excavation below the later level. Such excavation is not practicable where deeper digging would involve the destruction of mosaics, marble pavements, or other valuable material; nor, without unlimited resources, is it possible, except over a very long

[1] Ibid. 71.   [2] Ibid. 73 f.   [3] p. 34.

period indeed, to explore all the parts that are accessible. Procedure must be by sample tests, and the firmness of the conclusions will depend on the number and scale of the tests made, and on their distribution.

It has been already possible to explore in some detail long stretches of the main streets and the buildings that lined them; behind the buildings on the streets exploration has been much more limited. Moreover, certain crucial areas of the town are still covered. On the north excavation has not reached the river bank; on the south there are still large areas to be dug near the line of the walls, and in the west the line of ruins ends some 300 yards from where the river entered the sea in the second century A.D., though two groups of second-century buildings excavated in the nineteenth century can still be partly seen in the western area. Broadly speaking the periphery of the town is, with the exception of a few limited areas, completely unexplored; the sample investigation of republican levels has been more thorough in the centre and in the east of the excavations than in the west.

The main questions which we should like to answer are these: How soon and how fast did the fourth-century colony extend beyond its walls? How far does the building development suggest a carefully considered town plan? When the Sullan walls were built was their line virtually dictated by the area that was already built up or did they provide deliberately for an extension of the built-up area, large or small? Was the building of the new walls accompanied by a new or revised town plan? None of these questions can yet be answered with certainty. Between the Castrum walls and the new walls whose approximate date can be accepted with some confidence, we have no building on which the argument can be securely hinged. The best we can do is to survey the materials that are used and apply what is known of construction methods at Rome to the scanty remains that are found at pre-Sullan levels at Ostia.

The earliest traces of buildings within the Castrum show two types of construction. The walls under the Forum are built with small blocks of tufa, carefully cut and carefully coursed, without mortar.[1] Similar walls can be seen at the lowest level on the west side of the Via del Larario. Other early walls from the lowest level in part survive in large blocks of tufa, carefully fitted without mortar, *opus quadratum.* The first type of construction passed out of use when builders had fully grasped the potentialities of mortar; *opus quadratum* had a much longer

[1] Calza, *Topografia,* 71 with tav. xvii–xxi.

life and was still used in the early Empire for special purposes. The earliest work in this style, however, can be distinguished by the building level and the type of tufa used. The earliest walls in *opus quadratum* were built in soft tufa, similar to Roman capellacio; it is grey-green or sometimes reddish in colour, flakes easily, and wears badly. It was probably used first because, lying near the surface, it was easy to quarry; it was also easy to work. It was later superseded by harder and darker tufas.

The decisive change in construction comes with the introduction of concrete. At some point Roman builders discovered that a mixture of lime and the local volcanic ash provided a binder of immense strength; by pouring this mortar over an aggregate of random blocks of tufa or whatever other material was available they could produce a solid mass, capable of withstanding considerable pressure. It was logical to apply this discovery to the building of their walls. The concrete core carried the weight; for the sake of appearance a face was added, at first of tufa blocks, later of fired bricks. The facing blocks of tufa were originally large and irregular, but the size was gradually reduced and the shape of the blocks became more regular. In the final phase the blocks were regular squares, laid in a network pattern, *opus reticulatum*; the earlier phases are classified as *opus incertum* and *opus quasi-reticulatum*. This method of building—simple, effective, and flexible—became the dominant style of construction for permanent buildings, though *opus quadratum* was still used for the platform of temples, for piers, and occasionally for important walls.

Until recently it was generally thought that concrete construction was not introduced to Rome until near the end of the second century B.C. But Gatti's identification, from a fragment of the marble plan of Rome, of substantial walls that survive between the Aventine and Tiber with the Porticus Aemilia compels a revision.[1] The Porticus Aemilia was built in 191 and restored in 174 B.C.; the walls that survive show a mature use of concrete construction faced with *opus incertum*. These walls cannot reasonably be attributed to a later radical restoration of which no record survives. We must conclude that Roman builders were already familiar with the principles of concrete construction early in the second century B.C.; the experimental period should be sought in the third century.[2]

---

[1] G. Gatti, *BC* 62 (1934) 123.

[2] Lugli, *La Tecnica edilizia romana*, 375; M. E. Blake, *Ancient Roman Construction in Italy*, 324 ff.

There is an indication that it was not until the second century that the new style reached Ostia. This is primarily an inference from a series of walls that can be seen on the west side of the Via dei Molini (the external *pomerium* on the east). These walls run out at right angles from the Castrum wall, forming a line of deep rooms, perhaps shops: they are constructed of large well-coursed blocks of soft tufa, and their level approximates to that of the Castrum wall.[1] If concrete technique had been developed at Ostia, such walls would more naturally have been in concrete faced with *opus incertum*. On the other hand, these walls cannot be earlier than the early second century, for they destroy the defensive value of the Castrum wall.[2] While Hannibal was in Italy Ostia needed strong defences, for raids could be expected; any walls that interfered with these defences would have been destroyed.

These walls seem to be the earliest permanent construction outside the area of the Castrum and on historical grounds it is reasonable to believe that the first main expansion of Ostia came in the period of increasing Roman prosperity that followed the defeat of Carthage. Such extra accommodation as was needed during the war against Hannibal was probably provided by temporary constructions near the river.

The first stage of expansion was probably the conversion of the inner and outer *pomerium* into streets flanked by buildings. Along some of these lines blocks of the early tufas are indeed found, though not enough remain to determine the nature of the buildings that they supported. Most of this evidence has been recovered only by excavating below the imperial level. In two cases, however, substantial remains of these early buildings were incorporated in later work. The walls that run out from the east wall of the Castrum have been mentioned; a substantial section of wall, built in the same style from soft tufa, was also retained in a building on the east side of the Via del Larario (the western inner *pomerium*).[3]

Pre-Sullan walls show that the main arteries of the later town were established before the new walls were built. The line that the Decumanus was to take to the east was predetermined, for the Via Ostiensis already ran to the Castrum on this side. The other main streets make a more unexpected pattern. The Cardo, after passing through the southern

---

[1] *NS* 1914, 244; Pl. VII *a*.

[2] Becatti, *Topografia*, 98, dates these walls to the third century from their level and absence of foundations: neither feature would be inconsistent with an early second-century date.

[3] *NS* 1923, 183.

wall of the Castrum, instead of continuing the straight line followed within the Castrum, turns to the south-east. The Decumanus, instead of proceeding westward on its course, turns south-west. Where it changes course a third important street, the Via della Foce, runs north-west towards the river mouth. What dictated this departure from what we have come to regard as the standard Roman rectangular plan?

Becatti has offered an attractive solution of this problem. Emphasizing that Roman settlements were normally connected with a road system, he suggests that the siting of the Castrum was governed by two pre-existing routes leading to the mouth of the river; one track led from Laurentine territory, the other from Rome. The Castrum was built near the point where they crossed, using the track from Rome as its main axis—the Decumanus Maximus—and diverting the Laurentine track round the walls.[1]

Van Essen has pointed out an important objection to this theory. If these two tracks were both leading to the river mouth why did they cross and not converge? Why should the track from Rome be leading to a point to the south? An early track from Rome would either have followed the river closely or led directly to the mouth. The straight line of the eastern Decumanus outside the Castrum is the result rather than the cause of its line within the Castrum. Van Essen sees the reflection of the original track from Rome in certain unexpected lines that survive in imperial streets and buildings, notably the Via dei Misuratori and the *horrea* at the west end of the Via della Foce. These lines, he thinks, are the legacy of the original track; early property rights ensured their survival at certain points.[2] This modification is an improvement of Becatti's theory, but it is open to a more serious objection.

Van Essen names these early tracks the Via Salaria Sabina and the Via Salaria Laurens. If he were right in assuming that the salt-beds were at the mouth of the river his theory would be very tempting; but the firm sands in this area were not suited to the production of salt. The original *salinae* should be placed where they are found later, to the east of modern Ostia, at the edge of the Ostian marshes, on land that was below sea-level. If this is right we should not expect a well-worn track from Rome to the river mouth.

[1] Becatti, *Topografia*, 93. Air photograph, Pl. II.
[2] C. C. Van Essen, 'A propos du plan de la ville d'Ostie', *Hommages à Waldemar Deonna* (Collection Latomus, vol. 28, Bruxelles, 1957), 509–13. Apart from the Via dei Misuratori (Reg. i. 7 and 8), evidence for the early track from Rome is seen in i. 3. 6; i. 4. 5; i. 19 and 20.

Bradford has emphasized that the western Decumanus and the Via della Foce make identical angles with the main axis in the form of a regular Y, and suggests that this represents deliberate orientation, though he does not discount the possibility that the design was influenced by a Laurentine track.[1] An alternative possibility is that the line of the Cardo Maximus south of the Castrum represents the natural and quickest route to the good farming land of Piana Bella.[2]

While it is clear that the line of the main streets which were to serve the town throughout its history were established before the Sullan walls were built, it has not yet been possible to make sufficient soundings to know how far the secondary streets go back to this early period. The streets on the lines of the inner and outer *pomerium* were certainly formed early and some of them were continued beyond the lines of the Castrum. Thus the Via dei Molini, which represents the outer *pomerium* on the east, was extended in the Semita dei Cippi southwards to meet the Cardo. Similarly the Via della Fortuna Annonaria seems to be a continuation of the outer *pomerium* street south of the Castrum. To the north of the Castrum the outer *pomerium* street, which has been submerged by Hadrianic building, seems to have been continued westwards in a street that was suppressed much earlier, when the sacred area was formed round the temple of Hercules.[3]

There may also be traces in the later town of much more irregular development during this early phase; for it is difficult otherwise to account for the very odd lines of the area south of the Decumanus opposite the theatre, between the Via degli Augustali and the Via del Sabazeo.[4] We should expect to see here the rectangular planning of the area to the west and of the area on the opposite north side of the Decumanus, a series of streets at right angles to the Decumanus, joined by streets parallel with the Decumanus. Instead we find a series of awkward kinks in the walls and a tendency towards oblique lines converging in a south-easterly direction in a secondary gate in the walls. It is difficult to believe that this is the result of deliberate planning. The shift of direction in the west wall of the Horrea of Hortensius results in a series of rooms of very uneven size, some of them awkwardly small. The Horrea of Artemis to the west, following the same line with its

[1] J. Bradford, *Ancient Landscapes*, 240.
[2] The Cardo links directly with the westernmost of five parallel roads across the southern plain (pp. 473 f.).
[3] Becatti, *Topografia*, 106.
[4] Pl. II.

eastern wall, is left with an equally awkward shape. The very narrow second-century A.D. insulae beyond the *horrea* to the west do not look like deliberate planning. These irregularities are most easily explained if they result from uncontrolled private building at an early date, which preceded any attempt to form a coherent street plan for the area.

Most of the second-century walls that have been found seem to come from shops and houses, limited to one or two stories. The streets were not yet relieved by porticoes and some of them at least were very narrow. Traces of a large public building of obscure plan were found on the south side of the Decumanus in what was later to be the Forum,[1] but it seems that in the second century the main emphasis was on utilitarian building to meet an expansion of trade and population.

It is significant that the earliest temples to have survived are later than the Sullan walls, with the possible exception of the temple of Hercules and its two neighbours which might be a little earlier. Since, apart from the Hercules group, seven temples were built on or near the Decumanus before the end of the first century B.C. the contrast is very striking. At Rome many early republican temples retained their form and position long into the Empire: the fact that no temple earlier than the close of the second century has been found at Ostia strongly suggests that the early temples were modest in scale and light in structure. Fragments of painted architectural terra-cottas were found at a pre-Sullan level;[2] they may have decorated temples built mainly of timber.

Signs of more elaborate architecture and greater prosperity can probably be seen towards the end of the pre-Sullan period. The most outstanding evidence is a group of large houses, based on atrium and peristyle, datable by their *opus incertum* walls to the late second or early first century.[3] The house of Jupiter the Thunderer, on the west side of the southern Cardo, immediately beyond the Forum, remained a private house until the late Empire. Its peristyle was converted to other use, but the atrium, though adapted to changing tastes, retained its essential form. Of another similar house on the north side of the east end of the Via della Fortuna Annonaria a substantial wall and the outline of the peristyle survive through a later transformation of the building.[4] Remains of a third such house, of approximately the same date, are

---

[1] Calza, *Topografia*, 71.
[2] Ibid. 75, tav. xxii; for their date, p. 479.
[3] Becatti, *Topografia*, 107.
[4] Pl. XII *a*.

incorporated in the Mithraeum of the Painted Walls, on the south side of the Via della Foce. The building of houses with atrium and peristyle was continued through the first century B.C. and into the Julio-Claudian period near the centre of the city, and especially along the eastern side of the western Decumanus.

It may also be possible to identify a warehouse or granary of approximately the same period, the earliest of the *horrea* known to us. On the west side of the Via del Sabazeo, which runs south from the Decumanus some 300 metres west of the Porta Romana, can still be seen the so-called Sabazeum which Vaglieri excavated in 1909.[1] It is clear that the transformation of the room into a shrine is late. The original side walls are faced with *opus incertum* and this room was originally one of a series. The Sabazeum is closed at the east end by a Hadrianic wall in brick and reticulate which runs most of the length of the west side of the Via del Sabazeo: this seems to be a blind wall merely shutting off the buildings to the west. At the points where they meet this wall, traces of pre-Sullan walls can be seen parallel to the side walls of the Sabazeum. This line of deep narrow rooms seems to form part of a single building. West of the Sabazeum there is a corridor and beyond it, though the area is still covered, can be seen traces of further walls in *opus incertum*. It is probable that all these *opus incertum* walls formed part of a large building designed for the bulk storage of goods. It may be significant that the area to the west was later occupied by warehouses.

The temple of Hercules should also perhaps be dated to this phase that shortly precedes the building of the walls. It cannot be earlier than the closing years of the second century B.C. because it uses travertine for its frontal steps and for the two lowest courses of its surrounding stylobate.[2] The small tufa blocks used in the facing of the cella walls form a less regular pattern than the facing of the Sullan walls, and they are of soft granular tufa, whereas the new walls seem to have established the dominance of the harder tufas. Moreover, the temple is strictly oriented east–west, which sets it at an awkward angle to the Via della Foce and there seems to be no attempt to give the area an architectural framework to disguise the contrast of alignment, perhaps a sign of early date. A close contemporary of the temple of Hercules is the small tetrastyle temple near by to the north-east, which has a podium of very

[1] *NS* 1909, 20.
[2] For the introduction of travertine, Tenney Frank, *Roman Buildings of the Republic*, 32; Lugli, op. cit. 319–22.

similar profile and uses the same tufa for the facing of its cella. The third temple of the area is rather later, because it intrudes on the lowest step surrounding the temple of Hercules. It follows the line of the Via della Foce and may imply a later attempt to disguise the disharmony of the area.

If we are right in attributing these signs of a more ambitious architecture to a period shortly before the building of the new town walls we may perhaps see in them a reflection of the increased wealth and importance that came to Ostia from the Gracchan law providing for the distribution of cheap corn in Rome and from the wars at the end of the century against Jugurtha and against the Teutoni and Cimbri. To Rome these wars brought military and political crisis, but to Ostia armies fighting in Africa and Gaul meant good business.

Though the general lines of Ostian expansion in the second century can be traced along the main arteries, the extent of the expansion and the density of building remain very obscure. It is probable that expansion proceeded faster in the east than in the west. The area between the eastern Decumanus and the river, which was declared public by the Roman praetor Caninius, extends beyond the later line of the Sullan walls: this whole north-east quarter was presumably important to shippers and traders. The south-eastern district was nearest to the best agricultural land, and one would expect the men who worked in the plain south of Ostia to live there.

In the west the area between the Via della Foce and the river had a natural importance for traders and is likely to have been developed first. The south-western quarter of the town, towards the sea, was the least important in the town's economy and its development was probably much slower. There seems to have been no street running westwards from the western Decumanus until the Via degli Aurighi was opened in the early Empire.[1] Some such street was essential to the satisfactory development of the seaward side of the town. It is a reasonable inference that little importance was attached to the district in the Republic.

The problem of Ostia's westward expansion is complicated by the uncertainty of the line of the sea-shore throughout the Roman period. The line in the late Empire can be traced from the ruins; Tor Boacciana marks approximately the river mouth in the Severan period. If the average rate of coastal advance since attested were applied to the Roman period, the river mouth should have been not far from the Porta

[1] Becatti, *Topografia*, 109.

Romana in the fourth century B.C.[1] The siting of the Castrum shows that such calculations are valueless.

Our evidence suggests rather that there was no substantial change during the Roman period. The line of buildings nearest the sea includes some that are not later than the first half of the second century A.D.; the natural inference is that there was no marked advance of the coast-line for the next 300 years. There is even a little evidence that the sea was actually making inroads on the buildings after they had fallen in ruins.[2] If the sea had been steadily receding we should expect to find some record in literature. No Roman writer mentions it. The pleisto-cene sands on which the Castrum and the town that developed from it were built provided throughout the Roman period a stable coastline.[3]

How far and how fast Ostia expanded along the line of the Via della Foce is still uncertain. Meanwhile a negative point should be established. Immediately beyond the so-called imperial palace in the west of the town, near the river bank, a series of deep narrow vaulted rooms have been identified as republican docks.[4] An inscription of the second century A.D. records the restoration of a 'navale a L. Coilio aedifica-tum'[5] and the circumstantial evidence for the association of these rooms with the inscription seemed strong: the archaic form of the name suggested a republican date. From early accounts it seemed that these vaulted rooms ran to the river, and were used to house ships. In 1952 the low level of the river, which normally floods these bramble-covered ruins, gave opportunity for a closer examination. The walls are of mature reticulate, crowned by six courses of bricks from which the barrel-vaults spring. The date is very probably Augustan, and certainly cannot be earlier. Nor did these rooms house ships, for a small-scale excavation showed that they did not extend as far as the river and that on the river side the entrances to the rooms were no larger than standard doorways. This building, probably designed for the storage of goods, provides no evidence for the westward extension of the town in the Republic.

---

[1] The evidence for the rate of post-Roman coastal advance is tabulated by Le Gall, *Le Tibre*, 22–25.

[2] Bricks and stones worn smooth by the sea, west of the Piazza del Prospetto. The coastal Via Severiana needed protection from the sea under Maximinus (in 238): 'litus vicinum viae Severianae, adsiduis maris adluentibus fluctibus ad labem ruinae labefac-tatum, aggeribus marini operis a fundamentis, ut periculum commeantibus abesset, extrui curarunt' (*ILS* 489).

[3] p. 10.   [4] Paschetto, 346; Carcopino, *Mélanges*, 31 (1911) 214.   [5] 2.

Further excavation should throw more light on the westward expansion of Ostia; another important problem may be more difficult to resolve. If we accept only the evidence of permanent walls, there seem to be a large number of areas within the pre-Sullan town that were not occupied. In spite of widespread tests no republican walls were found under the public gardens north of the theatre, nor under the Grandi Horrea. No traces of pre-Sullan occupation were found under the Basilica; the earliest building on what would seem to be an important site at the north end of the western Decumanus, seems to date only from the end of the first century B.C.[1] On the southern Cardo, apart from the House of Jupiter the Thunderer, no second- or early first-century walls have been found.

If all construction at Ostia during the second century was in permanent material, pre-Sullan Ostia was not continuously built up and was probably a very small town. There are, however, indications, direct and indirect, that perishable materials were used on a substantial scale. The direct evidence is meagre. When Paribeni in 1914 excavated the four republican temples on a common platform west of the theatre he concluded that these late republican tufa temples had been preceded on the same site by earlier temples of sun-dried brick resting on light stone walls.[2] The material below the later podium which led him to this conclusion comprised a large quantity of clay and a scattered deposit of coins and pottery, including fragments of Rhodian amphorae. When recently these foundations were re-examined it was concluded that Paribeni's foundation walls were in fact contemporary with the tufa temples and had possibly served to provide a level surface for the podium. Becatti has also emphasized that the pottery found at the lower level reflects trade rather than cult.[3] All conclusions therefore based on the conception that four small temples had been built early in the second century more than 100 metres east of the Castrum must be abandoned. There remain, however, the pottery and the clay. Though there were no temples here the evidence strongly suggests some type of crude brick construction. The only other indication of such construction comes from a still earlier report. In 1912 Vaglieri found at the level of the sand near the Porta Romana a great quantity of clay, roof-tiles, and traces of a timber support; this material he took to be the remains

[1] Becatti, *Topografia*, 110.
[2] R. Paribeni, *MA* 23 (1914) 443.
[3] Becatti, *Topografia*, 105.

of two large huts.[1] It is unfortunate that his account is not more precise and detailed and that no photographs are available, but his report is adequate evidence for timber and clay construction.

It is legitimate also to argue from the analogy of Rome. There the use of sun-dried bricks, *opus latericium*, was widespread until the end of the Republic.[2] Most of Ostia's soil, unlike the clays round Rome, was predominantly sandy and unsuited to the making of bricks, but the heavier alluvial soil deposited by Tiber floods could have been used, as it was later used for fired bricks. Another early style of construction mentioned by Vitruvius, *opus craticium*, was based primarily on timber.[3] The framework was provided by stout beams; the walls were composed of wattle and daub or rubble. This style suited Ostian conditions better, for the district was well wooded. Timber probably remained in use as a main construction material even after concrete had been introduced. Its early importance in Rome is reflected in the terminology of the building trade. Stories remain *contignationes*, even when concrete vaults are common; the builder who is working almost exclusively in brick and tufa is still called the craftsman who shapes the beams, *faber tignarius*.

It is reasonable to infer that light structures in sun-dried brick or timber were common in pre-Sullan Ostia. They could be seen near the centre of the town, but were probably thickest on the outskirts. They included temples as well as commercial premises. The last century of the Republic saw their gradual replacement by more permanent construction.

LATE REPUBLIC AND EARLY EMPIRE

The Sullan walls have not yet been fully excavated, but Calza traced their line by a series of trial pits. The area that they enclose is not a regular rectangle, like the Castrum, but the main axis remains east-west. The factors determining the roughly trapezoidal shape are the river and the coastline. In the south-west the wall runs roughly parallel to the coast. Where the coast curves southwards the wall turns to run parallel to the river for 870 metres. From this point it reaches the Decumanus in three shorter stretches; north of the Decumanus it runs direct to the river.[4]

---

[1] Vaglieri, *NS* 1911, 207 f., 259; 1912, 162, 203.
[2] M. E. Blake, *Ancient Roman Construction in Italy*, 280.
[3] Vitruvius ii. 8. 20.   [4] Calza, *Topografia*, 79; *BC* 53 (1925) 232.

There were three main gates in the walls—the Porta Romana, where the Decumanus merged into the Via Ostiensis, the Porta Laurentina where the southern Cardo passed through the wall towards Laurentine territory, and the Porta Marina where the western Decumanus led to the sea-shore. Between these gates there were secondary gates or posterns of which the clearest example, demanded by street plan and discernible on an air photograph, comes where the Via del Sabazeo meets the wall. The main gates were flanked by strong squared towers, and small circular towers were added at the four angles in the walls.[1] A further squared tower was built north of the Porta Romana to command the river.[2]

There remain two problems to be resolved. The line of the wall was traced for 300 metres west of the Porta Marina, but its further course could not be discovered. It may have turned towards the river at this point, or proceeded farther towards Tor Boacciana, which is 380 metres distant. Until the line is established we shall not know how far the buildings at the west end of the town represent an expansion beyond the Sullan walls. It is also not yet completely certain whether the wall was carried along the river bank, but from Calza's exploration it seems that the riverside was not defended. A continuous wall would have interfered with trade; the fleet should have been able to protect the town from any attack by the river.

The new walls were not accompanied by important modifications of the town plan. The main arteries had already been established. The original form of the Castrum had dictated the rectangular street plan of the centre: the irregularity of the south-east side of the town had been due to uncontrolled development and was not corrected. It is, however, possible that the Forum was now laid out to provide a more imposing centre for the town. At some point the republican buildings south of the Decumanus were destroyed and the area left free. This step had been taken at the latest when the early Julio-Claudian temple of Rome and Augustus was built at the south end of the Forum, for that temple presupposes an open area in front. If our dating of the P. Lucilius Gamala concerned is correct, a Forum already existed under Augustus.[3] The building of the new walls provides an appropriate context.[4]

[1] Calza, *Topografia*, 86.
[2] Ibid. 83.
[3] 1[34]: 'idem tribunal in foro marmoreum fecit.' For the date, Appendix V, p. 493.
[4] The destruction of the early buildings under the Forum was not immediately followed by the creation of a Forum. At a higher level substantial concrete foundations were

The new buildings of the period between Sulla and Augustus brought interesting improvements in Ostian architecture. The development along the main street fronts of porticoes carried on tufa piers is probably to be dated to the late Republic. Compared with their imperial successors they were small in scale and the earliest served individual buildings rather than large blocks, but they gave a more lively and varied appearance to the streets. There is also evidence of more ambitious architectural compositions. The four Republican temples west of the theatre are small and unpretentious in their decoration; but together they form a coherent group. They were built to a common design on a common platform and surrounded by a large sacred area, enclosed on three sides by a portico, and open to the Decumanus on the south.[1] The original facing of the walls of these temples and of the portico resembles closely the workmanship of the Sullan walls and should be roughly contemporary. It is doubtful whether such a composite plan had been attempted before.

In the second half of the century a large area north of the Decumanus and immediately west of the Porta Romana was also developed to a common plan, which can still be seen in two blocks. The larger block to the west, the so-called Magazzini Repubblicani, has been readapted many times, but its original pattern can be recovered.[2] A portico supported by tufa piers surrounded rows of shops in reticulate; in the centre of the block, thicker walls supporting an upper floor suggest a building used for industrial purposes. This block is separated from its neighbour to the east by a street: the smaller eastern block repeats the pattern of portico and shops. These two blocks alone survive from the original plan, but sufficient elements were found to show that it extended westwards to two further blocks.[3]

It may be significant that both the group of republican temples and the blocks near the Porta Romana were built on land declared public by the Roman praetor. On this land between the eastern Decumanus and the river the orderliness of the planning, now and later, is in striking contrast with the irregularity and compromise in many other

---

found. There was no trace of any superstructure and it has been inferred that the building did not proceed beyond the foundation stage. No firm evidence is available for the date of these foundations, which I have assumed to be pre-Sullan. Becatti argues that the Forum was not created until the temple of Rome and Augustus was built, under Tiberius (*Topografia*, 115; fig. 21).

[1] R. Paribeni, *MA* 23 (1914) 441–84.
[2] Wilson, *BSR* 13 (1935) 77.   [3] Becatti, *Topografia*, 112.

quarters of the town. It may have been much more difficult to acquire large areas for coherent development where the land was private property.

The building of large houses with atrium and peristyle was continued during this period near the centre of the town. On the southern Cardo the House of the Mosaic Niche was built next to the House of Jupiter the Thunderer; and, like its neighbour, it was to remain a private house into the late Empire. A much larger house, on the western Decumanus, rebuilt during this period, was suppressed in the second century to make way for the Vicolo di Dioniso and the new buildings that this small street was designed to serve; but the rebuilding preserves the main form and dimensions of the earlier house.[1] This was the first of a line of such houses which was to spread along the east side of the western Decumanus.

Under Augustus important additions were made to the public buildings of the town. The development of the area reserved by Caninius was continued by the building of the theatre with its large colonnaded portico and public gardens. Radical changes were also made in the Forum, where, towards the end of the first century B.C., two temples were built on the north side of the Decumanus.[2] The larger (27 × 13·75 metres) replaced what was probably a secular public building; its smaller western neighbour may have replaced an earlier temple on the same site. In front of the larger temple are six squared holes lined with reticulate: they may have carried supports for an awning over part of the Forum.[3] In the angle between the western Decumanus and the Via della Foce the public market, the Macellum, was restored.[4]

Augustan building does not seem to have involved important modifications in the town plan, but it may have prepared the way for the development of the seaward district. The earliest known buildings outside the Porta Marina are two handsome public funerary monuments. One, to the south-east, commemorated C. Cartilius Poplicola, eight times duovir; the other, on the west side of the continuation of the Decumanus beyond the gate, remains anonymous for no inscription has been found. Both monuments probably date from the early years

---

[1] Ibid. 108. Below, p. 253.
[2] Ibid. 104. For the identification of these temples, p. 352.
[3] As suggested by Becatti, *Topografia*, 112.
[4] Bloch, 67. Though no republican elements can now be seen. *Topografia*, 118, must be mistaken in attributing the original building to the first half of the first century A.D.

of Augustus' principate,[1] and it was probably under Augustus or soon afterwards that the Via degli Aurighi was built, running westwards from the western Decumanus, and providing for the more systematic development of the south-western quarter of the town.[2]

The increase in the number of public buildings and the replacement of old buildings by new continued through the Julio-Claudian period. Shortly after the death of Augustus a temple of Rome and Augustus was built at the south end of the Forum, directly facing the larger of the two temples at the northern end. The temple cella was approached not from the front, but by stairs from the two sides, possibly, as Becatti has suggested, because the front of the temple was used as a platform for orators or judges.[3] The temple was completely dressed in marble and the quality of its architectural decoration can stand comparison with Augustan work in Rome, from which it probably derives.[4] This was the most elegant building yet seen in Ostia and it improved considerably the monumental character of the Forum. A little later a small temple of Bona Dea was built outside the Porta Marina.[5]

Two large granaries survive from the Julio-Claudian period. The Grandi Horrea of the mid-century added to the rectangular regularity of the area north of the eastern Decumanus.[6] The Horrea of Hortensius, perhaps a little earlier, were built on the south side of the eastern Decumanus, but the entrance lies opposite a street running from the Decumanus to the river.[7] The significance of these new *horrea* is uncertain, because no earlier buildings of the kind survive with which to compare them, but, though their plan may not be new, they probably exceeded their predecessors in scale and capacity.

The building of an aqueduct in the early Julio-Claudian period encouraged the development of public baths, which must have been severely restricted while they relied on wells. Remains of a handsome establishment of the mid-century were found under the Via dei Vigili;[8] another set of baths, partly excavated, remained in use in the south-

---

[1] Poplicola's monument can be approximately dated by the style of the relief, the lettering of the inscription, and comparison with Poplicola's other inscriptions. The other monument is assumed to be roughly contemporary owing to its liberal use of travertine. For a detailed discussion of the date, *Scavi di di Ostia*, iii (1) 169 ff.

[2] Becatti, *Topografia*, 109.

[3] Ibid. 115.

[4] Pl. xxxix *a*.

[5] Calza, *NS* 1942, 152.

[6] *NS* 1921, 360.

[7] Becatti, *Topografia*, 117 f.

[8] *NS* 1912, 204.

eastern district,[1] and the original nucleus of the Baths of Invidiosus, which were largely rebuilt in the first half of the second century, also seems to be Julio-Claudian.

THE ARCHITECTURAL REVOLUTION

So far as we can see, though individual buildings were replaced, there was no radical rebuilding of Ostia in the Julio-Claudian and early Flavian period. By the end of the second century Ostia had been transformed. Complete districts had been rebuilt, housing conditions had been revolutionized by the building of tall apartment blocks. New standards in scale and decoration had been applied to public buildings, and throughout the new building the level was sharply raised.

Reasons have already been given for regarding Domitian's principate as the first stage in the more radical transformation of Ostia.[2] The most important permanent contributions to the town's development were the 'Curia' and the Basilica, facing one another across the Decumanus on the west side of the Forum. The Basilica has suffered more heavily than any other public building in Ostia as a quarry for building material. Travertine foundation blocks as well as columns have been robbed; of the decorative elements very little has survived.[3] But the ground plan is clearly visible, showing an impressive scale, and the floor was covered by rectangular panels of Giallo Antico and Italian marble. Opposite the Basilica the 'Curia' had a handsome porch carried on six columns, the hall within had marble lining to its walls and floor.[4] These two buildings increased the dignity of the town centre. But it is with Trajan and his two successors that the rebuilding of Ostia is primarily associated.

Work of Trajan's principate can be seen in many quarters of the town; it is most conspicuous in the west. Between the Via della Foce and the river, westwards from the Via degli Horrea Epagathiana, the brickwork is predominantly Trajanic. In this quarter the Baths of Buticosus, the large Horrea of the Measurers, the radical reconstruction of the temple of Hercules and the buildings that lie to the north of this temple all date from this period.[5] The large isolated group of ruins at the far western end of the town by Tor Boacciana, excavated in the nineteenth century, and now partly overgrown, has Trajanic brickstamps.[6]

---

[1] Reg. v. 10. 3. [2] p. 64. [3] Becatti, *BC* 71 (1943–5) 31.
[4] *NS* 1923, 185. [5] Bloch, *Topografia*, 218 f. [6] Ibid. 226.

On the south side of the Via della Foce, opposite the Horrea of the Measurers, the large building which occupied the site where the Insula of Serapis was built under Hadrian and which was partly incorporated in the later building is Trajanic;[1] roughly contemporary is a row of shops on the western side of the building and beyond them a modest but well-planned housing estate, the Casette-tipo. Farther west, beyond the Serapeum, large *horrea*, not yet excavated, were probably originally built under Trajan. On the eastern side of the Insula of Serapis, between the Via della Calcara and the western Decumanus, the rebuilding was less radical; but substantial restorations were made under Trajan and some new buildings added, including small *horrea* on the Via degli Aurighi.[2]

In other quarters of the town Trajanic work is rarer, but it includes a handsomely built group of store-rooms on the Semita dei Cippi[3] and at least one further set of baths, the Baths of the Six Columns on the western Decumanus.[4] More important in the development of the town were the much larger baths south-east of the Porta Marina, by the sea-coast. They have not yet been systematically excavated, but there is reason to believe that they were at least begun under Trajan, and built at the emperor's expense.[5] Meanwhile at the eastern end of the town there seems to have been little new building.

When Trajan died Ostia was still in a transitional stage. In the west the new brick architecture was making rapid headway. Old temples were being reconstructed in brick and marble to match the growing prosperity of the town. New baths, small and large, had been built. But a visitor from Rome walking from the Porta Romana along the Decumanus to the Forum would have found the eastern half of Ostia old-fashioned. Along the line of the eastern Decumanus the buildings were still mainly Julio-Claudian or earlier; there was more reticulate than brick to be seen. The Forum had been enhanced by the new Basilica, but so long as the two late republican temples on the north side of the Decumanus retained their place the area would remain too

---

[1] Bloch, *Bolli laterizi*, 202; Pl. xl *d*.

[2] Bloch, *Topografia*, 222 (iii. 2. 6).

[3] No brickstamps recorded. Becatti (*Topografia*, 134) dates to Hadrian. The width of the bricks (averaging 3·7 cm.) and the dominance of brick in the combination of brick with reticulate favour a Trajanic date. The large bakery near by was also probably originally built under Trajan and there are further traces of Trajanic work on both sides of this street, incorporated in later building.

[4] Bloch, *Topografia*, 226 (iv. 5. 11).   [5] p. 407.

restricted to allow an imposing centre to the town. The new domestic architecture was providing apartment blocks for an increasing population, but the independent atrium house still held its own near the centre, particularly along the western Decumanus.

Hadrian's principate marks the decisive stage in Ostia's transformation. More than half the buildings that can now be seen date from this period and they are spread throughout the town. The piecemeal development of individual blocks was accompanied by the replanning of large areas. The two main streets assumed a new dignity, emphasized by continuous porticoes in brick; the Forum became a more fitting centre by the remodelling of its northern end. The building of tall apartment blocks was continued on a more intensive scale, and before their advance most of the independent atrium houses were swept away. Public baths increased in number and scale. New temples were built. Hadrianic work at Ostia is seen at its best in two large areas that were completely replanned. The first stretches from the Forum to the river and from the Cardo Maximus to the Via degli Horrea Epagathiana. The consistency of the brickstamps and the uniformity in the style of construction show that this area was rebuilt to a single master plan.[1] Only two of the new buildings incorporated earlier walls. The south wall of the Piccolo Mercato uses a stretch of the northern wall of the Castrum; the building to its west uses in its eastern wall an older wall of tufa blocks. All else was destroyed.

The northern stretch of the Cardo Maximus was an important highway. Emperors and other distinguished visitors coming to Ostia by river from Rome or arriving from overseas would naturally land at the quayside where the Cardo reached the river, and so proceed to the Forum. The street was now widened and made more impressive by continuous porticoes in brick on either side. Off the porticoes opened shops, with apartments above them, approached independently by solid stairs from the street. A narrow archway across the Cardo closed the northern entrance of the Forum to wheeled traffic.

The subsidiary streets in this newly planned area were similarly lined with shops, carrying apartments above them. Behind them were utilitarian buildings serving the needs of trade. The function of the Piccolo Mercato is uncertain.[2] Its series of twenty-seven large rooms surrounding an open court were probably used for the storage of goods. The

[1] Carcopino, *Mélanges*, 30 (1910) 397; Bloch, *Bolli laterizi*, 87.
[2] Paschetto, 310.

construction of ramps rather than stairs to the first floor suggests that the rooms on this floor also were used for storage. The building to the west is very similar in plan, but the raised floors of its rooms show that it was used for the storage of corn. On the opposite side of the street to the south is an entrance framed by brick pilasters; above it are inset a modius and a measurer's rod in terra-cotta.[1] The building into which this entrance leads has been largely lost by the erosion of the river, but the emblems of the corn measurers suggest another granary.

With the replanning of this large area was logically connected the transformation of the Forum. The republican temples at the north end would have been dwarfed by the new tall brick buildings. They were now destroyed and replaced by a single temple standing back from the Decumanus. To dominate the new buildings this temple, the Capitolium, was raised on a high platform, giving it a total height from the ground of some seventy feet. In front of the Capitolium a sacred area was reserved, extending the free area of the Forum; it was lined on either side by colonnades. Further changes were made south of the Decumanus, probably later in the reign. Two monumental arches, built on either side of the temple of Rome and Augustus, closed the Forum at its southern end; new porticoes framed it on east and west.

The brickstamps of the area north of the Forum show that this Hadrianic plan, including the Capitolium, was carried out at the beginning of the reign. The second comprehensive plan was developed in Hadrian's last years, and was probably not completed when he died. In the first plan brick and reticulate were used in combination except in the Capitolium, an all-brick construction. The second was carried out entirely in brick, and this remained the standard practice for the remainder of the century. The association of reticulate with brick in wall facing had probably been a measure of economy. It is likely that the tremendous expansion of the brick industry under Hadrian had lowered the cost of bricks enough to make brick facing cheaper than reticulate.

The area that was replanned towards the end of Hadrian's reign lies to the east of the theatre. It stretches southwards from the Decumanus, eastwards from the Via delle Corporazioni.[2] Its northern limit is probably marked by the Via della Fullonica and it extended at least a block eastwards from the Via dei Vigiles.[3] At the heart of the plan are two

[1] Paschetto, 314.
[2] Bloch, *Bolli laterizi*, 222.
[3] This area is only partly excavated.

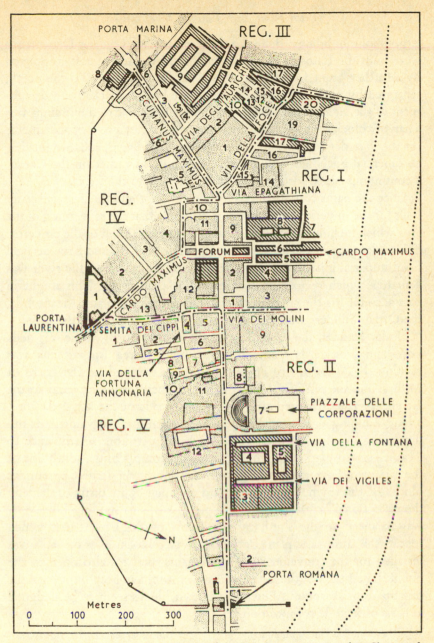

Fig. 2. Hadrianic building. I. 4: House of the Paintings, &c. I. 5 and 6: Shops and apartments. I. 7: Granary. I. 8: Piccolo Mercato and granary. I. 12: House of the Triclinia. I. 17: Baths of Mithras, shops &c. I. 20: Partly excavated *horrea* or market. II. 4: Baths of Neptune. II. 5: Barracks of Vigiles. II. 6: Shops and apartments. III. 9: Garden Houses. III. 10: Insulae of Serapis and of the Charioteers. III. 16: Baths of Trinacria. III. 17: Temple of Serapis, *horrea*, &c. IV. 1: Cybele and her associates. Forum: Capitolium.

large public buildings. Behind a frontage of shops on the Decumanus were built the Baths of Neptune, financed by Hadrian and completed by a further grant from his successor Antoninus Pius.[1] To the north, separated by a street from the baths, were built barracks for a detachment of the *vigiles* from Rome. To the west of these two buildings was a narrow block of shops and apartments: to the east a row of apartments on the Via dei Vigili, and behind them buildings probably serving commercial purposes. Along the Decumanus, as earlier on the Cardo, a continuous brick portico gave added dignity to the street.

Since the baths were financed by the emperor and the barracks were built for the imperial fire service it is probable that the replanning of the area which included them was initiated by or on behalf of the emperor. The replanning of the area north of the Forum may also have derived from imperial initiative, for the best use of the land near the river was a matter which concerned Rome no less than Ostia. This might in part account for the comprehensiveness of the two plans. Meanwhile, the Ostian builders were extremely busy in other parts of the town.

Under Hadrian the rebuilding of the district north of the Via della Foce and westwards from the Via degli Horrea Epagathiana was continued. To the many Trajanic buildings were added the Baths of Mithras and the rest of the block of which they form part,[2] and, at the far end of the excavated area, on the north side of the Via della Foce, a long building only partially excavated, with massive vaults.[3] Its full dimensions cannot yet be seen, but it bears a striking resemblance to Trajan's closed market above his Forum at Rome. On the south side of the Via della Foce the Insula of Serapis, one of the largest apartment blocks of the town, was built round an open court distinguished by the exceptional height of the brick piers of its surrounding portico. It was balanced to the south by the Insula of the Charioteers which repeats the same basic plan. Between the two blocks a set of baths was installed for the convenience of the tenants, perhaps also open to the public. The Insula of the Charioteers may not have been built until the principate of Antoninus Pius but the two blocks seem to be designed as parts of a single composition.[4]

---

[1] 98. For the identification, p. 409.   [2] Bloch, *Topografia*, 219 (i. 17. 2).

[3] Becatti, *Topografia*, 138.

[4] Bloch, *Bolli laterizi*, 202 f. The brickstamps of the Insula of Serapis are homogeneous (apart from a small Trajanic enclave) and point to a mid-Hadrianic date. A considerable number of stamps from the early years of Antoninus Pius were found among the ruins of the Insula of the Charioteers. Bloch concludes that there was an interval of at least ten

In the same district, west of the Casette-tipo, another new Hadrianic quarter was built, on either side of the Via della Trinacria which runs southward from the Via della Foce.[1] On the east side are public baths; on the west shops, houses, and the temple of Serapis. The Fasti record the building of the temple in A.D. 127; the building is identified by inscriptions and by brickstamps of the years 123–6.[2]

Along the eastern side of the western Decumanus the series of atrium and peristyle houses which had been built in the late Republic and early Principate had mostly been destroyed by the end of Hadrian's reign to be replaced by taller buildings that made more economic use of the space. Even the rich were moving into apartments as we can see in the residential area that was developed under Hadrian south of the Cardo degli Aurighi. This quarter of the town, far removed from the busy traffic of the riverside and within easy reach of the sea, must have been one of the most attractive for men of means. The enterprising owners who were responsible for the development invested in apartments and not in independent homes.

The architect of the development plan had a large, irregular, roughly trapezoidal area at his disposal; he reduced it to order with considerable skill.[3] At the centre of his composition were two long apartment blocks, each divided on the ground floor into four symmetrical flats. Independent stairs led to upper floors where the same plan was presumably repeated. These flats had no shops on their frontage but looked out on to gardens. Flats and gardens formed an inner rectangle, which was reconciled with the irregular shape of the building area in the varying depths of the buildings that surrounded the gardens. On the eastern side further apartment blocks were built, offering attractive residences. The House of the Muses at the north-east corner has twelve elegant rooms on its ground floor, and the House of the Dioscuri at the south-east corner, when later remodelled, was the most imposing house in the town. In this large architectural composition all the individual apartments are large; paintings and mosaics show careful workmanship.

years between the building of the two blocks. This is not certain. The two blocks, together with the baths between them, seem to form a coherent plan. Substantial modifications were made to the western wing of the Insula of the Charioteers not long after its completion. The Antonine stamps might come from these modifications. The blocks described, Calza, *Palladio*, 5 (1941) 8.

[1] Becatti, *Topografia*, 138.

[2] Bloch, *Topografia*, 225 (iii. 17. 4). A fuller discussion by Bloch will be published in *AJA* 1959.   [3] Pl. II e.

The owners undoubtedly expected high rents, but when population and prosperity decreased such properties may have become a liability.

Hadrian's principate also saw further modernization near the centre of the town. The brick-built 'Curia', opposite the Basilica, had replaced a reticulate building that was probably Augustan,[1] and must have presented a sharp contrast with its more old-fashioned neighbours in the block. These were one by one pulled down and replaced by Hadrianic buildings, but the irregular lines of the old building lots were retained.[2] The balancing block on the east side of the Forum was similarly rebuilt. Here the work may have begun under Trajan, but most of the buildings in the block are Hadrianic.[3] Opposite, on the south side of the Decumanus, next to the Forum, the large House of the Triclinia, built round an open courtyard, has early Hadrianic brickstamps.[4] Towards the middle of the reign the rebuilding of the area north of the Forum was extended by a block of apartments and commercial premises to the east.[5]

On the south side of the eastern Decumanus, east of the Semita dei Cippi, the long narrow block of apartments and shops which includes the House of Themistokles[6] was built under Hadrian, but no attempt was made to impose a new and more satisfactory plan on this area.[7] A more drastic treatment could have considerably improved the town.

Important changes were also made under Hadrian by the Porta Marina and the Porta Laurentina. Outside the Porta Marina and east of the gate is a large open square surrounded by a portico with an exedra at the eastern end; the brickwork associated here with reticulate is typically Hadrianic. On the sea-front itself fragments of columns remain from another small Hadrianic square, the Piazza del Prospetto. To the public funerary monument of C. Cartilius Poplicola was added a loggia in brick.[8] These improvements by the sea-coast, together with the new public baths near by, remind us that Ostia was not exclusively a trading city, but was making the most of the natural attractions of the sea.

By the Porta Laurentina a large triangular area was reserved for the cult of Cybele.[9] In front of her small temple was the ceremonial field of the Great Mother, where bulls were sacrificed in her honour. Within

---

[1] Becatti, *Topografia*, 105.   [2] NS 1923, 177.   [3] *NS* 1916, 399.
[4] Bloch *Topografia*, 217 (i. 12. 1).   [5] Ibid. 216 (i. 4. 2–4).
[6] Reg. v. 11, 2.   [7] p. 122.   [8] Bloch, *Topografia*, 227 (iv. 9. 1).
[9] p. 357. The date is not certain.

the area were also temples of Attis and Bellona and the headquarters of the guilds which administered the cults. The ample provision of open spaces by these two gates compensated in some degree for the intensive development of the rest of the town.

As population increased and the value of land rose the temptation to leave open spaces in the busier parts of the town was easily resisted. When the four temples on a common platform west of the theatre were built in the late Republic they were surrounded by a large open area enclosed on three sides by a colonnade. In the early Principate, buildings, probably shops, had invaded a large part of the free area. Similarly there had once been a considerable open space between the Via di Diana and the Decumanus, the Piazza dei Lari;[1] in Hadrian's principate buildings encroached on every side. The public gardens, however, behind the theatre were retained, a welcome oasis in an increasingly congested town.

By the time of Hadrian's death Ostia had become a modern city. Her wide main streets with their continuous porticoes and tall apartment blocks could stand comparison with those of Rome. Her new Capitolium provided a fitting architectural focus to the centre of the town. Her amenities had been improved by the sharp increase in the number of her public baths and the increasing emphasis on the seaward side of the town. The main lines of development had been laid down. There were, however, still many buildings which could be usefully replaced.

The street plan was to remain virtually unchanged for the rest of the Roman period. It does not present a tidy mathematical picture. The chequer-board pattern which we expect to find in Roman towns can be seen in the centre of the town, where it is inherited from the fourth-century Castrum, and in the area east of the Forum, between Decumanus and river, which had been reserved as public land in the Gracchan period. The opposite side of the Decumanus still preserved its oblique lines and awkward shapes, deriving from uncontrolled development in the pre-Sullan period. In the west of the town the main arteries, the Via della Foce and the western Decumanus, were deliberately planned. Practical needs dictated the development north of the Via della Foce: the main streets run at right angles to the river. South of the Via della Foce development had been more irregular. In some districts on this side Trajan and Hadrian imposed order, but the large area between the

[1] *NS* 1916, 411.

Via della Calcara and the western Decumanus remained a formless conglomeration of buildings.

The commercial activity of Ostia was mainly concentrated in the north of the town, between the eastern Decumanus and river and, in the west, between the Via della Foce and river. It is in these areas that most of the buildings for storing corn and other bulky goods are found, and the barracks of the *vigiles*, who were responsible for fighting fires. But utilitarian premises were not as concentrated as in a modern dock quarter. Public baths, shops, and apartments were liberally dispersed among the *horrea*: the important traders' exchange in the Piazzale delle Corporazioni was associated with the theatre.

The southern half of the town was more restricted, but the complete separation of residential from commercial and industrial areas was not the Roman pattern. In Ostia shops lined almost all the streets and even large independent houses were not ashamed to use their street fronts for the purpose. Industry was confined to small establishments and normally the producer sold his goods in the shop where they were made. There may have been social distinctions between different districts, but they are not very apparent. In the south-west district developed under Hadrian, the so-called Garden Houses, the apartments seem to be fairly homogeneous and designed for men of means, but normally rich and poor seem to be content to live close together, and no district that can reasonably be called a slum has yet been found.

Trade, religion, and recreation all profited from the great building activity under Trajan and Hadrian; but the tall apartment blocks were its most striking feature. They successfully solved the problem of accommodating a rapidly expanding population without a lowering of living standards, and their plain brick surfaces, relieved by rows of well-proportioned windows, provided an effective contrast to the marble of temples and other public buildings.

The concentration of a large population in a restricted area might have brought conditions as unhealthy as those which accompanied the first urban developments of the industrial revolution in Britain if due attention had not been paid to the prosaic problems of sanitation. In 1842 a Commission appointed to consider ways and means of improving the health of London included in their report a detailed description, with plans, of the sanitary arrangements in the Roman Colosseum and the amphitheatre of Verona.[1] This they did, not because the Roman

[1] Metropolitan Sanitary Commission (*First Report*, 1847) 135–9.

system was of interest to the antiquarian, but because it had much to teach the architects and builders of their day. Had they been able to study and report on the domestic architecture of Ostia they would have done even more useful service. For throughout the new building the necessity of good drainage was never neglected. In the tall buildings large pipes were provided to carry down the waste from the upper floors; small drains led from the blocks to the main drains under the streets, which ran in a gentle slope to the river. This system of drainage no doubt ruined the bathing prospects of the river, but a river port was no place for swimming and the sea was near at hand. The river current was swift enough to carry the refuse away. Wheeling flocks of seagulls must have been a familiar sight at the river's mouth.

The distribution of public latrines is, at first sight, less generous than might be expected. Of the three clear examples that survive one only can be dated as early as the second century; it is near the river on the east side of the Via della Fortuna, which runs parallel to and west of the northern Cardo. The handsome establishment behind the builders' guild house near the Forum replaces two Hadrianic shops and was probably installed when the Forum Baths were restored in the late fourth century.[1] The third was built behind a nymphaeum at the south end of the Forum. Inscribed tombstones are used for seats; the workmanship is very shoddy; it probably dates from the fifth century. This apparent scarcity of facilities in the hey-day of the Empire can, however, be understood if the latrines of public baths were also available. Most of them were placed near the street; they were probably used by the general public as well as by the users of the baths. The lack of privacy in these 'comfort stations' does not appeal to modern taste, but we can respect the provision of running water which carried the refuse away into main drains. Even less privacy was given to urinals. Large *dolia* were sunk in the ground beside streets, or stood in passage-ways or near the entrance of shops.

Water could not have been freely provided for latrines in the Republic when the town relied on wells, but in the early Empire an aqueduct had been built. A line of brick piers, perhaps of Severan date, shows where the aqueduct met the town wall, some 120 metres south of the Porta Romana. The water was carried from a distributing centre by the wall across the Piazza della Vittoria and along the Decumanus in a massive lead pipe. This can be seen at various points along the north

[1] Pl. ix *b*.

side of the street with the stamp which confirms public control 'colonorum coloniae Ostiense'.[1] Smaller pipes carried the supply into public buildings and into public cisterns on the streets, from which tenants of many of the large blocks drew their water. Some houses also had their own supply and the pipes that led to them were stamped with the owner's name. The consumption of water must have risen sharply in the second century, especially with the increase in the number of public baths, and the capacity of the aqueduct was overstrained. To supplement supplies in the baths water-wheels were installed to fill the cisterns from the subsoil;[2] in many private houses wells were still retained.

Hadrian's death seems to mark the end of large-scale replanning; new building continues under Antoninus Pius, but on a less extensive scale. The Hadrianic rebuilding of the area which includes the Baths of Neptune and the Barracks of the Vigiles was completed, and perhaps developed eastwards. A continuous portico in brick had been built along the Decumanus frontage of the new Hadrianic blocks. To balance it a similar portico was built on the opposite side of the street from the Via del Sabazeo to the Piazza della Vittoria. This portico has brick-stamps of Antoninus Pius' reign.[3]

The dignity of the town centre was increased by the building of a new set of public baths south-east of the Forum. They were the largest and most richly appointed in the town and the curving line of their southward-facing rooms contrasted attractively with the straightforward rectilinear planning that had hitherto dominated Ostian architecture. Associated with the plan of the baths was a small triangular palaestra on the south side, surrounded by a colonnade. The free area of the Forum, even after the Hadrianic remodelling, was small for Ostia's increasing population. The addition of further open space near by, however small, was valuable.

The Forum Baths and other buildings of this reign make it one of the most interesting periods in the architectural history of Ostia. The curving line is again prominent in the Schola del Traiano on the western Decumanus, probably a guild headquarters, built near the middle of the century.[4] Through an apsidal hall on the street one passes to a long open courtyard or garden with a nymphaeum running down the

---

[1] S 5309[2].

[2] The clearest traces of such water-wheels can be seen in the Baths of Mithras and in the Forum Baths; few sets of Ostian baths are without them.

[3] Bloch, *Topografia*, 227 (v. 14 and 15).   [4] Becatti, *Topografia*, 146.

whole length in the centre and a series of rooms at the far end. The shape of the hall and the length of the nymphaeum are highly original features. The House of Diana, roughly contemporary, makes more economic use of the space available than any other large building in Ostia.[1] The Horrea Epagathiana et Epaphroditiana combine utility and elegance to a remarkable degree.[2] The so-called 'Imperial Palace' includes baths, courts, and apartments on a scale not previously seen in Ostia.[3] Some of the less ambitious blocks of apartments, such as the House of the Sun, were also probably built in this reign, but none are yet securely dated by brickstamps, and it is not easy to distinguish late Hadrianic construction from what immediately follows. The House of Fortuna Annonaria, built for a single family round a garden court, seems like a gracious protest against the new tall blocks.[4]

Under the emperors who followed in the second half of the century the rhythm of expansion slowed down. Typical lines of shops with apartments above them continued the familiar pattern, as on the Via del Tempio Rotondo, south-west of the Forum; at the angle of the Via degli Horrea Epagathiana and Via della Foce; on the south side of the eastern Decumanus between the theatre and the Via degli Augustali, and the long line of the Caseggiato dell' Ercole on the western Decumanus.

More conspicuous and important were the changes in the area between the eastern Decumanus and the river. Even after the rebuilding under Hadrian and Antoninus Pius much remained here from the early Principate. It was probably under Commodus that the Julio-Claudian Grandi Horrea were completely rebuilt, to provide increased storage capacity by a higher building;[5] at approximately the same time another large granary was built to the east of the area replanned under Hadrian.[6] The Augustan theatre, rebuilt to provide increased accommodation, was dedicated at the beginning of Septimius Severus' reign.[7]

Two new temples were built during this period, and both were probably associated with guilds. The earlier, on the southern side of the eastern Decumanus near the theatre, cannot be identified. Inscriptions suggest that the second, on the western Decumanus, was built and maintained by the shipbuilders.[8] The handsome social headquarters of

[1] *NS* 1914, 244.
[2] *NS* 1940, 32. [3] Paschetto, 407; Becatti, *Topografia*, 147.
[4] Becatti, *Case Ostiensi del tardo impero*, 23. [5] *NS* 1921, 381.
[6] Becatti, *Topografia*, 143. [7] 114. [8] p. 327.

the *seviri Augustales*, on the eastern Decumanus, probably dates from the reign of Marcus Aurelius.[1]

THE SEVERAN PERIOD AND AFTER

The work of the early Severan period seems to be mainly confined to restorations, in *horrea*, baths, and in the Barracks of the Vigiles. The only new building of note so far known is a richly furnished set of baths on the line of the Sullan walls west of Porta Marina;[2] but we should probably add the semicircular 'emporium' reported at the west end of the town.[3] It is a surprise, after what seems to be a period of comparative sterility, to find one of the boldest and most interesting buildings in the town being erected towards the end of the Severan period or soon after. This round temple, on the west side of the Basilica, had a handsome pronaos supported on ten columns, and a large forecourt; early reports show that it was richly dressed in marble.[4] With it was rebuilt a small area to the west.

The Round Temple is the latest important building in the excavated area. The centre of gravity was by now shifting away from the river towards the sea coast. No new *horrea* can be seen and there are no signs of major late restorations in the old. But excavation has not yet extended to the western end of the town; it may be found that in the late Empire the shrinking volume of shipping was concentrated by the western quays.

The building of the late third and fourth centuries that can still be seen is more concerned with amenity than with the needs of trade. Public baths were kept in repair, and their number even increased. Fourth-century restorations can be seen in the Forum Baths and in the Baths of Neptune, and are recorded in an inscription from the Maritime Baths.[5] Two new sets were added, one on the Via della Foce, the other behind the House of Jupiter the Thunderer. Both are predominantly curvilinear in plan, in keeping with late-Empire taste. Towards the end of the century the theatre was adapted for the presentation of spectacles on water.[6] New public fountains and nymphaea were added.

Space was less precious within the city in the late Empire. The Piazza della Vittoria, the large open area at the entrance to the town

---

[1] Bloch, *Topografia*, 227 (v. 7. 2); below, p. 220.
[2] Paschetto, 304; for the date, Bloch, *Topografia*, 222 f. (iii. 8. 2).
[3] p. 80.   [4] Paschetto, 300.   [5] 137.   [6] p. 424.

inside the Porta Romana, is a late creation. Part of this area at least was once covered by buildings, and some of the walls that were destroyed were not earlier than the second century.[1] The dominant feature in this piazza is a long fountain against which is a strongly constructed wall, probably designed as a base for statues. Fountains and wall are faced with alternating courses of brick and tufa blocks. The workmanship is good; it probably dates from the third century.

Similarly an open square was cleared on the south side of the eastern Decumanus a little east of the Forum. When the Forum Baths were built the area between them and the Decumanus was occupied by a set of baths built under Hadrian.[2] These buildings were destroyed and the area left free. Colonnades framed the new square on east and west, and a brick portico provided its frontage on the Decumanus; in the centre of the square was set up a heroic statue. The shoddy character of the brickwork and the poorly assorted character of the old material reused suggest a date towards the end of the fourth century.

In domestic architecture the emphasis shifts back to the independent house. While the big apartment blocks show very little sign of late restoration and some were even allowed to fall into ruin, independent houses were maintained and new were built in the late third and through the fourth century.[3] These late houses are widely distributed, but the south and south-west districts remained the most popular for men of means.

Though the main lines of Ostia's development can already be approximately traced, there remain serious gaps in our knowledge, and not all of them can be filled by further excavation. The outline of the early history of the town will never be more than tentative, owing to the limits imposed on excavation below the imperial level, and the possibly widespread use of perishable materials; but it should be possible to trace the main stages of expansion to the west and south-west which at present can only be guessed. The important area on the river bank in the eastern half of the town, which was probably the main dock area in the early and middle Republic, will have been largely destroyed by the river, but there has been little change in the river course west of the Forum, and the exploration of this area should answer important questions. The partly excavated market on the Via della Foce is perhaps

---

[1] *NS* 1910, 251, 374.
[2] Becatti, *Topografia*, 159; this area has not been thoroughly explored.
[3] Becatti, *Case Ostiensi del tardo impero* (Roma, 1949).

the most impressive commercial building in the town, and farther to the west lies the semicircular 'emporium', which, according to early accounts, was a building of interesting design and large proportions. It may be found that, as the eastern end of the docks sank into neglect, the western end was kept in good repair. We may also expect to find a larger proportion of late construction along the line of the coast.

Of the south-eastern area of the town little is known. The earth cover is much lower here, suggesting that the buildings were lower, but it will be interesting to find out whether this was primarily a residential area, and whether the independent house held its own against the apartment block. The right bank of the river also remains unexplored; there are no reports of discoveries in this area, nor has account yet been taken of it. But even a casual stroll through the fields shows, as one might expect, that buildings lined the river on this side. Through a hole in the ground I have seen second-century walls still standing to a height of some 4 metres, and along the edges of fields are tell-tale piles of Roman brick and sherds of coarse pottery. But the built-up area on this side was not deep. The contour of the ground falls sharply some hundred metres from the river. Behind these buildings the land of Isola Sacra was probably reserved for market gardens.

8

PORTUS

THE history of the imperial harbours and the settlement that grew up around them cannot be studied in such detail as Ostia town because no part of the area has been systematically excavated. The scale of the harbours and of the ruins around them attracted antiquarians from the fifteenth century onwards. The earliest description preserved records the visit of Pius II in 1461;[1] the earliest plan is by Giuliano da Sangallo, between 1485 and 1514. But there is little precise detail in the early descriptions and the plans represent wishful thinking rather than a record of what could still be seen. None had greater influence than Ligorio's handsome reconstruction of 1554, but to make a convincing picture Ligorio drew heavily on his imagination. Some of his successors were considerably more restrained, but their plans are suspiciously schematic and none has stood the test of detailed investigation.[2] Not until the nineteenth century was the relative orientation of the harbours of Trajan and Claudius clearly shown; earlier plans set the two harbours on the same axis, though it is still clear on the ground that the outer harbour of Claudius lies to the north-west of the inner basin. The reproduction of the Claudian harbour on Nero's bronze coinage has also bedevilled crucial problems. It has clearly influenced both descriptions and plans, but, as will be seen, the nature and value of its evidence is far from clear.

There can never have been any serious doubt concerning the shape and size of Trajan's inner basin, but it is doubtful whether, even as early as the sixteenth century, an accurate plan could have been made of the Claudian harbour from what could be seen above ground. From the Renaissance onwards the history of the site of Portus runs for a long time parallel to that of Ostia. The ruins were exploited for building material and for the recovery of works of art. But the evidence for the excavations of the late eighteenth and early nineteenth century is even more meagre than at Ostia.

[1] The account quoted, A. Nibby, *Analisi de' dintorni di Roma*[2] (1848) 634.

[2] For the series of Portus maps, G. Lugli, 'Una pianta inedita del porto Ostiense', *Rend. Pont.* 23–24 (1947–9) 187.

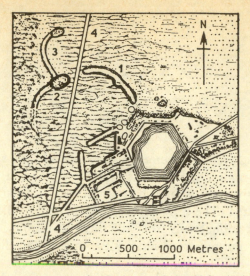

FIG. 3. Existing state, 1829, as seen by Canina. 1. Monte Giulio (right mole). 2. Monte dell' Arena (assumed to mark the site of the lighthouse). 3. Mole added in late Empire (p. 170). 4. Fronzino canal. 5. 'Darsena', basin for rowing-boats (p. 160).

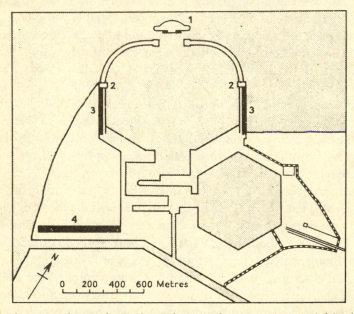

FIG. 4. Plan restored, 1858, by Texier, *Mémoire sur les ports antiques situés à l'embouchure du Tibre*. Details of buildings round Trajan's harbour (schematic) are omitted. 1. Island with lighthouse. 2. Balancing arches on moles (p. 159). 3. Texier assumes buildings on both moles up to the arches, but none on their seaward side. 4. Porticus Placidiana (p. 169). See also key to Fig. 3.

What little we know of them is due to Fea, who published in 1824 his valuable gleanings on the site,[1] and to Nibby, who in 1837 included

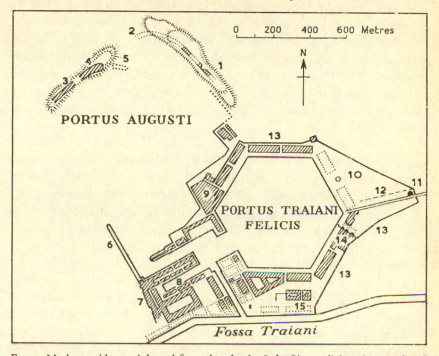

FIG. 5. Modern evidence. Adapted from the plan by Italo Gismondi (1935), reproduced in *Rend. Pont.* 23–24 (1947–9) 195; with additions. 1. Buildings partly excavated by Lugli on right mole (p. 158). 2. Turning-point of right mole towards entrance, traced by Carcopino (*NS* 1907, 735). 3. Parts of left mole, traced by Lugli (p. 155). 4. Widening of left mole from *c.* 50 ft. to *c.* 75 ft., revealed in 1957 (Pl. xix). 5. Wall, *c.* 15 ft. wide, first discovered by Carcopino (*NS* 1907, 736) and thought to be a late addition, at an angle to the left mole. Revealed in 1957 to be the termination of the left mole, almost certainly Claudian (p. 157). It is faced with well-coursed tufa bricks, excellently preserved. 6. Late Empire mole (p. 170). 7. Claudian portico (p. 160). 8. Darsena. 9. 'Imperial Palace' (pp. 163–5). 10. Temple of Liber Pater. 11. Temple of 'Portumnus'. 12. Aqueduct. 13. 'Constantinian walls'. 14. Defensive cross-wall (p. 170). 15. Tower shown in Pl. xxi *b*.

with his history and description of the ruins valuable information concerning what had come to light in his day.[2] Later excavations also followed a different pattern from those at Ostia. When Visconti excavated at Ostia for the Pope between 1855 and 1869 accounts and plans were

[1] C. Fea, *Viaggio ad Ostia* (1802) 30–39.
[2] A. Nibby, *Della Via Portuense e dell' antica città di Porto* (Roma, 1827), incorporated in *Analisi de' dintorni di Roma*, here cited in the 1848 edition as 'Nibby'.

published and the study of the town's history was steadily advanced. When at Portus substantial excavations were undertaken between 1864 and 1867 the contemporary record is virtually confined to a list of sculpture found. Lanciani visiting the site shortly afterwards found the ruins covered again, and, though local workers could give him a general impression of what had been seen, the information was inadequate to provide the basis for a plan. These excavations are particularly tantalizing, because they uncovered a large area between the two harbours and could have resolved important problems in history and topography.

Lanciani's thorough investigation of the site, however, marked a great step forward. Besides checking earlier accounts he was able to collect important evidence that had accumulated since Nibby wrote. Lanciani had a keener eye than his predecessors for the changing styles of Roman construction, and he appreciated the importance of brickstamps. His account, published in 1868 together with a more detailed plan of Trajan's harbour, for long remained the standard source of reference.[1]

While from 1870 onwards Ostia was being excavated by the state, Portus remained in the possession of the Torlonia family, who had acquired the site in 1856. In the course of agricultural work parts of buildings were occasionally uncovered but no accounts were published. In 1907, however, Carcopino, then Director of the French School in Rome, was authorized to make a limited series of tests in the Claudian harbour. Of the three specific problems which concerned him, the easiest only was satisfactorily resolved. Carcopino traced the line of the right mole to its approximate end, and confirmed the position and rough width of the entrance at this point. His more difficult problems eluded him. He was not able to establish the relation between the lighthouse and the left mole, nor to follow the course of the left mole to its junction with the land. The trial pits to which he was restricted were too limited in scope to resolve the problems, but useful new evidence, positive and negative, was obtained.[2] New evidence was also won from Trajan's harbour when the basin, which had degenerated into a reed-fringed marsh, was cleaned out and restored to its original form in 1923. Calza was able to study the structure of the quayside before the

[1] R. Lanciani, 'Ricerche topografiche sulla città di Porto', *Ann. Inst.* 40 (1868) 144–95 (cited as 'Lanciani').
[2] Carcopino, *NS* 1907, 734.

basin was refilled, and to leave an illustrated record of what can no longer be seen. At the same time he was able to describe and plan a substantial part of a large granary and a group of tombs which had been uncovered when the hydraulic pump used for drawing water into the restored basin was installed.[1]

Finally, in 1935 Lugli did for Portus what Paschetto had done for Ostia in 1912. In a volume handsomely illustrated by revised plans and photographs he collected the evidence available for a history of the site and described in considerably more detail than his predecessors the ruins that can be seen or of which some record has survived.[2] He also hoped to press to a conclusion Carcopino's investigation of the Claudian harbour, but once again, though valuable new evidence was secured, the scale of the digging was too restricted to provide decisive answers to the main questions.

The Claudian harbour was built some two miles north of the Tiber mouth, and the choice of site has been commonly criticized. The rate of coastal advance has been considerably more rapid to the north than to the south of the river, for the coastal current and prevailing winds sweep sand and silt northwards. By the eighth century, and perhaps earlier, the harbour was choked; today it is more than a mile inland. A harbour built to the south of the river, though exposed to the drift of sand, would not have been threatened by Tiber silt.

It has been suggested that Claudius deliberately avoided the more suitable area because he did not wish to expropriate the owners of coastal villas which stretched in a continuous line southwards from Ostia;[3] but such scruples would not have been decisive when Rome's corn supply was at stake. Nor should we lightly condemn his engineers for overlooking what seems to us a decisive factor. If we are right in believing that the coastline was comparatively stable during the Roman period the danger to the new harbour from Tiber silt would have been much less apparent than it became later.[4] The main positive advantage of the site chosen was that it provided the shortest and easiest communication with the Tiber; and there may already have been a small bay at this point on the coast.[5]

[1] Calza, 'Ricognizioni topografiche nel porto di Traiano', *NS* 1925, 54.
[2] G. Lugli and G. Filibeck. *Il Porto di Roma imperiale e l'agro Portuense* (Roma, 1935), a limited edition not available in England, cited as 'Lugli'.
[3] Carcopino, *Ostie*, 9 f.
[4] pp. 125 f.; Le Gall, *Le Tibre*, 129.
[5] Lugli, 9.

The general shape of the Claudian harbour is recorded by Suetonius and Dio, and can be partly confirmed on the ground and from air photographs. Suetonius gives a summary description in his *Life of Claudius*:

He constructed a harbour at Ostia. Two encircling arms were built out to sea: at the entrance where the water was deep a break-water was added. In order to provide more secure foundations for this breakwater he first sank the ship which had brought the great obelisk from Egypt . . . above he set a very high tower on the model of the Alexandrian Pharos, so that ships could steer their course by its burning light at night.[1]

Dio adds a little further detail:

First he excavated a not inconsiderable area of land; he built a retaining wall right round this excavated area and then let the sea come in. Next, in the sea itself he built great moles, one on each side, enclosing a large expanse of sea. He formed an island in the sea and built on it a tower with a beacon.[2]

A visit to the site still gives a vivid impression of the scale of Claudius' harbour. The modern road to Fiumicino runs close by Trajan's harbour. To the north of the road, less than a hundred metres distant, can be seen the hexagonal basin, once again filled with water; around it is an eighteenth-century classical landscape of open woodland and grass-covered ruins. When the road passes beyond this woodland the country is flat and comparatively featureless. But in the distance to the north-east a gently swelling rise can be seen, running in an unbroken stretch for roughly half a mile. This is Monte Giulio; it marks the line of the right mole. To the left of Monte Giulio, nearly a mile from the road, is an isolated hillock, rising up sharp from the ground. This is the sand-hill, Monte dell' Arena, growing good crops; it is generally assumed to hide what remains of the Claudian lighthouse. But from the road it is impossible to detect the line of the left mole; among the low undulations there is no single prominent contour. On the ground, however, its line can be followed westwards from Monte dell' Arena for some 500 metres, until it curves towards the land.[3] Beyond that point it is lost.

Carcopino's report in 1907 presented an intelligible reconstruction of

---

[1] Suet. *Claud.* 20. 3; 'portum Ostiae extruxit circumducto dextra sinistraque brachio et ad introitum profundo iam solo mole obiecta; quam quo stabilius fundaret, navem ante demersit.'

[2] Dio lx. 11. 4.

[3] J. Bradford, *Ancient Landscapes*, 253.

the main features of the harbour. Monte Giulio concealed the right
mole. Between the end of the right mole and Monte dell' Arena was
an entrance 120 metres wide. Monte dell' Arena marked the lighthouse
and beyond it was a second entrance of approximately the same width.
Nibby, however, had already reported that there was no room for
such an entrance between the lighthouse and the left mole,[1] and he was
confirmed when Lugli exposed a small stretch of the left mole almost
immediately below Monte dell' Arena.[2]

Lugli concluded that the lighthouse was built, not on an island, but
at the end of the left mole. For this view he found support in a passage
from the elder Pliny, who should be a reliable eyewitness. In a catalogue of trees of spectacular size Pliny digresses from the fir which
provided the mast to a brief description of the ship which was used for
the foundations of the lighthouse: 'longitudo spatium obtinuit magna
ex parte Ostiensis portus latere laevo. ibi namque demersa est.'[3] Lugli
takes this passage to mean that the ship occupied a large part of the left
mole; but since the left mole was at least 800 metres long and the ship's
length can hardly have exceeded 50 metres it is extremely difficult to
refer 'latere laevo' to the left mole. Like so much in Pliny this passage
is too obscure to carry decisive weight.[4] Dio explicitly states that the
lighthouse was on an island and Suetonius implies the same.

Nero's bronze coinage is also difficult to reconcile with Lugli's
thesis.[5] These coins show two curving moles, and the end of the left
mole is occupied by a temple. Between the moles is a colossal imperial
statue on a substantial base. The lighthouse itself is not represented, but
a relief found by Trajan's harbour, now in the Torlonia Museum, which
depicts some of the monuments of the two harbours, shows a colossal
statue on the penultimate story of the lighthouse.[6] It has not unreason-
ably been suggested that the artist of the coin design has chosen to
emphasize the statue at the expense of its background. More important
perhaps than this uncertain identification is the disposition of the ships
in the design. Through all minor variations in the different dies two

---

[1] Nibby, 643.   [2] Lugli, 24.   [3] Pliny, *NH* xvi. 202.
[4] In his description of a whale-hunt in the harbour of Claudius Pliny (*NH* ix. 14)
provides further ambiguous evidence. Nets were spread to prevent the whale's escape:
'praetendi iussit Caesar plagas multiplices inter ora portus.' This cannot mean 'between
the entrances', which would be nonsense. 'At the entrances' seems to me the least unlikely meaning but *ora* might be a poetic plural, implying a single entrance. Cf. Florus,
Epit. i. 33. 7: 'primusque Romanorum ducum victor ad Gades et Oceani ora pervenit.'
[5] Pl. xviii *a*.   [6] Pl. xx.

ships are seen in the same position; a merchantman in full sail is entering, a trireme is leaving the harbour: the colossal statue comes between them and they naturally suggest two entrances.

Nibby offered a plausible solution to reconcile the evidence of literary sources and of the coinage that the lighthouse was on an island with the archaeological demonstration which allowed no entrance between the Monte dell' Arena and the left mole. He suggested that in the late Empire the western entrance was increasingly threatened by the drift of sand and silt and was therefore closed.[1] He also noted a barely perceptible low ridge stretching for some 600 metres north-east of Monte dell' Arena and ending in a mound where he found scattered Roman material including fragments of marble decoration of a very late date.[2] This, he suggested, was a new lighthouse at the end of a new mole, built as a further protection against the sand, possibly in the time of Theodoric. Of this 'late mole' there is now no sign whatever and Lugli has discounted it; but Nibby was in good company when he visited Porto. Fea, Canina, and Rasi were with him and they discussed the main problems together. Canina showed the 'barely perceptible ridge' in his sketch of the existing state of the site.[3]

Nibby published his account in 1829. Nearly thirty years later the French engineer, Charles Texier, who had considerable experience both of harbours and of ancient construction, spent several days in an intensive study of the site.[4] From the literary evidence he was convinced that the lighthouse was on an island in advance of the moles; he satisfied himself that he had identified its position in remains of massive masonry some 100 metres in front of the harbour entrance. 'There still remain on the ground fragments of marble with mouldings, but the marshy nature of the ground made any attempt at excavation impossible. All I could do was to establish the centre of the mass of masonry.'[5]

The problems raised by these conflicting accounts cannot be resolved in the library, nor by walking over the site. Only excavation can furnish the answers and there are at last strong grounds for hoping that

---

[1] Nibby, 643.   [2] Nibby, 640.

[3] Lugli, 27. Canina shows this low ridge in the first edition of his plans (reproduced in Fig. 3, p. 150). He omits it in the plan of the Claudian harbour in his third edition. Lugli infers a change of mind. But in the first edition Canina was reproducing what he saw; in his third edition he was reconstructing the original form of the Claudian harbour. *

[4] C. Texier, *Mémoire sur les ports antiques situés à l'embouchure du Tibre* (= vol. xv, *Revue générale de l'architecture et des travaux publics*) (Paris, 1858).

[5] Texier, 31.

substantial excavations will be undertaken. The building of a new airport to the west of the Claudian harbour has involved subsidiary work
on roads and drainage within the harbour and some tracts of the left
mole near Monte dell' Arena have already been exposed. It is hoped
that the main lines of both moles will now be traced and that the relation of moles to lighthouse will be established beyond doubt. *

It is more discreet therefore at this stage to formulate the main questions that require answers. Was the lighthouse built originally on an
island or on the left mole? And, if it was on an island, was this island on
the same line as the moles or, as at Centumcellae, on the seaward side
of the moles? Recent work has narrowed but not resolved the problem.
It can now be seen that a little to the west of Monte dell' Arena the
left mole widens from roughly 50 to 75 feet.[1] How long it continues
eastwards at this enlarged width is not yet clear, but at some point it
narrows to a width of only some 15 feet and so continues to its end.
The full length of the narrow end of the mole cannot yet be measured,
but it is not less than 60 yards. There is nothing to suggest a late
closing of an original entrance to the west of Monte dell' Arena and
Nibby's attractive hypothesis should be abandoned. Either the lighthouse was near but not at the end of the left mole, where the width
was enlarged, or, more probably, it was on an island. No trace of the
massive platform that was expected under Monte dell' Arena has been
found.

Until the precise relation of moles to lighthouse is established we
cannot be certain which way the harbour faced. It is commonly assumed
that the harbour faced north-west to avoid the dangerous south-west
wind which often blows with gale force; but a passage in Ammianus
Marcellinus, if it can be trusted, indicates that corn ships could enter
harbour under full sail with a south-south-west wind behind them.[2]

The design of the right mole also remains in doubt. The left mole,
which faced the main force of the storms and the drift of sand and silt,
was built in a solid mass. Nero's coinage suggests that the right mole
was carried on arches, following the practice adopted at Puteoli.[3] This
would have allowed sand and silt drifting into the harbour to be swept
out instead of piling up against the mole. The interpretation of the coin

---

[1] Pl. xix.

[2] Amm. Marc. xix. 10. 4: 'dum Tertullus apud Ostia in aede sacrificat Castorum,
tranquillitas mare mollivit, mutatoque in austrum placidum vento, velificatione plena
portum naves ingressae, frumentis horrea referserunt.'   [3] Pl. xviii *a.*

M

design, however, is controversial and it is unprofitable to speculate when a clear answer can be expected soon from excavation.[1]

The total area of the harbour must also remain uncertain until the full line of the left mole is traced; but Texier's figure of 160 acres is probably not far from the truth.[2] The maximum diameter was perhaps nearly 1,000 metres, and in high storms this large expanse of comparatively shallow water could have been dangerous to shipping.

The lighthouse is the only building connected with Claudius' harbour whose outline we clearly know.[3] It was a spectacular building, the first of its kind in Italy, and it quickly caught the imagination. It is reproduced in mosaics and reliefs, on coins and on lamps: its rough outline is scratched on Ostian walls. It provided the model for the campanile of St. Paul's basilica and was used as a symbol on Christian and pagan sarcophagi. Though individual craftsmen introduced unorthodox variations there is sufficient agreement to confirm the main essentials. It rose in four stepped stories of decreasing height, the first three squared, the fourth, which carried the beacon, cylindrical. It had not the decorative grace of the Alexandrian Pharos, but its massive strength and good proportions made it an impressive building.

Nero's coins show three separate buildings on the left mole. At the seaward end is a small rectangular peristyle temple with a man in front of it sacrificing at an altar. The rest of the mole is occupied by two long buildings which may be porticoes. No buildings are depicted on the right mole, but there is an ample scatter of bricks and tufa on the surface of Monte Giulio, and Lugli in two of his trial trenches found walls of a late set of baths and of an earlier portico.[4]

It is tempting to associate another monument with the Claudian harbour. In the background of the Torlonia relief is a triumphal arch surmounted by an emperor in a chariot drawn by a team of elephants. The emperor is unbearded and should therefore be not later than Trajan. Domitian is the first emperor known to have set up an arch in Rome, surmounted by an elephant chariot.[5] He may be the author of

---

[1] K. Lehmann-Hartleben, 'Die antiken Hafenanlagen des Mittelmeeres' (*Klio*, Beiheft 14 (1923) 18), interprets the arches of the coin design as *navalia*, berths for ships, but one would expect ships to berth at the landward end of the moles; and the designer would probably have shown a ship berthed.   [2] Texier, 32.

[3] Lugli, 16–20; G. Stuhlfauth, 'Der Leuchtturm von Ostia', *RM* 53 (1938) 139.

[4] Lugli, 24–26.

[5] F. Matz, *Der Gott auf dem Elefantenwagen*, Ak. der Wiss. und der Lit., Mainz; Abhandlung der geistes. und sozialwiss. Klasse, 1952, n. 10, p. 31.

this arch at Portus and it might be one of a pair; for on a sarcophagus in the Vatican, which probably reflects some features of the Ostian harbours, two arches with elephant-drawn chariots on them are depicted.[1] Texier noted square foundations that would have been appropriate for such an arch at the point where Monte Giulio begins to curve and he claimed to have found corresponding foundations on the left mole exactly opposite, at a distance of 950 metres.[2]

On the landward side of Claudius' harbour, on the peninsula which separated it from Trajan's inner basin, were found at the end of the eighteenth century lead pipes stamped with the name of Messalina, wife of Claudius.[3] The evidence suggests that Trajan or Hadrian later built here a palace;[4] he had probably been anticipated by Claudius.

Claudius' new harbour to be fully effective needed communication by water with Rome. This, however, was a comparatively simple task since the Tiber was less than a mile distant. In a monumental inscription set up on a public building in 46 Claudius commemorated this side of his work: 'Ti. Claudius Drusi f. Caesar Aug. Germanicus pontif. max. trib. potest. VI cos. design. IIII imp. XII p.p. fossis ductis a Tiberi operis portus caussa emissisque in mare urbem inundationis periculo liberavit.'[5] From this inscription it seems clear that Claudius dug more than one canal from the Tiber to the sea, to provide communications for his new harbour: today there is only one canal and it is generally attributed to Trajan.

This problem, which raised considerable controversy in the nineteenth century, has been carried much nearer to a solution by Lugli's review of the critical area.[6] He points out that the Fiumicino canal runs in a roughly straight line from the Tiber parallel to the south bank of Trajan's harbour, but that, after passing Trajan's harbour, it changes direction. In this last stretch it runs parallel to the channel which communicated between the harbours of Claudius and Trajan, and to the so-called 'darsena', which lies between them. Lugli suggests that these three stretches of water are contemporary and Claudian, that Claudius built two canals, perhaps one for ships going upstream, the other for downstream traffic; and that these passed in a roughly straight line through what was later Trajan's harbour to join the Tiber nearly a

---

[1] Amelung, *Die Sculpt. des Vat. Mus.* ii. 49–62. Attributed to Ostia, K. Robert, *Hermes*, 1911, 249; but some details at least do not seem applicable. More probably a composite picture drawn from various harbours, Lehmann-Hartleben, op. cit. 232; Lugli, 42.

[2] Texier, 31. See Fig. 4, p. 150.

[3] Fea, *Viaggio*, 39.

[4] p. 163.

[5] 85.

[6] Lugli, 29 f.

mile above Capo Due Rami, where the two branches of the river now
join. Trajan maintained the end of Claudius' southerly canal but, to
have more space for his harbour, cut a new course from the Tiber and
oriented his harbour on the new line. The seaward end of the northern
canal was used for communication with his new harbour. Apart from
these surviving stretches the Claudian canals were swallowed up in
Trajan's new basin.

This general thesis, based on alignments, is strengthened by two
further points. The so-called 'darsena', though its present walling is
late, preserves traces of an earlier wall in a reticulate of large blocks
typical of Claudian building. It seems highly probable that this long
rectangular basin (45 × 24 metres), with a narrow entrance (9 metres)
goes back to Claudius and was intended as a harbour for smaller boats,
and in particular for the rowing-boats, *lenunculi*, used for auxiliary
services in the harbour.[1] Philostorgius, a late Christian writer, refers to
three harbours in his description of Portus;[2] the 'darsena' is included in
his reckoning with the main harbours of Claudius and Trajan. It was in
this area also between the two canals that substantial traces were found
of a monumental portico that is distinctively Claudian. Though it has
been largely concealed by incorporation in a later building, the rusti-
cated drums of the travertine columns, recalling at once Porta Maggiore
at Rome, proclaim its Claudian origin, as clearly as the new ephemeral
letters in a Claudian inscription. Lugli puts forward the very attractive
hypothesis that the inscription commemorating Claudius' canals was
once set in this portico.[3]

The Claudian harbour was connected by road and river with Rome.
Communication by road with Ostia was also essential and must have
been provided when the harbour was built or very soon afterwards.
This road ran straight across the island contained by the two branches
of the river; it left Ostia near the river mouth, opposite Tor Boacciana,
and ran in a direct line to a point on Trajan's canal roughly opposite
the 'darsena'. A short stretch has been excavated where it passes through
the Isola Sacra cemetery. It is considerably wider than the normal
Roman road (10·5 metres) and is designed for transport and pedestrians.
One side has typical paving blocks of *selce*, deeply rutted by heavy

[1] Lugli, 76.
[2] (τόν Πόρτον) μέγιστον δὴ νεώριον Ῥώμης λιμέσι τρισὶ περιγραφόμενον (*Die christlichen
Schriftsteller der ersten drei Jahrhunderte*, 21 (Bidez, Leipzig, 1913) 141).
[3] Lugli, 30 f., 116–18.

traffic; the other side is unpaved. In a late inscription this road is called 'Via Flabia' (Flavia). It was probably so named to honour Constantine, who gave Portus her independence under the title 'civitas Flavia Constantiniana', but Claudius or Nero must originally have been responsible for the road across the island.[1]

There is little evidence for the growth of the harbour area before Trajan's new building. Many of the workers probably lived in Ostia and walked each day to their work; but essential services could not be maintained unless there was from the outset some residential population. A group of pre-Trajanic tombs has been found near the south-east corner of Trajan's basin[2] and the earliest tombs in the cemetery that flanked the road to Ostia may be earlier than Trajan.[3] Both these cemeteries were separated from the harbour by Claudius' canals.

Claudius hoped that he had provided secure harbourage for the shipping that sustained Rome and that he had freed the city from the danger of flood. In 62, according to Tacitus, 200 ships were wrecked within the moles:[4] in 69 Rome suffered one of the worst floods on record![5] The flooding of Rome cannot be attributed to the failure of Claudius' engineers: no canal below the city could save Rome from floods. But the heavy loss of shipping within the harbour is surprising. So far as can be seen the general dispositions of the harbour were sound: under the lee of one of the moles there should have been adequate shelter from whichever direction the wind blew. The expanse of water, however, was large and the centre of the harbour could often have been dangerous. The easiest explanation of the catastrophe is to assume that an unexpected storm broke very suddenly when the harbour was particularly crowded. That the work of Claudius' architects and engineers was not considered a failure is shown by the handsome bronze coinage of 64, or shortly afterwards, publicizing the harbour from the mints of Rome and Lugdunum.[6]

But the danger sharply exposed by the crisis of 62 was probably one

---

[1] See *Note D*, p. 473. [2] *NS* 1925, 60.

[3] Degrassi, *Gnomon*, 26 (1954) 104, suggests an earlier date for Thylander, A 60 (tomb 49), a Claudian freedman married to a Julia Heuresis. Tomb 50 (Thylander, A 64) may also be earlier. The first large tombs date from Trajan, but some of the small, scattered tombs (including 49 and 50) may have preceded them.

[4] Tac. *Ann.* xv. 18. 3. [5] Tac. *Hist.* i. 86.

[6] For the date of this coinage, C. H. V. Sutherland, *Coinage in Roman Imperial Policy*, 162–72.

of the reasons that led Trajan to add to Claudius' harbour a land-locked inner basin. Of Trajan's work there is no clear record in the literary sources, but a restricted issue of coins from his sixth consulship (112) or one of the following years reproduces the harbour with the title 'portus Traiani',[1] and this title is completed by inscriptions, 'portus Trajani felicis'.[2] Trajan's main work was to excavate from the land a hexagonal basin in close relation to the outer harbour. It is possible that the position chosen for this basin was influenced by the development of building round Claudius' harbour and the economy in using in part the Claudian canals; the shape was a useful one for the distribution of shipping and warehouses. The entrance to the harbour was set in the centre of the south-west side. Claudius' northern canal was adapted to provide communication between the two harbours; his southern canal was redirected to run parallel to the south side of the new basin; the smaller canal linking the two Claudian canals was extended to the new line of the southern canal. Claudius' smaller harbour for small boats (the 'darsena') was retained.

The length of each side of the hexagonal basin was 357·77 metres, the maximum diameter 715·54 metres, and the total area 321·993 square metres.[3] The function of the harbour was severely practical and this is reflected in the buildings that surrounded it. Early accounts agree that on all sides large *horrea* ran parallel to the banks; they dominate Lanciani's plan and substantial remains have been uncovered at various periods. They conform to a standard pattern, long series of deep rooms of equal size opening on to portico or covered gallery. Space being more restricted than at Ostia, less use seems to have been made of the open central court, with four series of rooms round the four sides: more often two rows of rooms were grouped back to back. These *horrea* had normally at least two floors, and in one case at least the access to the first floor was by ramp. This particular building, at the southern end of the south-east side, was used for the storage of corn, as the raised floors of the ground-floor rooms indicate:[4] the ramp suggests that the first floor was also used for storage.

In the harbour retaining walls were set large blocks of travertine with a hole in the centre through which the mooring-rope could be tied. Their function is admirably illustrated by the harbour relief in the

[1] Pl. xviii *b*.   [2] 90, 408.
[3] Measurements by Texier, recorded by Lanciani, 163.
[4] *NS* 1925, 58.

Torlonia museum,[1] and similar mooring-blocks can still be seen at
Terracina and Aquileia. Calza found the series regularly disposed along
the south and south-west sides, twenty-four between the south-east
corner and the 'darsena'.[2] They probably ran round the whole basin,
except perhaps on part of the north-western side,[3] and will have provided mooring facilities for rather more than a hundred ships. Numbered
columns also have been found and reported round the basin:[4] they
probably indicated mooring-berths and will have been useful also for
the efficient distribution of unloading gangs.

Six metres behind the quayside runs a strong wall, shutting off the
horrea from the quay. Its construction is not uniform and Lugli has
suggested that the original wall was only 3 metres high and that it was
strengthened and raised under the Severi.[5] Early accounts report five
doorways in each side of this wall, and the width of a measured example
was only 1·80 metres.[6] Carts could not have passed through these
entrances: all goods must have been carried by the unloading gangs
from ship to warehouse. The purpose of this wall was probably to
maintain a closer control on customs and cargoes. Only a more
thorough examination could show whether it is Trajanic and an integral
part of the original plan, or added later when imperial control of trade
and shipping was being tightened.

The regular lines of the *horrea* round Trajan's basin were relieved by
other buildings and monuments. The craftsman who designed Trajan's
commemorative harbour coins was a very inferior artist whose work
cannot stand comparison with the Neronian bronzes depicting the
Claudian harbour; but he seems to have given special emphasis to the
buildings on the north-west side of the harbour. It is here, on the peninsula between the two harbours, that nineteenth-century excavations
produced a rich harvest of sculptures for the Torlonia Museum and discovered a series of richly furnished buildings.[7] These buildings included
a set of baths, maintained into the late Empire, a temple, a very small
theatre, and an 'atrium' with a large series of rooms; the richness of the
site is also reflected in the name that was given to it in the Renaissance,

---

[1] Pl. xx. [2] *NS* 1925, 55; Lugli, 70.

[3] They may not have been regularly disposed along the frontage of the 'Imperial
Palace' on this side (pp. 164 f.).

[4] *NS* 1925, 56; Lanciani, 164. These columns probably stood back from the basin; they
were later enclosed in a wall. Illustrated, Canina, *Mon. di Roma*, vi, tav. 134.

[5] Lugli, 68. [6] *NS* 1925, 57.

[7] Fea, *Viaggio*, 39; Lanciani, 171; Texier, 40–49.

'palazzo delle cento colonne'. Lanciani noted that what seem to be the original walls, in brick with reticulate, were of particularly fine workmanship; their approximate date is confirmed by brickstamps recorded

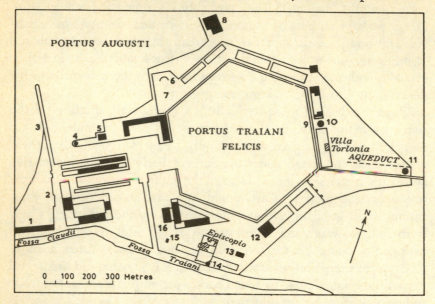

FIG. 6. Trajan's harbour. Blockings show buildings or parts of buildings for which there is reliable evidence. Other outlines show buildings reported or parts of buildings assumed. Post-Roman buildings are hatched. 1. Porticus Placidiana. 2. Porticus Claudii. 3. Late Empire mole. 4. Lighthouse. 5. Baths. 6. Theatre. 7. 'Imperial Palace'. 8. Baths, not included in the circuit of the walls. 9. Colossal statue of Trajan. 10. Temple of Liber Pater. 11. Temple of 'Portumnus'. 12. *Horrea*, partly excavated 1925, with Flavian tomb. 13. ?Barracks of Vigiles. 14. Tower (Pl. xxi *b*). 15. Unidentified temple. 16. ? Xenodochium of Pammachius.

by Lanciani from the last years of Trajan's principate.[1] Fragments of a dedication to Trajan were also found in this area; in it the new harbour is mentioned ('[port]us Traiani felicis'), though the context is obscure. The inscription was set up when Trajan was cos. VI, between 112 and 117.[2] It may, like the coins, commemorate the completion of the harbour.

In the nineteenth century this group of buildings was known as the 'Imperial Palace'. Lugli suggests instead that it probably marks the area of a Forum, surrounded by baths, basilica, and other public buildings.[3]

[1] Bloch, *Bolli laterizi*, 100. Allowing for a short period between production and use, building may not have begun until the beginning of Hadrian's reign.

[2] 90.

[3] Lugli, 98.

He considers that the peninsula between the two harbours, an area flanked by warehouses, was no suitable place for an imperial palace. Until the area is excavated afresh and the relative dispositions of the various groups of buildings established, caution is discreet, but on the present evidence the more romantic view seems to be nearer the truth. The site was an unrivalled one for seeing both harbours, and a good view of the shipping will have been the emperor's main concern when he visited the harbour. Nor is the site well suited for a civilian Forum. We should expect to find the Forum, if it existed, in one of the two areas where the main living-quarters developed, to the east and to the south of the harbour.

Confirmation of the identification of the area with Trajan's imperial palace may perhaps be found in a description of the boundaries of the diocese of Portus in 1019 which includes in a list of properties: *un palazzo detto Praegesta*.[1] The position of this property in the list suggests that it lay between the two harbours. The pipes already mentioned, bearing the name of Messalina, suggest that Trajan was rebuilding on a site previously used by Claudius for the same purpose. Both theatre and baths were probably attached to the 'Imperial Palace'. But though the buildings were planned for imperial visits they were also probably used by the imperial official, freedman, or equestrian procurator, who was responsible for the supervision of the harbour.

The Trajanic coins also show two tall columns surmounted by statues at either end of the side of the harbour facing the entrance, and possibly at other angles as well. A base, now in the Lateran Museum, probably belongs to this series. It records the restoration by Septimius Severus of a column broken by storm: 'L. Septimius Severus . . . columnam vii tempest[atis] confractam restitui[t].'[2] Other statues are seen in the Torlonia harbour relief, but only one of them can be clearly identified. That is a statue of Bacchus and it may have stood in or near the temple of Liber Pater, which was found in the centre of the north-east side of the harbour.[3] This temple, identified by inscriptions, was a small circular peristyle building. It is not certain that its original construction is Trajanic, but it was built not later than Commodus[4] and restored in the late Empire.

Trajan himself was handsomely commemorated. In the centre of the north side of his harbour were found a base and fragments of a colossal

---

[1] Nibby, 631.   [2] 113.   [3] Lanciani, 181.
[4] 30, a dedication to 'Liber pater Commodianus'.

statue of the emperor in military dress;[1] a life-sized bust was recovered by the harbour entrance.[2] These tributes he richly deserved. By increasing and substantially improving Rome's harbour capacity he had made it possible to maintain regular supplies to the capital and had removed a potential source of insecurity to the emperors that succeeded him. It remained only to ensure regular supplies by efficient administration.

Trajan's inner basin was primarily reserved for the unloading of ships. It is more difficult to say what was the function of the Claudian harbour in the new dispensation. Lugli believed that the left mole had already collapsed under the pressure of south-western gales and that this was the main reason for Trajan's new building.[3] While I have not been able to check all the detailed arguments adduced by Lugli I find the general objections to this thesis overwhelming. If the left mole had collapsed the harbour would have had no protection from the south-west winds and would have been little better than an open roadstead. The collapse of the mole would also have allowed the drifting sand to spread across the harbour; and the logical defence against incoming sand was a mole to protect the entrance to Trajan's inner basin. Such a mole can in fact still be seen, running out for some 300 metres at right angles to the entry canal; but Lugli's investigations have shown almost beyond doubt that this mole is not earlier than the fourth century.[4]

The standard description of the harbours in Ostian inscriptions as 'portus uterque' and the continuation of a cult of the *Lares portus Augusti*[5] would be anomalous if Claudius' harbour was no more than an entrance passage to the inner basin. Nor would this inner basin have been sufficiently large to harbour the shipping of peak periods. It is difficult to believe that Trajan, who was not easily deterred by difficulties, would have allowed a broken mole to threaten the security of Rome's shipping: indeed the scholiast on the passage of Juvenal quoted in an earlier chapter says that Trajan improved the Claudian harbour as well as adding his own: 'Traianus portum Augusti restauravit in melius et interius tutiorem nominis sui fecit.'[6] It is easier to believe that the Claudian harbour was efficiently maintained and that ships continued to unload at the Claudian quays, particularly perhaps on its south-west side.[7]

---

[1] Fea, *Viaggio*, 35.   [2] Ibid. 36.   [3] Lugli, 34.
[4] Lugli, 79–81.   [5] Thylander, A 19.   [6] Schol. Juv. xii. 75.
[7] The hero of Apuleius' fable disembarks in the outer harbour without entering Trajan's basin, Apuleius, *Met.* xi. 26: 'tutusque prosperitate ventorum ferentium Augusti portum celerrime ⟨pervenio⟩ ac dehinc carpento pervolavi'.

The improvements introduced by Trajan probably attracted an increasing number of settlers, but until the area is systematically excavated it will not be possible to tell how rapidly what under Constantine became the independent town of Portus developed. There has always been a tendency in descriptions of Portus to over-simplify chronology, and to divide buildings into Trajanic, Severan, and late Empire. The discovery of brickstamps of Marcus Aurelius' principate in large *horrea* that were assumed to be Severan is a salutary warning against such simplification.[1]

The shape and extent of the town in the fourth century is clear from the line of walls that can still be traced. These walls run parallel to the north-west and north sides of Trajan's basin and then diverge to enclose a large triangle east of the harbour. They return to run parallel to the south-east side until they meet the canal. Two areas give scope for civilian development, the eastern triangle and the area between the south side of the harbour and the canal, where the bishop's palace now stands. At the apex of the eastern triangle was the main gate through which passed the Via Portuensis. This road continued in a straight line to the eastern angle of the harbour; an aqueduct ran beside it to the north. Of the buildings in this area, apart from the temple of Liber Pater, very little is known; but one building in part survives, close to the site of the gate. This is a circular peristyle temple, the brickwork and style of which suggests a date early in the third century.[2] The settlement had presumably already developed to this point. In the second of these two areas the buildings included a late basilica to which a *xenodochium*, a rest-house for pilgrims, was added[3] and an unidentified temple.[4] Lanciani also inferred from a number of inscriptions found on the site that the Barracks of the Vigiles lay to the east of the site of the bishop's palace.[5]

On the south bank of the canal there seems to have been a thin fringe of buildings, shops or warehouses, towards the west,[6] but opposite the bishop's palace and to the east this bank seems to have been reserved as a dumping ground for marble. Melchiorri records that in 1839 more than fifty large blocks of marble were unearthed in this area, mainly Africano with a few blocks of Cipollino and of white

---

[1] Bloch, *Bolli laterizi*, 279.
[2] Lugli, 93; G. T. Rivoira, *Roman Architecture* (1925) 192.
[3] Lugli, 106.   [4] Lugli, 106; Lanciani, 181.   [5] Lanciani, 183–8.
[6] E. Gatti, *NS* 1911, 410. Walls of what may be a large warehouse have been recently revealed immediately north of the church of St. Hippolytus.

marble.[1] Further such blocks have been from time to time recovered, even as late as the winter of 1951. They are blocks rough cut from the quarry, some with consular date and quarry marks on them. They might lay there a long time: one was dated in A.D. 82, several others had second-century dates. It seems that the marble brought in from over-seas and from the Luna quarries was not unloaded in Trajan's harbour but brought to the south bank of the canal to await shipment upstream to Rome or carriage to Ostia.

Close by was one of the main cemeteries of the harbour settlement, flanking the road to Ostia. A very substantial group of tombs, in excellent state of preservation, was excavated here between the two wars. Calza, who devoted a special book to a record of the excavation, believed that the opening up of this cemetery followed the building of the inner harbour; but the earliest tombs may be earlier than Trajan.[2] The cemetery was a large one, extending far beyond the limits of excavation; tombs had been found in the nineteenth century more than 100 metres to the north. A vague record has been preserved of another cemetery near Capo due Rami where the two branches of the Tiber join.[3] Sufficient remains can be seen in the fields to show that tombs also lined both sides of the Via Portuensis as it proceeded in a direct line from the main gate to the river before turning east. In 1953 a large fragment of a figured sarcophagus in Greek marble lay in the grass of the river bank—but not for long!

The shape of the small town round Trajan's harbour is defined by its walls, but these walls represent a restriction. A large building or complex of buildings at the north-west angle was left outside the circuit[4] and earlier buildings have been incorporated in the wall or destroyed to make way for it, in a manner reminiscent of Aurelian's walls at Rome. It is not certain when the walls of Portus were built. They are commonly attributed to Constantine, who gave independent status to Portus, but they may be earlier, or even later. They were needed continuously from the end of the fourth century and reveal many signs of strengthening and reconstruction.

In spite of the very fragmentary nature of the evidence it seems clear that the building history of Portus in the fourth and fifth century was very different from that of Ostia. While most of Ostia's warehouses were redundant, Rome still depended on the storage facilities of Portus

[1] G. Melchiorri, *Bull. Inst.* 12 (1840) 43; Lanciani, 180; Lugli, 105 f.
[2] p. 161 n. 3.   [3] Nibby, 607 f.   [4] Lugli, 90.

for her supplies, and the *horrea* were maintained. The temple of Liber
Pater was restored in the fourth century,[1] but pagan temples were
soon overshadowed by Christian churches. A Christian basilica was excavated to the west of the bishop's palace in the nineteenth century, and
adjoining it was added an open court with fountain and a series of
rooms around: this was the *xenodochium* or pilgrim's rest-house, presented by the patrician Pammachius and praised by St. Jerome.[2] There
still stands to the south of the canal the medieval campanile which
marks the site of the church of St. Hippolytus, the first recorded martyr
of Portus.

The survey of the diocese of Portus in 1019 mentions churches of
S. Maria, S. Lorenzo, S. Pietro, S. Gregorio, S. Teodoro, S. Vito;[3] in 849
Leo IV had made gifts to a church of S. Ninfa.[4] Most, if not all, of these
churches will have been built in the fourth and fifth centuries. There is
evidence also that public baths remained in use into the late Empire,
and two of the sets that have been seen seem to be adapted from earlier
buildings used for a different purpose.[5]

Though Portus was captured and sacked by Alaric in 408, the dependence of Rome on her harbours ensured a measure of revival when the
invader was gone. Within a generation one of the town's most impressive public monuments was erected, the Porticus Placidiana, a colonnade which ran along the north bank of the canal as it approached the
sea; it seems to have been some 200 metres long. Part of the inscription
from the architrave survives, and the base of a statue set up by a *praefectus annonae*, 'ad ornatum porticus Placidianae'.[6] This monument commemorates Placidia, mother of the emperor Valentian III. It was built
in or near 425 and is the last building known to us.

Nibby in his account of Portus emphasized the prevalence of late
construction in the district between the south bank of Trajan's harbour
and the canal. It was here that he saw a large area paved with great
blocks of rough marble, probably taken from the dump on the south
bank;[7] it was here too that Calza saw remains of late buildings encroach-
ing on the quayside, and other late walls which followed lines different
from earlier constructions.[8] It seems likely that in time of increasing stress

---

[1] Lanciani, 181, inferring the date from the poor workmanship.
[2] Lugli, 106. But see Addenda.
[3] Nibby, 631.   [4] Nibby, 628.   [5] Lugli, 82, 90.
[6] Lugli, 119; Lanciani, 182. Inscriptions 140 (statue base), 141 (architrave).
[7] Nibby, 652.   [8] Calza, *NS* 1925, 65.

the population concentrated here for more secure protection. There is indeed a strong wall with towers that runs from the 'Constantinian' wall to the harbour basin near the northern end of its south-east side. This would have served admirably for an inner defence of the south side of the harbour. But though Nibby may be mistaken in calling this cross-wall Severan,[1] its workmanship certainly looks much better than that of the 'Constantinian' walls. If, however, it is substantially earlier it is difficult to see its purpose.

But though it seems likely that there was still a considerable amount of building in the late Empire at Portus the general standard of the work has the same character as at Ostia. Old material is reused, ill-assorted columns from different buildings are brought together for new building; the elementary requirements of coherent planning are ignored.

Meanwhile difficulties developed in the outer harbour. The first hint is an inscription which was found when Trajan's basin was restored. It comes from the base of a statue set up to Lucius Crepereius Madalianus, *praefectus annonae*, by the council and people of Portus and records the offices he had held.[2] At an earlier stage in his career Madalianus had been 'consul(aris) molium fari at purgaturae'. The office is not attested elsewhere in inscriptions nor in literary sources; Calza is probably right in regarding it as a special appointment. At some time between 337 and 341, when Madalianus was appointed, a thorough overhaul of the Claudian harbour seems to have been required, involving moles, light-house, and dredging operations. Not long afterwards the representation of Portus on the Peutinger map shows what seems to be an inner mole with a lighthouse at the end.[3] This may be identified with a line of wall that runs out for some 300 metres into the Claudian harbour at right angles to the communication canal. This line can be seen on the ground and is clear in an air photograph; at its seaward end is a modern build-ing. The nature and approximate date of this line has been established by Lugli.[4] It is a mole with mooring-blocks and a lighthouse probably stood at its end. It is of poor workmanship and seems to be not earlier than the fourth century. Its purpose is to protect the entrance to Trajan's harbour against sand. The natural inference is that the left mole had

[1] Nibby, 651. Lugli, 94, describes the brickwork as good and fairly regular, though some two-thirds of the bricks are taken from earlier buildings.

[2] **13.** *S* 4449; Calza, *NS* 1925, 73.

[3] Fig. 7. But the schematic design might merely be intended to represent the outer and inner harbour, K. Miller, *Die Peutingerische Tafel* (1887) 95.

[4] Lugli, 79 f.

collapsed and that sand was being swept in. Madalianus may in his special office, or later as *praefectus annonae*, have been responsible for the new mole.

Had it been possible to maintain regular dredging operations the harbour might still have had a long life. But wars and raids sapped the

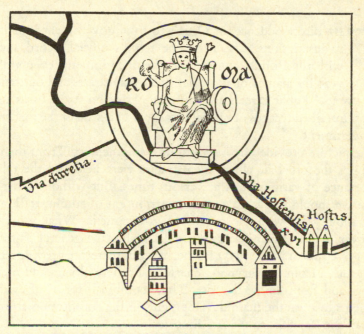

FIG. 7. Portus on the Peutinger map (*c.* A.D. 350).

resources of Rome and weakened the morale of Portus. The sand had probably won by the eighth century. It was easier to keep clear the mouth of the canal, and there is evidence that a ship passed out to sea as late as 1117. From the twelfth century even the canal was unnegotiable until it was reopened by Paul V in 1618.

9

THE CONSTITUTION

THE direct evidence for Ostia's form of government is confined to inscriptions. The Fasti, the town's official record, include with the Roman consuls and the main imperial events of the year the names of the chief local magistrates and outstanding local events.[1] Public careers are commemorated on statue bases and in tombs. Inscribed records of official acts show us a little of the machinery of government.

The picture provided by inscriptions is fragmentary. From them we can infer the order in which magistracies were held and the relative importance of various posts at various times. But without other evidence we should know little of the distribution of administration and responsibility between the organs of government. What we know, however, from Ostian inscriptions falls within the general pattern of local government imposed by Rome. We can therefore provide a fuller background from the surviving charters of other colonies and municipalities and from the legal codes. These combined forms of evidence enable us to trace the main developments in the constitution from the close of the Republic to the late Empire.

Our earliest document is a fragment of the Fasti which covers the years 49–45 B.C.; the last relevant inscription comes from the early fifth century. During this long period we can trace in outline the main changes in the forms and spirit of government; for the early and middle Republic we remain in the dark. The constitution as we first see it represents the revised model evolved by Rome for Italian colonies in the late Republic. Though the higher jurisdiction is reserved for Roman courts, the main responsibility for local affairs rests with the local authority. It was not always so.

Much has been written about the government of early Roman colonies; very little is known. The excavations at Ostia have done nothing to fill the gap, and detailed speculation is unprofitable, but it is reasonable to assume that early Ostia was more directly controlled from

[1] *Fasti*, edited by A. Degrassi, *Inscriptiones Italiae*, xiii. 173–241, cited as 'Degrassi'.

Rome than later. The Roman quaestor, first appointed to Ostia in 267 B.C., was primarily concerned with the provisioning of Rome, but he may also have had wider powers of jurisdiction. It was the Roman urban praetor, acting on the authority of the Roman senate, who ruled that a long stretch of land between the Decumanus and the river was public property. But routine administration must always have been a local responsibility and, since the main function of the fourth-century Castrum was to defend the coast, we should expect local officers to be responsible for leading the local levy against raiders.[1]

In the revised constitution the chief magistrates were duovirs, supported by aediles. They may have been preceded at Ostia by praetors and aediles; for these titles are found during the Republic in other Roman colonies, and their presence in early Ostia would be the easiest explanation of their survival through the Empire in the priesthood of Vulcan. The cult of Vulcan was the most deep-rooted of Ostia's cults. The *pontifex Volcani* exercised a general control over all temples; he was assisted by *praetores* and *aediles sacris Volcani faciundis*. There is no true parallel to such priesthoods in other towns, and Henzen was probably right in inferring that the titles were inherited from Ostian magistracies when Ostia's constitution was adapted to the colonial pattern that we find throughout Italy from the late Republic.[2] The main objection to this interpretation is the number of Vulcan's priests. We should expect two praetors and two aediles; there were three praetors, and there may have been three aediles, though records survive of no more than two.[3]

Two explanations are possible. De Sanctis derived the apparent anomaly from the early threefold tribal division of Rome.[4] The original Ostia had three praetors because, when it was founded in the regal period, Rome had three tribes. Alternatively it is possible, but less likely, that the original number was two, and only later increased. It may be significant that Vulcan's praetors and aediles are undifferentiated in the earliest inscriptions. The titles *praetor primus*, *secundus*, *tertius* are not known before the second century A.D.

A new constitution, embodied doubtless in a *lex coloniae*, had been granted to Ostia by the end of the Republic. It may have accompanied

---

[1] A. N. Sherwin-White, *Roman Citizenship*, 78.

[2] Henzen, *Ann. Inst.* 31 (1859) 197. Different interpretations discussed by L. R. Taylor, *The Cults of Ostia* (Bryn Mawr Monographs, xi, 1912) 17–19.

[3] p. 338.   [4] G. de Sanctis, *Storia dei Romani*, i. 383 f.

the building of the Sullan walls on Rome's initiative: both recognized the development of the small fourth-century Castrum into a substantial town. In its original form this constitution has a simple structure. Policy is controlled by the local council, executive authority is limited to two boards of magistrates, appointed for a year. The two aediles, who formed the junior magistracy, were responsible for the supervision of markets, the control of weights and measures, and the maintenance of the public services. To carry out the necessary work on drains, public latrines and, later, on the water supply, they had a body of slaves and freedmen belonging to the town. The senior magistrates were two duovirs who, like the consuls at Rome, gave their name to the year. They presided over meetings of council and people, administered justice except in cases which were in the reserved province of the Roman quaestor or had to be taken to Rome for decision. They are not in Ostian inscriptions entitled *duoviri iuri dicundo* as is the normal practice elsewhere, but the bare title *duoviri* without description is found, for example, also at Capua and Praeneste and there is no reason to believe that the chief magistrates of these towns were in an inferior position. The prestige of their office is reflected in the two lictors that attended them but, as can be seen from the public monument of C. Cartilius Poplicola, the rods that these attendants carried did not have the axe.[1] They were *bacilli* rather than *fasces*; the duovirs could not pass sentence of death.

Every five years the duovirate carried the fuller title *duovir censoria potestate quinquennalis*.[2] In these years the duovirs had censorial authority; the local register of property was revised, public contracts were allocated, and the council may have been brought up to strength by the incorporation of new members. The censorial duovirate conferred special distinction. On the public monument of Poplicola it was recorded that he had held the duovirate eight times, including three times with censorial authority; the higher honour is separately recorded.[3] It was normally in censorial years that emperors or members of their family accepted the compliment of office.[4]

---

[1] Cf. Cicero, *De lege agraria*, ii. 93 (speaking of the colony established at Capua in 83 B.C.): 'deinde anteibant lictores non cum bacillis, sed, ut hic praetoribus urbanis anteeunt, cum fascibus duobus.' Eight pairs of *bacilli* are depicted on Poplicola's funerary monument to represent his eight duovirates, *Scavi di Ostia*, iii (1), pl. xxx.

[2] An earlier form of the title, *duovir cens(or)* (or *censorius*), 4134, *S* 4710, Bloch, 61.

[3] 'octiens duomvir ter cens. colonorum iudicio . . . factus est'.

[4] 2⁶⁻⁷, 447 (= *S* 4674–5), *Fasti*, A.D. 126.

The attribution of censorial powers and duties to the chief magistrates of the year at regular five-yearly intervals is not an original element in the constitution. In the first preserved fragment of the Fasti, which covers the period from 49 to 45 B.C., no *II viri c(ensoria) p(otestate) q(uinquennales)* are recorded, though the title appears regularly later and should have appeared in 45 B.C. if the institution had already been established.[1] In the Fasti of Venusia *II viri quinquennales* are first recorded in 29 B.C.[2] It was probably at approximately the same time that the procedure was adopted at Ostia. Previously the censorship may have been a separate office; it is perhaps more probable that censorial duties were not separately defined and rested with the duovirs. The concentration of the work at stated intervals in the hands of men especially elected for their authority and competence would increase efficiency.

In the year that Caesar crossed the Rubicon an *interregnum* is recorded in the Ostian Fasti and no duovirs for the year are given. In the crisis of the Civil War, when party feeling at Ostia may have been strong and divided, no regular magistrates were appointed; and, following republican practice at Rome, a series of *interreges* probably filled the gap.[3] The term and the title are not found again, but we hear frequently later of *praefecti*, men appointed to take the place of the formally appointed chief magistrates. So when an emperor or a prince of the imperial house honoured Ostia by accepting the title of duovir the practical duties of the office were delegated to a distinguished Ostian.

In the record of A.D. 36 a rather different use of the office is seen. In that year T. Sextius Africanus and A. Egrilius Rufus entered office with censorial authority; but on or shortly before 17 July Rufus died and two *praefecti* were appointed. This was not the normal practice when one of the duovirs died in office, for in A.D. 30 when P. Paetinius had died, A. Hostilius Gratus was 'II vir pronuntiatus'. A special reason for the difference might be found in the censorial authority held in A.D. 36, for in Rome it was customary when one censor died for his colleague to resign; but a simpler explanation lies in the character of the surviving duovir. T. Sextius Africanus is probably the prominent senator who was to become consul in A.D. 59; his public career in Rome will have afforded him little time to carry out the routine duties of office in Ostia.[4] In 126, also a censorial year, the emperor Hadrian held the title

---

[1] The first attested censorial year is A.D. 6 (*Fasti*). Later dates in the five-yearly cycle are confirmed by the *Fasti* in 16, 31, 36, &c.   [2] Degrassi, 254.

[3] *Fasti*, 49 B.C., recording *interregnum*.   [4] Degrassi, 219.

for the second time.[1] The name of his colleague is lost, but he was a patron of the colony. Two *praefecti* are listed for the year. Degrassi suggests that they held office each for six months in Hadrian's place;[2] it is perhaps more likely that Hadrian's colleague was also holding the title as an honour without duties and that two *praefecti* were appointed for the whole year.

The financial office of quaestor was not included in the standard pattern of local government imposed by Rome in the late Republic. The magistrates of municipia were *quattuorviri*, later defined as *quattuorviri aedilicia potestate* and *quattuorviri iuri dicundo*; colonies had normally at first two duovirs and two aediles only. The Fasti of Venusia show that the quaestorship was there instituted in 34 B.C.;[3] the Ostian evidence is less secure. The earliest clear trace of the office is a fragmentary inscription dated not later than the principate of Tiberius;[4] the rapid growth of Ostia in the last century of the Republic makes it probable that it had been instituted much earlier. Unlike the aedileship the quaestorship does not seem to have been an essential stage in the *cursus honorum*, for the office is omitted in several careers recorded in full, both in the first and second centuries.[5] Its normal place is between the aedileship and duovirate; when Ostian prosperity declines it is often held after the duovirate, a mark of its increased importance.[6]

The function of the two quaestors was to administer the town chest, as the full title *quaestor aerarii* implies. They had to see that moneys owing to the town were paid and, under the authority of the council, to control expenditure. The chest that they administered was not well endowed. The town possessed certain properties,[7] but their extent is

---

[1] [Imp. Caesar Hadr]ianus Traianus Aug. II[—]. There is a break on the stone after the second stroke; III or IIII are formally possible, but it seems unlikely that Hadrian accepted the title more than twice.

[2] Degrassi, 233, quotes as a parallel Interamna, A.D. 73 (op. cit. 267), but the two *praefecti* were there replacing Titus and Domitian.

[3] Degrassi, 254.

[4] Bloch, 61, a man honoured by Augustus: 'II vir cens. q. d' (*or* p *or* r)? The supplement q(uaestor) is probable rather than certain. An earlier record may survive in *CIL* I², 2440 (with improved supplement in Degrassi, *Inscriptiones latinae liberae reipublicae*, Florence, 1957, n. 204), a republican dedication to Liber Pater: 'No(merius) Ofalius No(vi) f(ilius) q(uaestor) pro sed et familia soua Leibero donum dat meret(o).' This dedication passed to Vienna from the collection of Cardinal Pacca, which was derived mainly from Ostia. The quaestor, however, is more probably the Roman quaestor stationed at Ostia. If he were a local official the family name would probably have survived in other Ostian inscriptions.   [5] e.g. 332, 349, 415.

[6] p. 185.   [7] I⁴¹: 'cum respublica praedia sua venderet'.

unknown. The use by private individuals of the public water supply when the aqueduct had been built brought in a small revenue. Fines imposed by public authority went to the chest, and several funerary inscriptions record a penalty of 50,000 sesterces for the desecration of the tomb.[1] But it is probable that tombs were respected while prosperity lasted; when, in the period of decline, they were rifled and their material reused for restorations, it is doubtful whether penalties were enforced. Members of the council paid for their election and occasional windfalls came to the public chest from such rich men as Marcus Licinius Privatus, a freedman who made a bequest of 50,000 sesterces.[2] But no general rates, so far as we know, were levied on land or property. The financial system of local government was a fair-weather system, relying primarily on the public generosity of magistrates and patrons.

The public career of an Ostian was not limited to secular office. At Rome membership of one or more of the great priestly colleges was an integral part of the public career of leading statesmen. Cicero waited anxiously for the augurate; emperors, whatever other titles they refused, became *pontifex maximus*. So at Ostia a man who embarked on a career of office normally held an official priesthood. The charter given to the Caesarian colony of Urso in Spanish Baetica shows that the offices of pontifex and augur were a recognized element in the constitution of Roman colonies.[3] Neither augur nor pontifex unqualified is found at Ostia; their place is taken by an official priesthood whose roots almost certainly go back to the early days of the colony.

The cult of Vulcan, Ostia's patron deity, maintained until the late Empire the predominant place in the public religious organization of the town. The *pontifex Volcani* corresponded in function and prestige to the *pontifex maximus* at Rome. His post was the most honourable that an Ostian could hold and marked the climax of a public career: unlike the magistracies it was held for life. C. Antius Crescens Calpurnianus, who is recorded as *pontifex Volcani* in 194, still holds office in 203;[4] in 36 and 105 new appointments are recorded in the Fasti, and in each case the occasion is the death of the previous holder of the office.

The cult of Vulcan was also served by praetors and aediles, and both offices were graded. There seem to have been three *praetores sacris Volcani faciundis*, for several holders of this religious praetorship are styled

---

[1] e.g. 166, 307, 850.   [2] 15.

[3] *Lex Ursonensis*, 66: 'ita uti qui optima lege optimo iure in quaque colon(ia) pontif(ices) augures sunt erunt.'   [4] 325, 324.

pr(aetor) pr(imus);[1] another is praet(or) II;[2] and the P. Lucilius Gamala who lived under Marcus Aurelius is pr(aetor) tert(ius).[3] Fewer inscriptions recording the aedileship have survived, but M. Marius Primitivus, who lived under Antoninus Pius, is aed(ilis) II sac(ris) V(olc.);[4] there may also have been three aediles. Normally only one of these priesthoods was held by a man; and there is no evidence that the praetorship carried more distinction than the aedileship, for the Augustan Gamala, one of the most distinguished Ostians of his day, is aedile.[5] But Cn. Turpilius Turpilianus is both aedile and praetor[6] and the late-second-century Gamala is 'aed(ilis) sacr(orum) Volcani, eiusdem pr(aetor) tert(ius).'[7] While the post of *pontifex Volcani* was the climax of a career reserved only for the most outstanding public men, the praetorship and aedileship were normally the prelude to office, as is shown by their position in recorded careers.

Although the cult of Vulcan retained its pre-eminence in the religious organization of Ostia into the fourth century the imperial cult assumed increasing importance as the Empire developed. The building of the temple of Rome and Augustus at the south end of the Forum in the early Julio-Claudian period marks the adoption by the town of a public and official cult presided over by a *flamen Romae et Augusti*. This priesthood, though carrying less distinction than the pontificate of Vulcan, was reserved for men of standing and is normally recorded late in careers: its occurrence in inscriptions is sufficiently rare to justify the assumption that it was held for life.[8] To this central cult of Rome and the emperor was later added the cult of individual deified emperors. Vespasian is the first emperor known to us to have had a *flamen* at Ostia, but the absence of inscriptions recording priests of Augustus, Tiberius, and Claudius may be no more than coincidence. The holders of these priesthoods, like the praetors and aediles of Vulcan, were men at the outset of their public career.

The association of secular and religious office is illustrated in the only two careers recorded in full that have been preserved from the pre-Flavian period. The Augustan P. Lucilius Gamala was in turn aedile in the cult of Vulcan, co-opted decurion by decree of the decurions, pontifex of Vulcan, duovir with censorial authority.[9] C. Fabius Agrippa was

---

[1] 306, **II**, 432.　　[2] 341.　　[3] 2.　　[4] S 4553.　　[5] 1.　　[6] 3.

[7] **2.** Cf. 390: 'P. Nonio Anterotiano . . . aedili pr(aetori) sacr(is) Volk(ani)'; aedili pr(imo) is, however, a possible supplement.

[8] The assumption is strengthened by S 4674/5 (= 447): '[f]l(amini) perpetuo Rom[ae et Augusti].'　　　　　　　　　　　　　　　　　　[9] 1.

praetor in the cult of Vulcan, co-opted decurion by decree of the decurions, aedile, duovir.[1]

When public men were honoured with statues or commemorative tablets their careers were normally set out in full. On tombstones an abbreviated formula is frequently found: 'omnibus honoribus functus in colonia Ostiensi.'[2] The full public career implied by the phrase need perhaps cover no more than a priesthood, the aedileship and duovirate; it could also include the quaestorship and further priesthoods. The occasional omission of 'omnibus' from the formula is probably significant. We know from the inscription on his statue base that Q. Plotius Romanus had been aedile, *flamen Romae et Augusti*, and *flamen divi Titi*.[3] These offices are not recorded on his tombstone, where he is described simply as 'honoribus funct(us) in colonia Ostiensi'.[4] He died before his parents; probably he had not yet reached the duovirate.

In addition to magistrates Ostia, like other towns, appointed patrons. The title *patronus* was the highest honour that the town could confer. No formal duties were attached to the position, but patrons were expected to further the interests of the town, especially in relations with the central authorities. The local council, therefore, with whom the election lay, looked primarily to Roman senators and knights, particularly to Ostians rising in the imperial service. A man whose career was limited to Ostia could not expect election; no patron is known among the P. Lucilii Gamalae in spite of their long series of local offices and benefactions. The choice was not restricted to fellow townsmen. Prominent Roman senators and equestrian officials who had personal or official associations with the town and who could be expected to give useful service were honoured in this way.

Next in dignity to patrons and magistrates were the *decuriones*, the members of the town council. This council was the mainspring of government, framing policy, and controlling the work of the executive. In Ostian inscriptions we cannot expect to learn more than a fraction of the councillors' business. We find them voting public statues or commemorative tablets to distinguished men and public funerals to benefactors. They grant authority for the setting up of statues on public land, as the letters *l.d.d.d.p.* on statue bases from the Piazzale delle Corporazioni declare: 'locus datus decurionum decreto publice'. We assume that all matters concerning the town's administration were

---

[1] **8.**
[2] 294, 323*a*, 335, 354.
[3] 400.
[4] 401.

subject to the council's authority, and that the actions of the executive, apart from their routine duties, derived from council decrees, *decreta decurionum*.

For the qualifications governing entry to the council we have to rely on the general evidence concerning local government. Free birth was essential, unless a special exception was made in the town statute, as in Caesarian colonies which included a substantial admixture of freedmen. At Ostia the ex-slave could receive the honorary rank of a councillor, but not the full status.[1] The minimum age laid down by imperial regulation was twenty-five,[2] but this regulation was not always observed. In the second century P. Celerius Amandus had entered the council before he died at the age of eighteen;[3] M. Cornelius Epagathianus, also a councillor, was only twelve when he died;[4] the Antonine Gamala was admitted when he was a boy.[5] This dangerous symptom is found in many other towns, nor at Ostia is it limited to the period of decline; when Amandus was made a councillor the town was at the height of her prosperity. It was an unwise tribute to a family's public generosity. Of a census qualification for entry to the senate we have no evidence, but it is unlikely that Ostia was an exception to what seems to have been a general rule.[6]

The sole method of entry into the council recorded on Ostian inscriptions is by co-option; the new member is 'decurionum decreto adlectus decurio'.[7] We should expect ex-magistrates to be entitled to membership, and duovirs to have the power of enrolment in censorial years; but for these methods of entry there is no evidence. The Augustan Gamala was aedile before he became a councillor, but his entry to the council is by the council's decree, 'aedili, d(ecurionum) d(ecreto) allecto gratis decurioni'.[8] This Gamala was admitted *gratis*; normally an honorarium had to be paid. The same privilege was accorded to another Gamala, probably of the Julio-Claudian period;[9] in both cases it was perhaps a tribute to the benefactions of a long-established Ostian family. In the only other case known it was the reward for public generosity;

---

[1] 15.

[2] The minimum age before Augustus was 30, *Tab. Her.* 89; cf. Pliny, *Ep.* x. 79. 1. The Flavian charter of Spanish Malaca specifies a minimum age of 25 for councillors and magistrates (*Lex Mal.* 54). Cf. *Dig.* l. 4. 8: 'ad rem publicam administrandam ante vicensimum quintum annum . . . admitti minores non oportet.'

[3] 321.　　　　　[4] 341.　　　　　[5] 2.

[6] Pliny, *Ep.* i. 19. 2: 'esse autem tibi centum milium censum satis indicat, quod apud nos decurio es.'

[7] e.g. 321, **8,** 362.　　　　　[8] 1.　　　　　[9] 3.

C. Granius Maturus was accorded by decree of the senate 'gratuitum decurionatum et statuam ob munificentiam'.[1]

The normal strength of local councils was 100 members,[2] and such was probably the original Ostian establishment. An inscription, however, of the second half of the second century implies that there were then 110 members.[3] L. Fabius Sp. f. Eutychus left to the town a capital sum of 12,500 denarii, the annual interest on which at 5 per cent. was to be divided between the councillors, and the clerks and lictors of the town service. When the share of clerks and lictors had been deducted there remained 550 denarii available for the councillors who were to receive each 5 denarii. It seems unlikely that such an odd number as 110 had been laid down in the town statute. More probably the legal number had been exceeded, perhaps with special sanction from the central government.[4]

Magistrates and council were assisted in their work by a small establishment of clerks and attendants, divided into panels, *decuriae*. What is probably a full list is given in the career of Cn. Sentius Felix, a wealthy shipper who became duovir, probably in the late first century. He was 'patronus decuriae scribar(um) cerarior(um) et librarior(um) et lictor(um) et viator(um) item praeconum'.[5] Of these the most important were the *scribae cerarii*, the principal secretaries, who were responsible for keeping public records and accounts. The *scribae librarii* were inferior in grade and carried out the duties of junior clerks. The *lictores* were the official attendants of the duovirs and were present at public religious ceremonials; L. Antonius Epitynchanus is described as 'lictor dec(uriae) curiatiae quae sacris publicis apparet'.[6] The *viatores* were messengers in the service of the magistrates, who delivered their instructions and could be used to summon men to court. The *praecones* were the town criers.

Some light is thrown on the numbers and relative status of these grades in the charter of the Caesarian colony of Urso in Spain.[7] Each duovir at Urso was entitled to two lictors (at an annual salary of 600 sesterces), two *scribae* (at 1,200 s.), two *viatores* (at 400 s.), one *librarius* (at 300 s.), one *praeco* (at 300 s.). It is implied that appointment was annual and not permanent. That the numbers at Ostia were not

[1] 362.　　　　　　　　　　　　　　　[2] W. Liebenam, *Städteverwaltung*, 229.

[3] 14 (a funerary inscription repeating the terms of an honorary inscription, 353).

[4] Cf. Pliny, *Ep.* x. 112. 1 (written to Trajan from Bithynia): 'ii, quos indulgentia tua quibusdam civitatibus super legitimum numerum adicere permisit'.

[5] 59.　　　　　　　　　　　[6] 296.　　　　　　　　　[7] *Lex Ursonensis*, 62.

much larger is suggested by the already mentioned benefaction of
L. Fabius Eutyches, who had himself been *lictor*, *cerarius*, and *librarius*.
The councillors, numbering 110, were to receive each year 550 denarii,
the *cerarii* 37½, the lictors 25, and the *librarii* 12½.[1]

These minor officials were recruited from freedmen and free-born
citizens of humble class. Only one is known to have later held a
magistracy,[2] but three became presidents of the builders' guild.[3] They
were proud of their association with the government and on occasion
gave expression to their public loyalty. A commemorative tablet in part
survives which was probably dedicated to the *genius* of the *decuriones*; it
was set up by 'lictores, viator(es), et honore usi',[4] the last-named perhaps
being former lictors and *viatores* who combined with those in office for
the year. The same formula is found in the record of a restoration in the
area of the temple of Bellona;[5] the original inscription records that the
temple was built at the expense of the lictors and public slaves.[6] In
the guild house of the *hastiferi*, closely associated with the cult of Bellona,
was found a dedication to the *numen* of the imperial house by a *scriba
cerarius*.[7] Near by, probably also coming from the same building, was
found a dedication by the same man to the *genius* of the town councillors
and to the son of the emperor Antoninus Pius.[8]

In the building and restoration of the temple of Bellona the lictors
were associated with the public slaves and freedmen. These were needed
to maintain public services and they were organized in a guild. Cn.
Sentius Felix is 'patronus libertor(um) et servor(um) publicor(um)';[9]
and a guild roll of this *familia publica* survives, including eighty-one
slaves and freedmen.[10] As a reward for good service the public slave
received his freedom and took the town's name. A. Ostiensis Asclepiades,
who presented a figure of Mars to the guild,[11] had probably himself
received his freedom in this way. P. Ostiensis, *coloniae libertus Acutus*,
declares his status explicitly.[12]

In the structure of government the popular assembly was the least
important element. Rome in her expansion had learnt to distrust extreme
democracy. The pattern of government which she imposed was based

[1] 353, **14**.
[2] *S* 4641: '[A. Egri] lio Paterno | —[aedi]li lictor(i) curi | [atio flamini divi] Vesp(asiani)
sacr(is) Volk(ani) f(aciundis).'

[3] 296, 353, **15**.   [4] Bloch, 3.   [5] *AE* 1948, 27.
[6] Ibid. 26.   [7] Ibid. 28.   [8] Ibid. 30.
[9] 5[15].   [10] 255.   [11] 32.
[12] *NS* 1938, 63 n., 23*a*.

on oligarchic principles. But oligarchies of the Roman pattern were broadly based and did not in theory provide for the domination of a small minority. Power was centred by statute not in the magistrates but in the council, and ultimate control rested in theory with the people by virtue of their control of elections to office; for even where councillors were recruited by co-option, magistrates after their first public office normally entered the council. The importance of the popular vote in elections is nowhere better illustrated than in the painted notices on Pompeian walls in which farmers, traders, religious associations, neighbours, friends, press the claims of rival candidates.[1] This active concern of the people in who should govern them lasted at Pompeii until the town was destroyed in A.D. 79. By that time it is probable that the people had ceased to take part in elections at Ostia.

An inscription of the Augustan period suggests that the people then elected their magistrates. C. Cartilius Poplicola was elected and re-elected to the duovirate 'iudicio colonorum', by the verdict of the colonists; P. Lucilius Gamala was elected 'in comitis', but it is uncertain to which post he was so elected.[2] Three inscriptions from the end of the first century A.D., or the beginning of the second, suggest that elections had by then been transferred to the senate. M. Acilius Priscus owes his quaestorship or possibly his duovirate to the votes of the decurions;[3] Cn. Sergius Priscus is described on his tombstone as 'ex d(ecurionum) d(ecreto) aedili adlecto', appointed by decree of the council;[4] L. Calpurnius Saturus is similarly 'd(ecurionum) decreto aedili allecto'.[5] At Rome elections had been taken from the people at the beginning of Tiberius' principate; Ostia, always closely influenced by the capital, probably followed her example soon afterwards.[6] An exception to the general rule is the popular election of P. Lucilius Gamala to a financial commission in the late second century: 'idem curator pecuniae publicae exigendae et attribuendae in comitis factus cellam patri Tiberino restituit'.[7] But this was an extraordinary appointment.

[1] *ILS* 6398–438.

[2] 1[8-9]: 'IIvir(o) censoriae pot(estatis) quinquennal(is) in comitis facto curatori pecuniae publicae exigendae. . . .' See below, p. 501.

[3] 7: 'quaest(or) aer(ari) suffra[gio de]curion(um) IIvir.'

[4] 412. [5] 415.

[6] The evidence for the transfer of elections from popular assemblies in colonies and municipalities is insufficient to provide general conclusions. The Flavian charter of Spanish Malaca provides for election by the people (*Lex. Mal.* 51–58), but it does not follow that this was the practice throughout Italy in the Flavian period.

[7] 2[9].

When elections had been taken from the people it is doubtful whether they maintained an active interest in local politics. Popular assemblies can still be called, but the matters referred to them are not controversial. A formal meeting lies behind a dedication to Septimius Severus 'decreto colonorum';[1] similarly when Gallienus was honoured as 'protector of the Roman Empire and author of the security of all' by the whole citizen body at the end of ten years of his rule, a formal ceremony is implied: 'universi cives Ostienses decennii voti compotes.'[2] Other references to the people in inscriptions are more ambiguous. When a statue was put up to a famous pantomime by popular demand, 'postulante populo ob eximiam eius peritiam', it is uncertain whether a formal resolution was passed.[3] So too when a public endowment was commemorated 'decurionum decreto colonorum consensu'[4] the language need imply no more than an understanding by the council of the people's will.

The constitution that had been developed by the end of the Julio-Claudian period underwent little formal change before the third century. In the period of prosperity the only apparent innovations are the introduction of two new offices, those of the *quaestor alimentorum* and of the *curator operum publicorum et aquarum.*[5] The *quaestor alimentorum*, so defined to distinguish him from the existing town treasurer, the *quaestor aerarii*, is found in many other towns of Italy and is to be connected with the imperial alimentary system introduced by Trajan and continued by his successors.[6] By this system the imperial government lent money to Italian farmers on the security of their land, and the interest, charged at a low rate, was paid to the local authorities, who used it for the maintenance of poor children. The *quaestor alimentorum* seems to have been appointed to control this special fund, and any private benefactions made for a similar purpose. Only two holders of the post are known in Ostia and both are at the beginning of their careers.[7] It is doubtful whether the fund and the post were continued into the lean years that followed prosperity.

---

[1] S 5330.   [2] S 5334.
[3] 474.   [4] S 4450.
[5] The office of 'XXvir H.A.H.S.P.' is also recorded on an inscription (? second century A.D.), 340. I do not understand the form of the inscription, nor the meaning of the letters. No parallel is known.
[6] Hirschfeld, *Verwaltungsbeamten²*, 212–16; *quaestores aliment.*, Ruggiero, *Diz. Epigr.* i. 407. Attribution of the scheme to Trajan rather than Nerva, Mason Hammond, *MAAR* 21 (1953) 147–53.
[7] 298, S 4664.

The *curator operum publicorum* was responsible for the supervision of public buildings. C. Nasennius Marcellus, who was duovir for the third time in 111, is the first known holder of the office,[1] and only two others are recorded, the last in the third century.[2] It was a senior post, held by Marcellus after the duovirate, and was a permanent rather than annual appointment. The rapid growth of the town in the late first and early second centuries must have imposed an increasing strain on the small executive; the creation of a special responsibility for public buildings was a logical corollary to the rebuilding of the town.

Later in the second century a further new office was created. The Antonine Gamala was *tabularum et librorum curator primus*.[3] No other holder of the post is known and its function is obscure. The title is not found elsewhere; it may denote the control of public records. New public priesthoods were also added to those already established in the early Empire. The *sodales Arulenses* were probably instituted towards the end of the second century;[4] they were chosen, like the junior priests of Vulcan, from young men at the beginning of their public career; of similar status were the *sodales Herculani*, first found at this time.[5] More important was the *sacerdos geni coloniae*, who ranked in dignity with the *flamen Romae et Augusti*.[6] This priesthood was instituted, it seems, in the Severan period.

The building history of Ostia suggests a decline in prosperity in the second half of the second century. This may be reflected in the increased importance of the quaestorship. The normal position of the treasury quaestorship in a public career is between the aedileship and the duovirate; when the office is held after the duovirate we can infer that the duties carried greater responsibility and prestige. The first example known is the most striking. On the base of a statue set up towards the middle of the century P. Aufidius Fortis is described as '[d(ecurionum) d(ecreto) decu]rioni adlecto, IIviro, [quaesto]ri aerari Ostiensium III':[7] in a later dedication he is '[II]vir, q(uaestor) aer(ari) Ost(iensium) V'.[8] Fortis was appointed to the quaestorship after the duovirate and held the office five times. The natural explanation is that public finances are

---

[1] 9.

[2] 172 with p. 481 (dated 184), 373 (after the death of Septimius Severus).

[3] 2[8-9].   [4] p. 340.

[5] This priesthood is recorded in only two inscriptions, Bloch, 49 and 54. Neither is earlier than late second century, p. 79.

[6] 373, S 4452 with Bloch, 29, S 5340, Bloch, 49. Taylor, *The Cults of Ostia*, 35.

[7] 10.   [8] S 4621.

strained and need expert attention. The same emphasis on finance later
in the century is seen in the holding of the quaestorship after the duovirate by P. Lucilius Gamala and by M. Iunius Faustus.[1] A fragmentary
inscription, probably from the early third century, also records the
holding of the quaestorship by the same man more than once.[2]

Until after the middle of the third century the form of the constitution
seems to remain substantially unchanged. There are still *IIviri quinquennales censoria potestate* in 251 and they are sufficiently important to
be recorded on a statue base for dating purposes.[3] In the late third and
fourth centuries we lose all trace of local magistrates. The direction of
affairs is taken over by the central authority and the names of duovirs
no longer appear on public monuments.

In the administrative system of the late Empire Ostia and Portus
occupy a special position. The supervision of Italy rested in the north
with the *vicarius Italiae*, in the centre and south with the *vicarius urbis*,
both responsible to the *praefecti praetorio*. Under them *correctores* controlled the various districts. No sign of these officers survives at Ostia
or Portus until the fifth century; their place is taken by the *praefectus
annonae* who, from the middle of the fourth century at least, was
subordinate to the *praefectus urbi*.[4] The *praefectus annonae* is *curator rei
publicae Ostiensium* and his name is recorded on new buildings and
restorations;[5] even the dedication of statues is undertaken on his initiative
and in his name.[6] His headquarters may have been in the *praetorium* which
was built in Aurelian's Forum by the sea coast.[7] Flavius Domitianus,
commemorated by the council as 'praefecto annonae, curatori honorifi-
centissimo' is probably the first of the series known to us.[8] Not much
later is Hostilius Antipater, who, in the late third or early fourth century, set up a new altar before the temple of Hercules.[9] *

Curatores had been appointed to other Italian towns much earlier;

[1] **2**, 4142.
[2] Bloch, 54, a knight '[praef. divi] Pert(inacis) q(uaestori) aerar(ii) l[_____ .'
[3] 352.   [4] *RE, praefectus annonae*, 1270–4 (W. Ensslin).
[5] e.g. 134, 135, 157, S 4410.   [6] 131, S 4716.
[7] SHA, *Aurel.* 45. 2: 'forum nominis sui in Ostiensi ad mare fundare coepit, in quo
postea praetorium publicum constitutum est.'
[8] S 5342. A possible earlier example in the fragmentary S 4558, but context and restoration are very uncertain.
[9] *AE* 1948, 126. Before the death of Constantine, because Antipater is a knight
and under Constantine the *praefectus annonae* had senatorial status. After the mid-third
century, because his inscription reuses the base of a statue set up to P. Flavius Priscus
(Bloch, 29).

their main function had been financial supervision. But in the late first and early second centuries, when the institution was freely used, Ostia was enjoying her greatest prosperity and could continue to manage her own affairs. The decline of the third century had drained prosperity and undermined independence. A late fourth-century inscription on the base of an equestrian statue in the Forum records that 'the council and people of Ostia decreed and set up this statue to Manilius Rusticus . . . *praefectus annonae*, curator and patron of the most noble colony of Ostia, in recognition of his honour and services to the community, in order that the town should gain distinction from the record of his office'.[1] The language is in the spirit of the times, but it is a poor spirit.

Our main evidence for the position of local authorities in the late Empire derives from the Theodosian Code; the picture is extremely gloomy. Membership of a town council, which had once been highly honoured, has now become an intolerable burden. A continuous stream of regulations shows the anxiety of the imperial government and the unpopularity of the position. Increasing restrictions are imposed: the *curiales* must not evade their duties by trying to climb into the senatorial order; they may not hope for release by joining the legions.

The main reason for the government's anxiety was economic. The local councils were held responsible for meeting the government's requirements of men for the levy, horses for the public service, and supplies. The government stated its requirements from a town; it was the responsibility of the local council to see that they were collected. Some of these requirements were intermittent only, others were a standing commitment. From the middle Republic through the early Empire the towns of Italy had been freed from regular contributions to the central authority; in Diocletian's reorganization of the imperial economy Italy was no longer exempt and had to contribute in kind. What Ostia was required to contribute we do not know; she could perhaps best have supplied timber, pork, and salt.

The plight of the *curiales* in the late Empire is in sharp contrast with the powers and privileges of the senatorial order, particularly the great landowners. These were the *potentiores*, who could give protection or increase oppression. They were exempt from the *munera* of the local authorities, and it may well have been difficult to exact from them their due share of the town's obligations. In Ostia they formed a conspicuous minority.

[1] S 4455.

Throughout the fourth century the name of the *praefectus annonae* appears on all restorations of public monuments at Ostia and Portus; he was responsible for both centres. Early in the fifth century there may have been a change; for in the reign of Honorius and Theodosius (408–23) a public building, possibly the Curia, was restored at Ostia under the authority of a *vicarius urbis*.[1] At Portus the *praefectus annonae* still officiated; probably he was required to concentrate on the harbours themselves, while Ostia was merged in the general pattern of Italian organization, a formal confirmation that, unlike Portus, she was no longer of serious importance to Rome.

[1] S 4720: 'salvis (dominis nostris) Hon[orio et Theodos]io invict[is] | principibus Fl(avius) N[icius Theodu]lus v(ir) c(larissimus) | vicarius urb[is aeternae ? curia]m su[mptu] | [p]rinci[p]alium [coloniae Ostiensis] | totam renov[avit].'

IO

THE GOVERNING CLASS

THE character of a constitution depends not only on its forms but on the distribution of power, and the nature of the men who wield it. The inscriptions on which the history of the constitution is based are sufficiently detailed and numerous to invite a social analysis. They show that from the late Republic to the end of the Roman period the social pattern of the governing class underwent considerable changes. Four periods may be broadly distinguished.

The first period covers the transition from Republic to Empire and ends with the Civil War of 69, a period of steady but unspectacular growth in Ostia. It is marked by the concentration of power in a comparatively narrow aristocracy. The second period begins with the Flavian emperors and continues through the great rebuilding of Ostia in the first half of the second century; its main feature is the rise of a wealthy middle class, the wider distribution of office, and the infiltration of freedman stock into government. In the third period, which runs from the late second century to the middle of the third, the social tendencies of the previous period are further developed: old families die out and descendants of freedmen increasingly replace them in the council and in office. Prosperity is followed by growing economic strain. The last period extends to the end of the Roman period. It sees the collapse of the middle class, and a widening gulf between rich and poor. But the rich are no longer the directing force of government; the control of Ostia has passed to an imperial official. These periods correspond to general trends in the history of Rome, but any such divisions are to a certain extent arbitrary. Their primary justification is the historian's convenience; social changes in particular are gradual processes.

The building of an intelligible picture from a long series of individual inscriptions involves two main difficulties, that of dating the documents and of interpreting them. The Fasti are arranged chronologically and from them we know the names of a large number of chief magistrates and the dates when they held office; but where careers and other honorary inscriptions are not directly or indirectly dated, the only criterion available is the character of the script, and this criterion is frail. The series of dated inscriptions in Ostia is large enough to encourage hope that fairly reliable canons may eventually be fixed, but in the present stage of the study it is easy to make bad mistakes. In general it seems possible to distinguish pre-Flavian work from that which follows, and most inscriptions of the third century and later are considerably inferior to the workmanship of the second century, but it is still difficult to discriminate between the first and second halves of the second century, and the misdating of an important career can distort conclusions. Dating by script can at best be only approximate and should be used as a last resort.[1]

In a social analysis one of the main problems of interpretation concerns the tribe; for where a man's origin is not explicitly stated, his tribal affiliation is the surest indication of his family's origin, and in more than fifty Ostian inscriptions, many of them of important men, the tribe is recorded. Until the latter part of the nineteenth century it was assumed that Ostia was enrolled in the urban tribe Palatina, for that tribe clearly dominated the Ostian inscriptions then known. From this conclusion it was further inferred that Ostia was founded before the rustic tribes were instituted, an inference which seemed to confirm the tradition of a regal foundation. But by the time that Kubitschek published in 1889 his examination of the origin and distribution of the Roman tribes it was already clear that the rustic tribe Voturia was specially associated with Ostia.[2]

Voturia is the least widely distributed of all the Roman tribes. In Italy only Bergomum and Placentia are known to have been assigned to it; in the provinces it is not found. The fact that at Ostia it is the commonest tribe after Palatina cannot be coincidence. Kubitschek concluded that Ostia had two tribes, but he found no explanation for the anomaly. Dessau, studying the distribution more carefully while preparing the Ostian volume of the Corpus, noted that the members of Voturia included local magistrates, and suggested that the distinction between the two tribes was probably one of status.[3] He was clearly right. Puteoli follows the same pattern: there too Palatina is widespread, but Falerna not uncommon.

[1] Appendix X, p. 554.
[2] J. W. Kubitschek, *Imperium Romanum tributim discriptum*, 26.
[3] *CIL* xiv, p. 4.

The families enrolled in Voturia include some that played a long and distinguished part in Ostian life, others that are known to have been established in Ostia at least as early as Augustus. By contrast no man who is known to be of pure descent from a family resident in Ostia in the early Empire has as his tribe Palatina: indeed almost all the inscriptions recording this tribe can be shown to be of the second century or later. Normally the tribe denotes freedman origin. On what precise basis freedmen were allocated to this tribe we do not know. Sometimes at Ostia as elsewhere the patron's tribe was handed on to the descendants of his freedmen. Thus Cn. Sergius Cn. f. Vot(uria) Priscus,[1] the son of a freedman, presumably got his tribe from the Ostian family to which his father had been attached as a slave; but this was not an invariable rule. A. Egrilius Pal(atina) Hedoniacus and A. Egrilius A. f. Pal(atina) Magnus[2] derive their name from one of the oldest Ostian families known to us; they are both probably of freedman descent but do not inherit from the Egrilii their Ostian tribe Voturia.

Provisionally we assume that Voturia provides evidence for the Ostian origin of a family, though the individual concerned may not necessarily be of free descent. Palatina will probably signify servile blood in the family, though not necessarily recent; it will not, however, be decisive evidence for rejecting an Ostian family origin. The A. Egrilii, two of whom, as we have seen, are registered in Palatina, we know from other evidence to be Ostian; similarly L. Calpurnius L. f. Pal. Chius Felicissimus, the son of the rich freedman L. Calpurnius Chius,[3] may be connected with an Ostian family represented in an inscription by L. Calpurnius L. f. Vot(uria) Saturus,[4] himself possibly of freedman origin; though it is equally possible, since the name is common, that the L. Calpurnius from whom Chius received his freedom had once lived elsewhere. We are on firmer ground with tribes other than Voturia and Palatina. They invariably imply an origin outside Ostia.

THE ARISTOCRACY OF THE EARLY EMPIRE

The most striking feature of the early Empire is the strong hold on the duovirate of certain families and the persistent re-election of outstanding men. C. Cartilius Poplicola was elected no less than eight times,

---

[1] 412.   [2] 949, S 4899.   [3] 16.
[4] 415; he is associated in this funerary inscription with a freedman's descendants.

including three years with censorial authority;[1] Postumus Plotius,[2] probably of the late Republic and a P. Lucilius Gamala,[3] probably of the Julio-Claudian period, hold office four times and no less than nine others are known to have held the duovirate at least twice. Two families during this period overshadow all others in the Fasti. An A. Egrilius Rufus is duovir in A.D. 6, 34, 36;[4] the P. Lucilii Gamalae provided duovirs for at least three generations. There is probably a family connexion between Q. Vitellius, duovir in 47 and 45 B.C., and A. Vitellius, duovir in 46 B.C.;[5] Q. Fabius Longus, duovir for the third time in A.D. 37, is probably of the same family as C. Fabius Agrippa, duovir in the early Empire.[6] C. Naevius [—], duovir in A.D. 33, similarly may be connected with M. Naevius Optatus, duovir of 31 and *pontifex Volcani*.

As Wilson has pointed out, the cognomina of the duovirs of this first period have a respectable Roman ring:[7] Africanus, Agrippa, Bassus, Carbo, Dexter, Flaccus, Gemellus, Gratus, Longus, Montanus, Optatus, Pollio, Poplicola, Proculus, Rufus, Severus, Veiento. It is true that the cognomen alone is not valid evidence of origin, for we should never guess by their names that C. Silius Nerva and Cn. Sergius Priscus were the sons of freedmen;[8] but it was more common for men to retain their slave names when freed. If the descendants of freedmen were rising to the duovirate in significant numbers before the end of the Julio-Claudian period we should expect to find some trace of servile names among the cognomina.

It is probable that Ostia in this period was ruled by a comparatively limited aristocracy of free descent and that it was more difficult then than later for the new man to reach the highest office. Some of the families that held the key to office were of Ostian origin, and two of these produced senators. M. Acilius, duovir of 48 B.C., is probably related to,

---

[1] p. 476.

[2] S 4710: 'Postumus Plotius M. f. quarto | A. Genucius A. f. iter. duoviri | locum dederunt compiti aedificandi. | C. Cartilius C. f. Poplicol(a) duovir VII | cens. III compitum transtulit.' Poplicola probably died in the early Augustan period (p. 475).

[3] 3.

[4] The name could also be restored in the *Fasti* for A.D. 15, '[A. Egril]ius Rufus'; 16, '[A. Egrili]us Rufus'; 17, '[A. Egrilius] Rufus maior'; but no mark of iteration, normally recorded in the *Fasti*, is added, and Rufus is not an uncommon cognomen. See Degrassi, 214.

[5] Their relationship is made more probable by the name of a freedman on an Augustan tomb, Q. Vitellius, Q. A. Q. l. (*NS* 1938, 68 n. 29). This suggests that Q. Vitellius, duovir in 45 B.C., may be related to rather than identical with the duovir of 47 B.C.

[6] 8.

[7] Wilson, *BSR* 13 (1935) 45.   [8] 415, 412.

if not identical with, M. Acilius Caninus, Roman quaestor before 28 B.C. to whom the business men of the area by the temple of Saturn, the Roman treasury, set up a statue at Ostia.[1] From the same family, towards the end of the first century A.D., came M. Acilius Priscus, who had an equestrian military career;[2] his adopted son is enrolled in the Ostian tribe Voturia.[3] The other senatorial family recognized by its tribe Voturia as Ostian is that of the T. Sextii who provided in T. Sextius Africanus a duovir at Ostia in A.D. 36 and a Roman consul in A.D. 59.[4] The Egrilii also were Ostian: the name is extremely rare outside Ostia and more common than any other in the town. A new inscription has confirmed what was already virtually certain, that this family also belonged to Voturia.[5] The only other duovirs during this period whose tribe is known, C. Fabius Agrippa and C. Tuccius, were also registered in the Ostian tribe Voturia.[6] But there are already two important families at least in the governing class of Ostia in the early Empire who were probably not by origin Ostian.

The family whose elder sons took the name of P. Lucilius Gamala held office in Ostia for more than 200 years, but in not one of their many inscriptions is their tribe recorded; their cognomen, however, is distinctive and very rare. Since Mommsen published his reconsidered views on the two longest inscriptions of this family, the derivation of Gamala from the little town of Gamala in north Galilee has been accepted by all scholars who have made a special study of the family. A Roman Publius Lucilius acquired in the course of war or trade a slave from Gamala; the slave was named after his town of origin, and when he was given freedom he and his descendants clung tenaciously to the name. As Tenney Frank pointed out, it is unlikely that a slave from such an inconspicuous inland town came to Rome before Roman armies penetrated the region. The first Gamala, he suggested, came to Rome in the wake of Pompey's victorious army which, after crushing Mithradates, campaigned from Syria through Judaea.[7]

If this explanation of the name was correct we should have to modify our general impression of the Ostian governing class of the early Empire.

[1] 153. p. 507.   [2] 7.

[3] M. Acilius A. f. Vot. Priscus Egrilius Plarianus, 155, S 4442–4, Bloch, 24–26. For the relationship, p. 503.

[4] For the tribe of the Sextii, *AE* 1914, 141.   [5] 6.

[6] 8, 426. C. Aq(uilius), probably a duovir of the early Principate (Bloch, 66) may be of the same family as L. Aquillius L. f. Vot. (unpublished).

[7] Tenney Frank, *Class. Journ.* 49 (1934) 481.

For even if our attribution of the Gamala of the lost inscription to the principate of Augustus is incorrect, the family is well established in the Julio-Claudian period, providing duovirs in A.D. 19 and 33. Moreover, the climate could not have been unfavourable if the family made no attempt to conceal its eastern servile origin by a change of cognomen. There is, however, a more convincing explanation of the name. In one of his letters to Atticus Cicero mentions a Gamala whose father's cognomen or nickname was Ligus.[1] With this clue to guide us we can draw a natural inference from an inscription outside Ostia which records the rare name Gamala. A funerary stone with the name of C. Turselius Gamala is published with the inscriptions of Beneventum: it was found at Macchia, in the district where the Ligures Baebiani were settled by Rome in the early second century B.C.[2] The name Gamala may derive from Liguria or a neighbouring district.[3] How early the family came to Ostia we cannot tell, but its prominence under Augustus, and the honours that it continued to receive for two centuries suggest that its Ostian roots go well back into the Republic.

C. Cartilius Poplicola is the other outstanding public figure of this period whose family tribe is not recorded in surviving inscriptions. The name C. Cartilius is rare, and is perhaps of Etruscan origin.[4] It is found at Chiusi and it may be from that district that the family originally came.

To the leading families that can be securely dated to the pre-Flavian period three others may be tentatively added. The Fasti record the restoration in A.D. 94 of a 'crypta Terentiana'; the name must record a benefactor of the Julio-Claudian period or earlier. L. Terentius Tertius is the first holder of the name whose duovirate is known, in A.D. 92, but the dedication by a Terentia of a well-head in the area of an Augustan temple of Bona Dea confirms the earlier prominence of the family.[5] We have evidence also of early Volusii,[6] who may be linked with a name in the Fasti of A.D. 91: 'in f(undo) Volusiano arb[os ful] mine icta.'

---

[1] Cic. *Ad Att.* xii. 23. 3: 'de Gamala dubium non mihi erat. unde etiam tam felix Ligus pater?' The passage is very naked.

[2] *CIL* ix. 1491 with p. 125.

[3] The only other Gamala known to me is included in a fragmentary list of names from Etruscan Vettona, *CIL* xi. 5199.

[4] Schulze, *Geschichte lateinischer Eigennamen*, 145.   [5] Unpublished.

[6] An Augustan C. Volusius, *NS* 1938, 58 n. 19; L. Volusius, ibid. 73 n. 44; C. Volusius Flaccus, duovir II in A.D. 18 (*Fasti*).

More interesting and hazardous is speculation concerning the Rusticelii. In the imperial period a ferry service is named after this family, *traiectus Rusticelius*;[1] and a family estate, *praedia Rusticeliana*, is recorded in the Severan period as belonging to the emperor.[2] No duovir of the name is known from surviving records, but it seems clear that the family was once important in Ostia. It may be associated with the Rusticelii of the tribe Scantia, whose late republican tomb was discovered at the end of the seventeenth century under Monte Testaccio.[3] It is reasonable to infer from the siting of the tomb in the trading quarter of Rome outside the Porta Trigemina that the Roman Rusticelii were engaged in trade; the Ostian Rusticelii may have been a branch of the family with similar interests.

It would be interesting to know the occupations of this early local aristocracy. Some of its members at least must have had considerable wealth to incur the expense of repeated duovirates. For, though there is no explicit evidence from Ostia itself, we may assume by analogy with other towns that the duovir was required by statute to contribute substantially to the public expenditure of his year of office; and public opinion expected more than the law required. The large atrium houses of the late Republic and early Empire near the centre of the town also indicate wealth; their individual owners cannot be identified, but it is reasonable to associate them with the ruling class of the day. There is, however, little evidence to show the sources from which this wealth came.

C. Fabius Agrippa was descended from a family of soldiers; both his father and grandfather had been senior centurions.[4] The inscription on the public tomb of C. Cartilius Poplicola records that he was elected to the duovirate in absence as well as when he was present at the elections.[5] The frieze above the inscription depicts scenes of fighting; Poplicola may have been a military man. It is legitimate to infer that the family of P. Lucilius Gamala had no associations with trade, for in the long series of their inscriptions no honours from the trading guilds are included, nor are the descendants of their freedmen found in the rolls of the guilds. For the rest we lack even such indirect evidence.

Wilson has suggested that the comparatively small ring of ruling families of the pre-Flavian period represents a landed aristocracy in contrast to the growing domination of traders from the Flavian period

---

[1] *S* 4553–6.   [2] *S* 4570.   [3] *CIL* vi. 11534–5.   [4] **8.**   [5] p. 476.

onwards.[1] On general grounds this view does not carry conviction. Had there been a substantial group of wealthy landowners at Ostia we should expect to find more of them entering the Roman senate; nor was Ostian land well suited to large estates.[2] Some private fortunes, now as later, may have been based on the ownership of property in the town, which increased in value as Ostia developed, but the main source of wealth in Ostia must always have been trade. The distinction between the first and later periods is probably more of birth and origin than of occupation.

THE SOCIAL REVOLUTION

At Rome the Flavian period marked a decisive stage in the trans-formation of the Roman governing class. Caesar and Augustus had widened the basis of recruitment to the Roman senate by introducing new blood from the towns of Italy. Augustus' policy was continued by his successors, and extended to include on a small scale the western provinces. But in the senatorial debates recorded by Tacitus the descendants of old republican senatorial families still play a leading part during the period. By the death of Nero persecution had severely thinned their ranks. Vespasian, humble in origin, and severely practical in his approach to problems of government, used the censorship to recruit men of ability wherever he found them. Tacitus implies, perhaps exaggerating, that the new senators formed a sufficiently important nucleus to modify the living standards of the city.[3] Against this Roman background the Ostian evidence falls into an intelligible pattern. The holders of the duovirate from the Flavian period to the death of Antoninus Pius seem to form a much less homogeneous group than those of the first period. It is easier for new men to reach the highest office, but some of the old-established families retain their local leadership.

The most spectacular feature of this period was the rise of the Egrilii. In the first century A.D. they had played a leading part in Ostia's government. An A. Egrilius Rufus was duovir in A.D. 6; he, or perhaps his son, was appointed *pontifex Volcani* in 30. When he died holding the office of censorial duovir in 36 his son succeeded to the duoviral duties for the remainder of the year, as *praefectus*. In the next generation another A. Egrilius Rufus rose through the aedileship and quaestorship to the duovirate and held the important priesthood of Rome and Augustus.[4]

---

[1] Wilson, *BSR* 13 (1935) 45 f.   [2] pp. 262–5.   [3] Tac. *Ann.* iii. 55. 4.   [4] **6.**

It was probably this A. Egrilius Rufus, of the late Julio-Claudian or Flavian period who, by a judicious marriage, laid the foundations of the family's rise to imperial distinction. His wife Plaria Vera seems to have been indirectly connected with the Acilii Glabriones, who had provided Rome with consuls since the early second century B.C.[1] Her influence is seen in the change of the cognomen of the Egrilii from Rufus to Plarianus, in her appointment in Ostia as *flaminica divae Augustae*, and in the inscriptions set up in her honour.[2] She was commemorated as 'mother of A. Egrilius Plarianus, the father, consul, patron of the colony'.[3] This was her eldest son, who was one of the prefects of the public treasury before becoming consul at the end of the first or beginning of the second century. He was called 'father' to distinguish him from his son, who followed him in a senatorial career, was appointed to the military treasury, and became consul in 128.[4]* Both father and son kept alive their association with Ostia. Father and son became patrons of the colony; the son was appointed *pontifex Volcani*. What other honours they held in the town we do not know.

Of another senatorial member of the family we know much more, and his associations with Ostia seem to be closer. M. Acilius A.f. Vot(uria) Priscus Egrilius Plarianus combines the names of two old-established Ostian families, the M. Acilii and the A. Egrilii. He is almost certainly the adopted son of M. Acilius Priscus, who in the Flavian period held three military equestrian posts without proceeding further in the imperial administrative service. Instead he had a varied and distinguished local career, crowned by the two highest priesthoods in the colony; he was both *flamen Romae et Augusti* and *pontifex Volcani*.[5]

The Egrilius whom M. Acilius Priscus adopted saw service in many parts of the empire. His military tribunate took him to Moesia; he

[1] For the relationships of the Egrilii I have, with minor modifications, followed Bloch, *NS* 1953, 254. The evidence is summarized in Appendix V, p. 502.

[2] 399, S 5346, and perhaps 156 (Bloch, art. cit. 262).

[3] 399: 'Plariae Q. f. Verae, flaminicae | divae Aug(ustae), matri A. Egrili Plarian patris p(atroni) c(oloniae) cos.'

[4] S 4445: 'A. Egrilius Plarianus praef. aerari militaris p(atronus) c(oloniae) pontif. Volk[ani].'

[5] 7. His local career as recorded is anomalous: 'd(ecurionum) d(ecreto) d(ecurio) adle[ctus], quaest(or) aer(ari) suffra[gio de]curionum, IIvir aedil(is) II [quinq]uennal(is) pr[aef]ect(us) II, [praef(ectus)] colleg(i) fabr' . . . . *aedilis quinquennalis* is not an Ostian title, and the aedileship, always a junior office, seems out of place. Probably a cutter's error for *aedil. IIvir II*. . . . He was twice duovir, once with censorial authority, and twice he was *praefectus*, probably representing a member of the imperial family who had accepted the title.

served on the governor's staff in Sicily and Asia, himself governed
Narbonese Gaul, and then commanded a legion on the Rhine.[1] He was
appointed to the military treasury before 105 and, like his contemporaries Pliny the younger and L. Catilius Severus,[2] proceeded later to the
public treasury to which he was appointed in 106.[3]* From the Fasti we
know that he became *pontifex Volcani* in 105 and, almost certainly,
censorial duovir in the following year. He had already been elected a
patron of the colony. A commemorative tablet set up in his honour by
public authority pays tribute to his loyalty, his respect for religion, and
his generosity: 'pio ac religiosissim(o) . . . [mun]ificentissimo.'[4] His
loyalty is shown by the Ostian offices he held; his respect for religion is
reflected in his priesthood of Vulcan; and, as Bloch suggests, it may be
significant that the temple of Vulcan was restored in 112, during his
tenure of office. His generosity is attested by a handsome inscription on
an epistyle which records the dedication of a head of gold within a shield
in silver.[5] Two further inscriptions record his loyalty to his emperors.
In 106 he set up a commemorative tablet in honour of Trajan, perhaps
on the occasion of his appointment to the public treasury.[6] In 118 he
paid a similar tribute to Hadrian and in this he was joined by his son.[7]
When ugly rumours were circulating concerning the succession such
action was not without purpose or value.

The relationship of this adopted son of M. Acilius Priscus to the
Egrilii whom we have already considered is still a matter for conjecture
rather than demonstration. The most economic hypothesis, suggested
by Adams and accepted by Bloch, is that he is the younger son of
Plaria Vera, Quintus, brother of A. Egrilius Plarianus. It is equally
probable that his son is to be identified with Q. Egrilius who was consul in 143 or 144 and governor of Africa in 158/9.[8] The praenomen
Quintus derives from the father of Plaria Vera.

In two generations the Egrilii had provided at least three consuls.
Even more striking is their accumulation of treasury posts. The elder
A. Egrilius Plarianus was *praefectus aerarii Saturni*, his elder son *praefectus
aerarii militaris*; the younger held both posts. This is no coincidence. It
is almost certainly a tribute to the business capacity inherited from a
family which had grown rich on the profits of trade.[9] That the Egrilii

[1] S 4442, 4444.   [2] *ILS* 2927, 1041; and, a little later, *ILS* 8973.
[3] Bloch, 25.   [4] Bloch, 24.   [5] 72.
[6] Bloch, 25.   [7] Bloch, 26.   [8] *PIR*[2], E 49 (Groag).
[9] It is interesting to find three Egrilii of freedman stock among the few bankers
recorded, S 4644, Bloch, 53 (referring also to a third, unpublished, inscription).

derived their main wealth from trade cannot be proved, but it is strongly suggested by the wide distribution of the name in the trade guilds. Most of these men were freedmen, or of freedman stock. It is easier to understand the prevalence of the name in trade if the original patrons had trading interests.

Another Ostian family rose to the consulship in this period. C. Fabius Agrippinus, consul of 148, is almost certainly descended from C. Fabius Agrippa, of the Ostian tribe Voturia, whose career in the Julio-Claudian period or slightly later is preserved.[1] He was praetor in the cult of Vulcan, aedile and duovir, and his inscription records his free descent for four generations. The cognomen of his father and grandfather was Longus; Q. Fabius Longus, duovir in 31 and 37, *praefectus* in 36, probably comes from the same family; C. Fabius, colleague of C. Cartilius Poplicola,[2] may be a direct ancestor. C. Fabius Agrippinus, who brought the consulship to the family, is not known to have held office in Ostia, but two inscriptions show that he maintained his association with the town. The first was set up in his honour when, before his consulship, he held a praetorian post in a province.[3] The second is a public tribute by council and people to his daughter; she had left a capital endowment to provide for the maintenance of 100 Ostian girls and the celebration of annual games.[4]

In contrast no descendants of T. Sextius Africanus, the Ostian consul of A.D. 59, are recorded in any surviving inscription from Ostia after the Julio-Claudian period. This family remained prominent throughout the second century;[5] had it retained its links with Ostia some trace of one at least of its members should have survived. It had probably left the town.

The Lucilii Gamalae who held so many duovirates in the early Empire, unlike the Egrilii, did not rise above local government. They remained in Ostia through the second century and continued the family tradition of public service to the town. The member of the family of whom we know most, lived out his career into the reign of Marcus Aurelius. What part the two previous generations had played in public life is obscure. The name is not preserved in any surviving fragments of the Fasti though the record is particularly full for the reign of Trajan, nor does any statue base or commemorative tablet survive to record

---

[1] 8.   [2] 4134.   [3] Bloch, 28.
[4] S 4450 (= 350). The benefactress might be the consul's wife rather than daughter.
[5] T. Sextii are *consules ordinarii* in 112 (Africanus), 154 (Lateranus), 197 (Lateranus).

the career of a member of the family in this period. What little evidence
is available is controversial.

The only member of the family known in the first half of the century
was adopted into another family. Cn. Sentius Lucilius Gamala Clodianus commemorates two fathers, Cn. Sentius Felix[1] and Publius Lucilius
Gamala.[2] Dessau considered that Cn. Sentius Felix was his natural
father, and that he had been adopted by P. Lucilius Gamala.[3] The order
of names is not in itself decisive, for Roman practice varied, but the
contemporary Ostian parallel of M. Acilius Priscus Egrilius Plarianus
favours Mommsen's view that he was by birth a P. Lucilius Gamala.[4]
This also is the natural inference to be drawn from a comparison of the
two stones set up to commemorate his two fathers. The memorial to
P. Lucilius Gamala, now in the Florence Archaeological Museum, is a
short inscription in mean letters on a small undecorated funerary altar;
the memorial to Cn. Sentius Felix, in the Uffizi Gallery, is an elaborate
inscription excellently cut on a funerary altar richly decorated. The
inscription is framed at the sides by fluted pilasters with elaborate
capitals and, above, by a carefully carved scroll of acanthus with leaping
lions.[5] Cn. Sentius Felix is honoured as 'a most indulgent father'. The
conclusion seems inevitable that Cn. Sentius Felix had adopted P. Lucilius Gamala, and we may guess the reason. Cn. Sentius Felix was not an
Ostian by birth. His tribe was Teretina and his family came, almost
certainly, from Atina.[6] Though his inscription proclaims his free descent
for three generations his cognomen Felix is at best ambiguous and he
may be descended from a freedman of the family of Cn. Sentius Saturninus, the prominent Augustan marshal. But his rise at Ostia in the
Flavian period or slightly later was rapid. He was co-opted by the
council with the status of an aedile, was in the same year appointed
quaestor of the treasury and designated duovir for the following year,
an unprecedented honour, as his inscription emphasizes. Perhaps his
adoption of a member of one of the leading Ostian families was a
deliberate attempt to win local support in his new home. His other
claim to office was his wealth and his business associations. He became
a patron of many Ostian traders' guilds and was himself a shipper.

[1] 5.   [2] 377.
[3] Dessau, on 409.   [4] Mommsen, *EE* iii, p. 324.
[5] For the type of funerary altar, not uncommon in the Flavian period and early second
century, J. C. M. Toynbee and J. Ward Perkins, 'Peopled Scrolls: a Hellenistic Motif in
Imperial Art', *BSR* 18 (1950) 16.
[6] *CIL* vi. 2722: 'Cn. Sentius Cn. f. Ter(etina) Saturninus Atine spec. coh. VIIII pr.'

A Cn. Sentius Clodianus is recorded in the Fasti as duovir in 102, and is listed with Cn. Sentius Felix among the patrons of a guild in an inscription set up shortly before 135.[1] It is a reasonable economy to identify these names with the adopted son of Cn. Sentius Felix. It is possible that the Gamala adopted by Cn. Sentius Felix was an only son. It is more probable that, like the Q. Egrilius Plarianus adopted by M. Acilius Priscus, he had an elder brother. Perhaps some traces of the main branch of the family survive. The inscription set up on the temple of Bellona records the allocation of the site by the duovirs of the year: 'A. Livius Proculus P. Lucilius Gamala f(ilius) IIvir(i) praef(ecti) Caesar(is)'.[2] It is tempting to identify this Gamala with the late second-century holder of the name who was praefectus 'L(uci) Caesar(is) Aug(usti) f(ili)'.[3] This Caesar has been identified with Commodus, but the brickwork of the temple of Bellona and the style of the inscription seem to be earlier than Commodus.[4] It is possible that the Caesar in question was L. Aelius whom Hadrian adopted at the end of 136. Gamala is described as 'f(ilius)' to distinguish him from his father. It is tempting to believe, though the guess has no firm foundation, that the father's name should be restored in the Fasti of 126. In that year the emperor Hadrian held the title of duovir for a second time. His colleague whose name is lost was a patron of the colony, who may also not have been available for the routine duties of office. These were delegated to two *praefecti*, the first of whom is described as 'pater'. It may have been the senior P. Lucilius Gamala, elder brother of Cn. Sentius Lucilius Gamala Clodianus. It would be singularly appropriate for members of the imperial family to be represented in office by the same Ostian family in two generations.

In very few other duovirs of this period can continuity be seen with the past. L. Naevius Proculus, duovir in 95, and P. Naevius Severus, duovir in 110, may derive from the same family as M. Naevius Optatus and C. Naevius (—), who had held the office respectively in 31 and 33. P. Turranius Aemilianus, duovir in 145, is styled 'fil(ius)' in the Fasti; probably his father had also held the office. He may be from the same family as M. Turranius, colleague of the Augustan Gamala.[5] The family name may also be in part preserved in the Fasti of A.D. 14, [–Tur]ranius

---

[1] S 5374.
[2] 4. Pl. xxxviii
[3] 2.   [4] pp. 346 f.   [5] 1[30].

Pollio, and in the cognomen of M. Maecilius who paid for the building of the Julio-Claudian temple to Bona Dea, M. Maecilius [T]urr[anianus].[1]* The cognomina of the duovir of 112—[L]ongus Grattianus Caninianus—suggest connexions with the Fabii and Acilii. Longus and Grattus are among the ancestors of C. Fabius Agrippa; Caninianus recalls M. Acilius Caninus.

Many more of the early families seem to have left the town, died out, or lost their place in the governing class. The Vitellii who held office in 47, 46, and 45 B.C. do not reappear in the Fasti and only one later Vitellius is known, a freedman.[2] P. Paetinius Dexter, who was duovir for the second time and *pontifex Volcani* when he died in A.D. 30, was presumably living at Ostia, but no trace of any office-holder among his descendants is found. Even the family of C. Cartilius Poplicola, who was eight times duovir, and certainly had children, is not known to have produced any magistrates during this period, though the name is still found in the second century. *

Of the family names among the duovirs of the second period that are not known in office earlier, some seem to have been long established in Ostia. C. Nasennius Marcellus who is duovir for the third time in 111, a census year, and is patron of the colony, is probably of the same family as C. Nasennius Proculus who is known to be registered in the Ostian tribe Voturia.[3] He is probably not the first of his family to hold the duovirate; and he certainly was not the last. A. Livius Priscus, duovir in 105, seems from his name to be of free birth; the family is attested in the early principate at Ostia.[4] A. Livius Proculus, colleague of P. Lucilius Gamala when the temple of Bellona was built, is presumably from the same family.[5] The family name of [L.] Plinius Nigrinus, duovir in 147, is also found on a funerary stone of the early Empire.[6]

Business interests are well attested in the ruling class during this period and in several cases they are associated with non-Ostian tribes. The spectacular public career of Cn. Sentius Felix, whose family probably came from Atina, has already been mentioned. He was a member

---

[1] *AE* 1946, 221.

[2] L. Vitellius Calycand[er], *S* 4563, 1, col. ii. 7. Q. Vitellius Q.A.Q.l. (*NS* 1938, p. 68 n. 29) is probably a freedman of the magistrates of 47–45 B.C.

[3] *S* 5035. Career of Marcellus, **9**.

[4] 581, an A. Livius on the same inscription as a freedman of Antonia, mother of the emperor Claudius; 358, M. Livius M.f. Vot(uria) Rogatus and Iustus, early Principate.

[5] *AE* 1948, 26.

[6] *S* 5062: L. Plinius Euhodus, freedman. The letters seem to be not later than Augustus.

of the guild of shippers trading in the Adriatic and his wealth was probably mainly derived from wine.[1] P. Aufidius Fortis, who was duovir later in the second century, was president of the corn measurers and patron of the corn merchants; he was also councillor at Hippo Regius, an important centre of the corn trade in Africa.[2] Since his tribe is Quirina, the most widely distributed tribe in Africa, it might be inferred that he was a native of Hippo Regius who had come to settle in Ostia.[3] The order of the inscription makes it more probable that his membership of the council of Hippo Regius was conferred on him in view of his business associations with the town. The family origin may be African, but earlier Aufidii are known at Ostia.[4] It is probably because of his influence outside Ostia, particularly perhaps with the *praefectus annonae*, that he is made patron of the town; his holding of the quaestorship no less than five times after the duovirate is a tribute to his business experience. The approximate date of P. Aufidius Fortis is given by the Fasti, for he is recorded, as patron of the town, to have dedicated in A.D. 146 silver statues of Honour and Victory and to have celebrated games for three days to commemorate these dedications. His son followed him in the duovirate.[5]

C. Granius Maturus, who also became duovir, has probably a similar background.[6] His tribe is Quirina and, like P. Aufidius Fortis, he is concerned with the corn trade. He is patron of the corn measurers and of the curators of sea and river ships. His business interests probably explain his setting up a statue to Q. Petronius Honoratus, who had been promoted from the prefecture of the corn supply to the governorship of Egypt in 147.[7] Q. Plotius Romanus also belongs to the tribe Quirina. He may have died before he reached the duovirate, but he had become aedile and *flamen Romae et Augusti* when he was honoured with a public statue in 141.[8] There is, however, no evidence of his occupation.

The prosperity that followed the building of the imperial harbours led to the wider representation in office of families that were not of Ostian origin. It is clear also, from a study of names and from more

[1] 57⁻⁹; wine trade, p. 295.   [2] 10, S 4621.   [3] Wilson, *BSR* 13 (1935) 67.
[4] L. Aufidius from a tomb not later than Augustus, *NS* 1938, p. 48.
[5] S 4622: 'P. Aufidio P. fil. Quir(ina) Forti, Aufidi Fortis p(atroni) c(oloniae) fil(io), IIvir., q., aedil., flam. divi Titi.'
[6] 362, 363 (with S, p. 615), 364, S 4458, 4651, 4715; possibly also Bloch, 62. There are earlier Granii at Ostia, 707, 360, 361, 1094; but no earlier C. Granius is recorded.
[7] For the date, A. Stein, *Präfecten von Ägypten*, 79.   [8] 400, 401.

direct evidence, that there was by now a substantial admixture of servile blood in the ruling class. The cognomina in the Fasti of the period are less homogeneous than those of their predecessors. Celsus, Cinna, Clemens, Justus, Marcellus, Nigrinus, Priscus, Proculus, Severus continue the pattern of the early Empire. Such names as Aemilianus, Commianus, Manlianus, Pompilianus, Valerianus reflect the fashion of the age in perpetuating a mother's name, as the Egrilii kept alive the memory of the marriage of A. Egrilius Rufus to Plaria Vera when the family cognomen was changed from Rufus to Plarianus. But Augustalis, Euphemianus, and Orestes suggest descent from freedmen. These names are known from the Fasti.[1] To them may be added M. Aemilius Hilarianus, whose tomb outside the Porta Romana should probably be dated to the first half of the second century.[2] The suspicions aroused by his cognomen are strengthened by the name of his wife, Clodia Helpis.

C. Julius Proculus, duovir in 108, has been identified with the suffect consul of 109, but such a distinguished man would probably have accepted the honour only in a censorial year, and he seems to be the junior duovir.[3] More probably he is a local man, descended from an imperial freedman of the early Empire. Ti. Claudius (—), duovir in 115, probably has a similar origin, and the cognomen of M. Antistius Flavianus, duovir in 127, derives from a Flavian freedman.

These inferences from names are supported by more direct evidence. C. Silius C.f. Vot(uria) Nerva, who rose to the duovirate not later than the early years of the second century, is the son of the freedman C. Silius Felix and his son after him also held the office.[4] The family to which Felix owed his freedom was Ostian and that may have helped to secure his son's election. Such local loyalties may also help to explain the most surprising appointment of this period known to us. The Fasti for 105 record the appointment of the praetorian M. Acilius Priscus Egrilius Plarianus as *pontifex Volcani* in succession to P. Ostiensis Macedo,

---

[1] Augustalis (108), Euphemianus (109), Orestes (85).

[2] 332: 'M. Aemilius Hilarianus dec. flam. aedilis IIvir.' The tomb described, *Ann. Inst.* 29 (1857) 291 f.; Paschetto, 445 f. The approximate date is suggested by the character of the brickwork and the form of the tomb, which provides only for cremation. In the second half of the century some provision would probably have been made for burial (p. 464).

[3] Identified with the consul by Calza, *NS* 1932, 189, followed by Groag: I agree with Degrassi, 229.

[4] 415. C. Silius Felix, father of Nerva, was an *Augustalis*, and the *Augustales* were superseded by *seviri Augustales* not later than Trajan's reign (p. 218–20).

who had died.[1] Macedo owed his name to the town and must be descended, though perhaps remotely, from a public slave; however respectable his cognomen may appear, his contemporaries can have had no doubt as to the significance of his family name. Yet to become *pontifex Volcani* he should first have held the normal magistracies, for the pontificate was the most honoured post in Ostia and reserved for outstanding men. That a man of freedman descent should be followed in office by one of the most distinguished Ostians of the day, who represented two of the oldest Ostian families, is a striking commentary on the times.

If this study could be profitably extended to Ostian councillors who did not rise to the duovirate, we should probably be able to trace a much wider infusion of freedman stock at this lower level of government, but we do not even know the names of any such councillors from the Julio-Claudian period, and the number known from the late first and early second century is too small to justify generalization. The few, however, that can be dated before the death of Antoninus Pius, are either certainly or probably descended from freedmen. Cn. Sergius Cn.f. Vot(uria) Priscus became councillor and aedile but not duovir;[2] his father Cn. Sergius Anthus was an *Augustalis*, freedman priest in the imperial cult; but the family he served was registered in the Ostian tribe. L. Calpurnius L.f. Vot(uria) Saturus, aedile, probably has a similar background, for he is associated in a funerary inscription with the son and grandson of a freedman.[3] P. Celerius P.f. Pal(atina) Amandus was admitted to the council under the legal age.[4] His tribe, his cognomen, his mother's name (Scantia Spurii f. Lanthanusa) suggest servile blood in the background; a new unpublished inscription recording the same career confirms that his father was a freedman, P. Celerius P. libertus Chryseros. The family must have been wealthy, for the public funeral that was given to Amandus is more likely to have been a tribute to his parents' generosity than to his own services. On his tombstone are the tools of his trade; he was brought up to be a shipbuilder.

The chief magistrates of the period are of much more diversified origins than their predecessors. Old Ostian families are still represented; with them are business men attracted to Ostia by the rapid growth of trade at the imperial harbours, and descendants of freedmen. The

[1] The appointment of Macedo may be recorded in a further fragment of the *Fasti*, G. Barbieri, *Studi Romani*, i (1953) 369.
[2] 412.   [3] 415.   [4] 321.

exclusiveness of the early Empire has disappeared. Re-election to the duovirate, which was a marked feature of the earlier period, is now much rarer. Only one man is known to have held the duovirate as many as three times and, apart from the emperor Hadrian, only two others are known to have held it twice.[1] There are still very large gaps in the Fasti, but more entries are preserved for the second period than for the first: the general contrast is not likely to be seriously modified by new discoveries. And it may be significant that C. Nasennius Marcellus, who was three times duovir, is from an Ostian family. Such men as Cn. Sentius Felix did not hold office more than once: we suspect that they were too busy making money.

The number of town patrons known to us from this period reflects the increased importance and prosperity of Ostia. From the pre-Flavian period only one patron is recorded in surviving inscriptions. 'Glabrio, patronus coloniae' set up a statue to *salus Caesaris Augusti* outside the Porta Romana, perhaps commemorating an imperial visit.[2] He is a Manius Acilius Glabrio of the Augustan or Julio-Claudian period, member of a family which retained its consular distinction from the early second century B.C. to the late Empire and was associated with Ostia over a long period. From the following period no less than ten are known. A. Egrilius Plarianus, his brother, and his son were Ostians rising in the senatorial service.[3] C. Nasennius Marcellus, also an Ostian, had held four military equestrian posts.[4] P. Aufidius Fortis had trading connexions with Africa.[5] The names of two other patrons living in Ostia are known from the Fasti of 146, A. Egrilius Agricola and D. Nonius Pompilianus, who shared the censorial duovirate in that year. Agricola is presumably related to the senatorial Egrilii; Pompilianus is probably the son of the duovir of 110. It is likely that both men had made their mark outside Ostia, perhaps in equestrian careers.

More influential in imperial circles was L. Volusius Maecianus, distinguished lawyer and administrator, and teacher of Marcus Aurelius. Maecianus, after brief military service in Britain, had held a series of posts in the palace secretariat under Hadrian and Antoninus Pius, and had then been appointed successively *praefectus annonae* and governor of Egypt.[6] In 152 he was a patron of the guild of *lenuncularii tabularii*.[7]

---

[1] C. Nasennius Marcellus III (in 111), C. Valerius Iustus II (in 111), [—]vos II (in 84); probably also M. Acilius Priscus (p. 175 n. 5).

[2] S 4324. For the date, p. 508.   [3] p. 503 f.   [4] 9.   [5] p. 203.

[6] Bloch, 33.   [7] 250. Maecianus heads the list of equestrian patrons of the guild.

In 160–1, while he was governor of Egypt, two commemorative tablets were set up at Ostia in his honour as patron of the colony.[1] A further inscription was set up in Ostia when, after his governorship of Egypt, he was given praetorian status by Marcus Aurelius and designated consul.[2] Maecianus' association with Ostia may derive from his official duties in connexion with the corn supply,[3] but it seems likely that he became a guild patron before that appointment. It is not impossible that his family came from Ostia.[4]

The connexion with Ostia of the patron Q. Asinius Q. (filius) Trom-(entina) Marcellus, consul probably at the end of the first or the beginning of the second century, is unknown. He is commemorated in two Ostian inscriptions, by the council and by the *iuv[enes de]curion(um)*;[5] his name also recurs on an undated fragment of the Fasti, but the context is lost.[6] There is an elusive hint of a later connexion of the family with Ostia. A Q. Asinius Marcellus owned brickfields, which supplied Rome and Ostia under Hadrian and Antoninus Pius. Among the overseers of his production units was C. Nunnidius Fortunatus, whose name appears on brickstamps from 123 to 141.[7] This uncommon name recurs in an Isola Sacra tomb, and the date would fit.[8] Though several bricks with his stamp have been found in Ostian buildings, they cannot have been produced at Ostia for bricks with the same stamp are found in Roman buildings and Ostian bricks would not have been carried to Rome. There is no other trace of Nunnidii at Ostia; Fortunatus may have retired there owing to his patron's association with the town. Another inscription from Portus records a Q. Asinius in the early second century.[9] His cognomen is lost and much else; what little survives suggests

---

[1] *S* 5347, 5348. For the date of his governorship of Egypt, Stein, op. cit. 90.

[2] Bloch, 33. This inscription was set up by a relative or freedman.

[3] Stein, loc. cit., followed by Bloch, thinks that he was already *praefectus annonae* in 152; but this would imply an unusually long tenure of the corn prefecture, and the office would probably have been recorded on the guild roll.

[4] For earlier Volusii in Ostia, including a C. Volusius, duovir in A.D. 18, see p. 194 with n. 6; but the name is particularly widespread in Italy. There were also Maecii at Ostia.

[5] *S* 4447, 4448. Groag (*PIR*², A 1234) suggests a Julio-Claudian date on the ground that a patrician would not be *Xvir stlitibus iudicandis* in or after the Flavian period. The evidence is inadequate to justify such a rule; the lettering of the inscription cannot, I think, be earlier than Flavian. I identify with *PIR*², A 1235; cf. Degrassi, *Fasti Consolari*, p. 29.

[6] *Fasti*, frag. xxxv, p. 210, before 115 (Degrassi, 239). —m. Q. Asini Mar[celli—]. Wickert (*S* 4542) suggests 'in locum Q.A.M.—pontifex Volkani creatus est'. But see p. 514.   [7] *CIL* xv. 846–50, 860–1.   [8] Thylander, A 74.   [9] 622.

that he was a freedman. Perhaps the senatorial Asinii had a villa in the neighbourhood. P. Clodius Pulcher, who was responsible for the rebuilding of the Porta Romana at the end of the Flavian period or slightly later, is not, so far as we know, an Ostian and should therefore be a patron; but he is an embarrassment to the prosopographers and we know nothing of him.[1] *

The funerary inscription of another patron of the late first or early second century in large part survives, but his name is lost.[2] He was an Ostian who had held at least one equestrian military post and had become a *procurator Augusti*.[3] He was married to Egrilia Pulchra, who was almost certainly related to the senatorial Egrilii of the period.

THE ECLIPSE OF THE OLD FAMILIES

When we pass from the prosperity period to the second half of the second century the evidence at our disposal is inadequate. For the first two periods the Fasti provide a central structure of names and important chronological controls. The last dated surviving fragment of the Fasti gives part of the record for 154; after that date we have to rely on a much smaller range of inscriptions, many of them undated. Few traces of the leading families of the early Empire remain.

The only career recorded in full is that of the last known P. Lucilius Gamala, who died during or soon after the reign of Marcus Aurelius. His inscription is closely modelled on that of his Augustan ancestor and his career is in the family tradition. He is aedile and praetor in the cult of Vulcan, admitted to the council while still a boy, *praefectus* for an imperial prince, quaestor, *pontifex Volcani*, the first *curator tabularum et librorum*.[4] His public benefactions include the restoration of temples, public baths, and a *navale*. He spent more than the law required on all the public games he celebrated, and gave a gladiatorial display. But it is significant that, whereas the Augustan Gamala had built new temples, his work is confined to restoration.

---

[1] Of the inscription from the Porta Romana only small fragments survive, *S* 4707. The fourth line begins 'P. Cl[odius] P[u]lche[r co]nsu[l'. The fifth, and probably last, line begins 'p[ortam vetus]tate [c]orrupta[m]'. The natural inference is that P. Clodius Pulcher restored the gate. Degrassi, *Fasti Consolari*, p. 119, suggests, as possible alternatives to consul, *consularis filius* or *nepos*. No descendant of Cicero's enemy is known during this period. For the date of the restoration of the gate, p. 67.

[2] Unpublished. The date is inferred from the lettering and the layout. A.D. 50–130 are the approximate limits.

[3] His Ostian origin is shown by the fact that he makes provision in his tomb for his *maiores*.

[4] 2.

The family of C. Nasennius Marcellus, duovir for the third time in
111, also remains prominent. A C. Nasennius Marcellus, probably his
grandson, is duovir in 166,[1] *curator perpetuus operum publicorum* in 184,[2]
patron of the colony by 189;[3] he seems to have followed closely in his
grandfather's footsteps. Either he, or more probably his son, became
pontifex Volcani.[4]

The only evidence concerning the Egrilii during this period is controversial. Members of the family, together perhaps with a Fabius
Agrippinus, head the list of patrons in a Severan roll of a guild which is
probably to be identified with the *dendrophori*. It has been held that
M. Acilius Priscus Egrilius Plarianus and other distinguished members of
the family were retained in the list of patrons long after their death, but
it is more reasonable to regard the names as those of living men.[5] If that
is the case the Egrilii retained their associations with Ostia, but, unless
and until new inscriptions are found, we shall not know the last stages
of their Ostian history.

The other surviving names of men who rose to high office in this
period have no known associations with leading families of the past.
C. Antius Crescens Calpurnianus, who is attested as *pontifex Volcani*
in 194 and 203,[6] rose to the consulship, but there is no evidence that
his family had old roots in Ostia. M. Lollius Paulinus, colleague of
C. Nasennius Marcellus in the duovirate in 166,[7] is probably to be identified with M. Lollius M.f. Paulinus who commemorated his friend
C. Granius Maturus, duovir towards the middle of the century;[8] but the
name does not occur in surviving fragments of the Fasti. M. Iunius
M.f. Pal(atina) Faustus, who was duovir shortly before 173, seems from
his tribe and cognomen to be of freedman stock; a corn merchant, he
was honoured with a statue by the African and Sardinian shipowners.[9]
We may suspect that Q. Lollius Rufus Chrysidianus who held office in
the late second or early third century had a similar background;[10] his
colleague, M. Aemilius Vitalis Crepereianus, has a first cognomen that
usually denotes servile blood; but his second cognomen recalls the family
that probably produced a duovir as early as A.D. 6.[11] The cognomen of
C. Aemilius, who probably held his duovirate during this period, is
lost, but his tribe is Palatina.[12]

---

[1] 4148.   [2] 172 with p. 481.   [3] 460.
[4] 47; see p. 510.   [5] 281; see p. 504.   [6] 325, 324.   [7] 4148.
[8] 363.   [9] 4142.   [10] 47.   [11] L. Cre[pereius], *Fasti*, A.D. 6.
[12] Bloch, 49.

P. Licinius Herodes, who held no less than four public priesthoods and was successively aedile, quaestor, and duovir, probably in the early third century, belongs to the tribe Palatina, and his statue was set up by the freedmen *seviri Augustales*.[1] The father of Q. Veturius Firmius Felix, duovir in 251, a censorial year, had also been associated with the *seviri Augustales*, and the cognomen of his colleague, L. Florus Euprepes, suggests a similar background.[2] P. Flavius Priscus, who was duovir towards the middle of the century, was a man of distinction in his day. He rose to the second grade of imperial procurators and was made patron of the colony, but his tribe is Palatina.[3] He was followed by his son-in-law M. Aurelius Hermogenes, who similarly became a procurator and patron of the colony.[4] Only one *pontifex Volcani* is known from this period, Iulius Faustinus;[5] we know nothing of him.

From the little evidence that survives it seems likely that the tendencies operating in the prosperity period developed further in the period that followed, and that the representation of servile blood in the duovirate increased. It certainly permeated the council. More councillors are known from this period than from the last, and they present a consistent character. They are wealthy, as we should expect, and in most cases it can be shown that their wealth derives from trade, and that they are descended from freedmen.

M. Licinius Privatus is probably typical of his time.[6] Born a slave, he started his free career as a clerk in the town service, and became, shortly before the end of the second century, president of the builders' guild. His public generosity brought him the honorary rank of councillor and paved the way for his sons to a public career, from which he was himself debarred. The inscription on the base of his statue set up by his guild records that his sons became councillors, his grandsons councillors and Roman knights. The funerary inscription of T. Antistius Agathangelus follows the same pattern.[7] His cognomen suggests a servile origin; he provided in his tomb for himself, for T. Antistius Favor, his son, Roman knight and councillor, and for T. Antistius Favor Proculeianus,

---

[1] **11.** The date is inferred from his priesthood, *flam(en) divi Severi*.

[2] 352, 432.

[3] **12,** the base of his statue dedicated in 249. Another statue base, Bloch, 29. Priscus himself dedicated a statue at Ostia to Salonina, wife of the emperor Gallienus, *S* 5335.

[4] *S* 5340.   [5] 352, dated 251.

[6] **15.** Privatus was president of the builders' guild in their 29th *lustrum*, towards the end of the second century (pp. 330 f.). His name probably appears in their guild roll of 198, *S* 4569 (dec. xvi. 1).   [7] 294.

his grandson, also a Roman knight and councillor. His son was patron of the *lenuncularii pleromarii* in 200.[1]

L. Fabius Sp(urii) f. Eutyches followed closely the career of M. Licinius Privatus. At first employed as lictor and then clerk in the town service he too rose to the presidency of the builders and could launch his son on a public career. In this case adoption may have improved the prospect, for his son's full names are C. Domitius L.fil. Pal(atina) Fabius Hermogenes. He became councillor, *flamen divi Hadriani*, and died in the course of his aedileship. He was given a public funeral and an equestrian statue was set up in his honour in the Forum by decree of the council.[2] P. Cornelius Architectianus also probably owed his position in the council to money acquired in the building trade. His father Thallus was president of the guild and his grandfather's cognomen Architectus, from which his own was derived, suggests the same occupation.[3] It is doubtful from the names whether the family had been free for many generations. Sextus Carminius Parthenopius, Roman knight and decurion, was himself a president of the builders. His cognomen also is suspect, and his wife, Carminia Briseis, is presumably either a freedwoman or descended from a freedman of the family.[4] Two other decurions known from this period are also registered in the tribe Palatina, P. Nonius Livius Anterotianus[5] and D. Iunius Bubalus;[6] both were Roman knights.

SENATORIAL RESIDENTS IN THE LATE EMPIRE

In the late Empire we learn much less from inscriptions of Ostia's aristocracy. No records survive of local careers; we do not even know the names of any magistrates. Restorations of public buildings that in the second century would have been undertaken by local magistrates or ex-magistrates are now initiated by the *praefectus annonae*. The complete absence of surviving inscriptions recording public benefactions by local men is a sign that central control has dried up the springs of

---

[1] 252.

[2] 353, **14**. A date near the end of the second century is inferred from the lettering.

[3] 5. The father was president of the builders in their 27th *lustrum*, late second century (p. 331).

[4] 314. The tomb (*Ann. Inst.* 29 (1857) 298) is designed for burial alone; the brickwork is probably early third century.

[5] 390. Anterotianus was knighted by Marcus Aurelius.

[6] Bloch, 56 = S 4625. Bloch considers the lettering to be in or near the Severan period; it might be a little earlier.

public-spirited generosity. But the independent houses of the late Empire show that there were still wealthy residents in the town. How many of the owners of these houses were still actively concerned with the management of Ostian affairs we do not know; but the fragmentary evidence suggests that Roman senators, who had no long-standing associations with Ostia, dominated the social climate.

An inscription commemorates the celebration of a *taurobolium* by a certain 'Volusianus v(ir) c(larissimus) ex praefe(c)tis'. He is probably to be identified with C. Caeionius Rufus Volusianus Lampadius, praetorian prefect in 355, urban prefect in 365/6.[1] It is tempting to recognize his Ostian residence in the House of the Dioscuri. This is the largest and most handsome of the late houses in Ostia, the only one yet excavated which has a private suite of baths.[2] It takes its name from a mosaic depicting Castor and Pollux and this would be a singularly appropriate subject for Volusianus who, as urban prefect, would have celebrated the annual festival of the Dioscuri at Ostia.[3] A large coloured mosaic in the same house, depicting Venus and Nereids, has a motto which is particularly common in Africa;[4] this too would be appropriate, for the family had landed property in Africa.[5]

Another important family which had close associations with Africa is also found at Ostia in the late Empire. The Anicii share with the Acilii, who also have associations with Ostia, the distinction of maintaining their wealth and position by political tact and judicious marriages throughout the hazards of imperial persecution. They came originally from Praeneste;[6] Cicero mentions their African business connexions,[7] and African interests remained the mainstay of the family's wealth. In the late Empire they were one of the wealthiest families in Rome. Anicius Auchenius Bassus, in the late fourth or early fifth century, declared at Ostia the devotion of his family to God and the saints.[8] The name of Anicia Italica with her husband Valerius Faltonius, perhaps

---

[1] Bloch, 34. The identification was first proposed by H. Fuhrmann, *Epigraphica*, 3 (1941) 103–9.

[2] Becatti, *Case Ostiensi del tardo impero*, 14.   [3] For the Ostian festival, p. 344.

[4] 'plura faciatis meliora dedicetis.' Widespread, with minor variants, in Africa, *CIL* viii. 8510, 22774; *AE* 1931, 52; *AE* 1938, 130.

[5] *CIL* viii. 25990 (= *ILS* 6025). The family may have had an African origin, B. H. Warmington, *The North African Provinces from Diocletian to the Vandal Conquest* (Cambridge, 1954) 39.

[6] *RE*, Anicius (Klebs).

[7] Cic. *Ad fam.* xii. 21: 'C. Anicius . . . negotiorum suorum causa legatus est in Africam legatione libera.'   [8] 1875.

of the early fifth century, is found on an Ostian water-pipe, showing that she owned property in the town.[1]

When Augustine stayed at Ostia in 387 with his mother Monica before returning to Africa, he could move in congenial society. His own record of the short stay in his *Confessions* suggests that he was staying with friends and had other acquaintances in Ostia.[2] These were probably senatorials with African connexions. They included the Anicii; an Italica is among his correspondents,[3] and it was Anicius Bassus who set up his mother's epitaph.[4] He is likely to have known the Caeionii from their African connexions.[5] Augustine also writes to Pamachius, who dedicated a house of pilgrimage at Portus;[6] he too had African possessions.[7]

Symmachus owned a villa overlooking the Tiber and commanding a large estate in Ostian territory.[8] In one of his letters he adds another name to the list of Ostia's senatorial connexions. In 398 he attended the wedding at Ostia of the younger son of Sallustius,[9] who had been urban prefect and was one of the chief literary figures of the day.

The residence in Ostia of this senatorial aristocracy saved the town from more rapid decay. They lived handsomely and the shopkeepers at least must have been grateful to them. But Ostia was in no sense their real home, nor the main focus of their loyalty. They were no adequate substitute for the office-holders of the first and second centuries whose efficiency and public generosity had made Ostia great.

[1] Barbieri, 'Fistole inedite', *NS* 1953, 170 n. 32: 'Valeri Faltoni Adelfi v(iri) c(larissimi) et Aniciae Italicae.'

[2] That Augustine was not staying at an inn is clear from his account, *Confess.* ix. 12. 31: 'cohibito ergo a fletu illo puero psalterium arripuit Euodius et cantare coepit psalmum. cui respondebamus omnis domus . . .'. Other Ostian friends are suggested by ix. 11. 28: 'audivi etiam postea quod iam cum Ostiae essemus, cum quibusdam amicis meis materna fiducia conloquebatur (Monica)'.

[3] Augustine, *Epp.* 92, 99.

[4] De Rossi, *Inscr. Christ.* ii. 252.

[5] Augustine corresponds with a Volusianus, *Epp.* 132, 135, 137 (cf. 136, 138); he is probably the grandson of Lampadius, Seeck, *Symmachus*, clxxix. See p. 474 n. 1.

[6] Augustine, *Ep.* 58. For Pammachius' *xenodochium*, p. 403.

[7] Augustine, *Ep.* 58. 1: 'colonos tuos Afros.'   [8] p. 264.

[9] Symmachus (Seeck), *Ep.* vi. 35 (A.D. 398), with p. clvi: 'haec de nuptiis Ostiensibus, ad quas nos viri inlustris Sallustii filius iunior evocavit, contulimus in paginam.'

II

THE PEOPLE

FROM the Flavian period onwards there was an increasing infiltration of new-comers and of men of freedman stock into the council and public office. These tendencies are much more widely reflected in the population as a whole. The prosperity brought by the imperial harbours attracted men from other towns of Italy and from all parts of the Mediterranean world. If our evidence were fuller we should find men from the western provinces settled in Ostia in the late Republic, but their number was probably small. It was not until the harbours were built that easterners were attracted. Their early associations with Italy had been mainly through Puteoli, but, as the trade of Puteoli passed to the new harbours, they came in increasing numbers to Ostia. The rapid increase in population, however, which led to the concentration on apartment blocks in the second century, was due much less to such independent new-comers than to an increase in the number of slaves and consequently of freedmen and their descendants.

FREE IMMIGRANTS

Of all the provinces Africa, rich in corn, had the closest associations with Ostia. The Piazzale delle Corporazioni is dominated by traders from African towns,[1] who presumably had their representatives in Ostia to manage their business. One such representative is explicitly recorded: L. Caecilius Aprilis is *curator* of Carthaginian ships and he comes from Carthage, for he is registered in Arnensis, the Carthaginian tribe.[2] The origin of P. Caesellius Felix is given on his tombstone: he is a citizen of Sullecthum,[3] an African town whose traders have premises in the Piazzale delle Corporazioni.[4] L. Caecilius Aemilianus, a veteran of the praetorian guard, had been a decurion and duovir of African Aelia Ulizibbira, established by Hadrian.[5] He found it more attractive

---

[1] p. 283.   [2] S 4626.   [3] 477.
[4] S 4549²³.
[5] Bloch, *Epigraphica*, 1 (1939) 37.

to come to Ostia and engage in the wine import trade: 'corporatus in templo fori vinari importatorum negotiantium'. Valerius Veturius, who died at Portus, came from a farming background: he is described as 'civis Afer colonicus'.[1] The tribe Quirina, most widely spread of the tribes in Africa, is more common in Ostia than any other non-Ostian tribe.

From Hither Spain with his wife came the freedman trader L. Numisius Agathemeris:[2] M. Aemilius M.f. Malacitanus probably owes his cognomen to Malaca in Spanish Baetica.[3] M. Caesius Maximus was born at Aeminium in Lusitania.[4] Maecius Melo came from the district of Vienna in Narbonese Gaul: a record of his death at Ostia was set up in his native town.[5] L. Antonius Epitynchanus, who became president of the Ostian builders, was a *sevir Augustalis* at Aquae Sextiae in the same province.[6] P. Claudius Abascantus, who became prominent in the cult of Magna Mater, was a freedman of the three Gauls; he had been a slave of the provincial council, meeting outside Lugdunum, but left Gaul to settle permanently in Ostia.[7] In the harbour cemetery on Isola Sacra we find C. Annaeus, who came from the land of the Pictones in Aquitania,[8] and Samus Samifilus,[9] whose name suggests that he too came from Gaul.

The Greek east is also widely represented. T. Flavius Apollonius[10] and Aphrodisius, son of Arpocration[11] came from Alexandria; Asclepiades, son of Simon, from Cnidus;[12] Socrates, son of Astomachus, from Tralles.[13] Syrian Seleucia[14] and Miletus[15] are also recorded in Greek inscriptions. A guild roll of the shipbuilders of Ostia includes the names of eight free foreigners;[16] they all, to judge by their names, seem to be easterners. The inscription on a sarcophagus illustrating the shoemaker's trade is in Greek.[17] Most of these easterners were concerned with trade, but not all. T. Aelius Samius Isocrates, citizen of Nicomedia and Ephesus, who died at Ostia, was a sophist;[18] another sophist and

---

[1] 481. [2] 397: 'seviro Augustali, negotiatori ex Hispania citeriore.'
[3] S 4778. [4] S 4822. [5] CIL xii. 2211. [6] 296.
[7] 327. 'P. Cl(audius) trium Galliar(um) lib(ertus) Abascantus'; cf. 328, 326 with S p. 615. He came first to Ostia as a slave (328), presumably on some mission for the Gallic Council.
[8] Thylander, A 13: 'C. Annaei Attici Pict(onis) ex Aquitanica.'
[9] Thylander, A 170.
[10] 478. [11] 479. [12] 475. [13] 480.
[14] IG xiv. 934. [15] IG xiv. 938.
[16] Bloch, 43 (1 a 33; 1 b 10, 21, 22, 28; 11 a 15, 24, 28).
[17] NS 1877, 314. [18] AE 1947, 162.

rhetorician has his praises sung on his tombstone in elegant Greek hexameters.[1] Another Greek inscription records a doctor: 'Master of all wisdom here I lie, not dead. Say not that good men die.'[2]

The proportion of independent easterners was probably larger by the harbours than in Ostia town. The annual arrival of the Egyptian corn fleet brought ships' captains and crews from Alexandria; Egyptian resident agents probably watched their interests. This connexion attracted other settlers from Egypt. Two Egyptians are included in the shipbuilders' guild roll[3] and by the Severan period a Serapeum had been built and was attracting handsome benefactions. The citizens of Gaza resident at Portus set up a statue in honour of the emperor Gordian.[4] A Syrian trader made a dedication to Jupiter of Heliopolis on behalf of the emperors M. Aurelius and Commodus.[5] Cemetery inscriptions record a man from Phrygia,[6] a Rhodian,[7] and a worker in marble from Nicomedia.[8]

Other provincials came to Ostia to serve with the small detachment of the fleet; Thracians, an Egyptian, a Pannonian, Sardinian, Corsican are recorded on tombstones.[9] They merged in the mixed community and sometimes married local women and settled in Ostia after their discharge.

Roman citizens from other parts of Italy less frequently record their origin. Ravenna,[10] Praeneste,[11] and Vercellae[12] are attested; in far more instances we can only guess from the names that the families are not Ostian, but probably Italian. Veterans from the praetorian and urban cohorts are recorded in the cemeteries;[13] most of them were probably of Italian origin. The epitaph of a young soldier at Interamna recalls the marriage and settlement at Ostia of a man from Umbria. 'Umbria was my father's home, Ostia my mother's; there the Tiber flows glassy green, here the Nar flows white.'[14]

---

[1] *IG* xiv. 935.   [2] *IG* xiv. 942.   [3] 256[148] and 185.

[4] *IG* xiv. 926.

[5] 24. The dedicator is known as a Syrian from inscriptions in Rome, Taylor, *The Cults of Ostia*, 77.

[6] *IG* xiv. 933.   [7] Thylander, A 27.

[8] Calza, *Necropoli*, 279 (λευκοῦργος).

[9] 234–42, S 4496.   [10] 1170.

[11] Becatti, *Case tarde*, 54 n. 19.

[12] 230.   [13] 217, 221, S 4491.

[14] *CIL* xi. 4188: 'De genitore mihi domus Umbria, de genetrice | Ostia, Tybris ibi vitreus, Nar hic fluit albus.' I infer from the comparison of the Tiber with the Nar that the young man had probably been born and brought up in Ostia.

FREEDMEN

From these varied sources the population of Ostia increased, but a much more important element in the town's development was the liberality with which slaves were granted freedom. The freedman is at the very centre of Ostian society. He is indispensable to the town's trade and to the trading guilds; his descendants take an increasing part in local government. A mere glance at the inscriptions of Ostia will show how large a proportion of the population was provided by the freedmen, especially in the second century, and how widespread were their activities.

The most important factor in their rise to prominence was the institution of their special priesthood for the imperial cult. We first hear of such *Augustales* at Nepete in southern Etruria in 12 B.C., the year when Augustus became *pontifex maximus*.[1] It is probable that Ostia, owing to its close dependence on Rome and on the emperor, was one of the first towns of Italy to follow the precedent, though only one inscription survives before the death of Augustus; it commemorates Drusus, son of Tiberius, before he held the quaestorship in A.D. 11.[2] The priesthood of the *Augustales* was confined to freedmen; it focused their loyalty in the emperor and the imperial house and at the same time gave them an official standing in the town. Of their early organization we know nothing; we may guess that they were annually appointed, and perhaps were six in number, forming a small aristocracy within the large class of freedmen.[3] But at some time in the late first (or early second) century the institution was remodelled and developed an elaborate organization, resembling a trade guild much more than an exclusive priesthood.

The most obvious sign of the reorganization is a change in title from *Augustales* to *seviri Augustales*; more important is the new hierarchy of officers. The earlier *Augustales* had no grades within their ranks: *Augustalis* is the sole title found in inscriptions. In the inscriptions of individual *seviri Augustales* the title of *quinquennalis* and *curator* are common. But the new organization is more elaborate than the inscriptions of individuals might suggest. From the numerous fragments of registers that have survived from the late second and early third centuries we can see that there are four grades of dignity.[4]

---

[1] *ILS* 89. [2] *S* 5322.
[3] von Premerstein, s.v. Augustales, *Diz. Epigr.* 824 ff. esp. 826.
[4] See *Note E*, p. 473.

The *electi*, who seem by their position in the registers to have ranked highest in honour, were elected every two years, but could hold the position longer, and their number varies. There are three in 196 and 198, one in 210, 216, 239, and none in 208, 228, 234, 242: it seems that this position brought honour, and perhaps expense, rather than responsibilities. The *quinquennales*, who are probably the active presidents, come next on the lists. They form a board of four and are also elected for two years. Below them in standing are men described as *q.q.d.d.* In most Ostian inscriptions the last two letters stand for 'decurionum decreto', but if that were the meaning here we should expect the individual *sevir* in recording his career to refer, as decurions and aediles do, to his election by the council, an added dignity; it is more likely that Dessau was right in preferring 'd(ono) d(ato)':[1] these *quinquennales* have paid for the privilege. The title must have been easily obtained because the majority of *seviri* known to us are described as *sevir Augustalis idem quinquennalis*. The *seviri* also had treasurers whose names were drawn up on separate registers.[2] They were elected to office for a year, but could be reappointed, and A. Granius Atticus was treasurer for life.[3] Though most freedmen will have had good business heads, it seems doubtful whether special financial ability was required, for the annual number of appointments varies and the board is usually large: there are eight in 193, five in 201, and four in 239. At the end of each year's list was added 'ob h(anc) c(uram) HS$\overline{X}$': they paid 10,000 sesterces for the honour of the title and this may have been their main duty to the treasury. But the post was the normal stepping-stone to higher office.[4]

The registers that disclose this elaborate hierarchy come from the late second and early third centuries, but the main elements at least of the organization were introduced much earlier. The decisive change can be approximately dated.[5] L. Aquillius Modestus, who is described simply as *Augustalis*, was president of the builders' guild in Nero's principate:[6] the first undisputed reference to the new *seviri Augustales* is in an inscription commemorating a man who was honoured by the

[1] Dessau, quoted by Wickert (*S*, p. 693), followed by Wilson, *BSR* 14 (1938) 155.
[2] *S* 4560, Bloch, 40.
[3] 360. 'curator perpetuus'. Another, whose name is lost, was treasurer for five years, *S* 4641: '[se]viro Augustali idem q.q. [curato]ri eorum annis continuis v.'
[4] Cf. 316: 'L. Carullius Epaphroditus . . . post curam quinquennalitatem optul(erunt) qui egit continuis IIII.'
[5] Wickert, *S*, p. 611.   [6] 299; for the date, p. 331.

emperor Trajan;[1] but another inscription has been convincingly re-stored as a dedication to Nerva by the *seviri*.[2] Another argument, considerably more controversial, suggests a late Flavian date for the reform of the institution.

The majority of the fragments of the registers of the *seviri* were found in or near a building on the north side of the Decumanus, immediately west of the Forum and opposite the Basilica.[3] The building is comparatively small, but was handsomely decorated. Fronting on the Decumanus was a portico of six columns. Behind was a temple-like cella (11·7× 11·7 metres) whose walls and pavement were lined with marble. At the back of this room was a long high podium, in the side walls large niches, on the right side against the wall between the niches three statue bases. This building is admirably suited to the needs of the freedmen. The niches would have contained imperial statues; the podium was necessary for cult purposes and is found in the chapel of the *vigiles* and in the room converted into a chapel in the headquarters of the builders' guild. The fragments of the registers might have been brought from elsewhere for a late reconstruction, but it is more reasonable to believe that they were found where they originally belonged.

There is, however, a serious objection to this identification. Calza somewhat reluctantly concluded that this was the Curia, the meeting-place of the council,[4] and subsequent excavation has tended to strengthen his judgement. For the Curia is one of the most important public buildings of a town and has its natural place in or near the central Forum. That is where it is found at Rome, at Pompeii, at Timgad, and at other sites; but at Ostia excavation has now extended in all directions round the Forum and no other building has been found near the centre of the town, nor anywhere else, which can readily be identified as a council chamber.[5] It is true that there is no certain reference to a Curia in surviving inscriptions,[6] and we learn that on one occasion at least the council met in the temple of Rome and Augustus,[7] but it is inconceiv-

---

[1] *S* 4486a.

[2] *S* 4341, restored by Wickert: '[imp. Nervae Cae]sar[i] Aug. pontif. | [max. trib. po]test, p.p. c[o]s. ii [seviri] Augustale[s].'

[3] Calza, *NS* 1923, 185.   [4] Ibid. 186.

[5] A building at the south-east corner of the Forum, which in its present ruined state is featureless, is perhaps not to be ruled out.

[6] Possibly *S* 4720, but the restoration '[curia]m' is most uncertain.

[7] 353: 'in aede Romae et Augusti placu[it] ordini decurionum', perhaps because the man honoured was *flamen divi Hadriani*.

able that the main governing body of the town had no official headquarters.

In spite of the force of this objection, the so-called Curia of Ostia is
singularly unfitted to the needs of a council. It is small for a body of at
least 100 members; originally it had no attached rooms on the ground
floor or upper floor such as were needed for the keeping of records and
the work of the small civil service. Nor is there any sign of the triple
benches that are a distinctive feature of all Curiae of the Roman pattern.
On the other hand, the building is admirably adapted, as has been seen,
to the needs of the freedmen, and the inscriptions associated with the
building point the same way. We may tentatively conclude that this
is the headquarters of the *seviri Augustales*. The width and texture of its
bricks and a brickstamp found in the ruins indicate a Domitianic date
for the building.[1] The evidence of inscriptions and construction converge to show that the freedmen received their new organization at
approximately the same time as the rebuilding of Ostia on a new
scale at a higher level was beginning. *

From the start the *seviri* had their own presidents and treasurers;[2] but
the full elaboration that we meet at the end of the second century may
be a later development. It is probably significant that only one *electus*,
of the third century, is known from inscriptions other than the registers,[3]
whereas the title *quinquennalis* is very widespread and *curator* not uncommon. Probably *electi* represent a later refinement, as may the
increase in the number of *quinquennales*.[4]

That the *seviri* formed a wealthy corporation is clear, not only from
the contributions to their chest recorded in the registers and in other
inscriptions, but also from the premises that they occupied in the latter
half of the second century.[5] This building, on the south side of the
eastern Decumanus, resembles the builders' guild-house and the barracks
of the *vigiles* in plan. It is constructed round a central courtyard, surrounded by a portico carried on brick piers. A series of rooms open off

---

[1] p. 66.

[2] A. Granius Atticus may be one of the first, 360: 'dis manibus A. Grani Attici seviri
Augustali (*sic*) adlectus inter primos quinquennalis curator perpetus (*sic*).' Wickert
(*S*, p. 611), following von Premerstein (*Diz. Epigr.* i. 851), refers 'adlectus inter primos'
to his enrolment when the *seviri Augustales* were first established. I prefer Dessau's interpretation (*ILS* 6160): 'adlectus inter primos quinquennalis', implying that Atticus was
one of the first presidents.

[3] 461, dated 239.   [4] As suggested by Wilson, *BSR* 14 (1938) 154–6.

[5] G. Calza, *NS* 1941, 196.

the portico on the ground floor, and steps at the angles lead to upper floors. The building is attributed to the *seviri Augustales*, not from the direct evidence of a building inscription, but from the character of the sculptures that were found; they included portrait statues of a *sevir* and of an emperor in the formal dress of the *pontifex maximus*.[1] The most striking features of the building are the refinement of its decoration, the elaborate pattern of its mosaics, the plentiful use of marble on its walls, and its wealth of sculpture. But no registers of members and officers were found in or near this building. It is probable that the building by the Forum remained the official headquarters of the *seviri*, which was used for their official cult. The premises on the Decumanus were intended primarily to increase the social amenities of membership.

The change from a limited priesthood to a large and wealthy guild with its own officers and headquarters is of considerable importance in the rise of the freedman class at Ostia. It not only provided for former slaves the colourful satisfaction of a regular *cursus honorum* in their own organization, but made them members of one of the wealthiest, and therefore most influential, corporations in the town. It seems likely that membership of the *seviri* considerably improved the prospects of a freedman's advance in business and trade; it is clear at any rate that many of them rose quickly to prominence in the trade guilds. From them came presidents of the builders,[2] the shipbuilders,[3] the wine importers,[4] and there were in fact few trade guilds which did not have at some time freedmen among their officers.

Like the trade guilds, which they closely resemble in structure, the *seviri Augustales* attracted benefactions and honoured benefactors. Among them was P. Horatius Chryseros, to whom they set up a statue in 182 in recognition of his contribution of 50,000 sesterces to their chest.[5] Of this sum, 10,000 s. was to cover the appointment as *curator* of Sex. Horatius Chryserotianus, presumably son or nephew. The interest on the remainder was to keep alive his memory. Each year on his birthday his statue was to be decorated; 100 s. was to be given to the slaves who maintained the sevirs' headquarters, *familia Augustalium*; the balance was to be divided among those present. If these instructions were not carried out the endowment, with its attached conditions, was to be given to the town. Satisfied with the honour, Chryseros paid for

---

[1] R. Calza, *NS* 1941, 216.   [2] 296, 297, **15**, 418, S 4656, 4668.
[3] 372.   [4] 318.   [5] 367.

Q

the statue himself, a gesture that may have been anticipated. But the most interesting feature of the episode is the distribution that accompanied the dedication of the statue. Five denarii a head were given to the town councillors as well as to his fellow sevirs. Their inclusion might ensure that the terms of the endowment were respected; it confirms the standing of the *seviri Augustales*. This is further illustrated by their initiative, backed by popular demand, in publicly commemorating a famous eastern dancer.[1] In another fragmentary inscription they are associated in a very uncertain context with the town council.[2]

The most important official function open to freedmen was the maintenance of the imperial cult; but freedmen also administered the local cults of the wards (*vici*) into which Ostia, like Rome, was divided. Each ward had its own small shrine, at a crossroads or in some open space, where prayers were offered by and for the local community. The *magistri vici* who presided over these ceremonies were, as at Rome, freedmen. An inscription records the transference with due formality of one of these shrines in the late first century B.C.[3] A Julio-Claudian marble altar can still be seen in the Piazza dei Lari, depicting Hercules with Fauns and Lares. It was dedicated to the Lares of the district and was set up by the *magistri*.[4]

The freedman's main preoccupation was trade and business, but he had social ambitions also. He could not himself enter the council nor hold office, but he could hope to pave the way for his sons and descendants. In the first century this may have been more difficult, but by the second century money was a powerful persuader, and a judicious display of public generosity was perhaps as useful as the patronage of prominent men. Marcus Licinius Privatus bought his way to public recognition by a gift of 50,000 sesterces to the town chest; he was given a seat of honour in the theatre and, later, the honorary rank of councillor. His statue was set up by the builders' guild, of which he was president, in recognition of his affection and loyal services, and the site was authorized by the council.[5] It was in the Piazzale delle Corporazioni, where he was in good company, close to town patrons and important imperial officials. Two Ostian freedmen were members of the *seviri*

---

[1] S 4624.   [2] S 4558; possibly also S 4619.
[3] S 4710.
[4] *NS* 1916, 145; M. F. Squarciapino, *Arch. Class.* 4 (1952) 204. S 4298: 'mag(istri) d(e) s(ua) p(ecunia) f(aciendam) c(uraverunt) Laribus vicin(alibus) sacr(am) aram marmoream.' For vicin(alibus) cf. *AE* 1944, 56.
[5] 15.

Augustales at Tusculum as well as at Ostia.[1] They may be rich business men following the fashion of the Roman nobility and enjoying summer villas in the hills.

In literature we hear most of the freedman from the satirist, and the picture is not attractive. Juvenal's scathing outbursts against the hungry Greekling, ruthlessly depriving the free citizen of his livelihood, represent, in an exaggerated form, one side of the picture: the cemeteries of Ostia help to give a more balanced view. One does not expect to find realistic character sketches on tombstones and it is possible that the son of A. Egrilius Gelasinus, who, when he died at eighteen, is described as 'fili dulcissimi, piissimi, sanctissimi, amantissimi, incomparabilis adfectus erga parentes',[2] was a very ordinary young man, but certain inferences can reasonably be drawn.

It is clear that normally relations between patron and freedman were friendly and close. It was common practice for patrons to provide in their family tomb for their freedmen and freedwomen as well as for their own family. It was not unusual for a freedman or group of freedmen to provide for the patron's cremation or burial.[3] Marriages between a man and one of his former slaves were common. Gratius Centaurus commemorates his freedwoman Eutychia as 'coiunx merentissima';[4] Prastinia Quinta lived for eighteen years with her patron C. Prastinas Nereus, and, when he died, set up his tombstone 'coniugi et patrono optimo'.[5] It was very much less common for a freedman to marry into the family, as Q. Quintilius Zoticus, who married the daughter of his patron.[6]

Only rarely do we hear of strained relations. D. Otacilius Felix built his tomb for himself, Otacilia Hilara his fellow freedwoman, and Luria Musa his wife. With these he names two of his own former slaves who have been informally freed and adds 'ceteris libertis libertabusque meis omnibus posterisque eorum praeter quos testamento meo praeteriero'.[7] He is presumably not satisfied with the loyalty of his remaining freedmen and slaves, and is considering exclusions in his will. Scribonia Attice, in providing for her freedmen and freedwomen, expressly excludes two of them, Panaratus and Prosdocia.[8] C. Voltidius Felicissimus was more forthright: 'excepto Hilaro liberto meo abominando

---

[1] 372, 421.　　　　　　　　　　　[2] 936.
[3] e.g. 396, 518, 630.　　　　　　[4] 983.
[5] 1506.　　　　　　　　　　　　　[6] 1526.
[7] 1437, cf. 382.　　　　　　　　[8] Thylander, A 222.

ne in hoc monimentum aditum habeat';[1] Hilarus had apparently kicked
over the traces.

The bond between patron and freedman was often more than sentimental. An owner of an apartment block with shops along its frontage
would find it convenient when he had tested his own slaves to free
those whom he could trust to manage his shops for him;[2] the freedman
with his family would live over the shop and the main profits would go
to the patron. Iunia Libertas left her house property with shops to her
freedmen and freedwomen;[3] they may already have been managing the
shops while she was still alive. Freedmen who started working as slaves
for their masters in his trade were probably helped by him to rise in it
when they were freed. P. Aufidius Fortis, who was prominent in the
town government in the middle of the second century, was by trade a
corn merchant and president of the corn merchants' guild.[4] P. Aufidius
Faustianus and P. Aufidius Epictetus also held office later in the guild;[5]
they were probably his freedmen. Wilson has remarked that in several
of the guild rolls certain family names are particularly common, and
rarely found elsewhere;[6] the natural explanation is that freedmen were
following their patron's trade.

SLAVES

The wider distribution of freedmen presupposes a steady influx of
slaves, at least through the second century; we should like to know how
they came to Ostia. The origins of freedmen are not recorded in the
cemeteries and the only clue to guide us is the name which the slave
normally retained as his cognomen when he was freed. Certain names
are unmistakably Egyptian: Ammonius, Ammonianus, Hammonilla,
Sarapammon; Serapion, Serapio, Serapia sound Egyptian, but the cult
of Serapis was too widespread to make this a certain inference. Other
names are distinctively Semitic: Achiba, Malchio, Malchus, Sabda.
Ethnic names are also likely to give a fair indication of origin; we find
Antiochus, Armenus, Atticus, Bithynia, Byzantia, Chius, Corinthius,

---

[1] Unpublished.

[2] Cf. Gaius, *Inst.* i. 19: 'iusta . . . causa manumissionis est si quis . . . servum procuratoris
habendi gratia, aut ancillam matrimonii causa apud consilium manumittat.'

[3] Calza, *Epigraphica*, 1 (1939) 160.   [4] **10**, p. 203.

[5] 161 records their office. S 4621 is the base of a statue set up to Fortis their patron by
four freedmen, including Faustianus and Epictetus. The same freedmen set up commemorative tablets to Fortis' son, S 4622.

[6] Wilson, *BSR* 13 (1935) 65; cf. Bloch, *NS* 1953, 284.

Ephesia, Gaza, Miletus, Pergamis, Syrus. Of western ethnics only Hiberus and Baetica are known. But the great majority of freedman names are not distinctive. They are common Greek and Latin names such as Chryseros, Elpis, Agatha, Fortis, and, most common of all, Felix.

Since slave names could be arbitrarily conferred by the slave dealer or owner, a Greek name is not necessarily evidence for a Greek origin,[1] but the fact that Greek names are much more common than Latin among the freedmen of Ostia is probably not misleading. As we have seen, eastern ethnics are much commoner than western. We should also expect Ostia to reflect the Roman pattern, and it is the flooding of the Tiber by the Orontes, and the prevalence of the Greek-speaking element that most impresses Roman writers.

The means by which these slaves were acquired can only be guessed. In the late Republic and under Augustus, wars had flooded the market with prisoners; but when slave employment was at its height in Ostia, during the first half of the second century, the Roman world was enjoy-ing comparative peace. How did the slaves who were bought in such provinces as Asia, Achaea, and Syria come into the market? Brigandage was now restricted and discredited. The sale of children was practised, but apparently on a limited scale; Philostratus, in reporting that the Phrygians 'even sold their children as slaves', implies that they were exceptional.[2] There remain two other sources. The exposure of children was still widespread, particularly in the east,[3] and many of the exposed found their way into the slave market. There may also have been a trade in the breeding of slaves for sale. In the satire of Petronius the rich freedman Trimalchio receives a progress report on his properties: 'July 26. On the estate at Cumae, owned by Trimalchio, there were born 30 boys, 40 girls; there were carried to the granary from the threshing floor five hundred thousand modii of wheat; five hundred oxen were broken in.'[4] The numbers may be exaggerated, but the context is apt. Slaves were marketable produce; it paid to breed them.

---

[1] A good survey of the evidence, Thylander, *Étude sur l'épigraphie latine* (Lund, 1952) 134–85.

[2] Philostratus, *Vit. Apoll.* viii. 7. 12. There may have been cases of voluntary slavery; cf. Petronius, *Sat.* 57: 'quare ergo servisti?' 'quia ipse me dedi in servitutem et malui civis Romanus esse quam tributarius'.

[3] Pliny, *Epp.* x. 65 and 66.

[4] Petronius, *Sat.* 53. Cf. 76. 6, where slaves are included among Trimalchio's exports: 'oneravi rursus vinum, lardum, fabam, seplasium, mancipia'.

Slave households in Ostia were probably not large. No definite figures are recorded, but there are certain indirect pointers. A man's freedmen often held together in a quasi-family relationship, and lists of their names are found in the cemeteries. There are rarely more than six names in a list and never more than twelve. Nor are most living-quarters large enough to accommodate many slaves. In the early second century most of the traders and business men of Ostia were living in apartments of five to twelve rooms; slaves were no doubt crowded together at night, but it is unlikely that the largest quarters known to us had room for more than twenty slaves.

But, though few men owned large numbers, slave ownership was very widespread. One of the most striking features in the Ostian cemeteries is the large number of former slaves who themselves acquire slaves and make provision in their tombs for freedmen and freedwomen. Even in the cemetery of Isola Sacra, which is confined to people of the middle and lower classes, who were primarily concerned with the services of the imperial harbours, the formula 'libertis libertabusque posterisque eorum' recurs on a large proportion of the tombs.

A late republican lead tablet lists a number of female slaves who are described as *ornatrices*, lady's maids.[1] Their owners probably belong to the town's aristocracy and in such households slave services may have been specialized and extensive. But the main demand for slaves in Ostia was for cheap labour, to work for their masters in shops, at the docks, in warehouses and in river boats, as manual labourers, clerks, and accountants.

In addition to the slaves in private ownership, slaves were also owned by public bodies. The town had its own *familia publica* of public slaves, who had their own guild organization and could expect their freedom in return for good service.[2] We have seen how one of their descendants, L. Ostiensis Macedo, actually became *pontifex Volcani* in the Flavian period. The *seviri Augustales* also had their *familia*,[3] and some at least of the guilds corporately owned slaves.[4]

There was also a substantial number of imperial slaves at Ostia. Some were required to maintain the premises at Ostia and Portus which were reserved for imperial visits; others worked under imperial freedmen in the service of the Annona and in handling cargoes required for the imperial household in Rome. Imperial freedmen are recorded as *tabularii, dispensatores, tabellarii*; slaves worked under them. From these

[1] S 5306, probably a *tabula defixionis*.   [2] 255.   [3] 367.   [4] p. 318.

imperial slaves and freedmen comes the strikingly wide distribution of the imperial names in Ostia's population: Tiberii Claudii, Titi Flavii, Marci Ulpii, Marci Aelii, Marci Aurelii.

The imperial slaves formed the aristocracy of the slave world in Ostia, and sometimes they seem to act with the independence of free men. Euphrosynus and Herclianus, 'ser(vi) C(aesaris) n(ostri)', are granted by Flavius Rufinus the use of the right half of a divided tomb, with fourteen cinerary urns and three places for burial.[1] Similarly Hermes, 'Caesaris nostri verna tabellarius', imperial messenger, has the left part of a divided tomb with fourteen urns and a place for burial.[2] Trophimus, 'Caes(aris) n(ostri) ser(vus)' and Claudia Tyche provide for themselves, their two daughters, and their freedmen and freedwomen, having bought the site from Valeria Trophime.[3] Similarly Euhodus, 'Caesar(is) n(ostri) ser(vus)', and Vennonia Apphis provide for themselves and their freedmen and freedwomen.[4] Freedmen and slaves of the emperor Claudius share a large tomb outside the Porta Laurentina.[5] Olympus, slave of the imperial princess Matidia the younger, commemorates his Urbica, with whom he had lived one year, eight months, twenty-two days, three hours when she died, aged fourteen years.[6] Another imperial slave, Chryseros, married a free woman, Valeria Thetis, daughter of M. Valerius Italicus.[7]

A special place in the household was held by the *verna*, the slave born in the household, either from the union of two slaves or from the master's temporary union with a favourite. *Vernae* are commonly commemorated in family tombs with a warmth indistinguishable from that shown for free children; such epithets as 'dulcissimus', 'bene merens' frequently recur. Even when they die young they have sometimes received the names of their patrons as if they were free. The *verna* of Cornelia Charis is already called Cornelia Myrsine, though she is only five at death;[8] similarly Modia Justa, who died when she was fourteen, already has her patron's family name.[9] The little *verna* Melior, an infant prodigy, who lived only thirteen years, had clearly been given every encouragement to develop his natural abilities: 'his memory and knowledge were such that he outdid the records of all from olden times to the day of his end; and what he knew needed a whole volume rather than an epitaph to record, for such notes of his art as he left behind were

[1] 1636.　　　　[2] Thylander, A 256.　　　　[3] Thylander, A 251.
[4] Thylander, A 96.　　　[5] 482–9.　　　[6] Thylander, A 261.
[7] 1727.　　　　　　　[8] 886.　　　　[9] 1369.

made by none before him and he could only be rivalled if cruel fate had not envied the world for him.'[1]

The slave born in the household belonged to the patron, but he was normally brought up by his slave parents and often remained with them when they were freed. L. Calpurnius Chius provides a good example. On the inscription in his tomb he provides for himself and his wife, Calpurnia Ampliata, with whom he lived thirty-one years. Four children are listed: 'Calpurnia L.f. Chia vern(a), Calpurnius L.f. Ampliata vern(a), et L. Calpurnius L.f. Felix vern(a), L. Calpurnius L.f. Pal. Chius Felicissimus.'[2] His wife Calpurnia had been a fellow slave and their three eldest children were born in slavery; the fourth was born after Chius had won his freedom. The naming of his two eldest children after their slave parents shows the regard in which Chius was held by his patron. His subsequent career suggests that he could have given valuable service; after he had been freed he became president of the *seviri Augustales*, treasurer and president of the corn measurers, and treasurer of the *codicarii*.

Slaves born in the household, who were not needed by the owner, could be profitably sold. L. Naebius Chrysogonus makes provision in his tomb for himself, his wife, his two sons, grandsons, freedmen, and freedwomen.[3] His sons' names are M. Aurelius Augg. lib. Vitalis and M. Aurelius Augg. lib. Peculiaris. The natural inference is that his sons were born before he was freed and that they were transferred, presumably by sale, to the imperial service in Ostia.[4]

A large number of inscriptions affectionately record *alumni* and *alumnae*—adopted children.[5] A few of these are slaves,[6] probably foundlings. The majority have the names of freedmen or citizens. Normally they have the same names as their adoptive father[7] or mother[8] and may be slaves who have received their freedom very early, or children born free who have changed their names on changing homes. Some *alumni* have different family names, showing clearly that they were freedmen or citizens before adoption.[9] C. Modestius Theseus is the *alumnus* of

---

[1] 472.

[2] **16,** following Henzen, *Ann. Inst.* 23 (1851) 166; cf. Thylander, *Étude*, 150. Dessau (*CIL* xiv. 309) infers that the three children described as *vernae* were born after their parents were freed but still living in their patron's house.   [3] 1386.

[4] Sales of slaves may also explain cases where brothers and sisters have different family names, 585, 991, 1548.

[5] *Diz. Epigr.* i. 437–40.   [6] 222, 1006, 2055.   [7] e.g. 219, 530, 543, S 5084.

[8] e.g. 772, 1606. Cf. *Dig.* 40. 2. 14: 'alumnos magis mulieribus conveniens est manumittere.'   [9] 327, 60, S 5084.

P. Claudius Abascantus, who received his freedom from the Council of Gaul at Lugdunum.[1] While he was still a slave at Ostia he set up the tombstone of Modestia Epigone, *anima dulcissima*.[2] We assume that he had lived with Modestia and adopted her son. A. Egrilius Epitynchanus is commemorated on his tombstone both by his adoptive father and by his natural parents.[3]

WOMEN

There is little to be learnt from the inscriptions concerning the position of women in Ostia that we should not otherwise guess. We find them owning slaves and house property; there are two women among the owners of workshops for making lead pipes.[4] They build tombs and sell sites to others. They are commemorated in the most affectionate terms as wives, mothers, sisters, and daughters, and there is no trace in the cemetery inscriptions that girls received less affection than boys. The public funerals accorded to two women reflect a general respect for their importance in family life. Voltidia Moschis received this honour as a tribute to her husband,[5] Sergia Prisca as a tribute to her son.[6]

One benefaction is specially reserved for girls. A lady, whose name is largely lost, left in her will a capital sum to provide from the annual interest for the upbringing of a hundred girls.[7] The benefactress was probably the daughter of Fabius Agrippinus, the Ostian consul of 148; and she was following the precedent set by Antoninus Pius, who instituted 'puellae alimentariae Faustinianae' in honour of his wife Faustina when she died.[8]

In a harbour town we should expect to find prostitutes plying a brisk trade, and premises designed for their exploitation. It is one of the surprises of the excavations that there is extremely little evidence of this side of life in the ruins. No building, clearly designed as a brothel, such as is found at Pompeii, has been identified, and sexual professions on the walls are remarkably rare; but it would be naïve to infer that Ostia had higher moral standards than other towns of the day, or that visiting ships' crews behaved differently from ships' crews elsewhere.

Women had no place in the trade guilds, and the *seviri Augustales*

---

[1] 327.   [2] 328.   [3] 932.

[4] Barbieri, 'Fistole inedite', *NS* 1953, 172, 174 (nn. 38, 39).

[5] Bloch, 71: 'hanc decuriones in honorem Q. Vergili Mariani viri eius funere publico efferri censuerunt.'

[6] 413, voted by the duovirs and decurions, together with a statue. Her husband paid for the funeral.   [7] S 4450.   [8] SHA, *Pius*, 8. 1.

were confined to men; but they took a prominent part in the religious life of the town, particularly in the cults of Cybele and Isis, and they had their own special cult of Bona Dea, celebrated in at least two temples.

THE SOCIAL PATTERN

Free-born citizen, freedman, and slave had their separate legal status, but social distinctions were often blurred. A *verna* brought up in a rich household probably had as much affection and more material comfort than the son of a free citizen living in a crowded tenement. A rich freedman who became president of the builders' guild was as acceptable in society as a poor man who could trace his free descent from the Republic. A weakening of class barriers is to be expected in a trading city and it is clear that, in the second century at least, trading interests dominated Ostia. Trade was the natural outlet for ambition and dominated the social atmosphere. Veterans retired to Ostia, but they came to do business. There was little temptation to leave the town for the army. It is significant that in the long list of legionaries who record their towns of origin no Ostian is included. No Ostian members of the praetorian guard are known until the second half of the second century[1] and the decline in Ostian prosperity may account in part for their enrolment then: at approximately the same time they figure prominently in the lists of urban cohorts,[2] and perhaps for the same reason. But it would be a mistake to think of Ostia as a town where life was oppressed by hard work, and men thought of nothing but the profits of trade. The large number of sets of public baths show that hard work was balanced by recreation in plenty; and Ostia had her *bons viveurs*. C. Domitius Primus in his epitaph made no attempt to disguise his standards: 'I have lived on Lucrine oysters and many a time drunk Falernian. Women and wine and bathing have grown old with me through the years.'[3]

But trade was the dominant interest and this is clearly reflected in the scratchings on house walls which bring us closer than the formal language of funerary inscriptions to the daily life of the lower classes.[4] In striking contrast with Pompeii there are no Virgilian tags, and no literary quotations. There are a few obscenities, less than we should

---

[1] *CIL* vi. 2375–84.   [2] *CIL* vi. 3884.   [3] 914.
[4] Graffiti, *S* 5289–302. A larger number remain unpublished from the 1938–42 excavations.

expect. A careful drawing of Trajan's column, signed by the artist, reminds us how spectacular this monument must have seemed to contemporaries.[1] Rough drawings of gladiators confirm the popularity of the amphitheatre.[2] But far more common are series of numbers, rough accounts, records of debts and dates. One of the rare Greek graffiti, in the Insula of the Charioteers, invokes Hermes the just to bring the writer profit.[3] Most striking of all is the number of ships scratched on the walls, from large merchantmen to small rowing-boats. Some of these sketches are crudely drawn, but many of the merchantmen are drawn in considerable detail, showing close familiarity with the technicalities of the rigging.[4]

PRIVATE LIFE

While inscriptions enable us to reconstruct the broad pattern of the organization of trade, they tell us much less of the private lives of Ostian men and women. We should like to know the average age of marriage, the size of families, the stability of marriage, the expectation of life, the incidence and severity of disease. The inscriptions from the cemeteries furnish a little evidence on some of these points, but it is tantalizingly fragmentary.

In some 600 cases the age at death is recorded, often with the count of hours, as well as of years, months, and days.[5] But the proportion from the total number is very small; the figures do not provide a fair statistical sample. The fact that males who die before the age of 5 account for 23 per cent. of the male figures recorded, and those who die between 5 and 10 for a further 19 per cent. is not fair evidence for the rate of infant mortality since the age of very young children is more likely to be recorded than of those who died in middle age and later. Comparison with the figures for females, however, is legitimate: 19 per cent. of those whose age is known died before they were 5; 15 per cent. between 5 and 10. It would seem that the death-rate was higher among boys than girls. The relation is reversed between the ages of 20 and 30

---

[1] In the House of the Muses (iii. 9. 22).   [2] *MA* 26 (1920) 370.

[3] Ἑρμῆ δίκαιε, κέρδος εἰσ[. . .] δίδου. Cf. Ovid, *Fasti*, v. 672: 'te (Mercurium) quicumque suos profitetur vendere merces, | ture dato, tribuas ut sibi lucra, roget'. *

[4] *MA.* 26, 369. Good unpublished examples in the House of the Muses and in the Horrea Epagathiana (from the Garden Houses); p. 295, fig. 25.

[5] The statistics that follow are confined to the two Ostian volumes of the Corpus. The material available will be considerably more extensive when all the inscriptions discovered since are published.

(males 18 per cent.; females 25 per cent.), an indication perhaps of the strain of childbirth. The oldest man recorded was 95 when he died; eleven others are recorded to have lived beyond 60: the oldest known woman died at 85, and four others are recorded to have lived beyond 60. The sample, however, is too small to justify conclusions concerning the relative longevity of the sexes.

In the recorded figures the proportion of deaths under the age of 30 is very high, 82 per cent. for males, 86 per cent. for females. This conforms with better evidence from more representative statistics that the expectation of life in the Roman world was very much shorter than in modern western societies,[1] but the Ostian sample is too small to stress the figures. Evidence from a very different quarter presents a less gloomy picture. There were 125 members of the guild of *lenuncularii tabularii* in 152,[2] presumably adults of varying ages. The guild roll of 192[3] shows that forty years later 11 of them were still alive. Of the 258 members of 192 some 120 were still members when the guild roll of 213 was drawn up.[4]

The age of marriage is very rarely recorded, but three of the few instances known show girls marrying before fifteen.[5] Such early marriages, not uncommon in the Roman world, could turn out very well. Egrilia Storge married when she was fourteen: 'she lived forty-eight years, five months, twenty-six days: three children and three grand-children survived her'. Her inscription was set up by her husband, who had lived with her for thirty-four years 'without scandal and without quarrel'.[6] This is not the only record of a long marriage that has survived. A. Livius Restitutus, who also had three children, was married to Livia Helpis for fifty-eight years;[7] and L. Antonius Peculiaris described his wife, who lived with him for fifty years, as 'uxor rarissima'.[8] The adjectives *incomparabilis* and *bene merens*, which frequently recur, mean less than figures; seventeen marriages are recorded to have lasted more than twenty years. Prima Florentia was less fortunate. At the age of sixteen and a half she was thrown into the Tiber by her husband.[9]

It is not unreasonable to believe from the records of the cemeteries

[1] A. R. Burn, 'Hic breve vivitur', *Past and Present* (1953), n. 4, 2–31; R. Étienne, 'Démographie et Épigraphie', *Atti del III° Congresso internazionale di Epigrafia greca e latina* (1959) 415–24.   [2] 250.   [3] 251.   [4] Bloch, 42.

[5] 963, 1854, Thylander, A 261.   [6] 963.   [7] 1262.   [8] 297.

[9] Thylander, A 210: 'Primae Florentiae filiae carissimae . . . qui ab Orfeu maritu in Tiberi decepta est.'

that family loyalties were generally strong. When the elder Faustina died the Ostian council set up a tablet to commemorate the outstanding harmony of her marriage with Antoninus Pius and prescribed that all maidens in Ostia, when they married, should, with their husbands, offer prayers at a public altar.[1] They were probably following the lead of the Roman senate, but it need not have been an empty ceremony.

Sons and daughters are often included on tombstones with their parents. This is our only evidence for estimating the average size of family, and, since family lists normally include only those who were still living when the tomb was built, such statistics, taking no account of infant mortality, will tend to underestimate the number of children born. It is, however, significant that we have no trace of any family with more than five children, and that only four are known to have had more than three.[2] Small families, with one or two children only, were probably the general rule among the free population.

One death is explicitly referred to 'dira pestis',[3] but, apart from this, we learn nothing of the extent and nature of disease. We can assume that a harbour town attracting shipping from all quarters was particularly vulnerable to epidemics, but there is no evidence in the literary sources that the town was considered unhealthy and Strabo's account of the coastal district implies that it was not.[4] Malaria probably did not become the main enemy of life until the sea had receded and the land had fallen into neglect. Medical services were also probably better in the Roman period than in the Middle Ages. Galen reports that the doctors of Ostia and Portus kept him in touch with their most unusual cases;[5] they must have been familiar with Roman standards. A terracotta relief attached to an Isola Sacra tomb shows a doctor at work carrying out a surgical operation on a patient's leg;[6] it is a good advertisement of his skill. Other doctors are recorded in inscriptions.[7] In the tomb of one of them was found a bust of Hippocrates,[8] father

---

[1] S 5326: 'utique in ara virgines quae in colonia Ostiensi nubent item mariti earum supplicent.'

[2] Five children, S 5132; four, 380, 425, 436, possibly Bloch, 50.   [3] 632.

[4] Strabo, 231, who explicitly cites Ardea, and not Ostia, as unhealthy.

[5] Galen (Kuhn) xviii. 348.

[6] Calza, *Necropoli*, 248–51; P. Capparoni, *Due importanti raffigurazioni a soggetto medico* (Ist. naz. medico farmacologico 'Sereno', 1930, pp. 8).

[7] 468, 471, Thylander, A 158, *IG* xiv. 942. An Ostian doctor serving with the army on the Rhine, *CIL* xiii. 6621.

[8] Becatti, *Rend. Pont.* 21 (1945–6) 123; identification disputed by P. Mingazzini, *Rend. Pont.* 25–26 (1949–51) 33.

of medicine; the furnishing of the tomb suggests a man of standing and substance.[1]

Bad housing conditions usually accompany and largely account for a short expectation of life. So far as we can see, Ostian housing conditions compare favourably with those of any other society before the middle of the nineteenth century. Admittedly the density of population cannot be satisfactorily estimated, but we can at least be certain that the builders understood the importance of effective sanitation. A study of the houses throws further doubt on the reliability of the statistical evidence for the average span of life.

[1] Calza, *Necropoli*, 373–6. For the relationships in the tomb, Bloch, *AJA* 48 (1944) 217. See also Addenda.

12

THE HOUSES

DURING the nineteenth and early twentieth centuries, accounts of the Roman house were dominated by the excavations at Pompeii. These had revealed a standard house plan which admirably fitted the detailed description of Vitruvius and many more casual references in other authors. The mainspring of this plan was the atrium, a rectangular hall round which, on all four sides, were grouped the living-rooms of the house. This hall was roofed except at its centre, where it remained open to the sky. Through this opening in the roof, the *compluvium*, was collected the rain-water in a basin below, the *impluvium*; and through this opening escaped the smoke when a fire was lit. The atrium was not only the physical centre of the house; it was also the main source of light for its rooms. The house looks inward rather than outward and where windows are found on the street frontages of houses they are usually small and irregular.

Extra accommodation can be provided in such a house by adding attics over the ground-floor rooms, approached by inner staircases. But the height of the house is limited to the maximum height of the atrium, and upper floors tend to be irregular and cramped. The natural form of expansion is horizontal rather than vertical; and so to the atrium was often later added a peristyle, a garden surrounded by colonnade or portico around which a second series of rooms could be built. Such expansion was wasteful of space and in the later stages of Pompeii's life, when the pressure of population was being increasingly felt, more attention was paid to upper rooms and to balconies, which provided an extension of living space over the streets.[1] To provide more homogeneous upper floors internal balconies were sometimes built on brick piers at the corners of the *impluvium*. But these were improvisations to which the height of the atrium set a limit. Only by radically changing the character of the building and by abolishing the atrium could the maximum use be made of the building space available.

It is true that not all Pompeian houses conform to a stereotyped plan.

[1] A. Maiuri, *L'ultima fase edilizia di Pompei* (1942); R. C. Carrington, *Antiquity*, 7 (1933) 133.

By the Forum Baths and also by the Stabian Baths are a line of shops built to a common design with a regular first floor above them separately approached by stairs from the street.[1] In some small plots buildings are fitted in with no true atrium. But the atrium house remained the dominant type and it is doubtful whether any Pompeian building exceeded 40 feet in height. Meanwhile at Rome Augustus had imposed a building limit of 70 feet.[2] This alone is sufficient to show that different principles were being adopted in Roman housing. Vitruvius is more explicit:

In view of the imperial dignity of Rome, and the unlimited number of citizens, it is necessary to provide dwellings without number. Therefore . . . necessity has driven the Romans to have recourse to building high. And so it is that by the use of stone piers, crowning courses of burnt brick and concrete walls, high buildings are raised with several stories, producing highly convenient apartments with views. And so with walls raised high through various stories the people of Rome have excellent dwellings without any hindrance.[3]

Similarly Cicero contrasts Rome with its high houses to low-spreading Capua.[4]

High buildings were no novelty in Rome at the end of the Republic. In describing the portents of the first year of Hannibal's invasion in 218 B.C. Livy relates that an ox in the Forum Boarium found its way up from the street to the third story of a house;[5] and upper stories are sufficiently common in republican anecdotes to show that a large proportion of the population lived above the ground floor. High buildings were in fact, as Vitruvius says, the logical answer to the increase in population which began early in Rome and probably developed particularly rapidly in the century of overseas victories that followed the Punic Wars. When space was scarce and ground rents high the natural solution was for several families to live together in a single building and make the maximum use of the building plot by extending upwards rather than outwards. What was first a necessity for the poor became later also a convenience for the upper classes. Cicero has to defend his

---

[1] A. Boethius, 'Remarks on the development of domestic architecture in Rome', *AJA* 38 (1934) 166; A. Maiuri, *Atti del primo congresso nazionale di studi romani* (1929) 164.

[2] Strabo, 235.

[3] Vitruvius ii. 8. 17. In translating I follow the interpretation of A. Boethius, *The Art Bulletin*, 33 (1951) 136 n. 3.

[4] Cic. *De lege agraria*, ii. 96: 'Romam in montibus positam et convallibus, cenaculis sublatam atque suspensam'.

[5] Livy xxi. 62. 3.

irresponsible young friend Caelius Rufus against a charge of taking rooms in an insula owned by Clodius at a rent of 30,000 sesterces.[1]

The use by Cicero of the word 'insula' shows the emergence of a vocabulary to mark a fundamental distinction in house types. Henceforward insula and domus denote in common usage two very different forms of dwelling. The insula is the large, normally high, block divided into separate apartments which can be separately let. The domus is the house designed primarily for a single family. Suetonius, in describing the great fire of Nero's principate, clearly separates the two types: 'praeter immensum numerum insularum, domus priscorum ducum arserunt'.[2] Elsewhere he contrasts insulae with private houses: 'inquilinos privatarum aedium atque insularum pensionem annuam repraesentare fisco'.[3]

Vitruvius, as we have seen, gives a favourable picture of the large house-blocks in Rome. His contemporaries were much less flattering. Strabo emphasizes the general unsightliness of the city and the insecurity of the buildings, constantly threatened with fire and collapse.[4] Augustus attempted to stop one of the main abuses by limiting the height of buildings. Nero seized the opportunity afforded by the rebuilding of large parts of Rome following the great fire to improve general standards of building by more sweeping measures.[5] In particular the use of timber and inflammable tufas in the construction was severely restricted. Once the technique of concrete construction had been mastered, not later than the second century B.C., it should have been possible to build tall house-blocks that were reasonably secure, but it is probable that timber and sun-dried bricks remained for a long time the main building materials in the poorer parts of the city owing to their cheapness. The Neronian rebuilding set the standard for the future. From the Flavian period onwards concrete construction dominated the field, and the brick industry had developed sufficiently to make fired bricks and broken tiles the standard material for the facing of walls.

Rome had felt and satisfied the need for large house-blocks early in the Republic. They were common in Cicero's day and not confined to the poor; throughout the Empire they increasingly displaced the domus. Juvenal and Martial can look with envious eyes on the spreading mansions of wealthy patrons; they live themselves in insulae.

[1] Cic. *Pro Caelio*, 17. Cicero corrects the figure to 10,000 s.
[2] Suet. *Nero*, 38. 2.
[3] Ibid. 44. 2.   [4] Strabo, 235.   [5] Tac. *Ann*. xv. 43.

R

Martial is given a small farm on the Via Nomentana; at Rome he has only a third-floor apartment.[1] When the fourth-century regionary catalogues were drawn up, there were in Rome 46,000 insulae, and only 1,790 domus.[2] Ostia's housing development, dictated by the same basic causes, followed broadly the Roman pattern, but the need for vertical expansion was felt much later and the dominance of the insula came more abruptly.

There is no sign that space was unduly scarce in the late Republic or early Principate. The walls surviving from this period do not seem to be intended to carry heavy weight; there are no traces of large apartment blocks. The wealthy still lived in low spreading houses essentially Pompeian in type, and three small atrium houses on the Via delle Domus Repubblicane, which were probably built in the early first century B.C. and replaced by an insula in the early second century A.D., suggest that the 'Pompeian' house was not limited to the rich.[3] We may be certain that shops on street fronts carried living quarters above them, perhaps in two upper stories, but it is very doubtful whether any large areas were specifically planned or laid out in tall apartment blocks. It was probably the building of the new Claudian harbour, accentuated by Trajan's extension, that led to the revolution in housing. The increase of trade produced by the imperial harbours attracted a rapid influx of population into Ostia. It was for that reason primarily that the town was virtually rebuilt within three generations; in the rebuilding, insulae sprang up in every quarter. By the late Flavian period, when this rebuilding began, Ostian architects had Rome's experience to guide them; they could see the new streets of Nero's 'nova urbs' and the insula type had reached full maturity. They were able to plan even the largest areas on the new model and had soon mastered the principles involved.

The various types of Ostian insulae are not the original products of local architects; they reflect Roman models. This is clear both from ground plans preserved on the marble plan of Rome and from remains of Roman insulae that can still be seen. Two façades in particular serve to complement the Ostian evidence. One is incorporated in the Aurelian wall near the Porta Tiburtina,[4] the other in the church of St. John and

[1] Martial i. 117. 7: 'scalis habito tribus sed altis'.
[2] There are minor variations in the numbers recorded in different surveys, discussed by L. Homo, *Rome impériale et l'urbanisme dans l'antiquité* (Paris, 1951) 540, 638.
[3] *NS* 1923, 180.   [4] Calza, *MA* 23 (1914) 75 f. with tav. v (c).

St. Paul on the Caelian hill;[1] both show the same principles of construction as the insulae of Ostia, and would be completely in place in Ostian
streets. The striking ruin at the foot of the Capitol with traces of four
stories is like the cross-section of an Ostian insula,[2] and various series of
ground-floor rooms beneath Roman churches fit convincingly into the
Ostian pattern. But the evidence from Rome is scattered and fragmentary; it was the excavations of Ostia that first revealed the general
character of the dominant town house of the imperial period, and it
was Calza who first focused attention on the importance of the Ostian
evidence.[3]

Though the plans of individual insulae vary considerably, certain
general principles apply throughout. Space is used economically and
there are normally more than two stories. The upper stories are not
secondary and subordinate as in a Pompeian house, but regularly
planned and some of them at least no less attractive than the ground
floor. Separate access is provided for these upper stories by stairs
entered direct from the street: the staircase is wide and the steps solid,
either in travertine or in brick with wooden treads. The Pompeian
house turns away from the street and looks inward; the insula draws its
main light from the street through large windows. The disposition of
the windows is based on the needs of the rooms or corridors which
they serve, rather than the design of the elevation, but in the large
blocks the regularity of the plan results in a rough symmetry in the
façade. In some insulae light from the street is supplemented by light
from an inner court; and at all times the lighting of his building seems
to have been one of the architect's main preoccupations. The effectiveness, however, of the lighting was severely reduced by the lack of good
transparent glass; the selenite that was normally used dimmed the light
considerably.[4]

Although most insulae were divided into clearly distinct apartments,
some of the services were communal. Water could not be piped to the
upper floors, and tenants had to draw their supplies from a public

[1] A. M. Colini, 'Storia e topografia del Celio', *Mem. Pont.* 7 (1944) 164.

[2] A. Muñoz and A. M. Colini, *Campidoglio* (1930) 45.

[3] Calza's two basic studies: 'La preminenza dell'Insula nella edilizia romana', *MA*
23 (1914) 541–608; 'Le origini latine dell'abitazione moderna', *Architettura e Arti
decorative* (1923–4) 3–18 and 49–63. Supplemented later by 'Le case Ostiensi a cortile
porticato', *Palladio* 5 (1941) 1–33.

[4] Selenite, Calza, *Origini*, 13 f.; remains, *NS* 1908, 23. Many windows probably only
had wooden shutters.

source. In the House of Diana a cistern was provided in the central
court; in the Via della Fontana tenants had to go to the near-by cistern
in the street; in the Garden Houses fountains were supplied in the
gardens that surrounded the blocks of flats. In insulae which catered for
better-class tenants lavatories were probably provided for each apartment, or at least on every floor: the large size of the latrine near the
entrance of the House of Diana suggests that it was intended for the
whole block.

In appearance the insulae are simple and severe. There is no attempt
to dress them in superfluous ornament nor to disguise their character.
The brickwork of the façade is not covered by stucco, though relieving
arches are often picked out in bright red paint to add variety.[1] In better-
class blocks entrances are framed by brick pilasters or columns and
pediment, an inconspicuous but dignified feature.[2] Balconies also sometimes add liveliness to the street fronts. Some are in wood, carried on
projecting timber beams or travertine corbels: others are carried on
vaults springing from travertine corbels. On the south and west faces of
the House of Diana, as along the east side of the Via degli Horrea
Epagathiana, a continuous line of balcony supported by a series of
vaults runs along the whole street front, and has given its name to the
Via dei Balconi.[3] These are not true balconies. They are too narrow for
convenient use and, more important, they do not correspond with
floor levels; they were not accessible from within. Their purpose seems
to be primarily decorative, though they gave a little protection from
heat and rain to the pavement below.

The main effectiveness of the insulae comes from the lines of windows
and the plainness of the surface, and the larger the area planned the
more effective normally is the result. Thus the long narrow block
between the Via della Fontana and the Via delle Corporazioni, which
was built to a single plan, was probably always more attractive than the
south side of the Via di Diana where the building plots were comparatively small and irregular. Proportion also must have counted considerably in the total effect, but the evidence for the height of Ostian
insulae is insecure. The average height of the stories is 3·5 metres, and
in the House of Diana and some other buildings steps leading from the
first to the second floor can still be seen; the existence of fourth and
fifth stories, however, is disputed.[4]

The general arguments in favour of insulae with more than three

[1] Calza, *Origini*, 11.   [2] Pl. XI.   [3] Pl. VIII *b*.   [4] A. von Gerkan, *RM* 55 (1940) 161.

stories are strong. At Rome the building limit had been set at 70 feet by Augustus; Nero had also legislated in the matter and Trajan set a new limit of 60 feet.[1] This legislation clearly implies that building up to the limit was common practice in Rome and we should expect Ostia, at a time when the need for more accommodation was urgent, to follow Roman example. When most of the Ostian insulae were built, Trajan's reduced limit of 60 feet will have been in force. This height, rather more than 17 metres, could have provided four stories of average height and a lower fifth story.

That Ostian houses at least approached Trajan's building limit is also strongly suggested by the height of the Capitolium. It seems clear that this temple is set on such a high podium in order to raise it above the highest buildings behind and near it. The height from the ground of the pediment of the temple would have been roughly 70 feet, from which it seems reasonable to infer heights of over 50 feet in the neighbourhood. To such indirect argument may be added the more specific evidence provided by the House of Diana. Clear traces of three stories can still be seen in this house and the existence of the running balcony well above the first floor shows that there must have been at least one story above the second floor. A relieving arch thinner than the walls still standing, found among the ruins, seems also to have come from a floor above the second.[2] The standard width of weight-carrying walls in the insulae, 59 cm. (two Roman feet), is certainly sufficient to carry five stories, but provides no evidence for their existence, for the Romans notoriously often built more stoutly than was necessary. While some of the larger insulae like the House of Diana may have had four and five stories, narrow blocks such as that on the Via della Fontana were probably lower.

There is little evidence to determine the nature of roof construction. The distribution of pipes in the House of the Lararium suggests a terraced roof.[3] Elsewhere, as in the House of the Painted Vaults, many of the original roof-tiles have been found in the ruins; probably pitched roofs were more common than terraces.[4]

Though the insulae all conform to certain general principles they differ considerably in scale and plan and cater for a wide range of purses. The simplest plan is probably also the oldest, the building of

[1] *Epit. de Caes.* 13.
[2] *NS* 1917, 322. The thickness is 32 cm. compared with 59 cm. in the lower walls.
[3] P. Harsh, 'Origins of the insulae of Ostia', *MAAR* 12 (1935) 58.
[4] Calza, *Origini*, 8 f.

upper stories over a row of shops on the street front. The shops are high and vaulted and a mezzanine floor is added for the shopkeeper beneath the vault. This upper room, which could be subdivided by light partitions, is reached by a staircase from the back of the shop, the first four steps in brick, the rest in wood; it is lighted by a small window above the centre of the door to the shop. Staircases lead direct from the street to the upper stories. This type of dwelling developed naturally against such public buildings as basilicas: it is found at Pompeii by the Forum Baths, possibly introduced from Rome by Sulla's colonists.[1] It is frequently repeated at Ostia, as in the Cardo Maximus between the Capitolium and the river, and on the Decumanus frontage of the Neptune Baths. Narrow blocks of this type normally form part of a larger design, the main building developing behind them. The ground floor is used for shops, because shops brought in higher rents than apartments.

A simple development of this plan is to set two such narrow blocks back to back, as in the area between the Via della Fontana and the Via delle Corporazioni.[2] Passages joining these two streets divide the buildings into three groups. In the southern group a series of living-rooms occupies the ground floor on the Via delle Corporazioni: the corresponding frontage on the Via della Fontana is used for shops. In the centre group the distribution is reversed: shops line the Via delle Corporazioni; behind them is an apartment. The third group is occupied by industrial premises. The upper stories throughout the block are reached by independent stairs from the streets. The same basic principle underlies the so-called Garden Houses. Two large apartment blocks are laid out on a common plan in the middle of large gardens. A through passage divides each block into two halves. On each side of this central passage are two apartments, back to back, each independent of the other for its light. The Casette-tipo repeat the plan on a more modest scale.[3]

When the insula develops in depth and cannot be adequately lighted from street frontages an inner court is sometimes added. The utilitarian purpose of this device is best illustrated by the House of Diana.[4] The architect of this insula had a large building plot, 23·30 × 39·30 metres. He had two street frontages, the Via di Diana on the south, the Via dei Balconi on the west; but the north and east sides of his plot were

[1] A. Boethius, *AJA* 38 (1934) 166.   [2] Calza, *MA* 23 (1914) 599, Pl. IX *a*.
[3] Fig. 12.   [4] Calza, *NS* 1917, 312; Fig. 9.

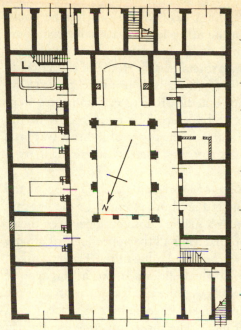

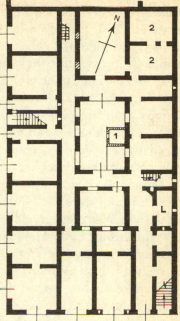

FIG. 8. House of the Triclinia (Builders' Guild House).

FIG. 9. House of Diana. 1. Cistern added in open court. 2. Rooms later converted to a Mithraeum.

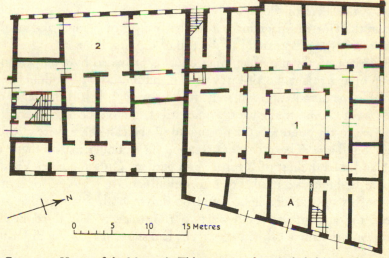

FIG. 10. 1. House of the Muses. A. This room was later included in the house by blocking the entrance from the street and opening a doorway in the west wall. 2. House of the Yellow Walls. 3. House of the Graffito.

already closed in by earlier buildings: from these quarters he could draw no light. He solved his problem by leaving a small open court (8·80× 5·80 metres) in the centre of his building, which directly or indirectly gave light to the rooms around it. The House of the Triclinia illustrates the same principle.[1] Light was available from the streets to the north and south of the building, but the areas to east and west were already built up, or shortly to be built up. The main rooms in the centre of the house had to have some other source of light; it was provided by a large open court (12·10× 7·15 metres) surrounded by a portico carried on brick piers.

Though the courts of the House of Diana and of the House of the Triclinia fulfil the same function and are both essential to the lighting of the buildings they serve, there is a marked difference between them. The small court in the House of Diana has all the appearance of a mere practical expedient: the larger court of the House of the Triclinia gives, as is intended, an aristocratic air to the building. It was in this type of building centred on a peristyle court that the insula came nearest to the domus, and, since it was comparatively uneconomic in space, it was probably accompanied by high rents. The most attractive example in Ostia is the House of the Muses,[2] where the careful paintings of the ground-floor rooms and the elegance of their mosaics suggest that the tenants were wealthy. Normally the portico of the ground floor reaches only to the level of the first floor, where it is repeated, as can still be seen in the Horrea Epagathiana.[3] In the Insulae of Serapis and of the Charioteers the piers extend to the top of the first floor.

A variant on the use of an inner court is provided by a garden in a group of apartments north-east of the Capitolium.[4] The building plot available measured approximately 70 × 27 metres. It had frontages on the Via dei Dipinti to the west, a quiet street, and on the more busy Via di Diana to the south; to the north and to the east there were already other buildings. The architect arranged his building in the shape of an L and used the rest of his space as a garden. On the quieter Via dei Dipinti he built two insulae to a common pattern, reserved for living apartments only. Since light could be drawn both from garden and street, the apartments could be two rooms deep. His third insula, occupying the angle of the two streets, had shops on the Via di Diana.

[1] P. Harsh, art. cit. 23; Calza, *Palladio*, 5 (1941) 3; Fig. 8.
[2] Calza, *Palladio*, 5 (1941) 6; Fig. 10; Pl. x *b*.
[3] Ibid. 19; Becatti, *NS* 1940, 32.   [4] Calza, *MA* 26 (1920) 321.

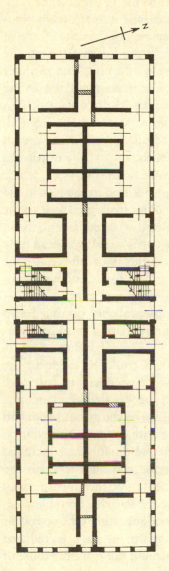

Fig. 11. Garden Houses.

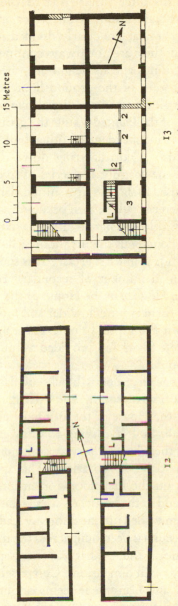

13

12

Fig. 12. Casette-tipo. Fig. 13. House of the Painted Ceiling. 1. Original entrance from street, closed when the apartment was reduced. 2. Light walls, no longer surviving. 3. Paintings described, p. 441.

It was larger and needed additional light; here he added a small open court. All three insulae shared the garden, and each insula had its separate stairs leading from street or garden to the upper stories.[1]

Most insulae are clearly divided into independent apartments, *cenacula*, but these are not always confined to a single floor. In the House of the Paintings and its neighbour, the House of the Infant Bacchus, the seven rooms of the ground floor are planned as a unit, but an inner staircase leads to an additional five rooms on a mezzanine floor. In the House of the Painted Vaults the ground-floor flat is self-contained. This insula is independent of other buildings and can draw light from all four sides. A corridor runs down the centre of the building: on each side of the corridor is a series of five rooms, the two at the north end being used as shops.[2] This simple plan is repeated on the first floor, where a kitchen can still be seen occupying the same position in the plan as the kitchen below. There is an outer staircase leading from the street to the upper floors, but the first floor is also connected with the second by an independent inner staircase. This staircase is narrow and may lead only to a small number of secondary rooms on the floor above. In the Garden Houses, in the House of the Muses and its two southern neighbours, there is a much wider and more imposing inner staircase leading up from the ground floor. These apartments probably occupied two complete floors and provided as much accommodation as an independent house.

But, as in modern blocks of flats, changes could be made in the distribution of rooms, and apartments could be reduced or enlarged. When the House of the Painted Ceiling on the Via della Fontana was originally built five living-rooms were provided on the ground floor and one of these had a doorway communicating with the shop behind it on the Via delle Corporazioni. This apartment presumably also included rooms on the first floor, for an inner staircase was built towards the south end of the house. As we see this apartment now, the inner stairway has been walled up, the doorway leading into the shop has been blocked, and a wall has been built across the main corridor cutting off two rooms at the north end.[3] What was once a spacious apartment has been reduced to very small dimensions. Conversely the ground floor of the House of Jupiter and Ganymede seems originally to have been a self-contained apartment; it was only later that an inner staircase was added, suggest-

---

[1] Fig. 14.   [2] Fig. 16.
[3] Excavation report, Vaglieri, *NS* 1908, 21; Fig. 13.

ing the incorporation of some rooms on the firts floor.[1] Similarly shops could be connected with or separated from the apartments behind them by the opening or blocking of a doorway.

Since no furnishings remain we cannot securely know to what uses the various rooms of an apartment were put, but it is clear that in the original planning the rooms were not all regarded as interchangeable. In all apartments that can be clearly recognized as independent units one room is substantially larger than the rest and in some cases its dominance is emphasized by its height. The room at the north-east corner of the ground floor of the House of Jupiter and Ganymede, for instance, is nearly twice as large as any other room in the apartment (6·80 × 8·30 metres) and its ceiling comes at the top of the first floor: in smaller apartments the distinction is less marked. The wall paintings and mosaic pavement of this room are usually the best in the apartment and it is particularly well lighted.

A standard plan is repeatedly used for the distribution of these rooms; it can be seen in its simplest form in the House of the Painted Ceiling. The ground-floor apartment of this insula is now entered at the south-west corner from a passage that connects two streets. Originally this was a secondary entrance only; the main entrance, subsequently closed, was on the street.[2] The rooms are served by a corridor which runs along the front of the building. The main room lies at the north end of the corridor and occupies the whole depth of the apartment: it is lighted from the street by three large windows. The second room in size and emphasis is at the south end of the corridor; it too is lighted direct from the street, but by only a single window. The three remaining rooms are smaller and open off the west side of the corridor. Their lighting is indirect, through the corridor, and their wall decoration is less elaborate; these are rooms of secondary importance, probably bedrooms. The corridor, liberally lighted from the street, is much wider than a corridor need be: it is both hall and corridor, as if it were the vestigial remnant of the atrium. This basic plan with a series of secondary rooms opening off a corridor and indirectly lighted through the corridor, and the two most important rooms directly lighted at the two ends of the corridor, can be seen also in the Garden Houses, the Casette-tipo, and the houses on the east side of the Via dei Vigiles. In every case the main room comes at the far end of the apartment from the entrance.

This standard plan is normally used when the apartment has no great

[1] *MA* 26 (1920) 360.   [2] Fig. 13; Pl. IX *a*.

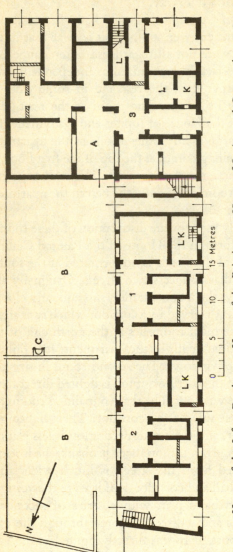

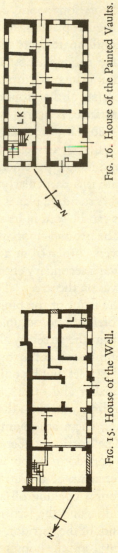

FIG. 14. 1. House of the Infant Bacchus. 2. House of the Paintings. 3. House of Jupiter and Ganymede. A. Open court. B. Garden. C. Small shrine with terra-cotta figure of Jupiter.

FIG. 15. House of the Well.

FIG. 16. House of the Painted Vaults.

depth, but in the House of the Paintings and its neighbour, which are substantially deeper than any of the houses mentioned above, the plan is based on the same general principles. The secondary rooms are in the centre, the more important rooms at either end. Where the plan is based on a central court the main room carries even more emphasis. Its logical place is at the end of the court facing the entrance, as in the House of the Triclinia, or in the social headquarters of the *seviri Augustales*. The House of the Muses forms an exception because the street entrance is not central, but to the side of the building: the entrance is from the east, the main room is in the centre of the south side. It is conspicuous not only by its size but also by its arcaded front.

The division of the insula into independent apartments is not always apparent. In the House of Diana certain small groups of rooms seem to be interdependent, but it is not easy to see how the first floor was divided. It seems likely that this large building catered for rather different needs and was more elastic in plan, providing for the renting of much smaller apartments and even single rooms.[1] There must indeed have been a large demand for temporary accommodation for visitors in Ostia, as well as many Ostians who could not afford to rent more than one or two rooms.

The main surprise perhaps in the Ostian insulae is the size of so many of the apartments. The House of the Paintings and its neighbour have twelve rooms, the House of the Painted Ceiling had originally five on the ground floor with further rooms on the first floor. The House of the Painted Vaults has eight rooms on its ground floor, and more than ten rooms in the apartment above. From Martial and Juvenal we expect darkness, squalor, and general discomfort in the insulae; only poverty can compel a man to lodge there. These Ostian apartments are well lighted, spacious, and cheerfully decorated with wall paintings and mosaic pavements. Certain amenities, it is true, are missing. No rooms yet found in insulae are heated, and upper floors could have no running water; but the size and decoration of their apartments show that the insulae were by no means confined to the poor. In the Augustan period the tenants of such blocks as the House of the Muses would almost certainly have lived in independent houses.

Nor do the buildings themselves correspond with what we should expect from the complaints of Seneca, Juvenal, and Martial. Like

---

[1] Becatti, *Mitrei*, 15, suggests that the building may have been the headquarters of a guild. The plan seems to be less well suited to this purpose.

Strabo before them, these writers emphasize the insecurity of life in the insulae of Rome.[1] Fire and collapse seem to be constant risks. In contrast, the insulae of Ostia seem solid and well built; their walls are sufficiently thick, at least on the ground and first floors, to carry the weight of the highest building that the law allowed; there are few signs of major reconstruction or restoration on the ground floors dictated by a need to strengthen the building. Nor do the brick-faced concrete walls of the ruins suggest an acute fire risk.

In this respect the ruins are perhaps misleading. Though external walls were of concrete, timber was widely used throughout the house, for doors, windows, and furniture. Some rooms were vaulted, but timber ceilings were equally common; and minor partition walls were also often of timber. The main danger came from oil lamps and open braziers, which were probably used in extreme cold. Carelessness in the use of fires was liable to summary punishment,[2] but enforcement must have been virtually impossible. The fire risk would have been less serious if the means of fire-fighting had been more adequate; as it was, there was great difficulty in controlling a fire once it had caught hold. Tenants in insulae were required to keep water in their apartments for use in the case of fire,[3] but the quantity available must have been totally insufficient if the fire was not tackled at once. The Fasti record a fire on 1 January 115 which destroyed a large number of properties.[4] Later, as excavation has shown, at least three large blocks were burnt to the ground. Both the House of Diana and the House of the Paintings, with its two neighbours, seem to have been abandoned by the beginning of the fourth century, though no evidence of fire was found.[5] The ground floors show no clear traces of collapse; the upper stories may have been more lightly and insecurely built.

The general amenities of the insulae, moreover, depended primarily on the number of people that they contained. In general the best apartments are probably the best preserved: it was not in such apartments as the ground-floor rooms of the House of the Paintings and the House of the Painted Ceiling that the poor people lived. Even in the most impos-

---

[1] Seneca, *De Ira*, iii. 35. 5; *De Beneficiis*, vi. 15. 7; Juvenal iii. 190–202.

[2] *Dig.* i. 15. 5: 'insularios et eos qui neglegenter ignes apud se habuerint, potes fustibus vel flagellis caedi iubere.'

[3] *Dig.* i. 15. 3. 4: 'praeterea ut aquam unusquisque inquilinus in cenaculo habeat, iubetur admonere (praefectus vigilum).'

[4] 'K. Ianuar. incendium ortum in v[ico—] et praedia complura deusta sun[t].'

[5] p. 85.

ing blocks the rooms beneath the roof were probably small and dark and the smaller insulae were probably much less comfortable than the larger. The mezzanine rooms over shops were certainly low and dark: in the strip-insulae that had only a narrow frontage of one or two shops on the street the apartments are likely to have been particularly small and poorly lighted.[1] Sometimes perhaps a ground-floor plan is misleading. The so-called Casette-tipo seem to be cheaply built: though reticulate and brick are used for the external walls, the internal walls are roughly faced with tufa blocks of irregular size. The stairs leading to an upper floor were of wood. The walls are not apparently designed to stand great weight and some of them are considerably out of line. The ground-floor apartments, however, closely resemble that of the House of the Painted Ceiling, with a large main room at the far end of the apartment, the second largest room at the opposite end of a corridor, and three other subsidiary rooms. Instead, however, of a small lavatory we find a large latrine with room for two seats. The natural inference is that the building was more crowded than its plan suggests.

The insulae were the response to the increase of population and a rise in ground rents. So long as demand for accommodation exceeded supply they represented the most attractive investment available, and during the period of prosperity the profits of trade and industry probably went largely into this type of building. Passages in the Digest confirm practices that even without evidence could be assumed: 'If I lease to you an insula belonging to another owner for 50,000 sesterces and you lease the same insula to Titius for 60,000 sesterces. . . .'[2] Another typical case is cited of 'a man who had rented an insula for 30,000 sesterces and so rented the individual apartments that his total revenue was 40,000 sesterces'.[3]

Between the late Flavian period and the death of Antoninus Pius few new independent houses were built, and many were pulled down to be replaced by insulae. These catered not merely for the poor, but also for families of substantial means. For some three generations the insula became the dominant house type at Ostia; its supremacy, however, did not long outlive the period of prosperity. At Rome the population did not decrease sharply as the wealth of the empire declined; the special steps taken by the emperors to feed and entertain the people ensured overcrowding. But when Ostia's commercial prosperity declined her

[1] For strip-insulae, A. Boethius, *Studies presented to D. M. Robinson*, i (1951) 440.
[2] *Dig*. xix. 2. 7.   [3] *Dig*. xix. 2. 30.

population declined also. In the third century there was almost certainly more accommodation than was needed or could be afforded: insulae were no longer a profitable investment and the standard of maintenance fell sharply as rents declined. It is clear at least that by the end of the third century some large apartment blocks had been abandoned.

But while in the late Empire the insula declined, the domus came back into its own. At the beginning of the second century independent houses were destroyed to make way for the building of apartment blocks. In the fourth century, and perhaps as early as the third, independent houses were reusing what had once been the walls of apartment blocks. But these houses of the late Empire differed considerably from their predecessors of the late Republic and early Empire both in plan and in decoration.

For the history of the Ostian domus in the fourth, third, and early second centuries B.C. there is no evidence; by the Sullan period, and probably earlier, the typical Pompeian house based on atrium and peristyle was fashionable. On the north side of the Via della Fortuna Annonaria there survived throughout the Empire the remains of a peristyle dating from the Republic.[1] This peristyle was once surrounded by tufa columns along its four sides and travertine columns at the corners. The columns were covered in stucco and fluted, and carried Doric capitals. On the south side the original columns remain; the rest were later replaced by brick piers. The date of the original building is approximately fixed to the early first century B.C. by the *opus incertum* face of the original walls. This peristyle probably formed the back of a house whose plan has been obscured by later rebuilding.

Pompeian affinities are more clearly recognizable in two houses on the west side of the southern Cardo, immediately beyond the Forum. The House of Jupiter the Thunderer has *opus incertum* walls of the late second or early first century B.C.; its neighbour, the House of the Mosaic Niche, was added some fifty years later. Though substantially modified and reconstructed more than once, these two houses had a continuous history as private houses into the late Empire and much of their original plan is still recognizable. The entrance from the street is flanked by two shops; between them a passage leads into a Tuscan atrium round which the living-rooms are grouped, with the main living-room of the house, the tablinum, facing the entrance. Each house originally had

[1] Pl. XII *a*.

a peristyle behind the atrium, but when space became more valuable these areas were taken over for other building.

But most of the evidence for the private houses of the late Republic and early Empire lies beneath the second-century level, for, when the town was rebuilt to meet a sharp increase in population, houses with atrium and peristyle were too extravagant in space to survive; most of them were pulled down to be replaced by insulae and public buildings. The eastern side of the western Decumanus was, before the rebuilding, lined with such houses. The street front was occupied by shops; passages led through to large atria, with peristyles behind them. These house plans have left their mark in the narrow frontages and considerable depths of the buildings that succeeded them, and nowhere can the contrast in the use of space be better seen than in the area of the Vicolo di Dionisio. This street is flanked by shops with living quarters above them; it leads to a large open area round which was built a series of insulae. What has become a populous district had been a single house; the area now surrounded by insulae was formerly a private peristyle.[1] Another such house has been replaced by the Baths of the Six Columns.

The latest of the atrium houses on the western Decumanus are not earlier than Augustus. By the Flavian period fashions have decisively changed. No new atrium houses are built; their place is taken by what for convenience may be called the peristyle house. The first clear example is a Flavian house on the western Decumanus outside the Porta Marina. The entrance on the street is flanked by shops; a passage leads into what was probably a garden, surrounded by a portico carried on brick piers. In the garden is a biclinium, recalling the open-air dining fashion familiar at Pompeii; the rooms open off the portico.[2] This is the commonest basic plan in Ostia; it is used for *horrea*, for the Barracks of the Vigiles, for insulae.[3] It becomes the dominant type of private house in the second century and continues into the late Empire. Sometimes the central area is paved with mosaic, sometimes it is laid out as a garden.

A more controversial early example of the peristyle house is to be seen in the House of Apuleius, which occupies a restricted and irregular area at the back of the group of four republican temples near the

---

[1] Becatti, *Topografia*, 108.

[2] Ibid. 121; Pl. XII *b*. The date might be late Neronian rather than Flavian, Bloch, *Topografia*, 221 (III.7.4).

[3] An analysis of the type, Calza, *Palladio*, 5 (1941) 1–33.

S

theatre.[1] Its walls date from a wide range of periods, but the original nucleus of the house is probably Trajanic. A long entrance passage, flanked by two rooms on either side, leads into what resembles a Corinthian atrium, with eight columns surrounding an open area in the middle of which is a sunk basin; from this 'atrium' a series of rooms leads westwards. This house has been called the last Pompeian house in Ostia, but the Corinthian 'atrium' is no true atrium. The area surrounded by columns is wider than the combined width of east and west corridors. It is in fact a small peristyle court.[2] This house, however, cannot be regarded as typical; its unusual shape is dictated by the shape of the area available.

Of the second-century peristyle houses the most elegant surviving example is the House of Fortuna Annonaria, built towards the middle of the century.[3] The central focus of the house is an open garden surrounded on three sides by travertine columns which were probably originally covered by stucco and fluted; on the fourth side a continuous wall runs the whole length of the building. The rooms open off the three sides of the colonnade, with the entrance from the street on the north and the main room at the west end. The central room at the eastern end of the garden was heated, the first example known to us at Ostia, and it probably served as a bedroom; for, while the rest of the mosaic pavement is divided into a series of figured octagonal panels, a large band against the east wall has only a simple geometric design; this is probably where the bed stood. Though changes were later made, especially in the main living-room at the west end of the garden, to meet the fashions of the late Empire, the plan of the house has remained substantially unchanged. A tasteful neo-Attic well-head was found in the garden[4] and, in its final phase at least, house and garden were liberally decorated with sculptures.

The House of the Columns, at the angle of the southern Cardo and the Via della Caupona del Pavone, is more orthodox in plan.[5] It was probably built in the third century and was continuously occupied into the fifth century. There are two entrances from the Cardo, a wide vestibule and, beside it, a narrow passage for the servants with a long narrow room off it for the doorkeeper. Both vestibule and passage lead into a long open court, surrounded by brick piers carrying a portico. In its final phase this court was paved with large cubes of variegated

---

[1] Lanciani, *NS* 1886, 163; Paschetto, 421.   [2] P. Harsh, *MAAR* 12 (1935) 29 f.
[3] Becatti, *Case Ostiensi del tardo impero*, 23.   [4] Pl. XXXVII *c*.   [5] Ibid. 15.

marbles and had a nymphaeum and a long shallow basin in the centre. This may be a later refinement; perhaps the court was originally paved with mosaic. The rooms open off the portico, the main room facing the entrance at the west end.

An open court is also the central feature of the charming House of the Round Temple.[1] This house in its present form probably dates from the late third century, but on its east side it incorporates much earlier walls. The main entrance is now from the Via del Tempio Rotondo to the south, but traces of an earlier entrance on the north side can still be seen; possibly the third-century house repeats the form of an earlier building on the site. This comparatively small building combines domus and insula.[2] The street frontage is occupied by two large shops, each with an inner staircase leading to a mezzanine floor. There are also two solid staircases leading up from the street to upper floors. On this side the walls have the standard insula thickness of two Roman feet (59 cm.), and presumably carried two or three stories above the shops.

A vestibule, between the two shops, leads to the domus behind, which is built round a small open courtyard with a fountain set in a sunk basin in the centre. On the north side the court admits directly to the main living-room of the house; on the other sides it is surrounded by a wide portico carried on brick piers. On the west side is a series of four rooms, three of them heated from a stoke-hole to the south;[3] on the east side there is a further series of four rooms. The walls of the domus are not designed to carry heavy weight. Those of the eastern wing are only 37 cm. thick, those of the west wing 44 cm.; since there are also no signs of an inner staircase, the house was probably limited to the ground floor. In its final phase marble was freely used to line court, brick piers, and many of the walls. Much of this may have been added later, but this house must always have been elegant.

The independent peristyle houses hitherto examined were built for wealthy families, but the plan could be adapted to a modest purse, and was sometimes used when the site available was not suited to the building of an apartment block. A good example can be seen near the temple of Hercules. This house was probably built towards the end of the

[1] Ibid. 3; P. Harsh, art. cit. 24; Fig. 17; Pl. XIII a.

[2] Cf. *Dig.* xxxix. 2. 15. 14: 'item quid dicimus, si insula adiacens domui vitium faciat, utrum in insulae possessionem an vero in totius domus possessionem mittendum sit?' *Dig.* xxxii. 91. 6: 'appellatione domus insulam quoque iniunctam domui videri.'

[3] Becatti, op. cit. 4 f., regards the heating system as a later modification. I believe that the stoke-hole, and with it the heating, is an original feature.

second century, but by the late Empire it had been abandoned. A series of seven rooms are grouped round a small open court and a light inner staircase in the north-west corner leads to upper rooms, probably over only one wing of the house. What remains of the paintings on the walls is unpretentious and unimpressive; in no respect does the house suggest social distinction.[1]

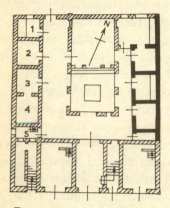

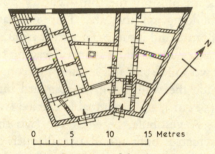

FIG. 17. House of the Round Temple. Rooms 2, 3, 4 were heated from 1 and 5.

FIG. 18. House of the Gorgons.

That the central open court had become the basic element in the independent house is well illustrated by the House of the Gorgons, which lies at the junction of the southern Cardo with the Semita dei Cippi, and was probably built towards the end of the third century.[2] The area available for the house was an irregular trapezoid of awkward shape and dimensions. The architect reduced his plan to some sort of order by building round an open court of very irregular shape. The plan, odd at first sight, in fact resembles that of the Round Temple House, with its main room leading off the court and two series of smaller rooms opening off porticoes on east and west. An inner staircase at the south end of the eastern corridor leads to upper rooms, probably over this wing only. The quality of the mosaics, the spaciousness of the vestibule, and the provision of two rooms, shut off from the rest of the house, for the doorkeeper, suggest that the owner was a man of means. But the house does not occupy the whole block. In the south-east corner are two rooms that have no connexion with the house, and on the Cardo one of the rooms is reserved as a shop, unconnected with the interior.

[1] Reg. I. 14. 3.   [2] Becatti, op. cit. 5; Fig. 18.

Among the independent houses of the second and third centuries there is one interesting exception to the open courtyard principle. The House of the Well has been adapted to the fashions of the late Empire, particularly in the lavish application of marble, but the plan of the original house, typically Hadrianic in its brickwork, has not been seriously modified.[1] It lies some distance south-west of the centre of the town and forms part of a long narrow block between two streets. The house plot is small, approximately 23×8 metres only. The long street front is well windowed in the manner of a contemporary insula. The main entrance, elegantly framed by applied brick columns, is roughly in the centre of the street front on the west; but there was originally a secondary entrance at the back in the north-east corner, later blocked up. The front entrance leads into a spacious hall, off which open three rooms. From the south-east angle of the hall a corridor leads to a small lavatory and, opposite, what was probably the kitchen. The main room lies left and north of the hall, well lighted by three windows on the street front. Two small rooms are entered from the east side of the hall. There was a further room at the north end which had originally two entrances from outside. Later these were blocked, the entrance from the hall was enlarged, and two columns of Giallo Antico gave additional emphasis to what had now become the main living-room of the house.

The façade and the ground plan of this building resemble those of a ground-floor apartment in an insula, but there are no outer stairs leading to upper floors, the walls are light, and there is no trace of an inner staircase. The house seems to be self-contained, and limited to a single floor. More such buildings may be found in the south-east quarters of the city, for in this area the general level of the ruins beneath the soil is conspicuously low.

Though the main tendency in the second century among the rich as well as the poor was to live in apartments in large insulae, independent family houses were still built. They were not confined to any particular quarter, but they are virtually excluded from the areas which were most important for Ostia's trade, between the river and the Via della Foce in the west and between the river and the Decumanus in the east. Some of them, such as the House of the Well and the House of the Round Temple, were no larger than some of the apartments in the insulae; others, such as the House of the Columns, could have accommodated

[1] Ibid. 25; p. 248, Fig. 15.

a substantial household of freedmen and slaves as well as the family; but none of them recall, except by contrast, descriptions of the palaces of the nobility at Rome. One important area, however, outside the town, has barely been touched by excavation. Pliny the Younger describes in detail his Laurentine villa, some five miles from Ostia.[1] It was one of a long line of villas that stretched southwards along the coast. All that can now be seen is a series of mounds, a few isolated walls, and, on the surface, bricks, roof-tiles, and a scatter of marble fragments.[2] Pliny was particularly proud of the elaborate plan that he had imposed on his builder; the form of his villa may not be typical, but we can be certain that these coastal villas were spacious and luxurious and that the main emphasis was on the ground floor. What concerns us more in a social study is to know how many of these coastal villas were occupied not by Ostians but by temporary residents, like Pliny, from Rome. This we may never know, even when the ruins have been excavated.

The domus within the town has been called an independent house. This conveniently distinguishes it from the insula, but it is not a completely accurate description. Even the largest late republican atrium houses had shops flanking their entrances. Shops rented or managed by the owner's freedmen brought good profits, and this arrangement withdrew the main living centre of the house from the street. The houses of the early Empire followed the precedent and incorporated shops in their street fronts; in the late Empire such shops are very rarely found. This may in some cases be a mark of widening social distinctions; but generally it is more easily explained by the decline in the value of shops when Ostia's prosperity declined.

The shift of emphasis from the insula to the domus in the late Empire was one of the most important revelations of the excavations begun in 1938. Earlier excavation, mainly concentrated in the area between the Decumanus and the river, had presented the picture of a general impoverishment from the third century onwards; the new campaign revealed a large number of houses that were handsomely maintained through the fourth century. These houses have been admirably described by Becatti and the generous supply of plans and photographs in his publication makes a detailed description of individual houses here unnecessary.

It is clear at once that the independent houses of the late Empire cannot be schematically reduced to a series of standard plans; what gives

[1] Pliny, *Ep.* ii. 17.   [2] Cf. Fea, *Viaggio*, 63.

them their common character is their style of decoration and the architectural forms that they use within the house. Some of the houses that flourished in the fourth century have a long continuous history behind them. The two houses on the southern Cardo still retain much of their original construction of the first century B.C.; others date from the second century A.D. and have received only minor modifications. But most of the late houses reuse walls of older buildings, and their plan is largely dictated by the serviceable walls that were available. When business declined, shops, industrial premises, and insulae were no longer profitable investments: ground rents probably fell and the rich could afford houses that were not economic in their use of space. But even the rich had no wish to spend money unnecessarily: if they could build their house by reusing old walls rather than by completely demolishing the buildings on their site they did so. Provided that the essential amenities were secured they seem to have been little concerned with the shape or symmetry of their houses. In the House of Amor and Psyche the re-used material is mostly confined to outer walls:[1] in the House of the Dioscuri the plan of the original insula is clearly recoverable.[2]

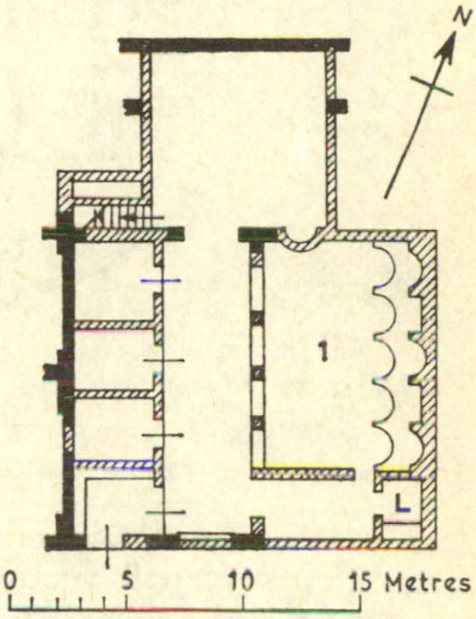

FIG. 19. House of Amor and Psyche. 1. Nymphaeum preceded by garden (Pl. XIV *b*).

In spite of the variety in plan the houses of the fourth century have much in common. They concentrate on the ground floor and when an upper floor is added it is secondary and approached by an inner staircase and not from the street: normally it does not extend over the whole house. Unlike the insula, the late domus draws away from the street, and looks inward rather than outward. The west wall of the House of the Dioscuri originally had a long line of regular windows: when the insula became a domus most of these windows were closed. Similarly on the east side which faced on the street a new peripheral wall was added to give greater privacy to the house. The other main changes in this conversion are the destruction of partition walls in order to provide larger rooms and the addition of a private set of baths. This last feature, however, is not typical, in fact no other example has yet been found;

[1] Becatti, op. cit. 6; Fig. 19. [2] Ibid. 14; Fig. 20.

but it is common for these late houses to have one or more rooms heated by hypocaust and hollow pipes running up the walls. Such heating is never found in the insulae.

But though the rich families of this period seem to be content to use the public establishments for their bathing, they set great store by

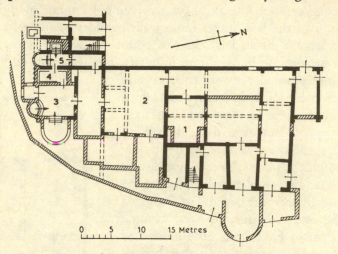

FIG. 20. House of the Dioscuri. The dotted lines indicate some of the walls destroyed when the house was remodelled. 1. Room with Castor and Pollux mosaic. 2. Room with coloured Venus mosaic. 3. Frigidarium. 4. Tepidarium. 5. Caldarium.

a display of water within their homes. In almost all these late houses there is a fountain or nymphaeum, which often assumes an elaborate form. In the small but richly decorated House of Amor and Psyche the nymphaeum and the small garden which precedes it occupy almost as much space as the combined area of the ground-floor rooms.[1] A wide corridor runs down the centre of the building with the main room at its end. On one side of the corridor is a series of four rooms with a light inner staircase at the north end leading to an upper floor over this wing. On the other side is a small room near the entrance leading to a small lavatory: the rest of this side is free of rooms. Behind a series of columns flanking the corridor is an open area probably used as a garden. Behind this, against the back wall, is a series of niches, curved and rectangular alternating, framed by arches in brick carried on small columns. From the foot of the niches marble steps lead down to the ground; water flowed over them. A variant on this scheme can be seen

[1] Fig. 19; Pl. XIV *b*.

in the House of the Nymphaeum, where the nymphaeum is again surprisingly large for the size of the house.[1] There is the same series of alternating curved and rectangular niches but the water flows down into a large marble basin. This strong emphasis on the play of water is possibly a late development. The large nymphaeum in the House of Fortuna Annonaria is not part of the original construction.

Both insula apartments and domus had always emphasized one main living-room by its size and by the quality of its decoration. In the later domus this emphasis is particularly marked. Frequently this room is raised by two steps above the level of the remaining rooms: it is also often emphasized by a pair of columns at its entrance. Originally this room was always rectangular in shape; in the late Empire it sometimes caught the fashion of the curving line. In the House of Fortuna Annonaria, for example, the room has been reconstructed to take an apsidal end;[2] the same change can be seen in the main room of the headquarters of the *seviri Augustales*.

New architectural fashions also appear in the late houses, looking forward to the Byzantine age rather than backward to the classical forms of Greece and Rome. The elaborately cut Corinthian capital which had become the prevailing fashion by the second century is now out of date: in these houses, as in the late restorations of public buildings, the capitals are stylized and schematic. In classical architecture columns were used to carry architrave and frieze; arches were carried on piers of brick or stone. In these houses the column is combined with the brick arch in a pattern that was to become common in the Middle Ages.

But the most striking common feature of these houses is the wealth of marble that they display. Framed marble panels form the dadoes on their walls, and many of their pavements have elaborate *opus sectile* designs in coloured marbles. To what extent this lavish use of marble represents a new fashion we cannot say, for even the oldest private houses changed with the times, but in pavements at least the widespread use of marble probably represents a change. The mosaics that can now be seen in the House of Fortuna Annonaria seem to be contemporary with the original building. Had marble floors been as fashionable in the second century as in the fourth more marble pavements would have been used. In the fourth century marble pavements were not confined to the wealthiest class; some of the most elaborate patterns are found in the smallest houses.

[1] Becatti, op. cit. 10.   [2] Pl. XIV *a*.

From late Republic to late Empire the housing of Ostia reflects the social and economic developments in the town. The large spreading atrium and peristyle houses are contemporary with the dominance of a limited aristocracy. The concentration on well-planned, solidly built insulae in the first half of the second century bears witness to the diffusion of prosperity that followed the building of the imperial harbours and the rise of the middle class. The decline of the insulae and the renewed emphasis on the domus are the results of the decline of trade, and the reopening of the gulf between rich and poor.

13

AGRICULTURE AND TRADE

AGRICULTURE AND FISHING

O<small>F</small> all the workers who contributed to the life of Roman Ostia the primary producers are the least conspicuous in the records that have survived; but they maintained the population before overseas trade developed and after it had collapsed. Even at the height of commercial prosperity, food crops, salt, timber, and fish were not unimportant to the town's economy.

Of Ostian agriculture we learn nothing from inscriptions, very little from literature. But from the nature of the land reasonable inferences can be drawn. There is a sharp distinction in character between the land to the east and to the west of the modern village.[1] To the east the plain between Ostia and Acilia had once probably been a lagoon. On its northern side there is an overlay of alluvium deposited by the Tiber and the land slopes gently down from the river until it reaches a point below sea-level. The southern half of the plain was almost certainly the marshland in which Nero proposed to dump Roman rubble after the great fire of 64.[2] Hydraulic pumps have now restored the land to agriculture, but through the Middle Ages and into the nineteenth century it was the *stagno di Ostia*. No traces of Roman occupation are to be found on this side of the plain. On the north-western edge of marsh were the salt-beds whose legacy can still be seen in the dejected look of crops and weeds.

The northern side of the plain was comparatively good agricultural land. The heavy soil deposited by the Tiber needs drainage in winter and irrigation in summer, but, when well cared for, it can produce grain and provide reasonably good pasture. Fragments of roof-tiles and brick, coarse pottery, occasional blocks of *selce* which do not seem to come from roads, can be seen at scattered points, suggesting

---

[1] p. 9.

[2] Tac. *Ann.* xv. 43. 4: 'ruderi accipiendo Ostiensis paludes destinabat utique naves quae frumentum Tiberi subvectassent onustae rudere decurrerent.' No trace of what should be a very large deposit of rubble has ever been reported. It may have been retained in Rome for use in concrete construction.

farm buildings and perhaps villas. There is other evidence to indicate that there were large estates in this area.

It is here that we should look for Symmachus' Ostian estate. He tells us that it was bordered by the river and he implies that his villa stood on high ground from which he could look down on the shipping going upstream: 'ergo de mei agri specula peregrinarum navium numero transcursus'.[1] The estate must have been large, for he complains of the military exactions on it: 'urget Ostiense praedium nostrum militaris impressio. nos legum inane nomen vocamus'.[2] There are two sites only which satisfy these conditions.

The present farm of Dragone stands on a small eminence overlooking the river, some two and a half miles upstream from Ostia. Roman bricks turned up by the plough in the fields, a large block of marble, fragments of columns, show that this was the site of a villa. More imposing is Dragoncello, less than a mile farther upstream. Occupying the site of ancient Ficana at the north-western end of the Acilia ridge, it stands on a high hill which drops sharply down to the river.[3] Walled within its buildings can be seen fragments of granite columns and Roman brick. Against a wall stands a somewhat dilapidated imperial statue, its head missing and its decorative breastplate pitted with the marks of bullets. This is the more imposing site, though the land is less productive than the farmland of Dragone. It was probably once owned by Symmachus.

There may also be other evidence of two large estates near the Tiber. Constantine is reported to have included in his endowment of the church which he built at Ostia two Ostian estates: 'possessio Quirinis, territorio Hostense, praest(ans) solid(os) trecentos et undecim; possessio Balneolum, territ(orio) Hostense, praest(ans) soli(dos) quadraginta duos'.[4] The name Balneolum survives in a modern agricultural settlement, Bagnoli, north of the Via Ostiensis, some two miles from Acilia.[5] It can be traced back to sixteenth-century maps, on which it seems to cover a large area below the Acilia ridge. It is tempting to associate the other estate, Quirinis, with a brickstamp VARAE QUIRIN which is found

---

[1] Symmachus, *Ep.* iii. 82. 2.

[2] Symmachus, *Ep.* ii. 52. 2; cf. *Ep.* vi. 72: 'Ostiense praedium nostrum frequens pulsat impressio.'

[3] Sites of Dragone and Dragoncello, Fig. 1, p. 112. For the identification of Dragoncello with Ficana, p. 17. Phot. B. Tilly, *Virgil's Latium*, 97.   [4] *Lib. Pont.* i. 184.

[5] G. Tomassetti, 'Vie Ostiense e Laurentine' (*Archivio della R. soc. rom. di storia patria*, xvii–xx, 1897) 100.

at Ostia and seems to have been locally produced.[1] If the association is valid the estate will have been near the river because only from the river clay could bricks be satisfactorily produced. Both these estates provided handsome revenues; they must have been large.

The extent of land available for large-scale farming is uncertain, because we do not know the eastern boundary of Ostia's territory. It is generally supposed that the high ground of Acilia marks the limit, and this is a natural geographical line; but we have no secure evidence, and an extension eastwards, perhaps as far as Malafede, is not impossible.[2] The land on the Romeward side of Acilia is better than the land to the west; there could have been profitable estates here.

To the west of modern Ostia, from Castel Fusano northwards across the Tiber to Trajan's canal, the soil is almost exclusively sand, except where on both its banks the river has deposited a layer of alluvial clay. This light soil becomes very parched in summer, but the phreatic table lies very little beneath the surface and there is no difficulty in providing water for crops. This land was best suited to the production of vegetables and a limited range of fruit. Ostian leeks were famous,[3] and lettuces, cabbages, beans, and turnips, the most popular of Roman vegetables, grow well in the district today. The younger Pliny, whose villa was some five miles from Ostia, tells us that figs and mulberries grew particularly freely,[4] and a chance record of the gluttony of the emperor Clodius Albinus suggests that Ostian melons were a delicacy;[5] they have a good name in the Roman market today. The island between the river and Trajan's canal was a dreary waste until its modern reclamation, but it could be called the garden of Venus in the late Empire,[6] and its proverbial fertility is confirmed by the vegetables and fruit it now produces.

---

[1] Bloch, *Harvard CP*, 56–57 (1947) 88 n. 440; cf. 439.

[2] Ostian boundaries reviewed, Dessau, *CIL* xiv, p. 9; Carcopino, 454–7. The evidence for the eastern boundary is not decisive.

[3] Pliny, *NH* xix. 110: 'laudatissimum (porrum) Aegypto, mox Ostiae atque Ariciae'.

[4] Pliny, *Ep.* ii. 17. 15: 'hortum morus et ficus frequens vestit, quarum arborum illa vel maxime ferax terra est, malignior ceteris'; Pliny, *NH* xv. 97: 'nec alio modo quam pomi magnitudine differunt mora Ostiensia et Tusculana Romae.'

[5] SHA, *Clod. Albin.* 11. 3.

[6] *Cosmographia* (Aethicus), Riese, *Geographi Latini minores*, p. 83, l. 24: 'insula vero quam facit (Tiberis) inter urbis portum et Ostiam civitatem, tantae viriditatis amoenitatisque est, ut neque aestivis mensibus neque hiemalibus pasturae admirabiles herbas dehabeat; ita autem vernali tempore rosa vel ceteris floribus adimpletur, ut pro nimietate sui odoris et floris insula ipsa Libanus almae Veneris nuncupetur.'

Vegetable production, both for the local market and for Rome, was probably the most profitable form of Ostian agriculture, and it was concentrated mainly in the plain south of the town and on the island north of the river. Such market-gardening does not encourage the growth of large estates, and the five parallel public roads that cross the plain helped no doubt to preserve the pattern of smallholdings.[1] Probably most of the workers lived in the town and went out daily to their work.

We should expect a local supply of pigs and poultry. Apicius preserves an elaborate recipe for an Ostian pork delicacy,[2] and there were ample supplies of acorns in the neighbouring woods. Varro has given us a glimpse of a poultry specialist in his allusions to the Ostian villa of M. Seius.[3] This villa was run as a strictly business concern. There were no elaborate paintings, bronzes, and marbles; nor the signs of olive and wine production normally associated with a rustic villa. Seius concentrated on bees and birds, making the maximum profit from the minimum space. Peacocks were his most lucrative line. He used his hens to hatch out the eggs, and then brought on the birds for the market, where they would fetch 50 denarii apiece. After Hortensius had set the example, peacocks became fashionable fare, and there would be eager buyers in the residential villas of the coastline and among the wealthier merchants in Ostia. On an Ostian relief we can see a shopkeeper at her stall catering for less luxurious tastes.[4] Behind her is a line of poultry, plucked and ready for sale; in a pen on the ground are live rabbits.

We can also assume that the local demand for mules and asses for the bakeries and mules and horses for carriages plying between Ostia and Rome was locally supplied and that oxen were bred for the plough, for sacrifice, and, later, for towing river boats upstream. Home-grown meat, which was not an important item in the Roman diet, could be supplemented by wild boar hunted in the Laurentine woods.[5]

Very little of Ostia's territory was suited to grain, and when imports from the provinces became available Ostia, like Rome, relied on them. For olives the soil was even less suited, but vines grow freely today and vineyards are marked in the earliest maps of the district. Ostian wine is

[1] See *Note F*, p. 473. [2] Apicius, *De re coq.* vii. 4. 1.
[3] Varro, *RR* iii. 2. 7–14; 6. 3–5.
[4] *Museo*, 134, phot. p. 53.
[5] Martial ix. 48. 5: 'inter quae rari Laurentem ponderis aprum | misimus: Aetola de Calydone putes.' Horace, *Sat.* ii. 4. 42, is less flattering: 'nam Laurens (aper) malus est, ulvis et arundine pinguis.'

not competitive; its consumption was probably confined to the leanest purses.

In the earliest and latest phases of Ostia's history the small population could have been self-supporting. When population increased with the growth of trade, agriculture played a minor part in the town's economy. In the early Empire the prospects of quicker money from trade may indeed have proved dangerously attractive to land workers, and it is perhaps for that reason that Vespasian, Trajan, and Hadrian settled imperial tenants on the land.[1] But if agricultural prices rose with a rising demand from an expanding population a smallholding should still have brought a good return.

The food which came from the land was supplemented by fish. Fishermen are recorded on only one inscription. Cn. Sentius Felix included among the many guilds of which he was patron the men who caught and sold fish, 'piscatores propolae',[2] and a large shop on the Decumanus near the Macellum can be identified as one of their shops. More revealing, however, are the representations of men fishing in mosaics and the exceptional prominence of realistic fish in mosaics and paintings throughout the town. Nor is this emphasis surprising. In addition to the local demand, which must have been heavy, Ostia's fishermen were in the best position to supply fresh sea fish for the Roman market.[3] Local waters, the younger Pliny tells us, were not well supplied with valuable fish but they yielded excellent soles and prawns.[4] Juvenal supplies a reason for the shortage of the connoisseur's requirements:

> mullus erit domini, quem misit Corsica vel quem
> Tauromenitanae rupes, quando omne peractum est
> et iam defecit nostrum mare, dum gula saevit,
> retibus adsiduis penitus scrutante macello
> proxuma, nec patimur Tyrrhenum crescere piscem.[5]

Ostian waters were being over-fished. Claudius, however, had added variety to the local catch by introducing *scarus* from the Hellespont.

[1] *Liber coloniarum* (Rudorff, 1845) i. 236: 'Ostiensis ager ab impp. Vespasiano, Traiano et Hadriano, in precisuris, in lacineis, et per strigas, colonis eorum est adsignatus, sed postea impp. Verus Antoninus et Commodus aliqua privatis concesserunt.' [2] 5[17].

[3] The same feature is found at Pompeii, where also fishing was an important trade. A. Palombi, 'La fauna marina nei mosaici e nei dipinti Pompeiani', in *Pompeiana* (Napoli, 1950) 425–55.

[4] Pliny, *Ep*. ii. 17. 28: 'mare non sane pretiosis piscibus abundat, soleas tamen et squillas optimas egerit.' [5] Juvenal v. 92–96.

The commander of the Misenum fleet was instructed to scatter them off shore from Campania to Ostia and they were to be given a chance to establish themselves freely. All that were caught in the first five years had to be put back; after that, says Pliny the elder, the supply was plentiful.[1]

Good fish could also be caught in the river. Varro even ranked Tiber fish with Campanian corn and Falernian wine, but Macrobius, who quotes him in the fourth century, regards Varro's encomium as a sign of the austerity of his times.[2] In the Empire the main delicacies came from the sea. The most prized of the river fish was the lupus,[3] similar to if not identical with the bass; eels were common enough, but little appreciated. Grey mullet, sturgeon, and shad are caught in the river today.[4]

While agriculture and fishing could be assumed without any explicit evidence, the production of salt is controversial. In the tradition reflected in Livy the main purpose of the original settlement at Ostia was the production of salt,[5] but in his account of Rome's fourth-century wars with the Etruscans the Roman salt-beds are those of the right bank.[6] That these were the beds from which Rome drew her main supplies in the Empire we know from an inscription discovered there towards the end of the last century, a dedication to the 'genius saccariorum salarior(um) totius urbis camp(i) sal(inarum) Rom(anarum)'.[7] In view of the absence of positive evidence Carcopino and Calza have assumed that the Ostian beds were early abandoned.[8]

There are two main reasons for believing that salt continued to be produced at Ostia through the Roman period. It seems unlikely that the impoverished Ostia of the Middle Ages would have turned to the production of salt if the beds had been abandoned for more than 600 years; medieval production suggests continuity from the Roman period.[9] Moreover, the frequent occurrence of Salinator as a family name on Ostian inscriptions is most easily explained as arising from

[1] Pliny, *NH* ix. 62.   [2] Macrobius iii. 16. 12.

[3] Horace, *Sat*. ii. 2. 31: 'unde datum sentis, lupus hic Tiberinus, an alto | captus hiet? pontisne inter iactatus, an amnis | ostia sub Tusci.'

[4] For Tiber fish, S. A. Smith, *The Tiber and its Tributaries* (London, 1879) 149–61.

[5] Livy i. 33. 9: 'in ore Tiberis Ostia urbs condita, salinae circa factae'; cf. Pliny, *NH* xxxi. 89.   [6] Livy vii. 17. 6.   [7] S 4285.

[8] Carcopino, 477. Calza, *Topografia*, 15, goes farther and thinks that they never existed, but were transferred from the right bank when the fourth-century operations of C. Marcius Rutilus were ascribed to Ancus Marcius (p. 17).

[9] A history of the salt-beds, C. Fea, *Storia delle Saline* (Roma, 1833).

the freedom given to slaves employed in the salt-beds. Similarly public slaves who had been freed by the town took the name Ostiensis, and Hadriaticus derives from the guild of shippers trading in the Adriatic.[1]

When the Ostian salt-beds were originally established they were probably on the edge of a lagoon, but, as the lagoon filled up, it will have been more difficult to maintain communication with the sea. The canal that now carries to sea the water pumped from what was previously marsh until recently carried a Roman bridge over it.[2] The broad canal which the Roman bridge presupposes may represent the widening and deepening of a natural outlet to the sea. The canal was maintained to feed the salt-beds.

The Ostian district had one other important natural resource of which surviving inscriptions tell us nothing. Scattered references in literature suggest that the coastal area was well supplied with timber. The wooded estates of Castel Fusano and Castel Porziano, where pine, oak, and ilex grow freely, recall the coastal woodlands that stretched from Ostia to Antium. Pliny speaks of the neighbouring woods that supplied his fuel;[3] Hortensius' Laurentine villa was in wooded country.[4] Virgil in his *Aeneid* counts timber among the resources of the king of the Latins,[5] and the tragedy of Nisus and Euryalus ends in a wood near Ostia.[6] Much later Procopius, in his account of the war against the Goths in the sixth century, describes the Via Ostiensis as hemmed in by woods.[7] In the early nineteenth century the hillside between Acilia and the coastal plain, now bare, was still covered by trees. They were probably descended from Roman woodlands; for these slopes are wooded in the earliest maps of the district known to us.

In the earliest days of settlement the local timber supply was most needed for construction. When concrete, tufa, and brick became the standard building materials, large supplies of timber were still needed for house fittings, furniture, and fuel. At both Ostia and Portus there were large guilds of boatbuilders, *fabri navales*, who probably drew their main supplies from local woods; for the coastal pine, *pinus pinea*, though comparatively worthless for general building purposes, is good ship timber. But in total volume the timber consumed as fuel, whether in the form of charcoal or wood, probably outweighed all other uses.

---

[1] p. 318.

[2] 126, recording the replacement of a wooden by a stone bridge in A.D. 284; phot. Carcopino, 488. The bridge was destroyed in 1943.   [3] Pliny, *Ep.* ii. 17. 26.

[4] Varro, *RR* iii. 13. 2.   [5] Virg. *Aen.* xi. 134 ff.   [6] Ibid. ix. 378 ff.

[7] Procopius, *Bell. Goth.* i. 26. 13: ὑλώδης τε ἡ ὁδός ἐστι καὶ ἄλλως ἀπημελημένη.

T

The growing number of baths in the second and third centuries must have imposed an increasing strain on diminishing resources and it is possible that by the fourth century the coastal woods were largely stripped. For in the Theodosian Code we find that there is considerable difficulty in maintaining the supply of timber for the baths of Rome.[1] Had adequate supplies still been available near Ostia the imperial government would surely not have been so anxious.

LOCAL TRADE AND INDUSTRY

In the period of prosperity boatbuilding was probably Ostia's most important industry, but small-scale production covered a wide field. The alluvial clay by the river provided the raw material for a modest production of bricks and lamps. Most of the bricks used in Ostian buildings came from the same clays near Rome that supplied the capital, but some stamps are confined to Ostia and seem to represent local production.[2] Among the owners are the two sons (or grandsons) of M. Petronius Mamertinus, praetorian prefect under Antoninus Pius;[3] among the foremen in charge is Egrilius Eutyches,[4] a freedman or the descendant of a freedman of the Egrilii, the most widespread family in Ostia. More direct evidence of small-scale local production is a deposit of roof tiles by a furnace towards the west end of the excavations.[5]

The production of lamps was also limited, and for the same reason, that the greater part of the soil being sandy was unsuited to the purpose. Though a very large number of lamps has been added by the new excavations to those already published, the general picture does not seem to have been modified. Most of them came from Rome or other popular centres of manufacture. There is, however, one local workshop that seems to have had a large output in the Severan period. The stamp of Annius Serapidorus is by far the commonest among those found in

---

[1] Fuel problems, *Cod. Theod.* xiii. 5. 13; Symmachus, *Rel.* 44: 'tunc urgente defectu navicularios aeque lignorum obnoxios functioni ad parem sollicitudinem vocare coeperunt' (*sc. mancipes salinarum*, who were responsible for providing fuel for the baths). *Cod. Theod.* xiii. 5. 10 (364): 'navicularios Africanos qui idonea publicis dispositionibus ac necessitatibus ligna convectant, privilegiis concessis dudum rursus augemus', has been taken (Waltzing, *Les Corporations professionelles*, iii. 55) to mean that African shippers were required to provide timber for the Roman baths. This, if true, would be a stronger indication of the shortage of Ostian supplies, but the reference is perhaps more probably to timber for construction.

[2] *CIL* xv. 2156–223; Bloch, *Harvard CP*, 56–57 (1947) 83 nn. 409–44.

[3] Bloch, art. cit. 84 n. 411.

[4] S 5308[20].   [5] Reg. i. 17. 1, near the Baths of Mithras.

Ostia, occurring on more than one hundred lamps and covering a variety of designs, both Christian and pagan.[1] With this workshop seem to be associated two others with a much smaller output.[2] Among imported lamps there are several examples of an African fabric.[3]

The plain coarse pottery used by the poorer people and the wide range of containers used in kitchen and larder may have been largely produced locally but the better-class ware of the middle and upper classes was imported. The earliest imports came from Athens and production centres in Etruria and perhaps south Italy, which were influenced by Attic models.[4] In the third and second centuries Italian black-glazed ware dominated the market. Soon after the end of the Republic it was superseded by the red-glazed decorated ware from the potteries of Arretium and other Italian centres. But the Arretine industry, in spite of its large output and wide distribution, had a brief life. Even before the Flavian period the less refined products of Gallic potteries had virtually won the market.[5] Glass also had to be imported: at first a luxury for the few, it became increasingly popular as Ostian prosperity increased.

The import of ready-made articles was, however, exceptional. A very large proportion of the goods that were sold in the shops were made on the premises. A terra-cotta relief from a tomb in the Isola Sacra cemetery shows a shopkeeper with a wide range of tools for sale: on the same relief a craftsman is shown making the tools.[6] This is a fair illustration of typical Roman practice, for production and distribution were normally in the same hands. Another Ostian relief shows a shoe-maker at work and suggests that he sold the shoes he made.[7] In a shop in front of the theatre was found satin spar that had been imported from Britain, but not yet made up into jewellery.[8] On inscriptions we find a metalworker, *vascularius*,[9] and a purple dyer, *purpurarius*.[10] They probably carried on their trades in small rooms behind shops such as can be seen lining most of the streets of the town. Even the lead pipes which

---

[1] *CIL* xv. 6296.   [2] Ibid. 6550, 6553 with Dressel's note on 6296.

[3] Ibid. 6643, from the factory of the Pullaeni. These lamps are widely distributed outside Africa, *Economic Survey of Ancient Rome*, iv. 61.

[4] *Topografia*, tav. xxiii. For the Attic fragments, p. 471.

[5] The increasing dominance of Gallic ware will become apparent when the detailed results of the 1938–42 excavations are published.

[6] Calza, *Necropoli*, 252, fig. 150; Pl. xxvii *a*.

[7] H. Blümner, *Technologie und Terminologie der Gewerbe und Künste bei Griechen und Römern*, i². 288 f., fig. 94.   [8] *NS* 1913, 393 f.   [9] 467.   [10] 473.

distributed the water supply from the aqueduct to public and private buildings throughout the town were not mass produced. That many of them were made locally is clear from their stamps, which, when fully preserved, include the name of the owner of the property which the pipe serves, the workshop (*officina*) and the *plumbarius*, the individual craftsman who made the pipe. Nearly half of those preserved come from imperial workshops, probably in Rome, but on the rest the craftsmen have familiar Ostian names, such as A. Larcius Eutyches, L. Caecilius Maximus, C. Ostiensis Felicissimus. Among the Hadrianic pipe-makers are C. Nasennius Musaeus[1] and C. Nasennius Fortunatus;[2] C. Nasennius Felix follows in the early Severan period;[3] C. Nasennius Thalamus, also a *plumbarius*, cannot be dated;[4] a Nasennius Fortunatus is recorded as the owner of a workshop in the joint reigns of Septimius Severus and Caracalla and under Alexander Severus.[5] The Nasennii were among the most prominent families of the local aristocracy in the second century; a freedman branch of the family probably carried on the manufacture of lead pipes over several generations. But they did not monopolize the trade; other workshops are recorded, and two were owned by women.[6]

Nor are there many clear signs of large-scale industry in the excavated area of the town. Nearly all the units are comparatively small and, since most of the buildings had been stripped bare before excavation, it is rarely possible to tell which shops were confined to the retail trade and which combined production with sale; for the typical form of shop suited either use. The large number of these shops is one of the most striking features of Ostia. They line nearly all the streets and cover a much larger proportion of the town than at Pompeii. This is partly because Ostia's population was much more concentrated, partly because the traders and ships' crews that came to the harbours provided good business for shopkeepers. They needed supplies for the homeward voyage.

The commonest form of shop resembles the Pompeian type and can still be seen in many Italian towns today. On the street is a large room in which the goods are stacked and sold; behind it there is a smaller room which can be used for production or for extra accommodation. In the corner a wooden staircase leads up to a small mezzanine

---

[1] *S* 5309[12, 13].   [2] Barbieri, 'Fistole inedite', *NS* 1953, 174, n. 40.
[3] Ibid. 159, n. 10.   [4] Ibid. 175, n. 41.   [5] Ibid. 160, nn. 12, 14.
[6] Ibid. 172, n. 38; 174, n. 39.

floor where the family live. The shop front during the day is completely open: at night wooden shutters are run across. There are minor variants. Some shops have no back room and were perhaps confined to retail trade; others have a back room as large as the shop, suggesting larger-scale production. Not all shops have living quarters above them.[1]

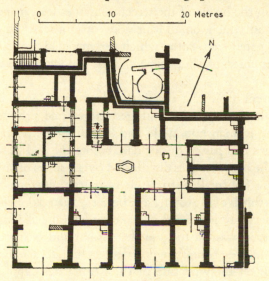

FIG. 21. Shopping market ('House of the Lararium').

Normally shops are set in rows along the frontage of public buildings and apartment blocks. Occasionally they are grouped together in independent architectural units. Such shopping bazaars are not found in Pompeii, but the conception of a self-contained block of shops is realized at Ferentinum and Tibur in the late Republic[2] and finds a more elaborate development at Rome by Trajan's Forum. The first example known at Ostia lies on the south side of the Via della Foce.[3] A passage from the street leads into a long open courtyard flanked by eight shops on either side. The east wall dates back to the first half of the second century B.C., but the earliest internal walls are in mature reticulate.[4]

[1] A catalogue and type-analysis of Ostian shops, G. Girri, 'La taberna nel quadro urbanistico e sociale di Ostia' (Ist. di arch., Milano, Tesi di laurea I, 1956). The total number of shops listed is 806.

[2] Boethius and Carlgren, *Acta arch.* 3 (1932) 181.

[3] Reg. iii. 1. 7; Becatti, *Topografia*, 110.

[4] The east wall is one of the earliest examples of *opus incertum*, faced with large irregular blocks, bound by very weak mortar. It was probably connected with other walls to the east.

This shopping market was probably established under Augustus, incorporating an earlier wall. It was substantially restored under Trajan. Under Hadrian the same principle was applied with greater refinement in the so-called House of the Lararium, built at the angle of the Decumanus and the Via degli Horrea Epagathiana.[1] Here too the shops are removed from the bustle of the streets. Passages lead from both streets into a court, off which, on all four sides, open a series of ten shops. A niche in variegated terra-cotta, which perhaps held figures of the *Lares* of this community of shopkeepers, adds colour and variety to the design.

Very different from the shops that have been considered are the premises of the bakers, which suggest large-scale production. In the early days the Roman housewife had baked her own bread at home; domestic ovens had passed out of date before the end of the Republic. At Pompeii the bread trade is distributed over a series of small establishments catering for small districts; at Ostia the units are much larger. Though two-thirds of the town have been excavated only two buildings that can be securely identified as bakeries have been found. The first to be discovered was on the Via dei Molini and occupies an area of 9,950 square metres, roughly equivalent in size to six normal shops.[2] The second is on the west side of the Semita dei Cippi, and its area is even larger.[3] Both probably date from Hadrian's reign and in both all the processes of bread-making were carried through on the same premises, from the grinding of the corn to the baking of the loaf. It is probable that one of these bakeries had a regular contract to supply the *vigiles*; both perhaps distributed their output through retailers. In the Severan period the Ostian bakers claimed privileges that had been granted to the bakers at Rome,[4] which might suggest that they were also supplying the Roman market. The distribution at Rome of *panis Ostiensis* in the fourth century implies the practice then.[5]

There are also signs of a wholesale trade in wine and oil. Immediately below the museum a large number of earthenware jars can be seen sunk in the ground.[6] The jars are over 4 feet high and their capacity is

---

[1] Calza, *NS* 1923, 183; Fig. 21.   [2] Id. *NS* 1915, 242.

[3] The date of this bakery (i. 13. 4) is not attested by brickstamps. Becatti, *Topografia*, 125, suggests a Trajanic date. The framing walls are probably Trajanic, but the internal walls associated with the bakery seem to be Hadrianic or later.

[4] *Frag. Vat.* 234 (Ulpian): 'sed Ostienses pistores non excusantur, ut Filumeniano imperator noster (Caracalla) cum patre (Septimio Severo) rescripsit.'

[5] *Cod. Theod.* xiv. 19. 1.   [6] *NS* 1903, 201.

marked on the lip. The size varies slightly but averages 40 amphorae, which is equivalent to some 230 gallons. Three other such deposits have been found, and the largest of them has over 100 jars, providing a total capacity of more than 20,000 gallons.[1] These *dolia defossa*[2] were not used for grain, which was stored on raised floors in buildings specially designed for the purpose. They contained wine or oil, which was stored in sunken jars to preserve a cool and even temperature.

These Ostian deposits were not serving Rome. Had they been intended for the temporary storage of Roman supplies they would have been near the Tiber bank, whereas one of them is more than half a mile from the river,[3] and the largest is also on the south side of the Decumanus. Almost certainly they are wholesale stores which sold to retailers, inns, and bars. Roman supplies remained in the containers in which they had been shipped until they could be carried up to Rome.

The business of the oil merchant, *olearius*, is well illustrated in the Insula Anniana. On the face of this Hadrianic block are three inscribed bipedales: 'omnia felicia Anni'. On two further bipedales reliefs have been roughly cut. One shows a vessel in full sail, loaded with jars of oil; the other shows a man standing between large jars, representing the oil arrived and stored for sale; there was a third, now lost. Next to the living quarters of the block is a large deposit of sunken jars. Perhaps the original Hadrianic owner of this block imported oil in his own ships and sold it to the trade. Inscriptions suggest that the wine trade was organized on the same general lines.

The wine trade at Ostia was centred in the Forum Vinarium and importers and merchants shared a common guild, 'corpus splendidissimum importantium et negotiantium vinariorum', whose members were concerned with the import and sale, probably in bulk, of wine. A dedication to the *genius* of the guild is made by an auctioneer, 'praeco vinorum';[4] we may infer regular auctions in the wine market. Some of the wine that was handled here came from the east coast of Italy and was probably carried by Ostian shippers. An inscription, now in the Vatican,

---

[1] The largest deposit, on the south side of the eastern Decumanus (v. 11. 5), next to the Horrea of Artemis; another next to the Insula of Annius (iii. 14, 3). The third was excavated at the end of the eighteenth century, near the Horrea of the Measurers, and is now overgrown, Paschetto, 344; Carcopino, *Mélanges*, 29 (1909) 360–4.

[2] For the term cf. *Dig.* xviii. 1. 76: 'dolia in horreis defossa si non sunt nominatim venditione excepta, horreorum venditioni cessisse videri.' [3] Reg. iii. 14, 3.

[4] Bloch, 2: 'genio corporis splendidissimi importantium et negotiantium vinariorum C. Septimius Quietus praeco vinorum d(ono) d(edit).'

records a wine merchant who was also a shipper in the Adriatic; 'nego-
tianti vinario item naviculario, cur(atori) corporis maris Hadriatici';[1]
and that the Adriatic shippers were an Ostian guild is confirmed by
other evidence. Cn. Sentius Felix, the wealthy duovir and patron of
many guilds at Ostia in the late first and early second century, was
'gratis adlect(us) inter navicula(rios) maris Hadriatici'; he was also a
member of a guild in the wine market, 'ad quadrigam fori vinari'.[2] The
family name Hadriaticus in Ostian inscriptions points the same way; it
was the name given to guild slaves when they were freed.[3]

Further confirmation was added when in 1953 a magnificently
inscribed tombstone of another officer of the guild was found at Ostia.
A. Caedicius Successus, a president of the *seviri Augustales* was 'curator
nauclerorum maris Hadriatici, idem quinquennalis'.[4] His wife's name
is Pontulena Pyrallis, and the family names of both husband and wife
are also found in an inscription in the cloisters of the Basilica of St.
Paul on the Via Ostiensis.[5] The A. Caedicius of this inscription was
married to Pontulena Iusta; his trade is not recorded, but the size of his
inscription shows that he was wealthy. Since many of the inscriptions
from St. Paul's come from Ostia we may suspect that we have in the
two Caedicii Ostian relations marrying into the same family. The
family name Pontulenus is not common, but names ending in 'enus'
are most widely distributed on both sides of the Adriatic.[6] It is probable
that the marriage connexion was made in the course of trade.

There is no evidence for this Adriatic trade before the second century
A.D., but Ostia had her own shippers early. The first record of them is
an Augustan dedication to the Roman quaestor at Ostia by the 'navi-
culariei Ostienses',[7] but, apart from the Adriatic trade, there is not yet
any evidence of their activities in the second century and later.

The pattern of the grain trade was probably similar. A large proportion of Ostia's storage capacity was used to hold reserves for Rome, but
the so-called Horrea of Hortensius, being on the far side of the Decumanus from the river, are ill sited for corn that was to be reloaded on to
river vessels; more probably they were built for Ostia's own needs. In
them the importers could store their stock.

---

[1] *CIL* vi. 9682 (origin uncertain, probably Ostian). For wine from this area, *CIL* vi.
1101: 'negotiantes vini supernat(is) et Arimin(ensis).'

[2] 5[8-9].   [3] p. 318.   [4] *Fasti arch.* 8 (1956) p. 272 n. 3680.

[5] *CIL* vi. 13876. The cognomen is lost.

[6] Indices *CIL* iii. v. ix. Pontuleni are recorded at Asculum in Picenum, *CIL* ix. 5232;
EE viii. 219.   [7] 3603; Bloch, 32.

The middlemen in the corn trade were the *mercatores frumentarii*, and the few inscriptions that record members of their guild suggest that they were men of substance. P. Aufidius Fortis, a life president, rose to the duovirate and was patron of the colony in the middle of the second century. He was also a member of the council at Hippo Regius in Africa, and it has been suggested above that this honour was associated with his trade visits to negotiate the purchase and shipment of corn.[1] He was also patron of the corn measurers and of the divers; a corn merchant would need the goodwill of the measurers; divers would be useful when salvage was needed. P. Aufidius Faustianus and P. Aufidius Epictetus, who also held office in the guild, were almost certainly his freedmen launched in business by their patron and owing their rise in the guild to his influence. Two other corn merchants are recorded. M. Iunius Faustus became both duovir and *flamen Romae et Augusti*.[2] He was also patron of the guild of curators of sea shipping and was honoured with a statue by the shippers of Africa and Sardinia, both corn-exporting provinces.[3] M. Caerellius Iazemis was president of the bakers' guild and a *codicarius*; he made a dedication to Hercules Invictus at Tibur.[4]

There may also be evidence of middlemen in the Horrea Epagathiana et Epaphroditiana. This large building is presumably a business investment by two enterprising freedmen. Its name, recorded above the monumental entrance, suggests that it is a warehouse for the storage of goods; and it is consistent with this purpose that the entry should have an inner as well as an outer door and that the stairways leading to upper floors should be sealed off by separate doors. The general dispositions of the building seem to be dictated by a desire for security. There are sixteen large rooms on the ground floor and at least two floors above.[5] Perhaps traders who bought in bulk could store their goods here before distribution to retailers.

Less ambitious *horrea* are scattered through the town. In places there is little to distinguish them from shopping markets such as the House of the Lararium. Some ten or twelve rooms are grouped round an open court, normally paved with *opus spicatum*; but the rooms do not have the wide-open doorways of shops and they are lit by slit windows. Good examples may be seen on the west side of the Semita dei Cippi and on the north side of the Cardo degli Aurighi. They were probably used for the storage of goods other than corn, oil, or wine, and operated by wholesalers. When trade declined some of these small *horrea* were

---

[1] **10**, p. 203.   [2] 161.   [3] 4142.   [4] 4234.   [5] Becatti, *NS* 1940, 32; Pl. xv *a*.

no longer needed for storage. One set, east of the Baths of the Six Columns, was converted to other use, probably in the Severan period, and a Mithraeum was installed in one of the rooms; in the fourth century a diminutive set of baths was carved out of the south-west corner of the *horrea* at the south end of the Via della Trinacria.

Such enterprises as the building of the Horrea Epagathiana required a considerable outlay of capital. We may suspect that the bankers played an important part in the development of Ostia. Unfortunately the inscriptions which record bankers, *coactores argentarii*, tell us nothing of their activities.[1] We should like to know how they invested the money deposited with them, to what extent they supplied capital for the rising middle class, and what rates they charged on their loans. It is doubtful, in view of the limited extent and general character of Ostian territory, whether much money was invested in land. Trade and building must have supplied the main demand for loans, and the banker's main hope of making his own money grow was directly or indirectly through trade.

During the second century there seems to have been no need for money to lie idle. When benefactors leave endowments to the town or to their guild they can specify the rate of interest to be realized on the capital and assume that it will accrue regularly and indefinitely.[2] The banker's business probably became much more hazardous in the economic decline of the third century.

OSTIA'S SERVICES TO ROME

By the second century Ostia was importing for her own population considerable quantities of corn, oil and wine, pottery, glass, and other finished products; and a wide range of raw materials for her craftsmen. This she could never have afforded to do on the resources of her own territory. Ostian prosperity depended primarily on the services she rendered to Rome.

In the complex structure of Rome's trade Ostia had three main functions to fulfil. She had to provide harbour facilities for Rome's imports from overseas; she had to provide storage capacity for Roman supplies that could not be immediately sent upstream; and, sooner or later, she had to send to Rome such cargoes as could not be carried in the ships

---

[1] Most are very fragmentary: 470, S 4644, 4659, 4967, 5197; Bloch, 53, a freedman Egrilius, president of the *seviri Augustales*. Cn. Sentius Felix is president of the *argentarii* (5¹¹), probably bankers. 405, a *stipulator argentarius* (for the trade, *Dig*. xlv. 1. 41; Suet. *Vit*. 14. 2; *Diz. epigr.* i. 660).   [2] 326 (12%), 353 (5%), 367 (6%).

that brought them to port. Ostia also was a more convenient centre than Rome for much of the business that had to be negotiated with shippers; for the larger merchantmen turned about at the harbour and could not make the river passage to Rome.

Before the building of the imperial harbours the most crucial problem was the difficulty of entry to the river mouth, owing to the silt carried down by the river. Local pilots were needed to guide incoming ships through the sandy shallows, and the larger ships had to unload part of their cargoes before they could enter harbour. In calm weather this need not have caused great difficulty, but the owners of tenders may not have been so ready to risk their boats in heavy seas. When Fiumicino had become the normal port of entry to the Tiber we find the same difficulties repeated. In 1826 twenty-seven ships' captains from Sardinia and other states sent a protest to the Pope because the river boats would not come out to sea to do their duty.[1] Earlier Sardinian ships' captains had probably made similar protests to the Roman quaestor at Ostia. Doubtless shipwrecks were not uncommon, both outside the river mouth and even in the river. An inscription records divers, *urinatores*,[2] presumably engaged on salvage work.[3]

When Trajan had added his inner basin to the Claudian harbour this main problem was solved. Even the great Alexandrian merchantmen could anchor in safety in the inner harbour. But the old river harbour was not completely neglected. The presence at Ostia of an office of the Spanish and Gallic export tax, 'statio Antonin(iana) XXXX Galliarum et Hispaniarum', suggests that goods from Gaul and Spain were still coming in at the Tiber mouth.[4] There may have been a lighthouse to guide them. Tor Boacciana in its present form is medieval, but its nucleus is Roman, of the late second or early third century, and its shape seems to have remained unchanged. There is no evidence of Roman remains beyond it; both shape and site suggest that it was a lighthouse or watch-tower.

It would have been impossible to send at once to Rome all the cargoes that arrived in harbour. Lucian describes an Alexandrian merchantman engaged in the transport of corn.[5] It was 150 feet long, 45 feet deep and

---

[1] G. B. Rasi, *Sul Tevere e sua navigazione da Fiumicino a Roma* (Roma, 1827) 70.

[2] 10.

[3] Cf. *Dig.* xiv. 2. 4. 1: 'sed si navis . . . in alio loco summersa est et aliquorum mercatorum merces per urinatores extractae sunt . . .'.

[4] S 4708; S. J. de Laet, *Portorium* (Bruges, 1949) 161.

[5] Lucian, *Navigium*, 5–6; L. Casson, 'The Isis and her voyage', *TAPA* 81 (1950) 43.

wide; and had enough corn on board to supply the whole of Attica for a year. When a fleet of such vessels[1] arrived in harbour the only practical solution was to store the corn in granaries and dispatch it to Rome by river boats over a period. It was also a wise insurance to spread Rome's reserves.

The most individual characteristic of a granary is the raising of the floor on low brick walls to keep the grain dry. By this criterion four large *horrea* can be identified as granaries in Ostia,[2] and the emblems of *modius* and measuring rod over the entrance to another building that has been largely destroyed by the river is a reasonably certain indication of a fifth.[3] One of these, the so-called Horrea of Hortensius, lies on the south side of the Decumanus, opposite the theatre, and may have served local rather than Roman needs.*The remainder are near the river. By the imperial harbours warehouses occupy an even larger proportion of the area than at Ostia. Trajan's inner basin is almost completely surrounded by them, but until they are excavated it remains uncertain how they were distributed between corn and other goods.

Three of the Ostian granaries conform to a common plan. The storage-rooms open off the four sides of a colonnade or portico which surrounds a large open area. Extra capacity is provided by adding a second story, repeating the ground-floor plan. Two at least of the *horrea* by Trajan's harbour are planned rather differently. The storage-rooms are built back to back in a series of blocks; the open area between the blocks is restricted.[4] A similar plan is used in the last of the Ostian granaries known to us, built towards the end of the second century.[5] This distribution of rooms makes more economic use of space; for that reason it probably superseded the earlier type.

The storage capacity for corn in Ostia's granaries was more than was needed for her own population, and part of it must have been designed to hold a reserve for Rome. That Roman corn should be stored in Ostia during the Republic and early Empire is natural; we should, however, have expected that, when the imperial harbours had been built, Rome's supply would be concentrated by the harbours. But the storage capacity of Ostia was substantially increased in the second century in spite of the addition of new *horrea* round Trajan's harbour. Two of the granaries were built shortly after the completion of the new harbour;[6] a third was

---

[1] For the volume, Casson, art. cit. 51; St. Paul's ship was comparable, Acts xxvii. 37–38.   [2] Reg. i. 8. 2; ii. 2. 7; ii. 9. 7; v. 12. 1.   [3] i. 7. 2; Paschetto, 314.
[4] *NS* 1925, 58; Lugli, *Porto*, 83.   [5] Fig. 23.   [6] i. 7. 2 and i. 8. 2.

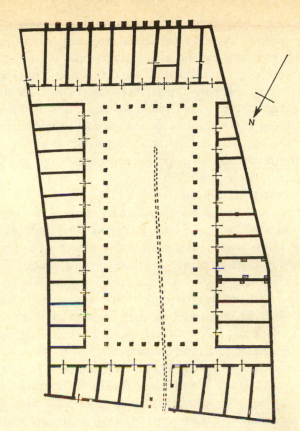

FIG. 22. Horrea of Hortensius.

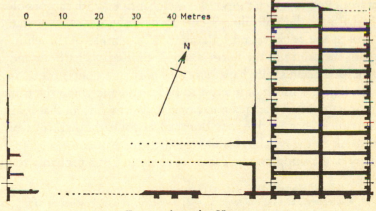

FIG. 23. Antonine Horrea.

rebuilt to double its capacity later in the second century,[1] and a fourth, probably the largest of the series, was added, probably under Commodus. The tremendous increase in the total storage capacity of Ostia and the harbours may in part be explained by the decision to bring the Alexandrian corn fleet to the new Ostian harbour rather than to Puteoli. Reserves that had previously been held at Puteoli now had to be stored by Trajan's harbour. It would seem uneconomic to transfer corn from the harbour to Ostia before dispatch to Rome, but this may have been done; it is more probable that the Roman corn stored in Ostia came in smaller vessels direct to the Tiber.

The efficient organization of the corn traffic depended in large part on the measurers, *mensores frumentarii*, who formed one of the most important guilds at Ostia, and later at Portus. The guild was divided into three sections, whose titles presumably reflect their different but related functions: there were *acceptores, adiutores, nauticarii*.[2] These titles are not self-explanatory, but we can roughly guess the division of responsibility. Cargoes had to be checked on arrival (? *acceptores*); quantities had to be registered as they entered and left the *horrea* (? *adiutores*); and further control was needed when river boats were loaded for the passage to Rome (? *nauticarii*).

Not all the *horrea* at Ostia and Portus were intended for grain. Temporary storage had also to be provided for oil and wine and other goods that arrived in bulk. In Ostia there is no sign that dock space was distributed according to commodities. The granaries are scattered and not concentrated. It is possible that the arrangements by Trajan's harbour were more deliberately planned, for in a well-known votive relief from Portus which shows two merchantmen with cargoes of wine in the harbour the unloading seems to be associated with a statue of Bacchus in the background.[3] Remains of a temple of Bacchus were found in the centre of the north-east side of Trajan's harbour and in it a statue of Bacchus.[4] Perhaps *horrea vinaria* were concentrated in this quarter. There is much of interest to be learnt concerning the planning of the storage when the area is excavated. Meanwhile all that is known for certain is that marble was dumped beyond the harbours on the south bank of the canal to await reloading for Rome.[5]

Many of the shippers who came regularly to Ostia probably found it

---

[1] Grandi Horrea, *NS* 1921, 381.

[2] *acceptores*, 2. 154; *adiutores*, 2. 154; *nauticarii*, 2. 289. Paschetto, 217.

[3] Pl. xx.   [4] p. 165.   [5] p. 167.

more convenient to do business there than at Rome and it is probable that Roman merchants came to meet them. In the Forum Vinarium the wine importers from Rome seem to do their business side by side with Ostian importers. An inscription records a *corpus vinariorum urb*(*anorum*) *et Ost*(*iensium*)[1] and Cn. Sentius Felix, whose career is centred in Ostia, is described as 'patronus negotiator(um) ab urbe'.[2]

A much more impressive illustration of such business is the Piazzale delle Corporazioni behind the theatre.[3] The large double colonnade is contemporary with the original construction of the theatre under Augustus. In its present form sixty-one small rooms open off the colonnade, and on the pavement in front of most of them mosaics illustrate the occupation of the owners.[4] One of these mosaics has the inscription 'stat(io) Sabratensium' and depicts an elephant.[5] A large proportion of the others illustrate the corn trade, and among the overseas communities represented Africa is the most conspicuous province.

But these mosaics are not set at the original level. Beneath them is an earlier series of which it has been possible to examine only four.[6] While the later mosaics mostly point clearly to overseas trade and especially the corn trade, the earlier mosaics are much more ambiguous. Three have designs which have no specific commercial association—Minerva and stag, a victor in the games, two Nereids; only the fourth is explicit. It has the letters 'S.R.' and probably depicts the instruments used by the *stuppatores restiones* in making rope.[7]

There has been much dispute concerning the original and later function of this public colonnade. Calza held that the traders and shippers who were most important for the supplies of Rome were concentrated here by imperial authority under Augustus, and that this was one of the main centres of official control, its function remaining virtually unchanged into the third century.[8] Rostovtzeff accepted this view and saw in the grouping of overseas shippers an early illustration of close imperial control.[9]

---

[1] 318; possibly also Bloch, *Epigraphica*, i (1938) 38: '[colleg]ium vinariorum impo[r-tatorum urb. et Ost.?]'.   [2] 5[11].

[3] Calza, *BC* 43 (1915) 178.   [4] A complete list, Calza, art. cit. 187; *S* 4549.

[5] *S* 4549[14]; Pl. XXIII *a*.   [6] *NS* 1914, 72 f., 98 f.

[7] *S* 4549[58], *NS* 1914, 72. The design of the mosaic rules out the suggestion (*Economic Survey*, iv. 63) that the letters represent 'statio Rusicadensium, Ruspinensium, or Regiensium'.   [8] Calza, art. cit. 196–206.

[9] Rostovtzeff, *Social and Economic History of the Roman Empire*[2] (1957) 159 and 607 f., n. 22.

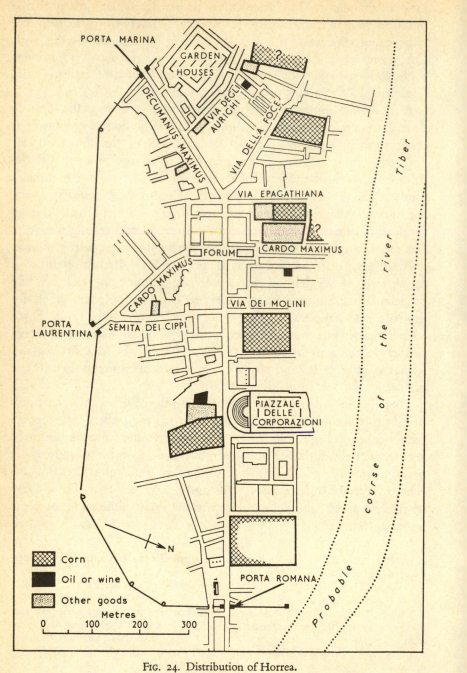

PORTA MARINA

GARDEN HOUSES

VIA DEGLI AURIGHI

VIA DELLA FOCE

DECUMANUS MAXIMUS

VIA EPAGATHIANA

FORUM

CARDO MAXIMUS

CARDO MAXIMUS

VIA DEI MOLINI

PORTA
LAURENTINA

SEMITA DEI CIPPI

PIAZZALE
DELLE
CORPORAZIONI

Tiber

Probable   course   of   the   river

N

Corn

Oil or wine

Other goods

Metres

0   100   200   300

PORTA ROMANA

FIG. 24. Distribution of Horrea.

The balance of argument has turned against this view, because it is not consistent with the rest of our evidence concerning the relation of traders and government in the early Empire. That evidence suggests that the control of shippers and trade developed slowly and only became rigorous in the Severan period and afterwards. Tenney Frank has emphasized that there is no evidence for the concentration of shippers in this colonnade until the raising of the level, which Calza has dated to the end of the second century, when the theatre was rebuilt. He concludes that not until then were the *stationes* designed as centres of control. Previously, he suggests, these were offices available to any who wished to buy the space.[1]

A more extreme reaction from Calza's view is advocated by Van Berchem. He suggests that the colonnade had originally no commercial significance, and was closely associated in function with the theatre. The small rooms off the colonnade were taken by guilds and other groups whose members congregated in them during theatre intervals. Perhaps they also paid for theatre performances.[2]

For this purpose the small rooms seem to be singularly ill fitted, and unless the colonnade had some ulterior function it is unlikely that it would have been so large. One of the earliest mosaics refers to the *stuppatores restiones*. It is likely that these spaces were rented to local trading groups and any others who wished to take space here. Ownership probably changed frequently; the rope-sellers occupy a different position in the colonnade when the level is raised.[3]

There is also now evidence that overseas shippers were represented here long before the end of the second century. A marble pediment, with the inscription 'naviculari Africani', was recently found on the east side of the colonnade.[4] The lettering is extremely good and cannot be later than the reign of Hadrian. Moreover, the chronology of the changes in the Piazzale as generally accepted from Calza is too schematic. It is tempting to associate the building of the temple in the centre of the gardens, and the raising of the level of the colonnade, with the rebuilding of the theatre, but a study of the various styles of construction suggests that the building history of the Piazzale was more complex.

[1] Tenney Frank, 'Notes on Roman commerce', *JRS* 27 (1937) 72–79, esp. 74 f. See also M. R. Étienne, 'Les amphores du Testaccio au IIIᵉ siècle', *Mélanges*, 61 (1949) 151.
[2] D. Van Berchem, *Les Distributions de blé et d'argent à la plèbe romaine sous l'empire* (Geneva, 1936) 111. [3] S 4549¹.
[4] Bloch, 44. This pediment is too heavy for the lightly built *stationes*. It may have been set up over the doorway to the rooms on the eastern side.

U

The brickwork of the central temple bears no similarity to that of the new theatre, nor to any other buildings in Ostia that can be dated to the reign of Commodus or later. It has every characteristic of a late Flavian building, including late first-century brickstamps, and was probably built under Domitian.[1] A series of large rooms behind the colonnade on the east side, but accessible from it, is of similar style and probably of approximately similar date. Nor are all the mosaics of the higher level contemporary. There is a considerable difference in the size of the tesserae used, a fair indication of a difference in date. The mosaics of the north-west corner may well be much earlier than Commodus.

We may even question the inference that in its later form this colonnade was under strict imperial control. It is perhaps not without significance that the authority for erecting statues in the public gardens round the temple was given not by the procurator, but by the local council.[2] It is also clear that, though the corn trade is extremely prominent, other trades are also represented, and among them some which would hardly seem to represent services vital to Rome.

One such *statio* is occupied by the tanners of Ostia and the harbours, *corpus pellion(um) Ost(iensium) et Porte(nsium)*.[3] Next to them on one side are the rope-sellers; on the other *navicularii lignarii*, timber shippers, who may have been catering for the Roman or Ostian market or both. Gaul is represented by Narbo[4] and probably also by Arelate, symbolized by a pontoon bridge over a river, which carries the combined flow of three smaller rivers, the confluence of the Rhône;[5] neither town was concerned primarily with the export of corn. The letters 'M.C.' are found in a mosaic between two jars of wine and date palms;[6] they may represent Mauretania Caesariensis, but there is no hint of corn. The Alexandrini of another *statio*[7] could be concerned with a wide range of goods other than corn.

It is true that the two Sardinian communities of Carales and Turris are corn exporters and the shippers of Carales add corn measures with ships in their mosaic to illustrate their business.[8] Most of the African towns represented are also concerned with corn. They include Carthage,

---

[1] p. 65.

[2] 'l(ocus) d(atus) d(ecurionum) d(ecreto) p(ublice)' on statue bases, e.g. 172, 4140. The point is emphasized by Van Berchem, op. cit. 113. But see Addenda.

[3] S 4549[2].   [4] S 4549[32].

[5] NS 1914, 288 with fig. 3; cf. L. A. Constans, *Arles antique*, 343.   [6] S 4549[48].

[7] S 4549[40]. The restoration '[Ale]xandrin[i]' is probable, but not certain, NS 1920, 166.   [8] S 4549[19, 21].

Misya, Hippo Diarrytus, Gummi, Curubis.[1] But the African elephant adopted by Sabrata[2] points to the trade in ivory which came up by the desert route from the south. Nor is Syllectum a corn centre; its shippers probably carried mainly oil.[3] Of the mosaics which carry no inscription, one depicts a boar, a stag, and an elephant, perhaps pointing to the supply of animals for the amphitheatre.[4]

In three inscriptions shippers are accompanied by traders, *navicularii et negotiantes*.[5] Presumably the *negotiantes* were concerned with orders for goods that they would buy in their home district and ship to Ostia. Even in the supply of corn it seems probable that in the early Empire arrangements for shipping were made by private contract.[6]

The offices in this Ostian colonnade cover a wide diversity of trades and traders. Since more than half of the mosaics are lost or cannot be identified, the full range is unknown to us: the absence of Spanish communities, for instance, may not be significant. But even among those that survive there is a sufficient range to lead us to doubt whether this is in fact a spectacular illustration of bureaucracy. More probably the colonnade was originally designed for the benefit of private traders from Ostia and overseas who found it convenient to have representatives in such a conspicuous setting. In their offices there was no room for the stocking and sale of goods; but here orders could conveniently be placed and progressed. The *procurator annonae* no doubt found it increasingly convenient to have so many representatives of the corn trade concentrated and easily accessible, but there is no reason to believe that they came here on his invitation or maintained their offices merely to receive his instructions.

Most of the shipping represented at the upper level in this colonnade probably came to the imperial harbours rather than to the river mouth. This would be a natural inference from the representation of large cornships; it is confirmed by the inclusion of the Claudian lighthouse in some of the mosaic designs.[7] The function of the colonnade was

---

[1] *S* 4549[18, 10, 12, 17, 34].   [2] *S* 4549[14].

[3] *S* 4549[23]; *Economic Survey*, iv. 63. But see Pl. xxiv *b*, note.

[4] *NS* 1914, 287, fig. 4.

[5] *S* 4549[21] (Carales). 15 and 16 have only 'navicularii et negotiantes de suo'; the name of the state may have been above the door.

[6] Columella, i *Praef.* 20: 'nunc ad hastam locamus, ut nobis ex transmarinis provinciis advehatur frumentum, ne fame laboremus.'

[7] *S* 4549[3, 23, 32]; 32 (Narbo), a ship in full sail, with lighthouse, wrongly interpreted (*NS* 1916, 326 f., followed by *CIL*) as a ship being loaded by a crane from a warehouse.

probably already established before Claudius built his harbour and it was natural to continue the use of facilities that were working well. Ostia's relation to the harbours was not dissimilar to that of London city to the London docks.

By analogy we may expect that the Forum Vinarium, which has not yet been discovered, is to be found near the Tiber and not at Portus. A recent attempt has been made to locate it near the temple of Bacchus by Trajan's harbour on the strength of the proposed identification of monuments depicted in the Torlonia harbour relief.[1] But the identifications are extremely speculative and the function of the Forum Vinarium seems to correspond so closely with that of the Piazzale delle Corporazioni that it seems more likely that it, too, should have been in Ostia.

The evidence of inscriptions confirms the inference. Material may have been taken from Ostia to Portus when Ostia was declining; but it is barely conceivable that inscriptions found in Ostia were originally set up in Portus. The finding of a dedication to the *genius* of the guild of wine importers at Ostia is adequate evidence that the guild head-quarters were at Ostia.[2] L. Caecilius Aemilianus is 'corporatus in templo fori vinari importatorum negotiantium';[3] the importers' headquarters were in the Forum Vinarium. Similarly, if their business was done by Trajan's harbour, the importers would have commemorated Marcus Aurelius there and not in Ostia.[4] The Forum Vinarium probably resembled the Piazzale della Corporazioni on a more modest scale. The temple and the sculptured group of a four-horse chariot[5] recorded in the inscriptions may have stood in a free area surrounded by colonnade.

Of the shippers that frequented the Ostian harbour we have a few further obscure glimpses from inscriptions. L. Caelius L. f. A[rn](ensis) Aprilis Valerian[us] is described as a *curator navium Carthaginiensium*.[6] The tribe Arnensis is the tribe of Carthage and we may assume that he is a Carthaginian resident in Ostia. We do not know what were his responsibilities, but there were guilds of *curatores navium marinarum*[7] and also of *curatores navium amnalium*.[8] Perhaps they acted as agents to secure docking facilities for shipping. While ship-owners from communities in the provinces seem to have congregated in the Piazzale delle Corporazioni and sometimes acted together, as when the owners

[1] M. Fasciato, 'Ad quadrigam fori vinari', *Mélanges*, 59 (1947) 65.
[2] Bloch, 2.   [3] Bloch, *Epigraphica*, 1 (1939) 37.   [4] Ibid. 38.
[5] 58-9.   [6] S 4626.   [7] 364, 5, 4142.   [8] 364.

of African and Sardinian ships, 'domini navium Afrarum universarum item Sardorum', set up a statue to a patron of the curators of sea-shipping,[1] it is possible that some big shippers had their own private representatives to watch their interests.

Sextus Fadius Secundus Musa is known as a rich Gallic shipper from Monte Testaccio sherds and the inscription on the base of a statue in his honour at Narbo.[2] His names and those of other Sexti Fadii are found on more than twenty amphora fragments from Monte Testaccio, showing that they were engaged in the shipment of Spanish oil to Rome. Héron de Villefosse has drawn attention to Sexti Fadii at Ostia and suggests that they may be descended from freedmen of the family sent to keep an eye on the passage of Fadian cargoes through Ostia to Rome.[3] Other shippers' names that are found on Monte Testaccio sherds also recur at Ostia, such as L. Antonii. D. Caecilii, Laberii; but all these names, including Fadii, are too widely spread in the Roman world to justify any secure inference from their presence at Ostia.

Concerning the transport of goods by river to Rome there is a considerable body of evidence in inscriptions, literary sources, and reliefs; but this evidence is not easy to interpret in detail. From the elder Pliny's description the river passage would seem to involve no serious problem. The Tiber is 'capable of carrying ships of the largest size from the Italian sea'; it is 'a most peaceful carrier of goods from every quarter of the world'.[4] Virgil's picture is very different; his Tiber is a dangerous river:

> verticibus rapidis et multa flavus harena,
> in mare prorumpit.[5]

Today one rarely sees a boat on the river between Rome and the mouth. The current flows swiftly and unexpected eddies increase the difficulties of light boats. Stories of incautious bathers being suddenly sucked down and drowned are repeated in Rome and Ostia.

Two American scholars who recently made the practical experiment of floating down the Tiber on a rubber raft have emphasized the difficulties of the river passage to Rome. They point out that Roman sails were square-rigged and therefore needed a following wind; in the winding course of the Tiber they would have been for much of the

---

[1] 4142. [2] *CIL* xii. 4393.

[3] Héron de Villefosse, *Bull. arch. du comité des travaux historiques et scientifiques* (1918) 264.

[4] Pliny, *NH* iii. 54: 'quamlibet magnarum navium ex Italo mari capax, rerum in toto orbe nascentium mercator placidissimus.' [5] Virg. *Aen.* vii. 31.

distance helpless. The current, they think, was too strong for oars. Their conclusion is that transport by river to Rome must have been confined to barges towed by oxen, that it was fundamentally uneconomic, and could only have been sustained by an imperial power with rich resources.[1]

This view would seem to be confirmed by Procopius' account of the Gothic war in the sixth century. After recording the capture of Portus by the Goths he briefly describes the relation of the harbour to Rome:

When traders arrive with their ships in the harbour they unload their cargoes, reload them on to barges and so proceed up the Tiber to Rome. They make no use of sails or oars. For boats cannot be carried by the wind owing to the winding course of the river which does not flow in a straight line; and oars are ineffective since the current flows continuously against them. Instead they attach ropes from the barges to the necks of oxen who drag the boats like wagons to Rome.[2]

A later passage, however, shows that oxen were not indispensable. Belisarius was besieged in Rome and could not bring in provisions by road. Portus had been surprised and occupied by the Goths; all hope of bringing food to Rome rested on Ostia and the Tiber. Supplies of food and military forces had been collected in Campania; all the ships that were available were loaded to capacity and sailed for the Tiber; the troops convoyed what remained by the coastal road; ships and troops met at Ostia.[3]

Procopius emphasizes the difficulty of proceeding farther. The tow-path on the left bank had long fallen out of use, since Rome's trade was concentrated in Portus. No oxen were available. The crisis was resolved by using the small boats attached to the largest of the merchantmen. They waited for a following wind and then set sail. 'Where the river flowed in a straight course they raised their sails and proceeded without difficulty; but where the river curved round and followed an oblique course, their sails got no benefit from the wind. The sailors took to the oars and with great difficulty forced their way against the current.' Procopius' evidence makes it clear that in the sixth century transport by river to Rome was normally confined to haulage by oxen, but that in a crisis a combination of oars and sail was practicable. Earlier evidence shows that Tiber transport was much more diversified in the Republic and early Empire.

[1] L. A. and L. B. Holland, *Archaeology*, 3 (1950) 87.
[2] Procopius, *De bell. Goth.* i. 26, 10–12.   [3] Ibid. ii. 7, 4–9.

When Virgil in the *Aeneid* described the dispatch of two biremes to Rome from the Trojan camp at the river mouth he was not straining his readers' credulity.[1] Warships frequently made the journey in the Republic. Ships stationed at Rome fought at sea and returned to Rome; and when Antium was conquered some of her ships were taken to Roman docks.[2] But warships relied on a concentration of oar-power and were better equipped than merchantmen for the journey.

The evidence of Strabo and Dionysius of Halicarnassus shows that merchantmen also could complete their journey by river. Dionysius speaks of ships of up to a capacity of 3,000 amphorae that are rowed or towed up to Rome.[3] Strabo adds that even ships which had to unload part of their cargo at sea could, when lightened, run inland as far as Rome.[4] Juvenal also seems to describe an African trader with a cargo of oil coming up the river.[5] It seems clear that merchantmen with a small capacity did not have to unload at Ostia: and probably many of them continued to use the river harbour even when the imperial harbours had been built. They made their way by a combination of sail and oars or haulage.

How much of Rome's trade was carried in small vessels we cannot determine, but the emphasis on grain transports has probably distorted the picture. The Alexandrian merchantman described by Lucian probably exceeded a thousand tons,[6] and this may not have been exceptional in the Alexandrian and later in Commodus' African fleet. But even grain carriers could often be much smaller. In offering privileges to ship-owners who carried corn for the Roman market Claudius set the lower limit at 10,000 modii, nearly 90 tons.[7]

But Claudius' regulation is poor evidence for the size of merchantmen carrying other goods. When in 218 B.C. it was decided that a position in the Roman senate was incompatible with mercantile trade, senators were forbidden by law to own ships of a capacity of more than 300 amphorae;[8] the natural inference is that men were trading with ships not much larger. Similarly when Cicero, speaking of the merchantmen collected by Dolabella in Asia in 43 B.C., says that they were all

---

[1] Virg. *Aen.* viii. 94: 'olli remigio noctemque diemque fatigant | et longos superant flexus.' [2] Livy viii. 14. 12.

[3] Dion. Hal. iii. 44. 3: 'μεχρὶ τῆς Ῥώμης εἰρεσίᾳ καὶ ῥύμασι παρελκόμεναι κομίζονται.'

[4] Strabo, 232.

[5] Juv. v. 88 f.: 'illud enim vestris datur alveolis quod | canna Micipsarum prora subvexit acuta.' [6] L. A. Casson, *TAPA* 81 (1950) 51–56.

[7] Gaius, *Inst.* i. 32 c. [8] Livy xxi. 63. 3.

over 2,000 amphorae (50 tons) in capacity he implies that ships of that
size were common enough.[1] It seems probable that much of the coastal
trade in Italy at least was carried on in small vessels. Petronius' genial
freedman Trimalchio built five ships, loaded them with wine, and sent
them, presumably from Campania, to Rome.[2] Had they not gone to
the bottom on the way they would have ended their journey in Rome
and not at Ostia. Trimalchio replaced his losses by bigger and better
ships: 'size, you know, means strength'. There may have been a general
tendency to increase the size of trading vessels.

Merchantmen that relied on sails alone had to be towed when the
wind was not behind them. The vessels best suited to make their way up
river were those that were equipped with oars as well as sails. Such
vessels had once been common. Little is heard of them in the Empire,
and it has sometimes been thought that they became obsolete when
sailing technique improved in the late Republic.[3] They probably had
a much longer life. When Ovid makes his melancholy journey to exile
at Tomi he changes ships at Corinth; for the first part of his journey at
least his ship relies on oars as well as sail.[4] One of the mosaics in the
recently discovered late Empire villa at Piazza Armerina in Sicily
depicts wild beasts being embarked. The ship, in addition to a central
mast and sail, is generously equipped with oars.[5] The type persisted
because it was still useful. It was less at the mercy of the winds and,
though its size was limited, it could travel more quickly than larger
ships completely dependent on sails.

While small merchantmen were probably a common sight on the
Tiber, it was rare for a large vessel to make the journey. Ammianus
Marcellinus describes the transport upstream of Constantius' obelisk
as a memorable occasion. The boat had 300 rowers, but even so it did
not complete the last winding stretch to the Roman docks; the obelisk
was unloaded at Vicus Alexandrinus and carried for the last three miles
by road.[6] This was not the first occasion that such a sight had been
witnessed. Augustus and Caligula had once brought obelisks nearly as

---

[1] Cic. *Ad fam.* xii. 15. 2.   [2] Petronius, *Sat.* 76.

[3] Le Gall, *Le Tibre* (Paris, 1953) 70–72.

[4] Ovid, *Tristia*, i. 10. 3: 'sive opus est velis, minimam bene currit ad auram | sive opus
est remo, remige carpit iter.' Cf. Fig. 25 *d*.

[5] G. V. Gentili, 'I mosaici della villa romana del casale di Piazza Armerina', *Boll.
d'Arte*, 37 (1952) 40, fig. 16. Cf. Dion. Hal. iii. 44: 'αἱ μὲν οὖν ἐπίκωποι νῆες ὁπηλίκαί ποτ' ἂν
οὖσαι τύχωσι'.

[6] Amm. Marc. xvii. 4. 13–14.

large to Rome and they too had been carried up the Tiber.[1] But the ships which carried them were specially designed and not kept in regular service.[*] The Augustan ship became an exhibit in the docks at Puteoli until it was burnt; Caligula's ship became the foundation for the lighthouse at the entrance to Claudius' harbour.

It was more normal to unload large cargoes and send them upstream by smaller boats. Of these river boats we hear most of the *naves codicariae*. Seneca raises the question who was the first to persuade the Romans to take to ships. It was Claudius, who was given in consequence the name Caudex—'quia plurium tabularum contextus caudex apud antiquos vocatur . . . et naves nunc quoque ex antiqua consuetudine, quae commeatus per Tiberim subvehunt, codicariae vocantur'.[2] This explanation does not describe clearly the form of the boats; their function was to carry Roman food supplies up river. This function is confirmed by other evidence. In the Theodosian Code the *codicarii* are closely associated with the *mensores frumentarii* who measured the grain.[3] The same association is seen in an inscription on the base of a statue set up to Ragonius Vincentius Celsus, *praefectus annonae*, in the late fourth century, by the measurers. They commemorate his high qualities in office; he resolved a long-standing feud with the *codicarii* so successfully that both parties to the dispute were satisfied.[4] They show their link with the harbour service when they commemorate a procurator of the imperial harbours.[5] One inscription records 'codicarii naviculari infernates';[6] another 'codicari nav(iculari) infra pontem S(ublicium?).[7] Both terms may be used to distinguish the *codicarii* operating from Ostia and those operating on the Tiber above Rome.[8] It is significant that the guild of the *codicarii* is one of the few Ostian guilds for which evidence survives through the third and fourth

---

[1] Pliny, *NH* xxvi. 69–70.

[2] Seneca, *De brev. vit.* 13. 4. Perhaps the name was originally used to distinguish a boat constructed with planks from the more primitive type hollowed from the trunk of a tree.

[3] *Cod. Theod.* xiv. 4. 9 (417): 'ad excludendas patronorum caudicariorum fraudes et Portuensium furta mensorum'; xiv. 15. 1 (364): 'sola ducenta milia modiorum frumenti integri adque intemerati iuxta priscum morem mensores et caudicarii levioribus pretiis pistoribus venundare cogantur.'

[4] *CIL* vi. 1759.   [5] 170.   [6] 131.   [7] 185.

[8] Le Gall, *Le Tibre*, 257, rejects this explanation on the ground that river traffic above Rome was confined to *lyntrarii*. This needs more independent confirmation; if there were *codicarii* only on the lower Tiber there would be no need for the descriptive qualification.

centuries. Being vital to Rome for the transport of food they were kept busy even when the total volume of trade was drastically reduced.

A representation of a boat used in this service may survive in a paint-in the Vatican, which was taken from a tomb in the cemetery outside the Porta Laurentina in the nineteenth century. The painting has been heavily restored, but the essential elements were clear when it was found.[1] The Isis Giminiana is being loaded with a cargo of grain. Standing on a cabin in the stern is Farnaces *magister*, the ship's master, ready to control the rudder. In the centre of the boat is a measure into which a man is pouring corn (*res*) from a sack; opposite him is a corn measurer checking the quantity. On his right stands a figure in black holding in his hand a branch. He is not, as has been suggested, the captain of the boat; the same figure appears on a mosaic design in the hall of the measurers and is connected with their work. In the bows sits a figure by a second measure on which is written 'feci', showing that he has finished his work. A planked gangway leads up from the quay (not represented) to the boat and two porters are shown carrying up sacks on their shoulders. The presence of the measurers shows beyond doubt that the loading of corn is being represented, and since the picture comes from an Ostian tomb this should be an Ostian scene, and the boat a river boat. Its shape is not perhaps what we would expect. It certainly could not be described as a low flat-bottomed barge, such as the *navis codicaria* has often been assumed to be. The stern rises high from the water; the keel has a curving line and the tapering prow also rises high. There is no sign of sails; the mast, near the prow, might be for a towing-rope.

Le Gall has convincingly identified two other boats as *naves codicariae*.[2] One is depicted on a relief from Rome, the other comes from a mosaic in the Piazzale delle Corporazioni. This mosaic shows two boats side by side; a porter is carrying an amphora of wine from one to the other.[3] The scene represents the transhipment from sea-going merchantman to river boat; the mast is a towing mast. The same crescent shape recurs in a boat incised with much less detail on the side of a dedication by the salt workers of the right bank.[4] Rome's salt was transported by river, not road, probably in *naves codicariae*.

The *navis codicaria* relied on haulage and, to keep the ropes clear of the deck, a haulage mast was normally used. In Procopius' day river boats

---

[1] B. Nogara, *Le Nozze Aldobrandini*, 71 (original state).
[2] Le Gall, op. cit. 228.   [3] Pl. xxv *a*.   [4] *S* 4285, now transferred to Ostia.

a

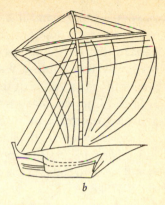

b

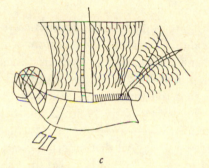

c

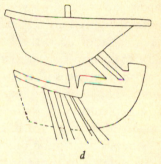

d

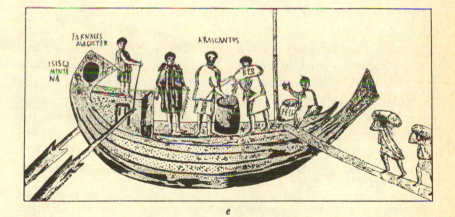

e

FIG. 25. *a–c.* Graffiti from house walls. *d.* From a tomb relief. *e.* From a tomb painting
the Isis Giminiana.

were towed by oxen and it has often been assumed that this was the general practice throughout the classical period. Le Gall has rightly emphasized that for the use of oxen there is no classical evidence; the sources imply that haulage was confined to manpower.[1] A relief on the base of the great statue of the Tiber, which probably came from the Iseum in the Campus Martius and is now in the Louvre, shows a boat being hauled upstream by three men, each straining on his own tow-rope.[2] Similar scenes are depicted on reliefs from Gaul.[3] Martial writes of hauliers, *helciarii*, on the upper Tiber.[4] Ausonius and Sidonius Apollinaris still refer to them in the fourth and fifth centuries on the Moselle and on the Saône.[5] Oxen were probably introduced after the fourth century, when manpower was short. Previously slave labour was the cheapest and most effective means of haulage.

In two inscriptions the *codicarii* are linked with the owners of a different type of boat, the *lenuncularii*. Together they honour a procurator of the imperial harbours;[6] and a Roman knight who is described as 'patronus et defensor' of the *lenuncularii* is a president of the guild of *codicarii*.[7] The association implies that the functions of the two trades were complementary or similar. The comparatively small number of references to *lenunculi* in Latin literature are scarcely more informative than Seneca's description of *naves codicariae*. All that emerges clearly is that they were small vessels; they were used at sea but also for fishing in rivers.[8]

At Ostia the *lenuncularii* were divided into five guilds, which sometimes combined. Together they are 'universi navigarii corporum quinque lenunculariorum'.[9] But each constituent guild had its own title and represented a separate function. Most important seem to have been the *lenuncularii tabularii auxiliarii*, for fragments of five separate rolls of their members have survived and between A.D. 152 and 192 the number of ordinary members rose from 125 to 258.[10] That they had Roman senators who were not Ostians among their patrons suggests, though

[1] Le Gall, op. cit. 257.

[2] Id. 'Les bas reliefs de la statue du Tibre', *Rev. arch.* 22 (1944) 41; *Le Tibre*, 219.

[3] A. Grenier, *Manuel d'Arch. Gallo-Romaine*, vi (2) 555, 557, figs. 178–9.

[4] Martial iv. 64, 21–25: 'quem nec rumpere nauticum celeuma | nec clamor valet helciariorum, | cum sit tam prope Mulvius sacrumque | lapsae per Tiberim volent carinae.' Cf. Ovid. *Tristia*, iv. 1. 10: 'cantat et innitens limosae pronus harenae, | adverso tardam qui trahit amne ratem.' The simile implies a common scene.

[5] Ausonius, *Idyll.* 10, 41–42; Sid. Apoll. *Ep.* ii. 10. 4.   [6] 170.   [7] 4144.

[8] Caesar, *BC* ii. 43. 3; Tac. *Ann.* xiv. 5. 7; Amm. Marc. xiv. 2. 10.

[9] 4144; cf. 170, 352.   [10] 250, 251.

it does not prove, that their work was of more than local significance. The *ordo corporatorum lenunculariorum pleromariorum* were considerably less important. In A.D. 200 they have only sixteen ordinary members and six of presidential rank, and neither of their two patrons seems to be a man of standing.[1]

One other guild of *lenuncularii* is recorded in inscriptions, *lenuncularii traiectus Luculli*.[2] The natural meaning of *traiectus* is the passage across the river.[3] The Tiber had no bridge near its mouth and ferry services were needed. In the Republic agricultural workers with holdings on Isola Sacra had to be carried across the river; when the imperial harbours were built the traffic in passengers and goods became more intensive. Four ferry services are recorded—*traiectus Luculli, marmorariorum*,[4] *togatensium*,[5] *Rusticelius*.[6] In two cases the type of boat is specified. Those who operated the Rusticelian ferry service are described as *scapharii*;[7] the *Lucullan* guild are normally described as *lenuncularii*, but, in one inscription, as *scapharii et lenuncularii*.[8] The *scapha* is a light rowing-boat, the word being used, for example, of the ship's boat carried by merchantmen; the *lenunculus*, in contrast, is presumably a heavier boat manned by several oarsmen. Perhaps the Rusticelian service was confined to passengers, while the Lucullan service provided for passengers and also heavy loads. If the two remaining ferry guilds were operated by *lenuncularii* we may have an explanation of the *quinque corpora lenunculariorum* in these three ferry services with the *tabularii* and *pleromarii*. They combined together because they used the same type of rowing-boat.

The functions of the *tabularii* and *pleromarii* can only be guessed. It has been suggested that *tabularii* is another form of *tabellarii* and that the members of this guild were concerned with a river messenger service between Ostia and Rome.[9] This is most unlikely. The Via Ostiensis and the Via Portuensis were the quickest means of communication; even the *classiarii* went on foot.[10] The addition of *auxiliarii* to the titles provides a better clue; it suggests auxiliary service to other boats.

The *lenuncularii tabularii* may be the owners of tug-boats. When the

[1] 252. Interpretation doubtful, perhaps only three presidents.

[2] S 5320; cf. 5380.

[3] Le Gall, *Le Tibre*, 224, rejects this meaning on the ground that one ferry service would have sufficed: he underestimates the traffic. His suggestion that *traiectus* represents services associated with different docks strains the meaning of the word.

[4] 425.   [5] 403.   [6] S 4553–6, 5327–8.   [7] S 5327–8.   [8] 5[13].

[9] Preller, *Rom und der Tiber* (1849) 149.   [10] Suet. *Vesp.* 8. 3.

harbour was crowded it would normally have been impossible for merchantmen to manœuvre into position under sail; more often they must have furled their sails and been towed to their berths by rowing-boats. The *navis codicaria* may also have been towed by boat to its loading point in the harbour and again out of the harbour before slaves started their tough journey along the river tow-path. That rowing-boats had an important part to play in the harbour service is confirmed by Nero's commemorative coinage; in many of the issues a small boat, manned by several oarsmen, is seen in mid-harbour among the merchantmen; and, as we have seen, a small basin was reserved for them by Claudius' harbour. They were also needed by the river docks at Ostia town.

A representation of one of these tug-boats may be preserved in a terra-cotta relief from an Isola Sacra tomb.[1] This roughly depicts a boat with curved prow and stern. Three men strain at their oars; a fourth stands in the stern wielding an extremely large rudder-oar. In the bows is a small mast, which may have carried an auxiliary sail, or perhaps a tow-rope; a rope is attached to the stern, but unfortunately the jobbing artist is not concerned with what his boat is pulling.

The *lenuncularii pleromarii auxiliarii* may correspond to the σκάφαι ὑπηρετικαί mentioned by Strabo in his account of the river harbour, small boats which went out to sea to lighten the larger merchantmen before they entered the river.[2] The provenance of the guild roll strengthens the identification a little; it was found near Tor Boacciana, which in the Roman period roughly marked the river mouth. Nor would the small size of the guild in 200[3] be surprising. By that time most of the big merchantmen preferred to sail to the imperial harbours, which they could enter without difficulty.

IMPERIAL CONTROL

In view of Ostia's importance as an essential link in Rome's overseas trade it is natural that the control of the harbours was not left to local authority. Supervision from Rome continued through the Republic; it was considerably extended as the imperial system developed. In the late Republic Rome's interests were safeguarded by a quaestor stationed at Ostia, whose primary function was to supervise the reception, storage, and reshipment of corn from the provinces. He had a tribunal

---

[1] Pl. xxviii *a*. Another example perhaps, incised on the face of a tomb, *NS* 1938, 47 (tomb 4).　　　　　[2] Strabo, 232.　　　　　[3] *S* 4459.

in the forum at Ostia[1] and perhaps his authority was backed by judicial powers greater than those normally associated with the quaestorship. This seems a reasonable inference from the inscription set up, probably under Augustus, by the shipowners of Ostia: 'Pacceio L. f. |q(uaestori) pro pr(aetore).'[2] This inscription was found at Tibur, but the recent discovery of fragments of a similar inscription to the same man at Ostia confirm that Pacceius was being honoured by the Ostian shipowners for his quaestorship at Ostia.[3] Perhaps all Roman quaestors at Ostia were given a praetor's judicial competence.

On the building of the Claudian harbour the senatorial quaestor was replaced by imperial officials responsible to the *praefectus annonae*. The most frequently attested of the new officials is the *procurator annonae Ostis*, many of whom are recorded from the second and early third centuries. But the first official known to us, an imperial freedman, Claudius Optatus, is 'proc(urator) portus Ostiesis'; he may be identified with the freedman of Claudius who was appointed to command the fleet at Misenum.[4] Later, in the third century, the title *procurator portus utriusque* is recorded.[5] From the evidence available when he wrote, Hirschfeld concluded that the two titles covered the same function, that the *procurator portus* was replaced, probably under Hadrian, by the *procurator annonae*, who in turn was superseded, probably under Septimius Severus, by the *procurator portus utriusque*.[6]

Since Hirschfeld wrote, new evidence has modified the dates he proposed for changes in organization. A new African inscription records a *procurator annonae* who held office under Trajan[7] and the last known member of the series must now be dated after 215.[8] Hirschfeld's main argument, however, remains unaffected since there is still no clear evidence of the two titles existing together.[9] Moreover, the title of the Trajanic *procurator annonae* might strengthen his argument. M. Vettius Latro is described as 'proc(urator) annonae Ostiae et in portu', which might seem to represent a transition between two titles.

---

[1] I[39] p. 499.   [2] 3603.

[3] Bloch, 32: '[— Pacceio L. f.] q. pr[o pr.] | naviculariei O[stienses]'.

[4] 163, Pliny, *NH* ix. 62.   [5] e.g. 125, 170.

[6] Hirschfeld, *Kaiserliche Verwaltungsbeamten*[2], 248–50.

[7] *AE* 1939, 81; H. G. Pflaum, *Les Procurateurs équestres* (1950) 56.

[8] 160. P. Bassilius Crescens was honoured by the builders' guild in their 34th *lustrum*, probably after 215 (see p. 331).

[9] The first known *procurator portus utriusque* is recorded in an inscription from Rome, *CIL* vi. 1020, a dedication to 'Vibia Aurelia Sabina d(ivi) Marci Aug(usti) f(iliae)'. This need not necessarily be earlier than 215.

On general grounds, however, it seems more likely that there were two offices rather than one. The control of the imperial harbours needed attention on the spot and should have occupied the full time of a responsible official. His main responsibilities will have been to see to the effective maintenance of harbour installations and to control the shipping. There was need for another official to attend to more general problems of supply and to serve as a link between the head of the department in Rome and the local authorities at Ostia.

The post of the *procurator annonae* belonged to the lowest of the three grades of equestrian procurators, carrying an annual salary of 60,000 sesterces.[1] Though holders of the post normally moved on to higher office,[2] they were at or near the beginning of their public career when they came to Ostia. Nor should they be regarded as experts replacing amateurs. There is little trace of specialized experience among them. Q. Petronius Melior, who had been *adiutor curatoris alvei Tiberis*[3] will have gained some relevant experience, but P. Aelius Liberalis is the only *procurator annonae* known to have served in the department earlier; he had previously been paymaster at Ostia: 'praepositus mensae nummul(ariae) f(isci) f(rumentarii) Ost(iensis)'.[4] Two others came to the work from the department of libraries.[5]

The honours paid to these procurators by Ostian guilds suggest something of the range of their work. That they should be commemorated by the corn measurers[6] and by corn merchants[7] is natural enough, for corn supplies were their primary responsibility, as their title implies. The frequent honours paid by the builders, *fabri tignuarii*,[8] are less expected. We may infer that the procurator was responsible for the maintenance of granaries and other warehouses used at Ostia and the harbours for Roman supplies. No inscriptions yet found record their relations with ship-owners, but this must have been an important part of their work. In the offices of the Piazzale delle Corporazioni they could deal conveniently with the carriers of overseas goods. In the early Empire the state's immediate concern seems to have been limited to corn; when oil and wine were also distributed free to the people at Rome the procurator's direct responsibilities were greatly increased.

The procurator had a small staff. His chief adjutant was a *cornicu-*

---

[1] *CIL* x. 7580: 'proc. ad annonam Ostis ad HS $\overline{LX}$.'
[2] Pflaum, op. cit. 340–2. [3] 172. [4] 2045. [5] S 5352; *CIL* x. 7580.
[6] 154, 172. [7] 161.
[8] 160, S 5344, 5345, 5351, 5352.

larius,[1] under whom were a number of *beneficiarii*.[2] Inscriptions throw a glimmer of light on the work of the department. The chest of the department, *mensa nummularia fisci frumentarii Ostiensis*, has already been mentioned; it presumably had to meet payments to shipmasters and for labour at the docks and in the warehouses. The head of this branch was an imperial freedman: under him, both at Ostia and at Portus, were a number of *dispensatores*, pay clerks, all of whom were imperial slaves;[3] they include one who worked at Puteoli as well as at Ostia, 'Chrysanthus Aug(usti) disp(ensator) a fruminto Puteolis et Ostis';[4] some of Rome's reserves were still stored at Puteoli.

In a dedication to the majesty of the imperial house two of these pay clerks join with an imperial freedman, whose title is obscure: 'Traiano Aug(usti) lib(erto) a X m̂.' It is possible that this freedman was 'a decem millibus modiorum'. Claudius had offered privileges to those who put ships of not less than 10,000 modii capacity in the service of Rome's corn supply. An imperial freedman at Ostia was responsible perhaps for investigating claims.[5]

Inscriptions also record *tabularii* at Ostia and at Portus.[6] They are all imperial freedmen, and there is an assistant grade, the *tabularius adiutor*.[7] A Flavian freedman, whose tomb has been found near the harbour, is *tabularius portus Aug(usti)*;[8] later, when Trajan's inner basin is added, P. Aelius Onesimus is *tabularius portus utriusque*.[9] An inscription from Rome gives the fuller title *tabularius Ostis ad annonam*; in his case the Ostian post was the first in a career that advanced through financial offices to the procuratorship of Belgica.[10] The function of the *tabularius* was to keep records and perhaps also to check imperial cargoes on arrival. A relief from Portus in the Torlonia museum may represent *tabularii*, or their assistants, at work.[11] It shows porters unloading wine jars from a ship; two men seated with tablets in front of them are probably recording quantities. Hispanus, *Aug(usti) lib(ertus) tabul(arius)*, makes

---

[1] 160.

[2] 5[16]. Cn. Sentius Felix is 'patronus beneficiarior(um) proc(uratoris) Aug(usti)'.

[3] At Ostia, 202; at Portus, 204, 207.   [4] *CIL* x. 1562.

[5] *S* 4319. The very improbable supplement suggested in *CIL*: '(a(nni) d(ecimi) m(agistr)o)' can be abandoned in view of a parallel from African Lepcis published by Miss Reynolds, *BSR* 23 (1955) 126 n. 4: 'Aurelio Caesari Antonini Aug. Pii f. Vitalis lib. verna a X m̂.' She suggests that both men were imperial officials, perhaps concerned with financial administration in harbours. It is an objection to my guess that Lepcis exports oil and not corn; but the privilege may have been extended.

[6] At Ostia, 200, 304, *S* 4316, *CIL* vi. 8450; at Portus, *S* 4482, *AE* 1948, 103.

[7] 49, 200.   [8] *S* 4482.   [9] *AE* 1948, 103.   [10] *CIL* vi. 8450.   [11] Pl. xxvi *a*.

a dedication to the imperial majesty to commemorate his promotion, presumably to the office of *tabularius*.[1] It was responsible work; he was proud to be appointed.

Other imperial procurators are recorded but their function is less clear, and they are known only from isolated inscriptions. C. Pomponius Turpilianus is 'procurator ad oleum in Galbae Ostiae portus utriusque'.[2] From this it has been inferred that *horrea* for the storage of oil had been built by the emperor Galba at the Claudian harbour. His rule, however, seems to have been too short to leave such a constructive mark; Wickert is more probably right in seeing here a reference to the well-known Horrea Galbae at Rome;[3] in which case Turpilianus was controlling the passage through the harbours of oil destined for Rome.

Dorotheus, an imperial freedman, is *proc(urator) massae Marian(ae)*,[4] presumably checking the passage of lead from the silver mines which Tiberius had confiscated in the south of Spain. The passage of iron may also have been under direct imperial control, for T. Petronius Priscus is described as 'procurator Aug(usti) ferrariarum et annonae Ostis'[5] and a dedication is made at Ostia by a slave in the service of a company producing iron, 'Hilarus socior(um) vect(igalis) ferr(ariarum) ser(vus).'[6] This division seems to have had an office in Ostia, for a lead token has been found inscribed: 'stat(ionis) ferr(ariarum) for(i?) Os[t(iensis)]'.[7]

A Flavian freedman on his tombstone is described as *praepositus camellorum*.[8] Below the inscription are roughly but vividly incised two camels and an elephant between them. T. Flavius Stephanus may have been responsible for the reception and sending on to Rome of camels and other animals for imperial displays. The inclusion of an elephant with the camels makes this a more natural interpretation of his function than a military post.

An imperial messenger service is suggested possibly by a *procurator pugillationis et ad naves vagas*[9] and, more clearly, by two *tabellarii* recorded on tombstones from Isola Sacra.[10] Evidence also comes from Ostia and from Portus of *frumentarii*, who were used in the imperial service both as messengers and as police. At Ostia two brothers dedicated

---

[1] S 4316: 'Hispanus Aug(usti) lib(ertus) tabul(arius) numini ob processus votum redd(idit).'   [2] 20.   [3] Wickert, S (2), p. 849.

[4] 52; cf. Tac. *Ann.* vi. 19. 1.   [5] S 4459.

[6] S 4326. Iron from Elba worked at Ostia, NS 1912, 387.

[7] S, p. 773, 4326 add.   [8] Bloch, 37.

[9] 2045. No parallel is known and the interpretation is very uncertain. Paschetto, 201; Le Gall, *Le Tibre*, 236.   [10] Thylander, A 256, 279.

a relief on a column on the south side of the Piazzale delle Corporazioni to the *genius* of the *castra peregrina*, their headquarters at Rome.[1] By the harbours a detachment of the *frumentarii* set up a commemorative tablet to Alexander Severus and the imperial family.[2]

The control of the Tiber and of its banks was also the responsibility of the central authority at Rome. Boundary stones have been found marking the right bank of the river. They were set up by the *curatores alvei Tiberis et riparum* in the Julio-Claudian period[3] and this board was probably responsible for the maintenance of embankments. In the nineteenth century ample traces of these embankments could be seen on both sides of the river between the Forum and Tor Boacciana.[4] Today only a small tract can be seen, which is not visible unless the Tiber is low, opposite Tor Boacciana on the right bank.[5] The wall is over 2 metres thick, built of concrete with an aggregate of large tufa blocks. Channels in the concrete can still be seen where the wall was laced with timber beams.

The Tiber authority had an office at Ostia, *statio alvei Tiberis*;[6] three inscriptions reflect its work. It is from the *curator alvei Tiberis et riparum* that the *lenuncularii traiectus Luculli* have to get authority to rebuild their premises early in the second century.[7] His authority is recorded in a more fragmentary inscription for the building or rebuilding of a *vigil[iarium]*,[8] perhaps by one the of ferry services. Of the third fragment all that can be said is that the authority of the *curator* is related to a guild, whose name is lost.[9] Whether these three inscriptions refer to the same guild or three different guilds is uncertain. That the *curator alvei Tiberis* exercised a general control over all the guilds of river boatmen seems unlikely, since in that case more evidence of his activity should have survived; it seems more probable that he controlled the use of the banks and that in all three inscriptions he is concerned with buildings. The *vigiliarium* of the second inscription may be a watch-tower.

The main work of the Tiber authority was at Rome and it is possible

---

[1] 7.   [2] 125.

[3] *S* 4704; *NS* 1921, 258. Two further stones have since been discovered: complete catalogue, G. Barbieri, *Topografia*, 62 n. 2.

[4] L. Canina, *Sulla stazione delle navi di Ostia* (1838) 3; Carcopino, 510. Le Gall, op. cit. 335, infers that there was no embankment in the eastern half of the town, but see p. 491.

[5] Pl. VI *d*.   [6] *S* 5384.   [7] *S* 5320.   [8] 254.

[9] Bloch, 46: '— permis[su - - - - Ma]ximi c(larissimi) v(iri) [curatoris | alvei] Tiberi[s et riparum | —] corp[us —.'

that the office at Ostia was in the charge of an assistant, related to the head of the board in the same way as the Ostian *procurator annonae* served the *praefectus annonae* at Rome. Le Gall identifies this assistant with the *praefectus curatorum alvei Tiberis*. When, in or shortly before the Flavian period, the Roman board of five was replaced by a single commissioner, the assistant's title became *adiutor curatoris alvei Tiberis*.[1] Only one *praefectus* is known, Sp. Turanius Proculus Gellianus, in the Claudian period,[2] and, as Le Gall has emphasized, it is probably significant that he was given a prominent part in the revived cult of the Laurentine Lavinates at Lavinium.[3] A large proportion of the officials in this cult were drawn from Ostia, for the good reason that they could attend the ceremonies without difficulty. Turranius Proculus was probably chosen because he was in office at Ostia, perhaps when the revival of the cult was inaugurated. While the Roman curator was a prominent senator, his assistant was a knight.

Two further imperial services were represented at Ostia, the fleet and the *vigiles*. During the Republic Ostia had been the main Roman naval base on the west coast of Italy. Augustus transferred the command to Misenum, but warships were still stationed at Ostia through the Empire. On Nero's harbour coins, though the field is mainly filled with merchantmen, a trireme is also shown leaving harbour,[4] and a dedication has been found at Portus to Iupiter Optimus Maximus Dulicenus by men serving in the Misenum fleet 'when they were at Ostia under the command of' a trierarch.[5] Tombstones also survive, both at Portus and at Ostia, of men who died on service and of others who lived on in the district when their service was completed.[6] From the distribution of inscriptions it seems that the ships of the Ostian detachment were divided between the imperial harbours and the Tiber. Their main duties, we may assume, were to police the harbours and control shipping. They may also have been used to carry governors to their appointments in western provinces and emperors when they sailed from Ostia. The presence of the Misenum flagship, the hexeres *Ops*, at Ostia is probably to be associated with such an imperial occasion.[7] The triremes at Ostia were normally a detachment from the Misenum fleet; but, as at Centumcellae farther north, there is also evidence at Ostia of ships from Ravenna.[8]

---

[1] Le Gall, op. cit. 182.   [2] *CIL* x. 797.   [3] Le Gall, op. cit. 183.
[4] Pl. XVIII *a*.   [5] 110, dated A.D. 186.   [6] 232–43, S 4496–8, Bloch, 39.
[7] 232; C. G. Starr, *The Roman Imperial Navy*, 53.   [8] S 4496, 4497; Starr, op. cit. 23.

Suetonius records that the ships' crews who had to come on duty from Ostia and Puteoli to Rome appealed to Vespasian for special boot money; they were instructed to dispense with boots altogether and meekly complied.[1] At Rome they were probably connected with imperial displays. We know that *classiarii* were in charge of the awnings in the amphitheatre; they are also likely to have been called on for naval displays in the *naumachia*.

There is more evidence concerning the organization of the *vigiles* at Ostia, for their barracks have been excavated. Claudius had detached an urban cohort to Ostia for fire service[2] but Hadrian seems to have been the first to station trained fire-fighters in the town. Towards the end of his reign a large new building was completed for a detachment of the Roman *vigiles*. A long series of inscriptions was found when the building was excavated.[3]

The Barracks of the Vigiles reproduces one of the commonest plans in Ostia. It is found on a small scale in the Horrea Epagathiana and the headquarters of the builders, on a large scale in several of the *horrea*. A fragment of the plan of Rome incised on marble suggests that the same plan was used for the barracks of the *vigiles* in Rome.[4] A large open courtyard is surrounded by a portico carried on brick piers. Off the portico open a series of eighteen rooms, and stairs at the four angles lead to the two or more upper stories, where the same plan was probably repeated. The building faced streets on three sides, and was closed on the fourth by a row of shops. There were subsidiary gates in the north and south walls, but the main entrance to the barracks was from the Via dei Vigiles on the east.

Most of the rooms round the courtyard seem to have been living-rooms for the men, and only two have a distinctive character. The room in the south-east corner was the men's latrine in which Fortuna presided. A small shrine attached to the wall carries the inscription 'Fortunae sanctae' and probably contained a marble or terra-cotta figure of the

[1] Suet. *Vesp.* 8. 3.   [2] Suet. *Claud.* 25. 2.

[3] Date of the barracks, p. 136. Description, Paschetto, 285; P. K. Baillie Reynolds, *The Vigiles of Imperial Rome*, 107–15.

[4] Baillie Reynolds, op. cit., pl. ii (p. 46). Lanciani (*NS* 1889, 19 and 77) thought that the building was originally a private house and that the change from large to slit windows in the ground-floor rooms marked a change of use: he was followed by Paschetto and Baillie Reynolds. But the change in windows took place in the course of construction. Brickstamps date the building to the last years of Hadrian and it was being used by the *vigiles* before Hadrian died.

goddess;[1] on the floor is a marble altar dedicated by C. Valerius Myron, who was attached to the staff of the commander of the *vigiles* at Rome, *beneficiarius praefecti vigilum*.[2]

At the western end of the courtyard, facing the main entrance, the room which carries most emphasis in the plan served as a chapel for the imperial cult. It was preceded by an antechapel occupying the space of the portico. Here was depicted in mosaic a typical sacrifice. The central scene shows a struggling bull with the axeman ready to strike; two balancing scenes at the sides show the dead bull about to be carved up.[3] The entrance to the chapel itself is emphasized by two columns and raised by a step above the level of the antechapel. In the centre were found traces of an altar and against the back wall is a podium which was originally lined with marble. On this were set five small 'bases' dedicated to the emperors Antoninus Pius, Marcus Aurelius, Lucius Verus, and L. Septimius Severus, and to Marcus Aurelius when he was heir apparent.[4] From this Antonine family party Commodus is noticeably absent, but the dedication to Septimius Severus is inscribed on an erasure. His names and titles probably replaced those of Commodus.[5]

At the side of the chapel was found the base of a statue of Lucius Aelius, adopted son of Hadrian, set up in A.D. 137.[6] Other imperial statues were set up between the piers of the portico, and many of their bases can still be seen in the building. Hadrian's base is not among those that have survived but his statue must surely have once occupied a prominent place.

Behind the imperial chapel was a group of five rooms, which may have been used for the officers, for there was originally a separate latrine in the north-west corner. There is, however, little evidence in the surviving remains to show for what purposes the various parts of the building were used. Fire drill was probably carried out in the open court; meals were taken in small units, for there is no sign of a large hall in the building. At the western end of the court are two water tanks feeding troughs, which at first sight suggest a drinking place for horses or mules. But there is no evidence for stabling in the building,

[1] S 4282. [2] S 4281. [3] Carcopino, *Mélanges*, 27 (1907) 227.
[4] S 4357, 4366, 4368, 4376, 4380. Two of these 'bases' are altars. Three carried small figures, presumably imperial, perhaps in silver.
[5] Paschetto, 294, suggests less probably that the base reused by Septimius Severus was originally dedicated to Hadrian. In style it corresponds very closely to that of Marcus Aurelius. [6] S 4356.

and the comparatively primitive equipment of the *vigiles* could have been carried in hand-carts. More probably this is where the men washed.

We see a little of the lighter side of the fireman's life. On each side of the main entrance there seem to have been bars, for the drinking cups in the mosaic floors point unmistakably to the sale of wine. They may explain why C. Pomponius cut his name twice on one of the pilasters that frame the door. On the walls and floors of some of the rooms traces of familiar games still survive.

The inscriptions found in the building tell us all we know of the organization of the detachment. At first there are no signs of a central-ized command and the number of senior officers seems to vary: there were apparently two tribunes in 168 and 190, only one in 181.[1] In 168 and 239 there were four centurions,[2] suggesting a total force of rather more than 400 men, and this was perhaps the normal size of the detach-ment. The four Ostian centuries, however, were composite forces drawn from different units at Rome. A group of men of the fifth cohort from the century of Respectus serve at Ostia under the command of Tettius Paulinus;[3] and while the tribunes of 168 are drawn from the fourth and seventh cohorts the centurions come from the first, second, sixth, and seventh.[4]

Detached duty at Ostia lasted only four months, and on the Ides of December, April, and August reliefs arrived: 'These men came down in the detachment to Ostia from the Ides of August to the Ides of December, when Pudens and Pollio were consuls (166) in the century of Claudius.'[5] Below comes a list of names followed by the letters 'f.p.a.d.', marking their admittance to state corn (*frumentum publicum accipit die . . .*) on a certain day of the month. For the *vigiles* were recruited partly from the Latini Juniani, whose citizen rights were restricted; by the second century such men received full citizenship at the end of three years' service in the force. The most tangible sign of their new status was the grant of state corn, and this they recorded care-fully. Most of the surviving lists are inscribed on stone, but some are less formal. Three soldiers, of whom two at least joined up on the same day and came down as comrades, have painted their record on a wall of one of the rooms.[6]

In A.D. 195 we hear for the first time of a tribune who is *praepositus*

---

[1] S 4500 (168), 4378 (190), 4503 (181).   [2] S 4500 (168), 4397 (239).
[3] S 4503.   [4] S 4500.   [5] S 4499.   [6] S 4509.

vexillationis,[1] pointing to a centralization of the command under Septimius Severus. A further change may also have been made in his principate, for on the bases of two statues set up in 207 he and his son Caracalla are described as 'restorers of the Ostian camp'.[2] It was probably at this time that the shops on the west side were incorporated in the barracks by the blocking up of their doorways on the street. From this time also the sub-prefect of the *vigiles* is regularly mentioned in inscriptions together with the tribune in command;[3] we may infer that he resided, for at any rate part of the year, in Ostia.

Inscriptions recording *vigiles* have also been found at Portus, and Lanciani reported that most of them came from a large building near the bishop's palace which he considered to be of Antonine date.[4] It seems likely that the harbour force was at first controlled from Ostian headquarters; for Cassius Ligus, tribune of the third cohort, who was *praepositus vexillationis* at Ostia in 195, made a dedication to Hercules by Trajan's harbour.[5] The subordination of a harbour detachment to a headquarters in Ostia town would conform with the general pattern of organization in the second century.

The latest inscription from the barracks of Ostia is on the base of a statue set up to Furia Sabinia Tranquillina, wife of the emperor Gordian III between 241 and 244.[6] The absence of later inscriptions is significant, for the series which begins in 137 is a long one. Later coins, extending to the reign of Julian, were found in the building,[7] but they merely show that the building was still used. The only later evidence connecting Ostia town with the *vigiles* is in an inscription of 386 from Portus which apparently mentions Ostia.[8] But the inscription is fragmentary and the context obscure. It cannot outweigh the absence of evidence in the place where evidence most naturally would have been found.

We may infer that shortly after the middle of the third century the Ostian detachment of *vigiles* no longer did duty in the old town. This is but one of many signs that Rome's overseas trade was now concentrated at the harbours and that Ostia herself was no longer regarded as of vital importance to Rome. It has already been remarked that most

---

[1] *S* 4380.   [2] *S* 4381, 4387.

[3] e.g. *S* 4388 (dated 211), the base of a statue of Caracalla: 'curantibus M. Firmio Amyntiano s(ub)pr(aefecto), M. Antonio Proculo trib. coh. VI vig. praeposito vexillationis.'   [4] 6, 13, 14, 15, Thylander, A 31; Lanciani, *Ann. Inst.* 40 (1868) 188; Fig. 6 (13), p. 164.   [5] Cassius Ligus at Ostia, *S* 4380; at Portus, 13, ?14.

[6] *S* 4398.   [7] *NS* 1889, 37.

[8] 231 = Thylander, B 236. The fragment which may have mentioned Ostia is now lost.

of the *horrea* show no signs of attention in the late Empire. The list of known *procuratores annonae*, whose headquarters seem to have been in Ostia, ends shortly before the middle of the third century. How long the Piazzale delle Corporazioni retained its original function is uncertain. The workmanship of some of the latest mosaics is crude, and several were very carelessly patched, but these are uncertain indications of date. It is more significant that no statue base from the area later than the Severan period has been found, though no less than twelve survive from the second and early third centuries, commemorating procurators, traders, and local dignitaries. It is doubtful whether shippers were doing business here in the fourth century.

The Theodosian Code does not mention Ostia. The *horrea* with which fourth-century emperors were concerned were the *horrea* of Portus and not of the old town. The corn measurers of the Code are the *mensores Portuenses*. Portus remains vital to Rome, but even at Portus the spring has gone out of the year. The *comes portus*, who has replaced the *procurator portus utriusque*, has an unenviable task. He controls less shipping, but he has more anxieties.

The Egyptian corn supply was transferred to Constantinople when Constantine established his new capital in the east. Rome relied increasingly on Africa and looked precariously for the balance to Sardinia, Sicily, and the other western provinces. The sea routes were no longer fully secure. When emperors repeated instructions that there was to be no interference with shipping bound for Rome[1] we may infer that such interference was not uncommon. Famine at Rome was a constantly recurring danger during the fourth century, especially when Africa was temporarily lost.

From the rescripts of the fourth-century emperors we see something of the growing difficulty of the administration. There is corruption in the management of the *horrea* at Portus and special precautions have to be taken against dishonesty; the *mensores* and the *codicarii* have to be reminded of their duties.[2] But the most conspicuous change lies in the position of the guilds. They had begun as free associations; they are now parts of the imperial machine. In the second century the trades which they represented were popular and no special measures were needed to man the services essential to Rome. By the fourth century numbers have to be maintained by a combination of pressure and

[1] *Cod. Theod.* xiii. 5. 4 (324); xiii. 5. 8 (336); xiv. 15. 3 (397).
[2] Ibid. xiv. 4. 9.

privilege. Membership of an essential trade has become hereditary. Claudius had been able to increase the volume of shipping by incentives, without compulsion. A little later the author of the Book of Revelation could write of 'the great city wherein were made rich all that had their ships in the sea by reason of her costliness'.[1] By the fourth century elaborate measures have to be taken to ensure that ship-owners keep their shipping on the seas.

A study of the Ostian guilds is an essential complement to any review of the trade of Ostia.

[1] Rev. xviii. 19.

14

THE GUILDS

WHEN Ostia was at the height of her prosperity, the men who worked at the docks and in the warehouses, in trade and industry, were no longer deeply concerned with local politics. The election of magistrates had passed to the council; the popular assembly rarely met, never for controversial business. The political and social life of the average Ostian was concentrated instead in the *collegia*, the guilds in which members who shared a common interest joined together for mutual benefit.[1]

Such associations had a long history in Rome. Welcome at first, they had come under increasing suspicion towards the end of the Republic when they were abused for political ends, and contributed handsomely to the organization of violence and intimidation. The natural reaction of the authorities was suppression. Only the oldest and most respectable *collegia* were allowed to continue; the remainder were dissolved. When stability was restored by Augustus greater tolerance could be shown, but the potential danger persisted and the guilds remained subject to central control. To maintain a secure existence every guild had to have the formal sanction of the Roman senate or the emperor. Without such formal sanction the guild was *illicitum*, having no legal rights, and was liable to suppression.

In some areas the new dispensation was no more tolerant than the old. In the east, where political faction persisted when power was lost, the guilds could still foment trouble. In spite of the danger of widespread fires, Trajan would not authorize a fire brigade in Nicomedia, though Pliny undertook to restrict the number of members.[2] In Pompeii the disturbances which culminated in bloodshed at the amphitheatre were attributed in part to *collegia*, and unauthorized guilds were suppressed as a result.[3] That the associations of traders were also playing an active part in local politics is clearly shown in the election appeals

---

[1] The basic account of the Roman guilds is by J. P. Waltzing, *Étude historique sur les corporations professionelles chez les Romains* (4 vols. Louvain, 1895–1900); cited as 'Waltzing'.

[2] Pliny, *Epp.* x. 33 and 34.

[3] Tac. *Ann.* xiv. 17. 4: 'collegiaque quae contra leges instituerant dissoluta.'

painted on street walls—farmers, wagoners, timber merchants, and others boldly champion their candidates for office.

At Ostia there were no such political dangers, and there is no sign of restriction. Nor are Ostian guilds confined to trades such as the corn measurers and owners of river boats that were vital to the service of Rome. They cover almost every aspect of the town's life and must have included a considerable proportion of the population. The list of trade guilds known from inscriptions is a long one, and we can be certain that it is not yet complete. Statue bases and commemorative tablets could be afforded by the large and prosperous guilds, such as the builders and those engaged in the corn trade; but the smaller guilds of local craftsmen and traders probably left very few such memorials. The career of Cn. Sentius Felix includes among the guilds of which he was patron, the *argentarii, olearii, piscatores propolae*.[1] We have no other record of these guilds. A tombstone found in 1908 was the first and remains the only hint of the guild of painters, *collegae pingentes*.[2] Very few of the trades of Ostia can have lacked a guild organization. Only a few of these guilds specifically record the authority which protected them, but these include the fullers, *fontani*,[3] who were only of local importance and not one of the most important trades. The number of their members in 232 was less than fifty and their premises, distributed through the town, are small.*We cannot assume that those guilds which do not record such authority were strictly illegal, for they include the powerful and prosperous guild of builders, and the *codicarii* who were indispensable to Rome's supplies.

Our evidence for assessing the nature and function of the guilds in Roman society is fragmentary. Of their legal status we know something from the great collections of Roman law. They could, from the time of Marcus Aurelius, hold property and inherit legacies;[4] they could own and free slaves;[5] they could collect subscriptions from members.[6] The gradual process in the later Empire of their virtual enslavement to the imperial government we can trace in outline from the same sources.

---

[1] 5.   [2] S 4699.

[3] S 4573: 'corpus fontanorum q(uibus) ex s(enatus) c(onsulto) coire lice(t).' Similar authority is recorded by the *fabri navales* of Ostia (168) and of Portus (256), and by the *pelliones* (10); also by the *mensores*, but on only one of their many inscriptions.

[4] *Dig*. xl. 3. 1 (Ulpian): 'divus Marcus omnibus collegiis, quibus ius coeundi est, manumittendi potestatem dedit'; cf. ii. 4. 10. 4. This does not exclude the practical exercise earlier of what now became a formal right.

[5] Waltzing, ii. 438.   [6] Id. i. 451.

For the rest we are mainly dependent on inscriptions. From these we can reconstruct the internal organization of the guilds and learn something of their activities. But inscriptions do not tell the whole story, and it is the things that were taken for granted and were not worth recording that we most want to know. The full record of a guild meeting or the conscientious diary of a *procurator annonae* at Ostia could resolve many problems.

It is on the professional side of the guilds' activities in the early and middle Empire that we are least well informed. How far did the guild press the common interests of its members in relations with other trades and with the authorities? When guild meetings were held, to what extent were trade matters discussed? Did the guilds ever bring pressure to bear by withholding services? Were they concerned with rates of pay and conditions of work? Did they in any sense adopt the principle of the closed shop, making guild membership a condition of exercising a trade?

For most of these activities there is no evidence in the ancient sources. The guilds certainly did not represent the interests of workers against employers, because employers formed the backbone of the guilds. The *lenuncularii* and the *codicarii* were owners of boats and not the oarsmen nor crew. The membership of the fullers' guild is so small that it was almost certainly confined to the owners and managers of fullers' shops. Here, as in the boats, the harder physical work was probably done mainly by slaves. Surviving inscriptions are largely concerned with the social side of the guild's life. It would be a mistake, however, to assume that the trade guilds were almost exclusively social clubs in origin.

In the late Empire the guilds were driven to protect their commercial interests owing to the increasing pressure placed on them by imperial officials. In the third century the *codicarii* and *lenuncularii* together set up a statue to the procurator of the imperial harbours: 'ob insignem eius erga se benevolentiam ac singularem abstinentiam'.[1] In the late fourth century Ragonius Vincentius Celsus, *praefectus annonae*, was commemorated by the measurers of Portus in fulsome terms on his statue base: 'he controlled the administration of the eternal city's corn supply with such fairness of judgement that all who approached him with disputes found in him a father rather than a judge. So it came about that we, the measurers of Portus, who had a long-standing feud with the *codicarii*,

---

[1] 170.

departed satisfied and each party congratulated itself on benefits received and victory won.'[1]

Such inscriptions, though in fact late, would not have been out of place earlier. When, in the second century, the builders honoured Q. Petronius Melior, *procurator annonae*, with a statue 'ob plurima beneficia eius',[2] they were probably thinking of public building contracts rather than private benefactions. C. Veturius Amandus, a Roman knight, described as 'patronus et defensor V corporum lenunculariorum Ostiensium', is commemorated by the *lenuncularii* 'ob insignem eius in defendendis se et in tuendis eximiam diligentiam';[3] it was probably the business interests of the *lenuncularii* that he defended. We see the same common business interests behind the taking of *stationes* by Ostian guilds in the Piazzale delle Corporazioni, as early as the first century.[4] Business interests played a part in the formation of the guilds; the social satisfaction that they provided was, however, an important factor in their growth and popularity. The guild was a miniature *res publica*. Each guild had its own set of rules, embodied in a *lex collegii*. But, though there was considerable variation in detail, the constitutions of the guilds conformed to a common general pattern. They were recruited, it seems, by election, and in some guilds at least membership involved an entry fee; for Cn. Sentius Felix is described as 'gratis adlect(us) inter navicular(ios) maris Hadriatici'.[5] The rank and file of the guild, normally designated *plebs* in the guild rolls, retained within the guild an active part that they had lost in their town assembly. They elected their officers by popular vote and it was by their decrees that honours were normally conferred and general business transacted.[6]

Office in the guild, as in the government of the town, was based on the collegiate principle, but there was variation in the numbers who shared office and in the titles they took. *Quinquennalis* was the standard title for the chief officers, and some, as their title implies, held office for five years; thus a president of the builders could be described as *magister quinquennalis lustri xx*, implying that he held his office in the twentieth five-year period of the guild's history. The chief officers of the *seviri Augustales* were elected for only two years. The number of presidents varied, but not according to the size of the guild. The *lenuncularii*

---

[1] *CIL* vi. 1759.   [2] *S* 5345.

[3] 4144. A similar phrase in a new fragment, Bloch, 48: '—corporis defend—'.

[4] The s(*tuppatores*) r(*estiones*) are among the earliest, above, p. 285; but the guild itself is not mentioned. Later, *S* 4549[2]: 'corpus pellion(um) Ost(iensium) at Porte(nsium) hic.'

[5] 57-8.   [6] *S* 4562.

pleromarii, who had only nineteen ordinary members, had at least three *quinquennales*;[1] the more important *lenuncularii tabularii*, who in 192 had 258 ordinary members, had only two.[2] The builders and probably the shipbuilders of Ostia had three;[3] the important corn merchants had two.[4] The shipbuilders of Portus were exceptional in having as many as six at their head.[5]

The *quinquennales* were the main executive. They presided over meetings, carried decisions into effect, and were responsible for the general conduct and discipline of the guild. In some guilds they were supported by treasurers, normally two, *quaestores* or *curatores*, who were responsible for controlling the income and expenditure of the guild chest. Their funds came from members' subscriptions and benefactions, especially under members' wills. When a man had held the presidency he could be elected to a life-presidency, becoming *quinquennalis perpetuus*; in some guilds ex-officers took the general title *honorati*.[6]

An inscription on the base of a statue set up by the corn merchants to a *procurator annonae* provides a typical illustration of a guild's procedure: 'Q. Calpurnio C. f. Quir(ina) Modesto, proc(uratori)Alpium, proc(uratori) Ostiae ad annon(am), proc(uratori) Lucaniae, corpus mercatorum frumentariorum per M. Aemilium Saturum et P. Aufidium Faustian(um) q(uin)q(uennales), ex decreto corporat(orum), q(uaestoribus) M. Licinio Victore et P. Aufidio Epicteto. l(ocus) d(atus) d(ecurionum) d(ecreto) p(ublice).'[7] The statue was voted by decree of the whole guild. Responsibility for carrying out its decision rested with the two presidents. The expenditure was met by the two treasurers. Since the statue was to be erected not in the guild centre but in the Piazzale delle Corporazioni, the authority of the town council was required.

Such honours were normally paid by the guild as a whole, but instances occur of action taken by part only of the guild. Two bases have been found which once carried statues of P. Martius Philippus, patron of the Ostian shipbuilders. Between the two inscriptions there is only one significant difference. The first is set up by the whole guild, *corpus fabrum navalium*,[8] the other by the ordinary members only, *plebes corporis [fabrum navali]um Ostiens(ium)*.[9] A statue set up by the builders

---

[1] 252; the interpretation is uncertain, possibly six presidents.   [2] 250, 251.

[3] Builders (128, 160); shipbuilders (169; possibly four presidents in a guild roll, Bloch, 43).   [4] 161.   [5] 256.

[6] Builders (128); *dendrophori* (67); shipbuilders of Portus (256).

[7] 161.   [8] 169.   [9] Bloch, 31.

to one of their presidents was decreed not by the whole guild but by the ex-officers: 'huic primum omnium universi honorati statuam ponendam decreverunt ob merita eius'.[1]

Like the town itself, the guilds also elected patrons, in recognition of services rendered or hopefully anticipated. Some patrons were already members of their guild when honoured, as T. Testius Helpidianus, who was 'patronus et q(uin)q(uennalis)' of the *corpus traiectus marmorariorum*.[2] Others were chosen from associated trades, as C. Veturius Amandus, who was patron of the *lenuncularii* and president of the *codicarii*;[3] or P. Aufidius Fortis, who was president of the corn merchants and patron of the measurers.[4] But such associations were not necessary; wealth and influence were the primary qualifications. Cn. Sentius Felix, who rose rapidly to the highest office in the town's government, and was himself a member of the guild of shippers who traded in the Adriatic, was patron of such widely varied guilds as the bankers, the fishermen, the wine merchants, and many others.[5]

Some of the Ostian guilds were even able to attract the patronage of Roman senators. The *lenuncularii tabularii* head their guild roll of 152 with the names of four senatorial patrons.[6] Three of these names recur among the patrons of two other Ostian guilds, one of which has in 140 no less then ten senatorial patrons.[7] But these guilds were perhaps exceptional. The patrons in the guild rolls of the *lenuncularii pleromarii* at Ostia and of the *fabri navales* at Portus seem to be local men.[8]

Within the guild there was no distinction between freedman and free-born citizen. The freedman could not be a member of the town council, nor hold a magistracy, but there was no restriction on his advancement in the guild and many of them rose to office. Nor was this late development. L. Aquillius Modestus, an *Augustalis*, was president of the builders before the death of Nero[9] and a large proportion of the many other presidents known to us from this important guild were also freedmen. They include Marcus Licinius Privatus, who, after rising to the presidency of the builders, became treasurer and then president of the bakers.[10] Office was in the reach of all who could afford the generosity

---

[1] 370.   [2] 425.   [3] 4144.   [4] 10.   [5] 5.   [6] 251.

[7] 246, 247. The names common to all these guilds are T. Prifernius T. f. Paetus Rosianus Geminus, M. Sedatius C. f. Severianus, M. Sedatius M. f. Severus Iulius Reginus. The reason for their close association with Ostia is unknown.

[8] 252, 256.

[9] 299. Modestus was president in the second *lustrum*. The guild was incorporated under Nero, p. 331.   [10] 15.

that was expected of them and a large proportion of members could look forward to a title which would add distinction to their tombstones. For the guilds were not large communities.

The builders who, from the number of surviving inscriptions seem to have been the wealthiest of the guilds, had only some 350 members at the end of the second century.[1] The *lenuncularii tabularii*, who had 128 ordinary members in 152, had increased their numbers to 258 in 192 and perhaps to 290 in 213.[2] The guild roll of the shipbuilders of Portus, probably from the Severan period, includes 353 names.[3] But many of the guilds were much smaller. The *lenuncularii pleromarii* have only 24 members in 200[4] and the fullers less than 50 in 232.[5] Nor does there seem to be any sign of the absorption of small guilds by the larger. The *lenuncularii*, for example, might have been expected to form a comprehensive guild; they preferred to maintain five separate guilds. The *quinque corpora navigantium* sometimes acted together; but they maintained their separate identities and set up independent guild rolls.[6] Similarly the corn measurers, *mensores frumentarii*, were divided into *acceptores, adiutores, nauticarii*; each had their own officers, though they too sometimes combined to honour benefactors.[7]

There were also two guilds associated with the Forum Vinarium, where a single comprehensive guild might have been expected. L. Valerius Threptus is *curat(or) negotiantium fori vinarii, q(uin)q(uennalis) collegi geni fori vinari.*[8] The first of these two guilds elsewhere has the fuller title *corpus splendidissimum importantium et negotiantium vinariorum.*[9] It seems to have combined Roman and Ostian merchants, for we hear of a *q(uin)q(uennalis) corpor(is) vin(ariorum) urb(anorum) et Ost(iensium).*[10] But the two groups may have preserved separate organizations within the guild, for Cn. Sentius Felix is *patronus negotiator(um) vinarior(um) ab urbe*. He was also member of a guild 'ad quadrigam fori vinari',[11] which is perhaps to be identified with the *collegium geni fori vinari*.

Even members who did not achieve office could have the satisfaction

---

[1] S 4569, the guild roll of A.D. 198. Some names are missing, but there are 16 *decuriae*, which average 22 members.   [2] 250 (A.D. 152), 251 (192), Bloch, 42 (213).

[3] 256.   [4] 252.   [5] S 4573.   [6] p. 296.

[7] Presidents of the three divisions are recorded in the dedication of a well-head in A.D. 197, 2. The *adiutores* and *acceptores* combine in setting up a statue to a *procurator annonae*, 154. Separate action by the *adiutores*, 4140. Several inscriptions record the *corpus mensorum frumentariorum Ostiensium*, presumably the combined divisions, e.g. 172, 363, 12. For their functions, p. 282.

[8] 430.   [9] Bloch, 2.   [10] 318.   [11] 5[11. 8].

Y

of rising in seniority among the *plebs*; for it seems that the order in which the names are listed in the guild rolls represents the standing of the members. Of the eleven members of the *lenuncularii tabularii* who survived in the guild from 152 to 192 two have become officers, the remaining nine have risen from near the bottom to the top of the list.[1] In the more recently found fragments of another roll of the same guild set up in 213 the practice is confirmed.[2] The first four columns of this list are missing, but the names at the head of the fifth column correspond with those at the foot of the last column in 192. If the length of the columns were the same in the two lists, some 120 members have remained in the guild since 192 and they are all listed before more recent entrants. Seniority depended apparently on the date of entry; in the record of the names no attempt is made to distinguish between freedman and freeborn. The shipbuilders seem to be exceptional in admitting a small number of free foreigners to their guilds, both at Ostia and at Portus; but there is no suggestion that they had an inferior status within the guild. They are not listed together in the rolls but are scattered through the lists, probably according to their seniority.[3]

Guilds could own slaves, but their names do not appear on the rolls. They were few in number and were probably used for the maintenance of guild headquarters and temples. If they were granted freedom they took their name from the guild which they had served, in the same way as a public slave of the town became Ostiensis. The family name Hadriaticus can have no other origin than the guild of shippers trading in the Adriatic.[4] C. Vinarius Sulpicianus,[5] a member of the *seviri Augustales*, probably owes his name to the wine merchants' guild. Similarly Q. Pistorius Ianuarius[6] may reflect the bakers' guild. But the only such name that is widely distributed in Ostia is Salinator, and the origin of this name is controversial. It has been suggested above that it derives from the workers in the *salinae*, the salt-beds near Ostia.

In some trade-guild inscriptions outside Ostia the titles *mater* and *filia* are found,[7] a strange intrusion in what were essentially masculine societies. Women with these titles are not patrons, but usually seem to be of the same social class as the ordinary members. Their appointments derive from social rather than religious reasons: for some reason they

---

[1] 250, 251, with notes on 251; cf. fragments of two intermediate rolls, S 4567, 4568.
[2] Bloch, 42.   [3] Id. 43; 256.
[4] S 4562 (2B, 1), 4569 (xii. 9), and in two unpublished inscriptions.
[5] S 4563 (5), 12.   [6] S 4975.   [7] Waltzing, i. 447.

had become particularly associated with the guild, perhaps in advising on practical matters in the guild headquarters. Though many guild rolls survive from Ostia, the title *mater* appears only once, in the shipbuilders of Portus. Maecia Menophile has a special heading to herself, and she is listed among the dignitaries, after the presidents of the year, and before the ex-officers, *honorati*.[1] The name Maecius does not recur in the long list; Maecia Menophile did not owe her position to relations in the guild.

Among the trade guilds of Ostia the builders, *fabri tignuarii*, were in several respects exceptional.[2] Unlike the other guilds they had a quasi-military organization, which was perhaps modelled on the pattern of the builders at Rome.[3] The ordinary members of the guild, in place of the colourless title *plebs*, were styled *numerus caligatorum* and were divided into sixteen sections, *numerus caligatorum decuriarum xvi collegii fabrum tignuariorum Ostiensium*.[4] Each section consisted normally of twenty-two members and was presided over by a *decurio*. The sixteen *decuriones* were in turn subordinate to the three presidents, *magistri quinquennales*, who held office for five years and were assisted by a secretary, *scriba*, who maintained the guild records.[5]

An inscription found at Tusculum may throw more detailed light on the organization of the builders' guild.[6] T. Flavius Hilario rose to the head of his section in the fifteenth *lustrum*; in the sixteenth he was chosen to help supervise the voting, *nungentus ad subfrag(ia)*; in the seventeenth he became president, and, after his five years of office, *honoratus*. In the following two periods he was *censor ad mag(istros) creando(s)*, presumably presiding over the elections to the presidency. Finally, in the twenty-second period he was appointed to a board of twelve judges, *judex inter elect(os) xii*, perhaps to settle internal disputes. For the titles *nungentus ad suffragia, censor, iudex* there is no evidence in inscriptions found at Ostia, but they are equally unknown among builders' guilds elsewhere. If Hilario was a freedman of a freedman of the Flavian house his date could fit the Ostian guild.

---

[1] 256²¹.

[2] Tenney Frank (*Economic Survey*, v. 250) suggests that the *fabri tignuarii* of Ostia are woodworkers, perhaps operating furniture factories. Their large size, their form of organization, and the honour they pay to imperial procurators make this view very unlikely. For the meaning adopted, *Dig.* l. 16. 235: ' "fabros tignarios" dicimus non eos dumtaxat qui ligna dolarent, sed omnes qui aedificarent.'

[3] For the Roman guild, Waltzing, ii. 117; for the date of its foundation, C. Pietrangeli, *BC* 67 (1939) 101.   [4] 160.   [5] 347, 418, *S* 4569, dec. iii. 2.   [6] 2630.

No patrons of the builders are recorded, and, in view of the particularly large number of their inscriptions that survive, we may assume
that they had none.[1]★ They were also unlike other guilds in having an
official who was not elected from the members. Three inscriptions
mention a *praefectus* of the guild. All three are men of importance in
local government, and seem to have no business connexion with the
builders. M. Acilius Priscus held equestrian military posts in or near the
Flavian period and, when he returned to Ostia, he became duovir and
pontifex Volcani.[2] P. Aufidius Fortis, in the middle of the second century, held the quaestorship five times as well as the duovirate.[3] Rather
later, M. Antonius Severus was in succession *quaestor alimentorum, quaestor
aerari*, and duovir; his tribe Menenia shows that he did not come from
an Ostian family.[4] M. Acilius Priscus, the first *praefectus* known to us,
is described in the record of his career as holding the post continuously
for three years; perhaps it was an annual appointment which could be
renewed. The title implies that the appointment was made from outside
the guild and not from within, perhaps by the town council.

The Ostian builders are not alone in having a *praefectus*. The title is
also associated with guilds of *fabri* and *fabri tignuarii* in other towns of
Italy and the western provinces. It is usually explained as a para-military
appointment connected with the use of the builders' guild as a fire
brigade.[5] That *fabri* were so used in other towns is clear enough from
the evidence; but there are two difficulties in applying this explanation
to Ostia. There is no positive evidence whatsoever from Ostia connecting the builders with a fire service, and it would be natural to
assume that this responsibility rested with the *vigiles*. There is also no
evidence at Ostia of a guild of *centonarii*, who seem to be an integral
part of the fire service in other towns.

It remains possible that the Ostian builders were required to deal with
fires in residential areas while the *vigiles* were responsible for the docks
and warehouses or that they were used as general auxiliaries to the

---

[1] In two inscriptions *patronus* is restored. 359, the career of a Roman knight, patron of
the colony: [*patrono*] | *collegi fab*[*rum*] | *Ostiensium*; I prefer [*praefecto*] | *collegi fab.* [*tign.*]
Ostiensium (for the office of praefectus, below); *S* 4656: *A. Livio A. filio Palatina* [*patro*]*no
collegi* | *fabrum* [*tignuar. Os*]*tis*. The conditions would be satisfied by *fabrum* [*navalium
Os*]*tis*.

[2] Bloch, 23 = **7**. The title is restored: [*praef(ectus)*] *colleg(i) fabr(um) Ostiens(ium)*
cont[*inuo t*]*riennio*. See Bloch's note.

[3] **10**, p. 203.

[4] 298. Possibly 359 (n. 1 above), also a public figure of standing.

[5] Waltzing, ii. 352–5.

vigiles. A simpler explanation might be that the special importance of the builders in the construction and maintenance of public buildings made it desirable to put them under the control of a senior official appointed by the town government. It is perhaps also possible that the absence of patrons is not the builders' choice. This may have been a precaution imposed from without against corruption. The ship-builders of Portus may also have been subject to official control. P. Martius Philippus, patron of the Ostian shipbuilders under Septimius Severus, is *tribunus fabrum navalium Portens(ium)*.[1] The title is recorded on only one inscription and is not included among the regular officers listed in the guild's roll.

To what extent Ostian trade guilds were confined to the trades they represented is uncertain. We happen to know from a chance inscription that the workers in ivory and citrus wood at Rome admitted to their guild only craftsmen in their own trade.[2] But this restriction was not applied by all the guilds. When the emperors gave privileges to the Roman bakers and to ship-owners they were careful to lay down that the privileges did not apply indiscriminately to all members of the guild, but only to those who were actually carrying on those trades.[3] But since one of the main functions of the guild was to safeguard trade interests it is reasonable to believe that men would most naturally seek election to the guild that represented their own trade. There are, however, several instances of Ostians who belonged to more than one guild.

By imperial regulation a man was not strictly allowed to be a member of more than one authorized guild. The original date of this regulation we do not know, but it was re-enacted by Marcus Aurelius and Lucius Verus.[4] It does not, however, seem to have been strictly enforced at Ostia. M. Caerellius Iazemis is president of the bakers, but also a *codicarius* and a corn merchant;[5] L. Calpurnius Chius, a corn measurer and *codicarius*, is treasurer of both guilds.[6] C. Granius Maturus is a curator

---

[1] 169. [2] *ILS* 7214.

[3] *Frag. Vat.* 233 (Ulpian): 'qui in collegio pistorum sunt, a tutelis excusantur, si modo per semet pistrinum exerceant.' *Dig.* l. 6. 6. 6: 'licet in corpore naviculariorum quis sit, navem tamen vel naves non habeat nec omnia ei congruant, quae principalibus constitutionibus cauta sunt, non poterit privilegio naviculariis indulto uti.' Cf. *Dig.* l. 6. 6. 12, applying more generally to important trade guilds.

[4] *Dig.* xlvii. 22. 1. 2: 'non licet autem amplius quam unum collegium legitimum habere, ut est constitutum et a divis fratribus: et si quis in duobus fuerit, rescriptum est eligere eum oportere, in quo magis esse velit, accepturum ex eo collegio a quo recedit, id quod ei competit ea ratione, quae communis fuit.'

[5] 4234. [6] 16.

of sea and river shipping and associated with the corn measurers.[1] Cn. Sentius Felix is president of the curators of sea shipping and also a member of the guild of shippers trading in the Adriatic.[2] The guilds to which these men belong represent interests that are closely allied. Sometimes there is no such connexion. The freedman Marcus Licinius Privatus worked his way up to the presidency of the builders, later he was treasurer and president of the bakers.[3] L. Valerius Threptus, another president of the builders, was treasurer of the traders in the wine market and president of the guild of the *genius* of the wine market.[4]

Did such men who belonged to more than one guild operate in more than one trade or were they admitted by guilds to which they had no natural claim? It is easy to believe that men who had acquired capital would spread their interests over associated trades. There is no reason, for instance, why a man who traded in corn should not also invest in its transport to Rome and in the bakers' trade which was the largest consumer of corn. It is more surprising to find builders as bakers and wine merchants, but there is nothing inherently unreasonable in a man who has accumulated capital in building trying to increase it by investment in very different occupations. His main responsibility would be to provide the capital for buying or extending the business; he could put the day-to-day management in the hands of freedmen.

There could, however, be a different explanation of such pluralism. Guilds may have been anxious to attract as members men of wealth whatever their occupation in the hope of benefactions. The instances that have been noted are all of men who held guild office, presumably men of substance. The evidence of the guild rolls suggests that such pluralism was not common; probably it was confined to the rich.

If pluralism were common among ordinary members we should expect to find clear traces of it in a comparison of the rolls of the builders of 198 and of the *lenuncularii tabularii* of 192.[5] The wealth of the builders is attested by their premises and by the number of statues that they erected; the *lenuncularii tabularii* had three senatorial patrons. Both guilds must have been very attractive. Yet though the roll of the builders contains some 350 names and that of the *lenuncularii* 258, no single name appears in both lists. A roll of the *lenuncularii pleromarii* also survives from A.D. 200;[6] it has no name in common with the

---

[1] 363, 364. If, as is probable, Bloch, 62, refers to the same man, he was patron and president of the corn measurers.
[2] 57.   [3] 15.   [4] 430.   [5] S 4569, 251.   [6] 252.

builders, and only two are shared with the *tabularii*, M. Cipius Ostiensis and M. Cipius Felix. Even here identity is not certain, for the M. Cipii are widely distributed in Ostia and the two cognomina are also extremely common. Of uncertain date, but probably not far from the end of the second century, is a large fragment of a roll of shipbuilders containing nearly one hundred names.[1] None of the names reappear on the other lists. Similarly, two long rolls survive, from the *lenuncularii tabularii* in 152 and from the contributors to a temple fund in 140; only one name is common to both lists.[2] None of the names recur in a substantial fragment from an unidentified guild roll, also set up near the middle of the century.[3]

In the late Empire the guilds became hereditary and members were tied to their trade. Such compulsion was new, but it had long been customary for sons to follow fathers in the guilds. It was also common for families and their freedmen to follow the same trade.[4] Among the *lenuncularii tabularii* there are 6 M. Cipii in 152, and 13 in 192; there are 10 M. Cornelii in 152 and 23 in 192; there are 5 M. Publicii in 152 and 28 in 192.[5] In the guild of contributors to a temple fund there are no less than 27 L. Naevii, though the name is not common in Ostia.[6] In another fragment of an unidentified guild roll more than a quarter of the forty-odd names preserved are T. Tinucii.[7] Similarly C. Vettii are common among the shipbuilders but otherwise rare.[8]

When the imperial harbours were built it was natural that those whose work was bound up with the harbours and the settlement that grew up round them should at first belong to the Ostian guilds. In some trades the two groups continued a common organization for a long time. The guild of bakers was still described as *corpus pistorum Ostiens(ium) et Port(ensium)* in the Severan period.[9] The tanners also had not yet separated, as their mosaic in the Piazzale delle Corporazioni shows: *corpus pellion(um) Ost(iensium) et Porte(nsium)*.[10] But it was inevitable that, sooner or later, independent guilds should be established

---

[1] Bloch, 43.

[2] 252, 246. P. Cincius Saturninus occurs in both lists (246. vii. 38; 250. iv. 25).

[3] 247. [4] Emphasized by Wilson, *BSR* 13 (1935) 66.

[5] 250, 251. [6] 246.

[7] *S* 5357 (dated 262); cf. *S* 4586, 5358, smaller fragments from similar lists in which T. Tinucii figure prominently, probably from the same guild.

[8] Bloch, 43 (note), perhaps over-emphasizes the point; there are 5 Vettii (no praenomen recorded) among the builders in 198 (*S* 4569), and Vettii in the *s(?tuppatores)* (257), but these are allied trades.

[9] 15. [10] *S* 4549².

by the new harbours; the process had begun long before the independence of Portus from Ostia had been made explicit by Constantine. The shipbuilders of Portus had their own guild, *corpus fabrum navalium Portensium*,[1] before the end of the second century, and a guild roll of *stuppatores*, earlier than the fourth century, has been found at Portus.[2] The *corpus saburrariorum* which honoured Marcus Aurelius in 156 by the harbours is also probably a harbour guild.[3]

Each guild had its own headquarters, *schola*, in which meetings were held, festivities such as the guild's birthday celebrated, and common religious observances maintained. To such *scholae* there are several references in Ostian inscriptions, but only one can be identified beyond doubt. The guild house of the builders occupies a valuable site on the south side of the Decumanus, immediately east of the Forum. It was built in the early years of Hadrian's principate when an intense building programme was being developed in the colony, and resembles in plan the Barracks of the Vigiles on a smaller scale. The rooms of the ground floor open on to a portico which surrounds an open court paved with plain white mosaic. Five of these rooms are clearly dining-rooms and can have been used for little else, for the couches on which the diners reclined are solidly built in concrete. The room which faces the entrance carries most emphasis in the plan and has a podium along its wall, showing that, like the corresponding room in the Barracks of the Vigiles, it was used as a chapel. The kitchen is in the south-west corner, and the latrine in the south-east, tucked away under the stairs. These stairs, with a corresponding set at the north-west angle, solidly built in travertine, still stand, but nothing remains of the upper stories to which they led. This building had already been largely stripped before excavation but it could be identified by the guild roll inscribed on the base of a statue of Septimius Severus.[4]

One other building can almost certainly be associated with a trade guild. On the north side of the Via della Foce is a large hall which was used by the corn measurers. A panel in the centre of the mosaic pavement shows measurers at work; in the hall was found part of a statue base set up by the corn measurers. This hall, however, is very different

---

[1] 169, Bloch, 31.   [2] 257.   [3] 102.
[4] S 4569. It is not certain that this was from the outset the builders' guild house. The podium of the chapel is considerably later, and one at least of the stone couches, in the north-east room, is not original, since it is built against an entrance which was later closed, p. 243, Fig. 8.

from the builders' headquarters. It is undivided and could not provide enough accommodation for an important guild's social headquarters. This was probably not their main *schola*; it may have been connected in some way with a temple that adjoins it.[1] Among unidentified buildings there are several others that may have belonged to guilds.[2]

The guild houses attracted gifts from members and patrons and among them representations of the imperial house predominate in the form of portrait heads, busts, and statues. Fragments of marble tablets recording dedications to the guild of the Rusticelian ferry service, *corpus scaphariorum traiectus Rusticeli*, illustrate the practice.[3] M. Marius Primitivus presents a head or statue of L. Verus to the guild in 145 on the birthday of the emperor Antoninus Pius;[4] in 166 he joins with a colleague in a similar bequest on the birthday of L. Verus.[5] Another fragment may record further bequests by himself and possibly his father to celebrate his appointment to the presidency of the guild under Marcus Aurelius.[6] The standard form of dedication became an imperial head of silver in high relief held up by an Atlas in bronze.[7] It seems clear from their records that this guild regarded imperial birthdays as important occasions. It is perhaps for the same reason that the ship-builders set up statues to patrons on 11 April 195. They probably deliberately chose the birthday of the emperor Septimius Severus for the dedications.[8]

Of another guild, which cannot be identified, we have a much fuller picture, from a well-preserved inscription recording the gifts presented by members to the guild house, which was dedicated in 143:[9]

M. Antonius Ingenuus (presented) a statue of the most true Caesar (M. Aurelius) with a Victory in painted wood and a silver bust of Antoninus Augustus, one pound in weight. To commemorate the dedication (he gave) to every member four sesterces.

A. Herenuleius Faustus (presented) a bust of Antoninus Augustus, two pounds in weight.

[1] Becatti, *Topografia*, 125.
[2] Notably the Schola del Traiano on the western Decumanus, Becatti, *Topografia*, 146. Less secure, Reg. iii. 2. 5, in which an altar to Mars was found, Bloch, 6 (with notes). Possibly the building in the centre of the south side of the triangular area south of the Forum Baths. See also Becatti, *Topografia*, 132.
[3] *S* 4553–6, 5327–8, with notes on p. 665.
[4] *S* 4553.   [5] *S* 4554.   [6] *S* 5327–8.
[7] 'imaginem ex argento cum clipeo et Atlante aereo'; the weight is added.
[8] 168, 169. W. F. Snyder, 'Public Anniversaries in the Roman Empire', *Yale Class. Stud.* 7 (1940) 223–317. esp. 253 f.   [9] Calza, *Epigraphica*, 1 (1939) 28.

C. Voltidius Martianus (presented) a bust of Aelius Caesar (L. Verus), one pound in weight.

C. Antistius Herme(s) (presented) a bust of Concordia, one pound and a half in weight.

C. Antistius Onesimus (presented) a silver bust of the most true Caesar, one pound and a half in weight.

C. Nasennius Felix (presented) a silver bust of Antoninus Augustus, one pound in weight.

C. Nasennius Felix iun(ior) (presented) a silver bust of the most true Caesar, one pound in weight.

P. Aelius Eutychu(s) (presented) six benches.

M. Cornelius Maximus (presented) four tables, two stools.

M. Aeficius Herme(s) and Cn. Sergius Feli(x) presented with their own money a painted wooden statue of L. Aelius Commodus (L. Verus).

Ti. Claudius Threptus presented a hot bath and with it a heating apparatus.

Q. Cornelius Hermes and L. Aurelius Fortunatus presented with their own money a bronze statue of Antoninus Augustus with a marble base and to commemorate the dedication gave to each member four sesterces.

L. Cornelius Euhodus presented a silver bust of Antoninus.

L. Aurelius . . . a pair of candelabra.

L. Cornelius Euhodus (presented) six ?mattresses, four ?cushions.

This catalogue probably covers bequests made over several years from the dedication of the guild house. It closes with a different, but no less typical form of benefaction: 'P. Sextilius Agripp(a) offered at a public meeting of the guild [. . .] on condition that from the interest of the above-mentioned sum the members of the guild should dine on 24 August, the anniversary of his birthday.'

Two of the dedications to this guild were accompanied by distributions of money to the members. Such distributions were not uncommon. On similar occasions the members of the Rusticelian ferry guild each received two or one denarii.[1] When the statue set up by the builders to P. Bassilius Crescens, *procurator annonae*, in the Piazzale delle Corporazioni was dedicated, his *cornicularius* distributed gifts in kind, *sportulae*, to the members.[2] Endowments to provide guild dinners are also recorded in other inscriptions. A. Egrilius Faustus left in his will a capital sum of 4,000 sesterces to his guild to provide an annual dinner on 27 November, presumably his birthday.[3]

A similar interpretation should probably be given to another Ostian inscription.[4] This lists under month headings the names of contributors.

[1] S 4554–6.   [2] 160.   [3] 246, col. 2, 24–29.   [4] 326.

Each name is preceded by the date of the contributor's birthday and is followed by his donation and the annual interest accruing at 12 per cent. There was no fixed contribution, for the sums range from 2,000 to 6,000 sesterces. Nor were all the names inscribed at the same time; it is quite clear from the arrangement on the tablet that the list grew. Probably it contains the names of benefactors providing money for their fellow members of the guild to dine on their birthdays. The list includes one woman and therefore belonged more probably to a religious than to a trade guild. The marble tablet which records the donations was provided by P. Claudius Abascantus and the list includes his son. Both were prominent members of the *dendrophori*; it probably comes from their guild house.

For the religious aspect of the trade guilds the evidence is less explicit, but it seems clear that it was an integral element in their organization. The cult of the guild *genius* and some form of imperial cult were common to all guilds, but most if not all had also their own patron gods or goddesses. The rope-sellers of Portus honour Minerva as *conservatrix et antistes*;[1] the measurers are described as *mensores frumentarii Cereris Augustae*.[2] In the builders' guild house was found a head of Minerva and the record of a dedication to Mars.[3]

It seems highly probable also that some guilds were particularly closely associated with certain temples which they built and maintained. Such guild temples are well attested in other towns;[4] at Ostia the evidence is less direct. No single case can be regarded as clearly proved, but the cumulative evidence is strong.

Opposite the so-called Schola del Traiano on the north-west side of the western Decumanus is a brick temple built probably towards the end of the second century.[5] The temple itself stands well back from the road and is preceded by a large open court enclosed by walls which shut it off from the streets. Such a court is not a common feature in temple architecture but it is well adapted for the purposes of a guild, providing a place for meeting as well as for worship. Within the temple

---

[1] 44.

[2] 5[12]: Cn. Sentius Felix is *patronus mensor(um) frumentarior(um) Cereris Aug(ustae)*; cf. 2, the dedication of a well-head by the measurers: 'monitu sanctissimae Cereris et Nympharum.'

[3] The dedication to Mars (*S* 4300), by a president of the guild, was reused to line the podium of the chapel. The stone was not recovered, but traces of the letters could be read on the plaster.

[4] A list of guild temples, Waltzing, iv. 439. [5] Bloch, 31.

area were found the base of a statue set up to a patron of the shipbuilders and a large fragment of a guild roll.[1] The title of the guild does
not survive on this fragment, but there are good reasons for attributing
it to the shipbuilders, for the list includes a number of free foreigners,
such as are found on the guild roll of the shipbuilders of Portus, but not,
so far as our evidence goes, in other guilds.[2] This then is probably
a temple built and used by the shipbuilders.

Two other temples repeat this plan. The earlier of the two stands on
the south side of the eastern Decumanus, a little west of the theatre.
Steps lead up from the street to an enclosed court. Against the back wall
is the temple, roughly similar in dimensions to that of the shipbuilders;
in front of the steps leading up to the cella is an altar. Little but the brick
carcase of temple and surrounding walls remains, and no inscription
was found within the building. The character of the brickwork and a
fragment of entablature point to a date in the second half of the second
century. Near by, on the opposite side of the Decumanus, was found
a fragment of a large inscribed epistyle; it has a dedication to the deified
Antoninus Pius and was set up probably by the builders.[3] It is tempting
to believe that this epistyle belongs to the temple and that the temple
was dedicated to Antoninus Pius after his death; but the temptation to
identify should probably be resisted. Farther west along the Decumanus,
beyond the Forum, was found a fragment of a very similar inscribed
epistyle.[4] It too carries a dedication by the builders to an emperor, but
during his lifetime, when a temple is not likely to have been built.
Both epistyles may belong to more modest monuments.* It remains
reasonable, however, to infer from its plan that the Antonine temple on
the eastern Decumanus was a guild temple.

The third courtyard temple was designed towards the middle of the
third century, and it has a strange history.[5] This temple lies a little west
of the Round Temple. The street entrance leads into an open court
surrounded by portico, and the temple was to have been built at the far
end of the court. But it seems that the temple itself was never completed. The podium was begun, but before the cella was added there
was a change of plan; the basement within the podium was modified
and converted into a Mithraeum. With this Mithraeum is associated an

[1] Bloch, 43; Becatti, *Topografia*, 149.
[2] Becatti, *Topografia*, 148.   [3] S 4365.
[4] S 4382. The height of the letters, in each line, is almost identical in the two epistyles.
[5] Becatti, *Mitrei*, 21.

inscription found near by, recording that it was built by Fructosus, the patron of a guild.[1] The natural inference is that the Mithraeum was designed for members of the guild; the plan of the area makes it probable that Fructosus was using guild premises. Only the first letter of the guild's name survives; it may have been the guild of *stuppatores*. Among such modest folk Mithraism was exercising a powerful attraction in the middle of the third century: the original intention may have been to build a temple to one of the traditional gods.

There may be a fourth example of a guild courtyard temple. On the east side of the Semita dei Cippi is an attractive building which centres on an open courtyard; by the late Empire a small set of baths had been installed. Two heads of a philosopher, perhaps Plotinus, found in the building, suggest that it may have been used for philosophical discussions. But originally there was a small temple at the end of the courtyard, which was later destroyed; the original plan suggests guild premises.[2]

Another temple may be associated with the measurers. This temple, which stands on the north side of the Via della Foce, has not the distinctive plan of the temple of the shipbuilders, but a hall which was occupied by the corn measurers immediately adjoins it. It is difficult to believe that they would have been allowed to build their premises against a temple unless they had some special relation to it.

In two further cases the evidence is confined to inscriptions. L. Caecilius Aemilianus is described as 'corporatus in templo fori vinarii importatorum negotiantium'.[3] The natural inference is that the wine importers were closely associated with the temple in the wine market. In the guild roll of the shipbuilders at Portus one member is described as *aediti(mus)*;[4] he may have served in a temple belonging to the guild.

It is tempting also to believe, as has often been suggested, that the temple in the middle of the public gardens of the Piazzale delle Corporazioni was a guild temple.[5] The colonnade round the gardens was occupied by *stationes* of Ostian guilds and traders and shippers from the provinces; many of the statues in the gardens were set up by guilds with the permission of the town council. It was here that the builders

---

[1] Bloch, 9: '—rius Fructosus patron(us) corp(oris) s[— | te]mpl(um) et spel(aeum) Mit(hrae) a solo sua pec(unia) fecit.'

[2] No detailed publication is available; Becatti, *Topografia*, 155.

[3] Bloch, *Epigraphica*, i (1939) 37. See also pp. 335 f.

[4] 256[179].

[5] Paschetto, 175.

honoured one of their presidents, Marcus Licinius Privatus;[1] Q. Acilius Fuscus, *procurator annonae*, was similarly honoured by two branches of the corn measurers.[2] The statue of Q. Calpurnius Modestus, also *procurator annonae*, was set up by the corn merchants.[3] The area was peculiarly associated with the guilds; it is not unlikely that they at least contributed to the building and maintenance of the central temple.

We do not know to what gods or goddesses these temples were dedicated, but, so far as our evidence goes, the guild cults in the second century were the old-established cults of the traditional religion. Though many of their members worshipped Isis, Mithras, and other oriental gods, there is no evidence to suggest that such cults were ever officially adopted by the trade guilds until the late Severan period. The building then of a Mithraeum instead of a temple on guild premises may be a sign of the times.

Their temples, their guild houses, their statues set up in public gave to the Ostian trade guilds a conspicuous place in the life of the town. It is possible that they also paraded with banners on ceremonial occasions. For this there is no evidence, but it is only from chance literary references that we know that the Roman guilds took part in such occasions as the triumphal processions of Gallienus and Aurelian.[4]

Any review of the trade guilds of Ostia must be based primarily on the inscriptions and buildings of the period from the Flavian to the Severan dynasties, when they were popular and prosperous. The evidence for their rise and consolidation and for their later decline is fragmentary and tenuous. Of trade associations under the Republic we know nothing and are likely to learn little from further excavation. Under Augustus the ship-owners of Ostia, *navicularii Ostienses*, acted together in honouring a Roman quaestor,[5] but they were not necessarily at the time formally united in a guild. The first guild whose formal incorporation we can approximately date is the guild of builders; their history starts in the Julio-Claudian period.

On the side of the base of a statue of the emperor Diocletian set up by the builders in 285 are recorded the names of the three presidents of the twenty-ninth *lustrum*.[6] This would suggest a foundation date for the guild near the middle of the second century, but it was long ago seen that such a late date was incompatible with many other inscriptions

[1] 15.   [2] 154.   [3] 161.
[4] *vexilla collegiorum*; SHA, *Gall.* 8. 6; *Aurel.* 34. 4.
[5] 3603, Bloch, 32.   [6] 128.

relating to the guild and its presidents. Formal proof that Diocletian's base had been used before and that the date referred to an earlier dedication was found when a membership roll was discovered in the builders' guild house. This roll is inscribed on the base of a statue of Septimius Severus which was set up in 198.[1] In it the three presidents of the twenty-ninth *lustrum* appear at the head of three of the sixteen sections, and since no presidents are separately recorded in the roll it is possible that they were in fact presidents at the time.[2] If 198 fell in the twenty-ninth *lustrum* the guild will have been established between 58 and 63.

On general historical grounds the principate of Claudius might seem a better context than that of Nero, but further correspondences confirm that this date is approximately correct. L. Antonius Peculiaris was president of the guild in the twenty-fifth *lustrum*.[3] In his period of office a commemorative tablet was set up to Q. Petronius Melior, *procurator annonae*,[4] who was honoured by the corn measurers in 184.[5] This also suggests a date near 60 for the formal incorporation of the guild.[6]

The only other evidence bearing on the first-century history of the guilds concerns a much smaller guild. Under Trajan the guild of the ferry service of Lucullus, *corpus lenunculariorum traiectus Luculli*, received permission from the Tiber commissioner to improve premises which may have been their guild house. The inscription records the completion of the work—'firmiori et cultiori opere fecerunt'—and its dedication to the majesty of the imperial house.[7] This guild must already have been well established at the time. From the evidence at present available no other trade guild can be proved to have been formed before the second century and one of the most important seems not to have been formed before the Antonine period. The *lenuncularii tabularii auxiliarii* had a large membership and powerful patronage. Fragments of no less than five of their guild rolls survive, but the earliest is from 152 and this roll includes with the presidents of the year only one ex-president,[8] whereas the roll of 192 has six. The first surviving roll seems to be near the guild's foundation.

The absence of evidence does not, of course, mean that no other guilds

---

[1] S 4569.
[2] Praenomina are not recorded in this roll, but nomen and cognomen correspond: (Cn.) Sergius Mercurius, dec. xv. 1; (M.) Licinius Privatus, xvi. 1; (T). Claudius Sosipolis, vi. 1.   [3] 297.   [4] S 5345.   [5] 172 with p. 481.
[6] For a fuller review of the evidence, Wickert, S, p. 611.
[7] S 5320.   [8] 250.

existed. First-century inscriptions are still comparatively rare, and very few Julio-Claudian buildings, apart from the temples, survived the rebuilding of the town in the early second century. But the contrast with the very large number of inscriptions from the early second century is striking and perhaps not without significance. It is doubtful whether the guilds were wealthy or powerful before the general growth of prosperity which is reflected in the intensive rebuilding of the town. In the second century they enjoyed wealth and prestige. They could afford handsome buildings, develop a colourful social life, and attract generous patronage. Their decline during the third century was probably abrupt. After the Severan period very few guild inscriptions survive. Even the builders in setting up a statue to Diocletian reused an old base and omitted to erase the earlier date.[1]

The main reason for the virtual eclipse of the trade guilds in Ostia was the shrinking of the total volume of trade and the shifting of emphasis to Portus. The guilds of Portus were still essential to Rome and could not therefore be allowed to disintegrate. In the Theodosian Code we hear of the *mensores*,[2] the *saccarii*,[3] the *codicarii*[4] of Portus. The *codicarii* set up a statue to the emperor Constantine,[5] the *mensores* to a *praefectus annonae* of the late fourth century.[6] When Portus can be excavated we are likely to find much more late evidence for the guilds than at Ostia. But the trade guilds of the fourth century are very different in character from those of the second; instead of free institutions they have become closely controlled departments of state.[7]

Not all guilds were connected with trade. Among the old-established guilds at Rome some were connected with public religion. Such religious guilds were not uncommon in imperial Ostia. Though serving a different purpose they closely resembled the trade guilds in organization, and offered similar social attractions in addition to their religious functions. They had their own guild houses, and a similar hierarchy of officers and patrons.

Attached to the cult of Magna Mater were the *dendrophori* and the *cannophori*. The cult which they served was popular among the ruling classes and the common people. A roll of the *dendrophori* from the Severan period records five patrons, including some of the most distinguished Ostians of the day.[8] When their guild house was rebuilt it

---

[1] 128. [2] *Cod. Theod.* xiv. 4. 9. [3] Ibid. xiv. 22.
[4] Ibid. xiv. 4. 9. [5] 131. [6] *CIL* vi. 1759.
[7] For the later history of the guilds, Waltzing, ii. 357. [8] p. 504.

was dedicated to the *numen domus Augustae*; gifts to it included figures of Mother Earth, of Mars, and of Silvanus. The *cannophori* had a similar organization and attracted similar benefactions. A high priest of the Great Mother presented statues of Cybele and Attis to the guild and dedications to emperors were made in the guild house by individuals and by the guild. In the area reserved for the cult of Magna Mater was a temple of Bellona; near by was the guild house of the *hastiferi*, who were especially associated with her cult.[1]

The *cultores Iovis Tutoris* also formed an association, but their headquarters may have been outside the town, for the only inscription referring to them was found near Acilia. It records a gift by two officials, a *quaglator*, whose function we do not know, and a *curator*.[2]

A record is also preserved of the *cultores Larum et imaginum Augustorum*.[3] They had petitioned an imperial procurator for the use of a site on an estate that had once belonged to the Rusticelii, but had become imperial property. His decision is commemorated as a charter of foundation:

This site was assigned by Callistus, imperial procurator, to the worshippers of the *lares* and *imagines* of our invincible lords on the Rusticelian estate for the celebration of due occasions under the care of Maximianus, slave born in the emperor's service, steward of the estate, as is provided in the letter sent by the above-named Callistus. The site was designated on the Kalends of June when the emperor Antoninus Pius Felix Augustus was consul for the second time (205).

There follows a copy of the procurator's letter to the steward of the estate:

Callistus to Maximianus. The petition sent to me by the worshippers of the imperial *lares* I have sent to you. In such a matter, where religious duty was so clearly involved, you should have shown every anxiety to see that the site which had been formerly consecrated should be used for meetings to promote the welfare of our lord emperors. Now, though the worshippers express their wish to do it themselves, see that you take the matter in hand and have the place cleaned without delay.

In the list of members added below at least three imperial slaves are included. The association was probably composed mainly of workers on the estate.

[1] For the guilds associated with Cybele, Attis, Bellona, p. 360.
[2] 25. Waltzing, i. 424, suggests that the *quaglator* was an arbitrator.
[3] S 4570.

In addition to trade and religious guilds individually sanctioned by the Roman senate or the emperor general authority was granted early in the second century by senatorial decree for the establishment of *collegia tenuiorum*.[1] These guilds of humble folk raised funds for the burial of their members and enjoyed the other social benefits of union. The decree which authorized them is quoted in an inscription from Lanuvium which contains also the rules of a local burial guild.[2] The conditions imposed were intended to ensure that the guild did not become a source of disturbance nor lose sight of its primary function. Monthly subscriptions could be collected, but members could meet only once a month. In the rules of the Lanuvium guild the special feast days of the guild are listed together with the contributions in kind due from members; precautions are also taken against unruly behaviour. A fragmentary inscription from Ostia seems to preserve in its heading a paraphrase of the senatorial decree;[3] it was probably set up by an Ostian burial club.

Similar in organization to the guilds were the *iuvenes*. The institution of the Juventus was widespread in Italy and the western provinces. It represented the young men of standing in the community, who had their own headquarters, paraded on ceremonial occasions, and gave their own special display, the *lusus iuvenalis*.[4] It is doubtful whether the institution had a long history in Ostia, for it is recorded in only two surviving inscriptions. Cn. Sentius Felix, who held the duovirate in the late first or early second century A.D., was *q(uaestor) iuvenum* and also *curator lusus iuvenalis*.[5] This latter office is recorded in another fragmentary inscription which is probably not much later in date.[6] Cn. Sentius Felix was also patron of the *veterani Aug(usti)*.[7] It is very doubtful whether Ostia attracted veterans from the legions, but several inscriptions record men who had settled in Ostia after serving in the praetorian or urban cohorts at Rome. *Veterani Augusti* also include men who had served in the fleet. They were of very different status and origin from the urban troops, but they probably belonged to the same veterans' guild.

---

[1] Waltzing, i. 141. [2] *ILS* 7212. [3] *S* 4548.

[4] M. della Corte, *Iuventus* (Arpino, 1924).

[5] 5[4, 17]. He is also *patronus iuven(um) cisianor(um)* (l. 15), perhaps a separate organization of *iuvenes* who raced in two-wheeled carriages.

[6] Unpublished.

[7] 5[16]; cf. *S* 4364, a commemorative tablet in honour of an emperor, probably Antoninus Pius, set up by '[cor]pus veter[anorum]'.

Freedmen had their own special organization, the *seviri Augustales*. Their official concern was the cult of the imperial house, but they had their own social headquarters and were organized as a guild. The main attraction of membership was almost certainly the prestige and practical advantage of belonging to a wealthy society, publicly recognized. The most distinctive feature of their organization is the elaboration of their hierarchy and the large number of their officials. The former slave was more conscious than the free citizen of the dignity of office.[1]

Even the public slaves and freedmen employed in the town service were allowed to form their own organization. Their guild roll is headed by a *tabularius*, a freedman, presumably responsible for keeping the records, and two *arkarii*, treasurers, who are both slaves. Of the 81 members, 21 are slaves, 35 have the name Ostiensis, showing that they are former slaves who have won their freedom in the town service, or freedmen of men so freed; the remainder are freedmen from other families.[2] It is significant that slaves are not separated in the list but are distributed among the freedmen. As in the trade guilds the order is probably based on seniority.

Two other guilds are more difficult to classify. The guild of the five districts, 'corpus V region(um) col(oniae) Ost(iensium)', is known from one inscription only.[3] Whether this association was religious or merely social we cannot know. The evidence for the other guild is fuller but hardly more easy to interpret. A large marble tablet, long since lost, records the names of guildsmen who contributed money for the enlargement of a temple, *ordo corporator(um) qui pecuniam ad ampliand(um) templum contuler(unt)*; it was set up in 140.[4] The guild has no less than ten senatorial patrons; in addition to life-presidents and presidents there are 181 ordinary members.

It would seem at first sight that the sole function of this guild was to raise subscriptions for the rebuilding of an important temple, and that its life would end when the temple was rebuilt. It is surprising therefore to see that one of the guild members left to the guild a capital sum to provide guild banquets on the anniversaries of his birthday.[5] Two further rolls of the guild, discovered more recently, confirm that the guild had a long life. The first was set up shortly before 135.[6] The guild

---

[1] For the *seviri Augustales*, p. 217. [2] 255.
[3] 352 (dated 251). [4] 246. [5] 246, col. ii. 24.
[6] S 5374. The title of the guild is lost, but the two *quinquennales* of 135 are listed in the roll of 140 as *quinquennalicii*. Other names occur in both lists. See Wickert's notes in *CIL*.

then had only three patrons and two at least, probably all three, were local men; perhaps this inscription marked the beginning of the guild. The second list is dated to 179, but records also the presidents for 182 and 187.[1] There are now only two patrons, a senator and a knight, but there are still more than 100 members. It seems unlikely that the rebuilding of a temple was spread over fifty years, for the earlier decades of the guild were years of great prosperity in Ostia.

There should be a clue to the identity of the guild in the career of Cn. Sentius Felix. He is recorded as a patron in the first of the guild rolls surviving, and his career is set out in great detail on his funerary altar.[2] There is no title in his career that directly reflects the heading in the guild rolls, but two titles remain unexplained. Felix was patron of the 'corpus togatorum a foro', a guild otherwise unknown; if, however, this was another name for the temple contributors, the temple should presumably be in the Forum. But it is almost inconceivable that either of the two temples in the Forum, the Capitolium or the temple of Rome and Augustus, should have been dependent on private subscriptions; nor does the list contain sufficient distinguished Ostian names to fit either of the two main temples of the town. Felix was also 'gratis allect(us) inter navicula(rios) maris Hadriatici et ad quadrigam fori vinari'. The reference seems to be to two closely associated guilds, the second at least having its headquarters in the Forum Vinarium. It is economic to believe that this is the guild to which L. Caecilius Aemilianus belonged, 'corporatus in templo fori vinari importatorum negotiantium'.[3] The guild rolls may belong to wine importers who were responsible for the maintenance of the temple in the Forum Vinarium. The interest of importers from Rome in the business of the wine market would help to explain the patronage of Roman senators.

The guilds of Ostia covered a very wide field and must have included a considerable proportion of the free population. They provided an outlet for the ambitions of the rich and, to those who were less well off, amenities which they could not individually afford. Their prosperity coincides with the rise of the middle class, and the dominance of the insula. When emphasis shifts to the domus, the self-contained house of the wealthy, in the late Empire, the guilds have become impoverished and inconspicuous in the old town. At Portus the trade guilds had a longer prominence under the mixed blessings of protection and control.

---

[1] S 5356. [2] Patron, S 5374 (a) 3. Career, 5.
[3] Bloch, *Epigraphica*, 1 (1939) 37.

15

RELIGION

WHEN Ostia was at the height of her prosperity, the Forum, which was the centre of public life, was framed at its northern and southern ends by temples, and the Capitolium, at the northern end, was the dominant building in the town. Temples were conspicuous in every quarter, built singly or in groups; a host of smaller shrines, less conspicuous, can still be seen in private houses and public buildings. The ruins and inscriptions suggest that religion pervaded public and private life, but the pattern is complex and changing. It reflects general changes of outlook in the Roman world, and particular changes in Ostia's social structure.

The study of Ostian cults is tantalizing, for more than half the temples that have been discovered are still nameless, and many of those known from inscriptions have yet to be identified. But sufficient evidence is already available to attempt an historical survey. The traditional cults of the Roman people dominated Ostian religion in the Republic and early Empire; the rise of the middle class and the growing cosmopolitanism of second-century prosperity was accompanied by a deep penetration of oriental cults. The spreading of Christianity coincides with the period of economic stress, and the stubborn resistance of paganism to the domination of Christianity in the fourth century probably derives from a wealthy aristocracy. Every aspect of Ostian religion can be paralleled elsewhere in the Roman world, but the total pattern is distinctively Ostian.

REPUBLICAN CULTS

The most distinctive feature in the history of Ostia's religion is the pre-eminence of the cult of Vulcan.[1] His high priest has a general supervision over the temples of the town; he is *pontifex Volcani et aedium sacrarum*. His authority is recorded in inscriptions for the setting up of a statue to a priest of Isis;[2] he also authorizes statues in the field of

[1] L. R. Taylor, *The Cults of Ostia* (Bryn Mawr Monographs, xi, 1912) 14. Cited as 'Taylor'.　　　　　　　　　　　　　　　　　　　　[2] 352.

the Great Mother,[1] and dedications to Serapis by the imperial harbour.[2] He is chosen from the leading citizens of Ostia and his appointment, which is for life, is recorded in the town Fasti.[3] He is assisted in the cult of Vulcan by three praetors and two (possibly three) aediles, *praetores (aediles) sacris Volcani faciendis*.[4]

While the *pontifex Volcani* was always a man who had won distinction, local or imperial, the praetors and aediles of the cult were normally appointed before they entered the local Council; and they could be appointed very young. A. Fabius Felicianus died at the age of nineteen;[5] L. Aurelius Fortunatianus, *praetor primus*, was only four and a half years old when he died;[6] P. Lucilius Gamala similarly was probably only a boy when he was appointed *praetor tertius*.[7] Normally only one of these junior priesthoods was held; Cn. Turpilius Turpilianus and P. Lucilius Gamala are exceptional in holding both.[8] It seems likely that the office was held for one year only and was regarded as a preliminary step in a public career. Of the duties of this college of junior priests we have only one echo, in a fragment of the Fasti for A.D. 91: 'in [fundo] Volusiano arb[os ful]mine icta; cond[itum per] aedilicios'. It seems that the aediles of Vulcan were responsible for the laying of the god's anger when lightning had struck. A small marble tablet found in the Via della Fullonica, with the inscription 'fulgur divum',[9] and similar tablets in an Ostian house and on the wall of a *crypta*[10] may record the propitiatory action of Vulcan's aediles.

One Ostian inscription mentions a *patrius deus* of Ostia. Cn. Turpilius Turpilianus, aedile and praetor in the cult of Vulcan, offered an image of Vulcan 'patrio deo'.[11] It is a reasonable inference that the offering was in fact made in the temple of Vulcan. Even if this inference is wrong, the offering of an image of Vulcan would still emphasize the importance of Vulcan's cult in Ostia.

The origin and early nature of Vulcan's cult remain obscure. The Romans themselves could not explain the name and the derivation is still far from certain. In historical times Vulcan was primarily a god of fire and had been largely assimilated with the Greek Hephaestus; he was important, but not one of the major powers. Earlier it may have

---

[1] 324, 325.　　　　　　　　　[2] 47.　　　　　　　　　[3] *Fasti*, A.D. 36 and 105.
[4] For the number, p. 173.　　　　　　　[5] 351.　　　　　　　　[6] 306.
[7] 2³⁻⁵. His priesthoods of Vulcan are listed before his election to the council, when he is *infans*.　　　　　　　[8] 3, 2.　　　　　　　　　[9] S 4294.
[10] C. Pietrangeli, 'Bidentalia', *Rend. Pont.* 25–26 (1949–51) 37–52 (Ostia, 39, 41).
[11] 3.

been very different. Before Jupiter came to dominate the Roman
pantheon, tradition suggests that Vulcan had a more important place
than later in Roman cult.[1] Of this there is an echo in the ritual of
devotio described by Livy: 'qui sese devoverit, Volcano arma sive cui
alii divo vovere volet, ius est.'[2]

In what form and by what means did Vulcan come to Ostia?
Wissowa considered that the special importance of Vulcan in Ostia is
explained by the overriding danger of fire among the granaries.[3] To
this there are strong objections. When fourth-century Ostia was built,
her main function was to protect the coast; it was not until much later
that the storage of corn and other goods became her chief concern. We
may doubt whether, if Wissowa's explanation is right, Vulcan would
have displaced the patron god of the fourth century. It is reasonable
to look for deeper roots.

Carcopino, who has made the most detailed study of the problem,
has offered the most comprehensive solution.[4] In his view Vulcan was
originally the god of water as well as fire and pre-eminently the god of
the Tiber. His cult was a federal cult of the Latins at the river mouth.
Like the cults of Lavinium it was taken over by Rome when she conquered the area, but the cult was maintained at its original centre. The
priesthood of Vulcan at Ostia is to be compared with the *Laurentes
Lavinates* of Lavinium and the *sacerdotes Caenin(i)enses*. Pontifex, praetors,
and aediles were appointed by Rome, but since Ostia was a populous centre, unlike Lavinium, it was unnecessary to look outside Ostia
to fill the posts. The main festival of Vulcan at Ostia, the Volcanalia on 23 August, remained a Roman concern. The emperor or his
representative presided and stayed at Ostia for a series of associated
festivals, including those of Castor and Pollux. Virgil, according to
Carcopino, glorified this cult in his *Aeneid*. His Thybris is the Ostian
Vulcan and the federal centre is clearly prophesied in a well-known
passage:

> hic mihi magna domus, celsis caput urbibus exit.[5]

The 'magna domus' is the temple of Vulcan at Ostia; the high cities
are the Latin cities of the Alban hills who share the cult at the river
mouth. The name of this cult centre is preserved in a priesthood

---

[1] Wissowa in Roscher, *Lexikon der griech. und röm. Mythologie*, vi. 357.
[2] Livy viii. 10. 13; cf. i. 37. 5; xxx. 6. 9; xli. 12. 6.
[3] Wissowa, *Religion und Kultus der Römer*[2], 230; still maintained in Roscher, *Lexicon*,
vi. 362.   [4] Carcopino, 39–167.   [5] Virg. *Aen.* viii. 65.

recorded in Ostian inscriptions, the *sodales Arulenses*. Arula was the name of the pre-Roman religious centre at the Tiber mouth.

Carcopino's identification of Vulcan with the god of the Tiber has won very little support. The arguments marshalled against the view by Rose seem decisive,[1] and they have been further strengthened by Le Gall's more recent study of the Tiber cult.[2] There is no real evidence in the *Aeneid* to suggest that Virgil's Thybris is any other than *pater Tiberinus*, who had a shrine at Ostia and was also worshipped at other points on the river. The crucial line from which Carcopino drew such sweeping inferences admits more easily a completely different meaning. The contrast is between the lower and upper Tiber; the high cities are the hill-top towns near the headwaters of the river.[3]

But though Carcopino's identification of Vulcan with the Tiber cannot be accepted, his view that Roman Ostia was preceded by a federal cult centre of Vulcan is not thereby discredited: Rose finds this interpretation reasonable and probably right.[4] The case rests on two main arguments, the interpretation of the *sodales Arulenses* and the control by Rome of the Ostian priesthood. In the present state of our evidence neither argument can be more than a hypothesis; each has its difficulties.

The *sodales Arulenses* are recorded in five inscriptions and in four cases certainly, in the fifth possibly, the holders of this priesthood also held a junior priesthood in the cult of Vulcan. But four of the inscriptions come from the late second or the third century and there is no reason to believe that the fifth is substantially earlier.[5] In this late period the priesthood seems to be a normal stage in a public career. Had it existed in the first half of the second century some record of it should have survived, for those years, corresponding to the peak of Ostia's prosperity, are particularly rich in inscriptions. It is natural to infer that the *sodales Arulenses* were instituted after the middle of the second century; it is unlikely therefore that their roots lie so deep in Ostia's history. If the memory of a pre-Ostian Arula had survived so long, we could expect to find some echo in a literary source.[6]

---

[1] H. J. Rose, 'The Cult of Volkanus at Rome', *JRS* 23 (1933) 46.

[2] Le Gall, *Recherches sur le culte du Tibre* (Paris, 1953) 40.

[3] Ibid. 43 f.   [4] Rose, art. cit. 51 f.

[5] 341, **11**, 432, *S* 4671 are approximately dated by clear internal evidence. Bloch, 56 = *S* 4625 has to be dated by script alone.

[6] Arulenses might possibly be derived from *arula* = a little altar; cf. *CIL* xiii. 939: 'sacerdos Arensis'. In a second-century hall opposite the temple of Hercules (Reg.

The relation of Rome to the Ostian cult of Vulcan remains equally obscure. In the Fasti 'creatus' is used of the appointment of the pontifex; the word, embarrassingly wide in connotation, would be applicable to appointment by a Roman authority, by the Ostian council, by the Ostian people, or by the priests of Vulcan. Among praetors and aediles in the cult the method of appointment is specified in only one case, and even there the restoration is controversial. M. Marius Primitivus was probably appointed by the Ostian council: 'decur(ionum) dec(reto) aed(ilis) | sac(ris) Volc(ani) fac(iundis)';[1] but his case might be so recorded precisely because it was exceptional.

We are on no firmer ground when we look for the presence of emperors or their representatives at the Volcanalia at Ostia. Carcopino points out that the tradition of a third-century Christian persecution at Ostia records that the investigations were carried out on the emperor's instruction either by the *praefectus urbi* or by a *vicarius urbis*, and that he was at Ostia from roughly 8 to 28 August. Carcopino assumes that the dates are significant and that the investigation was timed to coincide with the Volcanalia on 23 August over which the emperor's representative was to preside.[2] It is easier to assume that the investigation took place in August, because the trouble came to a head in August.

A second instance is rather stronger. When Messalina made her bid for power in 48, she waited, according to Tacitus, until Claudius was to leave for Ostia to celebrate a sacrifice.[3] That this was not the only object of his journey is suggested by the account of Dio, who says that Claudius went to examine the corn supply;[4] and Claudius was certainly accompanied by his *praefectus annonae*.[5] But the two accounts are compatible and, if the dates fitted, the Volcanalia might be implied in the reference. Tacitus gives a mark of time in his description of Messalina's celebrations: 'adulto autumno simulacrum vindemiae celebrabat.'[6] The Romans regarded autumn as beginning on 8 or 11 August; the Volcanalia were on 23 August. This might possibly be described as 'adulto

---

1.15.3, the Aula delle Are) were preserved four republican tufa altars, which may have been in the care of the *sodales Arulenses*.

[1] *S* 4553. Carcopino (64) refers his appointment by the council to his membership of the council: 'Primit[ivus d(ecreto)] decur(ionum) dec(urio), aed. || sac. Volc. fac.' But the standard formula for appointment to the council is 'decurionum decreto decurio adlectus', e.g. 321, 349, 362, 390.   [2] Carcopino, 156.

[3] Tac. *Ann.* xi. 26. 7: 'nec ultra expectato quam dum sacrificii gratia Claudius Ostiam proficisceretur.'

[4] Dio lxi. 31. 4.   [5] Tac. *Ann.* xi. 31. 1.   [6] Ibid. 4.

autumno', but the natural interpretation of the phrase requires a later date, in September, or possibly October. And if Claudius was concerned for the corn supply he is more likely to have sacrificed to Castor and Pollux, to whom we later find an urban prefect praying for calm weather.[1]

If it could be demonstrated that the festival of Castor and Pollux was closely associated with the Volcanalia, Carcopino's thesis would be strengthened, for we know that this festival was presided over in the late Empire by the urban prefect or consul, and earlier by the urban praetor. But Carcopino's general arguments for dating the festival in August are insufficiently strong to outweigh the only piece of positive evidence available, which dates the festival to 27 January.[2]

Nor should any inference concerning the importance to Rome of the Ostian cult of Vulcan be drawn from the propitiatory ceremonial prescribed by the Sibylline books in 64 after the great fire at Rome.[3] Tacitus records that supplication was to be made to Vulcan, Ceres, and Proserpina; and that Juno was to be propitiated by the matrons of Rome, first on the Capitoline hill, then at the nearest point on the coast; water was taken from the sea and sprinkled over the temple and image of the goddess.[4] Ostian Vulcan is not here concerned; purification by sea-water was a standard prescription, which had been earlier applied in a more drastic form to Cybele.[5]

Until more definite evidence can be found it is easier to believe that Vulcan came to Ostia from Rome rather than to Rome from Ostia, and that when he came he was a god of wider powers than he enjoyed in the late Republic and Empire. It is not impossible that he was the main god of an early settlement by the salt-beds and that he retained his preeminence and an elaborated priesthood when that settlement was absorbed by the fourth-century colony. If that is so, his temple may have been east of Ostia, near the salt-beds, and that would help to explain why no trace of it has been found. We learn that it was restored by the Augustan Gamala,[6] and the Fasti record a further restoration under Trajan in 112, but no temple within or near the Castrum can be identified as Vulcan's. The problem is further complicated by a series of fragments ingeniously associated by Barbieri. This inscription records

---

[1] As suggested by Taylor, 24; Amm. Marc. xix. 10. 4. For the beginning of the Roman autumn, Pliny, *NH* xviii. 271, Varro, *RR* i. 28. 1.

[2] Calendar of Polemius Silvius, *CIL* i², p. 257.   [3] Carcopino, 77.

[4] Tac. *Ann.* xv. 44. 1.   [5] Dio xlviii. 43. 5.   [6] I²¹.

an *aedes Volcani* and *pronaos*, but seems to refer to a new building sanctioned by the Roman senate.[1] The size of the letters suggests a small building and the date is probably Julio-Claudian. This may be a secondary temple within the city.

Vulcan's is not the only cult associated with the origins of Ostia. L. Calpurnius Chius, a rich freedman living in or near the Severan period, was *magister ad Martem Ficanum*.[2] The title has been associated with Ficana, which, in the tradition, was conquered before Ostia was established.[3] It was the conquest of Ficana, the last high point between Rome and the sea, which gave Rome control over the mouth of the river and the coastal plain. This inscription is insufficient evidence for a public cult of Mars Ficanus, for L. Calpurnius Chius might have been an official of a *vicus* named after a statue. New evidence, however, shows conclusively that such a cult was maintained. The new evidence is a small base carrying an inscription. The relief above the inscription, probably a figure of Mars, has been almost completely lost, but the inscription is well preserved. It records a dedication to Mars Ficanus by an imperial slave, *vilicus saltuariorum*, probably in the late second century A.D.[4] This inscription was found in 1952 in the grounds of an agricultural establishment on the Via Ostiensis, roughly half a mile east of Roman Ostia; it had been brought there some five years previously and was said to have been found at Malafede, roughly a mile on the Romeward side of Acilia. If this was the original site of the dedication, it might mark the assumed position of a battle that preceded the capture of Ficana.[5]

Among the other cults of republican Ostia the worship of Castor and Pollux had special importance. The Fasti of Polemius Silvius include among Roman festivals 'the games of the Castors at Ostia' on 27 January, which was the day of the dedication of the temple of Castor and Pollux in the Roman Forum.[6] At Rome the Dioscuri were associated with the cavalry: they had taken part in the Battle of Lake Regillus and

---

[1] *S* 4724. With the help of new fragments Barbieri restores: '[ae]dem Vo[lc]ano ex s(enatus) c(onsulto) faciund[am] cur[avit] | —Proculus [duo]vir II [cum] pronao—'. The letters of the first line are 8 cm. high, of the second 6·5 cm.

[2] **16**[10].   [3] p. 17.

[4] 'Marti Ficano | Agathon | Caesaris ser(vus) | vilicus saltua | riorum cum | suis voto | libens | d(ono) d(edit).' The base is now in the Museo della Via Ostiense (M. F. Squarciapino, *Il Museo della Via O.* 31). The *saltuarii* were probably employed on the imperial Laurentine estate; cf. Carcopino, 255, who quotes a further record from the district.   [5] See *Note G*, p. 474.   [6] *CIL* 1², p. 257, 232; Taylor, 23.

miraculously appeared on horseback by the Fountain of Juturna to give the news of victory. But in Greece and southern Italy Castor and Pollux had long been associated with navigation, and it was this aspect of their cult that Rome observed at Ostia.

Each year on 27 January the Roman *praetor urbanus*, succeeded in the later Empire by the *praefectus urbis* or consul, celebrated on behalf of the Roman people games in honour of the twin gods, and a praetor of the late second or early third century A.D. has left a record in indifferent verse of the festivities:

> litoribus vestris quoniam certamina laetum
> exhibuisse iuvat, Castor venerandeque Pollux,
> munere pro tanto faciem certaminis ipsam,
> magna Iovis proles, vestra pro sede locavi
> urbanis Catius gaudens me fascibus auctum
> Neptunoque patri ludos fecisse Sabinus.[1]

Catius Sabinus, urban praetor, who was to hold a second consulship in A.D. 216, commemorated his official visit to Ostia by a representation in sculptured relief or in painting of the games over which he had presided.[2] The versifier does not record the nature of the contests of the *ludi Castorum* at Ostia, but the close association of Castor and Pollux with the cavalry suggests horse-racing. A glimmer of light on the spectacle may possibly be derived from a poem of Statius. The second poem of the fifth book of the *Silvae* is composed in honour of the sixteen-year-old Crispinus, son of Vettius Bolanus, distinguished consular of the Julio-Claudian period. Amid the obscurely rhetorical catalogue of his virtues there is a probable Ostian reference:

> ipse ego te nuper Tiberino in litore vidi,
> qua Tyrrhena vadis Laurentibus aestuat unda,
> tendentem cursus vexantemque ilia nuda
> calce ferocis equi, vultu dextraque minacem
> —si qua fides dictis, stupui armatumque putavi.[3]

The most recent editor of Statius sets this scene in the Campus Martius, where young men of quality certainly rode when Strabo

---

[1] I.

[2] Carcopino, 80, and R. Paribeni, *Rend. Pont.* 15 (1939) 97, thought that Catius Sabinus officiated as *praefectus urbis*, a forced interpretation of the Latin. That the games were at this period conducted by the *praetor urbanus* is confirmed by Bloch, 10, a dedication at Ostia to Neptune, Castor, and Pollux by an urban praetor. Catius Sabinus made a similar metrical dedication as praetor to Hercules at Rome, *ILS* 3402.

[3] Statius, *Silvae*, v. 2. 113–17 (éd. H. Frère, Collection Budé, 1944).

wrote.[1] A Silver Latin poet might refer to the Campus Martius as the Tiber shore, but not even the most rhetorical of poets would picture the river in these terms. The two banks of the river might possibly be titled Laurentine and Tyrrhenian, but the description of the meeting of Tyrrhenian waters with Laurentine shallows is inapplicable to the Tiber flowing through Rome. Transferred to Ostia the description has convincing point. The meeting of two waters aptly describes the contrast between the open sea and the outflow of the river. The Laurentine shallows stretch south from the Tiber's mouth, and it is on this coastline that the scene should be set. What was Crispinus doing there? He might have been merely taking exercise on his horse, his family might even have had a villa by the shore. But why was Statius looking on? It is not far-fetched to regard him as a spectator at a formal occasion, a *certamen* in the *ludi Castorum*; Crispinus may have been taking part with other young nobles in a ceremonial horse-race.

There is a further literary reference to the cult in the late Empire. In 359 Tertullus, city prefect, when storms prevented the grain ships entering harbour and there was serious danger of riots in Rome, left hurriedly for the coast. 'While Tertullus sacrificed at Ostia in the temple of the Castors, the wind dropped and the sea was calmed; then the wind changed to a gentle breeze from the south and the ships in full sail entered the harbour and filled the granaries with corn.'[2]

The temple of Castor and Pollux at Ostia has not yet been found, though an inscription records that it was restored in the second century by P. Lucilius Gamala.[3] None of the temples yet excavated seems appropriate, and the ambiguous wording of a fifth-century writer has been held to imply that the temple was on the right bank of the river. 'The river dividing into two branches makes an island between the city harbour (Portus) and the town of Ostia, where the Roman people come with the city prefect or consul to honour the Castors with genial solemnity.'[4] The passage is clearly not decisive, and better evidence suggests that the temple was on the left bank. A small base carrying a dedication to Neptune, Castor, and Pollux by L. Catius Celer, urban

---

[1] Strabo, 236.
[2] Amm. Marc. xix. 10. 4.
[3] 2[13].
[4] *Cosmographia Julii Caesaris* (Aethicus), Riese, *Geographi Latini minores*, 83: '[Tiberis] in duobus ex uno effectus insulam facit inter portum urbis et Ostiam civitatem, ubi populus Romanus cum urbis praefecto vel consule Castorum celebrandorum causa egreditur sollemnitate iocunda'.

praetor, was found near the centre of the city;[1] it probably once stood in the temple area. Like so many Ostian inscriptions it was not found in its original setting, but it is unlikely to have been carried across the river. A dedication to the Castors in honour of Jupiter Optimus Maximus Serapis probably stood in the temple area of Serapis, for it was found near by.[2]

From an inscription of Severan date we know that oracles were given in the temple: the three that have survived do not inspire confidence. Septimius Nestor, an epic poet from Laranda who had a wide reputation in Asia Minor, commemorated on a marble tablet the oracles given him by the Dioscuri. The first recognizes him as a renowned poet, the second assures him that his fame will survive throughout the ages. From the little we know of his works it is no injustice that this prophecy, probably composed by the poet himself, was unfulfilled. The third bids him set up his statue in the temple.[3]

Jupiter also was worshipped at Ostia from early days, for Livy in his account of 199 B.C. records that envoys brought news from Ostia that the temple of Jupiter had been struck by lightning.[4] This temple, perhaps dedicated to Iupiter Optimus Maximus, will have been within the walls of the fourth-century colony.[5] Outside the walls of the Castrum Iupiter Optimus Maximus is attested by four boundary stones in the area of the four republican temples, near the theatre. These stones delimit at the corners an irregular but roughly square area: on each are the letters 'I(ovi) O(ptimo) M(aximo) S(acrum)'.[6] This was an open area sacred to Jupiter: later it was enclosed by a wall but it still remained open to the sky. A small altar set up to Iupiter Optimus Maximus by a corn measurer as the result of a dream may be republican.[7] A further dedication of two silver Lares by a prominent freedman, also prompted by a dream, was found in the guild house of the builders and belongs to the second century.[8] There was also an association of *cultores Iovis*

---

[1] Bloch, 10. G. Barbieri, *Athenaeum*, 31 (1953) 166, suggests that the small temple at the angle of the Decumanus and the Via dei Molini (iii. 9. 4), near which this inscription was found, is the temple of Castor and Pollux. This temple, however, was not built until the late Republic and seems to have had no predecessor on the site. We should expect a larger temple. More probably it was on the seaward side of the town.

[2] Unpublished.

[3] R. Paribeni, *Rend. Pont.* 15 (1939) 97–102. For the text of the third oracle and the identification of the statue, G. Barbieri, *Athenaeum*, 31 (1953) 158.

[4] Livy xxxii. 1. 10.　　　　　　　　　　[5] For a possible identification, p. 352.

[6] S 4292.　　　　[7] 23, 'fortasse rudis potius quam antiqua' (Mommsen).

[8] S 4293, president of the *seviri Augustales*.

Tutoris; its cult centre was probably outside the town, for the only inscription recording the cult was found near Acilia.[1]

Among the earliest cults of Ostia may also have been that of Liber Pater. The only certain evidence of his cult is an inscription of the Empire,[2] but there is reason to attribute to Ostia a dedication to the god in archaic lettering and style: NO.OFALIUS NO.F.Q.PRO | SED.ET.FAMILIA. SOUA.LEIBERO | DONUM.DAT.MERET. This dedication, now in Vienna, came from the collection of Cardinal Pacca, and, since his collection was formed primarily though not exclusively from excavation at Ostia, an Ostian origin was suggested by Mommsen.[3] The quaestor who made the dedication was probably the Roman quaestor stationed at Ostia.[4]

To these early cults was added later that of Hercules Invictus. The finding of a large temple to Hercules was one of the great surprises of the excavation programme begun in 1938;[5] for there was little to suggest in the inscriptions and earlier excavation of Ostia that Hercules held an emphatic position in the religious life of the town.[6] Some 200 metres west of the Forum, on the north side of the Via della Foce, is a roughly triangular area reserved for religion. Dominating the area is a large temple, strictly oriented east–west. The faces of the podium are constructed of large blocks of tufa, carefully fitted, with a severe cornice above and below. Below the podium, providing a firmer base, are two steps of travertine, and the eight wide frontal steps which lead up to the temple on the east are also in travertine. The walls of the original cella were of small tufa blocks, approaching regularity in shape, an early example of *opus quasi–reticulatum*. Of the further decoration of the original temple nothing survives.

The type of workmanship of the cella walls and the substantial use of travertine indicate that this temple dates from the last quarter of the second century, or the first half of the first century B.C. The large altar in front of the temple is dedicated to Hercules Invictus. A most attractive relief in marble found near by raises interesting speculation on the nature of the cult.

This relief has been admirably described, illustrated, and explained by Becatti, and what follows is based on his account.[7] The relief is 0·71 metre high and was probably 1·40 metres long originally, but the left side has been broken away. Three scenes are depicted, of which the

---

[1] 25.   [2] S 4299.   [3] *CIL.* 1². 2440.   [4] p. 176 n. 4.
[5] Becatti, 'Il culto di Ercole ad Ostia', *BC* 67 (1939) 37.   [6] Taylor, 36.
[7] Becatti, art. cit. 39. Other interpretations examined, *BC* 70 (1942) 115. Pl. xxx *a*.

third on the left is largely lost. On the right two groups, each of three fishermen, are pulling hard at a net. Within the net are an empty boat and three fishes (one of them perhaps a dolphin), representing the sea. In the centre of the net is a figure of Hercules, his right hand with club upraised and his left hand stretched in front. He is bearded and his hair is tightly curled. He wears a corslet and a chiton, but his sex remains emphatically exposed. To his left and below is a box or chest. The figure of Hercules represents not the god himself, but a bronze statue of the god in the style of the late archaic period.

The central scene shows Hercules in movement, turned to the left. On a truncated pyramid stands a box or chest which seems to be identical with the box figured in the net in the first scene. From the box Hercules takes a folded tablet which he hands to a small boy standing to the left: on the tablet are the letters '[s]ort(es) H(erculis)'. Above these figures is an open tablet.

In the final scene to the left, a male figure in toga turns left and holds a tablet half open; to his left, above, a small figure of a winged victory holds out a wreath; below can be seen traces of a boy's head; another figure to the left is needed to balance the design. Above the relief is the dedicatory inscription 'C. Fulvius Salvis haruspexs d(edit) d(edicavit)'. The style of the lettering of this inscription, the style of the relief itself, and the form of the toga jointly suggest a date approximately between 100 and 50 B.C. for the dedication.

These scenes Becatti interprets in relation to the Ostian cult. The statue of Hercules in the net is the cult statue in the temple at Ostia: the scene records a myth otherwise lost which may be compared with the legend of Albunea whose image was found in the Anio holding in her hand a book of prophecies. The chest in the net contains oracles and is seen again in the central scene. Here a small boy, as was the Roman practice in oracular shrines, takes an oracle written on a folded tablet which is presented, symbolically, by Hercules. The third scene, which must be more conjectural since it is partly lost, may record the interpretation by the *haruspex* of an oracle to signify the promise of victory to a consultant. So interpreted the three scenes form an intelligible and convincing narrative: we may at least feel certain that the Ostian Hercules in the late Republic gave oracles.

The most difficult scene to interpret is the scene on the right. There is no trace of an appropriate myth in the story of Hercules elsewhere in the Greek or Roman world. Becatti suggests as an alternative the literal interpretation that the cult statue was in fact recovered from the sea, a Greek original brought to Italy and lost off the Tiber mouth in a ship-wreck.[1] This interpretation, which Becatti rejects, is attractive, and is perhaps the easiest way of explaining the presence of what seems to be an archaic Greek statue in an Ostian temple. During the late Republic there was a brisk traffic in sculpture from Greece to Italy, and not all of it arrived at its destination. One ship went down off African Mahdia; another might have been lost in bad weather while waiting to negotiate the sand-bar at the Tiber mouth. Such treasure trove in fishermen's nets would not be without parallel at Ostia. Suetonius records among school debating themes drawn from actual life the story of some youths who went down to Ostia and agreed a price with fishermen on the shore for their catch. When the nets were pulled in there were no fishes but a bar of gold. Both sides claimed the gold; to whom did it belong?[2]

If an archaic Greek statue of Hercules was fished out of the sea at Ostia it would indeed have been a portent and a *haruspex* was the man to interpret it. Perhaps C. Fulvius Salvis was responsible for the establish-ment of the oracular shrine to hold the statue and recorded the story in stone, adding the illustration of a successful prophecy which he had interpreted.

Part of the original dedicatory inscription of the temple may, as Bloch has suggested, survive on a fragment of travertine found near by.[3] If the identification is sound the inscription records the names of the two men, probably magistrates, who were responsible. The first of these names begins 'C. Ca . . . '. It is an attractive guess that this is a C. Cartilius, possibly the father of the C. Cartilius Poplicola for whom the town built a public tomb in the early Augustan period outside the Porta Marina.[4] For at an early stage in his public career Poplicola dedi-cated to Hercules an idealized portrait statue of himself, rather larger than life, represented as Theseus.[5] The inscription on the base has been much altered.[6] It was originally dedicated when he was duovir for the second time: as this honour was repeated the inscription changed until

[1] Becatti, *BC* 67 (1939) 54.   [2] Suet. *De rhet.* 1.

[3] Bloch, 64, reads: 'C. CA— | P. DO— | EX S(ENATUS) [C(ONSULTO)]', implying that the building was authorized by the Roman senate: he infers that the names are of Roman magistrates. I am very doubtful whether any trace of the letter S remains on the stone* and, even if the authority came from Rome, local magistrates could have been made responsible for the work. The combination of senatorial authority and local executive is attested in a small temple of Vulcan at Ostia (p. 343 n. 1).

[4] p. 39.   [5] R. Calza, *Scavi di Ostia*, iii (1) 221, *Museo*, 121.

[6] Bloch, *Scavi di Ostia*, iii (1) 209 f.

'duovir iterum' became eventually 'duovir V iterum q(uin)q(uennalis)'.★
He is also associated with Hercules in another inscription of which
only a fragment survives.[1] Later dedications to Hercules Hermogenia-
nus[2] and Hercules Turranianus[3] show a similar attachment of families
to the cult. More difficult to interpret is the inscription on an altar:
'aqua Salvia Herculi sac(rum)'. This altar was already broken when the
larger part of it was reused in a Mithraeum, in or near the Severan
period, and the decoration largely erased.[4] But the original inscription
is probably not later than Augustan and there may be some connexion
between Aqua Salvia, possibly a well near the temple, and the C. Fulvius
Salvis who dedicated the relief that has been discussed.

In the same area with the temple of Hercules are two other smaller
temples; one to the north-east, probably contemporary, another to the
south, fitted in awkwardly a little later between the Via della Foce and
the Hercules temple: neither temple can be identified.

Not long after the laying out of this religious area five further small
temples were built. One stands alone on the north side of the Decumanus immediately outside the east gate of the fourth-century walls, and
remains anonymous.[5] The suggestion that it was the temple of Vulcan,
placed outside the colony walls, as was the normal custom, must be
abandoned in view of the exploration of the foundations:[6] it seems that
there was no earlier temple on this site, and the temple of Vulcan must
date back long before the first century B.C.

The remaining four temples of this period were built on a common
tufa platform to a common plan, on the north side of the Decumanus,
west of the theatre. They stood in a large reserved area, enclosed on
three sides by a portico, and open towards the Decumanus.[7] They were
small in size and unpretentious in decoration, confined to tufa and
stucco. In the easternmost a small altar was found, dedicated to Venus;[8]
and it has been suggested that these four temples are those built by the

---

[1] 'C. CARTILIO— | DUOVIR(O) SE— | HERCULA—', 315, *Scavi di Ostia*, iii (1) 212 n. 4,
with tav. XXXV. 3. Dessau, following C. L. Visconti, read a stop after HERCUL. I agree
with Bloch that the mark is probably not original. He suggests for the last line
'HERCULA[NI PATRONO P(OSUERUNT)]'.

[2] *S* 4287.   [3] Unpublished.

[4] *S* 4280; revised and discussed, Becatti, *BC* 70 (1942) 120. On one face the inscription
was later changed to *aquae Salviae et Hercli sacr.*

[5] *NS* 1918, 133.

[6] Wilson, *BSR* 13 (1935) 56 n. 4. But perhaps the partial exploration is not decisive.
A suggested identification, p. 351.

[7] R. Paribeni, *MA* 23 (1914) 441.   [8] 4127.

first P. Lucilius Gamala to Ceres, Fortuna, Venus, and Spes.[1] This suggestion was first made in 1907 by Van Buren;[2] it was accepted by Carcopino, who further proposed that the house built behind the temples belonged to Gamala the donor.[3] The view seemed even more attractive when in 1911 an inscription was found immediately behind the temples recording a Gamala.[4] Carcopino also noted the finding in the area of an inscribed fragment probably referring to Ceres.[5]

For those who date this Gamala, as most do, to the second century A.D. the identification is inadmissible, because the temples were clearly built much earlier and *constituit* cannot be regarded as an alternative for *restituit*. Even for Carcopino, who dated the death of this Gamala to the early years of Claudius, the construction of the temples is too early, for a date scratched on plaster shows that they were completed, at the latest, by 23 B.C.[6] In style the workmanship seems to fall between the Sullan walls and the Augustan work in the theatre.[7] A date towards the end of the Republic suits our chronology of the Augustan Gamala.

In Gamala's inscription the fourth temple, that of Spes, is separated from and comes later than the remaining three. We should infer that Gamala was responsible for only three of the four temples on a common platform. His temple of Spes, built a little later, may perhaps be identified with the small temple on the Decumanus outside the east gate of the Castrum; the style fits the context. The house, however, behind the four temples should probably not be attributed to Gamala's family. It was not built before the Flavian period, and the name on the water-pipe leading to the house, dating perhaps from the second century, was P. Apuleius.[8]

The cults that can be assigned to the republican period in Ostia are those of Vulcan, Castor and Pollux, Jupiter Optimus Maximus, Hercules, and probably Liber Pater, but the number of unidentified temples indicates that there were several others. Among them was undoubtedly Silvanus, not perhaps honoured with a separate temple—that was not his custom—but by altars and small shrines. His cult was still popular in the Empire and will have been strong in the Republic.

Near the end of the first century B.C. two temples were built on the Decumanus, at the north end of the Forum, but no evidence has been

---

[1] I 23–28, 32. [2] *AJA* 11 (1907) 55.

[3] Carcopino, *Mélanges*, 31 (1911) 224–30.

[4] S 4657. I have not been able to find this inscription.

[5] Carcopino, loc. cit. 227; 4146.

[6] S 5289[1]. [7] pp. 538 f. [8] S 5309[29].

found to identify them. Since they were both destroyed when the Hadrianic Capitolium was built, their cults were probably taken over by the new temple and this should limit the field of inquiry. The eastern temple seems to have replaced a secular building and may be the original Capitolium.[1] The western temple might be the temple of Jupiter, mentioned by Livy,[2] replacing perhaps an earlier temple on the same site.

To the Augustan period should probably also be assigned a small temple at the south end of the Via degli Augustali, enclosed in a trapezoidal area.[3] The wall enclosing this area has been rebuilt in neat reticulate, but the lowest section of the wall in the south-east corner is much earlier; the large irregular tufa blocks suggest a date early in the second century B.C. It is possible therefore that the Augustan building replaces a much earlier temple on the site. The inscription on a well-head found near the temple identifies the cult with Bona Dea,[4] goddess of fertility whose rites were confined to women. It is appropriate that the temple is withdrawn from public view by the wall which surrounds the area.

Another temple of Bona Dea was later built just outside the Porta Marina on the east side of the Decumanus.[5] The temple area was surrounded by an enclosing wall open only at the north-east corner. Here a doorway led into a room containing an altar. From this room a passage led to the centre of the area, in which was the small temple itself, prostyle and tetrastyle, with four columns in brick or tufa covered with stucco. In front of the temple was an altar, and a three-winged portico ran round the wall enclosing the area opposite the temple and to the south. To the north of this temple three rooms, whose function was not indicated by excavation, completed the complex. Though the form of the temple itself was similar to many others in Ostia, it was not raised up on a podium and it was not immediately accessible to the public. The wall that surrounded the area was unbroken, except for the doorway, and entrance to the temple was indirect, at the end of a corridor. A serpent coiled round a phallus in marble, found near the temple, reflects the main focus of the cult.[6]

The style of construction of this temple complex, in *opus reticulatum* with tufa quoins, brick being used only in decorative external pilasters

---

[1] Becatti, *Topografia*, 104.   [2] Livy xxxii. 1. 10.
[3] Reg. v. 10. 2; Becatti, *Topografia*, 119.
[4] Unpublished.   [5] Calza, *NS* 1942, 152.   [6] Inv. 985.

on the west and south walls, suggests a date in the early Julio-Claudian
period. To the same period points the lettering of the dedicatory inscription, which records that the temple was the gift of a duovir.[1] The
cult of Bona Dea is also probably illustrated in a small statuette found
between the western Decumanus and the Via della Foce. It represents
a seated matron holding in her left hand a cornucopia. Head and right
arm are lost, but what remains strongly resembles representations of the
goddess.[2]

Ostia was also concerned with a cult revived at Lavinium to the
south. According to tradition Lavinium had once housed the Di
Penates of Rome, and in the Republic Roman magistrates regularly
visited the town to attend religious ceremonies. By the end of the
Republic Lavinium was becoming depopulated and the religious links
with Rome may have lapsed. It was probably the antiquarian Claudius
who created a new priesthood, including *pontifex, augur, salius*, to revive
the cult.[3] The members were appointed mainly from knights; Ostians
of the upper classes figure prominently, because they were near enough
to attend the ceremonies.[4]

THE INTRODUCTION OF THE IMPERIAL CULT

While the principate of Augustus probably saw at Ostia an increase
in the number of cults long established at Rome, it saw also the introduction of the imperial cult which was gradually to pervade the whole
life of the colony. As in many other Italian towns, the imperial cult first
took official shape in Ostia in the organization of the priesthood of
Augustales, confined to freedmen. The first inscription recording the
office known to us is probably to be dated shortly before A.D. 11,[5] but
the institution is known elsewhere as early as 12 B.C. and Ostia, closely
associated with Rome and with the imperial house, is likely to have
been one of the first towns to adopt the institution.

For the citizen population the cult of Rome and Augustus was more
important. A temple, almost certainly eclipsing all other Ostian temples
of the day in magnificence, was built at the south end of the Forum
not long after the death of Augustus.[6] At the head of the temple cult

---

[1] *NS* 1942, 163 (*AE* 1946, 221): 'M. Maecilius M. f. [T]urr[anianus] | aedem Bonae
Deae ex sua [pecunia constituit] | idemq(ue) prob[avit].'   [2] Ibid. 152 and fig. 1.
[3] G. Wissowa, 'Altlatinische Gemeindekulte', *Hermes*, 50 (1915) 21–33.
[4] A list of Ostians associated with the cult, Le Gall, *Le Tibre*, 183 n. 2.
[5] *S* 5322, in honour of Drusus, son of Tiberius, before his quaestorship in A.D. 11.
[6] Becatti, *Topografia*, 115.

was a *flamen Romae et Augusti*, always a man of distinction, and appointed for life. In the temple was found a statue of Roma with her foot resting on a globe representing the world,[1] for the cult combined with the new imperial house the greatness of Rome herself: it is appropriate that a temple servant should make a dedication to *Imperium*.[2] Individual emperors who were deified were also, at least from the Flavian period, honoured with *flamines* in Ostia and may have had temples. For the Julio-Claudians no evidence survives, though record is preserved of a *flaminica divae Augustae*, priestess of Livia; she was Plaria Vera, the distinguished wife of the distinguished A. Egrilius Rufus, who, after rising to the duovirate, was himself *flamen Romae et Augusti*.[3]

Much humbler is the cult of the Lares Augusti, first introduced, so far as our knowledge goes, under Claudius. The inscription on the marble panels which once formed the outer face of a circular chapel gives the date of the ceremonial dedication of the building, 26 June 51, and names the three *magistri* of the first year who paid for the building: 'Laribus Augustis sac(rum) magistri anni primi de s(ua) p(ecunia) f(ecerunt).' The benefactors are not men of great standing in the colony; all three are probably freedmen or of freedman stock; they have the same praenomen and nomen and probably came from the same household. But they were allowed a good site for their building. The marble panels fit precisely a small round brick building on the south side of the Decumanus in the Forum.[4]

THE RISE OF ORIENTAL CULTS

If we followed the prejudices of Tacitus and Juvenal we should regard all the cults attested at Ostia before the Flavian period as respectable. The absence of evidence for oriental cults at Ostia during this earlier period may be accidental, for the number of inscriptions surviving from the first century A.D. is substantially smaller than from the second. But though it might seem that the flowing of the Orontes into the Tiber should proceed first by the mouth of the river, it is to be remembered that Ostia during the Republic looked west rather than east: Rome's main gateway to Asia Minor and Egypt was Puteoli. There were probably many slaves and freedmen of eastern origin in

---

[1] *Topografia*, tav. ix.

[2] 73: 'imperio | Q. Ostiensis | Felix | aedituus | aedis Romae et Aug(usti) | fecit'.

[3] 399. For the identification of her husband, Bloch, 22.

[4] The identification of the fragments with the building is due to Gismondi. The inscription is not yet published.

Ostia by the end of the Republic, but this stock had not yet risen to challenge the ruling classes of Roman and Italian origin. Devotees of oriental cults there must have been,[1] but, until secure evidence is found, it may be doubted whether these cults, with the possible exception of Cybele, had won the recognition of temples and priesthoods in Ostia. After the building of the imperial harbours the social climate changed. In the period of prosperity that began under the Flavians and lasted through the Antonine age eastern trade was attracted to Ostia, and freedman stock played an increasingly important part in local government. It was against this background that the oriental cults won recognition and began to leave a significant mark in the records of the town.

Of these oriental cults the worship of Cybele, the Great Mother, held a unique position in the Roman state.[2] In the crisis of the second Punic War the black stone of the goddess had been brought to Rome from Pessinus, at the prompting of the *Libri Sibyllini* and with the authority of the priestly college of the *decemviri*. This was a state act and the goddess was given a worthy reception by the state. Formally met at Ostia by leading senators and noble ladies, the goddess was ceremonially brought to Rome and lodged in the very heart of the city on the Palatine hill near to the hut which still commemorated Romulus. Here an impressive temple was built to house the goddess, and dedicated with much pomp and ceremony on 9 April 191 B.C.

The cult itself was orgiastic and not to Roman taste; the embarrassment was solved by a typical Roman compromise. The goddess, if she was to protect the Roman state, had to be worshipped in her own way; native priests were brought with her, to perform the necessary ceremonies. These, however, were highly emotional and were confined to the temple area. The priests were allowed once a year to collect offerings in Rome but they were forbidden to parade their religion through the streets. Rome paid her respects to the goddess in a more Roman way. In the days between the anniversary of the carrying of the goddess to Rome and the dedication of her temple, from 4 to 9 April, special games of a traditional Roman pattern were held in Cybele's honour, Ludi Megalenses, and presided over by curule aediles. As an additional compliment the leading nobles of Rome formed dining clubs in honour

---

[1] A painting of Isis, or of a priestess of Isis, on an Augustan tomb, *NS* 1938, 56 (tomb 18); *Scavi di Ostia*, iii (i) 86.

[2] For a detailed account of the cult of Cybele, H. Graillot, *Le culte de Cybèle* (Paris 1912).

of the goddess, and the nobility retained a special attachment to her cult until the late Empire.[1] This is to be explained in part by the initiative that the senate had taken in summoning the goddess to Rome; it was strengthened by the association of Cybele with the home of Rome's Trojan ancestors. Though Pessinus was always regarded as the original centre of the cult, Cybele in Italy and the west was always the Idaean mother of the gods, 'mater magna deum Idaea'.

Cybele was a goddess of nature and fertility: with her cult was associated that of Attis, the shepherd of the hills. The story of Cybele and Attis was commemorated in an annual festival in March, when winter was over and the new year beginning. On 15 March the festival opened with a parade of reed-bearers, *cannophori*, perhaps recalling the finding of Attis by the river bank; there followed nine days of fasting and continence during which, on 22 March, came the procession of the *dendrophori*, the tree-bearers, carrying to the temple each year a pine tree symbolizing the death of Attis. The period of fasting was ended on 25 March by the day of rejoicing, Hilaria, when the rebirth of Attis was celebrated; devotees at this climax of the festival cut themselves with knives and some even sacrificed their manhood to become *galli*, dedicated for life to the service of the goddess.

In the Republic the public performance of these ceremonies had been forbidden, and, since only eunuchs could be priests of the goddess, the priesthood was barred to Roman citizens. This dualism in Rome's attitude to Cybele was ended by the emperor Claudius. The priesthood, which no longer was confined to eunuchs, was opened to Roman citizens, and the March festival was officially recognized and performed in public.[2] How soon and in what form did this cult reach Ostia?

For Cybele the evidence from Ostia is fuller than for any other of the oriental cults. The area reserved for the goddess was largely excavated by Visconti in the middle of the last century and yielded a rich harvest of cult buildings, sculptures, and inscriptions.[3] By the beginning of this century the area had again become overgrown with grass and bramble, but it was included in the 1938 programme. Calza was able to check and modify Visconti's report in important respects and to

[1] S. Aurigemma, 'La protezione speciale della gran madre Idea per la nobilità Romana', *BC* 37 (1909) 31.

[2] Carcopino, 'La réforme romaine du culte de Cybèle et d'Attis' in *Aspects mystiques de la Rome païenne*, 49–171, modified by J. Beaujeu, *La Religion romaine à l'apogée de l'Empire*, i (1955) 316 f.

[3] C. L. Visconti, *Ann. Inst.* 40 (1868) 362; 41 (1869) 208.

complete the investigation of the whole area, at least at its imperial level. Though much had been taken from the site in the earlier excavation, new shrines, important inscriptions, and sculptures were found.[1]

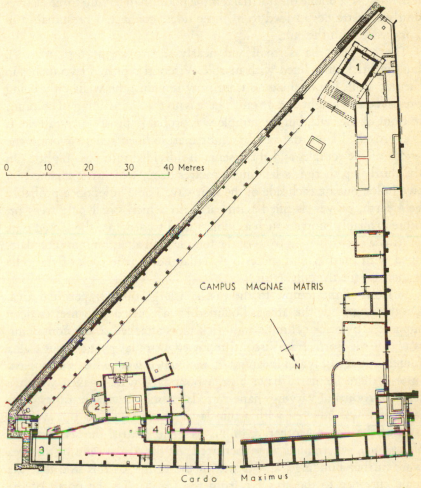

FIG. 26. Cybele and her associates. 1. Temple of Cybele. 2. Shrine of Attis. 3. Temple of Bellona. 4. Guild House of *Hastiferi*.

The area reserved for Cybele and her associates lies on the south side of the town by the gate that leads to Laurentine territory. It forms a large triangle, approximately 4,500 square metres in extent, bounded on the east by the Cardo Maximus, on the south by the Sullan walls,

[1] G. Calza, *Mem. Pont.* 6 (1947) 183.

on the north by a set of public baths and other buildings. The actual temple of Cybele lies at the western apex of the triangle and faces east. The podium is constructed in reticulate and crowned by a brick cornice; it is, however, unlike the normal temple podium in having three alcoves nearly 1 metre deep added to its three sides, connected presumably in some way with the cult.

The temple cella is small and nearly square (7·30 × 6·50 metres), built in brick once lined with marble. Visconti reported two niches in the side walls but of these no trace now remains, the walls only being preserved to a height of *c.* 70 cm. There is no trace remaining of columns in front of the cella, but the temple was probably prostyle, tetrastyle. It is approached from the east by eight marble-lined stairs covering the width of the temple, and these stairs are divided into two flights. On the third step there is a landing 2 metres deep, which is explained by two holes, one on each side of the stairway. These holes once probably held earth, or vessels filled with earth, in which small pine trees or, more probably, flowers such as violets used to decorate the sacred pine of Attis were grown. In front of the temple is an altar, built in reticulate, lined with marble, and successively enlarged. At the back of the cella is the base for the cult statue.

In front of the temple to the east is a large open trapezoidal area. On the south side this area is bounded by a portico 4·50 metres deep supported by brick columns and brick piers attached to the containing wall; on the north side Visconti reported a similar portico, but Calza found no trace of it and it cannot be reconciled with what is now seen. Instead there seems to have been a boundary wall, against which a series of rooms of varying shape were later built at various times. This large area was covered with a thin layer of sea sand, for this was the field of the Great Mother, Campus Magnae Matris, the scene of the *taurobolium*, where bulls were sacrificed. At the eastern end of the area were further buildings, and it was in the centre of this side that the main entrance to the area lay from the Cardo. To the north of the entrance was a series of shops: to the south, behind a wall that screened them from the street, was a series of shrines and associated buildings.

One of the most dramatic triumphs of Visconti was his discovery of three dedications excellently preserved (which can now be seen in the Lateran Museum)—an admirably executed reclining life-sized Attis in marble, the gift of C. Cartilius Euplus, a bronze Venus half life size, and a small cippus in the form of a chest crowned by a cock, dedicated by M. Modius Maximus, high priest of Cybele, *archigallus coloniae Ostiensis*.[1] These dedications were found together in the portico on the south side of the campus, and it seems that they were taken here in Roman times, perhaps to be hidden. They probably came from the shrine of Attis that Calza discovered in 1940, among the buildings at the east end of the area.[2]

This shrine is a roughly square enclosure, entered on the south side. The doorway is framed by two Pans emerging in high relief from half-columns of marble. They hold in one hand a shepherd's crook, in the other a six-reeded pipe. Though the workmanship is rough, the effect is striking. Within the enclosure is a small chapel, oriented south–north with two rectangular niches in the side walls and a large apse facing the entrance. A number of dedications were found in or near this chapel of Attis. Seven statuettes were given by C. Cartilius Euplus, who also presented the large reclining Attis found by Visconti.[3] They include with small figures of Attis a frieze of animals associated with Cybele, and a figure of Venus Genetrix who, as the goddess of the Julian house, of Trojan origin, has a natural place in the cult of Idacan Cybele and is associated with her in Rome.[4] The syncretism of the cult is also seen in the symbolism of the reclining Attis:[5] his head is crowned with the rays of the sun and on his Phrygian cap is a crescent moon, suggesting the influence of astrological doctrines borrowed from the cult of Anatolian Men. With Men Attis became identified under the title Attis Menotyrannos, which is applied to him in a late Greek dedication from Ostia.[6]

To the east of Attis' shrine is a temple to Bellona of modest dimensions, whose dedicatory inscription has survived. The temple was presented and paid for by the lictors and town slaves: the site was assigned by the two duovirs of the year.[7] Later the area of the temple was improved and the work was again paid for by the lictors and town slaves, together with the colony's freedmen.

---

[1] Visconti, *Ann. Inst.* 41 (1869) 210. Photos: Paschetto, 163 (Attis), 377 (Venus), 378 (cippus).

[2] Calza, art. cit. 193. It is difficult to understand their excellent state of preservation unless they were hidden.

[3] R. Calza, *Mem. Pont.* 6 (1947) 207. But see Ch. Picard, *Rev. Arch.* 48 (1956) 84, who argues that one of the figures, identified as Mars, is more probably a Corybant.

[4] A. Bartoli, 'Il culto della mater deum Idaea e di Venere Genitrice sul Palatino', *Mem. Pont.* 6 (1947) 229.   [5] Graillot, op. cit. 210.

[6] *IG* xiv. 913.   [7] Calza, art. cit. 198. The inscription, 4.

The cult of Bellona, goddess of war, had been introduced to Rome in the early Republic, probably from the Sabine country; but in the late Republic and increasingly in the Empire the Roman cult was submerged in the more orgiastic cult of a goddess who, under various names, was widely worshipped through Asia Minor, and who was identified at Rome with Bellona. It was this oriental goddess of war and fertility who was commonly associated with Cybele.[1] An essential part in the cult of Bellona was played by the *hastiferi*, who originally perhaps celebrated a ceremonial war dance; their guild house was built at the north end of Bellona's temple area. A dedicatory inscription is preserved in which the *plebs* of the guild honour the emperor Caracalla in A.D. 203[2] and there is a record of the restoration of a shrine in A.D. 211 by three patrons of the guild, two men and a woman.[3]

But the most important guilds in these associated cults were the *dendrophori* and *cannophori*, attached to the ceremonial of Cybele. Both had guild houses and both attracted benefactions from patrons, officers, and members. Visconti found huddled together in the central niche of the back wall of the temple of Cybele a group of bases of dedications to the *cannophori*.[4] Q. Caecilius Fuscus, high priest of the cult in Ostia, had presented to the guild a small silver image of the Great Mother with a representation of Nemesis.[5] There is a separate record of his gift of a silver image of Attis to the guild with a representation in bronze of the sacred fruit of the goddess.[6] Calpurnia Chelido had presented a silver image of the stone fetish of the goddess.[7] Q. Domitius Aterianus with his wife Domitia Civitas, described as *pater* and *mater*, honorary titles conferred by the guild, had presented a statuette of Attis.[8]

Near by were found inscriptions of the guild of *dendrophori*. C. Atilius Felix, attached to the ceremonial cult as an *apparator* and freedman of a priest of the goddess, records the gift of a statuette of Silvanus.[9] Sex. Annius Merops, an ex-officer of the guild, *honoratus*, presented in A.D. 142 a statuette of Mother Earth;[10] Iunia Zosime, *mater*, a small silver representation of Virtus.[11]

Small imperial heads in silver were also presented to the guild. The first, of Antoninus Pius in 139, was given by the guild itself.[12] A head of

[1] Cumont, *Les Religions orientales dans le paganisme romain*[4] (1929) 50 f.
[2] Calza, 200 (n. 3).   [3] Ibid., n. 5. The *aedes* is not identified.
[4] Visconti, *Ann. Inst.* 40 (1868) 390.   [5] 34.
[6] 35: 'imaginem Attis argentiam p(ondere) i cum sigillo Frugem aereo.'
[7] 36. 'typum matris deum argenti p(ondere) ii.'
[8] 37.   [9] 53.   [10] 67.   [11] 69.   [12] 97.

L. Verus was presented by a member, to commemorate the grant of immunity to him by the guild.[1] A head of Septimius Severus is also recorded.[2] In another inscription the guildsmen record that they 'restored with new expenditure the guild house which they had built with their own money, and dedicated it to the majesty of the imperial house', 'numini domus Aug(ustae)'.[3]

From these discoveries Visconti inferred that the small irregular area behind Cybele's temple was the headquarters of the two guilds.[4] This view seemed confirmed by his report of two altars in the area, the larger attributed to Cybele, the smaller to Attis, and of a stone bench built against the wall. When the area was again investigated, no trace of the stone bench was found and the two 'altars' were seen to be brick piers. The walls which to Visconti seemed to divide up the area were of a much earlier date than the temple and had probably been destroyed down to the new level when the temple was built.[5]

Visconti's interpretation of this area must therefore be rejected. The guilds of the *dendrophori* and *cannophori* were wealthy, as the dedications presented to them show; they were also probably large. The roll of the *dendrophori* dating from the Severan period has five patrons and no less than eleven officers and ex-officers: the number of the *plebs* is not known but it cannot have been small.[6] Such guilds can hardly have been content with premises so restricted; their guild houses must be sought elsewhere in the neighbourhood.

The patrons of these two guilds, and particularly of the *dendrophori*, included men of great distinction in the town. The Severan roll is unfortunately fragmentary, and only the ends of the names of the patrons which head the list survive, but it is clear that three at least and probably four are members of Ostian senatorial families.[7] They had at least two distinguished predecessors, Cn. Sentius Felix, who rose quickly to the duovirate and was patron of many guilds,[8] and C. Granius Maturus, duovir, patron of the corn measurers and of two shipping guilds.[9] Their relation to the cult was probably very similar to that of the Roman nobility. A fragment of a roll of the *cannophori* is headed by a senatorial patron.[10]

But the officers and members of the guilds and the priests of the cult do not seem to have been men of great standing. None is known to

---

[1] 107. [2] 116. [3] 45. [4] *Ann. Inst.* 40 (1868) 385.
[5] Calza, art. cit. 189. [6] 281. [7] p. 504.
[8] 5[14]. [9] 364. [10] Unpublished.

have held public office in Ostia, though many were wealthy. One unknown *dendrophorus* is described on his tombstone as *sevir Augustalis idem q(uin)q(uennalis)*;[1] probably there were many other rich freedmen in the guild. Publius Claudius Abascantus, for example, had been a public slave in Gaul, attached to the council of the Three Gauls, from whom he secured his freedom. He came to Ostia late in the second century, probably made money in trade or business, and became a prominent member of the *dendrophori*;[2] he may have been a devotee of Cybele's cult in Gaul. In 203 he proudly set up a statue to his young son, P. Claudius Abascantianus, to commemorate his appointment for a second term to the presidency of the *dendrophori*. On the side of the statue base is recorded the authority given by the *pontifex Volcani* for the setting up of the statue in the field of the Great Mother.[3]

At the head of the cult was the *archigallus coloniae Ostiensis*; he was assisted by priests and priestesses. The sarcophagus of a priestess, Metilia Acte, wife of a president of the builders' guild, illustrates the main objects used in the ritual—lighted torches, cymbals, and double flute.[4] Inscriptions add a little colour. Calpurnius Iovinus commemorates on his tomb 'his dearest brother, Iulius Charelampes, priest of the mother of the gods of the colony of Ostia, who led in nineteen trees and lived 48 years, 2 months'.[5] For nineteen years Charelampes had ceremonially, as priest, accompanied the *dendrophori* as they carried a new pine tree, symbolizing the dead Attis, to the temple of Cybele. More interesting, because more individual, are the fragmentary records of the *taurobolium*.

The sacrifice of a bull or of a ram was not an original element in the cult of Cybele, but it was common to many Anatolian cults. At some time in the second century it was grafted on to the cult of Cybele, and probably by official inspiration;[6] for the commonest form of the *taurobolium* in the cult of Cybele was a public ceremony on behalf of the emperor. The earliest recorded example that has been found at Ostia is in honour of Marcus Aurelius and his family, celebrated between A.D. 170 and 174;[7] a second is perhaps 'for the preservation and safe return and victory of Severus Alexander and Iulia Mamma';[8] another is for the preservation and victory of the emperors Trebonianus and Volusianus (251–3).[9] A *criobolium* was celebrated for the preservation of

---

[1] 33. [2] Wickert, S, p. 615 ad 326. [3] 324.
[4] Amelung, *Die Sculpturen des vatican. Mus.* i (3) (Museo Chiaramonti), p. 429 n. 179.
[5] S 4627. [6] Graillot, op. cit. 150. [7] S 4301 = 40.
[8] S 4303. [9] 42.

Commodus, though his name was erased when his memory was damned.[1] Other fragments cannot be attributed to specific emperors.

What makes the Ostian series particularly interesting is the fullness of their formula in contrast with the records of other towns. Elsewhere the imperial house and the state concerned alone are recorded.[2] At Ostia blessings were invoked on all the main organs of imperial government: 'a *taurobolium* was celebrated in honour of the great Idaean mother of the gods for the preservation of the emperor Caesar Marcus Aurelius Antoninus Augustus and L. Aurelius Commodus Caesar and Faustina Augusta and all their other children; for the senate, the *xvviri sacris faciundis* (the Roman priestly college responsible for the control of foreign cults), the equestrian order, the army of the Roman people; for all that sail the seas . . . for the decurions of the colony of Ostia, for the *cannophori* and for the *dendrophori*'.[3] The contrast with other towns is explained by the intimate connexion between Ostia and Rome.

Such public ceremonies were normally held on the prophetic prompting of the high priest of Cybele, 'ex vaticinatione archigalli':[4] this formula has not yet been found at Ostia, but the ends of all the inscriptions are lost or only partially preserved. On one perhaps the concluding formula is 'by decree of the decurions in public session',[5] but the Ostian council even in this case may have merely given formal authority at the suggestion of the high priest.

Bulls could also be sacrificed for individuals. In such cases the person concerned stood in a deep trench specially dug, which was covered by a board pierced with holes. Through the holes poured the blood of the sacrificial bull and the initiate covered his whole person with the blood. This baptism of bull's blood, which originally was thought to transfer the power of the bull to the initiate, came to have a symbolic meaning. The blood of the sacrifice purified the initiate and if repeated after twenty years could confer everlasting blessedness. Aemilia Serapias records her baptism on 15 May 199 and her commemoration of the event by an altar.[6] The names of the two priests who presided at the ceremony are added.

Calza, assembling the evidence of his excavations, concluded that the large area by the Porta Laurentina was adapted to the cult of Cybele and her associates in the time of Antoninus Pius.[7] The earliest evidence

---

[1] S 4302. [2] A list of *taurobolia*, Graillot, 159. [3] S 4301 = 40.
[4] Graillot, 153. [5] S 4302: '[decurionum decret]o publ[ice].'
[6] 39. [7] Calza, art. cit. 202.

for the religious guilds came from his reign: the brickwork of the
temple of Cybele was appropriate: there was no evidence to associate
Hadrian with the cult in Ostia. The original walls of the sanctuary of
Attis are of much earlier date, their large reticulate suggesting the Julio-
Claudian period, but the preserved dedications to Attis, the Pans which
flanked the entrance, and the large apse are almost certainly not earlier
than the Antonine period; before this the building might have been
used for another purpose. The temple of Bellona in Calza's view fitted
this general dating. Identifying P. Lucilius Gamala f(ilius) praef(ectus)
Caes(aris) with the P. Lucilius Gamala who restored baths built by
Antoninus Pius, and who is described in his inscription as *praefectus L.
Caesar(is)*, Calza concluded that the temple of Bellona was built in the
second half of the second century when Commodus was Caesar.[1]

The attribution of the large-scale conception in Cybele's honour to
the reign of Antoninus Pius would on general grounds be appropriate,
as Calza emphasized.[2] The concern of Pius for the cult of Cybele is
emphasized in his biography and in his coinage; and the first public
taurobolium of which record has survived dates from his reign.[3] But
there is perhaps a stronger case for preferring a Hadrianic date. The
earliest surviving inscription in the area of the temple dates from 139,[4]
the very first year of Antoninus Pius, and though Hadrian is nowhere
explicitly connected with the Ostian cult of Cybele, a head of Hadrian
and a large number of coins of his reign were found by Visconti near
the temple.[5] A water-pipe stamped with Hadrian's name shows that
there was at least some activity in the area in his reign.[6] Hadrianic brickstamps were reported by Visconti from the area of the temple of
Cybele,[7] and the southern colonnade with its pattern of brickwork
and reticulate fits the context. Hadrian's sympathy for Cybele is
shown in his restoration of Cyzicus, one of the great centres of the
cult.[8] His concern for Ostia, as has been seen, was serious and continuous: the replanning of this area would match the other great
composite building plans of the reign.

An earlier date than Calza has chosen may also be preferred for the
temple of Bellona. The brickwork is regular and well coursed and the
width of the bricks is larger than the standard brickwork of the second

---

[1] Calza, art. cit. 198. Temple inscription, 4; 'praef. L. Caes.'; 2[6].
[2] J. Beaujeu, op. cit. 312 ff.   [3] Graillot, 150.   [4] 97.
[5] Visconti, *Ann. Inst.* 40 (1868) 369.
[6] Ibid. 376.   [7] Ibid. 369.   [8] *RE*, 'Kyzikos' (Ruge), 231.

half of the century: the dedicatory inscription also is better than one would expect at such a date.[1] Brickwork and lettering both point to a Hadrianic or early Antonine date. Moreover, a recently published inscription shows that the guild of *hastiferi*, which presupposes a cult of Bellona, received a dedication from one of its members as early as 140.[2] If we are right in identifying the Caesar of the temple inscription, for whom P. Lucilius acted as *praefectus* with L. Aelius, the adopted son of Hadrian, the temple will have been built at the end of Hadrian's reign, in 137 or 138.[3]

For the general history of Ostia an uncertainty covering little more than a generation is not a critical issue. It is more important to decide whether the development (Hadrianic or Antonine) of the area marked the first introduction of an organized cult of Cybele to the town. Calza concluded that it did, and the absence of any earlier evidence makes any other answer rash. Yet doubt must remain. In Rome the cult had been established since the end of the third century B.C. and the goddess had passed through Ostia on her way to Rome. By the Augustan age a legend was even established of a miracle at Ostia. The vessel carrying the goddess had grounded on the river mud and efforts to float it were unavailing. Claudia Quinta, daughter of a noble house, whose reputation was in question, solemnly invoked the goddess to prove her innocence, and was able to free the boat by the lightest of efforts. Ovid records the legend, and a relief later commemorated it.[4] Nor was this Ostia's only recorded connexion with Cybele before the Empire. In 38 B.C. Roman public opinion was shocked by portents. The hut of Romulus burnt down; a statue of Virtus which stood before one of the gates fell to the ground. 'Certain persons, inspired by the mother of the gods, declared that the goddess was angry with them.' The Sibylline books gave the same interpretation and prescribed that the image of the goddess should be taken down to the sea and purified by its water. It was presumably at Ostia that Cybele received her ritual bath, and caused no little consternation, for 'she went out from the shore to the deep water, remained there a long time, and was only brought back with difficulty'.[5]

---

[1] The bricks average 3·4 cm. in width; the joints are carefully raked. The only feature that would be unusual at such a date is the thickness of the mortar between bricks, often exceeding 2·5 cm.: the other criteria are more important. Inscription, Pl. xxxviii *a*.

[2] Bloch, 7.   [3] p. 201. L. Aelius was adopted in 136 and died in Jan. 138.

[4] Ovid, *Fasti*, iv. 291; for the relief, Graillot, 65.

[5] Dio xlviii. 43. 5.

Ostia had earlier associations with Cybele than with other oriental cults: we should expect Cybele to be established in the town before the second century A.D., if not already in the Republic, at least under Claudius, who was responsible for the transformation of the cult at Rome and was a frequent visitor to Ostia. Perhaps the evidence does not exclude the possibility of a cult of Attis and Cybele on or near the site of the second-century rebuilding. There were certainly earlier buildings at both ends of the field, but their function we do not know.

One other piece of evidence may be relevant. In the Lateran Museum is a funerary stone commemorating L. Valerius Fyrmus, *sacerdos Isidis Ostiens(is) et M(atris) M(agnae) D(eum) Trastib(erinae)*.[1] In high relief above the inscription is the figure of the priest, now headless, and on each side of the figure the symbols of the two cults, including a cock representing the *galli* of Cybele and lotus flowers of Isis. What is the significance of *Trastib(erinae)*? Dessau interpreted the term to refer to the cult of Cybele at the harbours, but Paschetto was surely right in rejecting this explanation.[2] It would not perhaps be anomalous for the priest of Isis whose cult was in Ostia itself to serve also a cult of Cybele some two miles distant: probably many of the workers at the harbour still lived in Ostia town. What would be anomalous would be the description of the harbour area as *Trastib(erinus)*. The standard term used after the building of Trajan's harbour was *portus uterque*. The bakers of the joint guild are *pistores Ostienses et portus utriusque*:[3] Culcia Metropolis, cymbalist in the cult of Cybele by the harbours, is described as *tympanistria m(atris) d(eum) m(agnae) utriusq(ue) portus*.[4] Paschetto would seem to be right in interpreting *Trastiberinus* as the right bank of the river opposite Ostia town. The memorial of L. Valerius Fyrmus cannot be precisely dated, but the lettering is good and, with the style of the relief, points to a date in the second century, possibly in the first half, certainly well before the end. The right-bank cult is not therefore necessarily earlier than the main cult by the Laurentine gate, but it is possible that it was the first centre of the cult to be established. It may have marked the place where legend said that the vessel carrying Cybele to Rome was grounded on the river mud.

Though Cybele was the first of the oriental goddesses or gods to be formally adopted by Rome, it was the Egyptian cults of Serapis and

[1] 429; Benndorf und Schöne, *Die antiken Bildwerke des lateranischen Museums*, p. 53 n. 80. Phot. Graillot, 246.　　[2] Dessau in *CIL*; Paschetto, 164.

[3] 101.　　[4] Thylander, A 92.

Isis that had the widest international following in the Hellenistic period. The political acumen of the Ptolemies, aided by the interested patronage of Greek philosophers, had transformed the old Egyptian cults for export and they had spread rapidly and widely throughout the Greek world. There were temples of Serapis and Isis in Puteoli, Pompeii, and other Campanian towns by the end of the second century B.C.,[1] and the cult of Isis was strong enough in Rome in the middle of the first century B.C. to attract intermittent persecution. It was persecuted because it offended against Roman manners, being emotional, orgiastic, and liable when misused to undermine morals. The support given by Cleopatra to Antony and, more especially, the emphasis laid by Octavian's propaganda on the danger of the east to Rome stiffened the official opposition to the Egyptian cults; but under Gaius a temple was built to Isis in the Campus Martius, and from that time the cult enjoyed wide popularity at Rome. It was probably not until the prosperity period that the Egyptian cults secured a firm hold in Ostia. A fragment of the Fasti records that a temple of Serapis was dedicated on 24 January A.D. 127,[2] and we may assume that no earlier temple to Serapis preceded it. Though included in the town record the temple was not built by the town authorities nor by its magistrates: it was the gift to the town of a member of the Caltilian family. Since his cognomen is missing it is idle to speculate whether he was a rich freedman, but there is no reason to believe that he was prominent in Ostian government.

This temple of Serapis may be identified with a small brick-built temple standing back in its sacred area from a street which runs south from the Via della Foce at the far end of the excavated area.[3] At the entrance from the street is a bull in black mosaic on a white ground. Within is an open court paved with a black-and-white mosaic of Nilotic scenes, of which little remains. The temple is approached by a flight of steps at the west end of the court and preceded by a pronaos paved with a black-and-white unfigured mosaic, variegated by square and triangular insets of various coloured marbles. The court was originally connected, to north and south, with two other buildings, which must have been associated with the cult; they may have been the living quarters of the temple warden and the priests. But in the late Empire, probably in

---

[1] *RE*, 'Isis' (Roeder), 2103, 2107.
[2] *Fasti*, 127: 'VIII k(alendas) Febr. templum Sarapi, quod [.] Caltilius P[—] | sua pecunia exstruxit, dedicatum [es]t.' Bloch, in an article published in *AJA*, 1959, reminds us that the day of dedication was Hadrian's birthday.   [3] p. 139.

the fourth century, the entrances from the temple court were closed and these buildings passed into other hands. The cult of Serapis was in decline.

The dimensions of the temple are modest, but the evidence is inadequate to provide a fair impression of its architectural decoration and wealth; for the site had already been plundered, and many of its dedications were probably dispersed, before the end of the Roman period. Inscriptions and sculptures, however, tell us a little of the cult. In contrast to the practice in the Serapeum by the harbours, where Greek was the normal language of dedications, most of the inscriptions concerning Serapis at Ostia are in Latin; probably the association with Egypt was less strong. Of the temple hierarchy we have evidence only of a temple warden, *neocorus*, mentioned in two inscriptions.[1] Serapis was not an exclusive deity. His association with Egyptian Isis was to be expected; he could also come to terms with Roman cults. Not far from the temple were found two bases, which once carried dedications to Hercules and to the two Castors in honour of I(upiter) O(ptimus) M(aximus) S(arapis).[2]

Representations of Serapis have been found at many points in the town, in private houses and in public places. Most conspicuous of the private statues preserved is the terra-cotta figure of Serapis, nearly life-size, seated within a small shrine that was added to the south side of the main court of the Insula of Serapis, probably in the Severan period.[3] A similar statue, which was found near the temple in the garden behind the theatre, was probably a public dedication.[4] In the interesting dialogue of Minucius Felix the discussion of Christianity is introduced when the pagan Caecilius salutes Serapis with a ceremonial kiss;[5] we imagine a head of Serapis on a herm, or a free-standing statue by the side of the street.

No temple of Isis has yet been found, but the distribution of inscriptions and dedications referring to her cult suggests that it was on or near the river bank, west of the centre.[6] Inscriptions record three priests of

[1] 188; *IG* xiv. 920. Taylor, 73, refers both inscriptions, said to have been found at Ostia, to Portus, since, when she wrote, there was no evidence of a separate Serapeum at Ostia.

[2] Unpublished. For the title of Serapis (I.O.M.S.) cf. *ILS* 4393. A similar abbreviation, I.O.M.D(olichenus), *ILS* 4296 (cf. 4287).

[3] *Arch. Anz.* 52 (1937) 385.

[4] Paschetto, 370, describes the statue before the head was found. Signora Calza was able to fit a head, found later, to the statue, inv. 1210.

[5] Min. Felix, *Octavius*, 2, 4.   [6] Paschetto, 401.

Ostian Isis, *sacerdotes Isidis Ostiensis*: L. Valerius Fyrmus, who was also priest of the Great Mother,[1] M. Ulpius Faed[imus],[2] and one whose name is lost but who may have been a decurion of the colony.[3] To these may be added D. Flavius Florus Veranus 'priest of the revered queen', *sacerdot(i) sanct(ae) regin(ae)*, decurion of the Laurentine *vicus Augustanus*. He was commemorated by a senator, Flavius Moschylus, himself a devotee of the cult, who made provision in his will for a statue of the priest to be set up, 'mindful of his reverence and purity'.[4] This interesting inscription is dated to A.D. 251, when social currencies were considerably debased. There is nothing in the surviving evidence to suggest that the cult attracted men of such standing in the second century.

Records of dedications to Isis survive. P. Cornelius Victorinus, a clerk in the town government service, presented, presumably to the temple, a statuette of Mars on horseback 'to Queen Isis who restored health to him'.[5] Caltilia Diodora, whose family name is that of the builder of Serapis' temple, presented a silver Venus, one pound in weight, with two wreaths, one of gold.[6] C. Pomponius Turpilianus, an imperial procurator, dedicated an altar to Isis, and, with her, to the numen of Serapis, to Silvanus, and to the Lares: 'aram sanctae Isidi, numini Sarapis, Silvano, Laribus', and his dedication was made in honour of the imperial house: 'pro salute et reditu Antonini Aug(usti), Faustinae Aug(ustae), liberorumque eorum'.[7]

Two inscriptions which record an *Anubiacus*[8] and a *Bubastiaca*[9] show that in the general religious syncretism of the middle Empire Isis assimilated the cults of the dog-headed Anubis, conductor of souls in the underworld, and of Bubastis, whom the Romans identified with Artemis: Caltilia, herself titled *Bubastiaca*, makes her dedication to Isis Bubastis. Of the *pastophori*, the religious brotherhood normally associated with the cult of Isis, there is no trace in surviving Ostian inscriptions, but in the area by the river, where the cult of Isis has left most evidence, was found a statuette of a kneeling *pastophorus*, holding in his hand a little shrine containing an image of Isis with hieroglyphs above.[10]

In the cemeteries devotees of the cult are recorded on tombstones, *Isiaci* and *Isiacae*;[11] and the terra-cotta epistyle over the tomb of Flavia

---

[1] 429. [2] 437. [3] S 4672. [4] 352; revised, *ILS* 6149.
[5] S 4290: 'signum Martis cum equiliolo Isidi reginae restitutrici salutis suae.'
[6] 21. [7] 20. [8] S 4290, cf. 352. [9] 21.
[10] Paschetto, 165. [11] 302, 343, 352, S 4290.

Caecilia and Q. Maecius Iuvenalis reflects the cult of Isis no less clearly
in its imagery.[1] On one side is the sacred Apis bull lying to the right,
with sistrum above and in front a basket laden with fruit; on the other
side, a second Apis lying to the left, with sistrum above and situla in
front. On the situla is cut in relief the head of a man or boy.

A different aspect of the cult of Isis is recalled by a large terra-cotta
hanging lamp with ten burners in the form of a ship.[2] Within the field
of the boat are three figures, each represented within a sanctuary framed
by two columns: Isis is in the centre, above is Harpocrates, below, Serapis. This lamp reflects Isis' function as goddess of the seas, protector of
voyagers, celebrated by the festival of the *navigium Isidis* on 5 March.

To judge by the evidence that has survived, the cults of Cybele and
of the Egyptian gods enjoyed their widest support in Ostia from the
Antonine to the Severan periods: by the later third century the religion
of Mithras seems to have eclipsed them in popularity. Mithraism, of
Persian origin, had assimilated in its contact with Mesopotamia a strong
Semitic and astrological background, and during the Hellenistic period
had spread widely through Asia Minor. Plutarch records that it was
brought to Rome in Pompey's day, but it was not until the Flavian
period that it made any headway in the west.[3] No less than eight Mithraic shrines could be seen at Ostia when the 1938 excavation campaign
was launched; when the campaign was completed the number had
risen to at least fifteen, and others no doubt will be found when the
remaining third of the town area is uncovered.[4]

Some of the Ostian Mithraea have individual features, but in general
they conform to the common pattern. There is usually a small room or
pronaos leading into the shrine itself: this is a long and narrow room
shut off from the light, representing the rocky cave in which the god
was born: in two inscriptions the shrine is actually called a cave,
spelaeum.[5] On both sides of the room are long podia sloping slightly
upwards from the wall; on these the worshippers kneeled to pray.
Between the two podia is a corridor, along which the celebrating priest
passed to an altar.

---

[1] 1044; Benndorf und Schöne, op. cit. 386 nn. 556–9.

[2] *NS* 1909, 118 n. 7, fig. 2.

[3] F. Cumont, *Les Mystères de Mithra*[2] (1902) 31.

[4] A detailed identification, description, and analysis of the Ostian Mithraea, G. Becatti,
Scavi di Ostia II, i Mitrei (Roma, 1954), cited as 'Becatti'. The monuments and inscriptions
are catalogued by M. J. Vermaseren, *Corpus inscriptionum et monumentorum religionis
Mithriacae* (1956) 216–321.   [5] S 4315, Bloch, 9.

Some of the altars are hollowed to take a lamp, and the front of the altar is pierced so that the light could shine through in the form of a crescent or illuminate a relief applied to the altar.[1] In the Mithraeum of the Painted Walls a bust of the sun was dramatically lighted in this way.[2] Behind the altar the central mystery of the cult is represented, normally in a relief applied to the wall. In the scene depicted there is little variation from shrine to shrine except in the quality of the workmanship and the material used. Mithras is figured in Phrygian dress, mounted on a bull, which he kills with a large knife, looking backwards as his knife is plunged into the bull's neck. A dog jumps towards the blood flowing from the wound, and on the other side a serpent stretches up towards it; a scorpion attacks the bull's genitals. Above, a crow watches the scene. At the entrance to the shrine, or on either side of the altar, Cautes and Cautopates are portrayed in small statues or in mosaic. Cautes, with torch upraised, represents day and light; Cautopates, with torch lowered, darkness and night.

One shrine, which adjoins to the west the House of Apuleius, behind the four republican temples, is particularly well preserved and rich in astrological symbolism.[3] At the heads of the two podia are Cautes and Cautopates in mosaic. In the white mosaic of the corridor seven semicircles in black at regular intervals represent the seven planets, which are also represented by figures in black-and-white mosaic on the faces of the podia. Above, on the narrow ledge in which the podia end, are depicted, also in black-and-white mosaic, the twelve constellations of the zodiac. In the Mithraeum of Felicissimus the planets are explicitly related to the seven grades of initiates in mosaic panels along the central corridor between the podia.[4]

The astrological background is reflected again in a small statue of the god of time found in another Mithraic shrine. He is represented with a lion's head, for time devours all things, and his body is six times encircled by a serpent, representing the tortuous course of the sun in the sky. Wings, symbolizing the winds and decorated with symbols of the seasons, spring from his shoulders and hips. In his hands he holds two keys, each pierced with twelve holes, which open the gates of heaven, and, in his left hand, the sceptre of rule. The thunderbolt of Jupiter is cut on his chest, and on the base of the statue are represented the hammer

[1] Becatti, 136.
[2] Becatti, 61 f.
[3] Lanciani, *NS* 1886, 163; Becatti, 47.   [4] Becatti, 108.

and anvil of Vulcan, the wand of Mercury, and the cock and pine-cone of Aesculapius or possibly Attis. Time is the parent of all things.[1]

More exceptional is the representation of a footprint in the mosaic pavement near the entrance of one of the smaller shrines. This feature is unknown in Mithraea elsewhere and may, as Becatti suggests, have been adopted from the cult of Serapis, whose temple was near by. It was probably an invocation to the faithful to follow in the footsteps of the god.[2]

The Mithraea of Ostia do not suggest great wealth. The largest are far smaller than many at Rome, holding at most some forty worshippers; some have room for less than twenty. Most of the shrines are improvised within existing buildings. One of the largest makes use of a service corridor under a set of public baths;[3] another takes over a *crypta* in the imperial palace;[4] another uses the face of the tower in the Sullan town wall by the Tiber and the wall itself.[5] In the House of Diana two small rooms in the north-east corner of the ground floor are adapted to the cult by blocking windows and installing podia.[6] In the near-by Mithraeum of Menander rooms in a house are similarly taken over and no attempt is made to change the paintings on the walls and the mosaic pavements, though they have no Mithraic reference.[7] The incorporation of a large painting of two crested serpents and a *genius* from a private lararium in another Mithraeum was a useful economy, but the subject was appropriate, for the serpent figures prominently in Mithraic representations.[8] Such economies were not always practised. In the Mithraeum of the Painted Walls new paintings were superimposed on the old and they illustrate the cult, though too little remains for their significance to be clear.[9]

In contrast to most of the Ostian Mithraic sculpture, which is undistinguished in quality, one cult group suggests, at first, good taste and a long purse.[10] This fine group is remarkable in three respects. It is a free-standing group instead of the normal relief; it is signed by the artist, Kriton of Athens; and Mithras is represented not in Phrygian but in Greek dress, which has no parallel in the whole range of Mithraic monuments. The style of the sculpture seems to place it in the first half

---

[1] Becatti, 119. The type probably derives from Egypt, R. Pettazzoni, *Essays on the History of Religions* (Leiden, 1954) 180–92 = *Ant. class.* 18 (1949) 267.

[2] Becatti, 80; M. Guarducci, 'Le impronte del *Quo vadis*', *Rend. Pont.* 19 (1942–3) 323 ff. 　　　　　[3] Becatti, 29. 　　　　　[4] 66, p. 374.

[5] *NS* 1924, 69; Becatti, 39. 　　[6] *NS* 1915, 327; Becatti, 9. 　　[7] Becatti, 17.

[8] Becatti, 102. 　　　　　[9] Becatti, 63. 　　　　　[10] *Museo*, 149; Becatti, 32.

of the second century,[1] and the Greek dress would admirably fit the strong hellenizing flavour of Hadrian's reign. But it is difficult to date the Mithraeum in which the group was found as early as this: moreover the insignificant base on which it was set, and the crude ancient restorations to the figure of the bull suggest that this impressive group was acquired for the Ostian shrine after it had already been damaged.[2]

Most of the inscriptions that have survived record the gift of the essential furnishings of the shrine. In addition to the main cult scene of Mithras slaying the bull, the altar, the marble or mosaic furnishings of podia and corridor, and the figures of Cautes and Cautopates, the commonest form of dedication is a head or statuette of Mithras. But in one case a representation of Ahriman, *signum Arimanium*, the principle of evil, is recorded,[3] recalling that the Mithraic cult envisaged a dualism in which the god of light and sun strengthened his followers against the evil in the world.

Of the various grades in the cult Ostian inscriptions record only the highest, *pater*. Each shrine was presided over by a *pater*, who is sometimes described as *pater et antistes*, sometimes as *pater et sacerdos*. The title *pater patrum* is also found once. It occurs elsewhere, but is not common before the fourth century and its meaning is far from certain. It might mean no more than highest in the highest grade; the Ostian example may invite a different interpretation. The inscription commemorates 'Sextus Pompeius Maximus, sacerdos solis invicti Mithrae, pater patrum' and was set up by the priests of Mithras, 'sacerdotes Solis Invicti Mithrae ob amorem et merita eius'.[4] Pompeius Maximus in another inscription found *in situ* is recorded as *pater* to have restored a Mithraeum.[5] Perhaps his fuller title, *pater patrum*, implies that he was the head of the cult in Ostia; the *sacerdotes* who honoured him may have been the heads of individual shrines.

The *patres* do not seem to be important public figures. Sextus Pompeius Maximus, *pater patrum*, was president of one of the ferry-service guilds,[6] but no other record of his guild has yet been found and it may

---

[1] Becatti (37) prefers a later date, identifying the sculptor with a M. Umbilius Criton who is recorded on a late-second-century dedication from another Ostian Mithraeum (Becatti, 83); he suggests that the sculptor received his citizenship through M. Umbilius Maximus, a Roman senator who was patron of the Ostian *lenuncularii tabularii* in 192 (*CIL* xiv. 251). It is difficult to date the sculpture late enough to allow the identification.

[2] Becatti, 37.

[3] S 4311. For Ahriman's place in Mithraism, Cumont, *Textes et monuments . . . de Mithra*, i. 139, ii, nn. 27, 323, 324.   [4] 403.   [5] S 4314.

[6] 403: 'q(uin)q(uennalis) corp(oris) treiectus togatensium'.

be assumed that it was comparatively unimportant. Fructosus, who built a guild Mithraeum, to be described below, was also president of one of the smaller guilds.[1] M. Cerellius Hieronymus may be identified with 'Cerell(ius) Ieroni(mus)', an ordinary member of the builders' guild in 198.[2] The rest are mere names to us, but most of the cognomina suggest freedman stock. No worshipper of Mithras is known to have held public office; the majority seem to have been men of humble means and modest social standing.

Very few Mithraic inscriptions are dated, and the chronology of the cult's development remains largely conjectural. The earliest firm evidence dates from 162, when the Mithraeum in the so-called 'Imperial Palace', excavated by Visconti in 1857, was furnished.[3] The combined evidence of paintings, mosaics, and coins found in the building suggests that the Mithraeum of the Seven Gates is roughly contemporary;[4] on similar grounds the Mithraeum of the Animals has been dated to the same period.[5] None of the surviving Mithraea can be securely dated before the middle of the second century; most of them are demonstrably later.

The great majority of surviving inscriptions seem by their lettering to date from the end of the second or from the third century, and on historical grounds the reign of Commodus forms an appropriate context for the expansion of the cult. For Commodus was both a follower of Mithras and closely associated with Ostia.[6] It was perhaps because of the emperor's personal concern for the cult that a group of worshippers could ask for and receive authority to use a cellar or back room in the palace designed primarily for imperial visits.[7] The expansion of Mithraism continued through the Severan period and probably reached its peak near the middle of the third century.

The Mithraea are not concentrated in any one district, but are evenly distributed over the town.[8] Most of them probably served the initiates

---

[1] Bloch, 9. Only the first letter (S) of the guild survives, but this is sufficient to exclude the most important guilds.   [2] 70, 4313; in builders' roll, *S* 4569, iii. 7.

[3] 56, 57; Becatti, 54.   [4] Becatti, 99.   [5] Becatti, 92.

[6] SHA, *Commodus*, 9. 6. For his association with Ostia, p. 79.

[7] 66: 'C. Valerius Heracles pat[e]r e[t] an[tis]tes dei iu[b]enis incorrupti So[l]is invicti Mithra[e, c]ryptam palati concessa[m] sibi a M. Aurelio—.' A possible restoration is 'a M. Aurelio Commodo Antonino Aug.', but the authority may have been given by an imperial freedman. This Mithraeum is later than that excavated by Visconti in the 'Imperial Palace' (which has inscriptions of 162), but it may have been in an unexplored part of the establishment, Becatti, 120.

[8] Distribution map, Becatti, 132. Fig. 27, p. 382.

of a restricted area round the shrine, but one seems to be closely associated with a guild. A little west of the Round Temple is a building
complex of mid-third-century date, which closely resembles the courtyard temple of the shipbuilders. The plan seems to be typical of guild
temples. Two shops open on the street; a passage between them leads
into a courtyard, at the end of which was to have been built a
temple of orthodox form. But the plan to build the temple was abandoned, and the basement, which had been begun, was modified and
converted into a Mithraeum.[1] Fragments of an inscription found near by
record the building of a Mithraeum by the president of a guild, possibly
the *stuppatores*;[2] it comes almost certainly from this shrine. The building
of a Mithraeum instead of a temple to one of the traditional gods on
guild premises, presumably for members of the guild, is striking evidence of the popularity of Mithraism towards the middle of the third
century.

An interesting graffito on the wall of a small room in a living apartment behind a row of shops has been interpreted by Becatti as a private
tribute to Mithras: 'Dominus Sol hic avitat.'[3] The letters are large and
carefully written, high enough (1·90 metres) to avoid damage; the
words were a serious declaration of faith. Becatti sees here a follower of
Mithras invoking the god in his own cave-dark room. But the language
of Mithraism requires 'invictus Sol' or 'Invictus Deus Sol', and the room
is no darker than many in Ostia. 'Dominus Sol' reflects more probably
the general cult of the sun, which grew in strength during the third
century, especially under Aurelian. There may be further evidence of
this sun cult in the name of a priest of the Sun and Moon on a brickstamp found at Ostia.[4] But the unobtrusiveness and the uncertainty of
this evidence for a cult which, if Ostia followed the Roman pattern,
should have been strong in the third century is surprising.

In contrast to the widespread evidence of Mithraism, Christianity,
which in the third century was to become its chief rival, is not firmly
attested before the end of the second century and will be discussed in
a later setting. The known list of oriental cults recorded may be briefly
completed. Iupiter Dolichenus is normally associated with the armies

---

[1] Becatti, 21.

[2] Bloch, 9: '—rius Fructosus patron(us) corp(oris) S[— | te]mpl(um) et spel(aeum)
Mit(hrae) a solo sua pec(unia) fecit'. For the guild, *saburrarii, susceptores, scapharii* are also
possible. [3] Becatti, 125.

[4] 4089[7]: 'ex oficin(a) L. Aemili Iuliani | solis et lunae | sac|erd(otis)'. For a further
possible reference to the sun cult at Ostia, Becatti, 127.

and the fleets, but he had a shrine on the Janiculum at Rome, and at Ostia there survives a dedication by a civilian. In the republican tetra-style temple near the temple of Hercules was found a small base: 'Iovi Dolicheno L. Plinius Nigrinus q(uin)q(uennalis)'[1] and near it a magical alphabet.[2] This temple cannot have been dedicated to Jupiter Doli-chenus. It is possible that the base, like so many of Ostia's inscriptions, was not found in its original setting; or perhaps the dedication was made in the temple of another god. The dedicator was a man of stand-ing and is probably the Plinius Nigrinus who is recorded in the Fasti as duovir in A.D. 147.

Jupiter Sabazius, a Thracian god who had a wide vogue in the im-perial period, is also attested in a dedication, possibly of the second century, by a L. Aemilius, 'ex imperio Iovis Sabazi'.[3] This inscription was found in a sanctuary which has the main characteristics of a Mith-raeum.[4] Near by was found a further dedication: 'numini caelesti P. Clodius Flavius Venerandus vivir Aug(ustalis) somnio monitus fecit.'[5] *Numen caeleste* has been identified with Carthaginian Caelestis, whose cult is associated with that of Sabazius in Rome.[6] Caelestis had spread her influence widely in the Empire as queen of the sky, earth, and under-world. She protected travellers, and foot imprints were commonly dedicated to her; two *ex-voto* footprints, found under the corridor of this sanctuary, might seem to strengthen the identification.[7] But in another Ostian inscription 'caeleste numen' is applied to 'Invictus deus Sol omnipotens';[8] it was found near by and may have been set up by the same man in this same shrine. Becatti is probably right in regarding both inscriptions as Mithraic.[9] The building, in its final form, and especially the two podia flanking the central corridor point to a Mith-raeum. We may infer either that a Sabazeum was later converted into a Mithraeum or, perhaps more probable, that the cults were associated. There is evidence also for the cult of the Thracian rider god at Ostia in two reliefs of the second or third centuries.[10] In each case the name of the dedicator is in Greek; the cult probably did not spread widely.

[1] Bloch, 4.   [2] Bloch, 5.   [3] S 4296.

[4] Vaglieri, *NS* 1909, 20: Becatti, 113.   [5] S 4318.

[6] Taylor, 93; M. Guarducci, 'Nuovi documenti del culto di Caelestis a Roma', *BC* 72 (1946) 11–25 (*Ostia*, 19).   [7] *NS* 1909, 21.

[8] S 4309; Becatti, 116: '[Invicto] deo Soli | [omnip]otenti | [—]o caelesti | n[u]m[ini p]raesenti | fo[r]tu[na]e laribus | tut[ela]eque | [sa]c. | [Venera]ndus.'

[9] Becatti, 116.

[10] *NS* 1912, 439, (inv. 764) and another unpublished example (inv. 865). For this cult, G. I. Kazarow, *Die Denkmäler des thrakischen Reitergottes in Bulgarien* (Budapest, 1938).

Unidentified cults from the east are reflected in the Shrine of the Three Naves on the east side of the Insula of the Charioteers, which has the long podia normally associated with a Mithraeum but a distinctive mosaic which is not Mithraic, and in an altar from the Piazzale delle Corporazioni showing a seated female figure between two griffins, with a standing Hermes beside her.[1]

To this list of oriental cults may tentatively be added the festival of Maiumas. John Lydus, whose account is repeated by Suidas, records that 'the festival was celebrated in Rome in the month of May. The leading men of Rome came down to the coastal town of Ostia and gave themselves up to enjoyment, splashing one another in the waters of the sea.' The main centre of this festival in the late Empire was at Syrian Antioch, though it originated perhaps from Gaza. The name Maiumas probably means a harbour and Maiumas may have been a ship festival. At Antioch it had a bad reputation and was frequently suppressed. In the Theodosian Code are included rescripts of the fourth century threatening penalties for abuse, but the Roman celebration, in Lydus' account, seems harmless enough. The reliability of Lydus' testimony has been doubted, since there is no other reference to the Roman festival; but such argument from silence, in a field where so much is unknown, carries little weight. That the festival, which certainly was not confined to Syria, should have been adopted by Rome is not improbable and, since it was concerned with the sea, Ostia was the natural place for its celebration: Castor and Pollux had already established the precedent. The festival, however, was probably not introduced before the Severan period, and perhaps later.[2]

Oriental cults were widely represented in Ostia; and the most important of them, the cults of Cybele, of Isis and Serapis, and of Mithras, had a large following. They became firmly established in the prosperity of the first half of the second century and expanded in the late Antonine and Severan periods. Our evidence consists in the ruined shells of buildings and unemotional inscriptions. To clothe the dry bones with flesh we must imagine colourful processions in the streets; crowds thronging the field of the Great Mother when the *taurobolium* was celebrated; the cymbal, flute, and drum of Cybele's ritual; and the rattle of Isis.

---

[1] Becatti, *Mitrei*, 69. For the altar, *NS* 1914, 289, fig. 6, wrongly interpreted as Cybele with her lions (I owe the correction to Signora Calza).

[2] Lydus, *De mens.* iv. 8 (Wuensch, p. 133, 1–8); *RE*, 'Maiumas' (Preisendanz); Taylor, 80.

THE DIFFUSION OF THE IMPERIAL CULT

By the second century the imperial government had no reason to distrust the oriental cults: they were loyal to the empire and invoked the blessings of their gods on the imperial house. Bulls were sacrificed to Cybele on behalf of emperors, and the guild house of the *dendrophori* when rebuilt was dedicated to the majesty of the imperial house. A dedication could be made to Isis for the preservation and safe return of the imperial family.

The imperial cult meanwhile pervaded Ostia more widely than in the pre-Flavian period. *Flamines* of Vespasian,[1] Titus,[2] Hadrian,[3] Antoninus Pius,[4] Marcus Aurelius,[5] Pertinax,[6] Septimius Severus[7] are recorded; it is no doubt by chance alone that Trajan is until now missing from the list. And some at least of these individual cults were maintained for a long time. A *flamen divi Titi* was still alive in 173,[8] and a *flamen divi Hadriani* towards the end of the second century.[9] The temple of Rome and Augustus was probably the original centre of this form of imperial cult; other temples may have been added later. Bloch has convincingly interpreted a large inscribed architectural fragment as the inscription over a *templum divorum*, set up by decree of the council under Antoninus Pius.[10] The names of Hadrian and Trajan survive; the measurements admit the addition of Nerva, Titus, and Vespasian. A combined cult of all the deified emperors is also attested by a *flamen divorum*.[11] Fragments of two epistyles come from buildings in honour of emperors. Both were probably set up by the builders, and the very close correspondence in the height of the letters suggests that the buildings were of similar form and function. The first commemorates *divus Pius*,[12] but the second was set up to an emperor, Septimius Severus or possibly Pertinax, in his lifetime.[13] They were probably not temples.

In view of Hadrian's generous patronage of the colony it is not surprising that his favourite, Antinous, should have been honoured at Ostia. When Antinous died in Egypt in 130 his cult spread widely, with imperial encouragement, through the empire.[14] At Ostia two statues

[1] 292, 298, S 4641, Bloch, 63.   [2] 400, 4142, S 4622.   [3] 390, 391, **14**.   [4] Bloch, 49.
[5] S 4671, Bloch, 54.   [6] S 4648, Bloch, 60.   [7] **11**, Bloch, 60.   [8] 4142.   [9] **14**.   [10] Bloch, 16.
[11] Only one instance known, 444. For parallels elsewhere, F. Geiger, 'De sacerdotibus Augustorum municipalibus', (*Diss. Phil. Halenses*, xxiii, 1913) 25. *Flamen* alone occurs three times (301, 332, 341); it may imply *flamen divorum*, as Taylor (47) suggests.
[12] S 4365. The builders also set up a commemorative tablet to *divus Traianus*.
[13] S 4382.
[14] Dio lxix. 11. 4: 'καὶ ἐκείνου ἀνδριάντας ἐν πάσῃ ὡς εἰπεῖν τῇ οἰκουμένῃ, μᾶλλον δὲ ἀγάλματα, ἀνέθηκε'; P. Marconi, 'Antinoo', *MA* 29 (1923) 161–300.

have been found, closely corresponding in measurements and attributes. Antinous is represented as a god of the countryside, possibly Vertumnus, carrying in a fold of his dress the flowers and fruits of the fields. One of these statues was found in the Baths of Porta Marina,[1] in company with heads of Trajan's sister Marciana and another lady of the imperial house, perhaps Sabina;[2] the other comes from a building near Tor Boacciana, and with it were found heads and busts of emperors and fragments of statues larger than life.[3] More puzzling is a head found in the field of Magna Mater.[4] Antinous is crowned with a diadem on the front of which are two medallions with male busts. Other parallels suggest that Antinous is here represented as a priest in the service of the two male figures of the medallions.[5] These have been identified as Hadrian and Nerva, the founder of the dynasty,[6] but this can be little more than a guess, for the features are unrecognizable.

The imperial cult during this period was freely extended to the wives of emperors. Sabina and Iulia Domna are represented as Ceres,[7] Sabina and the younger Faustina as Venus.[8] No explicit record of a formal cult survives, but a veiled statue of the elder Faustina points to her deification,[9] and a statue found in the social headquarters of the *seviri Augustales* may represent the priestess of a dead empress.

The cult of the Lares Augusti, first attested at Ostia under Claudius, has left wider traces in the second century. P. Horatius Chryseros, in whose honour the *seviri Augustales* set up a statue in A.D. 182, is described as *immunis Larum Aug(ustorum)*, exempt from payments in an association of worshippers of the imperial Lares.[10] Another similar association, centred in the estate that had once belonged to the Ostian Rusticelii and had passed to the emperor, has been mentioned in an earlier chapter.[11] Other inscriptions record a small shrine, '[aedic]ulam Larum Aug(ustorum)',[12] and a dedication by a certain Primigenia.[13] The priests of the deified emperors were chosen from men destined for a public career; the worship of the imperial Lares was reserved for humbler folk.

---

[1] Marconi, op. cit. 194 n. 86.   [2] p. 408.
[3] Paschetto, 490–3; Marconi, op. cit. 170 n. 16; A. Giuliano, *Catalogo dei ritratti Romani del museo profano Lateranense*, 50 n. 55.
[4] Marconi, op. cit. 171 n. 19; B. M. Felletti Maj, *Museo Nazionale, Romano, i Ritratti*, 100 n. 191.
[5] G. Blum, *Mélanges*, 33 (1913) 65–80.   [6] Ibid. 67.   [7] *Museo*, 25, 21.
[8] *Museo*, 24 (Sabina); Felletti Maj, op. cit. 119 n. 236 (Faustina).   [7] *Museo*, 30.
[9] *Museo*, 22.   [10] 367.   [11] p. 333.   [12] 26.   [13] 2041.

There is no trace at Ostia of any cult of the emperor's *genius*, but the *numen domus Augustae* is widely venerated, in the guilds, in the religious associations, and in private dedications. Hispanus, an imperial freedman and *tabularius*, set up a small statue to commemorate his promotion, perhaps to the position of *tabularius*, 'ob processus votum redd(itum)'.[1] Another dedication to the *numen domus Augustae* was made by two slaves and a freedman of the imperial house.[2] Two dedications also survive to imperial Victory.[3]

THE SURVIVAL OF TRADITIONAL RELIGION

The imperial cult expressed a recognition of the material advantages brought by imperial rule: the oriental cults appealed to the emotions and held out confident hopes to initiates of a blessed life beyond the tomb. It might be expected that the traditional cults would be eclipsed. This conclusion, however, is not justified by the surviving evidence.

The temple at the north end of the Forum which dominates the ruins of Ostia is almost certainly the Capitolium, centre of the supremely Roman cult of Jupiter, Juno, and Minerva, whose temple on the Capitoline hill at Rome dated back to the beginning of the Republic and was rebuilt, after its destruction by fire in 69, with great magnificence and imposing ceremony by Vespasian. The direct evidence that this Ostian temple was a Capitolium is not strong. There is no evidence in the building of a triple cult such as is found in almost all Italian Capitolia.[4] The cella was undivided and there is no means of determining how many statues stood on the podium at the north end. But A. Ostiensis Asclepiades is described as *aeditu(u)s Capitoli* when he presents a statuette of Mars to the guild of public freedmen and slaves.[5] The inscription was found at Rome, and Asclepiades might have been a servant in the Roman Capitolium; but, since the name recurs in the roll of members of the *familia publica* of Ostia,[6] and since his dedication was made to them, it is reasonably certain that the Capitolium in question is Ostian. If Ostia had a Capitolium, its natural place was in the Forum.

A further argument can be derived from the earlier history of the area. Recent excavation has revealed that towards the end of the first century B.C. two temples were built on the north side of the Decumanus in the Forum. These temples were destroyed when the Hadrianic

---

[1] *S* 4316. [2] *S* 4319. [3] 68, *S* 5321.
[4] M. Cagiano de Azevedo, 'I "Capitolia" dell' impero Romano', *Mem. Pont.* 5 (1941) 1–36. [5] 32. [6] 255, col. 1. 5.

temple was built. It is reasonable to infer that the new temple combined the cults of the two older temples which it replaced. We have suggested above that one may have been the original Capitolium, the other a temple of Jupiter.[1]

Until recently it was possible to believe that the new temple might have been dedicated to Vulcan, whose cult was historically the most important in Ostia, but it is now known from a fragment of the Fasti that the temple of Vulcan was restored on a handsome scale under Trajan and rededicated in 112 on 22 August, the eve of the Volcanalia.[2] It is barely conceivable that it should have been completely rebuilt within twenty years, and the evidence of brickstamps shows conclusively that the great temple in the Forum was built in the early years of Hadrian's reign.[3]

Vulcan's was not the only republican temple to receive attention in the prosperity period. The temple of Hercules was substantially restored under Trajan,[4] and its immediate neighbours at about the same time. Traces of second-century restoration can also be seen in the four republican temples on a common foundation near the theatre.[5] When a small corner of the area reserved for Bona Dea outside Porta Marina was taken to provide room for a nymphaeum, the goddess was compensated by a small addition to her area and a more imposing entrance.[6] Later, in the second century, P. Lucilius Gamala restored the temple of Venus that his ancestor had built, the temple of Castor and Pollux, and the cella of pater Tiberinus, whose cult is not otherwise attested but may date back to the Republic.[7]

The natural inference from all these restorations that the old cults were far from moribund is confirmed by other evidence. The games of Castor and Pollux were still being celebrated by Roman praetors at the beginning of the third century. The *pontifex Volcani* maintained his primacy in the religious organization of the town. Records from the second or early third century survive of dedications made to Jupiter Optimus Maximus,[8] Hercules,[9] Mars,[10] Apollo,[11] Spes Augusta,[12] Fortuna.[13] An association of *cultores Iovis Tutoris* is found outside the town.[14]

---

[1] p. 352.

[2] *Fasti*, 112: 'xi K(alendas) Sept. aedis Volkani vetustate corrupta, [restituta or]nato opere, dedicata est.'   [3] Bloch, *Bolli laterizi*, 346 f.

[4] Bloch, *Topografia*, 219 (i. 15. 5).   [5] *MA* 23 (1914) 475.

[6] Calza, *NS* 1942, 164.   [7] 2[16].   [8] S 4293.

[9] S 4287–9.   [10] 31, S 4300, Bloch, 6.   [11] S 4279.   [12] S 4330.

[13] 2040, 4281–2; Fortuna Praestita, Bloch, 1 (cf. *ILS* 4030).   [14] 25.

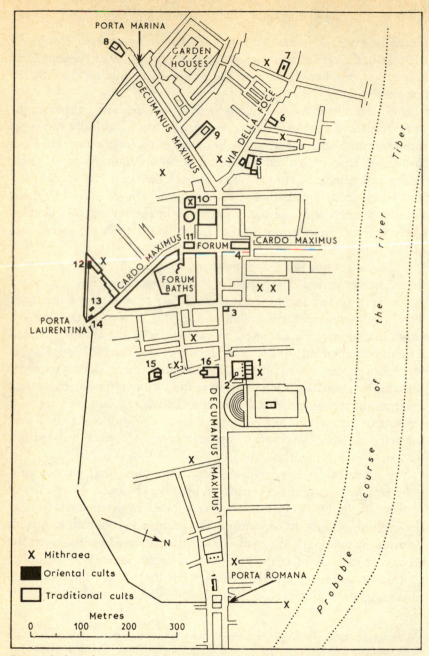

FIG. 27. Ostian cults. 1. ? Venus, Fortuna, Ceres, and another (p. 351). 2. Jupiter Optimus
Maximus. 3. ? Spes (p. 351). 4. Capitolium. 5. Hercules. 6. Temple associated with the
measurers (p. 329). 7. Serapis. 8. Bona Dea (Julio-Claudian). 9. Guild temple of the shipbuilders. 10. Guild temple converted to Mithraeum (p. 328). 11. Rome and Augustus.
12. Cybele. 13. Attis. 14. Bellona. 15. Bona Dea (Augustan). 16. Guild temple. Temples
not numbered are not yet identified.

The cult of the Nymphs remained popular into the Empire. D. Hostius Heraclida made a dedication to 'the divine Nymphs'.[1] Titus Amerimnus 'made a gift' to the Nymphs.[2] Ammonius, an imperial slave, built them an altar, for he had been 'freed by their divine power from a critical malady'; below the inscription is a roughly sculptured scene, depicting a man lying on the ground with his hands raised in terror and a dog running away. It seems that Ammonius owed to the Nymphs his recovery from hydrophobia.[3] A well-head was set up in A.D. 197 by the presidents of the corn measurers, 'at the prompting of Ceres and the Nymphs'.[4] The cult of the Nymphs is perhaps a tribute to the excellence of the natural water supply which, in spite of the close proximity of the sea, was pure and sweet.[5] Old religious beliefs are also reflected in an altar to the goddesses of the cross-roads, 'deaes Tribiaes sanctaes et loco divino'.[6]

The peculiarly Roman cult of the *genius* is also still widespread in the Empire. Dedications are made to the *genius* of trade guilds,[7] of the *seviri Augustales*,[8] of the decurions,[9] of the colony itself,[10] of the Roman people,[11] of 'the place'.[12] But the most widely attested cult among the common folk is the deep-rooted cult of Silvanus. On the right bank of the river was found an inscription recording the restoration of a shrine of Silvanus: 'Anteros Aeliorum et Theodora Silvano sancto aedem dirutam a solo restituerunt.'[13] Temple would probably be a misnomer, for it was not the custom to build temples to Silvanus: probably the *aedes* was a small shrine, perhaps at a cross-roads. More commonly Silvanus is honoured by small altars and statuettes of the god holding billhook and cornucopia, the symbols of his agricultural origin.

Silvanus is invoked to protect the emperor[14] and the *numen* of the imperial house.[15] He is associated with cults old and new. One dedication he shares with Hercules;[16] another with Isis and Serapis.[17] His image is presented to the *dendrophori* of Cybele,[18] and is represented in coloured mosaic in a room that is probably associated with a Mithraeum.[19] Silvanus also finds his way into the trade guilds. He is especially associated

---

[1] 46a.　　　　　[2] S 4321.　　　　　[3] NS 1920, 163 n. 1 = S 4322.

[4] 2.　　　　　　　　　　　　　　[5] Pliny, *Ep.* ii. 17. 25.

[6] Bloch, 12; cf. ILS 3271. For the form of the dative, Sommer, *Handbuch der Laut- und Formenlehre*, 326.

[7] 10, S 4285, Bloch, 2.　　　[8] 12.　　　　　[9] AE 1948, 30; Bloch, 3.

[10] 8, 9. In the late second century a *sacerdos geni coloniae* was appointed, p. 185.

[11] S 4284.　　　　[12] 11.　　　　[13] S 4327. For Silvanus at Ostia, Taylor, 37.

[14] S 4327.　　[15] S 4326.　　[16] 17.　　[17] 20.　　[18] 53.

[19] Visconti, *Ann. Inst.* 36 (1864) 174; Becatti, *Mitrei*, 56.

with the weighers, *sacomarii*, whose guild takes his name;[1] he takes pride of place in the paintings of the small chapel in a large bakery.[2] The wide distribution of such a rustic cult in a commercial city is a reminder that the products of the farm land and of the woods were not unimportant in the life of the town. The dedications known to us are made by slaves, imperial freedmen, and humble folk: they are found in public places and in private houses. Silvanus triumphantly survived the concentrated urbanization of the second century and the invasion of the oriental cults.

In considering the position in the town's life of traditional religion it may also be significant that there is very little surviving evidence that during the second century the ruling classes were closely associated with the oriental cults. The position of Cybele, as we have seen, was exceptional. She had from the outset enjoyed the patronage of the nobility at Rome; it is consistent that some of the patrons of the Ostian *dendrophori* should have been among the most prominent men of the town. But, so far as our evidence goes, the devotees and officials of the other cults did not include men of great standing. L. Plinius Nigrinus, who made a dedication to Jupiter Dolichenus, is the only chief magistrate of Ostia known to have been associated with any of these cults.[3] The sterility of the traditional cults has often been exaggerated by an undue emphasis on the contractual nature of Roman religion. The Capitoline cult had all the emotional associations of a national anthem. The cult of Hercules was capable of new significance against a changing moral background: the idea of superhuman physical force merged into the higher conception of self-sacrifice, Hercules devoting his own life to make the world a better place for others to live in. Many of the older gods and goddesses still had the emotional appeal of patron saints.

THE CULTS BY THE HARBOURS

A further warning against underrating the strength of the traditional cults is given by the development of the area round the imperial harbours. When the Claudian harbour was built, there seems to have been no intention to provide for the growth of a substantial living settlement, but the addition of Trajan's inner basin led to a change. In the reign of Constantine Portus had become a small town and was made indepen-

---

[1] 309; cf. 51.　　　　　　　　　　　　　　　　　　　　　　　[2] NS 1915, 246.

[3] p. 376. The oriental cults are conspicuously absent in the long list of benefactions of the Antonine Gamala, **2**.

dent of Ostia; it was already growing fast through the second century. Excavation in this area has not been systematic or extensive. The argument from silence, therefore, which has some validity, if discreetly used, at Ostia, has none at Portus; but sufficient inscriptions and buildings have been at various times recovered to give a partial glimpse of the cults established, and the harbour settlement has special importance for our purpose because it had no roots. Traditional cults might be continued at Ostia because they had become an integral part of the fabric of the town's life; if they were introduced by the harbours and received temples, the natural inference is that they still had an attractive power. And while Ostia town had a long-established local aristocracy and a significant element of men who earned their living from the land and from the woods, and might therefore be more conservative in religious observances, the new population by the harbours was essentially a population of traders and harbour workers. The establishment of traditional cults in such a centre is significant.

The first of these cults for which evidence survives is that of Bona Dea. An early second-century statuette in the Villa Albani portrays a seated matron with a serpent twined round her right forearm and cornucopia held in her left hand.[1] This is the standard representation of Bona Dea and is probably a dedication offered to her temple, for the back of the figure is left rough, suggesting that it stood against a wall. That a temple to Bona Dea existed is confirmed by a later inscription mentioning Bonadienses, a district named presumably after the temple.[2] This later inscription is a dedication to Silvanus made by a priest of Liber pater Bonadiensium and the cult of Liber pater centred near Bona Dea is also attested by further dedications, including an image of the god set up by Cn. Maelius Epictetus 'in aria sua', on his own private property.[3] Another dedication commemorates the association of Commodus with this god, showing that the cult was established by the late second century: 'pro salute imp. M. Aureli Commodi Antonini Aug. pii felicis Libero patri Commodiano sacrum.'[4] The temple itself has been identified in a small round Corinthian peristyle structure just north of the Torlonia villa, near the north-east corner of Trajan's harbour.[5]

Hercules, whose cult became so important in Ostia town, is also

---

[1] A. Greifenhagen, *RM* 52 (1937) 235.   [2] S 4328.
[3] 28. Other dedications, 27, 29; cf. *IG* xiv. 925: 'ἱερεῖς ἱέρειά τε θεοῦ μεγάλου Διωνύσου'.
[4] 30.   [5] Lanciani, *Ann. Inst.* 40 (1868) 181.

commemorated in three inscriptions from Portus. The earliest is from
the base of a statue dedicated to Hercules Invictus in the early second
century, and set up near the south bank of Trajan's canal.[1] The other
two inscriptions probably commemorate statues in the Barracks of the
Vigiles. One was set up towards the end of the second century by
Cassius Ligus, commander of the detachment of *vigiles* at Ostia;[2] the
other was in honour of Septimius Severus.[3] Remains of the temple of
Hercules were thought to have been found in the late eighteenth and
mid-nineteenth centuries between the harbours of Claudius and
Trajan, but the evidence recorded is not decisive.[4]

It is Minerva, not an eastern god, who was the patron of the guild of
stuppatores: 'numini evidentissimo Minervae Aug(ustae) sacrum con-
servatrici et antistiti splendidissimi corporis stuppatorum.'[5] Diana is
mentioned in an inscription of uncertain meaning.[6] An altar is set up to
Fortuna Domestica for the preservation and safe return of Septimius
Severus and Clodius Albinus by a centurion of the *vigiles*.[7] Silvanus
is honoured with a small altar by an imperial freedman who was a
tabularius,[8] and by a priest of Liber Pater who makes a dedication in
thanksgiving for his success in hunting: 'Silvano sancto cui magnas
gratias ago conductor aucupiorum.'[9]

Even in the scanty evidence that has survived the traditional cults
hold a significant place, and with them we may include the cult of
Cybele, which, as has been seen, held a special position in the Roman
state. There is no doubt that the cult of Cybele became well established
at the harbours in the second century. The earliest record is a funerary
altar from the Isola Sacra cemetery, dated by its style to the early second
century. It commemorates Culcia Metropolis, cymbalist in the cult,
tympanistria m(agnae) d(eum) m(atris) utriusq(ue) portus.[10] A second cymbalist is recorded in a slightly later inscription from the same cemetery,
and she is the wife of a priest, *sacerdos m(agnae) d(eum) m(atris) et Ae-
sculapis*.[11] Another priest is recorded later, and in the same tomb was
buried a ceremonial flute-player, *tibico m(agnae) d(eum) m(atris) portus
Aug(usti) et Traiani felicis*.[12] From the third century dates the tomb of a
high priest, who reclines full length in his ceremonial dress on the lid of
his sarcophagus and is represented in two separate reliefs, sacrificing to

---

[1] S 4288.   [2] 13.   [3] 16.   [4] Fea, *Viaggio*, 39.   [5] 44.
[6] 4 = Thylander, B 287: 'Diana iobens iub. Traianensium.'   [7] 6.
[8] 49, set up by a Flavian freedman.   [9] S 4328.
[10] Thylander, A 92: for the altar, G. Ricci, *NS* 1939, 63.
[11] Thylander, A 142.   [12] 408.

Cybele and Attis.[1] Special importance was attached to the cult by the harbour: 'is qui in portu pro salute imperatoris sacrum facit ex vaticinatione archigalli a tutelis excusatur.' The rite in question is perhaps the *taurobolium*.[2]

But though the traditional cults were not unimportant by the harbours, the new settlement probably felt the impact of the east more strongly than Ostia town. For it was not until Trajan's harbour was built that eastern trade moved sharply away from Puteoli and, when Ostia itself began to decline, easterners will have done their business and normally stayed at the harbour rather than in the old town.

Of all the oriental cults at Portus those of Egypt have left the most prominent mark. The cult and temple of Serapis were probably inspired by the close association of the Alexandrian corn fleet with the imperial harbours in the second century. In the Severan period we find an official of this fleet as temple-warden,[3] and it may be significant that all the inscriptions that can be certainly attributed to the Portus cult are in Greek,[4] in contrast with the Latin inscriptions from the Ostian Serapeum. In the Torlonia Museum is a large capital with volutes in Egyptian style, carved in a dark granite which probably came from Egypt.[5] It may have originally crowned one of the columns of the Serapeum of Portus.

The little that we know of the elaboration of the cult has to be inferred from a single inscription. From this we learn that the retainers of the temple included an ἀρχιυπηρέτης, who may be the head of the religious hierarchy under the temple-warden; ἱερόφωνοι, ritual singers; and καμεινευταί, whose function is uncertain but presumably concerned with ritual fire. There were also slaves attached to the temple, ἱεροδουλεία.[6]

Most of the dedications that have survived are in the name of the temple-warden. Two, both of the Severan period, are in honour of the imperial house,[7] and in one of them with the prayer for the preservation and safe return of Septimius Severus and Caracalla is coupled a prayer for the safe voyage of the whole (Alexandrian) fleet.[8] Another inscription records the dedication by a temple-warden of three altars,

---

[1] Calza, *Necropoli*, 205, figs. 108–11; *Museo*, 158–60; Pl. XXXI *a, b*. [2] Graillot, 153 n. 1.

[3] *IG* xiv. 917: 'Γ. Οὐαλέριος Σερῆνος νεωκόρος τοῦ μεγάλου Σαράπιδος, ὁ ἐπιμελήτης παντὸς τοῦ 'Αλεξανδρείνου στόλου.' For the title, cf. *S* 4626: 'curator navium Karthag(iniensium).'

[4] *IG* xiv. 914–21. A possible exception in Latin, 123 = Thylander, B 308. Portus Serapis inscriptions discussed, Dessau, *Bull. Inst.* 54 (1882) 152; Taylor, 72.

[5] Visconti, *Catalogo Museo Torlonia*, n. 13.

[6] *IG* xiv. 914. [7] Ibid. 914, 917. [8] Ibid. 917.

a large lamp, a censer, and other furnishings, presumably for the temple, and the authority of the *pontifex Volcani* is added.[1] One private memorial, a small marble column, commemorates an athletic victory at Sardis and is set up in honour of his grandfather by a wrestler and his father, who was 'a senator of the renowned city of Alexandria'.[2]

Two inscriptions refer to the cult of Isis and both are concerned with her *megaron*. One records a restoration by a priest of Isis and the *Isiaci*;[3] the other, an enlargement by two women.[4] In a third inscription of uncertain restoration Isis may be associated, as at Ostia, with Cybele.[5]

Mithraism, which has left such a prominent mark in the ruins of Ostia, is attested by only two inscriptions from the harbour area,[6] but no inference can be drawn as to the comparative popularity of the cult in the two centres, for Mithraea are not conspicuous monuments, and excavation by the harbours has not yet touched the main living quarters. Jupiter Dolichenus is commemorated in two inscriptions, one dedication set up on behalf of Commodus by the commander of a cavalry squadron,[7] another, also from the reign of Commodus, by a group of sailors of the Ostia detachment from the Misenum fleet, perhaps celebrating their discharge.[8] From farther east comes Jupiter of Heliopolis; he was invoked by a Syrian to protect Marcus Aurelius and Commodus.[9]

CHRISTIANITY AND ITS RIVALS[10]

In the Severan period, both in Ostia town and by the harbours, while the oriental cults and the cult of the imperial house grew in popularity, many at least of the traditional cults held their own. The religious pattern of the later third and early fourth century is much more elusive. The small number of inscriptions surviving from Ostia is a reflection of the sharp decline that set in during the third century. Some thirty inscriptions are associated with the Ostian cult of Cybele between the accession of Antoninus Pius and the end of the Severan dynasty: from that point until the middle of the fourth century only one dated inscription survives, the record of an imperial *taurobolium* celebrated between

---

[1] *IG* xiv. 915. [2] Ibid. 916. [3] 18 = Thylander, B 293. [4] 19.

[5] 123 = Thylander, B 308, as restored by Lanciani: '[numini Isid]is et | [magnae deum] matris | [Idaeae sac]rum | [cultores Ser]apis scholam | [constituta]m sua pecunia | [dedicave]runt . . .'.

[6] 55; 286 = Thylander, B 295, is an 'album sacrat(orum)'. Thylander suggests Isis worshippers. Cumont, noting the titles *pater* and *leo*, rightly associates with Mithras, *Textes et monuments . . . de Mithra*, ii. 117 n. 140.

[7] 22 = Merlat, *Répertoire des inscriptions . . . du culte de Iupiter Dolichenus*, 265.

[8] 110 = Merlat, 264. [9] 24 = Thylander, B 297. [10] See also Addenda.

251 and 253.[1] In the cult of Isis a devotee of senatorial status honours 'the priest of the revered queen' in the middle of the third,[2] but most of the Isiac inscriptions belong to the second century. Similarly most at any rate of the evidence for the cult of Serapis comes from the second half of the second century or the early years of the third. So far as our limited evidence goes, only one of the original cults shows signs of strength in the third century. Mithraism, which had expanded vigorously under Commodus, continued for some time to exercise a strong attraction. Few Mithraic records are dated, but to judge from the lettering of the inscriptions, the physical remains of the buildings, and the style of paintings, mosaics, and sculptures, the cult was still flourishing through the third century. It was against Mithraism that the Christian apologists of the third century launched their keenest attacks and it is possible that at Ostia the rivalry between the two creeds was sharp.

One of the most surprising features of Ostian excavations has been the comparative insignificance of explicit Christian evidence. Though a substantial proportion of Ostia's tombs have been fully or partly explored, less than a hundred Christian epitaphs have been found and most of them seem to belong to the fourth century or later. If M. Curtius Victorinus, whose funerary inscription is clearly Christian—'M. Curtius Victorinus et Plotia Marcella viventes fecerunt si deus permiserit sibi'— is to be identified with the *lenuncularius* of the same name who is listed in the guild's roll of A.D. 192,[3] he is the earliest of whom we know.

On general grounds it would not be surprising if Christianity was slow to gain a firm hold in Ostia. It was at Puteoli that St. Paul landed when he brought his appeal as a Roman citizen to Rome, and Christianity grew roots most easily in towns such as Puteoli, Naples, and Pompeii which had had a long and close association with the Greek-speaking world. It was only when the building of Trajan's harbour drew the eastern trade more and more from Puteoli and the southern ports that Christian influence was likely to be strongly felt at Ostia.

Christianity also spread most easily where large Jewish communities were already established, and there is no good evidence to suggest that the number of Jews in Ostia or by the harbours was ever large. The evidence for a Jewish organization at Ostia is confined to a restoration in a single inscription, which was found some miles outside Ostia.[4]*

---

[1] 42.   [2] 352.   [3] 1900; 251, col. I. 25.
[4] *NS* 1906, 410 (found at Castel Porziano): '[universitas] Iudaeorum | [in col(onia) Ost(iensium) commor]antium.'

Unless and until more evidence of Jewish names or Jewish monuments is found within the town, no conclusions should be drawn from the restoration.*A large number of Jewish inscriptions including reference to a synagogue and an organized community have been attributed to the harbours, but convincing arguments have recently been put forward to show that the most important inscriptions in the series were almost certainly taken to the bishop's palace at Portus from Rome.[1]

But it is too early to speak confidently of the early growth of Christianity in Ostia. Most of the Christian epitaphs so far found come from tombs near the church of S. Ercolano; earlier Christian cemeteries may yet be discovered. If they existed they are likely to have been some distance from the town, and in such areas there has been no systematic exploration. Brief consideration of the third-century evidence confirms the warning. Within the walls there are few certain traces of Christianity, and the number of Christian epitaphs remains small. But the literary tradition suggests that, by the middle of the third century, Christianity was firmly rooted, for in the later records of a third-century persecution Ostia already has her bishop, presbyters, and deacon.

The story concerns the Christian activities of Aurea, an imperial princess who was banished to Ostia for her refusal to abandon the faith; Censorinus, a high Roman official, who was committed to prison in Ostia; and the bishop Cyriacus, with other leaders of the Ostian church.[2] When Censorinus is visited in prison by a presbyter, his chains are miraculously loosed, and the soldiers on guard, overwhelmed by the miracle, are converted and baptized. The climax comes when news reaches Rome that a cobbler's son has been brought back from the dead. An official is sent down to investigate. The soldiers, refusing to recant, are executed 'by an arch in front of the theatre'; Aurea, Cyriacus the bishop, a presbyter, and a deacon are put to death. Alexander Severus, Claudius Gothicus, and Trebonianus Gallus are named as the emperors concerned in variant versions. We can probably eliminate Alexander Severus who, in Church tradition, was sympathetic to the Christians.

Much of the detail in the story is unacceptable. Different martyrdoms have probably been conflated, but that the tradition of this persecution

---

[1] H. J. Leon, 'The Jewish community of ancient Porto', *Harvard Theol. Rev.* 45 (1952) 165.   [2] Further discussed, p. 518.

was firmly rooted in actual events is confirmed by its commemoration
in Ostia. In the early Middle Ages a small oratory was built near the
south-east corner of the theatre area. The walls were poorly constructed
of miscellaneous material from other buildings and collapsed when the
town was deserted; but near the ruins were discovered a number of
sarcophagi.[1] One has a figure of Orpheus, commonly adopted in early
Christian monuments to represent the good shepherd, and on its lid is
the simple inscription 'hic Quiriacus dormit in pace'.[2] Perhaps, when
the oratory was built, the remains of the martyrs were collected and
laid to rest near the scene of their martyrdom. As late as the twelfth
century a priest from Ostia still celebrated mass in this oratory of the
martyrs, known as the church of St. Cyriacus, though the Via Ostiensis
by which he came from medieval Ostia to the theatre was overgrown,
and grass and brambles covered mounds of ruins on either side of the
road.[3]

Aurea's memory is preserved in the church dedicated to her in Ostia.
The present building dates from the fifteenth century, but it was not
the first church on the site. A basilica of S. Aurea was in ruin, 'distecta
vel disrupta', at the end of the seventh century.[4] Her name has recently
been found on a half-column in the church;[5] the lettering is not later
than the fifth century.

Other Christian martyrs are recorded in similar traditions and in the
lists of martyrs,[6] and some of them may have died in the third century.
There is independent evidence that a basilica had been built by the tomb
of one of these martyrs, Asterius, before the time of Pope Damasius
(366–84), and this may provide an important clue.[7] It is probable that,
before Christianity prevailed in the fourth century, the Christians met
and worshipped in the cemeteries outside the walls. This will help to
explain why there is so little evidence within the town itself.

That the Christian community of Ostia was firmly established before
the reign of Constantine is clear also from the presence of Maximus,
bishop of Ostia, at the council summoned by Constantine to Rome in
October 313 to heal the divisions in the African Church.[8] Inscriptions
add a little substance to the picture; most of them come from tombs
near to the modern cemetery by the church of S. Ercolano. Very few of

---

[1] Vaglieri, *NS* 1910, 126; *Nuovo bull. arch. crist.* (1910), 57.
[2] Phot. *NS* 1910, 137. [3] p. 520 n. 3. [4] *Lib. Pont.* i. 376.
[5] M. F. Squarciapino, *Museo della via Ostiense* (1955) 35.
[6] See Appendix VII, p. 518. [7] p. 524.
[8] Duchesne, *Histoire ancienne de l'église*, ii[4] (1910) 110 f.

the epitaphs give any indication of status or occupation, but one commemorates an official of the mint established in 309 by Maxentius;[1]
another a presbyter,[2] but his date is uncertain. Recurrent formulas are
found, and some of them are distinctively Ostian. The comparison of
death to sleep, so common later, is in Roman times rare outside Ostia.[3]
Similarly the phrases 'si deus permiserit', 'cum deus voluerit', 'quando
deus voluerit' are not commonly found elsewhere.[4] To the evidence of
inscriptions may be added a large number of Christian lamps found at
scattered points in the town and a Christian glass with the words 'bibe,
zeses' in gold lettering at the bottom, and the Christian symbol of a
fish in relief on one side.[5] But of Christian meeting-places in this period
there is no secure evidence.

The list of Ostian martyrs is not long. In the present state of our evidence it seems probable that Christianity made little headway at Ostia
during the second century, but spread widely during the economic
distress of the third century. By the time of Augustine it was a well-
established tradition that the Pope should be consecrated by the bishop
of Ostia.[6]

While Christianity and Mithraism were struggling for supremacy in
the third century, how fared the traditional cults? The evidence is
extremely slender and does not afford a clear answer. Only one temple
is demonstrably later than the end of the second century, but it is one
of the most imposing in the town. This 'Round Temple', as it must be
called until it is identified, adjoins the Basilica to the west and is built
on a monumental scale with a handsome forecourt. Though it has been
attributed to the fourth century it is almost certainly to be placed, by
the character of its brickwork, towards the middle of the third century.[7]
It would be of particular interest to know to what cult it was dedicated.

The dedication, towards the end of the third century or a little later,
of a large new altar in front of the temple of Hercules by the prefect
of the corn supply, who was by then responsible for supervising the
government of Ostia, shows that the cult of Hercules was still main-

---

[1] 1878.　　　　　　　　　　　　　　　　　　　　　　　　　　　　　[2] 1879.

[3] De Rossi, *Bull. arch. crist.* (1875) 104; M. B. Ogle, 'The Sleep of Death', *MAAR* 11
(1933) 109 f.

[4] De Rossi, *Bull. arch. crist.* (1873) 143.　　　　　　　　　　[5] Paschetto, 183.

[6] Augustine, *Breviculus collationis cum Donatistis*, coll. 3. 16 (Migne, *PL* xliii. 641): 'sicut
nec Romanae Ecclesiae ordinat aliquis episcopus metropolitanus, sed de proximo
Ostiensis episcopus.' *Lib. Pont.* i. 202: 'hic (Marcus, A.D. 336) constituit ut episcopus
Hostiae qui consecrat episcopum palleum uteretur et ab eodem episcopus urbis Romae
consecraretur.'　　　　　　　　　　　　　　　　　　　　　　　[7] p. 550.

tained.[1] But one traditional cult at least was declining. At some point the temple area of Bona Dea outside Porta Marina was drastically reduced. The colonnade that surrounded an open court in front of and to the south of her temple was suppressed, and the southern half of the area was converted to other purposes. A new wall cut the area in two and the southern end was divided into a series of rooms, perhaps used as shops.[2] The new construction, in block and brick, probably belongs to the third century. The festival of Castor and Pollux, attested for the early third century and for the fourth, was still no doubt maintained through the third, and the *pontifex Volcani* preserved his authority in religious matters. Some of the unpretentious dedications to Silvanus are probably also from this period, but of the other traditional cults we learn nothing.

It is possible that, in this period of difficult transition from a commercial to a residential town, philosophical speculation played a bigger part than it had done hitherto among the more leisured class of Ostians. Even when the town was expanding vigorously from the profits of trade, philosophers could find Ostia congenial. Aulus Gellius reports a visit by the learned Favorinus in the early second century. He was joined by two leading representatives of the Peripatetic and Stoic schools from Rome, and a lively discussion developed as they strolled along the shore towards dusk.[3] Minucius Felix' dialogue between pagan and Christian has a similar setting. But, when prosperity had passed, the climate was more favourable. In an attractive building on the east side of the Semita dei Cippi, equipped with a small set of baths, two heads were found representing the same man. He was almost certainly a philosopher, and the style is not far from the middle of the third century. Perhaps the building was used as a meeting-place for philosophical discussions; it has been persuasively argued that the man they honoured in this striking way was Plotinus, the great leader of the neo-Platonists.[4]

The evidence for the harbour district is less fruitful for the third century than for the second. The cult of Serapis was certainly flourishing in the Severan period, and the close contact with the Alexandrian corn fleet probably ensured its continuity; it is likely to have declined when Constantine transferred the corn of Egypt from Rome to his new eastern

---

[1] *AE* 1948, 126.   [2] Calza, *NS* 1942, 164.   [3] Aul. Gell. xviii. 1.
[4] The suggestion, first made by H. P. L'Orange, *Les Cahiers archéologiques*, 5 (1951) 15, is supported, with further argument, by R. Calza, *Boll. d'Arte*, 38 (1953) 203. A third head of the same man probably also comes from Ostia.

capital. To the oriental cults attested in the second century can be added the cult of Syrian Marnas, for the city of Gaza honoured the emperor Gordian as benefactor 'at the prompting of their ancestral god and through Tiberius Claudius Papirius, keeper of the temple'.[1] The dedication was made at the harbours, and the temple of which Papirius was keeper was presumably a temple of Marnas in the harbour area. One of the dedications of Silvanus is probably to be dated to this period;[2] of other pagan cults no evidence has yet been found.

The evidence of the growth of Christianity by the harbours before Constantine is scarcely more satisfactory than for Ostia. According to a late tradition Hippolytus was bishop of Portus in the middle of the third century; but much that is recorded of him applies with little doubt to the Roman Hippolytus, a dangerous thinker whose place in the Papal succession it was convenient to obscure.[3] However, though the confused threads cannot now be disentangled, it is probable that a Hippolytus was among the martyrs of Portus. The site of his church on Isola Sacra is still marked by a medieval campanile, and an earlier church was largely destroyed by the Vandals in the fifth century.[4] He was, however, probably not a bishop. When Christianity was first developing, the harbour settlement was controlled from Ostia, and the bishop of Ostia probably presided over both Christian communities. The first bishop of Portus who is firmly attested was present at the Council of Arles in 314.[5] It may be significant that the Christian formula 'hic dormit in pace', characteristic of Ostia but not found in this period at Rome, is shared by Portus, though each centre also has individual expressions which are not found in the other. Such phrases as 'cum deus voluerit', 'cum deus permiserit', are not found at Portus; 'in deo (*or* in domino) vivas', common at Portus, is not found at Ostia.

In the cemetery of Isola Sacra there are no Christian records in the main phase of development in the first half of the second century. When earlier tombs were reused in the late third and early fourth centuries, three Christian inscriptions and a Christian sarcophagus are found.[6] Most of the Christian inscriptions come from a cemetery on the north side of Trajan's canal, near its junction with the Tiber;[7] it probably did not develop before the third century.

---

[1] *IG* xiv. 926; Taylor, 79. [2] *S* 4328. [3] p. 526. [4] p. 98.
[5] Duchesne, *Histoire ancienne de l'église*, ii⁴ (1910) 113.
[6] Thylander, A 283–5; Calza, *Necropoli*, 215.
[7] De Rossi, *Bull. arch. crist.* (1866) 45–49.

Early Christian tradition records a long list of martyrdoms at the harbours in the periods of persecution, in contrast with the comparatively lean record from Ostia.[1] They include Bonosa, who was put to death with fifty soldiers whom she had converted. In 1837 a large fragment was found near the junction of Tiber and canal of an inscription commemorating 'the holy and most blessed martyrs Eutropius, Bonosa, and Zosima'. It records the enhancement of a tomb and the building beside it by Bishop Donatus of a basilica 'for the holy people of God'.[2] Twenty years later a random search for marble revealed at the same site a large fragment of an inscription recording in hexameters the triumphant reception of Zosima in heaven.[3]

The list of Portus martyrs also includes Taurinus and Herculanus. Their memory was still revered on a fifth-century sarcophagus: 'Deo patri . . . sanctis martyribus Taurino et Herculano omni ora gratias agimus.' This inscription may have been found at Ostia rather than Portus, but it seems to refer to the Portus martyrs.[4] That Christianity was stronger by the harbour than in the old town during this period is probable but cannot yet be proved.

By the end of the third century Christianity had permeated all ranks in Roman society. When Constantine accepted the sign of the cross and professed himself Christian he gave a powerful incentive for further conversions. When later he declared Christianity to be the state religion it might have been thought that pagan cults, old and new, would quickly disintegrate. But at Rome the magnificent churches of Constantine and his successors are balanced by *taurobolia*, celebrated by the Roman nobility, and a continuous pagan polemic. Neither toleration nor persecution at first succeeded, and for a brief period in the middle of the fourth century the empire once again fell under a pagan ruler. It was not until the closing years of the century that the final victory of Christianity was won.

Of this struggle between faiths old and new there are tantalizing glimpses at Ostia. Anastasius in his life of Pope Silvester records that Constantine built at Ostia a basilica to the blessed apostles Peter, Paul,

---

[1] p. 526.

[2] 1937 = Thylander, B 234; De Rossi, *Bull. arch. crist.* (1866) 46.

[3] 1938 = Thylander, B 235; De Rossi, art. cit. 47. See also p. 529.

[4] 1942, reported by Marini to have been brought to Rome 'ex agro Ostiensi'. These martyrs were said to have been buried at Portus (p. 528), but the little church of S. Ercolano at Ostia may have commemorated them. The earliest work in this much restored church may date from the fifth century.

and John.[1] No trace of this basilica has been found, and it has been suggested that the basilica was in fact built at Portus, for a church, of unknown date, of the blessed apostles Peter and Paul is there attested.[2] But the text of Anastasius is precise: 'in civitate Hostia, iuxta Portum urbis Romae', an interesting reflection on the comparative importance of the two centres in the late Empire. Moreover, the endowment of Constantine's basilica is specified: it includes two properties 'in the territory of Ostia', one of which, 'Balneolum', is recalled by the modern Bagnolo, a farm on the northern side of the Ostian plain, west from Acilia. The endowment is generous, and the basilica should have been built on a substantial scale. Until the remaining third of the town has been excavated the evidence of the Pope's biographer should be accepted.

In the excavated area, which includes the central and most important part of the town, there are no Christian buildings of impressive stature. On the north of the eastern Decumanus two small basilicas have been associated with Christian worship, but neither was built originally for a Christian community and, if they were converted to Christian use, the conversion was probably late. For one, the so-called Aula del Buon Pastore, the evidence is limited to a figure of the Good Shepherd, holding a lamb on his shoulder, with two sheep at his feet: the figures are sculptured on a cut-down column of Cipollino and probably date from the late third or early fourth century.[3] Though the representation is clearly Christian it is possible that it was not found in its original setting. The so-called Aula di Marte e Venere[4] has no better claim. Its final form, reached after many modifications, with two balancing apses and a raised eastern end, is suited to Christian worship, and in it was found a richly ornamented pagan funerary altar from which the decoration had been erased and the top removed; Moretti suggests that it may have been used as a stoup for holy water.[5] It is, however, an embarrassment that in this building was also found a life-size group of Mars and Venus.[6] Traces can also be seen of a water-pipe running round the northern apse, which would have been out of place in the church.

Two Christian buildings of the late Empire are, however, beyond controversy. At some point the western wing of the Baths of Mithras

[1] *Lib. Pont.* i. 183 f. [2] Paschetto, 86 f.
[3] R. Paribeni, *NS* 1916, 143 and 410 f.
[4] G. Moretti, *NS* 1920, 41–66. [5] Ibid. 48 f., 58.
[6] Ibid. 59; B. M. Felletti Maj, *Museo Nazionale Romano, Ritratti* (1953), n. 236.

was converted to Christian use. A large apse was added at the northern end and a choir or presbytery was marked off by a wooden or metal railing flanked by two marble posts with the Christian monogram.[1] The pavement of this Christian church had already been restored with a miscellaneous collection of pagan epitaphs while it still belonged to the baths: from this restoration and from the style of the apse and the Christian monogram the conversion can be dated with some probability near the middle of the fourth century.[2] It is significant that underneath the wing of these baths taken over by the Christians was a large Mithraeum. The sculptured group of Mithras slaying the bull was found in scattered fragments; it had been deliberately broken.[3]

The only building known to us which was from the outset designed for Christian use has attracted sharp controversy. It has been fully described by Calza and a brief summary will here suffice.[4] The building lies on the west side of the western Decumanus. It is built over an earlier street, whose entry to the Decumanus it closes. This street was flanked by shops on the south side and on the north by public baths. The shop entrances were closed to form the south wall; on the north side three rooms were incorporated from the baths. The shape of the new building, governed by the earlier walls it used, is long and narrow, divided by a row of columns; and it has three rooms, possibly chapels, on its northern side. At the west end the southern half of the building is separated from the main building. Its entrance is marked by two columns supporting an architrave on which is inscribed:

> in ☧ Geon Fison Tigris Eufrata
> ⟨Ti⟩ Cri[st]ianorum sumite fontes.[5] *

There has been much dispute about the nature, date, and identification of this building. On its nature Calza's judgement still seems to be right, that it was a Christian basilica and that the inscription marks the entrance to a baptistery.[6] Calza is less convincing when he identifies the building with Constantine's basilica. The evidence available for assessing the date is not substantial; it consists of the inscription over the 'baptistery', the style of construction, and a name on one of the columns.

---

[1] Calza, 'Nuove testimonianze del cristianesimo a Ostia', *Rend. Pont.* 25–26 (1949–51) 129; Becatti, *Topografia*, 160. [2] See also p. 552.

[3] Becatti, *Mitrei*, 32, 139. [4] Calza, *Rend. Pont.* 16 (1940) 63.

[5] I assume, with Calza, that 'Ti', at the beginning of the second line, is a cutter's error, a mental echo from the first line. The surface for two letter spaces following 'ri' is lost. If it had been damaged before the inscription was cut, the cutter may have written TIGRIANORUM. [6] See *Note H*, p. 474. See also Addenda.

None of these clues is decisive; together they point to a date not earlier than the middle of the fourth century.

On one of the columns used in the basilica is the name Volusianus, which recurs on other similar columns in a dump in the area of the near-by temple of the shipbuilders. Presumably the pagan temple had been abandoned and its area was being used by a dealer in marble. Calza identified this Volusianus with Rufus Volusianus, city prefect in 310; the identification confirmed his view that this was Constantine's basilica. But the style of construction and the plan of the building make this view untenable. Constantine's building was richly endowed; this small basilica is squeezed in between secular buildings. It uses existing walls wherever possible, and its new walls are constructed from miscellaneous material, without pattern or form.

In closing the shop entrances on the southern side no attempt was made to provide a continuously straight line for the new wall; and the backs of these closures and of the baptistery apse were left unfaced. This suggests either that they backed on to ruins or that no attempt was being made to keep up appearances in the area. Such miserable conditions do not fit the early fourth century. Similarly the inscription on the architrave above the entrance to the baptistery is poorly cut and poorly centred; and the stone had already been used for two different purposes, originally in a building carrying an inscription, later as a threshold.[1]

Fuhrmann's identification of Volusianus with C. Caeionius Rufus Volusianus Lampadius, praetorian prefect in 355 and city prefect in 365, carries greater conviction.[2] The association of this Volusianus with Ostia is attested by the record which he has left of a *taurobolium* celebrated in honour of the Great Mother;[3] his name on columns used for a Christian basilica need not necessarily imply that he had himself become a Christian. Fuhrmann sees confirmation in the character of this Volusianus. Ammianus Marcellinus describes the man as a creature of vanity who blazed his name on buildings throughout Rome, obliterating all traces of the original builders.[4] In having his name inscribed on columns Fuhrmann thinks that he was acting in character. But the comparison has little force. When Volusianus advertised himself he did it in monumental inscriptions on public buildings; the rough

---

[1] Pl. xxxvii *b*. This was first observed in 1957. The original inscription has not yet been published.

[2] H. Fuhrmann, *Epigraphica*, 3 (1941) 103, accepted by Bloch, *NS* 1953, 273.

[3] Bloch, 34. [4] Amm. Marc. xxvii. 3. 5–7.

inscriptions on these columns are merely marks of ownership. The identification should therefore be left open. The shoddiness of the building makes a later date, in the late fourth or in the fifth century, more probable, and the inscription cannot be dated within narrow limits. A Roman aristocrat who proclaimed his pagan sympathies by a *taurobolium* is not likely to have allowed his columns to be used by the religion he was fighting. The Volusianus of the basilica's columns was probably a Christian, perhaps the grandson of Lampadius.[1]

A lead pipe stamped with the word 'aeclesiae' was found during the 1938 excavations.[2] The building served by this pipe was either a church or church property. The lettering is very poor, not earlier than the late fourth century and probably from the fifth; but, since it is not known where the pipe was found, it would be dangerous to associate it with the basilica on the western Decumanus.

One other document might possibly have a Christian context. On one of the columns at the west end of the Macellum an inscription was cut, probably in the fourth century: *lege et intellige mutu loqui* (or *mutuloqui*) *ad macellu*. Calza, in noting the text, assumes that the cutter made a slip and intended to write 'multu loqui', warning the passer-by that there was much gossip in the market.[3] This interpretation is most improbable. The inscription is carefully cut in large letters;[4] the cutter evidently attached importance to what he was saying, and must have taken considerable time in the cutting. Could this refer to a Christian miracle, the recovery of speech by a dumb man in the market? The formula 'lege et intellige' is used in Christian writing,[5] but we should expect also the Christian monogram, or some other explicit Christian reference. The cryptic utterance at least deserves reinterpretation.

Of all the Christian associations of Ostia the most moving is the death of Monica, mother of Augustine. She had come in 388 from Milan with her son and was resting a few days at Ostia, away from the crowded area of the harbours, to recover from the long journey before returning to her native Africa. Augustine describes in his *Confessions* how they stood alone together, leaning out of a window which looked onto an inner garden, and speculated on the nature of the life eternal of the saints. But within five days Monica was overtaken by a fever

[1] p. 474 n. 1.
[2] Barbieri, 'Fistole inedite', *NS* 1953, 162 n. 15. The place of finding is not recorded.
[3] *Ostia* (1954) 43.
[4] The inscription is 1·27 m. long; the letters decrease in height from 8 to 5 cm.
[5] Matt. xxiv. 15; Marci xiii. 14; Act. Ap. viii. 30.

and, after a short illness, died in perfect peace. Though she had always set her heart on being buried by her husband in her African home, she asked, as death approached, to be buried where she died: 'nothing is far from God; there is no fear that at the end of time He will not know where to raise me from the dead'.[1] A manuscript copy survived of a verse epitaph that was said to have been added to Monica's tomb by the consular Anicius Bassus.[2] In the summer of 1945 two boys, playing in a small courtyard beside the church of S. Aurea in Ostia, began to dig a hole to plant a post for their game. They disturbed a fragment of marble; it contained part of the original inscription.[3] Perhaps Anicius Bassus may be identified with the only senatorial Christian securely attested in Ostia on a late dedication: 'Anicius Auchenius Bassus v(ir) c(larissimus) et Turrenia Honorata c(larissima) f(emina) eius cum filiis Deo sanctisque devoti.'[4]

But when all the Christian evidence of the fourth century is assembled it is far less impressive than we should at first expect. The Christian buildings in particular are improvised, poorly built, and lacking any signs of wealth. Yet there was wealth in Ostia, as the large number of houses richly decorated with marble and mosaics in the fourth century demonstrates beyond a doubt. It is significant that only one of these houses shows traces of Christian decoration. The so-called House of the Fishes takes its name from a mosaic in which the association of fish and chalice has a very probable Christian reference;[5] in none of the other houses does the surviving decoration have a specifically Christian character. We cannot from this infer that none of the other late houses excavated were occupied by Christians but, had they been predominantly Christian homes, some further traces of Christianity would surely have been apparent. A fine Christian bowl was found in the House of the Porch, on the east side of the Semita dei Cippi.[6] But the bowl dates from the late fourth or early fifth century: when the

[1] Augustine, *Confess.* ix. 10–13.

[2] De Rossi, *Inscriptiones Christianae*, ii. 252; Paschetto, 184.

[3] A. Casamassa, 'Ritrovamento di parte dell' elogio di S. Monica', *Rend. Pont.* 27 (1952–4) 271.   [4] 1875; Paschetto, 181; Symmachus (Seeck) xciii.

[5] Becatti, *Case Ostiensi del tardo impero*, 18, 51; Calza, *Rend. Pont.* 25–26 (1949–51) 126. In addition to the mosaic a fish in relief on marble (now lost) was incorporated in a semi-circular basin in the court, which Becatti (p. 51) identifies as a baptismal basin. Though the fish is commonly used as a Christian symbol, both mosaic and relief could be pagan decoration. H. Schaal (*Ostia, der Welthafen Roms*, 153) rejects any Christian reference, but he has not, I think, fully met Becatti's argument.

[6] M. F. Squarciapino, *Boll. d'Arte*, 37 (1952) 204.

house was built, not earlier than the late third century, it had an underground pagan chapel.

It is at least a tenable hypothesis that a large section of the upper classes remained pagan for much of the fourth century and that Christianity flourished mainly among the poor. Symmachus, one of the leaders of the pagan opposition in the second half of the century, had a villa outside Ostia; we could gladly sacrifice much of his dreary epistolary exercises for a realistic report on the attitude of his Ostian neighbours in the long-drawn-out struggle.

A few indications of this pagan opposition survive. At Rome the cult of Cybele formed a rallying-point for the nobility; at Ostia an inscription on a statuette, now headless, of Dionysius, records a *taurobolium* celebrated by the mid-century Volusianus, who had held the two great prefectures at Rome.[1] A small altar, of the late third or early fourth century, records another *taurobolium* by a Roman senator: 'Marcarianus v(ir) c(larissimus) taur(oboliatus) m(atri) d(eum) d(edit) d(edicavit).'[2]

The finding of the cult statue of Attis in perfect condition far away from its original setting suggests that it was deliberately hidden. Similarly dedications belonging to the *cannophori* were walled in behind the temple of Cybele.[3] Mithraism had been the main challenge to Christianity among the middle and lower classes. The building of a Christian church above a Mithraeum in the Baths of Mithras was probably deliberate policy; the cult group was violently destroyed. It is probably also significant that another Mithraeum seems to have been sacked and destroyed by fire.[4] Christian tradition records a persecution in the brief reign of the pagan Julian; no official persecution is attested in any reliable source, but there may well have been a strong local reaction at Ostia. It was at this time, according to the story of Gallicanus, that Hilarinus, who used his home as a rest-house for Christian travellers from overseas, was put to death.[5]

The final glimpse of paganism at Ostia has a fitting context.[6] Julian's attempt to revive paganism was followed by a strong reaction. The

---

[1] Bloch, 34; *Museo*, 165: 'Volusianus v(ir) c(larissimus) ex praefe(c)tis taurobolium d(ono) d(edit).'

[2] *AE* 1948, 25; cf. *ILS* 4094 (from Rome): 'Virius | Marcarianus v.c. Deam Cybeben p.s.'   [3] Visconti, *Ann. Inst.* 40 (1868) 390.

[4] Becatti, *Mitrei*, 28.   [5] p. 523.

[6] Bloch, 'A New Document of the Last Pagan Revival in the West', *Harvard Theol. Rev.* 38 (1945) 199. For a further reflection of this pagan reaction see p. 588.

emperor Gratian in 382 withdrew a grant of public funds for the old public cults and ordered the removal of the altar of Victory from the Roman senate house. In spite of vigorous protests this policy was maintained, largely under the influence of Ambrose, bishop of Milan, but not for long. By 389 Ambrose had temporarily lost his influence and pagan leaders were again given positions of high responsibility; but in February 391 Ambrose was again in the ascendant. A decree was issued outlawing pagan cults and the great Serapeum of Alexandria was destroyed. This, however, was not the end. Eugenius, declared emperor in August 392, was nominally a Christian but had pagan sympathies. When his attempt to remain on terms with his colleague in the purple, Theodosius, failed, he appealed to the pagan nobility for support and paid subsidies for pagan cults as a personal gift. Theodosius named his son Honorius Augustus and Eugenius was forced to fight. Flavianus, leader of the pagan opposition, was in command of his army, Jupiter and Hercules accompanied him on the battlefield. The decisive battle at the Frigidus, in August 394, was lost.

In this brief interlude of Eugenius' reign, the prefect of the corn supply restored the cella of Hercules at Ostia:[1] it is likely that the gesture had local support. But the defeat at the Frigidus meant the end of open opposition, at Ostia as at Rome. Pagan undercurrents doubtless survived into the fifth century,[2] but the growing insecurity of property further weakened the class which had kept paganism alive. The Ostia which survived the fifth-century invasions was probably a dominantly Christian community.

Christianity met strong pagan opposition at Ostia during the late Empire; the atmosphere at Portus was probably different. The pagans at Ostia, it has been suggested, came primarily from the wealthy residents in the well-appointed private houses of the fourth century; they reflected the temper and behaviour of the senatorial aristocracy at Rome. Portus was more directly influenced by the emperors; and, unlike Ostia, it never became a residential town. Portus was also more open than Ostia to influences from the provinces, and of all the provinces Africa was most closely linked with Rome. African Christianity was particularly vigorous in the fourth century; traders were accom-

---

[1] Bloch, ibid. 201.
[2] At the end of the fifth century the cult of Castor and Pollux was attacked by Gelasius. It survived in Rome, and probably therefore at Ostia. *Gelasii Papae epistulae et decreta: Adversus Andromachum*, PL 59, col. 114: 'Castores vestri certe, a quorum cultu desistere noluistis.'

panied by pilgrims on their way to Rome. Already in the third century Cyprian writes of the many confessors of the faith who came from Africa, and of their reception at Portus.[1] It was for such pilgrims that the Roman senator, Pammachius, friend of Jerome and Augustine, at the end of the fourth century, built a large rest-house, *xenodochium*, at Portus.[2] The rooms were built round an open court surrounded by a colonnade.

Attached to the *xenodochium* was a basilica with three naves. Finely worked glass bowls and plates decorated with Christian scenes were found in the building;[3] they suggest wealthy patronage.

Portus was probably won for Christianity more quickly and completely than Ostia.

[1] Cyprian, *Ep.* 21. 4.

[2] Jerome, *Epp.* 66. 11; 77. 10: 'xenodochium in portu Romano situm totus pariter mundus audivit. sub una aestate didicit Britannia, quod Aegyptus et Parthus agnoverant vere.' For the archaeological evidence, De Rossi, *Bull. arch. crist.* (1866) 50; Lugli, *Porto*, 44. But see Addenda.

[3] De Rossi, *Bull. arch. crist.* (1868) 37; M. F. Squarciapino, 'Vetri incisi Portuensi del Museo Sacro del Vaticano', *Rend. Pont.* 27 (1952–4) 255.

16

RECREATION

BATHS

'BALNEA, vina, Venus, mecum senuere per annos. . . .' The order of pleasures in this Ostian epitaph is not significant.[1] The hexameter had to begin with dactyl or spondee and *balnea* fitted the purpose admirably. The emphasis, however, is not ridiculous: in the Empire a visit to the baths was the favourite recreation of almost all classes of society.

The building of baths for public use was introduced into Italy in the second century B.C. from the Greek world. At first they were small in scale, modest in decoration, and primarily utilitarian in purpose. By Cicero's day they were becoming more popular and more elaborate, but it was the imperial purse that developed their full magnificence. Agrippa set the precedent in the great new baths he built in the Campus Martius: Nero, Titus, Trajan, and a long succession of emperors down to Constantine followed him. They competed in the size and costliness of their buildings. Seneca had deplored the growing extravagance; Martial rejoiced in it. The public were with Martial.

Baths were popular because they met a variety of needs. Very little washing was done in the home; it was in the public baths that the Romans kept clean. Proper use of the baths was also considered to be good for health, as statues of Aesculapius and Hygia from two sets of Ostian baths suggest.[2] But it was the social pleasures rather than the utilitarian services of the baths that accounted for their impressive development in the Empire. At the baths the gossip and scandal of the town could be exchanged. They combined the amenities of swimming bath, gymnasium, and community centre; and there was no need to hurry away, for food and drink could be bought on the premises. Since we are apt to associate sculpture, mosaics, and marble-lined walls such as are found in the ruins of Ostian baths with solemn or at least expensive occasions, we need to be reminded by the writers of the realities

[1] 914. The beginning of the verse had a wide currency, cf. *ILS* 8157, *CIL* iii. 12274.
[2] Porta Marina Baths (p. 104). ? Forum Baths, Paschetto, 152.

of the crowded scene. Seneca, who once took lodgings over a set of public baths, describes his experience vividly:

Picture to yourself the assortment of sounds, which are strange enough to make me hate my very powers of hearing! When your strenuous gentleman, for example, is exercising himself by flourishing leaden weights; when he is working hard, or else pretends to be working hard, I can hear him grunt; and whenever he releases his imprisoned breath, I can hear him panting in wheezy and high-pitched tones. Or perhaps I notice some lazy fellow, content with a cheap rub-down, and hear the crack of the pummeling hand on his shoulder, varying in sound according as the hand is laid on flat or hollow. Then, perhaps, a professional comes along, shouting out the score; that is the finishing touch. Add to this the arresting of an occasional roysterer or pickpocket, the racket of the man who always likes to hear his own voice in the bath, or the enthusiast who plunges into the swimming-tank with unconscionable noise and splashing. Besides all those whose voices, if nothing else, are good, imagine the hair-plucker with his penetrating shrill voice,—for purposes of advertisement—continually giving it vent and never holding his tongue except when he is plucking the armpits and making his victim yell instead. Then the cake-seller with his varied cries, the sausageman, the confectioner, and all the vendors of food hawking their wares, each with his own distinctive intonation.[1]

The baths were not designed for swimming. The cold baths were no larger than small plunge baths and were substantially less than 2 metres in depth; there was no deep end. The sea, however, was near at hand and in the summer months attracted bathers. Minucius Felix, in his description of the sea-shore, speaks of a breakwater to protect them from the waves.[2]

The normal time for the bath was the afternoon. By then most men had probably completed their work, for the Roman day began much earlier than ours. It is certain at any rate that public baths were not the prerogative of a leisured class. The large number of establishments at Rome and Ostia suggest that they catered for a widespread popular demand; Roman writers confirm it. A charge was made for entry, but the normal fee at Rome seems to have been a quarter of an *as* only;[3] very few can have been excluded by poverty. The provision of free bathing in perpetuity or for a limited period, which was a common form of endowment in the Roman world, is not specifically attested yet

[1] Seneca, *Ep.* 56. 1–2 (trans. R. M. Gummere: Loeb, 1925).
[2] Minucius Felix, *Octavius*, 4.
[3] Horace, *Sat.* i. 3. 137; Seneca, *Ep.* 86. 9; Martial iii. 30. 4; Juv. vi. 447.

in Ostia, but it would be surprising if Ostia's poor did not occasionally benefit from such windfalls.

When public baths were first introduced, separate baths were built for men and women. So at Pompeii the two earliest, the Stabian and the Forum Baths, have each two series of rooms and separate entrances for the two sexes. In the central baths, however, at Pompeii, which were still unfinished when the town was destroyed, no such distinction is made; and in Martial's day at Rome, though certain baths were particularly frequented by women, mixed bathing seems to have been the general rule.[1] At Ostia there is no evidence in any of the ruins of special provision for women. The bathing together of the sexes, however, was not always tolerated. Hadrian forbade it, and Marcus Aurelius repeated the ban.[2] During periods when the ban was strictly enforced it is probable that special hours were reserved for women.[3]

The earliest Ostian bathing establishment attested by an inscription dates from the late Republic or early Principate,[4] but no physical remains earlier than the Julio-Claudian period have yet been found. Such baths as existed earlier were probably small and their water had to be drawn from wells. It was only when an aqueduct was built, in or shortly before the principate of Gaius, that the full amenities could be developed. Probably the first establishment to exploit the new supply of water was the set of baths that can be partly seen under the Via dei Vigiles. The area covered by these baths is not yet known, but a mosaic pavement, illustrating the trade of empire, and a large marble basin show that they were handsomely appointed.[5] Two other establishments probably date from the Julio-Claudian period, but in neither can we see the full plan. One, in the south-east district, has only been partly uncovered;[6] the other, the Baths of Invidiosus, on the Semita dei Cippi, was largely rebuilt in the first half of the second century.

The number and scale of the baths of the early Empire will only be known when excavation has been in due time extended to the lower levels throughout the town. What we see now are the baths that were built in the great rebuilding of Ostia from the late Flavian period onwards or which survived through that rebuilding. The most extensive baths date, as we should expect, from the great period of prosperity in the second century; but in contrast to commercial and industrial

[1] Martial iii. 51. 72. 87; vii. 35; xi. 75.   [2] SHA, *Had.* 18. 10; *Marc. Aur.* 23. 8.
[3] Carcopino, *La Vie quotidienne*, 298 f.   [4] S 4711.
[5] NS 1912, 204–8.   [6] Reg. v. 10. 3; Becatti, *Topografia*, 117.

premises, the number of baths continued to swell into the late Empire.

The fourth-century regional catalogues of Rome draw a distinction between the great imperial *thermae* which are individually named, and the considerably larger number of *balnea* for which only a total number is given. Martial reflects the same distinction:

Titine thermis an lavatur Agrippae
an inpudici balneo Tigillini.[1]

This distinction between *thermae* and *balnea* is not consistently maintained by writers or in inscriptions, but it serves a convenient purpose and will be used here. For the same contrast is seen at Ostia as at Rome. Three public baths eclipse all others in scale. All three probably derive from imperial subsidy, and all three can be associated with monumental inscriptions. In addition, there are at least eleven other establishments of varying size, plan, and elegance. They can be approximately dated by the style of their construction, but we do not know to whose initiative they are due; there are no inscriptions to shed light on their history.

The earliest of the three *thermae* are probably the baths south-east of the Porta Marina, which are still largely buried. The Scottish painter, Gavin Hamilton, in a letter of 1775 already quoted writes:

I got as near the sea as possible, judging it the most probable place to find objects of taste. We opened ground on a spot now called Porta Marina. From the figure of the ruins they proved to be the remains of publick Thermae Maritimae, and from the inscriptions which were found of an unusual size, it seems those Baths had been restored by different emperors down to Constantine. I gave a very elegant one of the time of Trajan to Carlo Albagine. . . .[2]

An inscription which can now be seen in the Capitoline Museum records the restoration and enlargement of *thermae maritimae* in the late fourth century:[3] it may be the inscription which gave to Hamilton his name for the building. The name might imply no more than that they were built by the sea-shore; it is more probable that they were called 'maritimae' because their water was drawn from the sea.[4]

These inscriptions and Hamilton's excavations have been commonly associated with a set of baths partly excavated in the middle of the nineteenth century by Visconti, which have been duly marked on plans as *thermae maritimae*. This identification should be abandoned. Visconti's

[1] Martial iii. 20. 15. [2] *JHS* 21 (1901) 314.
[3] 137: 'thermas maritimas intresecus refectione cellarum, foris soli adiectione'.
[4] Cf. *ILS* 5724 (Pompeii): 'thermas M. Crassi Frugi aqua marina, et baln. aqua dulci'.

baths are built on the line of the Sullan walls, some 100 metres from the
sea. The rooms excavated, which form the main functional part at least
of the establishment, are Severan in date, and there is no trace of large-
scale fourth-century reconstruction. Moreover, Hamilton's indications
are specific. While most of Ostia was buried, two tall brick piers stood
out in isolation on the south side of the town; a very little distance
beyond them the swollen contour of ruins ended, where the ancient
shore-line ran. Porta Marina was the name naturally given to these
isolated piers,[1] and it was here that Hamilton tried his luck. He found,
as we can now see, that the brick piers were in fact part of a large
apsidal room belonging to a set of baths. Of the 'Trajanic inscription'
which Hamilton gave to a Roman dealer no trace has survived, but
there is no good reason to doubt its existence. It is possible that Hamilton was misled by the inclusion of Trajan's name in the titulature of a
later emperor, but the natural explanation is that Trajan's name was in
the nominative. It is possible that these baths were included in the building programme at Ostia that followed the completion of Trajan's
harbour towards the end of the reign, and that they were financed by
the emperor.

It was in these baths that the head of Marciana, sister of Trajan, which
is now in the Ostia Museum, was found;[2] and the head of another
imperial princess may also have been found here. This general area was
included in the excavations of Campana (1831–5). In the ruins of a
large room in a set of baths he found a head which is now in Copenhagen.[3] It was first identified as Plotina, wife of Trajan, later as his
sister Marciana, but Signora Calza may be right in preferring the
younger Sabina, wife of Hadrian.[4] If these baths were begun at the end
of Trajan's reign, their construction is likely to have extended into the

[1] A. Nibby, *Viaggio antiquario ad Ostia* (1829) 76.
[2] Wegner, *Arch. Anz.* 53 (1938) 290; *Museo*, 20.
[3] *Bull. Inst.* 6 (1834) 133. The excavation took place 'near the sea coast, where there
were traces of magnificent ancient buildings'. No ruins were more conspicuous and
tempting than the Baths of Porta Marina. It is not strange, after Hamilton's earlier
exploration, that, apart from this imperial head, only fragments of statues were found.
[4] Plotina in the report of the discovery. F. Poulsen, *Catalogue of ancient sculptures in
the Ny Carlsberg Glyptotek* (1951), n. 675 (Billedtavler (1907) lv), identifies with Marciana,
but does not exclude her daughter Matidia. The identification will remain doubtful, but
the hair style shows the portrait to be not later than the first half of Hadrian's reign. For
the imperial ladies of this period, not easily distinguished, M. Wegner, 'Datierung
römischer Haartrachten', *Arch. Anz.* 53 (1938) 276. A cast of the head is now in the
Horrea Epagathiana at Ostia.

reign of Hadrian. For such a building history the statues of Marciana and the young Sabina would be very appropriate.

No brickstamps have yet been found in the construction; two dating from Trajan and one from Hadrian, found among the ruins, are an inadequate basis for argument. Becatti dates the construction to Antoninus Pius,[1] but the brickwork of the earliest walls seems to be earlier, and could be Trajanic. A detailed study, following the complete excavation of the building, should resolve the problem. The original plan of the building cannot be recovered from what is now visible. What is clear is that the area covered was large, that the walls were freely lined with marble, and that some of the sculpture in the building was of distinguished quality. The plan was, so far as can be seen, rectangular throughout. The apsidal Frigidarium to the north and two apsidal Tepidaria in the south wing are later refinements.

These Maritime Baths were followed within a generation by the Baths of Neptune on the north side of the eastern Decumanus. These baths were an integral part of a comprehensive plan under which a large district was rebuilt. The brickwork of the district is homogeneous, and brickstamps indicate the last years of Hadrian's principate for the execution of the plan.[2] The Barracks of the Vigiles, separated from the baths by a street, were in use before Hadrian died. The completion of the baths was delayed, if, as seems virtually certain, an inscription whose precise origin is unrecorded is to be associated with these baths. This records that Antoninus Pius, in the first year of his reign, completed what his predecessor had begun. Hadrian had promised two million sesterces for the building of the baths; Antoninus Pius added the extra money that was required and the marble to complete the decoration.[3] It is probably these baths also that are referred to in the career of a second-century P. Lucilius Gamala: 'idem thermas quas divus Pius aedificaverat vi ignis consumptas refecit porticum reparavit.'[4] In the Baths of Neptune brickstamps dated to the reign of Marcus Aurelius have been found in two of the heated rooms,[5] and evidence remains of the restoration of the portico on the Decumanus. Most of the brick piers of this portico date from a later reconstruction in the fourth century, but two of the series are much earlier than the rest and probably represent Gamala's restoration. In the record of Gamala's career the

---

[1] Becatti, *Topografia*, 146. Brickstamps, Bloch, *Topografia*, 227 (iv. 10. 1).

[2] Bloch, *Bolli laterizi*, 222.

[3] 98.   [4] 2[18-26].   [5] Bloch, *Bolli laterizi*, 243.

credit due to Hadrian, which was confirmed by the finding in the baths of a portrait statue of his wife Sabina in the dress of Ceres, is obscured, and the building is ascribed to Pius alone. Bloch is therefore probably right in identifying the Baths of Neptune with the *lavacrum* said by his biographer to have been presented to Ostia by Antoninus Pius.[1]

The Baths of Neptune are built to a square plan, each side measuring approximately 67 metres. The baths proper develop from south to north on the east side of the building. An entrance from the Via dei Vigiles leads into a large hall, off which open several rooms which may have been used as dressing-rooms. Adjacent to the north is the Frigidarium, with two baths at its eastern and western ends. The larger of these baths, at the eastern end, received decorative emphasis from two grey granite columns, with Corinthian capitals in Greek marble, which, with two pilasters attached to the side walls, once carried architrave and cornice. Both baths have niches in their walls for statues. From the Frigidarium the bather proceeded through rooms heated with hot air by hypocausts under the floor and hollow pipes lining the walls to the Caldarium, which, in its present form due to a later restoration, has three small baths for hot water. A service passage ran along the west side of this wing, from which the bath attendants fed the furnaces under the floors through stoke-holes. The water for the baths was stored in the north-east corner in upper cisterns to increase the pressure.[2]

In the centre of the building is an open Palaestra in which exercise could be taken before or after the bath, with a foot-bath in the south-east corner. Blocks of travertine bedded in the ground, with holes in them, were probably used to fix apparatus. The Palaestra is surrounded on three sides by a colonnade of Porta Santa columns. On the south and east sides is a series of rooms which, with one exception, have preserved no distinguishing character. The exception is the central room on the west side; this is larger than the rest, has a marble pavement, and a statue base against its back wall: it was probably here that the portrait statue of Sabina with the attributes of Ceres, found in this room, originally stood.[3] These rooms were presumably used for less energetic recreation; the latrine was tucked away in the north-west corner. The building was served by an entrance on each of its four sides.

---

[1] SHA, *Ant. Pius*, 8. 3; identification, Bloch, *Bolli laterizi*, 245, 267–9.
[2] Description, with reference to excavation reports, Paschetto, 265.
[3] Paschetto, 274, fig. 59; *Museo*, 25.

The entrance to the baths proper was from the Via dei Vigiles on the east; the other three entrances led into the Palaestra.

These baths, though dwarfed by the imperial establishments at Rome, were spacious for Ostia, and they were decorated handsomely. The sculpture found in the ruins included, besides the statue of Sabina, a charming head of a girl, a male bearded head of competent workmanship, and the figure of a youth with fruit and cornucopia.[1] The mosaics from the rooms in the south-east corner, and particularly the vigorous composition which centres on Neptune driving through his watery kingdom, are the product of a highly skilled and inventive craftsman or workshop.[2] Marble was freely used, not merely in columns, but on floors and to line baths. Of the original paintings which covered the walls of the main hall and other rooms virtually nothing survives. The fragments still visible in the latrine come from a redecoration in the late second or third century: it is, however, interesting to note that this severely utilitarian room was painted with no less care than the living-rooms of the period.

The generous outlay on the baths was accompanied by sound economies. The building has no façade on the Decumanus; it is there fronted by a line of shops opening on a portico supported by brick piers. Probably more money was spent in the shops of the eastern Decumanus than in any other quarter of the town: shops on this frontage could therefore command high rents. The urgent need for accommodation, which is reflected in the contemporary building of so many insulae, was also capitalized. On south and west sides solid stairways led from the streets to upper stories. Rent from these apartments and from the shops might help to bridge the gap between bath receipts and the cost of maintenance.

The third of the series of imperial *thermae* was built immediately to the east of the south end of the Forum. The general character of the brickwork seems to be Antonine; brickstamps suggest a date near the death of Antoninus Pius.[3] These Forum Baths cover a larger area than the Baths of Neptune; their scale and decoration were more imposing; their plan is more adventurous. But their setting and their disposition have been radically changed since their construction. In the late Empire, and as we see the ruins now, a large open square, with colonnades along east and west sides and a statue in the centre, covered the area between the Decumanus and the eastern half of the north wall of the baths. On

---

[1] Paschetto, 268, 272, 275.   [2] p. 449.   [3] Bloch, *Bolli laterizi*, 268–76.

this side the baths had two entrances, one of them, towards the west, monumental. These features are the result of fourth-century changes. When the baths were built, what became later an open square was still a block of buildings, separated from the baths by a street.[1]

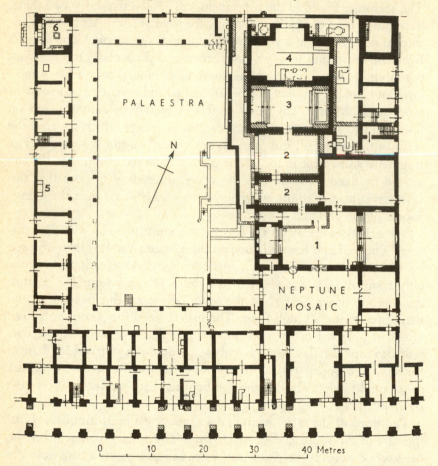

FIG. 28. Baths of Neptune. 1. Frigidarium. 2. Tepidaria. 3. Caldarium. 4. Original Caldarium, later abandoned. 5. Statue of Hadrian's wife Sabina as Ceres. 6. Latrine.

The baths were originally entered by a main entrance from the west, or a subsidiary entrance from the south-east. The northern block was orthodox in plan, rectangular and symmetrical. At either end was a large entrance hall, through which one passed to a further hall, off which opened what may have been dressing-rooms. In the centre of the

[1] Becatti, *Topografia*, 159.

block was the Frigidarium with two baths, on the north and south sides, flanked by small rooms that had sufficient heating in their floor

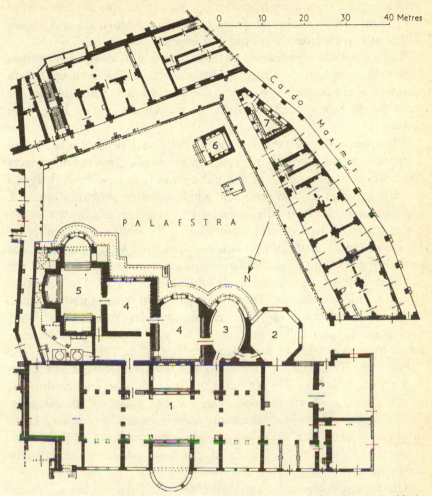

FIG. 29. Forum Baths. 1. Frigidarium. 2. ? Heliocaminos. 3. ? Sudatorium. 4. Tepidaria. 5. Caldarium. 6. Unidentified temple in Palaestra. 7. Latrine.

and walls to take the chill from the air. The northern bath in its present form has an apse at its northern end, but this is a fourth-century refinement.

In sharp contrast to the rectangular symmetry of the northern block is the series of heated rooms on the south side of the building, stepping out from west to east. These rooms present an interesting variety in

E e

design and an ingenious adaptation to function. They were substantially restored more than once, and important changes were made in the fourth century, but, apart from the insertion of an apse in the southern wall of the eastern room, the shape of the rooms remained unchanged. The southern elevation was bold and original.

The most distinctive feature of these rooms as now seen is the series of very large windows in their southern walls, dating from the fourth century. Their purpose is to make the maximum use of sunlight, for these rooms face south,[1] and some of the windows may have been unglazed.

The room at the west end is a regular octagon. The floor is heated by a hypocaust, but there are no pipes in the walls. This room receives more sun than any other in the building and may have been designed for sun-bathing; its wide and tall windows were probably open. A heated passage leads to an elliptical room which is the hottest in the baths, heated by hypocaust, by pipes lining the walls, and probably by pipes in its vault; artificial heat was supplemented by the sun. This was probably a sweating room, Sudatorium, and a stone seat ran round the wall for those who preferred to sit while they sweated. The next two rooms are more orthodox. Their floors and walls were heated, but they received much less sun and their temperature was considerably lower; they were Tepidaria. The western of the two has a slightly curving south wall; its neighbour is rectangular.[2]

From the Tepidaria one passes to the last room of the series, the Caldarium. This has three hot baths on its north, east, and south sides, whose water was heated in boilers in a service room on the east side. Floors, walls, and probably the vault were heated. The southern bath, originally rectangular, was changed to an apsidal form in the fourth century and enjoyed the benefit of the large windows immediately above it.

The Forum Baths had a roughly triangular Palaestra behind them,

---

[1] Cf. Vitruvius v. 10. 1: 'ipsa autem caldaria tepidariaque lumen habeant ab occidente hiberno; si autem natura loci impedierit, utique a meridie, quod maxime tempus lavandi a meridiano ad vesperum est constitutum.'

[2] E. D. Thatcher, in a valuable detailed analysis of the heating system of these baths (*MAAR* 24 (1956) 170–261), has concluded that all the southern windows were originally unglazed, though glass was later added in one of the rooms. Vivid memories of long spells of cold winds and low temperatures in Ostian winters undermine my confidence, but the argument needs more expert judgement than mine. The absence of archaeological evidence for the fixing of glass might be accounted for by the use of timber frames. I would tentatively suggest that only the eastern, octagonal, room had open windows.

surrounded by a colonnade in which the architect seems to have deliberately selected a contrasting variety of marbles and granites for his columns. Off the colonnade opened shops and other premises, perhaps including a guild headquarters in the centre of the south side. At the west end was a small temple.

These baths had already been explored at the beginning of the nineteenth century and probably on other occasions also; for their ruins stood high, and were a natural temptation to the treasure hunter. Very little therefore was found of their sculptures, paintings, and mosaics when they were excavated. But the tall Cipollino columns of the great hall and architectural fragments of Proconnesian marble show that the decoration matched the boldness of the building. Strong, emphasizing the mixture of styles and the unorthodox carving of the motifs, suggests that this is the work of foreign craftsmen, whose influence he also finds in work of the period at Rome.[1]

The Forum Baths were almost certainly not built with Ostian money. Like the Maritime Baths and the Baths of Neptune they are imperial *thermae*, but probably not the gift of an emperor. Among the fragments of inscriptions recording a late fourth-century restoration undertaken by Ragonius Vincentius Celsus, *praefectus annonae*, the name of the baths may be recorded: '—mis Gavi Ma—'. Bloch suggests the attractive restoration 'thermis Gavi Maximi', implying that these baths were built for Ostia by M. Gavius Maximus, who served Antoninus Pius as his praetorian prefect for twenty years.[2] This hypothesis may receive confirmation from an unexpected source. A fragment of entablature formerly in the Vatican, now removed to the Lateran, has the same decoration as surviving fragments in the Forum Baths at Ostia. The block is inscribed and the inscription begins 'Maximus has olim therm[as]', referring to the original builder.[3] An honorary inscription to M. Gavius Maximus is also preserved at Ostia; it was probably found in or near the baths.[4] *

Whether Commodus, Septimius Severus, or any other of the later emperors added to the imperial *thermae* of Ostia we cannot know for certain until the whole area of the town has been uncovered. No traces have been recorded from earlier exploration. No conspicuous ruins

[1] D. Strong, 'Late Hadrianic Ornament', *BSR* 21 (1953) 138.
[2] Bloch, 'The name of the Baths near the Forum of Ostia', in *Studies presented to D. M. Robinson*, ii (1953) 412.
[3] See *Note J*, p. 475; Pl. xxxviii *b*.   [4] Bloch, art. cit. 416.

remain which seem likely to be *thermae*; but the long history of surprises in Ostia's excavation is a warning against premature assumptions. It is certain at any rate that the provision of smaller baths did not end with the decline in public prosperity.

The main distinction between *thermae* and *balnea* is one of scale. The architect of the *thermae* has a comparatively free hand. His plan is not restricted by competing demands; he has a generous purse behind him and can afford magnificence. The smaller establishments, *balnea*, are probably the result of private enterprise and represent investments. Such is the natural inference concerning practice at Rome from the poems of Martial. The *balnea* he mentions carry the names of private individuals—*balnea* Phoebi, Stephani, Tigillini. These are presumably the men who built the baths or who owned them. For Ostia there is no explicit evidence, but two possible hints. In the Baths of Mithras (so called from a striking sculpture of Mithras) two portrait heads within *clipea* were found. Their style shows them to be at least roughly contemporary with the baths, which are Hadrianic.[1] They may record the original builders. Under the Pharos Baths water-pipes were found stamped with distinguished names, a second-century consul and Cornificia, daughter of the emperor Marcus Aurelius.[2] The natural inference is that these baths were private property, and did not belong to the local authority.

While *thermae* stand free and dominate the block in which they stand, the plan of *balnea* is largely dictated by the size and shape of the building plot available. They are often built in the middle of blocks and usually enclosed on at least two sides by other buildings. The Baths of Buticosus have shops and commercial premises to north and south. The block in which they stand is comparatively narrow; their main development follows the block plan and runs from south to north, though their entrances are from east and west. The long narrow shape of the Baths of the Six Columns is dictated by the earlier plan of the houses on this stretch of the Decumanus, which had a narrow frontage on the street but developed through atrium and peristyle to a considerable depth. Such restrictions were common also at Rome; Martial speaks of the Baths of Stephanus 'joined to' his living quarters.[3] A case is also quoted

[1] Becatti, *Le Arti* (1941) 172; *Museo*, 56, 57.
[2] Barbieri, 'Fistole inedite', *NS* 1953, 154 n. 5: Cornificiae (sister of M. Aurelius); 167 n. 28: Scipionis Orfiti, probably a late-second-century consul. Presumably the property had changed hands.
[3] Martial xi. 52. 4: 'scis quam sint Stephani balnea iuncta mihi.'

in the Digest which is typical of Ostian conditions: 'a certain Hiberus, who owns the insula behind my *horrea*, built a bathing establishment using a party-wall: he may not put hot pipes against the party-wall'. This was an essential regulation, 'for through the pipes the wall is scorched by the heat'.[1] Traces of burning and reconstruction can be seen in almost all the heated rooms of Ostian baths: perhaps the use of pine with its high resin content increased the risk.

It may at first seem odd that if the entry fee was low the building of baths should have been considered a satisfactory investment. The answer probably lies in the additional profit that the baths brought from miscellaneous sales, including food and drink. Nor was space used uneconomically: the street frontages were normally reserved for shop rents, and provision was made for apartments in upper stories. Perhaps some baths were able to charge a considerably higher fee which guaranteed greater exclusiveness. The baths excavated by Visconti on the line of the Sullan walls west of Porta Marina may have been of this type.[2] The figured mosaics and the lavish use of marble would have been attractive to a select clientele such as might be expected from this district, which was primarily residential. So in Rome it is difficult to believe that the same fee was charged for the Baths of Claudius Etruscus with their rich display of Phrygian and Numidian marble[3] as for the dark gloom of Gryllus' establishment.[4]

During the period of prosperity the building of *balnea* developed briskly. The baths by the Christian Basilica are probably late Flavian, possibly Trajanic:[5] the Baths of Buticosus and the Baths of the Six Columns are Trajanic.[6] Three sets at least were added under Hadrian, the Baths of Mithras,[7] of Trinacria,[8] and a third set on the south side of the eastern Decumanus near the Forum, which were destroyed in the fourth century to make way for an open square.[9] The Baths of Invidiosus, which incorporate a Julio-Claudian core, may be a little later.[10]

The Baths of the Seven Sages, built between two large apartment blocks, the Insula of Serapis and the Insula of the Charioteers, were designed primarily for the tenants of these apartments, but they may

---

[1] *Dig.* viii. 2. 13. [2] Paschetto, 304; cf. *ILS* 5723.

[3] Martial vi. 42; Statius, *Silvae*, i. 5.

[4] Martial i. 59. 3: 'tenebrosaque balnea Grylli'.

[5] Becatti, *Topografia*, 127, dates to Trajan.

[6] Bloch, *Topografia*, 218 (i. 14. 8); 226 (iv. 5. 11).

[7] Ibid. 219 (i. 17. 2). [8] Ibid. 225 (iii. 16. 7).

[9] Becatti, *Topografia*, 159. [10] Ibid. 144.

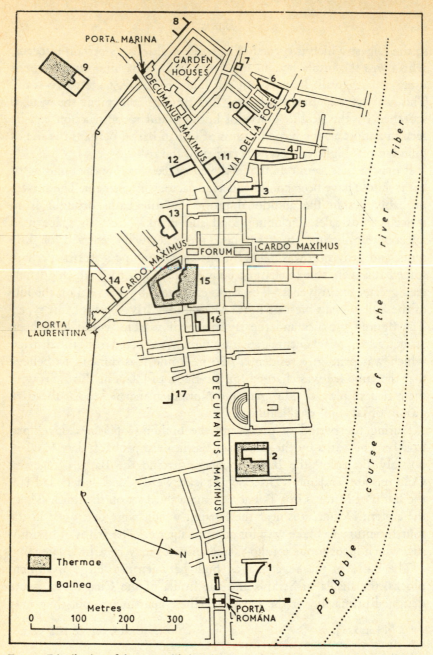

FIG. 30. Distribution of *thermae* and *balnea* (p. 407) in the late Empire. 1. Drivers (Third century). 2. Neptune (Hadrian). 3. Buticosus (Trajan). 4. Mithras (Hadrian). 5. Fourth century. 6. Trinacria (Hadrian). 7. Fourth century. 8. Sullan walls, partly excavated (Severan). 9. Porta Marina (? Trajan–Hadrian). 10. Seven Sages (Hadrian). 11. Basilica (Domitian or Trajan). 12. Six Columns (Trajan). 13. Fourth century. 14. Pharos (? Trajan). 15. Forum (Antoninus Pius). 16. Invidiosus (Julio–Claudian, largely rebuilt). 17. Julio–Claudian, partly excavated. ★

also have been open to the public.[1] In their present form they are Severan,[2] but their original plan goes back to Hadrian. The handsome suite of baths in the 'Imperial Palace' was more probably private.[3]

The original walls of the Pharos baths near the Porta Laurentina are Trajanic or Hadrianic, but the building may only have been converted to baths later, towards the end of the second century.[4] Similarly several walls in the Baths of the Drivers on the north side of the Decumanus near the Porta Romana date back to the late Republic or very early Empire. They once belonged to industrial premises; the baths probably represent a third-century adaptation.[5] A further set of baths was added in the early third century west of the Porta Marina on the line of the Sullan walls, richly furnished with marble and mosaics.[6] *

The plan of these small sets of baths is dictated by their site and, as we should expect, there is considerable variety in their disposition. None of them had exercise grounds, as the large *thermae* had, but all provided the essential sequence of cold bath, heated rooms, and hot bath. By the Severan period they were distributed through all the districts of the town.

The imperial *thermae* may have been neglected in the difficult period that followed the end of the Severan dynasty. Certainly large-scale restorations were carried out in the early fourth century, and building activity is attested still in the baths when there is little sign of it else-where, down to the end of the century. These restorations are often shoddy work. Old material is reused, mosaics are patched with marble without any respect for the design, floors are paved with funerary

[1] I assume, in the absence of inscriptions, that the Insulae of Serapis and of the Charioteers were private and not public buildings. Two Greek graffiti (unpublished) and the nearness of the Serapeum suggest that this may have been something of an oriental quarter. The baths were richly furnished with sculpture as well as paintings and mosaics. The ruins do not suggest that these blocks catered for the wealthy, for the individual apartments are not particularly large or handsome. If the use of the baths was confined to the tenants they would surely have been uneconomic. Some at least of the rooms on the ground floor were used as shops, entered from the inner courts and not from the street; this makes it reasonable to believe that the baths also were open to the public.

[2] Bloch, *Bolli laterizi*, 203.   [3] Paschetto, 414.

[4] Mosaics, paintings, and stucco decoration are not earlier than late-second century, but there has been much reconstruction. A more detailed study, with some digging, is needed to establish the original function.

[5] The decoration of the baths, including mosaics, and the hypocausts (Bloch, *Bolli laterizi*, 279) date from the third century. Wilson, in a detailed study of the block (*BSR* 13 (1935) 82–84) argues that the baths in their original form were Flavian. The evidence is, I think, insufficient. *   [6] Paschetto, 304; Bloch, *Bolli laterizi*, 278.

inscriptions. But it is clear that the population clung tenaciously to their baths. We even find two new sets added; one, west of the Trajanic *horrea* on the north side of the Via della Foce, is very modest in scale.[1] The other, only partially excavated, south of the Round Temple, is as large as the average *balnea* of the second century and exploits the late Empire fashion of the curving line in its rooms more fully than any other Ostian building known to us.[2] * Both are almost certainly from the fourth century.

It was not only in the interests of the poor that bathing facilities were maintained with such determination. In spite of the wealth of their decoration and the heating of many of their living-rooms, the House of the Dioscuri is the only late house known in Ostia which has its private suite of bath rooms. When there was such ample provision of public facilities for a declining population there was no need for the rich to provide their own.

THEATRE

At Rome it was a recognized part of the duties of the lesser magistrates to provide shows and games for the people, and the same policy was followed in colonies and municipalities. The expense was borne partly by the town treasury, but the magistrate was compelled by statute to contribute and expected by custom to contribute generously. The charter of the Caesarian colony at Urso in Spain prescribes a maximum that the duovir may draw from the treasury for the public shows that he presents in his year of office and a minimum which he must add from his own pocket.[3] The Antonine Gamala's generosity in his interpretation of such a clause is commemorated among his many services to the town: 'hic ludos omnes quos fecit amplificavit impensa sua.'[4] Social ambition or public spirit might also encourage wealthy individuals to provide entertainment in the theatre. Fabius Hermogenes, once a municipal clerk, boasts that he was the first who in his priesthood (he was *flamen divi Hadriani*) gave at his own expense *ludi scaenici*;[5] and a wealthy woman in the second century left money to provide annual shows in memory of one of her family.[6] The common phrase *ludi scaenici* gives little idea of the nature of these theatre shows, but con-

---

[1] Becatti, *Topografia,* 155. [2] Loc. cit.
[3] *Lex Ursonensis,* 70.
[4] 2[20]. [5] 353, 14.
[6] S 4450. The nature of these *ludi* is not specified.

temporary literature shows that stage fashions had changed considerably since the days of the Republic.

In Cicero's lifetime there was still a popular demand for tragedy and comedy, but the Roman theatre was already living on the past. There were no contemporary dramatists of note; most of the productions were adaptations of Greek plays or revivals of Roman favourites. The audiences, according to Cicero, were enthusiastic; every allusion that could be given a topical twist was seized on. One suspects that they enjoyed their political demonstrations more than the play; that may be one of the reasons why no important new writers of tragedy or comedy appeared in the Augustan revival.

The wall paintings and the scribblings on Pompeian walls show that through the first century of the Empire the standard Greek and Roman classics were still well known and probably performed,[1] but we hear little of them in literature after the first century; in popularity they were eclipsed by other forms. The refinements of comedy could not compete with the vulgarities of Atellan farces.[2] These plays, which had grown in popularity in the late Republic, maintained a strong hold into the late Empire. A loosely constructed plot was built round a series of stock figures—Maccus, the fool; Pappus, the dotard; Manducus, the glutton; Dossenus, the cunning hunchback; Bucco, the braggart. Such titles as *Maccus miles*, *Bucco adoptatus* suggest the pattern. For their appeal they relied not so much on the intricacy of the plot as on their broad humour and grotesque situations. Mistaken identities, disguises, riddles, were, as in the modern pantomime, an essential part of their stock-in-trade.[3]

Towards the close of the Republic the Atellan farce was rivalled by the mime, which catered for broadly the same tastes. The mime had been introduced to Rome from the Greek cities of the south and had become considerably vulgarized in its new home. It had several advantages over its rival: the number of its characters was not limited by tradition, it could use actresses for female roles, and the actors, dispensing with masks, had freer play for facial expression. The mimes of Laberius and Publilius Syrus, Cicero's contemporaries, could be quoted as literature, but they were exceptional. The mime that appealed most to popular taste was as ephemeral as a sketch in a modern revue. The

[1] M. Bieber, *The History of the Greek and Roman Theatre*, 391–400; M. Gigante, 'La cultura letteraria a Pompeii', in *Pompeiana* (Bibl. della Parola del Passato, 4; Napoli, 1951) 125.

[2] W. Beare, *The Roman Stage*[2] (1955) 127–38.

[3] Ibid. 139–48.

actors were more important than the script, and improvisation was tolerated, even expected. Their stock characters were the cuckold, the pander, the procuress, the parasite. Ovid in exile feels very self-righteous when he thinks of the mimes that were drawing the crowds in Rome:

> quid si scripsissem mimos obscena iocantes,
> qui semper vetiti crimen amoris habent:
> in quibus assidue cultus procedit adulter:
> verbaque dat stulto callida nupta viro?[1]

There seems every reason to believe that they became less rather than more refined. Even Martial can claim that his verses at their frankest are no franker than the mimes.[2] The authorities of Massilia banned them from the local stage,[3] but Massilia still retained something of the Hellenic taste which it owed to its original colonists from Phocaea.[4] There are not likely to have been such scruples at Ostia.

Farce and mime appealed primarily to the lower and middle classes. The art of pantomime satisfied all tastes. The dramatic dance first became a recognized art form under the patronage of Maecenas and Augustus. Pylades and Bathyllus were the pioneers of the period, and left the new form firmly established. The art of the *pantomimus* was to accompany a song or recitation and interpret it by dance and gesture.[5] He wore a mask and adapted his dress to the character he was presenting, often changing mask and dress several times during a single performance. With no play of features to help him he had to rely entirely on the movements of his body and cover an immensely wide range of expression with his gestures. His subjects were usually drawn from tragedy and retold the old stories of gods and heroes, among them the madness of Hercules, the sorrows of Niobe, the judgement of Paris.

These *pantomimi* roused even fiercer passions among the audience than the mimes, and measures had to be taken against popular disturbances in the theatre. Upholders of Roman tradition regarded their popularity as a social danger, and Tiberius issued an edict forbidding senators to enter their houses and knights to accompany them in public.[6] But official decrees and the attacks of the satirists made little impression. Few actors during the Empire attained the social standing of a Roscius, but the successful *pantomimus* often found his way to court. Augustus had patronized Pylades and Bathyllus: Mnester, freedman of

---

[1] Ovid, *Tristia*, ii. 497.
[2] Martial iii. 86. 4.
[3] Val. Max. ii. 6. 7.
[4] Tac. *Agricola*, 4. 3.
[5] *RE*, s.v. pantomimus (E. Wüst).
[6] Tac. *Ann.* i. 77. 5.

Tiberius, was intimate with Gaius and Messalina; Paris turned the head of Domitian's wife. It was common also for wealthy people to have *pantomimi* in their households for the entertainment of guests: even when she was nearly eighty Pliny's friend Ummidia Quadratilla found their performances a pleasant diversion.[1] But their main place was the public stage, and the successful *pantomimus* was the film star of his day. So, if a poet wished to make money, his quickest means lay in a libretto for a dancer. Statius may fill a hall to hear a reading of his *Thebaid*, but if he is to keep the wolf from the door, he must cater for more popular tastes:

> sed cum fregit subsellia versu,
> esurit, intactam Paridi nisi vendit Agaven.[2]

There was fierce competition among the towns to attract the great dancers of the day to their stage, and numerous inscriptions record the public and official recognition that was offered to them. A base from Ostia records the council's decision, backed by popular demand, to set up a statue to a dancer 'in recognition of his outstanding skill'.[3] Another dancer, in the third century, was commemorated by the *seviri Augustales*; he came from the East and is described as 'the leading *pantomimus* of his day, honoured by Valerianus and Gallienus'.[4] Both dancers had probably performed on the Ostian stage. Performances at Ostia are probably also reflected in the simple marble tablet set up to L. Aurelius Apolaustus Memphius, freedman of the emperors Marcus Aurelius and Lucius Verus.[5] Only his name is recorded, but he was famed as a dancer. The first two of these inscriptions emphasize the skill of the dancer, his *peritia*. The libretto counted for little; it was the subtlety and range of the dancer that caught the imagination. The dancing could also satisfy less exalted appetites. The stories of gods and goddesses gave ample opportunity for suggestive and erotic contortions; the opportunities were liberally taken.

Recitations, singing, and various forms of spectacle also had their place on the Ostian stage, and an odd story in the historian Dio may here be relevant. Dio records that when Septimius Severus found the senate less than lukewarm at his decision to deify Commodus, he pointed out their inconsistency by a very pertinent illustration.[6] One of their number, a former consul, he reminds them, had recently in a

---

[1] Pliny, *Ep.* vii. 24. 4.   [2] Juvenal vii. 86.   [3] 474.
[4] *S* 4624, fragments of twin marble tablets. The dancer was a member of the council at Ascalon and Damascus.   [5] *S* 5375.   [6] Dio lxxvi. 8. 2.

public exhibition at Ostia sported with a prostitute dressed as a leopardess. There is no good reason to doubt this story, for Dio at this stage in his history is writing from personal experience in the senate. Behind the story may lie a spectacle under Commodus in honour of the wine god, who at Portus is described in an inscription as 'Liber pater Commodianus'.[1] The natural setting for the performance would be the theatre.

There seems little doubt that theatre standards had been considerably debased by the Severan period. There was still in the third century no doubt an element of the broad humour which has always justified the music hall. The general temper of the day, however, was not the robustness of the Shakespearians, but the immorality of Restoration Drama without its style, descending often to a mere parade of sex. The rebuilding of Ostia's theatre is almost contemporary with Tertullian's treatise on Public Spectacles, and this strong appeal to Christians to give up the theatre, the arena, and the circus contains a vivid denunciation of the stage. It is 'immodesty's own particular abode, where nothing is in repute but what elsewhere is disreputable'.[2] Another Christian writer of the third century can speak of the theatre as 'the brothel of public shame and the school of indecency'.[3] We do not look to Christian polemics for an unbiased picture of pagan customs, and we can safely allow for considerable exaggeration; but we should not ignore their evidence.

Whatever we may think of the developments of the Roman stage, the Ostian theatre remained popular. When it was rebuilt under Commodus its seating capacity was increased roughly from three to four thousand. It survived the severe economic depression of the third century and was kept in repair throughout the fourth. At the end of the fourth century indeed the Ostian theatre took on a new lease of life; aquatic displays were added to the attractions.

The evidence for this late adaptation of the theatre at Ostia has in part been lost by modern restoration, but Gismondi has ingeniously collected the clues from Lanciani's report on the original excavation.[4] The decisive indication, however, has always been visible; its significance had been overlooked. At some period the two rooms on either

---

[1] 30.   [2] Tertullian, *De spectaculis*, 17. 1.
[3] Pseudo-Cyprian (ed. Boulanger; Paris, 1933) 6. 2.
[4] Gismondi, 'La Colimbetra del teatro di Ostia', in *Anthemon* (Scritti . . . in onore di Carlo Anti; Firenze, 1955) 293–308.

side of the central entrance from the Decumanus, originally shops, were converted to cisterns. Doorways were blocked, walls and floor were lined with cement. These cisterns had been regarded as medieval improvisations to collect water when the aqueduct had failed. But, as Gismondi has pointed out, medieval Ostians lacked either the heart or the competence for such large-scale reconstruction; for their water supply they relied on old wells, or new wells clumsily constructed. Gismondi has also drawn attention to the original apertures, still visible in the walls, where the water from the cisterns was fed into the central passage to flood the orchestra. The southern end of the passage was also converted into a cistern, but the original traces of this conversion are more difficult to distinguish. Cisterns were needed for storage, because the demands on the aqueduct exceeded supply; they could be filled at night when the needs for houses, baths, and public fountains had died down. To flood the orchestra from these cisterns was a simple task; it was no less simple to drain off the water when the theatre reverted to its normal function.

The people of Ostia had grown accustomed to Nereids in the mosaics of their baths. They could now see them in the flesh.[1] Choreographic displays of nymphs and goddesses provided splendid opportunities for enterprising producers, but one wonders whether the bishop of Ostia approved the innovation.

AMPHITHEATRE AND CIRCUS

At Rome the spectacles of the theatre were eclipsed, as forms of popular entertainment, by the wild-beast shows of the amphitheatre and the chariot races of the circus. Both appealed strongly to popular passions, and most of the emperors met the demand with extravagant displays. That the amphitheatre was not regarded as a luxury which only a capital city could afford is shown by the number that survive in the towns of Italy and the provinces: the evidence for circuses is less widespread.

If such a comparatively unimportant town as Pompeii had its own amphitheatre before the end of the Republic, Ostia should have felt and satisfied the need in the prosperity of the second century if not before. Gladiatorial shows were certainly presented at Ostia. The record of the career of the Antonine Gamala includes an instance: 'idem munus

---

[1] For aquatic displays, G. Traversari, 'Tetimimo e Colimbetra', *Dioniso* 13 (1950) 18.

gladiatorium ded(it).'[1] An entry in the Fasti probably recorded a hunting display to commemorate the dedication of a basilica in 152.[2]
The three days' games which P. Aufidius Fortis, patron of the town,
celebrated in 146 on the occasion of the dedication of silver statues of
Honour and Virtue were also probably gladiatorial displays.[3] That the
common people were familiar with the gladiator's technique is suggested by rough scratchings of gladiators on a wall in the House of
Jupiter and Ganymede[4] and on an Ostian slab of marble on which
some of the principal Roman diversions are roughly incised.[5]

Wild beasts and gladiators are also widely represented in a large hoard
of terra-cotta moulds found in a series of sunken dolia near the centre of
the town.[6] These moulds were made in pairs, fitting together; they are
elaborately figured and represent scenes associated with the circus, the
theatre, and the amphitheatre. The subjects include a giraffe being
attacked by a lion and a leopard, and a hunter coming to grips with a
lion which has attacked a bull. The excavator's attractive conclusion that
these moulds were used for the baking of cakes or bread to be distributed at public spectacles should probably be abandoned. None of the
moulds show signs of having been used in this way, not all the scenes
are appropriate, and in some the detail is extremely elaborate. Dr.
Squarciapino is probably right in removing the moulds from the kitchen
to the studio. She suggests that they were used for reproduction in some
perishable material, which would explain why no positives have been
found.[7] The hunting scenes at least confirm the popularity of such shows
at Ostia.

For displays such as are recorded in the inscriptions there is no suitable open area in imperial Ostia. The Forum was too restricted and too
crowded with statues, the theatre orchestra was too small. The field of
the Great Mother could have been adapted to the purpose, but it was
too closely associated with the ceremonial of Cybele. No amphitheatre,
however, has been found, and none is recorded in any surviving inscription. To explain the absence of an amphitheatre by the nearness of Ostia

[1] 2[12].

[2] *Fasti*, 152: 'famili[a | glad(iatoria) munus venatio]ne legitima edidit, in qua [— |
— fu]erunt duo.' See Degrassi's note, p. 238.

[3] *Fasti*, 146: 'ludos per triduum sua pec(unia) edidit.' Theatre performances fit Virtus
and Honos, military qualities, considerably less well.

[4] Calza, *MA* 26 (1920) 370.

[5] *NS* 1914, 290.

[6] A. Pasqui, *NS* 1906, 182, 357–73.

[7] M. F. Squarciapino, *Arch. Class.* 6 (1954) 83, who adds further Ostian examples, and
cites parallels from other towns.

to Rome is not convincing. Fifteen miles is a long distance for men who have to walk, and if her own theatre was given to Ostia under Augustus there seems no reason why an amphitheatre should not have been demanded later.

In this dilemma the single positive reference to an Ostian amphitheatre should not be neglected, though it comes from a source which many historians would condemn on principle. The reference is contained in the story of the martyrdom at Ostia of Asterius.[1] The Acts of the Christian martyrs, with a few remarkable exceptions, are notoriously unreliable and this is not one of the exceptions. The story is late and melodramatic and as a record of judicial procedure it has no more value than most of its kind. But even the most sensational of these acts of the martyrs usually derive from local tradition, and though their chronology may be inconsistent and their narrative romanticized, they often preserve valuable details of local topography. The trial of Asterius at Ostia ends in his condemnation to the amphitheatre. He was led out 'ad locum qui appellatur Ursariae . . . quia ibi ferae nutriebantur'. With his followers he was taken into the arena, presumably near by, and the wild beasts were sent in. There is a genuine ring about 'the place of bears, so called because it was there that the wild beasts were kept'.

It is then possible that there was an amphitheatre outside the walls, but we should like to have firmer evidence. An amphitheatre should have become a conspicuous ruin, and at least we should expect some record from the eighteenth or nineteenth century. The dilemma could be formally resolved by assuming that the building was completely stripped before the Renaissance, or that it was constructed in timber;[2] but neither solution is satisfactory. The main reason for retaining an open mind is the difficulty of believing that a town as crowded, rich, and important as Ostia lacked suitable provision for the most popular form of entertainment in the Roman world.

No trace of a circus has been found or reported, and no clear mention is made in inscriptions or wall scribblings of chariot races. Reliefs in terra-cotta and marble illustrate circus scenes, but such themes were part of the sculptor's stock repertoire. Local races are suggested, but not proved, by the inclusion of a horse crowned with victory palm among the diversions crudely illustrated on the marble slab referred to

---

[1] p. 524.
[2] Timber amphitheatres: Tac. *Ann.* iv. 62 (Fidenae); *AE* 1926, 78 (Pisidian Antioch); Suet. *Nero*, 12. 1 (Campus Martius).

above.[1] There was no permanent construction for the purpose, but races may have occasionally been held near the sea coast on the southern plain. A Roman praetor commemorating his celebration of the games of Castor and Pollux describes them as 'certamina';[2] they may have included races for chariots or horses.

INNS AND BARS

In modern societies the inn, the bar, and the café are the main rivals of organized entertainment in the pattern of social recreation. The *caupona* and the *popina* took their place in Roman life.[3] A gossip over a drink of wine was doubtless part of the daily routine of the middle class, and many establishments on the street fronts catered for a quick drink or more leisurely refreshment. Most of the shops had been stripped bare before excavation and can no longer be identified, but we get a glimpse of the variety of setting available to men who liked to take their wine or food in public.

One of the most vivid buildings in the town is the largely restored 'Thermopolium' on the Via di Diana.[4] It dates from the economic decline of the third century, when second-hand marble was easily acquired, and could be used even for shelving and cupboards. At the entrance is a wide counter with shelves attached to the wall behind, on which glasses, dishes, and food for sale were set. Beneath the counter are two basins for washing glasses and dishes. Even these are lined with marble, and the panels include a tablet commemorating C. Fulvius Plautianus, consul, praetorian prefect, father-in-law of the emperor Caracalla.[5] When he was purged his name was erased: one wonders whether the man who washed the glasses in this basin ever gave a thought to the history of the stone.

Within the shop against the east wall is a marble cupboard and, above it, further shelving. Over the shelving is a large painting, a still life illustrating some of the goods that were for sale; they include ? olives swimming in brine, a bunch of grapes, two pomegranates (?).

---

[1] NS 1914, 290.   [2] 1; p. 344 f.

[3] The *caupona* provided lodging as well as food and drink; the *popina* covered a wide range from drinking den to respectable restaurant, J. Kleberg, *Hôtels, restaurants et cabarets dans l'antiquité romaine* (Uppsala, 1957). Ostian evidence, 45–48, 53–56.

[4] NS 1915, 29; 1916, 415; Pl. xxix a. *Popina* would be a better title; *thermopolium*, borrowed from the Greek, is rarely used, Kleberg, op. cit. 14, 16.

[5] S 4392. See Addenda.

The shop is connected with a room to the west, which may have been used as a kitchen; in it is a large *dolium* sunk in the ground, which may have contained wine.

Food and wine could be consumed on the premises. Behind the shop is a small open court, with a plain mosaic pavement and a small fountain in the middle. Along the eastern wall is a stone bench where the customer could bring his food and wine; or he could sit on one of the two stone benches that flanked the entrance on the street and watch the passers-by.

There is a less leisurely atmosphere in the *popina* which is strategically placed at the junction of the eastern Decumanus with the Via della Fontana.[1] This is no larger than a single small shop and was probably somewhat like an espresso bar in function. The shopkeeper has made his business clear, by the invitation to drink inscribed on his mosaic pavement.[2]

Another *popina*, of less orthodox character, can be seen in the Via della Calcara. As we see it now, it is a dressing-room incorporated in the set of baths between the Insula of Serapis and the Insula of the Charioteers; but originally this room was wide open to the street. It formed part of the small Trajanic nucleus of this large Hadrianic block,[3] and the paintings are original. There are two zones of figures on the walls. The lower was largely destroyed when the shop was taken over and transformed, but the upper zone was unaffected and three of the figures are still well preserved. They represent the seven sages of Greek tradition, seated and half life-size, with their names inscribed in Greek lettering below; the names of Solon, Thales, and Chilon are clearly legible.[4] These sages were noted for their pithy maxims, but not for those recorded here: 'Solon rubbed his stomach to ease his motions'; 'Thales advised determined effort as a cure for constipation.' All the inscriptions that survive are similarly concerned with what a French scholar has discreetly called 'les dernières péripéties de la digestion'.[5] But in typically Roman spirit the coarseness of the humour is accompanied by great care in the painting and lettering. There are few more skilfully painted figures on Ostian walls than these philosophers, and it is not surprising that they were allowed to remain. On the ceiling are

---

[1] *NS* 1909, 92.

[2] *S* 4756: '[hospes, inquit] Fortunatus, [vinum e cr]atera, quod sitis, bibe.'

[3] p. 134.

[4] Calza, 'Die Taverne der sieben Weisen in Ostia', *Die Antike*, 15 (1939) 99–115; Pl. xxix *b*.   [5] Ch. Picard, *Rev. Arch.* 12 (1938) 252.

painted wine flagons and against one of them *Falernum* can still be read, the connoisseur's Falernian wine. This was clearly a wine shop.

The humour of these walls is essentially masculine. We are in a different atmosphere when we visit the Inn of Helix by the Porta Marina, if the mosaics are a fair guide. A nude Venus with a cupid might be purely decorative, but there is nothing pure about another mosaic that certainly would not pass the modern censor. One suspects that this inn did a very mixed business.[1] The elegance of the paintings in the Peacock Inn, on the other hand, suggests a more refined clientele.[2]

In their widely distributed baths, in the theatre and at other public spectacles, in their inns and bars Ostian men and women had ample opportunity to relax and enjoy themselves.

---

[1] Cf. *Dig.* 23. 2. 43: 'palam quaestum facere dicemus non tantum eam, quae in lupanario se prostituit, verum etiam si qua (ut adsolet) in taberna cauponia vel qua alia pudori suo non paret.' Juvenal (8. 171 ff.) has been understood (Kleberg, op. cit. 55) to refer to low company in an Ostian *popina*: 'mitte Ostia, Caesar, | mitte sed in magna legatum quaere popina. . . .' Lateranus is to be sent to Ostia to take ship for a provincial command. The *popina* from which he must first be extracted is in Rome.

[2] Reg. iv. 2. 6. The paintings illustrated, *Ostia* (1954), fig. 57.

17

THE ARTS

Few features point the contrast between the ancient and the modern world more sharply than the wealth of sculpture, painting, and mosaics from Roman sites. The contrast is in part misleading. Much of the painting should be compared with the work of the internal decorator rather than the original artist; changing tastes have replaced mosaics by carpets. But the sculptor is governed by the same conditions and to a large extent uses the same tools now as then.

SCULPTURE

The quality and quantity of Ostian sculpture that can still be seen in the museum on the site is impressive; it represents, however, but a small proportion of what once existed. Much was destroyed in medieval lime kilns; more has been taken from the site. The earliest excavators dug for treasure, and the statues, reliefs, and busts which they found were dispersed throughout Europe. The rich harvests of nineteenth-century excavations were reaped primarily by the Papal Collections in Rome. Two rooms of the Lateran Museum, devoted exclusively to Ostian discoveries of the mid-century, suggest something of the richness of the site. To wander through the Vatican galleries with a list of Ostian origins is even more revealing.

If today a local authority in Britain commissions a group of sculpture for a fountain or a public building, the gesture is news, and the seeds of a nice controversy are sown. In Ostia, as in other Roman towns, the sculptor was regarded naturally as the architect's colleague. To compare Ostia with a British town perhaps exaggerates the contrast. Sculpture has rarely been at home in Britain; temperament and climate are uncongenial. But even in modern Mediterranean ports we should find considerably less sculpture, and a considerably lower average of achievement.

Sculpture at Ostia was widely displayed in public places, public buildings, and private houses. The two main fields for commemorative statues were the central Forum and the public gardens within the

Piazzale delle Corporazioni behind the theatre. In the Forum two bases only survive, and one of these was transferred to the Forum in the fourth century when the district in which it was originally set up had lapsed into slum conditions.[1] The other carried an equestrian statue of Manilius Rusticus, a *praefectus annonae* of the late Empire.[2] No bases survive from the early and middle Empire, but inscriptions record two Ostians honoured with statues in the Forum[3] and there were doubtless many more. Commemoration in the Forum was the reward of outstanding public service to the town; the Piazzale delle Corporazioni was primarily reserved, as was appropriate, for those who had benefited the traders and business men of Ostia. More bases survive here, for they were used in a late reconstruction of the theatre; their inscriptions show that they once carried statues of imperial officials concerned with Rome's supplies and their passage through Ostia, presidents of Ostian guilds, and other men of local distinction.[4]

Though commemorative statues seem to have been mainly concentrated in these two centres, it is probable that no public square was completely free of sculpture. An inscription records a chariot group in the Forum Vinarium;[5] statue bases were found in the field of the Great Mother.[6] Individual monuments could also be seen at the street side. Immediately before he entered the Porta Romana the visitor to Ostia in the Empire saw a statue of Hygia dedicated by a patron of the town to *salus Caesaris Augusti*.[7] When he had passed along the Decumanus beyond the theatre he could see a more than life-size statue which had stood beside the street since the late Republic or early Principate.[8]

Public buildings were rich in sculpture, perhaps overcrowded. The temples had cult statues and subsidiary dedications. In the Capitolium each side wall has three large niches reserved for statues: statues stood also in the seven large niches of the Round Temple. From the Basilica probably came the series of imperial heads now in the Sala a Croce Greca in the Vatican, which were found by Petrini in the early nineteenth century.[9] The court of the Barracks of the Vigiles contained a veritable portrait gallery. Sculpture also played an important part in the decoration of public baths. Chancing his luck at a promising ruin

---

[1] *S* 4721. [2] *S* 4455. [3] I[38], 353.
[4] Texts collected, Paschetto, 335. [5] 5. [6] 324, 325.
[7] *NS* 1910, 60; *S* 4324. For the date, p. 508.
[8] The core of the base remains; the approximate date is inferred from the level. There is a fragment of an arm from a statue *c.* 10 ft. high lying near the temple in the Piazzale delle Corporazioni. It may come from this base. [9] p. 106.

near the Roman line of the sea shore, the Scottish painter Gavin Hamilton found in a set of baths 'a fine Antinous, an indifferent Aesculapius, a large statue of Hygea and a most excellent torso', and he would have found more if others had not been there before him.[1]

The guilds also were good customers for the sculptor. Since they depended increasingly on imperial favour they concentrated primarily on imperial statues and busts, but their guild houses were also decorated with statues of their own distinguished officers and patron deities. Particularly striking is the wealth of sculpture from the social head-quarters of the *seviri Augustales*.[2] Though probably much had already been taken away, there remained, when the building was excavated, nine substantial figures. They included a full-length statue of a *sevir Augustalis* dedicated by one of his freedmen, a late third-century em-peror dressed in the robes of the *pontifex maximus*, a Venus Genetrix with a portrait head of Sabina, wife of Hadrian, part of a figure of Diana, and a fountain figure of a reclining nymph[3]

In private houses sculpture needs space for display. In the large apart-ment blocks terra-cottas and small bronzes have been found, but little sculpture. This little, however, includes an impressive Roman copy of an early Greek head of Themistocles.[4] It was found in an unpretentious block with comparatively small rooms and, if it once belonged to a tenant of the house, it is interesting to speculate why and how he acquired it. It would have caused less surprise if it had been found in one of the well-appointed houses of the late Empire. For the owners of these houses were clearly wealthy, and their walls and floors show their passion for marble. Unfortunately most of the furnishings have long since been robbed, but the sculptures found in the House of Fortuna Annonaria are probably typical.[5]

In the central niche of the main room of this house was a statue of Artemis, copied from a Hellenistic figure, which combined features of fifth- and fourth-century work. A statuette of Hera (or Demeter), copied from a late classical work, was found in the niche in the southern wall of the garden court. A statuette of Venus is a small-scale copy of the third-century original by the Greek sculptor Doidalsas. A headless

---

[1] *JHS* 21 (1901) 314. For the identification of these baths, p. 407.

[2] R. Calza, *NS* 1941, 216.

[3] It is not certain that all this sculpture came from the building: some of it may have been collected for conversion to lime.

[4] *Museo*, 385 (with references); G. M. A. Richter, *Three Critical Periods in Greek Sculpture* (Oxford, 1951) 6.   [5] Becatti, *Case tarde*, 24.

Athena derives from a fifth-century original. Such copies of Greek works, competently but somewhat lifelessly reproduced, were the hall-mark of respectability throughout the imperial period. More interesting is the figure which gives its name to the house. On a base against the south wall of the garden court, at its west end, was a large seated female figure on a throne. She wears a girdled chiton and himation and holds in her left hand a cornucopia and an oar; her head is turreted.[1] Though horn of plenty and oar are appropriate to Fortuna, the turreted head would seem to be out of place. It is normally the mark of a city. Rather than Fortuna we probably see here a personification of Ostia; but, even if this identification is right, the figure derives ultimately from a Greek original. The only specifically Roman sculptures found in the house were two portrait busts of the third century A.D.

In other late houses niches and nymphaea show where sculpture was once displayed, but very little remained for the excavators. The few pieces that were found, such as the copy of a Hellenistic group from which the House of Amor and Psyche takes its name[2] and the Perseus from a suburban villa outside the Porta Laurentina,[3] confirm the Roman lack of originality in decorative sculptures.

There was also a steady demand for sculpture for the tomb. Trimalchio was a true representative of his age and class when he designed his tomb to represent the trade he had followed.[4] At Ostia modest reliefs in terra-cotta or marble depict the toolmaker, the boatman, the water-seller, the marble-cutter, the innkeeper, and many others, all plying their trades.[5] When cremation was the rule, the container of the ashes was often elaborately carved in marble; when burial succeeded cremation, the sarcophagus, with its mythological reliefs and symbolic scenes, gave wider scope to the sculptor. Marble doors decorated in relief sometimes gave emphasis to the tomb entrance; portrait heads or statues were often placed inside.[6]

How much of this widespread demand for sculpture, public and private, was satisfied by local craftsmen? The only three signatures preserved are of Greeks. A small base in black marble preserves the name of a Rhodian sculptor of the late Republic.[7] The free-standing

---

[1] The head was stolen from the site soon after discovery.
[2] Becatti, *Arti figurative*, 1 (1945), tav. x; *Museo*, 180.
[3] *Arch. Anz.* 49 (1934) 436; *Museo*, 99.   [4] Petronius, *Sat.* 71.
[5] Calza, *Necropoli*, 249–57.   [6] Ibid. 221–47.
[7] NS1880. 478 n. 16: '[ʼΑθαν]όδωρος ʼΑγησάνδρου [ʼΡ]όδιος ἐποίησε'. The restoration of the name is based on other examples of the signature in Italy, identified by some scholars

group of Mithras and the bull, from the Baths of Mithras, was the work of Κρίτων Ἀθηναῖος;[1] a figure of Ganymede, now in the Vatican, has the name Φαίδιμος.[2] These works could have been bought outside Ostia; or they could have been produced in Ostia by travelling sculptors temporarily resident; they were not the work of sculptors locally trained. One sarcophagus came from an Attic workshop;[3] two others, of a well-known columned type, are made from Phrygian marble and came from Asia Minor.[4] Copies of Greek and Hellenistic works could have been imported, but copy books were freely circulating and local workshops are likely to have competed for the demand. The prototypes of imperial portraits originated normally in Rome, but many of the cruder copies found in Ostia are almost certainly local work; and perhaps not only the cruder copies.

But although there is a wide range of sculpture from Ostia, the origin of which will probably remain uncertain, there remains a large output which can be attributed to local workshops. The portraits of local men and women from tombs and public places, or at least the great majority of them, were carved at Ostia. They form an impressive series from the late Republic to the fourth century A.D., and the best of them can compare with the best from Rome. Some of the best can be seen in the museum on the site: the late Republican head of an old lady, severe, economic, expressive, resembling a death mask;[5] the sensitive mid-second-century portrait bust of C. Volcacius Myropnous;[6] a striking full-length fourth-century figure, redeeming with its very individual head the careless cutting of the toga.[7] The heads of two members of the Caltilian family cut in low relief on a funerary monument, now preserved in the Lateran Museum,[8] are among the most impressive Trajanic portraits that have survived. *

In narrative reliefs Ostian sculptors were perhaps slower in catching up with the best work of the day. The aetiological scenes from the

with one of the sculptors of the Laocoon; but see G. M. A. Richter, *Three Critical Periods*, 67. [1] Becatti, *Mitrei*, 32; *Museo*, 149; Pl. XXXI c.
[2] Ganymede or Narcissus, Amelung, *Die Skulpturen des vatican. Museums*, i (i) n. 388, p. 56. [3] Calza, *Necropoli*, 210, fig. 112; *Museo*, 34; Pl. XXXVI a.
[4] Marion Lawrence, 'Additional Asiatic Sarcophagi', *MAAR* 20 (1951) 141, 158.
[5] Wessberg, *Studien zur Kunstgeschichte der röm. Republik* (1941) 251; *Museo*, 63; Pl. XVII a.
[6] Calza, *Necropoli*, 225, figs. 123–4; *Museo*, 38; Pl. XVII c.
[7] R. Calza, *BC* 69 (1941) 113; *Museo*, 55. ? Symmachus (R. Calza), ? Ragonius Vincentius Celsus (Becatti, *Case tarde*, 46).
[8] Bendorff und Schöne, *Die antiken Bildwerke des lateranischen Museums* (1867) 376 f., nn. 535, 567.

temple of Hercules are interesting for their story, but less impressive as compositions. The frieze on the public monument of Cartilius Poplicola outside the Porta Marina is crude and provincial by comparison with contemporary work at Rome. Nor can high artistic claims be made for the series of reliefs which illustrate Ostian trades, whether coming from tombs or business premises. These were mainly commissioned by humble folk and were not the work of the leading sculptors of the day. Their purpose was to tell a story; their merit lies in the realism and vigour with which they told it. An exception may be seen in the relief, attributed to the late Flavian period, which depicts two marble-cutters at work. In this relief the sculptor has arranged and executed his figures with considerable care, and not without success.[1]

Local workshops have also been traced in Ostian sarcophagi. The finest were probably imported, but two types at least seem to be specifically Ostian. Reference has already been made to the sarcophagus of Quiriacus found in the Christian chapel by the theatre. In the centre of the strigilated face is the figure of Orpheus playing the lyre; at each end is another figure. Two other examples have been found at Ostia showing the figure of Orpheus treated in precisely the same style. It is a reasonable inference that a further example, from Porto Torres in Sardinia, comes from the same Ostian workshop; it was probably in the return cargo of a corn ship.[2] Some of the strigilated sarcophagi with central medallions containing portrait busts of the dead are also probably Ostian products. The general type is common elsewhere, but some of the Ostian examples have distinctive decoration round the medallion.[3] We may also attribute to a local sculptor the elaborate sarcophagus of a priestess of Cybele, which represents the restoration of Alcestis from the dead by Hercules; for some of the heads are clearly portraits.[4]

PAINTING

Painting has naturally suffered considerably more than sculpture from weather and neglect, and it is only recently that paintings have been found in sufficient quantity at Ostia to justify even the most

[1] Calza, *Necropoli*, 257; *Museo*, 138.

[2] G. Pesce, *Sarcofagi romani di Sardegna* (Roma, 1957) p. 102 n. 57. The Ostian examples, collected by Signora Calza, are quoted, p. 103 n. 4. Other sarcophagi found in Sardinia are tentatively attributed to Ostian workshops by Pesce (p. 13) on grounds of varying strength.   [3] Signora Calza has drawn my attention in particular to inv. 856, 919.

[4] p. 469.

guarded generalization.[1] When, in the late nineteenth century, a block of apartments north-east of the Capitolium was excavated, the paintings that survived on the walls at once gave the name 'House of the Paintings' to the building. For, though considerable areas between the Decumanus and the Tiber had already been uncovered, and though paintings from tombs outside the Porta Laurentina could be seen in the Vatican and Lateran Galleries, this was the only building at Ostia where the visitor could form some idea of the decoration of house walls. The name is now an embarrassment; it could apply with equal force to more than twenty buildings.

Ostian painting should not be approached too solemnly. Very little of the best has survived, and only the very best Roman painters can stand comparison with the sculptors and mosaicists. For refinement of taste and craftsmanship we turn naturally to public buildings and the private houses of the aristocracy. But from basilicas, temples, the largest of the imperial baths, and other major public buildings almost nothing survives; in the independent houses too little remains to judge the quality of the work. When the spreading houses of the late Republic and early Empire were pulled down, their paintings were lost for ever; in the late houses the lower part of the wall was normally reserved for marble panelling, and only small fragments of painting survived. We are left, therefore, in the main to judge Ostian painting by the survivals in the large insulae, designed for the middle class. In these great apartment blocks the ground floors have often been protected by the ruin of upper floors above them: when exposed by excavation they steadily deteriorate, and only an unlimited purse could give complete protection for all. Sufficient, however, remains to judge the standard wall decoration of the middle class in the second and third centuries.

In most of the insulae the work is not of high quality. Rarely are the outlines of the design incised before painting; often the painter does not even use a guide for his straight lines; the surface which is to receive the paint is generally much coarser than at Pompeii. On very

---

[1] Very little has been published on Ostian paintings. F. Fornari, *Studi Romani*, i (1913) 305–18, reviewed the examples then known. F. Wirth, *Römische Wandmalerei* (1934), made ample use of Ostian material, but his dating of Ostian walls, based exclusively on brick measurements, is very unreliable. The 1938–42 excavations added considerably to the quantity and range, but very little of the new material has been published. A chronological classification with brief analysis, C. C. Van Essen, *Meededingen van het Nederlands hist. inst. te Rome*, 8 (1954) 33–55. See Addenda.

few walls is the true technique of fresco employed; more often the craftsman, though painting his background colour while his surface is wet, imposes his figures on a dried wall, a less exacting but less effective and less durable technique. For his more wealthy patrons he works with care, as in the House of the Muses, but in more modest apartments such as the House of the Sun he works with a quick brush carelessly. If his lines are not straight, if he carries his stroke too far, the explanation is usually economic and not aesthetic; he is doing a cheap job.

How much should be attributed to careless workmanship is perhaps a matter of dispute. Fornari, the first of the few who have made a special study of Ostian paintings, considered that the minor irregularities in the paintings he saw (in 1913) were so widespread that they must be deliberate.[1] But the features he noted—arches not truly centred, lines slightly oblique, garlands unequally divided, irregular frames to minor scenes—have no clear aesthetic intention or effect and are more easily ascribed to the speed with which the painter worked. He was more concerned with the total effect of the wall than in the painstaking execution of detail; such irregularities do not at once catch the eye. Not all irregularities, however, are due to carelessness. It has often been remarked that many of the figures in the main living-room of the House of Jupiter and Ganymede ignore the frames that surround them. The head of a philosopher breaks the line of the top of the frame;[2] the feet of other individual figures come below their frame. This is very different from a failure to draw lines strictly parallel or to centre an arch. The irregularity must be deliberate; perhaps the intention is to make the figures more lifelike. It is also possible that in some rooms where all the vertical lines are noticeably oblique the painter has deliberately avoided the perpendicular.

Ostian painting has not the wealth of mythological interest that compensates for the immediate unattractiveness of much of the painting at Pompeii; but for the study of Roman art it has its own special importance. The changing styles of Pompeian painting, which should not be too rigorously schematized, are reflected in Rome and elsewhere; in the abundant material from Pompeii and Herculaneum we have a point of reference for the fashions in wall decoration of Roman Italy. But Pompeian painting ends abruptly in the middle of the Flavian period. Though discoveries of later paintings in Rome are steadily in-

---

[1] Fornari, art. cit. 306 f.
[2] Ibid. 310 f.; Wirth, op. cit. 109, Taf. 25 and 26.

creasing, there is barely yet from Rome itself sufficient material for an historical survey of Roman painting in the imperial period. Ostia helps to fill this gap.

In painting as in sculpture and architecture Ostia reflected Rome. On Ostia's walls we can see the changing currents of Roman taste, and within broad limits we can date some of the changes; for a considerable proportion of Ostian walls are securely dated by brickstamps and where this evidence is not available a comparative study of construction suggests an approximate context. A painting will not necessarily be contemporary with the wall on which it is painted, but the wall gives at least the earliest possible date, and it is usually clear when the painting is not original. In many cases, even when a new surface has been added and a new painting imposed, it is the original painting that has survived.

The clearest signs of changes in taste are the shifting dominance of different colours, and the painter's changing methods of organizing his wall space. It would, however, be unwise to expect rigid uniformity. Within any period we should expect differences not only of quality but of style among Ostian painters. In an apartment where red and yellow are the dominant colours, a white room will not necessarily have been painted later than the rest. A rich man's house is likely to use cobalt blue when it is absent from middle-class flats, because it is an expensive pigment. When styles are changing, an older painter may not change at once with his younger contemporaries. But such differences should not be exaggerated. The painters of Ostia formed a guild, *collegae pingentes*,[1] and in what survives of their work there is little trace of individualism.

Though small fragments of painting from the early Empire survive, it is only from the reign of Hadrian that the study of Ostian painting can usefully begin. One of the most striking features of his reign in Ostia, as has been seen, is the intensive development of large apartment blocks to house a rapidly increasing population. In many of these Hadrianic blocks the original paintings survive. It is clear at once that they cannot be compressed within any of the four recognized Pompeian styles. There are echoes of Pompeian treatment and of Pompeian motifs. Some of the figured scenes recall the second and third Pompeian styles: architectural elements, such as colonnades in perspective, framing columns, and ornamental doors can be paralleled at Pompeii, and the flowering candelabra and garlands on Ostian second-century walls are common in the Flavian period at Rome and elsewhere. But to discuss

[1] S 4699.

Ostian painting in terms of distinctive Pompeian styles is irrelevant and confusing. The total effect of an Ostian wall in the Hadrianic or early Antonine period is at once recognizable and different from any of the standard styles of Pompeii. The wall is still divided into horizontal zones, but the divisions are less emphatic; vertical divisions in the main living-rooms are only rarely indicated, by columns cutting across the horizontal divisions. Architectural forms fill out the design, especially in the upper zone, but they never dominate the wall and become increasingly subordinate until they eventually disappear.

There is a difference of treatment, as one might expect, between the more important living-rooms and secondary rooms and corridors. In the former the dominant colours until the latter part of the century are red and yellow, supplemented by white, green, dark red, violet. The wall is divided into three horizontal zones, of which the central is the largest and most emphatic. The lowest zone is reserved for panels of colour; the central zone is divided into a series of framed panels, each containing one or more figures. The colouring of the figures, in which white, green, and violet predominate, contrasts with the dominant yellow and red of the background. In the smaller rooms each panel normally contains a single figure; scenes with two and three figures are sometimes found on larger walls; there are no large-scale compositions. The scenes are taken from mythology: Jupiter caressing Ganymede, with a somewhat solemn seated female figure in the background,[1] the young Bacchus being presented to one of the nymphs,[2] the desertion of Ariadne.[3] Single figures represent gods, muses, dancers, philosophers, often floating insubstantially in mid-air. The upper zone, very subordinate in the design, is completed with panels of colour accompanied sometimes by architectural forms, fanciful but not so completely unrealistic as in the flights of imagination of the Flavian period.

In looking at these walls the eye focuses first on the contrast of colour masses, and particularly the contrast of red and yellow panels. This effect is a little misleading, because the figures, which were an important element in the original decoration, have suffered much more than the background colours. Being painted on a dry surface they flake away when exposed and on many walls they have entirely disappeared. But even when the paint was fresh, the large panels of colour must have been the dominant feature of the design, and the figures secondary.

[1] *MA* 26 (1920) 397; Wirth, 109, Taf. 25, 36.
[2] *MA* 26 (1920) 381.   [3] Ibid. 376.

Sometimes there is a contrast of shape as well as of colour, the regular rectangles being offset by panels with curving lines.

When the rooms are comparatively small and the client has an adequate purse, this style of decoration can be attractive; but it was not well suited to large surfaces. In the small main living-room of the House of the Painted Ceiling in the Via della Fontana the painter can claim a modest success.[1] The emphasis is concentrated on the central zone, which is distinguished by three large vertical panels of colour, red in the centre, flanked on each side by panels of yellow. In each panel is a single floating figure in white, green, and violet. The lowest zone, occupied by small panels of red and yellow, remains inconspicuous; the upper zone has at each angle a columned portico in perspective with architrave and cornice, and, in the centre, a further single figure. More coherence is given to the wall by two white columns which extend from the ground through the horizontal zones. Much less successful is the main room of the House of Jupiter and Ganymede. Here there is no point of rest for the eye, and no coherence in the design. Although individual scenes and figures are carefully painted, the panels of colour remain unorganized.[2] The painter, possibly accustomed to much smaller surfaces, was unable to adapt his style to the scale of the wall.

The less pretentious decoration of corridors, bedrooms, and other secondary rooms is often more attractive to modern taste. On these walls the low dado found in the main living-room is omitted, and the surface is divided at roughly two-thirds of its height into two horizontal zones. It is, however, the vertical zones that carry the main emphasis. A series of light architectural features, resembling elongated stands to carry vases, divide the surface into vertical fields.[3] These features are linked together by light garlands, while in the field minor decorative forms are added, such as a Medusa's head, flying bird, or fish. In the Hadrianic period the background colour is usually white or yellow, the decoration in red and yellow; sometimes the foliage of garlands is painted green, but there is no strict adherence to naturalistic colours. The general pattern is maintained over a long period, but the fashion in colour changes. Sometimes the painting is rough and rapid, as in the

[1] Vaglieri, NS 1908, 24; Wirth, 104 (his date, *c.* 160–70, should be rejected. This house is included in a large area built at the end of Hadrian's reign (p. 136); the paintings are almost certainly contemporary.

[2] Wirth, taf. 25. The original construction is Hadrianic. Calza (*MA* 26 (1920) 363) dates the paintings in this room to a later phase, possibly Severan; Wirth (109) dates them *c.* 180. I am not convinced that a Hadrianic date is excluded.   [3] Pl. XVI *b*.

House of the Sun and in the original painting of the corridor of the House of Jupiter and Ganymede; sometimes the design is painted with considerable care and precision, as in the House of the Muses.

In some secondary rooms a variant on this standard pattern is found. In the field between the architectural dividers, small scenes are painted, sometimes free, sometimes within dark frames. The painting is done with a quick brush, and the scene is composed of blocks of contrasting colour, white, brown, and green. No attempt is made to represent detail, but from a distance the little landscapes add distinction to the wall.[1]

The Hadrianic style of wall decoration in main rooms, characterized by the contrast of large masses of colour, particularly red and yellow, had gone out of fashion by the end of the second century. In the House of Lucretius Menander we meet a very different style.[2] In the rooms later converted into a Mithraeum the background is white. The central zone is divided into a series of large panels framed by a thin band of red, within which are three bands of different colours. In the white field of each panel is painted a scene in green and brown, only one of which remains clearly recognizable, a landscape with shrine. The dado below this zone is now concealed by the benches of the Mithraeum but probably was filled by horizontal panels of colour. The upper zone, now lost, is separated from the central zone by a delicately painted stucco cornice in red, black, and blue. Architectural motifs, which had already become very subordinate in the Hadrianic style, have here been completely omitted. Another room in the same house is similar in style and may be from the same workshop. The house was built under Hadrian, but the paintings follow the reconstruction of some of the walls: they also precede the Mithraeum, which was inserted in the house not later than the early third century. The paintings probably are to be dated shortly after the middle of the second century.

Perhaps we should date to roughly the same period a group of paintings in the west wing of the Insula of the Charioteers. Here the background is white; the decorative effect is achieved by simple means. Thin lines of garlands break the monotony of the surface, but the main emphasis is on a series of small unframed scenes, of which the best are a hunter and stag in brown and green,[3] and a panther. The painters of Ostia, never completely happy with the human figure, are at their best in such quick renderings of animal life.

---

[1] Wirth, Taf. 30*b*.   [2] Wirth, 134.   [3] Pl. XVI *a*.

Towards the end of the second century there is a clear change in fashion in the decoration of secondary rooms both in colour and in subject. Red becomes the dominant background colour, and the change is too widespread to be coincidence; the explanation is not that red was a more practical colour and showed the dirt less, but that the colour had become fashionable. In one case we can see and approximately date the change. The ground-floor corridor of the House of Jupiter and Ganymede had originally, when the block was built under Hadrian, a white background with its decoration in red and yellow; later, though the east end of the corridor, used as a separate room, remained unchanged, the rest of the corridor was given a red background with yellow and green decoration. The new coat covers an original entrance to the street which was later closed, and the chance scratching of a date shows that the new painting was completed before the death of Commodus. The man who wrote 'vii Kal(endas) Commodas'[1] did not realize that the month would retain the emperor's name for less than two years.

As a variant on what we may call the standard corridor pattern, new motifs appear under the Severi. It becomes a common practice to paint stalks with foliage,[2] or cups on a red background. The foliage is painted in green with a broad brush and in a free style; the cups are large, painted in yellow to represent bronze or gold. This form of decoration can be seen on brick piers, as in the Insula of Serapis, in corridors, as in the Baths of Invidiosus, and in larger rooms, as in the Baths of Buticosus. It shows a reaction from the earlier practice of dividing the wall up into panels and treats the surface more as a unity. The same conception lies behind the large unframed figured scenes that date from approximately the same period. Two ambitious examples can be seen decorating the walls of Frigidaria. In the Baths of the Seven Sages Venus is depicted rising from the sea, at her toilet. On one side of her a Cupid holds up a mirror, a second Cupid at her other side holds a toilet box. Realistic fishes swim around, but the large lobster in the foreground strikes an incongruous note.[3] In the Pharos Baths Europa rides her bull accompanied by a miscellaneous assortment of fishes. The two pictures are very similar in style; they may be by the same painter, or at least from the same workshop. The colouring is not unattractive, but the drawing of the figures is weak and the compositions lack design.

While adequate evidence is available for classifying Ostian paintings

[1] *MA* 26 (1920) 369.   [2] Pl. xvi c.   [3] *Ostia* (1954), fig. 41.

of the second and early third centuries, it is more difficult to select what
properly belongs to the period that follows the Severi. There was little
new housebuilding in these years of anarchy, and much of the repaint-
ing in the insulae has disintegrated as a result of the method employed.
To secure an enduring surface in redecoration the wall must be stripped
and a fresh start made, or the old painting must be picked over so that
a new bed of plaster can be bound into the old; a fresh surface is then
built up. But it was much cheaper merely to cover the old surface with
a very thin layer of stucco. The immediate effect of painting on such a
surface was satisfactory, but, since it was not securely bound to the old,
it was extremely fragile and liable to flake away. Such shoddy redecoration was found in the House of the Paintings and its two neighbours[1]
and in the House of the Painted Ceiling.[2] At the time of excavation a
little of the later decoration could be distinguished, but no traces now
remain; the original paintings are comparatively well preserved. The
proper use of this technique was for notices on brick walls, where the
writing or decoration was not required to endure, and the quickest and
cheapest method was the best for the purpose. Its application to interior
walls is a typical mark of the third-century decline in living standards
of the middle classes.

The linear style which pervaded the catacombs through the middle
of the third century is represented at Ostia in the little that survives from
this period; it was probably the fashion of the day.[3] The surface of the
wall and ceiling is covered by a pattern, rarely symmetrical, of thin
lines, straight and curved, painted in red and green with a subsidiary
use of yellow on a white background. Small figures, human and animal,
are often included but they are never conspicuous. There is little rest for
the eye in such decoration, and if the painter is trying to carry experi-
ments in spatial illusion to their logical conclusion he has failed in his
purpose. This is not a triumph of abstract art; it seems to reflect the
disintegration and insecurity that followed the end of the Severan
dynasty.

Towards the end of the third century and through the fourth a new
fashion sweeps the field. On the lower zones of walls the imitation of
marble becomes the dominant theme. The taste derives no doubt from
the increasing use of marble dadoes and *opus sectile* pavements in the

---

[1] *MA* 26 (1920) 347 f.   [2] *NS* 1908, 23.
[3] For the style, Wirth, 165. At Ostia, *NS* 1908, 23 (no longer visible); a good example
on a wall near the Caupona del Pavone (Reg. iv. 2. 6).

houses of the wealthy. Where marble itself cannot be afforded or where, as in corridors or unimportant rooms, it would seem unduly extravagant, the painter does his best to give the appearance of marble. Not content with whites and greys, he paints panels of Giallo Antico, Pavonazzetto, and Cipollino with the same perverted ingenuity and relish with which a modern craftsman imposes an aristocratic oak grain on a door of Canadian pine. Sometimes the framed marble panels of the dado are his model, as in the Insula of the Eagle; sometimes, as in the north-east room of the Schola del Traiano, he reproduces the geometric pattern of a marble floor. That the fashion is late in development is shown by its absence from the original paintings on Hadrianic and Antonine walls and its appearance in various rooms where it replaces earlier paintings, as in the House of the Muses. In the main room facing the entrance of the guild house of the builders it is later than the podium, which in turn is later than the original Hadrianic construction.

The widespread imitation of marble dominates the painting of the period that has survived, but it was accompanied by large-scale figured scenes. The almost total disappearance of such late paintings is one of our most serious losses. Isolated figures that have survived in Rome suggest that perhaps the painters were not far behind when the sculptors were producing their striking series of late portraits. Fragments of a large composition from the House of the Nymphaeum suggest a higher standard than Ostian painters reached in the period of prosperity.[1]

Not all the paintings that have survived in Ostia submit to easy classification. Two in particular deserve attention, for they have few parallels in Italy, and anticipate modern principles of wall decoration. Both use a recurring pattern. The first was found in the north-east room off the garden court of a house near the sea coast outside Porta Marina. On a background of cobalt blue the painter has imposed a maze in white. At the crossings of the maze are sheafs from which stream swags of foliage, or graceful little figures in white within a red circle. While the main pattern is repeated, the figures are varied. Colour and design combine to make this one of the most attractive paintings to be seen in Ostia.[2] The wall on which it is painted dates from the construction of the house in the Flavian period; the painting itself may be contemporary, for there is no sign of an earlier coat underneath. The second

---

[1] Becatti, *Case tarde*, 38, figs. 37–39.

[2] Reg. iv. 8. 6 (Domus Fulminata). The painting has been transferred to the Horrea Epagathiana.

painting based on a recurring pattern is not earlier than the third century. It forms the upper zone of a room in the Insula of the Eagle. The lower zone imitates marble, and is divided from the upper zone by a band of red. Above, on a brown background, the painter has drawn with compass a series of concentric and intersecting circles with colouring of red, green, and blue-grey. The design has the restfulness of a Victorian wallpaper in moderately good taste. A similar but more attractive pattern, based on compass-drawn circles, was later found in an apse near the temple of Serapis and has been moved to the Horrea Epagathiana; it may have come from the same workshop.

MOSAICS

The decorators of pavements have fared much better than the painters in the chances of survival.[1] When walls are pulled down their paintings are lost. Pavements are not torn up; they are simply replaced at a higher level. Ultimately, by careful excavation at lower levels, it should be possible to trace in some detail the history of Ostia's pavements. For even what can now be seen gives a much more representative impression of the pavement worker's quality than of the painter's. Most of the insulae still retain on the ground floor their mosaics; a large series of ambitious decorations survive from the floors of baths and other public buildings, and we can still judge the quality and style of the pavements in the late houses of the rich. What is most needed to complete a general survey is a series of representative samples from independent houses of the early Empire.

The black-and-white mosaic pavement is already well established by the early Empire. It is, however, only from the second century that a sufficient number of pavements can be seen to form a general impression of the mosaicist's work. One of the most striking characteristics of the insulae is the free use of black-and-white mosaics to pave the floors. Normally the kitchen and lavatory are differently treated, with floors of cement or *opus spicatum*, but all other ground-floor rooms and corridors are paved with black-and-white mosaic, even in such humble blocks as the Casette-tipo. In corridors and courts the mosaic is often, but not always, in plain white with a black border; in rooms the pave-

---

[1] The widest illustration and discussion of Ostian mosaics is by M. E. Blake, 'The Pavements of the Roman Buildings of the Republic and early Empire', *MAAR* 8 (1930) 1–159; 'Roman Mosaics of the Second Century in Italy', ibid. 13 (1936) 67–214. A chronological classification of mosaics, including many from Ostia, C. C. Van Essen, *Meededingen van het Nederlands hist. inst. te Rome*, 8 (1954) 64–94.

ment is patterned, and the design is almost invariably geometric. The basic shapes are simple and often repeated, the square, the star, the lozenge, the circle, the pelta, and the hexagon. What makes the pavements interesting is the combination of shapes and the building up of the design. One might have expected that in large blocks, in which the plans of individual apartments often corresponded precisely, the craftsman would have worked to a limited number of selected designs and repeated the pavements of one apartment in the next. It is clear that he approached his job in a very different spirit. In the block which contains the House of Jupiter and Ganymede, the House of the Paintings, and the House of the Infant Bacchus, twelve mosaic floors have in part survived on the ground floor; though many are composed from the same elements, they are all different.[1]

The simple designs, such as the key or meander pattern, though unexciting, are always effective. In some of the more complicated arrangements of shapes the design is lost in over-elaboration. But, as a class, these pavements compare very favourably in taste with the floor decoration of a modern middle-class home, and they were practical as well as decorative. Most of them seem to have remained in good condition with comparatively minor repairs for more than a hundred years.

In the insulae there are no figured mosaics, coloured mosaics, or marble pavements. In these respects they are very different from the houses of Pompeii. The contrast might be less striking if we could see the pavements of the Julio-Claudian independent homes at Ostia; for it is perhaps significant that in the only domus preserving pavements that are roughly contemporary with the Hadrianic insulae the pavements are not limited to geometric designs. This house, the so-called House of Apuleius, was probably built under Trajan, but it had a long life and underwent several modifications.[2] At least two periods can be seen in its pavements, and in two rooms both original and later pavements survive. The original pavements include a simple design of squares, triangles, and hexagons in a small range of coloured marbles; and a black-and-white mosaic design with a figured scene in the centre. This design is composed of rectangles, peltae, and curvilinear squares surrounding a central hexagon: in the centre was once a charioteer raising the palm of victory over his successful chariot.[3] Two other figured mosaics can be seen in the west wing of the house. One shows two sea-monsters ridden

[1] Blake, *MAAR* 13 (1936) 90; *MA* 26 (1920) 366.
[2] *NS* 1886, 163; Paschetto, 421.　　　　　　　　　　[3] Blake (1936) 88–90.

by Nereids, the other a maenad and satyr; both are later than the original construction. This house is built in a very restricted area; the pavements of the more spacious houses on the western Decumanus were probably more ambitious.

By the early second century Ostian craftsmen were familiar with laying pavements of marble and reproducing elaborate figured compositions in black-and-white mosaic. Of the marble pavements only small fragments survive. The Basilica was paved with alternating rectangular panels of Giallo Antico and Luna; the design of the Capitolium pavement, as reported in the early nineteenth century, was a simple pattern in more varied marbles of squares enclosing rhombs.[1] In the more modest examples that survive from private buildings there is the same simplicity. Only the simplest geometric forms are used, and the range of marbles is limited.

Figured compositions in mosaic are much more widely represented, and especially from the baths. The earliest large-scale composition known to us was found in a set of baths which was constructed in the middle of the first century A.D. and pulled down before the district was rebuilt at the end of Hadrian's reign.[2] The field is divided into a series of squares, with a central panel occupying the space of six squares. In this central panel are four dolphins, representing the sea. At each end of this centre-piece four squares contain representations of provinces and winds. At one end is Spain, a female head bound with a wreath of olive, for oil was the province's main export; diagonally from Spain is Sicily, represented by the triskeles. Balancing the two provinces are male winged heads. One is bearded, the other beardless; they represent winds. At the other end two similar winds are balanced by female heads representing Egypt and Africa. A crocodile's head and tail denote Egypt; the elephant's head and tusks which form her head-dress is the badge of Africa. Around these central features of the design run two rows of squares, in which a simple geometric pattern alternates with crossed shields, or shield and spear, symbolizing the fighting that won the provinces. The whole composition is framed by a meander border. There is little subtlety in the technique of this mosaic; the heads are roughly drawn, the representation of beard, hair, and other details is still crude, but the craftsman has organized a large area (13 × 9 metres) into a simple but effective composition. The pavement illustrated the

[1] Paschetto, 360.
[2] Calza, *BC* 40 (1912) 103; Blake (1930) 123 f.

trade of empire and may have been inspired by the building of the Claudian harbour.

At approximately the same time the colonnade of the Piazzale delle Corporazioni was providing ample scope for figured compositions on a smaller scale. Most of those that can now be seen date from the second century or later, but four mosaics from the lower Claudian level have been preserved. They include a Nereid on a sea-horse accompanied by two dolphins, a man crowning himself for victory over a fallen bull, and Diana with a stag.[1] But it was the great increase in the number and scale of public baths in the second century that gave the Ostian mosaicists their richest opportunity. Here were large surfaces to be decorated, and at least during the first half of the century handsome fees could be afforded. Scenes from marine life were the fashion of the day, and they provided good opportunity for invention.

The finest of Ostia's mosaics paves the floor of the Frigidarium in the Baths of Neptune.[2] In the centre Neptune is swept along by four galloping sea-horses; in his left hand is his trident, his right holds the reins loosely. His mantle is blown by the wind to form an arc over his head. Around this central group are two bands of swimming figures. The inner band is comparatively restrained and realistic, composed of human figures, cupids riding dolphins, and very plausible fish. In the outer band, fantastic sea-monsters and Nereids in undulating coils prance gaily through the sea.

This is an extremely effective composition, and however much he may have owed to a model in a copybook, the craftsman has imposed his own individuality on the work. His most striking success is to have filled in such a large composition with so many figures without a sense of crowding or monotony, and to have infused the whole with such a sense of movement and high spirits. The interest extends to detail. Rarely do mosaicists show such concern for the anatomy of their sea-monsters, and in his particular formula for expressing the transition from front to hind part of his hybrid creatures he seems to have left his individual mark.[3] It recurs in the mosaic in the next room of these baths, a quieter composition, and less fully preserved. Amphitrite rides a sea-horse through the waves, preceded by Hymen and accompanied by sea-monsters, some of whom make music for the approaching

[1] *NS* 1914, 72, 98; Blake (1930) 101.
[2] Calza, *Boll. D'arte*, 6 (1912) 199; Blake (1936) 145; Wirth, 144 (with Taf. 35).
[3] I am grateful to Professor A. D. Trendall, to whom this observation is due.

marriage. The coiling monsters are unmistakably from the same work-shop as the Neptune mosaic.

These mosaics have been dated to the mature Antonine period, and their style has been thought to reflect particularly well the spirit of that age.[1] But the baths in which they were laid were virtually completed by the end of Hadrian's principate,[2] and it is reasonable to regard the mosaics as contemporary with the building. Some slight support for this earlier date may be found perhaps in a mosaic from the Baths of Buticosus. This mosaic is now half hidden by a hot bath built when the function of the room was changed in a reconstruction; but the marine monsters that figure in the design strongly resemble those of Neptune's Baths and repeat the individualistic formula for expressing the joining of two different forms. The Baths of Buticosus were built under Trajan[3] and their decoration may be an earlier work of the Neptune mosaicist.

Scenes taken from marine life are also found in the Severan Baths on the line of the Sullan walls south-west of Porta Marina.[4] The best pre-served shows in the centre a head of Oceanus; at each of the four angles is a triton blowing a horn and holding an oar in the other hand. The design is neat and balanced, but lifeless. There is a similar dullness in the heated rooms of the Baths of the Seven Sages. More interesting is the mosaic that paves the circular room in the latter baths, the so-called hunter's mosaic.[5] It depicts a series of hunters and wild animals, and the field is divided up by acanthus scrolls. The scale of the figures is small, producing an effect of crowding, and the scrolls, following an undeviat-ing pattern, become monotonous. On grounds of style the mosaic has been attributed to the Severan period, but the present structure of the room is Hadrianic: unless another pavement is found underneath, this mosaic should logically be attributed to the period of Hadrian.

The figured mosaics so far considered were designed primarily as decoration. The main purpose of others is to tell a story. The scene on the pavement of the vestibule of the chapel in the Barracks of the Vigiles depicts the sacrifice of the bull, the central element in the im-perial cult.[6] The mosaic is divided into three scenes. In the centre, the bull has been brought in. He awaits the executioner's blow but struggles

---

[1] Wirth, 144, followed by Doro Levi, *Antioch Mosaic Pavements*, 530.

[2] p. 409.　　　　　　　　　　　　　[3] Bloch, *Topografia*, 218 (Reg. i. 14. 8).

[4] Paschetto, 304; Blake (1936) 146 (but her Antonine dating should be changed to Severan, p. 419).　　　　　　　　　　[5] Phot. *Ostia*, 86, fig. 35.

[6] Carcopino, *Mélanges*, 27 (1907) 227; Blake (1936) 166. For the more common representation of this scene, O. Brendel, *RM* 45 (1930) 196.

to escape. Behind him, with stick upraised, is the man who has led him in, and the executioner, with long-handled axe ready to strike. To the right is a lighted altar, and to the right of the altar a flute-player in the background; in the foreground is the officiating priest. The two scenes on left and right balance one another; they show the bull stretched out dead, and a man with axe raised preparing to cut up the sacrificial meat. The drawing of the figures is rough, but the total effect is impressive. There is a nice balance in the design and a fine contrast between the struggling bull of the centre and the dead bull of the side scenes. The date of the barracks is late Hadrianic, but the mosaic is part of a later modification.[1] Somewhat later, probably from the Severan period, is the mosaic of the hall of the corn measurers. In a central panel their measuring trade is depicted; but the figures are crowded and the scene somewhat lifeless. The series of mosaics from the Piazzale delle Corporazioni are less concerned with the composition of the design than in setting out the business of the traders they represent; but the ships which are the dominant theme in most of the scenes are drawn with considerable care and skill. There is no doubt that even if we consider only such work as this or the average product on the floors of insulae, shops, and smaller baths, the mosaicist made much better use of his medium than the painter.

How soon and how widely coloured mosaics were used in Ostian pavements is still uncertain, owing to the absence of adequate material from the first century. Some coloured tesserae were used in one of the mosaics from the Claudian level in the Piazzale delle Corporazioni,[2] but the first mature example that survives probably dates from the reign of Antoninus Pius. It was laid in a small shrine on the north side of the Decumanus near the Porta Romana. The shrine is divided into a vestibule and main room. In the first a simple geometric pattern is used; the main room is covered with interlacing ribbon-like scrolls. The colours used are soft tones of red, yellow, green, black, white.[3] Roughly contemporary is the finest of the series known to us. It was discovered by Visconti in the middle of the last century in the baths of the so-called 'Imperial Palace' and preserved for the Pope. The mosaic was carefully lifted, brought to Rome in thirty journeys, restored, and relaid in the

---

[1] The vestibule itself is not original. It was carved out of the portico by two side framing walls, probably Commodan.

[2] *NS* 1914, 99.
[3] Blake (1936) 126.

Hall of the Immaculate Conception in the Vatican galleries, where it can still be seen.[1] The border is modern, the size of the mosaic has been considerably reduced to fit the room (from 18 × 13·37 metres to 14·50 × 8·40 metres), and the surface has been in places heavily worn by visitors. But even now one can understand Visconti's enthusiasm. The basis of the design is provided by rows of large squares and rectangles framed by borders of two-strand guilloche. The scale and the interlace patterns of the squares contrast with naturalistic patterns in the rectangles. Colour and design blend well, and Visconti's comparison with an oriental carpet is apt.

In another room in the Vatican an Ostian mosaic combines coloured panels with a black-and-white field. In the centre is a charming scene showing two birds pecking at a basket of flowers. This central square is flanked on each side by a small square containing a simple rosette. These coloured squares are set against a black-and-white background in which a grape-vine curls gracefully over the field.[2] Coloured mosaics were also occasionally used to decorate walls. The simple acanthus scrolls on the piers and vaulting of a small room in the Baths of the Seven Sages probably date from Hadrian's reign;[3] rather later in the century is the brightly coloured Silvanus which was found lining a niche near the Mithraeum in the 'Imperial Palace' and removed to the Lateran Museum.[4]

For the second and early third centuries we have a wide range of pavements from private and public buildings. In the late Empire no bath or temple pavements survive, and in private buildings our evidence is confined to the domus. In such insulae as were still occupied it seems that the old pavements were crudely restored; only where a domus was carved out of an insula, as in the House of the Dioscuri, were the pavements renewed. From the late houses we can get a clear impression of the fashions of the wealthy in the fourth century. What we cannot yet fully know is how far the fashions reflected in their pavements differed from those of the wealthy classes of the two preceding centuries.

The dominance of marble pavements is probably a new development. They were certainly used earlier, as in the House of Apuleius,

---

[1] B. Nogara, *I mosaici antichi conservati nei palazzi pont. del Vaticano e del Laterano* (Milano, 1910) 33; Blake (1936) 125.

[2] Nogara, op. cit. 33 (who suggests that two mosaics may be combined); Blake (1936) 130.   [3] Doro Levi, *Antioch Mosaic Pavements*, 498.

[4] Nogara, 32; Becatti, *Mitrei*, 56 f.

but the fact that in that house an *opus sectile* pavement was succeeded, probably in the second century, in the same room by a black-and-white mosaic suggests that they were less widespread than later. In the fourth century *opus sectile* is normally applied in the main living-room of the house. This emphasis on marble pavements thus corresponds to the popularity of marble dadoes on walls and painted panels imitating marble, which seem to be a late development. The designs of these *opus sectile* pavements are more elaborate than those of the early Empire; rectangular shapes, particularly squares, triangles, and hexagons, have been largely replaced by circles, curving lines, and rosettes; also the range of marbles used is wider.

Black-and-white mosaic geometric designs are still used, particularly in rooms of secondary importance, but their design is normally more complex than in the Hadrianic insulae. Such motifs as Solomon's knot and the Greek Cross are not uncommon, and, consistent with the fashion in architecture, curvilinear patterns tend to replace the square, hexagon, and triangle of the earlier period. Coloured mosaics also appear in the fourth-century houses, both unfigured and figured. It is perhaps socially significant that the only parallel in the fourth century to the impressive black-and-white figured compositions from the public baths of the second century are found in two large mosaics in colour from private houses. One, in the largest room of the House of the Dioscuri, represents Nereids on sea-monsters and shows in the centre Venus at her toilet in a setting of sea-shells.[1] There is a calm resignation about the sea-monsters that contrasts strongly with the liveliness of second-century work, and there is little unity in the design, but the total effect is not unpleasing. The other has been only in part preserved: it was found in the bath wing of a suburban villa and has now been set up on the garden wall of the House of the Paintings. It depicts in a series of panels the months of the year, of which only March and April survive.[2]

Ostia's mosaics do not rival, in quality and range, those of Antioch or of the wealthiest towns of Africa and Gaul; but there is at least one masterpiece among them, and the general standard of taste and execution is higher than we might expect in a town concerned primarily with trade and commerce.

Neither literature nor inscriptions tell us anything of the social status

---

[1] Becatti, *Case tarde*, 36, figs. 42–45.   [2] *Arch. Anz.* 51 (1936) 460.

or national origin of Ostia's sculptors, painters, and mosaicists. We should think of them as craftsmen rather than artists, normally working in small premises on street fronts, similar to those of the shoemakers and jewellers, mixing freely with traders and shopkeepers. Theirs was not a luxury trade. Even the meanest household had its walls painted, and the demand for mosaics reached at least to the lower middle classes. Only wealthy homes could afford sculpture, but the people expected to see statues in their public places and their public buildings; it was the tradition of public life that the governing class should meet the need.

During the great rebuilding of Ostia in the second century painters and mosaicists must have been hard pressed to find enough assistants to meet the rush of work in the new apartment blocks. At the same time new public buildings and the headquarters of the more prosperous guilds provided opportunities for the decorators and sculptors such as they had never known before. But the depression of the third century fell no less heavily on them than on those whose living depended more directly on the flow of trade. Through the fourth century there was a brisker demand for work of good quality in the houses of the rich; the unpretentious decorator, who had once done a thriving business in the insulae, must have had a much leaner time.

18

THE CEMETERIES

WHEN Juvenal announces his intention to attack the dead he describes his victims as men 'whose ashes lie buried by the Flaminian and Latin roads'. A law of the twelve tables forbade burial or cremation within the city, but the strong desire to be remembered after death required a place for the tomb where it could be easily seen and easily visited. Roman custom was followed in Roman colonies and municipalities; most of their cemeteries are on or near roads.

At Ostia tombs were built along more than seven miles of road. Along the Via Ostiensis they reached eastward as far as Acilia and a little beyond; south of the town they lined long stretches of the five roads that crossed the Piana Bella. At Portus the two main cemeteries were associated with the roads that led to Rome and to Ostia. Inscriptions, sarcophagi, and sculptures have been taken over a long period from tombs in widely dispersed areas, but the early excavators left no record of the tombs themselves. Only two small compact areas have been systematically excavated at Ostia, on the Via Ostiensis immediately outside the Porta Romana,[1] and along a short stretch of the continuation of the Cardo Maximus towards Laurentine territory, some 200 metres outside the walls;[2] at Portus a larger section of a cemetery has been excavated on Isola Sacra by the road that links the imperial harbours with Ostia.[3]

These three areas between them cover a long period from the end of the Republic to the fourth century A.D., and reflect the changing customs of the middle class; but among the tombs that have been excavated none belonged to the most distinguished layer of society. The Laurentine and Isola Sacra cemeteries were primarily used by small traders and craftsmen; in neither are the tombs of any magistrates or even councillors found. The tombs outside the Porta Romana represent

---

[1] Paschetto, 441–61. The evidence re-examined, M. F. Squarciapino, *Scavi di Ostia*, iii (1) 11–60.

[2] Paschetto, 461–77; Calza, *NS* 1938, 26–74; *Scavi di Ostia*, iii (1) 62–127.

[3] Calza, *La Necropoli del Porto di Roma nell' Isola Sacra* (1940).

a rather higher social level. The inscriptions include records of knights and a few magistrates, but no men of distinction are among them. It was probably more fashionable to build the tomb farther from the town. The finest sarcophagus from Ostian territory was found at Acilia, some three miles to the east.[1] It was also at Acilia that a relief showing six consular *fasces* was found; it probably came from an Ostian consul's tomb of the early Empire.[2] The area to the south near La Toretta also proved a happy hunting-ground for elaborate sarcophagi in the early nineteenth century.[3]

One of the most striking features of the cemeteries that we can now see is the apparent absence of public control in their development. On Isola Sacra we should expect the earliest tombs to be concentrated near to the canal, and then a systematic extension of the cemetery towards Ostia; but it is clear that some of the earlier tombs were built at least a quarter of a mile from the canal.[4] Small groups of tombs follow a common alignment, but there are too many variant alignments to be reduced to a rational plan.[5] Tombs 88 and 90 follow a building line already established, but, unlike the others in their row, which have their entrance from the front, these two tombs are entered at the side, and between them was left an open space. This space the owners had presumably bought, for later a new tomb was built here by permission of their heirs.[6] The Laurentine cemetery is a little more orderly but it does not suggest a development plan.

The earliest burials so far discovered were found outside the Porta Romana at the level of the sand, but all had been disturbed when later tombs were built over them, and it is impossible to form a clear picture from the evidence that has been recorded.[7] It seems that normally the ashes were placed in an urn which was laid in the ground, together with a few personal belongings of the dead. In one case certainly, and possibly in others, ashes and belongings were contained in a wooden

[1] *Boll. d'arte*, 39 (1954) 200.

[2] Fea, *Viaggio*, 10. Now in the cloisters of St. Paul's basilica. Dated to the first half of the first century A.D. by A. M. Colini, *Il Fascio littorio di Roma* (1933) 84 f. Perhaps from the tomb of T. Sextius Africanus, Ostian consul of A.D. 59.

[3] Paschetto, 477–81.

[4] The Vatican cemetery provides an interesting parallel, J. Toynbee and J. Ward Perkins, *The Shrine of St. Peter*, 30.

[5] Thylander (*Étude sur l'épigraphie latine*, 27–37) explains the difference in alignments by changes in the road system, but some lines (particularly tombs 10 and 11) would still be unexplained.   [6] Thylander, A 180; Calza, *Necropoli*, 350.

[7] *NS* 1911, 83, 448; 1912, 95, 202, 239, 274; *Scavi di Ostia*, iii (1), 11–20.

coffin decorated with applied reliefs in bone.[1] No inscriptions were found to mark those early burials, nor even tufa markers, but the names of the dead might have been recorded on wood. There is no evidence for inhumation as distinct from cremation, but the sample is too small to exclude the possibility. The evidence for dating is inadequate, but a Boeotian coin gives a *terminus post quem* of the early second century B.C. for one burial,[2] and the general description of the pottery and other associated objects is consistent with a second-century dating of the series. These tombs precede the Sullan walls, but are considerably later than the establishment of the Castrum in the fourth century.

We come to firmer ground towards the end of the Republic. The tombs of the Laurentine cemetery are well enough preserved to allow general conclusions, and the style of construction, together with the lettering of inscriptions, provides a reliable basis for dating the earliest of the tombs to the principate of Augustus or perhaps a little earlier. When the Laurentine tombs had been examined it became clear that the contemporary tombs outside the Porta Romana, which were much less well preserved owing to the more intensive building history of the area, were being built in the same style.

In the early Augustan period two main types of tomb are found and both are already well established. The simpler takes the form of a plain rectangular enclosure with plain reticulate walls some 2 metres high. In this enclosure the body was normally burnt, recalling Festus' definition: 'bustum proprie dicitur locus, in quo mortuus est combustus et sepultus . . . ubi vero combustus quis tantummodo, alibi vero est sepultus, is locus ab urendo ustrina vocatur'.[3] The ashes were then collected in an urn and the urn was sunk in the ground, usually in the corner or against a wall of the enclosure. There was no entrance to the enclosure and one assumes that ladders were used.

The second type differs from the first in having a massive monument, normally rectangular, in the face of the enclosure.[4] Those who could afford it used travertine, at least for the façade; the cheaper alternative was tufa. Of these monuments only the lowest courses, in plain *opus quadratum*, survive. How they were finished we do not know, but Pompeian examples offer possible parallels. The public tomb of C. Cartilius Poplicola outside the Porta Marina conforms to this type; one contemporary tomb has a different character. Instead of a solid

[1] *NS* 1911, 83; 1912, 95.
[2] *NS* 1911, 448.
[3] Festus (Lindsay), 29.
[4] Fig. 31, p. 458; Pl. XXXII *a*.

rectangular monument in the face of the enclosure there was in the centre some form of light structure supported on columns; within it were found a number of urns containing ashes.[1]

The ownership of a tomb is indicated by an inscribed travertine panel or cippus inserted in the wall. The inscriptions are extremely simple. They specify, as tombstones continue to do later, the precise area covered in frontage and depth, and they give the names of those by whom and for whom the tomb is built. In marked contrast with later practice, the

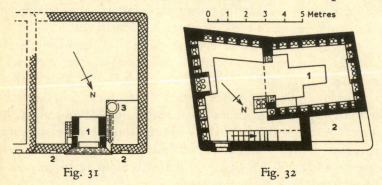

Fig. 31   Fig. 32

FIG. 31. Augustan tomb. 1. Tufa monument in reticulate façade (Pl. XXXII *a*). 2. Inscribed cippi, embedded in wall. 3. Well.

FIG. 32. Early Julio–Claudian columbarium (Pl. XXXII *b*). 1. Triclinium. 2. Ustrina.

owners seem to be concerned only with the immediately foreseeable future. The individuals for whom the tomb is intended are listed and there is no indication in the text that the tomb will receive other burials after their death. But in two cases it is laid down that the tomb shall not pass to the heir;[2] we assume that normally it remained the burial place of the family or passed with the rest of the dead man's property to his heir. In only one Augustan inscription is provision explicitly made for a man's freedmen and freedwomen.[3] Later *libertis libertabusque suis posterisque eorum* became a standard formula ensuring a long continuity of occupation. It is not surprising that several Augustan tombs were built over at a higher level before the end of the Julio-Claudian period.

Before Augustus died a new type of tomb, found considerably earlier at Rome, was emerging at Ostia, the so-called columbarium.[4] The

[1] Tomb 23, *NS* 1938, 39.   [2] *NS* 1938, 63 (n. 23), 64 (n. 24).
[3] *NS* 1938, 62 (n. 22).

[4] Pl. XXXII *b*. Tomb 18 in the Laurentine cemetery, one of the earliest columbaria, may be dated to the Augustan period by the specially fine quality of its stuccoes and the style of its reticulate facing, *NS* 1938, 56.

central feature is a rectangular barrel-vaulted tomb chamber. The urns containing the ashes of the dead are no longer placed in the ground but in niches built in the wall. Some tombs have open enclosures added to them, whose walls are also lined with niches, and occasionally narrow stairs lead to an upper room. In the early stages of development of the type a small area is sometimes walled off in the corner of the outer enclosure for the burning of the body as in the previous period;[1] but this custom soon died out. By the Flavian period, and probably earlier, the bodies of the dead were always cremated in public *ustrinae*, a more economic and probably more efficient system.

The columbarium remained the dominant type of family tomb for more than a century. Early examples, such as the tomb of the Claudii,[2] can be seen in the Laurentine cemetery and outside the Porta Romana, but a more comprehensive impression of the type can be derived from the Trajanic and Hadrianic tombs of the Isola Sacra cemetery. The columbaria reflect the rising standards of the middle class; and the clearest signs of the growing prosperity are the general replacement of travertine by marble for funerary inscriptions and the refinement of the construction and decoration of the tomb.

In contrast with the plain severity of earlier tombs, the columbaria were rich in decoration within and without. The inner wall faces were usually finished crudely, for they were to be plastered; the side and back walls received no emphasis, for they were inconspicuous; but the tomb face was intended to impress the passer-by. In the reticulate period the work was carefully finished; when fired bricks came into general use specially thin bricks were usually selected, deep pink or sometimes yellow, and the layer of mortar between rows and between joints was reduced to a minimum, providing a much more elegant surface than in contemporary insulae. Sometimes pilasters were added to the face in a contrasting colour, red pilasters against a yellow brick wall, or yellow against red.[3] While most tombs followed the current building style of reticulate or brick, or a combination of both, others were more original. In one tomb outside the Porta Romana variety was given to the reticulate surface by alternating rows of tufa and *selce* blocks. A stranger experiment was made in one of the Isola Sacra tombs, in which *opus spicatum*, a herring-bone pattern of bricks, normally reserved for floors, was used for the walls.[4]

---

[1] *NS* 1938, 42, fig. 15.
[2] Fig. 32, Pl. xxxii b.
[3] Calza, *Necropoli*, 76, fig. 26.
[4] Ibid. 83, fig. 31.

The door of the tomb chamber, much lower than a house door, was framed by massive travertine imposts surmounted by a simply moulded lintel. Above was inset the inscription providing the title-deed for the tomb. This inscription was made an effective element in the general design by its decorative framing cornice, in which pumice, tufa, and brick were often used to provide contrasts of texture and colour in a rich variety of patterns.[1] Many tombs also had terra-cotta tablets inserted in their walls, illustrating the owner's trade. Above was a plain entablature surmounted by a pediment usually triangular but sometimes curved.[2]

The tomb chamber was dimly lit by slit-windows, but the interior was elaborately decorated. Rows of niches, each normally containing two urns, were built into the wall and formed the basis of the general design. Special emphasis was given to the central niches, which were larger and more ambitiously decorated; semicircular and rectangular niches were co-ordinated in a comprehensive pattern. The surface of walls, niches, and ceiling offered wide scope for the painters. The larger niches were filled with individual figures or mythological scenes; in the smaller niches floral, animal, or geometric decoration predominates. In many of the tombs stucco was combined with paint. The central niches, sometimes others also, were framed by fluted pilasters, more rarely columns, and stucco shells were widely used to line the semi-domes. Stucco mouldings divided the ceiling into panels of varied shape, which were filled with further paintings. Most tomb floors were paved with mosaic and in a small minority sculpture was added.

The ashes of the dead were normally placed in a plain urn already embedded in a niche, but those who could afford it preferred a more individual memorial. For them decorated marble coffers, or funerary altars, inscribed with their names and epitaph, were used. A similar distinction is seen later, when cremation gives place to burial, between the marble sarcophagus and the simple recess in the wall or grave in the floor.

Columbaria differed considerably in size and capacity, but many of them contained more than a hundred urns, anticipating long-continued use. When all the niches were filled, an enclosure could be added to the front of the tomb, providing new walls for niches, or, in rarer cases, another row of niches could be made in the tomb chamber itself at the expense of the general design. It was the responsibility of the family

---

[1] Calza, *Necropoli* 89, fig. 37.   [2] Pl. XXXIII *a*.

to maintain the tomb and pay due rites to the dead. The funeral was followed by a banquet at the tomb and birthday anniversaries were similarly celebrated. Regular libations also had to be made. In some tomb chambers permanent *triclinia* are found;[1] others have *biclinia* on either side of the entrance. A few ovens survive, in which meals were prepared. Wells are much more widespread; the water was needed not merely for meals but for keeping the tomb clean.

The inscriptions of the earliest columbaria in the Laurentine cemetery preserve the same simple form as those of the enclosures that preceded them. By the second century many of them have become more elaborate. The addition of the standard formula *libertis libertabusque suis posterisque eorum* on most tombs is an indication that most of the middle class, even among the small traders and craftsmen of the imperial harbours, have slaves in their household who will probably receive their freedom early. There is also a widespread anxiety that the integrity of the tomb should be preserved and that it should not pass out of the family. This is expressed in its simplest form by the letters *h(oc) m(onumentum) h(eredem) e(xternum) n(on) s(equetur)*, 'This tomb shall not pass to an heir who is not of the family.' But many preferred to be more explicit.

Marcus Antonius Vitalis and Marcus Antonius Verus his son built this tomb for themselves, their freedmen, freedwomen, and their descendants. But if, after the death of M. Antonius Vitalis, anyone should sell or give or in any other way alienate this tomb, or if anyone introduces the body or bones of anyone with a name other than is contained in this inscription, then as penalty he shall pay for each body 3,000 sesterces to the worshippers of the Lares of Portus Augusti.[2]

The penalty prescribed was usually stiffer.

L. Cocceius Adiutor made this provision for himself and declares that no one should burn or bury any body on the left side as you enter this tomb. If he does so he shall pay 50,000 sesterces to the Ostian government; the informer shall receive the fourth part.[3]

At Ostia the fine was normally to be paid to the Ostian treasury, at Portus to the public treasury of Rome.[4]

---

[1] Fig. 32.   [2] Thylander, A 19.   [3] 850.

[4] Ostia, e.g. 166, 307, 850; Portus, Thylander, A 245, 328, B 210. The distinction between the two centres is embarrassing. One would have expected Portus fines also to go to the Ostian treasury, since the harbour settlement seems to have been controlled by the Ostian government (p. 62). 166 is unique in prescribing fines to be paid both to the Ostian and to the Roman treasury.

Not all were so exclusive. In the Isola Sacra cemetery Valeria Trophime had a large tomb with an attached enclosure.[1] Within the enclosure four separate little tomb chambers were later built. 'C. Galgestius Helius, having bought the ground, not yet used, from Valeria Trophime, built for himself and his descendants a tomb chamber joined to the wall on the right side as you enter, in which are fourteen urns.'[2] The urn-filled niches can still be seen. The other three small tombs were similarly built on ground bought from Valeria Trophime in the enclosure.

Tombs were also sometimes divided after they had been built, to secure family independence. Tomb 75 in the Isola Sacra cemetery is a large tomb, combining chamber and enclosure, with a frontage and depth of 40 Roman feet. The inscription over the entrance records that it was built by M. Cocceius Daphnus for himself, his dependants, his freedmen, freedwomen, and their descendants, and also for M. Antonius Agathias and M. Ulpius Donatus with their dependants and freedmen.[3] A second inscription set in the face of the enclosure shows that one of the beneficiaries preferred to be independent. 'M. Antonius Agathias built for himself, his freedmen, freedwomen, and their descendants a tomb from the monument of M. Cocceius Daphnus whose heir he is, having made a division between himself and his coheirs, adding himself a dividing wall and an independent entry.'[4] There were originally two tomb chambers, of which Agathias took one. He divided the enclosure by a new wall and added a new doorway in the face of the enclosure to allow independent access. His inscription was set in the wall above his new entrance.

The expenses of a tomb could also be shared. M'. Acilius Marianus and Cognita Optata both made provision for their dependants in the same tomb. Their inscriptions are set out side by side on the same tablet and underneath each is the reciprocal record: 'this tomb is shared with Cognita Optata', 'this tomb is shared with M'. Acilius Marianus'.[5] An Isola Sacra inscription records a similar partnership. L. Domitius Callistion and Domitia Eutychia shared their tomb with M. Ulpius Artemidorus, *p(ro) p(arte) dimidia recepti in soccietate ab Ulpio Artemidoro*.[6]

It was also possible to secure niches or graves within the tombs of others. 'Primitivianus and Volusia his parents made this provision for

[1] Calza, *Necropoli*, 359–61.   [2] Thylander, A 124.
[3] Ibid. 83.   [4] Ibid 16.
[5] S 4761, cf. S 5176.   [6] Thylander, A 253.

L. Kacius Volusianus, who lived 19 years, 1 month, 26 days; the place was granted to them by A. Gabinius Adiectus, best of friends.'[1] 'M. Cascellius Diadumenus provided 3 niches and 6 urns for himself, for Cacia Euhodia, his wife, and their descendants.'[2] Presumably Diadumenus acquired the right to use a limited number of urns in a friend's tomb. Another inscription from the same tomb records that Cacia Euhodia, his wife, gave one of the niches with its two urns to Herennuleia Primilla.[3] Graves for burial could later be acquired in the same way: 'Flavia Marcellina provided this grave for Flavia Hilaritas, her well-deserving sister, on the right side as you enter the tomb. It was granted to her by A. Plotius Hermes and Valeria Saturnina.'[4]

The inscriptions set up over tomb entrances are almost always a plain statement concerning the dispositions of the tomb. Within the tomb individuals were commemorated in more varied style. The majority of the epitaphs record only names, relationships, and, in many cases, the age at death; but there is a tendency in the second century for the language to become less restrained, particularly in what we may loosely call the lower middle class. The records of the aristocracy are almost invariably confined to a list of offices held. Sentimental superlatives, 'dulcissimus', 'pientissimus', 'dignissimus', 'sanctissimus', are not uncommon lower down the social scale, and most of the verse epitaphs that survive come from the same class. One of them laments a recruit to the army from Carthage who died young;[5] another tells the sad story of a small child run over by a cart;[6] two commemorate flamboyantly men who, without holding office, have enjoyed the good things of life.[7] Metre and grammar have proved too much for most of these amateur poets; two of them are virtually illiterate.[8]

The columbarium was the dominant form of family tomb, but in both the Laurentine and Isola Sacra cemeteries more modest tombs can be seen, built for individuals or small groups. The commonest type is the *tomba a cassone*, shaped like a chest;[9] others take the form of an *aedicula* or a pedimented pillar.[10] The monument of C. Annaeus Atticus from Gallic Aquitania was a small brick pyramid.[11] Some imperial slaves were sufficiently important to have their own tombs, but no provision was made for slaves in the family tomb. Their burials are

---

[1] 705.   [2] 777.   [3] 1106.   [4] 1051
[5] Thylander, A 125.   [6] 1808.   [7] 480, 914.
[8] 510 = Thylander, A 3, S 5186.   [9] Calza, *Necropoli*, 78, fig. 29.
[10] Ibid. 79, fig. 30.   [11] Thylander, A 13 (tomb I); Calza, op. cit. 285 f.

marked in the Isola Sacra cemetery by amphora necks projecting from the ground.[1] The ashes were buried and over them was placed the neck of an amphora through which libations could be poured to the dead. Such burials were not confined to slaves, but it is doubtful whether in Ostia and Portus there were many free men who could not afford some modest memorial.

Cremation remained the general practice at Ostia until the reign of Hadrian, when burial is introduced. The two rites continue side by side through the remainder of the second century with the emphasis gradually moving to burial. By the early third century no provision seems to be made in new tombs for cremation. It is difficult to find an adequate explanation for this change in custom.[2] It comes too early to reflect the influence of Christianity. It does not seem to derive from the oriental cults, for their devotees had for a long period been accustomed to cremation. The view that it represents a spiritual respect for the human body[3] finds no echo in contemporary literature nor in the language of funerary inscriptions. It has been suggested that it was the appeal to the rich of the sarcophagus, with its scope for elaborate decoration, that was responsible,[4] but rich men could find ample scope for ostentatious display before cremation was abandoned. Logically we are driven to the conclusion that it was a change in fashion and feeling.

One of the first persons known to have adopted the new fashion at Rome was Domitian's secretary Abascantus, and we owe our knowledge to the facile hexameters of Statius. When his wife Priscilla died, Abascantus embalmed her body with costly unguents. Had the motive been religious or deeply spiritual Statius would have developed the theme at length. His words suggest that Abascantus rejected cremation because it was too crude, and the accompanying scene too emotional.

> nec enim fumantia busta
> clamoremque rogi potuit perferre.[5]

[1] Calza, *Necropoli*, 80, 46 (fig. 10).

[2] The main explanations that have been offered are convincingly refuted, in a detailed review of the evidence, by A. D. Nock, 'Cremation and Burial in the Roman Empire', *Harv. Theol. Rev.* 25 (1932) 321–61.

[3] Toynbee and Ward Perkins, op. cit. 113: 'The change of rite may well have expressed a vague, perhaps, but deepening intuition of the human body's meaning and purpose *sub specie aeternitatis*, which the Christian doctrines of the Incarnation and Resurrection of the Body were to clinch and clarify.' I should like to believe this, but can find no support for it in the Ostian evidence.

[4] Nock, op. cit. 358. See also Addenda.

[5] Statius, *Silvae*, v. 1. 226.

The wish to preserve rather than destroy the body is also implied,[1] but it is not associated with Priscilla's destiny in an after life.

The change in custom affects tomb design. At first there is little modification in the form of the columbarium. Decorated niches are still the dominant element, but recesses in the walls are added at floor level for burials. As the century advances niches are replaced by recesses in some of the older columbaria, and in new tombs the proportion of recesses to niches increases; by the early third century the transition seems to be complete. The latest of the Isola Sacra tombs, on the west side of the Roman road, and the tombs on the south side of the Via dei Sepolcri outside the Porta Romana at Ostia are designed exclusively for burials. Recesses take the place of niches in tomb chambers. At first they had been confined to floor level; now they occupy the whole height of the wall. But they are uneconomic in space, and to provide accommodation on the scale of the columbaria full use has to be made of the floor area. In a tomb on the Via dei Sepolcri the whole area of the floor is divided by brick walls into a series of graves. When these were filled another row could be built on top. An inscription from Isola Sacra records the practice: 'A. Plautius Primitibus and Iunia Hieronis, having bought the ground from the two Tiberii Iulii, Zoticus and Aetetus, heirs of Julius Prosdocimus, have made two burial places, one above the other, for themselves and for Plautius Mascellio their sweetest son, who lived 3 years 4 months, 20 days.'[2]

The change in the form of the tomb led naturally to a change in the style of decoration. The figures and scenes that were well adapted to the niches of the columbarium did not suit the long recesses which were the dominant element in the new tombs. Their place was taken by scenes of hunting, water fowl with cupids,[3] and other frieze-like compositions.

The form of burial was dictated primarily by cost. Those who could afford it were laid in marble sarcophagi ranging in elaboration from a simple strigilated pattern to finely detailed mythological scenes. Much more widespread was the use of a plain terra-cotta sarcophagus. In both it is interesting to note that a head-rest was provided so that the dead could lie comfortably, and in one sarcophagus found at Ostia a glass panel was found in the lid over the position where the head would

---

[1] Ibid. 228: 'nil longior aetas | carpere, nil aevi poterunt vitiare labores: | sic cautum membris, tantas venerabile marmor | spirat opes'.

[2] Thylander, A 198.

[3] Pl. xxxv *b*.

rest,[1] perhaps for the benefit of the dead rather than the living. But the majority were laid in recesses in the wall or in graves in the floor. Recesses were sealed after burial either by a rough wall, sometimes plastered to imitate a sarcophagus, or by a marble slab, plain or decorated. Graves were sometimes covered with a mosaic or marble slab, but most of them merely with earth.

In the limited areas that have been excavated there seem to be no new tombs after the middle of the third century, and it is significant of the leaner economy of the times that many of the older Isola Sacra tombs should be reused for late burials. By this time it is probable that the families for whom the tombs had been originally built had died out; it was cheaper to readapt than to build anew. Even more significant is the wholesale pillaging of tombs which is characteristic of the fourth century and may begin earlier. A large proportion of the funerary inscriptions found at Ostia have been recovered from the floors of public baths and private houses; nor had the new users always the modesty to hide the inscribed face.

No Christian cemetery has been systematically excavated, but the majority of Christian inscriptions from Ostia were found in the region of the little church of S. Ercolano,[2] and at Portus there were Christian burials near Capo Due Rami.[3] From the little evidence that is available it seems that the form of their tombs followed contemporary pagan fashion, but the language of their epitaphs is very different. There is a striking contrast between the fulsome language of many of the second-century pagans and the simple formulas of these Christian inscriptions, showing a calm confidence in death and a submission to God's will. 'Caelius sleeps here. Decria will join him when God wills.'[4]

While the attitude of Christians to death is clear from their inscriptions as well as their literature, it is much more difficult to understand the feelings of Ostian pagans, even in the imperial period. How many of them felt that death would lead to a better existence or even to an intelligible existence at all? We might expect to find the answer in their epitaphs and in the decoration of their tombs.

In this inquiry the inscriptions are extremely disappointing. One, recording an easterner, points clearly to a Pythagorean conception of

[1] Information kindly supplied by Signora Calza.
[2] Paschetto, 482.
[3] De Rossi, *Bull. arch. crist.* (1866) 47.
[4] 1893. Christian formulas, p. 394.

the after-life.[1] The dead youth 'has left men and the wickedness of men and has found in exchange a place in heaven', where he will appear in the starry firmament. But this is an isolated example. The idea that death is a release, however, lies behind a mosaic in front of an Isola Sacra tomb. The design shows two ships and between them the Claudian lighthouse. Below is inscribed in Greek ὧδε παυσίλυπος, 'So end all cares'.[2] Death means leaving the storms of life for a safe refuge. The same basic idea is expressed in an Ostian epitaph, which has many parallels elsewhere: 'securitati aeternae A. Egrili Thalli.'[3] There is no evidence that this attitude is widely shared.

One verse epitaph, which is barely intelligible, suggests that a virtuous life removes the fear of such punishment as afflicted Tantalus, Sisyphus, and Ixion,[4] but the idea is conventional and negative. Nor can we attach any profound feeling to the Greek epitaph of a doctor: 'Master of all wisdom here I lie. Say not that good men die.'[5] Very few inscriptions indeed throw any light on the questions that interest us here. The great majority record nothing but names, ages, and relationships. The rest, with very few exceptions, record the affection of husbands and wives, of parents and children; they catalogue the virtues of the dead, and they lament the sadness of early death; but they give no hint of what follows death. The traditional formula 'D(is) M(anibus)' continues to preface every epitaph; it had become a mere convention.

Our other main source of evidence is the decoration of the tombs, and here the main difficulty lies not in finding evidence but in interpreting it. The sample, however, is a very small one. The Isola Sacra tombs are the only ones in which we can study the decoration as a whole. Individual paintings have been found in the Laurentine cemetery, but the interpretation of a painting may depend on the other paintings with which it is associated. By the time that the Isola Sacra tombs were built tomb painting had developed a traditional symbolic repertoire. The peacock was a symbol of immortality; birds, and particularly doves, represented the souls of the dead; and roses evoked the gardens of the blessed. These motifs were all fully exploited, but their treatment is

[1] M. Guarducci, 'Tracce di pitagorismo nelle iscrizioni Ostiensi', *Rend. Pont.* 23–24 (1947–9) 214. Two other inscriptions which Prof. Guarducci interprets in a Pythagorean sense can be explained more naturally otherwise, A. Barigazzi, *Cretica Chronika*, 7 (1953) 97–109.

[2] Calza, *Necropoli*, 169. [3] 949. [4] 510.

[5] *IG* xiv. 942.   Ε—5 εἰητὴρ ὁ [π]άνσοφος | [ἐ]νθ[ά]δε [κ]εῖμαι
οὐχὶ θανών. | θνή[σ]κειν μὴ [λ]έγε τοὺς ἀγαθούς.

Cf. Callimachus, *Epigr.* 9 (Pfeiffer).

conventional. Unless they are associated with more individual subjects with a more clear-cut meaning we can infer very little concerning the hopes and fears of those who commissioned the painter.

In one tomb the paintings do seem to be consistently centred on the Dionysiac cult and may represent religious beliefs held by a worshipper of Liber Pater,[1] but in most of the tombs the subjects seem to have little deep spiritual content.[2] We see figures of the gods, particularly Hercules and Venus, but also Mars, Apollo, and Hermes the conductor of souls. The popularity of Hercules may derive partly from the local importance of his cult, but his triumphal restoration of Alcestis from the underworld after overcoming Thanatos made him a natural patron of the dead. In one tomb his twelve labours are represented in stucco;[3] more commonly his figure is painted in a niche. The heads of the Seasons and the figures of the Fates recur more than once, but they, too, are part of a common repertoire. Such scenes as the Rape of Persephone or the Visit of Orpheus to the underworld to bring back Eurydice have a natural association with death, without necessarily implying any profound meaning.

It is strange that the oriental cults have left so very little mark on the Isola Sacra tombs. We should have expected the worship of Isis, Cybele, Serapis, and Mithras to be widely reflected, but a single painted head of Serapis is the only clear reference to an oriental cult in the tomb paintings. The high priest of Cybele whose sarcophagus was found in the cemetery was anxious that his religious office should be commemorated. He reclines on his sarcophagus in his priestly robes and two reliefs show him sacrificing to Cybele and to Attis. In his hand he holds an evergreen branch suggesting that like Attis he will live again after death.[4] It would be interesting to see whether his beliefs affected the subjects painted in his tomb, but his tomb cannot be identified.

The sculpture found in tombs seems, like the paintings, to have no deep significance. The commonest subjects are portrait statues and busts of the dead. In a doctor's tomb were found a head of Hippocrates from a herm, and a life-size portrait of his stepdaughter, represented as Hygia, both recalling his profession.[5] Figures of the gods and conventional representations of the seasons repeat in marble the painter's subjects.

---

[1] *NS* 1928, 151–64; Wilamowitz, *Stud. It. Fil. Class.* 7 (1929) 89–100.
[2] The tomb paintings from Isola Sacra are discussed by Calza, *Necropoli*, 97–156.
[3] Ibid. 108.　　　　　　　　　　　　　　　　　[4] Ibid. 205–9.
[5] Ibid. 222, 245. For this tomb see also Addenda.

But some of the sculpture of the Isola Sacra cemetery seems to be purely decorative, notably a light-hearted group of a young child on horseback with a rustic servant in attendance, and a Pan and satyr. Calza thought that such sculpture, having no symbolic significance, had been brought from the town of Portus to be hidden for safety in a tomb.[1] The distance is too great and the motive unconvincing.[2] It is easier to believe that the owner thought that such subjects were attractive and could add distinction to his tomb chamber.

Sarcophagi also present problems of interpretation. The sculptors, like the painters, developed their own repertoire, and certain mythological scenes became particularly popular. These scenes could mean a great deal or very little. They could be deliberately chosen by the purchaser because of the symbolic meaning he attached to them, or they could be bought because they were fashionable and looked expensive.[3] The most popular theme on Ostian sarcophagi is the story of Endymion, the shepherd who sleeps for ever and is visited by the Moon Goddess.[4] This could to some symbolize the reunion in an after-life of husband and wife,[5] or it could be chosen because it was popular and the comparison of death to sleep was generally appropriate. We must at least be careful not to press its symbolism too narrowly when we find the subject used for a young boy[6] and also for a mother.[7] One sarcophagus at least, however, was chosen with great care. It was provided by a president of the builders' guild for himself and his wife, who was a priestess of Cybele, and represents the death of Alcestis and her restoration from the dead by Hercules.[8] The sarcophagus has the emblems of the cult of Cybele above the relief, and several of the faces are portraits. Almost certainly it was specially ordered and made by an Ostian sculptor. It is reasonable to interpret the scene as a belief in the triumph over death inspired by religion.

More conspicuous in the tombs than any clearly held views about an after life is the strong desire to be remembered by the living. This is

---

[1] Ibid. 233. Pl. xxxvi *b*.   [2] Bloch, *AJA* 48 (1944) 215

[3] F. Cumont, *Recherches sur le symbolisme funéraire des Romains* (1942); A. D. Nock, 'Sarcophagi and Symbolism', *AJA* 50 (1946) 140–70.

[4] Ostian examples, C. Robert, *Die antiken Sarkophag-Reliefs*, iii (1), p. 68 n. 49; 73 n. 56; 79 n. 64; 103 n. 83; iii (3), add. p. 568 n. 41 = *NS* 1909, 202 n. 2; F. Matz, *Metropolitan Mus. of Art. Bull.* (Jan. 1957) 123. There may be a link between the popularity of sarcophagi illustrating the sleep of Endymion and the adoption by Ostian Christians of the sleep formula in their epitaphs.

[5] Cumont, op. cit. 247.

[6] 662.   [7] 565.   [8] 371. Robert, op. cit. iii (1), p. 31.

reflected in portraits of the dead, in paint or sculpture, and especially in the many representations in terra-cotta reliefs or painting of the dead man's occupation. Tomb 29 in the Isola Sacra cemetery is of particular interest in this context.[1] When the tomb was first built a terra-cotta tablet was inserted in the face showing a man grinding a knife. Later an enclosure was added in which a small tomb was built with an upper tomb chamber. In the face of the enclosure two terra-cotta tablets were inserted. One shows a man making and selling tools; in the other we see a tool-grinder. The grinding machine is also depicted in mosaic on the floor of the upper tomb chamber. It seems that the same trade was carried on by the same family over more than one generation. Other terra-cotta reliefs depict doctor, miller, water-seller, and boatman.[2] In the Laurentine cemetery two similar scenes are depicted in paint. One shows a river boat being loaded with corn;[3] in the other a man taps a large *dolium* with a stick to see how much liquid it contains.[4] It has been suggested that these realistic scenes from daily life convey the belief that useful toil merits personal immortality.[5] It is surely better to regard them as an extension of the portrait. This is what the dead man did in life; this is how he wished to be remembered. Trimalchio was not thinking of a new life beyond death when he designed his tomb. There were to be ships in full sail on his monument, to recall his prosperous trading ventures, and lavish illustration of his public generosity.[6] His main concern was that he should not be forgotten.

[1] Calza, *Necropoli*, 303.

[2] Ibid. 247–57.

[3] p. 298. Fig. 25 e.

[4] NS 1938, 68, fig. 26.

[5] Toynbee and Ward Perkins, op. cit. 111.

[6] Petronius, *Sat.* 71.

NOTES

NOTE A, p. 21. I am greatly indebted to Sir John Beazley, who has generously examined the Attic fragments in detail. The references in his notes which follow are to fragments illustrated in *Topografia*, tav. 23.

'Lower group, right.

'*Left*. Fragment of an Attic lekanis. On the right, part of a woman seated to left on a small table. On the left, the arms of another figure, with a fan in the left hand: probably Eros flying towards the seated woman. Egg-pattern in the border below. Between the two figures an ornamented ball. Belongs to a large class of lekanides, complete examples of which are: two in Leningrad (*Otchët*, 1913–15, 86, fig. 135; ibid., p. 95 fig. 154), one in Stuttgart (Schefold, *Untersuchungen zu den kertscher Vasen*, pl. 15. 1), and (without Erotes) one in Salonica, from Olynthos (Robinson, *Olynthus*, 13, pl. 87), and one in Toronto (Robinson and Harcum, pl. 83, no. 451); see also Talcott and Philippaki, *Small Objects from the Pnyx*, ii, pp. 40–42. For the woman, table-seat, ball, compare the Salonica lekanis (*Olynthus*, 13, pl. 87); for the fan, the Toronto vase; for the woman, a lekanis-fragment in Salonica (*Olynthus*, 5, pls. 110, 213).

'The fragment in the top left-hand corner of pl. 23 is also from a fourth-century lekanis.

'*Middle*. Fragment of an Attic bell-krater symposion. Part of a man or youth reclining on a couch to left, with his left elbow resting on a cushion, and of a woman seated on the couch, to right. The man's himation is let down to his waist. The finger-tips of his left hand are preserved. Compare the bell-kraters by the Black-Thyrsus Painter in Barcelona (Garcia y Bellido, *Hispania Graeca*, pl. 110, left: Beazley *ARV*, p. 879, no. 11) and in the Louvre (*CV*, III I e, pl. 5, 9–10: Beazley, *ARV*, p. 879, no. 10); also the fragments of bell-kraters, with symposion scenes, from Olynthos, in Salonica (Robinson, *Olynthus*, 5, pls. 81–82).

'*Right*. Fragment of an Attic (? bell-)krater. Lower part of a satyr wearing a panther-skin; on the left, part of a thyrsus. By the Black-Thyrsus Painter: compare his bell-krater in Madrid (Garcia y Bellido, *Hispania Graeca*, pl. 136, right: Beazley, *ARV*, p. 879, no. 8). Several vases or fragments by him were found at Olynthos (Robinson, *Olynthus*, 13, pls. 48–50; 121 b; 137, 361; *Olynthus*, 5, pls. 104, 163).

'Upper group, left.

'*Lower left*. Fragment from the reverse of an Attic krater. Head of a youth.

'*Lower right*. Fragment from the inside of a kylix, most probably Attic. Part of a maenad seated to right; behind her a tympanon.

'Vases at the same stage of development as all these were found at Olynthos. The destruction of Olynthos in 348 B.C. indicates a date *ante quem*. 375 to 348 or a very few years later would be safe.'

NOTE B, p. 32. *S* 4703. I have followed the generally accepted interpretation. F. Maroi (*Studi in onore di Pietro Bonfanti*, ii. 621) rejects it on two grounds: (1) In addition to the inscribed cippi on the Decumanus, a further cippus was found a little to the west, on the east side of the Via dei Molini. It had been deliberately cut down so that the inscription, if it was inscribed, is lost. It strongly resembles the other stones, and Paribeni (*NS* 1921, 258) was right in suggesting that it belongs to the series; but it lies west of the privatum-cippus. (2) The accepted interpretation is wrong on legal grounds. While strictly the banks of rivers can be private, the use of them is public. Land in such a vital area would not have been allowed to pass into private hands. M. interprets the inscription to signify a right of access to the river by a path through public land, and he compares 'privatum iter' on various inscriptions. In his view, the privatum-cippus precedes the Caninius-cippi.

I do not think that the legal argument is decisive, though I am not competent to judge. I believe that the lettering of the privatum-cippus is unmistakably later than that of the Caninius-cippi. It is a simpler hypothesis to believe that, after the original demarcation, a small area at the west end was made private. The westernmost cippus was then cut down to remove the inscription; the privatum-cippus was set up to confirm the new status of what had hitherto been public land.

NOTE C, p. 50. L. Casson, in an interesting article on the grain trade in the Hellenistic world (*TAPA* 85 (1954) 182–7), concludes that Egypt was already one of Rome's main suppliers in the late Republic. If Egypt, he argues, was not supplying Rome, how were the cities she was supplying kept alive when Augustus directed the Egyptian harvest to Rome? And if Rome's supply still remained precarious after Augustus, how could she have survived earlier without substantial imports from Egypt? Casson also emphasizes the close association of Pompey with Ptolemy Auletes in 57 B.C., when Pompey was *curator annonae* and Ptolemy was pressing nervously for his restoration to the Egyptian throne.

The main objection to this thesis is the silence of Cicero. Had Rome depended on Egyptian corn we should expect some clear reference in the public speeches or correspondence. In praising Pompey's energetic clearance of the seas under the Lex Gabinia of 67 B.C. Cicero emphasizes the liberation of Africa, Sicily, Sardinia. These are the 'frumentaria subsidia reipublicae'; Egypt is not mentioned (*De imperio Cn. Pompeii*, 34). In his letters describing senatorial debates concerning the restoration of Ptolemy Auletes there is no word of Egyptian corn. When he defends Rabirius Postumus for his alleged irregularities in Egypt (*Pro Rabirio Postumo*) we should expect some reference to corn ships if Egyptian corn was vital to Rome.

Appian (*BC* v. 67) attributes the acute shortage of corn at Rome when Sextus Pompeius controlled the seas to the cutting off of supplies from the east as well as from the west. Shipments from Egypt might also be inferred from a passage in Cicero's attack on Verres: 'cum civitatum Siciliae vulgo omne frumentum improbas, num ex Aegypto aut Syria frumentum Romam missurus es?' (*Verr.* ii. 3. 172). But if supplies from Egypt were large and regular we should find more direct evidence. It is doubtful whether it would have paid private merchants to carry the corn such a long distance except in times of shortage when prices were high; when Egypt became a Roman province the Egyptians had no option. I assume that large-scale annual import from Egypt was an innovation by Augustus.

The absorption of this large increase in supply at Rome may be explained by an increase in purchasing power deriving from Augustan prosperity, and perhaps also by an increase in the city population. It is more difficult to assess the effect of the Roman monopoly on other consumers. The exportable Egyptian surplus will have been substantially smaller before the Roman army was set to work on the canals. If most of this surplus was sold in the Aegean, Egypt may have been replaced by the kingdom of Bosporus, for which Rome showed a continuing concern.

NOTE D, p. 161. Both the name and the history of the road raise difficult problems. It is certain from the heavy traffic marks that the road now seen through the cemetery was in the late Empire the main road from Portus to Ostia. It is certain also, from an inscription, that its official name was then Via Flavia (Thylander, A 90). It is most uncertain when this name was given, when this road was built, and whether it represents the original road across the island or a change in route. It has by some been identified with the Via Severiana, but on the Peutinger map that road starts at Ostia and not Portus. This we should expect since there must already have been a road between Ostia and Portus by the Severan period, whereas a coastal road south of Ostia was needed. The name 'Via Flavia' might commemorate one of the late first-century Flavian emperors, but we should expect the road to have been built earlier; more probably the name is a tribute to Constantine who gave independence to Portus. It is possible that the road now seen marks a change in course and that it was not built before the third century, but, though the level is high, the large reticulate blocks of the retaining wall fit the first century better. The line of the road seems to me consistent with its being built before Trajan's harbour (Pl. v). Admittedly the earlier tombs are not aligned on this road, but I am doubtful whether secure inferences can be made from the disposition of tombs to changing road plans, as is argued by Thylander (*Étude*, 27–36). Not all the tomb alignments fit the reconstruction (p. 456). See also Calza, *Necropoli*, 21–27; Bloch, *AJA* 48 (1944) 213.

NOTE E, p. 217. *S* 4560–3, three series, the first two confined to officers. The third (4563) merely gives lists of names. Wickert (p. 673) refers these lists to the earlier *Augustales*, since one fragment includes L. Rennius Philodoxus (4563, 1; ii. 10), recorded in another inscription (407) as Augustalis. If he is right, the *Augustales* will not have been a small priesthood, as suggested above, and they will have had presidents, since the letters Q Q are added to some of the names. There are serious objections: (1) No president of the *Augustales* is otherwise recorded. (2) The lettering of the lists is not earlier than the middle of the second century and it is unlikely that a list of first-century *Augustales* would be drawn up so late. (3) The name M. Aurelius Priscus (*S* 4563, 5. 42) probably derives from a second-century imperial freedman. It is more probable that the lists comprise the full membership of the *seviri Augustales*. The name L. Rennius Philodoxus may have recurred many times. (See also Addenda.)

NOTE F, p. 266. Roads across the southern plain ('Piana Bella') are indicated, though not accurately mapped, by Canina (reproduced in *Topografia*, 50 (fig. 12)). I am grateful to John Bradford, who studied them with me from air photographs and on the ground. Swollen contours, probably covering tombs, indicate five parallel north–south roads. The westernmost is a continuation of the Cardo Maximus emerging from the Porta Laurentina; it is not yet possible to establish the relation of the others to the town plan. The roads are not evenly spaced, the distances between them varying from 500 to

750 ft. One transverse road, running east–west, can also be followed on the ground. Though these roads do not preserve the formal framework of standard centuriation they may be connected with a division of the land. Their date and purpose could be discovered by digging. For a more detailed description, J. Bradford, *Ancient Landscapes*, 242.

NOTE G, p. 17. I have accepted above (p. 343) the identification of Ficana with Dragoncello. Geographically this identification is convincing, but it does violence to our only evidence, which places Ficana by the eleventh milestone on the road from Rome (Festus (Lindsay) 298): 'Puilia saxa esse ad portum, qui sit secundum Tiberim, ait Fabius Pictor: quem locum putat Labeo dici, ubi fuerit Ficana via Ostiensi ad lapidem undecimum.' The eleventh milestone was at least a mile east of Dragoncello, at Malafede. Since an altar to Mars Ficanus was said to have been found in this area it is possible that Ficana should be located near the Tiber at this point.

NOTE H, p. 397. Different interpretations are given to the inscription and to the building by A. von Gerkan, 'Die christliche Anlage in Ostia', *Römische Quartalschrift*, 47 (1939, published 1942) 15–23; T. Klauser, 'Die Inschrift der neugefundenen altchristlichen Bauanlage in Ostia', ibid. 25–30. The former sees the building as a 'Katechumenschule', the latter as a library. The plan does not seem to me suited to either use, but my knowledge of comparative material is negligible. The history of the building deserves more detailed study. It is, I think, more complex than Calza's account suggests.

NOTE I, p. 399. If this conjecture is right the Ostian history of the Caeionii becomes more interesting. Lampadius, *praefectus urbi* in 365, was a stubborn pagan and left a record of a *taurobolium* at Ostia in honour of Magna Mater. It has been suggested above (p. 212) that he owned the House of the Dioscuri near the Porta Marina. His son, if we follow Seeck (*Symmachus*, clxxviii), was Publilius Caeionius Caecina Albinus. Like his father he was a pagan by conviction, but he married a Christian wife (Hieron. *Ep.* 107. 1). Of the two children of this marriage the son, Volusianus, followed his father; the daughter Albina was, like her mother, a Christian; and her daughter in turn, Melania, became particularly famous for her faith and works.

Volusianus is recorded in the Theodosian Code (v. 16. 31) as *comes rerum privatarum* in 408. At about this time his mother asked Augustine, by now bishop of Hippo, to use his influence with Volusianus to persuade him to become a Christian. Augustine writes, somewhat coldly, to Volusianus urging him to study the Scriptures and refer any difficulties to him (*Ep.* 132). Volusianus sets out various difficulties (*Ep.* 135; cf. 136). Augustine replies at great length, but one has the impression that he felt considerably less at ease with this side of the family than with the female side. He writes warmly to Albina, sister of Volusianus (*Ep.* 126), and had every reason to be pleased with Melania's rigorous interpretation of the faith.

At the time of his correspondence with Augustine, Volusianus was still pagan, but prepared to listen to Christian argument. In 429 he is *praefectus praetorio* (*Cod. Theod.* xi. 6. 32). We hear later of his conversion by his niece Melania in 434, while he was on official business at Constantinople (*Analecta Bollandiana*, 8 (1889) 51; 22 (1903) 35). He was critically ill, and died very soon afterwards.

The name Volusianus on the column of a Christian building, very near the House of the Dioscuri (which we have attributed to the family), might reflect his conversion.

NOTE J, p. 415. Amelung, *Die Sculpturen des vatican. Museums*, i (2) n. 160b, Taf. 29. This block (Pl. XXXVIII b) was found near the church of S. Pudentiana in Rome and was thought to have come from the Thermae Novatianae (*Bull. crist.* 1867, 55). I am grateful to Donald Strong, who drew my attention to its marked similarity to the fragments in the Forum Baths, and to G. V. S. Corbett, who confirmed that the measurements allowed the identification. The naming of the original builder recalls the Ostian inscription discussed by Bloch.

The beginning of another hexameter is preserved below the first: 'divinae mentis ductu cum o (possibly c or g)—'. It may not have immediately followed the first, the length of the inscription being unknown. The language of the line recalls the inscription on Constantine's arch, set up 'instinctu divinitatis' (*ILS* 694). Constantinian restorations in the Forum Baths are reflected in brickstamps. This inscription may commemorate them. *

A further link between Roman and Ostian fragments may be found in a Greek inscription, now lost, which Marini associated with this Latin inscription; it presumably came from a similar fragment: '—ειξεν Βικτωρ αρχος εωι[ας]'. This text, difficult to interpret, and perhaps incorrectly recorded, is to be associated with an unpublished Greek text which can still be seen in the Forum Baths on two large fragments of this distinctive entablature. The first (Pl. XXXVIII c) reads 'λουτρον αλεξιπονο'; the second 'ν κυδιμος Αυσονιης'. A further fragment from a different architectural member found in the Forum Baths has '—nte Fl. Octavio V—'. This should indicate a restoration supervised ([cura]nte) by a *praefectus annonae*. He may be identified with a Flavius Octavius Victor recorded in another, unpublished, Ostian inscription. Tentatively I identify him with the Βικτωρ of the lost Greek inscription. Together, Greek and Latin texts record a restoration of the baths, which must be different from that of Ragonius Vincentius Celsus. The lettering of both Greek and Latin texts is carefully done and not later than the fourth century. Whether they refer to a Constantinian or later restoration is uncertain.

The Greek inscription has a further interesting association. The term 'λουτρον αλεξιπονον' is, I think, unparalleled in bath inscriptions. It recalls, however, a passage in Augustine's *Confessions* (ix. 12. 32). After his mother's death at Ostia, he tells us, he went to the baths 'because I had heard that baths were called *balnea* from the Greek βαλανειον, which means driving away care from the mind'. This is, I think, our earliest record of this most unconvincing etymology, though it could have been invented much earlier. It is at least interesting to find the same idea reflected on stone in Ostia. It is not unlikely that Augustine went to the Forum Baths. (The texts of Latin and Greek inscriptions from Rome, *CIL* vi. 29769; Diehl, *ILCV* 1901 A.)

NOTE K, p. 40. In the third volume of *Scavi di Ostia* (Le Necropoli, Parte 1), which reached me too late to be used in my text, Poplicola's monument and the inscription on its face are published in detail (169 ff.). From converging lines of evidence a date in or shortly after the twenties B.C. is inferred. The inscription, as restored by Bloch (214 ff.), runs:

Po[bli]c[e].
[C. Carti]li[o C.f. Pop]licolae [—8 or 9]
[— c. 24 — et] libereis pos[tereisque eius]
    [decurionum decreto co]lonorumque con[sensu]

5   preimario viro pro eius meriteis
               hoc m[on]umentum constitutum est
                 eique merenti gratia rellata est,
               isque octiens duomvir, ter cens(or) colonorum iudicio
                 apsens praesensque factus est,
10   ob eius amorem in universos ab
               universieis – – – – – – – – (erasure)
                 Humaniae M.F. (added later).

There remains a gap of *c.* 32 letters at the end of the second and at the beginning of
the third line. In view of the military subject chosen for the frieze some reference to
military service is needed. I assume that in this space was recorded either a normal
military post or special service in a special campaign. A military tribunate would be
appropriate, but the normal epigraphic formula 'trib. mil. leg. [—]' would be too
short; 'trib. militum legionis [—]' is not impossible.

The erasure of 15 or 16 letters at the end of the original text presents a more difficult
problem. Bloch considers that lines 10 and 11 might be part of the clause which begins
in l. 8, and that the erasure might reflect an error by the cutter or the executive official
responsible. This is possible but unattractive. After *colonorum iudicio, ab universieis*
would be redundant, though stylistically the addition would be intelligible with *in
universos*. We should, however, from the rhythm of the preceding clauses, expect the
main verb *factus est* to be placed at the end. The balance of the text is better preserved
if *ob eius amorem* begins a new and final clause.

After analysing this inscription Bloch reviews the career of C. Cartilius Poplicola
in the light of all the inscriptions in which the name is recorded (315, 4134, S 4710,
4711, 4712, and two unpublished texts). He gives good reasons for believing that the
public career of Poplicola, covering some twenty years, fell between 44 B.C. and A.D. 5,
and adds colour to his career by the interpretation of the inscription on the statue which
he dedicated in the temple of Hercules (above, p. 349). This inscription, now fully
published for the first time, requires special explanation. In its final form it runs: 'C.
Cartilius C.f. | duovir V tertio | Poplicolae'; but it can be seen that the original text of
l. 2 was *duovir iterum.**At a second stage *iterum* was changed to *tertio*, though traces of
the original letters remain; subsequently *V* was added after *duovir*, but *tertio* was not
erased. The third line is also unorthodox; the cognomen appears in the wrong place
and in the wrong case. Bloch is also convinced (though this is perhaps a little less
certain from the script itself) that it is an addition to the original text in a different hand.

The changes in the second line are easy to explain: they were made to celebrate
further appointments to the duovirate. The reason for the addition of *Poplicolae* is
less evident. Bloch infers that C. Cartilius had no cognomen when he was duovir for
the second time. The name Poplicola, 'friend of the people', was, he thinks, conferred
later by the people in recognition of his outstanding services to the town, and the
honour was commemorated on the statue.

This attractive hypothesis is very tempting and it might even be suggested that the
words erased on Poplicola's tomb were *cognomen datum est*. We should expect such an
outstanding honour to be recorded on his tomb; the words would fit the space. But
certain objections must be considered.

1. The cognomen Poplicola (or Publicola) is extremely rare. According to Roman tradition it was conferred on C. Valerius at the beginning of the Republic for his services to the people (Livy ii. 8. 1); it remained hereditary in the family, who seem to have exercised a monopoly. I have been able to find only three examples in Italy of the name attached to other families, and in all three cases a link with the Valerii can be proved or reasonably inferred. For L. Gellius Poplicola, cos. 72 B.C., there is no evidence, but his son, cos. 36 B.C., is stepbrother of M. Valerius Messalla (Dio xlvii. 24, 5; Syme, *Roman Revolution*, 198 n. 8). Q. Pedius Poplicola, mentioned by Horace (*Sat.* i. 10. 28) is almost certainly the son of the consul of 43 B.C.; his mother was a Valeria (Pliny, *NH* xxxv. 21). L. Vipstanus Publicola Messalla, cos. A.D. 48, shows by his second cognomen that he is connected with the Valerii, for Messalla is also hereditary in the family. If Bloch's hypothesis is correct C. Cartilius Poplicola becomes a very striking exception.

2. I can find no parallel for the conferment of a cognomen by a colony or municipality. If this were done at Ostia it should have been done elsewhere. Such an honour would be commemorated on statue bases and tombstones. The argument from silence is not conclusive, but it reinforces doubt.

3. The inscription *S* 4712 (op. cit., pl. xxxvi. 1) records a C. Cartilius Poplicola in large letters (height, m. 0·125–0·13) on an epistyle. It was found by the Via Ostiensis near Acilia. Other inscriptions from this area (*S* 2, p. 823) come from tombs which lined the road; we should expect this inscription also, from its form and site, to come from a tomb. But it cannot come from the tomb of our Poplicola, for his ashes were placed in his public monument outside Porta Marina. The lettering seems to be earlier than the other inscriptions of our Poplicola. The tail of R starts from the vertical stroke and the stop is within the circle of the C; in the other inscriptions the tail of R starts from the curved line, and the stop comes between the two ends of the C. I had believed that the Acilia inscription referred to our Poplicola's father. There are, however, two inscriptions from this area, which probably do not come from tombs. One is on an altar to Jupiter Tutor (25); the other refers to an altar, probably to Ceres (74). Our inscription might come from a temple or smaller shrine, and the argument from letter forms cannot be pressed.

If we hesitate to accept Bloch's hypothesis, an alternative explanation is required for the name and its anomalous appearance on the statue. Tentatively I suggest that a C. Cartilius, probably in the late Republic, married into the Valerii and named his son Poplicola. Valerius is, in the Empire, one of the commonest family names in Ostia. Almost all known Ostian Valerii are of freedman stock, but the wide distribution of the name suggests that there were once Valerii of some importance at Ostia. Pliny the elder mentions a C. Valerius Ostiensis who roofed a theatre at Rome, probably in the late Republic. From the Fasti we know that a M. Valerius (—) was duovir in A.D. 20, and it is a nice coincidence that M. Valerius Messalla was *consul ordinarius* in the same year. An association between the Cartilii and a junior branch of the Valerii settled in Ostia would not be surprising.

It is much more difficult to explain the addition of *Poplicola* to the statue from the temple of Hercules, but not impossible. In the Republic the cognomen was not an essential element in the official name; more often than not it is omitted in formal documents (Thylander, *Étude*, 68 ff.). Under Augustus, a transitional stage, it gains ground. After Augustus it is very rarely omitted. Poplicola might have omitted it when he was near the outset of his public career, and duovir for only the second time. Later, when his public services had emphasized the relevance of his cognomen, it may have been added. The use of the dative, implying that his statue is a dedication to rather than by Poplicola, is odd, but the cutter may have been misled by *tertio*.

This explanation would be more plausible if parallels could be quoted from Ostia. In the mosaic pavement of the westernmost of the four republican temples west of the theatre there is an inscription recording at the top the duovirs of the year and, below, the names of four freedmen and one free citizen, who may have paid for the pavement (Bloch, op. cit. 210, revising 4134). The duovirs are recorded as C. Cartilius Poplicola and C. Fabius (the line is partly restored, but there is no space for a cognomen after Fabius). In a Julio-Claudian inscription (8) a C. Fabius C.f. Agrippa records his free descent for four generations; all his recorded ancestors, clearly stretching back into the Republic, have cognomens. It is at least possible that C. Fabius of the mosaic pavement had a cognomen, though it is not included in the inscription. Similarly M. Acilius, recorded without cognomen in the Fasti as duovir in 48 B.C., may possibly be identified with M. Acilius Caninus, who was quaestor at Rome before 28 B.C. (153) and honoured with a statue at Ostia (but see p. 507).

Bloch's hypothesis offers a much easier solution of the inscription on the statue, but the objections outlined above convince me that another explanation should be sought.

Dr. Squarciapino adds a further interesting hypothesis (op. cit. 205). The relief found near the temple of Hercules (above, p. 347) probably commemorates the interpretation of an oracle which was successfully fulfilled. The figure of the person to whom the oracle was given is missing. She suggests that it may be C. Cartilius and that the statue which he dedicated in the temple may be a thank-offering for the fulfilment of the oracle. I should like to believe this, but must remain sceptical. Becatti gave good reasons for dating the relief between 80 and 65 B.C. (*BC* 67 (1939) 55), and Dr. Squarciapino accepts these limits. It would be very difficult to date Poplicola's second duovirate, when the statue was dedicated, earlier than 40 B.C. The interval between relief and statue would be too long.

Appendix I

THE EARLIEST OSTIA

THE view adopted in the text that there was a Roman settlement at Ostia before the fourth century rests primarily on the early Roman tradition of a foundation by Ancus Marcius. Other arguments require further consideration.

1. The statement that there is no archaeological evidence of settlement before the fourth-century Castrum might be questioned. Carcopino drew attention to a fragment of Attic pottery of the mature classical style of the second half of the fifth century, which is reported to have been found at Ostia.[1] No record, however, survives of the context in which it was found and Carcopino rightly dismisses it as evidence. Somewhat earlier is an archaic bronze lamp in the form of a boat which was found at Portus. It was briefly reported soon after its finding in 1869 and the accompanying illustration shows that it belongs to a well-known Sardinian series.[2] This early bronze might support early contact with Sardinia but, since the exact context of the find was not reported, any historical inference would be dangerous.

A pre-Castrum date has been given to some terra-cotta architectural fragments which were found at the lowest level within the Castrum. Andren regarded these fragments, which once probably decorated Ostian temples, as archaistic and dated them to the third century.[3] Mingazzini has argued that some at least go back to the sixth and fifth centuries.[4] This is a problem for specialists. Professor Trendall, who kindly examined the fragments with me, was satisfied that none need be earlier than the fourth century. The head of a Maenad,[5] in particular, which looks genuinely archaic in a photograph, is much less convincing in the original, and is almost certainly not earlier than the third century.

It remains a reasonable inference from excavation within the Castrum that this site was not occupied before the fourth century. But if, as tradition implies, the earliest settlement was near the salt-beds, this evidence does not

[1] Carcopino, 10.

[2] *Archaeologia*, 42 (1869) 487, pl. xxviii. 2. Cited by F. W. von Bissing, 'Die sardinischen Bronzen', *RM* 43 (1928) 32, who attributes it to Ostia and refers to a similar lamp, possibly two, from Portus. This reduplication probably derives ultimately from the original publication, which was headed 'Lamp from Ostia', but describes the find-spot as 'on the Torlonia estate'.

[3] A. Andren, 'Architectural terra-cottas from Etrusco-Italic temples', *Acta inst. rom. regn. Sueciae*, 6 (1940) 369, pl. 113.

[4] P. Mingazzini, 'Esisteva un abitato Ostiense anteriore a la colonia romana?', *Rend. Pont.* 23-24 (1947-9) 75-83.   [5] *Topografia*, tav. xxii.

affect the present issue. It has been held that, if an earlier Ostia existed to the east, some trace would have been found during building operations in the modern village or in farming operations on the plain. Such argument from silence has no force. Between the salt-beds and the river there is ample evidence of Roman buildings in tiles, bricks, and pottery thrown up by the plough, which have not been investigated. On one of the larger sites suggested by such evidence I have seen fragments of black-glazed pottery probably dating from the second century B.C.[1]

2. Festus records that the Via Salaria was so called because by it the Sabines carried their salt from the sea.[2] He implies a continuous route from the seacoast. In later times the road that led from Rome to Sabine country was still called the Via Salaria, but of the roads that led from Rome towards the coast, the road on the right bank was called the Via Campana, the left-bank road was the Via Ostiensis. If the Via Salaria had run along the right bank the name should have persisted; it is much easier to see how it lapsed if the road was on the left bank. For by the middle of the fourth century at the latest Rome and the Sabines drew their salt from the beds on the right bank.[3] The main function of the road on the left bank was no longer to carry salt; it was logical that when Ostia became more important Via Ostiensis should supersede Via Salaria. It is a reasonable inference that originally the Via Salaria ran from Sabine country through Rome to the river mouth on the left bank. This does not necessarily presuppose a Roman settlement, but it makes the tradition of Ancus Marcius' settlement more plausible.

3. Another passage of Festus has been used to support the tradition: 'Quiritium fossae dicuntur quibus Ancus Marcius circumdedit urbem quam secundum ostium Tiberis posuit, ex quo etiam Ostiam.'[4] If this was the consistent interpretation of 'fossae (or fossa) Quiritium' it would carry weight, but different versions are found in other sources. Livy introduces the name (in the singular), without further explanation, in his account of Ancus Marcius, but he seems to associate it with the Janiculum: 'Quiritium quoque fossa, haud parvum munimentum a planioribus aditu locis, Anci regis opus.'[5] Dionysius of Halicarnassus, whose account of Ancus Marcius' operations resembles Livy's, does not translate the name, but he says that the king surrounded the newly incorporated Aventine hill with wall and ditch, and this ditch may correspond to Livy's 'fossa Quiritium'.[6] The much later author of

---

[1] On the east side of the Via delle Saline, immediately before it meets the Via del Collettorio Secondario.

[2] Festus (Lindsay), 437: 'Salaria via Romae est appellata, quia per eam Sabini sal a mari deferebant'; cf. Pliny, *NH* xxxi. 89.

[3] For the view that the Via Salaria was on the right bank, T. Ashby, *The Roman Campagna in Classical Times*, 219; L. A. Holland, 'The Primitive Roman Bridge', *TAPA* 80 (1949) 281–319 (esp. 313).   [4] Festus (Lindsay), 304.

[5] Livy i. 33. 5–7.   [6] Dion. Hal. iii. 43.

the *De viris illustribus* attaches the name to the *cloaca maxima* built by Tarquinius Superbus.[1]

From this conflicting evidence we may infer that there was no continuing association of the name with any definite place. But the name was handed down and had to be explained. The antiquarians of the late Republic may have inherited a tradition which connected it with Ancus Marcius, but not with any particular event. The main achievements of Ancus Marcius in the tradition were the incorporation of the Aventine and of the Janiculum at Rome and the foundation of Ostia. All provided a suitable context: the various attributions may be no more than guesses. Unless we can prove the superiority of Festus' source this passage cannot be regarded as independent confirmation of the main literary tradition concerning Ostia.

4. I have accepted the evidence of Livy and Dionysius of Halicarnassus for Roman corn imports by sea in the early Republic because I see no good reason to question them. The primary document, however, concerning Rome's interest in the sea routes is her first treaty with Carthage, quoted in full by Polybius and dated by him to the foundation of the Republic.[2] This dating has been repeatedly attacked, but Polybius is well aware that his date will surprise his readers: he is explicit and deliberate. The new situation created in Latium by the expulsion of the Etruscan dynasty from Rome provides a sound historical context. Polybius' dating should be accepted.[3] Rome, though not yet a sea power, already had interests at sea. Ostia is not mentioned in the treaty, but that does not affect our problem. If, as we think, a settlement already existed, it was little more than a salt-workers' village on Roman territory, controlled by Rome; it needed no independent guarantee against Carthaginian interference.

Apart from the tradition of the foundation by Ancus Marcius only one passage in literature mentions Ostia explicitly before the fourth century, and that is the story of Sp. Maelius, sketched briefly by Livy and Dionysius of Halicarnassus.[4] There was a serious famine in 440 which L. Minucius, specially appointed *praefectus annonae*, was unable to relieve. Sp. Maelius, a rich knight, seized the opportunity to buy corn privately on a large scale in Etruria and Campania and sell it cheaply to the people. This brought him wide popularity which led him to hope for the consulship; it might even be necessary, since the senate's opposition could be expected, to become king. He became the storm centre of a popular party threatening the constitution. The senate in alarm appointed Cincinnatus dictator. Servilius Ahala, *magister equitum*, was sent to summon Maelius; he resisted arrest and was put to death.

---

[1] *De viris illustribus*, 8. 3. [2] Polybius iii. 22.

[3] H. Last, *CAH* vii. 859; J. H. Thiel, *A History of Roman Sea-power before the Second Punic War* (1954) 6 n. 10; a review of the controversy, F. W. Walbank, *A Historical Commentary on Polybius*, i (1957) 337. [4] Livy iv. 13–16; Dion. Hal. xii. 1–4.

There is probably a core of truth in the story and we may accept the famine and the import of corn. But the political colouring is affected by later events, and particularly by the conflict between the senate and the Gracchi. Dionysius says that the corn from Etruria and Campania was brought to 'Ostia, Rome's harbour'; this too might be a reflection of later conditions. But, if we are right in believing that ships were coming up the Tiber in the early Republic, it is reasonable to infer a settlement of some kind near the river mouth to provide water, food, and other services for ships' crews. In our view a settlement already existed.

5. The tribal affiliation of Ostia may not be irrelevant. Ostia was enrolled in Voturia, one of the original rural tribes. The precise date of the formation of these rural tribes remains controversial, but it is at least agreed that they precede the conquest of Veii in the early fourth century. If Roman territory had not extended to the coast before the fourth century we should have expected a new tribe to have been created when the new territory was won. The enrolment of Ostia in Voturia suggests that Ostia was established before the fourth century.

Such arguments from Ostia's tribe, from the history of the Via Salaria, from Rome's early trade, add a little support to the tradition of a regal settlement, but they are by no means decisive. The rejected rubbish of a small hut of the regal period would carry more weight than any such inferences from our literary sources. Doubts will remain until unambiguous archaeological evidence is found. It should be sought not on the firm sands where the Castrum was built in the fourth century, but in the alluvial soil deposited by the Tiber, north of the salt-beds.

An important argument is added on p. 566 (add. p. 481). For more recent evidence see p. 579.

Appendix II

VIRGIL AND OSTIA

IN Virgil's *Aeneid* Aeneas lands at the Tiber mouth. It is there and in Laurentine territory to the south of the river that the action of the last six books of his *Aeneid* unfolds. The legend was not yet fixed, but in most accounts the landing was placed farther south.[1] It is reasonable to ask whether Virgil had any purpose other than a literary purpose in elaborating his version of the legend, whether he was influenced by what he knew of the Ostia of his day, and whether his account can throw light on geographical and historical problems that concern the development of Ostia.

A great deal has been written on these topics; most of the writing is singularly unconvincing. There is little doubt that Virgil was generally familiar with the landscape, but it is dangerous to press his verses rigorously for topographical detail. It is outside the scope of this book to examine his description of Laurentine territory, but certain opinions on his use of Ostian material require examination.

Tenney Frank believed that Virgil in his description of Aeneas' building of a new Troy at the mouth of the Tiber was strongly influenced by what he saw of the walls of the fourth-century Castrum.[2] These are 'the very walls, in my opinion, which Virgil, with a slight license, intended the reader to have in mind when he mentioned Aeneas' first city in Latium'. Aeneas' city, unlike the Castrum, was unwalled on the river side. The discrepancy can be explained, because 'most of the north wall has disappeared down to a very low level, . . . presumably torn down before Virgil's day'. This reconciliation is forced. A substantial stretch of the north wall can still be seen incorporated in the south wall of the Piccolo Mercato, which was not built until Hadrian's reign. Before this rebuilding more of the wall may well have survived. Aeneas' foundation, like the Castrum, has walls, ditches, and towers. But these are the normal Roman means of defence, though they would not be found in Italy as early as the days of Aeneas. There is no good reason to believe that Virgil's description was influenced by what he saw at Ostia.

Miss Tilly attached more importance to the sacred area west of the theatre. When she wrote, its four tufa temples were thought to have been preceded on the same site by earlier temples in more perishable materials. The traditional sanctity of the area, she thought, may have made a deep impression on the poet, and its cults may be reflected in his *Aeneid*.[3] A later examination of the

---

[1] Carcopino, 392.   [2] Tenney Frank, *AJP* 45 (1924) 64.
[3] B. Tilly, *Virgil's Latium*, 21 (Virgil's Ostia background, 1–30).

archaeological evidence has made it much more probable that the temples we now see were the first temples on the site; in Virgil's day they were still comparatively modern.[1]

More important is the comprehensive and coherent hypothesis elaborated by Carcopino. One central aspect of this hypothesis has already been considered (p. 339 f.). His view that pre-Roman Ostia was a federal centre of the Latins focused on the cult of Vulcan should be regarded as unproved and unlikely; no support can be legitimately drawn from Virgil on the nature or antiquity of Vulcan's cult. It remains to consider the topographical arguments that have a bearing on Ostia's history. The central argument[2] may be briefly summarized:

It is clear that the advance of the coastline at the Tiber's mouth is not a modern problem. It has advanced more rapidly since the sixteenth century, but the measurable annual advance from the late Roman Empire to the sixteenth century was 1·50 metres. If this average measurement be applied to the Roman period, the river mouth in Augustus' day was not far from the so-called *navale* just west of the 'Imperial Palace'. Primitive Ostia must have been considerably farther to the east. There are indications in Virgil's Aeneid and Ostian buildings that pre-Ostian Ostia was sited by the bend of the river.

This bend is attested in Ovid's account of the journey of Cybele to Rome:

> fluminis ad flexum veniunt: Tiberina priores
> atria dixerunt, unde sinister abit.[3]

Today the river turns northward considerably to the west, but this is the result of a flood in 1557. Before that date the bend was farther east. Early maps and drawings show the river's course before the flood, turning to form a loop by the fifteenth-century castle in the modern village; the *fiume morto*, which was not filled in until the nineteenth century, marked its course. This line, however, was not the river line in Roman days, but was the result of changes that resulted from the neglect of embankments after the collapse of Rome. That it was not the Roman line is proved by the fact that had the river followed the course shown in the earliest maps, the Decumanus, emerging from the Porta Romana as the Via Ostiensis, would have had to cross the river. The bend was farther west, not far from the line of the Porta Romana. Here on the north side of the Decumanus in Virgil's day were republican *horrea*, which, through a further four centuries of adaptation, preserved their original tufa piers and some of their original reticulate walls. The obvious reason is that they were regarded with veneration as marking the site of the original Ostia. It is in this neighbourhood that the temple of Vulcan should be found.

Virgil's *Aeneid* shows that it was at this bend of the river that Aeneas built his city and protected his ships. He emphasizes the harbour in his account; it was here that ships coming into the Tiber first won shelter from the west and south-west winds. The siting is confirmed by the description of the city when Turnus attacks and the

[1] p. 538.
[2] Carcopino, 391–780.
[3] Ovid, *Fasti*, iv. 329.

heads of Nisus and Euryalus, killed while trying to break through to recall Aeneas, are displayed to the Trojans:

> Aeneadae duri murorum in parte sinistra
> opposuere aciem, nam dextera cingitur amni.[1]

The passage appears to give two sides only instead of four to the new Troy. This is explained by its setting on the bend of the river. Left and right are to be understood from the point of view of a spectator coming down-river from Rome. The left side, that is the south, was marked by a wall running eastwards from the river curve, and here alone defence was needed; for the northern side was protected by the river and the eastern side was protected by marsh. This marsh is implied by Virgil

> huc turbidus atque huc
> lustrat equo muros aditumque per avia quaerit.[2]

There are fatal objections to this thesis. The real reason why the republican *horrea* were readapted rather than rebuilt has already been given (p. 339). It was the prosaic need for economy. The rebuilding of Ostia started in and near the centre; had prosperity lasted longer this area would also have been rebuilt at a higher level and to a greater height. Original walls were preserved because it was cheaper to reuse them. Nor were they of any great antiquity in Virgil's day; their near-reticulate shows that they were roughly his contemporaries. Nor did the river make its bend where Carcopino's thesis requires. After he wrote, boundary stones of the Julio-Claudian period were discovered farther east, showing that the Roman river line was little different from that shown on the earliest maps.[3]

We cannot even infer securely from Virgil that he visualized his city of Aeneas at the bend of the river. Carcopino's illustration of the river's bend comes from Ovid; in Virgil's account there is no word of it. The somewhat odd description of the camp in the passage quoted is quite insufficient to stand the weight imposed on it; poetic licence rather than detailed topography should be invoked. The marsh on the eastern side, regarded as a continuation of the river, is essential to Carcopino's thesis. It is not mentioned by Virgil, nor can it be inferred from the passage quoted: the simple meaning of 'aditumque per avia quaerit' is that Turnus 'sought for an entrance where no way could be found'. Livy is a better guide than Virgil for the siting of the earliest Ostia.

Carcopino has also given a positive answer to the other main inquiry provoked by the *Aeneid*.[4] He suggests that Virgil chose Ostia as the scene of the new Troy to popularize Augustus' plans to create a new harbour. The work, he thinks, was in fact begun, but was abandoned when Agrippa died in 12 B.C., and Claudius had to begin afresh. The evidence for this solution of the problem is unimpressive. There is no direct hint in the *Aeneid*, though an

---

[1] Virg. *Aen.* ix. 468.
[2] Ibid. ix. 57.
[3] NS 1921, 258. See also p. 115.
[4] Carcopino, 729–54.

appropriate prophecy could have been fitted in without serious strain. The inferences drawn from other sources are invalid. The first is a comment on a passage in the *Ars Poetica*:

> sive receptus
> terra Neptunus classes Aquilonibus arcet,
> regis opus, sterilisve diu palus aptaque remis
> vicinas urbes alit et grave sentit aratrum,
> seu cursum mutavit iniquum frugibus amnis
> doctus iter melius: mortalia facta peribunt.[1]

Carcopino is probably right in following those who see in these lines specific reference to historical works or projects rather than general illustrations of man's control over nature. We cannot follow him when he identifies Horace's allusions with works undertaken by Agrippa for Augustus. The argument from the date of the poem must remain very uncertain. Carcopino accepts 12 B.C., the year of Agrippa's death, and sees in these lines a lament for Agrippa.[2] But even if the date were right, the association of these lines with Agrippa would need to be independently established; in themselves they need not necessarily apply to recent works. The independent evidence is found by Carcopino in the scholiasts Acron and Porphyrion. Their record on the passage inspires no confidence, and Carcopino's interpretation of what they say is special pleading. We cannot follow him in finding in their comments evidence that Augustus built a harbour at Ostia.

Acron quotes Augustus as the creator of the harbour envisaged by Horace: 'Augustum dicit . . . divus Augustus res divinas fecit.' But he names 'portus Iulius' in Campania, not Ostia: 'portum Lucrinum munivit.' Porphyrion has a different interpretation: 'divus Caesar duas instituerat res facere: portum Ostiensem munire et Pomptinam paludem . . . emittere in mare'. According to Carcopino Porphyrion by 'divus Caesar' means Augustus; 'instituerat facere' means not that he had planned to build, but had begun to build. This is not the natural meaning of 'divus Caesar' nor of 'instituerat facere'. We should follow the majority of commentators, who see here a reference to Julius Caesar's project to build a harbour at Ostia.

The chronographer of 354 records: 'hoc imp(eratore) (Octaviano Augusto) navis Alexandrina primum in portu Romano introivit nomine Acatus.'[3] This passage, Carcopino thinks, shows that Augustus' work at Ostia was sufficiently advanced for an Alexandrian merchantman to anchor in the new harbour. This interpretation would create more difficulties than it solves. If the work was so far advanced before it was abandoned, the complete silence of contemporary authors, particularly of Strabo, would be inexplicable. The continuation of the passage quoted shows beyond reasonable doubt that 'in portu Romano'

---

[1] Horace, *Ars Poetica*, 63–68.   [2] Carcopino, 732.

[3] Mommsen, *Chronica minora*, i. 145.

refers to Rome and not to Ostia: 'qui attulit frumenti modios CCCC, vectores MCC, piper, linteamen, carta, vitria et opoliscum cum sua sibi base, qui est in circo maximo, altum pedes LXXXVIIS'. This was the ship that brought the great obelisk to Rome. Like its successor in the fourth century it came up river, as Pliny indicates,[1] and docked at Rome. *

Carcopino finally infers that the name of the Claudian harbour, 'portus Augusti', was chosen to commemorate the initiative of Augustus in creating a new harbour. This explanation of the name would be probable enough if there were any other firm evidence that Augustus had begun the work. The name, however, need imply no more than that the harbour was an imperial construction.[2]

Further evidence of Augustus' active interest in Ostia is shown, according to Carcopino, by the establishment of a colony of veterans; but the only evidence for this colony derives from a doubtful interpretation of a passage in Pliny the elder. In his survey of Italy Pliny has been thought to be limiting the title of colony to Augustan foundations, and he includes Ostia. It seems clear, however, that in describing the coastal areas he follows a *Periplous* and includes colonies that were not Augustan; his obscure reference to Augustan colonies is associated with his description of the interior.[3] The establishment of veterans by Augustus at Ostia cannot be accepted without independent confirmation.

That Augustus, who fully understood the political importance of Rome's corn supply, was closely concerned with Ostia's efficiency is certain. That he began to realize Caesar's project of a new harbour is most unlikely. Suetonius implies that he did not. In his brief catalogue of the major works of Claudius he includes 'the outlet to the Fucine lake and the Ostian harbour, though he knew that the first of these schemes had been rejected by Augustus in spite of insistent appeals from the Marsi, and that the second had often been projected by the divine Julius but not tackled owing to its difficulties'.[4] The clear inference is that Augustus, while considering the drainage of the Fucine lake, had accepted the general judgment that the building of a new harbour at Ostia was not a practical proposition.

I do not believe that a minute scrutiny of Virgil's text or intentions will make any substantial contribution to our understanding of Ostia's history.[5]

[1] Pliny, *NH* xxxvi. 70.
[2] Cf. Macellum Augusti, dedicated in A.D. 59: BMC Emp. I, Nero, 191–7, 335–7.
[3] Pliny, *NH* iii. 46 and 56. Mommsen, 'Die italischen Bürgercolonien von Sulla bis Vespasian', *Ges. Schrift.* ii (1908) 250; R. Thomsen, *The Italic Regions*, 41.
[4] Suet. *Claud.* 20. 1.
[5] See Addenda.

Appendix III

TRAJAN'S CANAL AND THE DATE OF TRAJAN'S HARBOUR

IN the nineteenth century there was considerable dispute whether the present Fiumicino canal was in origin the work of Claudius or Trajan. I have followed Lugli in believing that this was a new canal cut by Trajan, replacing two Claudian canals which passed through what was to become Trajan's inner basin.[1] This thesis is supported not only by the alignments noted in the text, but also by a passage in Pliny's correspondence: 'Tiberis alveum excessit et demissioribis ripis alte superfunditur, quamquam fossa, quam providentissimus imperator fecit, exhaustus, premit valles, innatat campis, quaque planum solum, pro solo cernitur.'[2]

Trajan had cut a canal from the Tiber which, Pliny implies, was expected to reduce the danger of flood. A canal with this purpose should have been drawn from the upper river above Rome; but no trace of such a canal has ever been found. Claudius, as his inscription of 46 shows,[3] thought that canals near the mouth would be effective. Trajan seems to have shared the illusion. For Pliny's reference should almost certainly be associated with a monumental inscription now in St. Paul's monastery, which records Trajan's action in connexion with a canal.[4] The provenance of the inscription is unknown, but, since a large proportion of the inscriptions in St. Paul's come from Ostia, an Ostian origin is probable.

Very little of the inscription survives, but there can be no doubt about the restoration of the emperor's name, and 'fossam' is clear on the stone. Dessau in the Corpus adopted Mommsen's restoration: 'fossam [fecit | q]ua inun[dationes Tiberis | a]dsidue u[rbem vexantes | rivo p]eren[ni arcerentur].' Thylander rightly pointed out that 'fossam fecit' gives too short a line, and suggested 'fossam restituit'.[5] If this restoration were right, the inference would be that Trajan preserved and restored Claudius' canal. 'fossam [novam fecit]' is, however, a possible alternative and accords better with the language of Pliny. Mommsen's other restorations also are too long, but the general sense is probably right.

The inscription cannot be dated; Pliny's letter was probably written in 107; by that date the canal had been cut. When the rest of the work was begun and ended is less certain. Until recently it was generally thought that work was started on the harbour at the beginning of the reign and

[1] p. 159. [2] Pliny, *Ep.* viii. 17. 2. [3] 85 = Thylander, B 310.
[4] 88. [5] Thylander, B 312.

completed by the middle.[1] This was primarily an inference from some of the commemorative coins which were dated to a year when Trajan was cos. V, from 103 to 112. A reference was also seen to the harbour in a passage from Pliny's *Panegyric*, delivered in 100. Pliny is praising Trajan for the flourishing state of the corn supply, and comparing his achievement with Pompey's: 'nec vero ille (Pompeius) civilius quam parens noster auctoritate, consilio, fide reclusit vias, portus patefecit, itinera terris, litoribus mare [litora mari] reddidit diversasque gentes ita commercio miscuit, ut, quod genitum esset usquam, id apud omnes natura videretur.'[2] Such commonplace flattery is too general to cover new construction. Had Trajan started work on a new harbour Pliny would not have missed the opportunity to make the contrast with Pompey. Nor can the coin evidence now be accepted. Strack has argued convincingly that cos. V is a misreading from a worn surface of cos. VI, which is clear on the best specimens.[3] Trajan was consul for the sixth and last time in 112. The coinage commemorating the completion of the work was issued between 112 and his death in 117, probably in 113.[4]

An inscription survives in part at Portus recording the bequest by Trajan probably of a building to the colony of Ostia in the year 101 or 102.[5] This need not be connected with his reconstruction of the harbour system. At the outset of his reign Trajan, while doing enough in Rome to consolidate his popularity, was preoccupied with frontier problems. Work on the new harbour was probably not begun until Dacia had been finally reduced in 106. By then Trajan had more time and more money for major schemes.

[1] R. Paribeni, *Optimus Princeps* (1927) ii. 108.

[2] Pliny, *Panegyric*, 29. 2.

[3] P. L. Strack, *Untersuchungen zur röm. Reichsprägung des zweiten Jahrhunderts* (1931) i. 212.

[4] 112 is excluded because the completion of the harbour is not recorded in the fully preserved entry for the year in the Ostian *Fasti*. Trajan left Rome for Parthia in 114.

[5] *S* 4342.

Appendix IV

A PASSAGE IN MINUCIUS FELIX

MINUCIUS FELIX, in his dialogue *Octavius*, gives a vivid picture of the Ostian shore. His language, however, is difficult and his meaning is not always clear.

II (3) . . . placuit Ostiam petere, amoenissimam civitatem, quod esset corpori meo siccandis umoribus de marinis lavacris blanda et adposita curatio: sane et ad vindemiam feriae iudiciariam curam relaxaverant. Nam id temporis post aestivam diem in temperiem semet autumnitas dirigebat. (4) itaque cum diluculo ad mare inambulando litori (litore)[1] pergeremus, ut et aura adspirans leniter membra vegetaret et cum eximia voluptate molli vestigio cedens harena subsideret, Caecilius simulacro Serapidis denotato, ut vulgus superstitiosus solet, manum ori admovens osculum labiis pressit.

III (2) . . . cum hoc sermone eius medium spatium civitatis emensi iam liberum litus tenebamus. (3) ibi harenas extimas, velut sterneret ambulacro, perfundens lenis unda tendebat; et, ut semper mare etiam positis flatibus inquietum est, etsi non canis spumosisque fluctibus exibat ad terram, tamen crispis tortuosisque ibidem erroribus delectati perquam sumus, cum in ipso aequoris limine plantas tingueremus, quod vicissim nunc adpulsum nostris pedibus adluderet fluctus, nunc relabens ac vestigia retrahens in sese resorberet. (4) sensim itaque tranquilleque progressi oram curvi molliter litoris iter fabulis fallentibus legebamus. Haec fabulae erant Octavi disserentis de navigatione narratio. (5) sed ubi eundi spatium satis iustum cum sermone consumpsimus, eandem emensi viam rursus versis vestigiis terebamus, et cum ad id loci ventum est, ubi subductae naviculae substratis roboribus a terrena labe suspensae quiescebant, pueros videmus certatim gestientes testarum in mare iaculationibus ludere. . . .

IV (5) 'modo in istis ad tutelam balnearum iactis et in altum procurrentibus petrarum obicibus residamus, ut et requiescere de itinere possimus et intentius disputare.'

We decided to visit Ostia, a most attractive town, since the sea baths would provide a soothing and fitting treatment for drying the humours of my body. The holidays for the vine harvest had brought an end to the anxieties of the courts; for after the summer heat the autumn was moving to a cooler mood.

[1] In II (4) the Teubner editor rightly prefers *litori* to the alternative manuscript reading *litore*. 'inambulando litore' would imply that the morning walk begins on the coast. It is clear later that the friends have to walk through the town before they come to the sea. The dative expresses purpose.

So daybreak found us making towards the sea to walk up and down the shore so that the breeze gently blowing might refresh our limbs and we might experience the great pleasure of feeling sand give way gently beneath our feet. Caecilius noticed an image of Serapis and, following the superstition of the common people, moved his hand to his lips and impressed a kiss. . . .

This talk brought us through the middle of the town and we had now reached the open shore. There the water was gently lapping the edge of the sand, as if it was levelling it for our walk; and restless as the sea is even when the winds have dropped, though it did not come in white and foaming waves, yet it trickled in, curling and winding, in a way which delighted us. We dipped our steps in the edge of the sea itself, which washed the waves against our feet and then withdrew them and sucked them back. Leisurely and peacefully we made our way along the gently curving shore with beguiling stories. These came from Octavius on the subject of sailing. But when we had walked as far as our talk took us, we turned and retraced our steps. When we came to the place where the little boats drawn up from the sea rested on their oak frames which raised them from the dangers of rotting that contact with the ground would bring, we saw some young boys competing eagerly at ducks and drakes. . . .

'Let us sit down on this breakwater built to protect the bathing place and running out to sea, so that we can rest from our walk and converse more seriously.'

I assume that the friends lodge in the town. At daybreak they walk, perhaps along the western Decumanus, to the coast, and proceed south along the curving shoreline away from Ostia towards Castel Fusano. They then retrace their steps to the point on the coast from which they started, where they sit on a breakwater built out to sea to protect bathers.

Le Gall[1] has drawn inferences from this passage which need reconsideration:

1. He thinks that the morning walk begins at the east end of the town near the Porta Romana. The friends first proceed along the Tiber bank until they come approximately to the Grandi Horrea; they then leave the river and cross the town by the western Decumanus. Since at the beginning of their walk they are treading on sand, he infers that the Tiber had no embankment east of the Forum. This interpretation rests on a different text in II (4): *itaque cum diluculo ad mare in amnis ambulando litore pergeremus.* For this text there is no manuscript authority and the order of words would be strained even for Minucius Felix. The existence of large Antonine *horrea* at the east end of the town makes it virtually certain that the embankment extended eastwards from the Forum.

2. He suggests that the *balneae* of the passage should be identified with

[1] Le Gall, *Le Tibre*, 333–7.

the small set of baths on the ancient shoreline immediately south of the Baths of Porta Marina. These baths, however, are almost certainly later than the date of the dialogue, and enclosed baths would not need a breakwater to protect them. The reference is presumably to bathing in the open sea.

3. He sees in the small boats evidence for tunny fishing. The inference is too specific. There is nothing odd in small fishing boats being drawn up on the sand in September.

For minor differences of interpretation see Becatti, *Scavi di Ostia*, vi, 51.

Appendix V

SOME OSTIAN FAMILIES

The Publii Lucilii Gamalae

AMONG the families which played a leading part in Ostia's public life the P. Lucilii Gamalae have a unique record. Before 1938 their history was based on eight inscriptions; each presented difficult problems. The excavations begun in 1938 added three further inscriptions; these introduced new problems without resolving the old.

CIL xiv. 375 (**1**) and 376 (**2**) are the key to the family history. They record in detail distinguished careers and they mention a large number of public buildings. Few Ostian inscriptions have been more often quoted, and many false deductions have been made from them. Lively controversy has continued intermittently since 1849 and the main issues are not yet resolved.

Though **1** is no longer extant, its genuineness has not been seriously questioned. It was discovered in the sixteenth century at Porto and there are too many divergences in the copies that have survived to suggest a forgery. Fea could find no trace of it at the beginning of the nineteenth century, but a hundred years earlier Fabretti had seen a large fragment from the stone.[1] It was then much worn; variations in the text show that it was always difficult to read.

Mommsen was the first to draw attention to this inscription, in 1849.[2] On grounds that still seem cogent he dated the career to the Augustan age, but, when he wrote, **2** was unknown to him. This second inscription had remained unnoticed in the Vatican until it was published by Visconti in 1857;[3] but it was almost certainly known in the sixteenth century, for Ligorio seems to have used it for two of his less successful forgeries.[4] In every respect it is a puzzling document. In spite of the distinction of the career recorded it is cut in small letters on a very narrow block of marble.[5] The letters of the opening lines are neat and regular; the rest of the inscription (from l. 12) is cut meanly on an erasure and by a different hand; these letters are even smaller, irregular, and influenced by cursive script. The first part of the inscription is studded with accents; the second has only one. **2** is clearly related to **1** and seems to be a conscious imitation.

[1] Fea, *Viaggio*, 38; R. Fabretti, *Inscriptionum Antiquarum . . . explicatio* (Rome, 1699) 529 n. 381.

[2] Mommsen, *Berichte königlich sächs. Gesell. des Wiss. zu Leipzig.* 1 (1849) 290.

[3] C. L. Visconti, *Ann. Inst.* 29 (1857) 325.   [4] *CIL* xiv. 13*, 15*.

[5] Width 19 cm., height preserved 54 cm. The bottom of the stone is lost, but the inscription seems to be almost complete. Pl. xxxviii *d*.

Visconti and Homolle[1] rejected the second part of the inscription as a forgery, possibly the work of Ligorio. We may safely follow Mommsen in accepting the whole text as we now see it. The meanness of the second hand is an argument against forgery; a forger would naturally have copied carefully the style of the opening lines. The content is decisive. An early forger is not likely to have known that Ostia had a Forum Vinarium (24). *Navale a L. Coilio aedificatum* (25) also has a genuine ring: the archaic spelling of the name and the absence of cognomen suggest that it is taken from the original monument. A learned forger such as Ligorio could have known from the emperor's biography that Antoninus Pius presented a *lavacrum* to Ostia. He might well have added a restoration after fire to make his text more circumstantial; he is most unlikely to have added *porticum reparavit* (18–20). Any lingering doubts are removed if, as is almost certain, these baths are to be identified with the Baths of Neptune on the Decumanus (p. 409). Brickstamps provide evidence of reconstruction in the main wing of these baths under Marcus Aurelius.[2] Contemporary restoration in the portico on the Decumanus can also be seen.[3]

Mommsen revised his views in the light of Visconti's publication.[4] Emphasizing the close similarity of the texts he assumed that they referred to the same Gamala and could be regarded as complementary. He identified L. Caesar Aug. f. (2. 6) as L. Aelius Caesar, adopted by Hadrian at the end of 136. The *bellum navale* of l. 42 he referred to the fighting of M. Aurelius against the Marcomanni. According to Mommsen this Gamala's career stretched from the end of Trajan's reign to the reign of Marcus Aurelius.

It is a striking testimony to Mommsen's authority that his main conclusion held the field for more than fifty years, even surviving an attack which should have been fatal. It was accepted by Dessau[5] and by von Premerstein[6] and has been many times repeated. Seeck challenged briefly Mommsen's identification of the two careers, and returned to Mommsen's original Augustan date for I.[7] It was Carcopino who made the detailed demonstration that the two inscriptions must refer to different men.[8]

There can be no doubt that Carcopino is right in rejecting Mommsen's revised view. As he points out, though the two careers are superficially very similar, there are important differences. The Gamala of I is aedile in the cult of Vulcan (I. 4); the Gamala of 2 is both aedile and praetor (2. 3–4). The first

---

[1] Homolle, *Rev. arch.* 34 (1877) 234–53, 301–15.

[2] Bloch, *Bolli laterizi*, 243.

[3] Most of the brick piers of this portico probably date from the fourth century, but two of the series are much earlier.

[4] Mommsen, *EE* iii (1877) 322 = *Ges. Schrift.* 8 (1913) 329.

[5] *ILS* 6147. [6] von Premerstein, *Klio*, 12 (1912) 139.

[7] Seeck, *Gesch. des Untergangs der ant. Welt II*, 156 (with II. Anhang, 523).

[8] Carcopino, *Mélanges*, 31 (1911) 143.

is made a decurion *gratis* (**1**. 6); the second, *infans* (**2**. 5). The games of **1**. 11 are a special occasion; those of **2**. 23 are a series of games spread over a whole career. The first Gamala builds a new temple of Venus (**1**. 23); the second restores a temple of Venus (**2**. 21). Nor is there any valid reason why important benefactions mentioned in **2**, such as the restoration of the temple of Castor and Pollux (**2**. 12) and of the baths of Pius (**2**. 18), should be omitted in **1** and why others equally important should be present in **1** and absent in **2**. The inscriptions refer to two members of the family; it remains to date their careers.

The approximate date of **2** is determined by internal evidence. This Gamala restored a set of public baths after the death of Antoninus Pius in 160. A further clue should be provided in his appointment as *praefectus L(uci) Caes(aris) Aug(usti) f(ilius)* (**2**. 6). Mommsen and Dessau identified this Lucius Caesar with Lucius Aelius, Hadrian's adopted son. Carcopino challenged this identification on two grounds. He argued that, since Lucius is styled *Augusti filius*, his father should be living when the inscription was cut, especially since Antoninus Pius is described as *divus*. He also held that the appointment was in a censorial year, which excluded Lucius Aelius. The dates of censorial years are established by the Fasti; they fell in 131, 136, 141, but not between the end of 136, when Lucius was adopted, and his death in 138. Carcopino concluded that Lucius Caesar must be Commodus, and that the inscription was set up after 12 October 166, when he became Caesar, and before the death of M. Aurelius on 17 March 180.

Neither of these objections is decisive. If Lucius was the adopted son of the reigning emperor when he accepted the title of office at Ostia, *Augusti filius* could still be used after Hadrian's death, just as in the record of public careers emperors under whom a senator or knight has served are not necessarily styled *divus* if they are dead when the inscription is cut.[1] The second objection involves a difficult point of interpretation in the text (6–7): *iivir. praefecto L. Caesar. Aug. f. cens. q. a.* Carcopino suggests for the last three words *cens(um) q(uinquennalem) a(gentis)*. Such abbreviations are unparalleled and unacceptable; at the least we should expect *cens. quinq. ag.* The last two letters must stand for *q(uaestor) a(erarii)*. Carcopino resisted this solution on the ground that there was only one parallel at Ostia for the bare letters to describe the quaestor's office (5), and he thought that such abbreviations were incompatible with the recording of an important career in full. The parallel, however, is a good one, the career of Cn. Sentius Felix, adoptive father of a Gamala, whose distinguished career is also fully recorded. A further Ostian example has been added since Carcopino wrote.[2]

The use of *cens.* without qualification for the censorial duovirate is, as Carcopino emphasizes, unexpected. The full title of the office is *duovir censoria*

---

[1] Cf. *ILS* 986. [2] *S* 4648.

potestate quinquennalis, often shortened to *duovir quinquennalis* or *quinquennalis*. The form *cens.* (whether *censor*, or *censorius*) is found early in the Principate,[1] but not, apart from this inscription, in the second century. More difficult is the problem of punctuation. It is formally possible that one, two, or three offices are concerned. Gamala could have been *duovir praefectus* for Lucius in a censorial year; he could have been duovir, and then subsequently *praefectus* in a censorial year; or he could have been duovir, then *praefectus*, and later censorial duovir. Normal usage strongly favours the separation of the offices of duovir and *praefectus*.[2] It is more difficult to decide whether *cens.* stands for *censoris* (*censorii*) or *censori* (*censorio*). The first usage is common; for the second a parallel can be found at Ostia (Bloch, 23). M. Acilius Priscus is described on his statue base as *iivir aedil. ii quinquennal. praef. ii*. It has been suggested earlier (p. 197, n. 5) that the office of aedile has been misplaced. Priscus was probably duovir twice, censorial duovir once, and *praefectus* twice. Similarly Gamala may have been duovir, *praefectus*, and, later, *quinquennalis*.

This possibility should be kept in mind in the light of the opening two lines of the inscription recording the assigning of the site for the building of the temple of Bellona: 'A. Livius Proculus P. Lucilius Gamala f. iivir praef. Caesar.'[3] This Gamala was *praefectus Caesaris*; we have argued above that the Caesar he represented was L. Aelius (p. 201). It is an attractive economy to identify him with the Gamala of **2**. That Hadrian's adopted son was called Lucius Caesar we know from literary and epigraphic sources;[4] the name is not attested for Commodus who, so far as our evidence goes, was called either L. Aurelius Caesar or Commodus Caesar.[5] I therefore incline to the view that the Gamala of **2** was born towards the end of Trajan's reign. In view of his family tradition he was probably elected to the duovirate early; his father was still alive when in 137 he represented L. Aelius, since in the inscription on the temple of Bellona he is distinguished as *f(ilius)*. He will have become *pontifex Volcani* probably under Antoninus Pius and continued his public benefactions into the reign of Marcus Aurelius. He will have died either under M. Aurelius or Commodus. If we accept Carcopino's identification of Lucius Caesar with Commodus he will have been born some twenty years later and have died not later than 180.

Carcopino, while dissociating **2** from **1** decisively, did not accept an Augustan date for **1**. He based his view on the mention of *tribunal quaes(toris)* (39), the *bellum navale* (42), and the place of discovery, Portus. The discovery of the inscription at Portus suggested a date after the beginning of the Claudian harbour in A.D. 42; the *bellum navale* was the conquest of Britain; the inscription was set up between 42 and 44, when the quaestor was replaced by an imperial procurator.

---

[1] *S* 4710, Bloch, 61. [2] *RE*, 'duovir' (Liebenam), 1819. [3] 4.
[4] *CIL* xiv. 2486; SHA, *Marc. Aur.* 5. 1; *Verus*, 2. 1. [5] *PIR*[2], A 1482.

These controls are too stringent. It is doubtful whether important inferences should be drawn from the finding of the stone at Portus. The buildings and bequests of the inscription seem to concern Ostia and not the harbour area. If the inscription was originally set up by the harbours we should expect the fact and the reason to be stated on the stone. It is more likely that it once stood on the same site in Ostia as the other (2), which it seems to have closely resembled in form and style. In the fourth century and later, Ostia, in sharp decline, was the cheapest source of bricks and marble for the builders of Portus. Gamala's proud inscription may have been used to line a pavement or restore a wall.

The identification of the *bellum navale* with the British expedition should be rejected. It was well known that the tribes of Britain had no war fleet; no naval fighting can have been anticipated. Nor can we believe that the conquest of Britain was financed by Italian towns. Mommsen's view that the war in question was against the Marcomanni and that the money was needed to strengthen the Pannonian and Moesian fleets has the same weakness; in the northern campaigns of Marcus Aurelius the fleets played a very subordinate part and the war could not reasonably be described as a *bellum navale*. von Premerstein's identification with a war against the Moorish pirates in the western Mediterranean or against the Kostoboki under Marcus Aurelius,[1] or Mancini's with Commodus' projected expedition against the Moors,[2] suit the language better, but their attractiveness rests on the false assumption that **1** and **2** refer to the same Gamala. The fighting against the Moors falls within the career of the second; the *bellum navale* occurs during the career of the first.

In view of the striking similarity of the records it is tempting to assign both inscriptions to the second century. This was the view briefly stated by Wilson, who suggested that they commemorated father and son.[3] It was developed more fully by Miss Taylor in an interesting re-examination of **1**.[4] Miss Taylor found an important clue in a piece of evidence not known to her predecessors. A fragment of the Fasti records the restoration of the temple of Vulcan in 112. This temple was restored by the elder Gamala, who was aedile in the cult of Vulcan and, later, *pontifex*: *idem aedem Volcani sua pecunia restituit* (21 f.). 'It seems very likely that this restoration (of 112) was identical with the one made by the *pontifex* P. Lucilius Gamala of no. 375.'

If this identification were right, *bellum navale* cannot mean a naval war, for there was no serious naval engagement under the Flavians, Trajan, or Hadrian. Miss Taylor revived a suggestion made long ago by Cavedoni that *bellum navale* is here used instead of the normal *naumachia* for a naval display.[5] She

[1] von Premerstein, *Klio* 12 (1912) 141.

[2] Mancini, *Atti Reale Acc. Nap.* 13 (1887–9) 170.   [3] Wilson, *BSR* 14 (1938) 152.

[4] L. R. Taylor, *AJP* 57 (1936) 183, followed by Thylander, *Étude sur l'épigraphie latine* (1952) 6–9.   [5] Cavedoni, *Bull. arch. Nap.* NS 6 (1858) 195.

suggested that Gamala's contribution to a *bellum navale* may have been made for the *naumachia* of Trajan recorded for 109 in the Fasti of Ostia: *III id. Nov.* [*i*]*mp. Traianus naumachiam suam dedicavit* [*in*] *qua dieb. VI pp. CXXVIIS et consumm. VIII k. Dec.* The duration of the celebration for six days justified the use of *bellum* instead of *proelium.* Miss Taylor further suggested that the spectacle was held in Trajan's new hexagonal basin at Ostia, following the precedent of the great *naumachia* of Claudius on the Fucine lake. The contribution promised by the colony of Ostia was not for the expenses of the spectacle, which the emperor himself probably defrayed, but for the entertainment of the visitors who would have had to come from Rome and the surrounding towns for a stay of some days. His public-spirited contribution to the fund for the *bellum navale* caused the decurions of Ostia to vote Gamala a bronze statue at Ostia beside the quaestor's tribunal, and a gilded statue (**1**. 30), the location of which is not specified. Miss Taylor tentatively suggests that the lost inscription (**1**), found at Portus, may have been cut on the base of this second statue, set up near the scene of the *bellum navale.* Miss Taylor's conclusion is that this Gamala reached the peak of his career under Trajan and was probably grandfather of the Gamala of **2**. Carcopino's point that the mention of a *tribunal quaes(toris)* sets a lower limit of A.D. 44 Miss Taylor meets by suggesting that the tribunal belonged to the chief officer of the local treasury, the *quaestor aerarii Ostiensis.*

These arguments are extremely vulnerable. It is very unlikely that a public *naumachia* would have been held in Trajan's harbour at least three years before the issue of the commemorative coinage celebrating the completion of the work, and Strack has shown convincingly that the coins were issued when Trajan was cos. VI, that is, in or after 112 (p. 489). It is also virtually certain that the entry in the Fasti for 109 records the dedication of a building in Rome.[1] This does not, however, rule out the possibility that a naval display was given in the harbour at Ostia in one of the later years of the reign not covered in detail by the Fasti; but would the town in those expansive days have sold its properties to raise the promised contribution? We are also still left with the difficulty of accepting *bellum navale* as an alternative for *naumachia. Bellum* is certainly used for *proelium* in poets and late prose, but I can find no convincing example of the use of *bellum* for a mock battle or series of mock battles.[2]

The argument on which the dating hinges, the date of the restoration of the temple of Vulcan, has now lost much of its force. A further fragment of the Fasti, unknown to Miss Taylor when she wrote, records that M. Acilius Priscus Egrilius Plarianus was made *pontifex Volcani* in 105; he was still alive in 118 (Bloch, 25). Gamala cannot have been *pontifex* when the temple was restored in 112. This does not exclude the possibility that he paid for the

---

[1] Degrassi, *Fasti,* 229 (on 109, l. 15).   [2] *Thesaurus ling. lat.* ii. 1824-7, 1851.

restoration, but it makes the suggestion much less convincing. Nor is it easy to fit in Gamala's period as *pontifex* in this period. We know that M. Acilius Priscus Egrilius Plarianus was immediately preceded by P. Ostiensis Macedo (Fasti, 105); by 128 (*S* 4445) the office was held by his nephew, A. Egrilius Plarianus the younger. Gamala was appointed *pontifex* before he became duovir (**1**. 7–8), presumably fairly early in life; he should have held the office a long time. Nor is it easy to accept Miss Taylor's suggestion that the Ostian quaestor had a special tribunal, unless other municipal parallels can be found. If the inscription was originally set up at Portus it was not on the base of Gamala's gilded statue. The stone is variously described as a *cippus* or a *columna quadrata*; it was not a statue base.

These difficulties disappear if we return to Mommsen's original view that the elder Gamala is Augustan. The arguments may be briefly tabulated:

1. *Bellum navale* can have its natural meaning. It is the war against Sextus Pompeius of 38–36 B.C. This war, on which corn supplies depended, concerned Ostia vitally. Appian records that Octavian was promised help by friends and cities.[1] Ostia's promised contribution in such a context needs no explanation. The need to sell public property to raise money accords much better with the difficult years of civil war than with the great prosperity of the early second century. It must be admitted that after *pollicitatio* we should expect an objective genitive of the thing promised, but there is no great difficulty in understanding *belli navalis* as a substitute for a prepositional phrase which would have been less elegant, the promise arising from, associated with, or in the time of the naval war.[2]

2. *Tribunal quaes(toris)* can also have its natural meaning. It is the tribunal from which the Roman quaestor stationed at Ostia administered justice. That he had powers of jurisdiction might be assumed from his function of controlling the passage through Ostia of corn for Rome. It is confirmed by the full title, *quaestor pro praetore*, recorded on two inscriptions.[3] The natural inference is that the inscription was set up before the quaestor was withdrawn in A.D. 44.

3. The colleague with whom Gamala presented weights to the Macellum, M. Turranius, has no cognomen. The absence of cognomen is common in the late Republic and under Augustus.[4] In the second century when the emphasis had shifted decisively to the cognomen it would have been a very strange anomaly.

4. Gamala shared in a presentation of weights to the Macellum (29–31).

---

[1] Appian, *BC* v. 92; cf. Dio xlviii. 49.

[2] Cf. Cicero, *Tusc. disp.* i. 30, 'deorum opinio (= de deis)'; id. *Ad fam.* viii. 8. 4 (Caelius), 'exspectatio Galliarum (= de Galliis quid decernatur)'. On this and other points of Latinity I owe much to my colleague, Mr. G. W. Williams.

[3] 3603, Bloch, 32.   [4] *Fasti*, 48, 47, 45 B.C.; 426, *S* 4710. See p. 477 f.

The entry comes towards the end of the inscription and therefore probably records one of his last benefactions. An inscription records the restoration of the Macellum under Augustus (Bloch, 67). This would have been a particularly suitable occasion for presenting new weights. Similarly the weights presented by the Gamala of **2** may have accompanied a large-scale restoration which can be dated in the later part of the second century (p. 549). There is, however, clearly no necessary association between new weights and new building.

5. It is unsatisfactory to argue from the form of an inscription that has never been described in detail and is now lost; but we can accept the length of line as recorded. The number of very short lines seems out of place in the second century, but much less surprising under Augustus.

6. There are not sufficient early forms in **1** to argue strongly from the spelling. *Ahenea* (38), *proxume* (39), *trichilinis* (17) would be unusual in the second century; but, since **2** has *peq(unia)* for *pec(unia)* (27), it would be dangerous to argue from such evidence.

7. The style of the Latin is perhaps closer to Caesar than to the second century. In particular the use of *propterea quod* is still common in Caesar and Cicero, but is very rarely used in the Empire.[1]

If these arguments are sound, the Gamala of **1** was born in the late Republic, probably between 80 and 60 B.C. He had reached maturity when Caesar crossed the Rubicon and was a leading figure in Ostia during the difficult years of civil war. He lived to see the new order established after Actium and deserved the public funeral that was voted to him when he died under Augustus. His descendant of the second century (**2**) was very conscious of the family tradition of public service and even the inscription that commemorated him was closely modelled in form and style on that of his Augustan predecessor.

Some further notes of interpretation which do not affect the central issue should be added:

1. 5–6. *aedili d(ecurionum) d(ecreto) allecto gratis decurioni*. His admission by the decurions might formally apply to the aedileship or the decurionate. For the first there is a rough parallel in Cn. Sergius Priscus, *ex d(ecreto) d(ecurionum) aedili adlecto* (412), but, since *gratis* almost certainly applies to his admission to the council, the preceding phrase should accompany it. The order of words is unusual, the standard formula being *decurionum decreto decurio adlectus*.

---

[1] K. Reisinger, *Über Bedeutung u. Verwend. Praep.* propter, i (Landau, 1897) 75, ii (Speyer, 1900) 60. The order of words in l. 12, 'in ludos cum accepisset public(um) lucar remisit', has more parallels in Caesar than in second-century prose. Mommsen originally held that *lucar* suggested an early date, but the word is still used by Tacitus (*Ann.* i. 77. 4).

9–12. *iivir(o) censoriae pot(estatis) quinquennal(i) in comitis facto curatori pecuniae publicae exigendae . . . . In comitis facto* might qualify what precedes or what follows. Normal usage favours the first alternative, but the close parallel in **2**. 13–16, *idem curator pecuniae publicae exigendae et attribuendae in comitis factus*, favours the second. The office of *quinquennalis* was a normal magistracy; it is more likely that the form of appointment was specified in the financial office, which was an extraordinary appointment. The order of words resembles the entry in lines 5–6.

15–16. *idem sua pecunia viam silice stravit quae est iuncta foro ab arcu ad arcum.* All streets leading to the Forum have now been excavated and there are no arches at the Hadrianic level that fit this context. Tentatively I suggest that the street paved by Gamala is the Decumanus Maximus where it passes through the centre of the town and that the 'arches' are the original east and west gates of the fourth-century Castrum. These were probably not destroyed until the sharp raising of the level in the late first or early second century.

23 sq. This Gamala built temples of Venus, Fortuna, Ceres, and, later, of Spes. They have been tentatively identified with three of the four small temples on a common platform west of the theatre and the slightly later temple at the corner of the Decumanus and the Via dei Molini (p. 351).

43. It should be emphasized that the sum of money contributed by Gamala is variously recorded and must be regarded as most uncertain.

2. 25. *idem navale a L. Coilio aedificatum extruentibus fere collapsum restituit.* On the stone one can read EXTRU-NTIBUS. The spacing of letters in the second half of the inscription is irregular, and either one or two letters could be missing. Mommsen's *extruentibus* is to be preferred to *extrudentibus*; the *navale* was for the building of ships. Carcopino identified this *navale* with a building some 200 metres east of Tor Boacciona, but a limited excavation showed that this building did not extend to the river (p. 126).

The Gamalae remained prominent in the Julio-Claudian period. A P. Lucilius Gamala is recorded in the Fasti as 'iivir II' in A.D. 19, and two new inscriptions record members of the family in the early Principate. The first (3) honours a Gamala for pleading the case of Ostia in the Roman senate.[1] He had been aedile at Ostia, military tribune, decurion, duovir four times. The letters of the inscription are deep and carefully cut. They suggest an Augustan or early Julio-Claudian date. Other signs of an early date are the abbreviations *trib. milit.* without the name of the legion, and the archaic form *grateis*. The first two lines, recording the name, are on a lower level, suggesting that the original surface has been cut away, but there is no reason for dissociating the career from the man.

---

[1] This inscription was first published by F. Grosso in *Atti del III° Congresso internazionale di Epigrafia greca e latina*, 1959, 133.

This career has certain resemblances to the Augustan Gamala already considered (**1**). Both are co-opted to the council without fee; both are aedile before becoming councillor. It is not impossible that they refer to the same man; it is, however, unlikely. The Gamala of **1** becomes *pontifex Volcani* before he reaches the censorial duovirate; the Gamala of the new inscription is not yet *pontifex Volcani* when he has held the duovirate four times. In the career of the Gamala of **1** the military tribunate, having no Ostian reference, might have been omitted; but the pleading of Ostia's case in the Roman senate would have been included. The Gamala of **3** is better identified with the duovir II of A.D. 19.

The second new inscription of an early period is a mere fragment. Only the beginnings of four lines are preserved: 'P. Lucilio— | P. nep.— | Ga— | pon—'. This inscription would seem to honour a Gamala who is *pontifex Volcani.* The letters are good and early. This Gamala might be Augustan; he might even be the Gamala of the lost inscription (**1**).

The history of the family in the Flavian period and in the early second century is elusive. A Gamala was adopted by Cn. Sentius Felix, the wealthy patron of so many guilds, and became Cn. Sentius Clodianus Lucilius Gamala. It has been suggested that he may be the Cn. Sentius Clodianus, recorded in the Fasti as duovir for 102, and as patron with his adoptive father of an unidentified guild under Hadrian (p. 201). A bolder conjecture has also been made, that possibly his elder brother served as *praefectus* for Hadrian in 126, and that it was this man's son who served for Lucius Aelius Caesar in 137 (p. 201). Spanning the next half-century we have the detailed career of the last Gamala known to us (**2**).

For some 200 years at least the family had held high office in Ostia. Two at least of its members had been *pontifex Volcani*; they had built and rebuilt temples and been generous to the common people. Like M. Acilius Priscus Egrilius Plarianus (Bloch, 24) they were 'pii ac religiosissimi', loyal to their town and family, and upholders of the traditional cults. We have suggested that the family had no connexion with the east and that its roots were in Italy, but probably outside Ostia (p. 194). There is no evidence connecting them with trade, and their freedmen are not found in the guild rolls. They were probably landed gentry. Doubtless they could have made their way in the imperial service; it seems that they deliberately preferred the less anxious honours of local government.

The Senatorial Egrilii

The chronology and relationships of the senatorial Egrilii have been much disputed since the middle of the nineteenth century. None of the earlier reconstructions, however, have withstood the crucial test of new discoveries. Further inscriptions found in the excavations begun in 1938 have provided firm chronological controls and added much new evidence for the history of the family. These new inscriptions were admirably published by Bloch in 1953; what follows is based on his Italian commentary.[1]

M. Acilius Priscus A. f. Egrilius Plarianus was already known to have been *praefectus aerari militaris* before his appointment as *pontifex Volcani* (S 4444). We now know from the Fasti that he became *pontifex* in 105. He was *praefectus aerarii Saturni* in 106 (Bloch, 25),[*] and was still alive in 118 when, with his son, he set up a commemorative tablet to Hadrian (Bloch, 26). We do not know whether he reached the consulship; he will have been born about 70 or rather earlier. His adoptive father was a M. Acilius Priscus whom, following Bloch, we may identify with the M. Acilius Priscus of an inscription on a statue base found in 1938 (Bloch, 23 = 7). The lettering of this inscription suggests a date in or near the Flavian period. Priscus was dead by or soon after 100, because he was *pontifex Volcani*, and this post, which was held for life, was filled by M. Acilius Priscus Egrilius Plarianus from 105, and by P. Ostiensis Macedo before him (Fasti, 105).[2] His connexion with the Egrilii is established by the inscription itself, for Priscus left instructions in his will for his statue to be set up 'per A. Egrilium [?Primi]genium'. His adopted son, now rising in his senatorial career, may not have been in a position to act.

Before his adoption M. Acilius Priscus A. f. Egrilius Plarianus was an Egrilius Plarianus; his father, like the earlier Egrilii recorded in the Fasti, was an Aulus Egrilius. The cognomen Plarianus, which replaced Rufus in the main branch of the Egrilii, clearly comes from Plaria Q. f. Vera, *flaminica divae Augustae*, who is honoured as 'mater A. Egrili Plariani, patris, p(atroni) c(oloniae), co(n)s(ulis)' (399). Bloch is also probably right, following a suggestion made by Freeman Adams, in identifying her husband with an A. Egrilius Rufus whose career is recorded in a new inscription (Bloch, 22 = 6).[*] He was aedile, quaestor, duovir, and *flamen Romae et Augusti*. The style of the lettering seems to be too late to commend identification with A. Egrilius Rufus recorded in the Fasti as *praefectus* in 36.

Bloch rightly insists that, since M. Acilius Priscus Egrilius Plarianus is given all his names in the Fasti and in at least five other Ostian inscriptions, he cannot be identified with A. Egrilius Plarianus, pater, consul, son of Plaria Vera (399). He was probably his younger brother. The clue comes in a later Q. Egrilius Plarianus, who served as staff legate in Africa towards the end of Antoninus Pius' reign, when an Egrilius Plarianus, probably his father, was governor.[3] As Bloch points out, the praenomen Quintus, like the cognomen

[1] Bloch, *NS* 1953, 254–64.

[2] Priscus may not have been the immediate predecessor of Macedo. Barbieri (*Studi romani*, i (1953) 369) restores a probable fragment from the *Fasti*: 'in locum Q. Do[miti P. Ost]iensis Ma[cedo pontif(ex) . . . creatus est.']

[3] *CIL* viii. 110260; *AE* 1942–3, 85.

Plarianus, should have come to the family from Plaria Vera Q. f., and from this it is a logical step to infer that M. Acilius Priscus Egrilius Plarianus started life as Q. Egrilius Plarianus, younger son of Plaria Vera and A. Egrilius Rufus. Bloch offers an attractive restoration of an inscription which would make Plaria Vera honoured as his mother. Two friends, L. Vettius Felix and P. Novellius Atticus, who commemorated M. Acilius Priscus Egrilius Plarianus (155), also commemorated one of his relations (156): 'Plariae Q. f. Verae matri' would admirably fill the gap. It was probably his son, reverting to the father's original family name, Q. Egrilius Plarianus, who was governor of Africa in 158/9 after holding the consulship in 143 or 144.[1]

The elder son of Plaria Vera, A. Egrilius Plarianus, was, like his brother, prefect of the public treasury (Bloch, 27); he became consul in or near the early years of Trajan.* In his inscriptions he is described as *pater* (399 and Bloch, 27) to distinguish him from his son, who was appointed to the military treasury before becoming consul in 128 (*S* 4445; Fasti, 128). The son was *pontifex Volcani* while he was at the military treasury (*S* 4445). Probably he directly succeeded his uncle, who held the office from 105 at least until 118.

We may have a record of a near relation of these senatorial Egrilii in an unpublished funerary inscription set up by an Ostian *procurator Augusti* who was also a patron of the colony (above, p. 208). His wife was Egrilia Pulchra, and the fine lettering of the inscription suggests the Flavian period or the early second century.

One inscription still remains very controversial. A fragment from a roll of the members of an Ostian guild, probably the *dendrophori*, includes distinguished names among its patrons (281): '[patr]oni | —cus Egril(ius) Plarian(us) | —f. Larcius Lepidus | —Plarianus | —Agrippinus.' It is tempting to restore the first name as M. Acilius Priscus Egrilius Plarianus, but the guild roll is firmly dated in the Severan period.[2] Bloch, following Wickert, believes that the name of M. Acilius Priscus Egrilius Plarianus was retained among the patrons owing to his special distinction long after his death, and with him his son, Q. Egrilius Plarianus, and C. Fabius Agrippinus, the Ostian consul of 148.[3] This is difficult to accept. There were other and better ways of honouring dead patrons than in listing their names on an active roll. The names should be those of living men.

The second patron on the list seems to be a Larcius Lepidus adopted into another family. The senatorial Larcii were not Ostian, but it is interesting to

[1] For the date of the consulship, Syme, *JRS* 36 (1946) 167; Degrassi, *Fasti consolari*, p. 41.

[2] If P. Claudius Abascantus qq II (281, col. 2, 15) is, as seems certain, to be identified with P. Claudius Abascantus qq II corp(oris) dendrophorum Ostiens(ium), honoured with a statue in 203 (324).

[3] Bloch, 264; Wickert, 'Zur Geschichte der Gens Egrilia', *Sitz. Preuss. Ak. Wiss.* (Berlin, 1928) 6.

note that A. Larcius Eutyches was manufacturing water-pipes at Ostia under Hadrian,[1] and the name is not uncommon in the town later. Perhaps the family had a villa in the neighbourhood. The association of the Larcii Lepidi with the Egrilii is probably reflected in the cognomen of A. Larcius Lepidus Plarianus, mentioned in the record of the Arval brothers for 145 (*ILS* 5038); and, more clearly, in the presence of a Larcius Lepidus on the staff of Q. Egrilius Plarianus when he was governor of Africa. The patron might be the son, of this Larcius Lepidus, adopted by Q. Egrilius Plarianus the governor's son, who served as his colleague on the staff in Africa.[2] The third patron could be a Q. Egrilius Plarianus, grandson of the governor of Africa. C. Fabius Agrippinus, if this is the right restoration, could be the son or grandson of the Ostian consul of 148. The first name is the most puzzling, but it might represent an association of the Egrilii with another branch of the Larcii, the Larcii Prisci: A. Larcius Priscus Egrilius Plarianus. Precise identification cannot be pressed. It is sufficient to show that there is no insuperable objection to regarding the Severan patrons of the *dendrophori* as living men. They witness the continued concern of the senatorial Egrilii for Ostia.

There are further tantalizing glimpses of the influential connexions of the Egrilii. An inscription on a statue base from Pisaurum commemorates Arria L. f. Plaria Vera Priscilla, *flaminica*, wife of M'. Acilius Glabrio, consul (*CIL* xi. 6333). She should be related to Plaria Vera, wife of A. Egrilius Rufus. The association of the Egrilii with the L. Arrii at a lower level is attested by an Ostian inscription set up to L. Arrius Hermes, *vascularius*, by an A. Egrilius Plarianus (467). It is also tempting to link a dedication by M. Acilius Priscus Egrilius Plarianus to Diana Nemorensis (*CIL* xiv. 2212) with the name of Arria Priscilla (? = Arria Plaria Vera Priscilla) on a water-pipe in Diana's sanctuary (*CIL* xv. 7830). The date of the Pisauran statue base is not recorded. The letters are well shaped, the organization of the text simple and severe. The identification of Priscilla's husband with M'. Acilius Glabrio, consul of 152, adopted by Groag[3] and commonly accepted, cannot be ruled out, but an earlier Glabrio, the consul of 91 or his son, the consul of 124, is to be preferred; such an earlier dating, better suited to the lettering of the monument, would have the additional advantage of bringing Arria Plaria Vera Priscilla nearer to Plaria Vera.

An inscription from Rome suggests that an Egrilia married into the Vibii Maximi (*CIL* vi. 1538): 'C. Vibio, C. fil. Maximo Egriliano laticlavio'. This Maximus may be descended from C. Vibius Maximus, friend of Statius, prefect of Egypt in 104 (*PIR*[1] V 389), and, perhaps before that, *praefectus*

---

[1] 1996.

[2] The town of Gigthi set up three statues to patrons, the proconsul (whose name is only partly preserved), his son Q. Egrilius Plarianus, and – Larcius Lepidus. *CIL* viii. 11030, 11026, 11027.

[3] *PIR*[2] A 73, A 1120.

annonae.[1] The marriage of a *praefectus annonae*, whose work will have taken him to Ostia, or of his son to an Ostian Egrilia is an attractive hypothesis. Two other inscriptions may probably be dismissed. In Parma was discovered an inscription set up to his wife Asicia Frontine by O. Aegrilius Plarianus (*CIL* xi. 1075). Perhaps the cutter should have written Q, but the Asicii were not, so far as we know, socially distinguished or politically prominent; it is unlikely that this is a senatorial Q. Egrilius. Similarly A. Egrilius A. f. Plarianus, *decurialis scr(iba) cer(arius)*, married to a Claudia Hermione (346), must, in spite of his name, be descended from a freedman of the family.

The senatorial Egrilii may have acquired philosophical interests in their rise to imperial distinction. Among Fronto's letters addressed to his friends is one to an Egrilius Plarianus;[2] Groag has also suggested that Q. Aelius Egrilius Euactus, *philosophus* (*ILS* 7776), the friend of Salvius Junianus, may have derived his citizenship from Q. Egrilius Plarianus, governor of Africa, or his son (*PIR*[2], E 49).

The Egrilii and the Lucilii Gamalae are the two outstanding families in Ostia's local history during the early Empire. They were both well established by the time of Augustus and they maintained their pre-eminence in the town through the second century. Both families proudly emphasize their long line of free ancestors. Both respected Ostia's religious traditions, providing each at least two members who became *pontifex Volcani*. Both accepted the informal responsibilities of public generosity attached to public office. But the contrast between them is sharp. The Gamalae confined their ambitions to Ostia; the Egrilii seized their chances when further opportunities were given to new men under the Flavian and second-century emperors, and gave distinguished service to the empire, without forgetting their town of origin. The contrast may be explained by the background of the two families. We have suggested that the fortunes of the Egrilii were based on trade. This is an inference from the wide distribution of their freedmen in the trade guilds and their own accumulation of treasury posts. It may be significant that of the few Ostian bankers recorded three are freedmen of the Egrilii.[3] The Gamalae were probably conservative landowners.

Against this background the adoptions from the two families in or near the Flavian period have an air of irony. The conservative Gamalae give one of their members to Cn. Sentius Felix, a rich trader, who has probably only recently come to Ostia. From the progressive Egrilii Q. Egrilius Plarianus is adopted into an old Ostian family by M. Acilius Priscus, who gave up imperial ambitions for a long period of public office in Ostia, and who seems to

[1] Syme, 'C. Vibius Maximus, Prefect of Egypt', *Hist.* 6 (1957) 483 f. The Roman inscription is probably not earlier than the late Antonine period (Syme, art. cit. 487 n. 40). [2] Fronto, *Ad amicos*, 1. 4 (MS. Accri[lio Pl]ariano).
[3] *S* 4644, Bloch, 53 (referring also to a third, unpublished, inscription).

have had no connexion with trade. Perhaps the unexpected alliance of the Gamalae with business interests was dictated by financial stringency. As the standard of living rose and the cost of public benefactions increased, their land revenues may have proved inadequate. The Egrilii, on the other hand, were wealthy; their main concern in the adoption was to increase their social prestige.

The Acilii

That M. Acilius Priscus, the Flavian knight (Bloch, 23), assumed to be the adoptive father of M. Acilius Priscus Egrilius Plarianus, was an Ostian living in Ostia can be regarded as certain in view of his long record of local office. It is natural to associate him with M. Acilius, duovir of 48 B.C. (Fasti). To the same family should belong M. Acilius M. f. Caninus (153). As Roman quaestor he was honoured with a statue at Ostia by the *negotiatores ex area Saturni*. We may infer that he was an Ostian and that he held the quaestorship when quaestors still presided over the public treasury, that is, before 28 B.C. He is probably not to be identified with the duovir of 48 B.C. since the latter has no cognomen in the Fasti and the lettering of Caninus' inscription seems later; there should, however, be some relationship. He should also be related to M. Acilius, legate of Caesar in 48 B.C. and proconsul of Sicily in 46/45, whose cognomen is variously given by different manuscripts as Caninus, Caninius, Caninianus.[1] No M. Acilii during the Empire rose to imperial distinction, and the M. Acilius Priscus who adopted Q. Egrilius Plarianus may be the last of the line. Freedmen of the family and their descendants, Aciliae and M. Acilii, are not uncommon in Ostia.

Very different were the Manii Acilii. Two brothers, Glabrio and Aviola, were raised by P. Scipio Africanus to the consulship at the beginning of the second century B.C.[2] A M'. Acilius Aviola was consul in A.D. 239; M'. Acilii Glabriones also held consulships in the third century. They weathered the storms of civil war and avoided dangerous prominence under the Julio-Claudians. The consul of 91 and his father were both members of Domitian's *consilium*;[3] the son, a too successful performer against wild beasts at the emperor's Alban villa, was killed in 95 on suspicion of plotting revolution.[4] He had been consul with the future emperor Trajan and would have been one of the leading figures of his reign. But his son survived him to be consul in 124, and consulships came to his descendants in 152 and 186 (for the second

---

[1] For Caesar's legate of 48 B.C. the manuscripts give only the cognomen and record it differently. The Oxford text (1900) and the Teubner text (1950) print M'. Acilius; that his praenomen was Marcus is shown by Dio xlii. 12. 1. As governor of Sicily he was hard pressed for favours by Cicero (*Ad fam.* xiii. 30–39).

[2] F. Münzer, *Römische Adelsparteien und Adelsfamilien*, 91.

[3] Juv. iv. 94–98.   [4] Dio lxvii. 14. 3; Suet. *Dom.* 10. 2; Juv. iv. 94 with schol.

time). The Manii Acilii had been a new family when they rose to the consulship; by the end of the second century few could match their nobility. The consul II of 186 boasted descent from Aeneas, and was offered the throne by Pertinax.[1]

This great family had associations with Ostia. 'Glabrio p(atronus) c(oloniae)', who set up a statue of Hygia outside the Porta Romana to *salus Caesaris Augusti* (*S* 4324), is clearly a M'. Acilius Glabrio, recalling in the form of his dedication his family's association with the introduction of Greek medicine to Rome;[2] but his identification is uncertain. Groag, emphasizing the title Caesar Augustus, which, though still found under Claudius and Nero,[4] points more naturally to Augustus, suggested identification with the proconsul of Africa of 25 B.C. (*PIR²*, A 71). The lettering of the inscription seems to me too mature for this date,[3] and M'. Acilius Memmius Glabrio, Tiber curator under Tiberius (*PIR²*, A 75), perhaps his son, is to be preferred. M'. Acilius Aviola, consul in 54 A.D., who may also have been called Glabrio (*PIR²*, A 62), cannot be ruled out. The level of the base shows that it is earlier than the rebuilding of the Porta Romana under Domitian or Trajan and virtually excludes the consul of 91 or any later member of the family. The economy in material also confirms an early date. The marble base rests on two steps in travertine. While the higher step projects on all four sides, the lower step is flush with the upper step at the back; such an economy would be surprising in the Flavian period or later.

Arria L. f. Plaria Vera Priscilla, wife of M'. Acilius Glabrio, consul (*CIL* xi. 6333), should be related to Plaria Vera, wife of A. Egrilius Rufus.[5] We have suggested that her husband may be the consul of 91 or his son (p. 505). A later connexion of the family with Ostia is attested by an inscription found near Acilia and now in St. Paul's monastery: *Thiasus Acili Glabrion(is) inperatu aram fecit dominae* (74). The script is mean and difficult to date. It probably belongs to the second century, and perhaps to the latter half.

There are also traces of freedmen and descendants of freedmen of this branch of the Acilii in Ostia, one not later than the early second century.[6]

---

[1] Herodian ii. 3. 3 f.

[2] Pliny, *NH* xxix. 12; cf. coinage with head of Salus issued by M'. Acilius *c*. 55 B.C., E. A. Sydenham, *The Coinage of the Roman Republic*, n. 922.

[3] Phot. *NS* 1910, 60.

[4] The title Caesar Augustus is applied to Claudius (*CIL* vi. 5539) and to Nero (*ILS* 1838).

[5] The association at a lower level of the family of Plaria Vera with the Acilii is reflected in a funerary inscription from Rome (*CIL* vi. 24260) which records the marriage of Q. Plarius Trypho to Acilia Nebris; a Plaria Vera, presumably their daughter, is included in the inscription.

[6] 287 records an *Augustalis* and is therefore earlier than the institution of the *seviri Augustales* under Domitian or a little later (p. 219). *S* 4761, to judge from the lettering, is also not later than the early second century.

Two of these Manii Acilii are registered in the tribe Voturia, M'. Acilius M'. f. Vot. Marianus, and M'. Acilius M'. f. Vot. Restitutus.[1] A natural inference would seem to be that Voturia was the tribe of the Manii Acilii Glabriones and that Ostia was their town of origin. Other evidence, however, raises serious doubts. In an inscription from Tibur (*CIL* xiv. 4237) Glabrio, consul of 152, has the tribe Galeria; in a republican inscription a much earlier Glabrio has the tribe Voltinia.[2] In face of this embarrassing conflict the origin of the family must remain uncertain until more decisive documents are found. It is, however, reasonable to infer from the Ostian evidence that the Acilii Glabriones had a residence in Ostian territory.

The Nasennii

I have inferred (p. 202) that C. Nasennius Marcellus, duovir III in 111, a censorial year, was from a family long established at Ostia on the strength of the Ostian tribe Voturia recorded for C. Nasennius Proculus (1395 + S 5035). I have found no traces of the family, however, before the Flavian period. The name does not appear earlier in surviving fragments of the Fasti, and none of the inscriptions of freedmen C. Nasennii or their descendants that I have seen is pre-Flavian.

The argument from silence cannot, however, be pressed, since the record of the Fasti is very incomplete and pre-Flavian inscriptions are considerably less common than those of the succeeding period. It is reasonable to believe that a man who is duovir for the third time in 111 is not a newcomer. The inscription recording C. Nasennius Vot(uria) Proculus may also be significant. Its lettering suggests a Flavian or slightly later date, and the association of names in the family group is interesting. Proculus makes the tomb for himself, C. Nasennius Agathyrsus his father, Lucilia — his mother, Terentia Acris his wife (a freedwoman), and C. Nasennius Proculus his son. His father's cognomen Agathyrsus suggests that he is a freedman; his wife is a freedwoman of the Terentii. Both Lucilii and Terentii are old-established families.[3] Freedmen are likely to follow the associations of their patrons.

The full career of the duovir of 111 is recorded in one complete inscription (171) and another that is fragmentary (S 4457). Though the lettering is radically different in the two inscriptions[4] the identity cannot be questioned. The same posts are set in the same chronological order. This Marcellus was

---

[1] S 4761, 1073.

[2] *S.C. de Thisbensibus*, Riccobono, *Fontes iuris Romani* (1941) i. 243. Münzer (op. cit. 92) infers from their Hellenic interests a family origin in the south of Italy.

[3] Lucilii, p. 493; Terentii, p. 194.

[4] S 4457 is typical of public inscriptions of the period. 171 comes from the tomb and was set up by a freedwoman; its style derives from painting and the letters resemble rustic capitals (p. 557).

duovir III, curator operum publicorum et aquarum perpetuus, patronus coloniae (171). He is described as *senior*, an alternative to *pater*, to distinguish him from his son.

The next record is of a Marcellus who was duovir with M. Lollius Paulinus in 166, a census year (4148). In 184 a Marcellus is recorded on the base of a statue as assigning the site in virtue of his office as *curator p(er)p(etuus) oper(um) pub(licorum)* (172 + p. 481). Since the elder Marcellus held this office after the duovirate and it was a life appointment we may identify the duovir of 166 with the *curator operum publicorum* of 184. It is presumably the same man who is recorded as *patr(onus) col(oniae)* on 4 January 189 (460). He is more probably the grandson than the son of the duovir of 111, and the similarity in the two careers recalls the strong resemblance in the careers of the two Gamalae.

A C. Nasennius Marcellus is also recorded as *pontifex Volcani* on an inscription from Portus (47). Dedications were made to Serapis 'permissu C. Nasenni Marcelli pontificis Volcani et aedium sacrarum et Q. Lolli Rufi Chrysidiani et M. Aemili Vitalis Crepereiani IIvir(orum)'. This inscription cannot be precisely dated. If the patron of 189 was *pontifex Volcani* he can have lived very little longer, for by 194 at the latest M. Antius Crescens Calpurnianus held the office (325). This inclines me to believe, without strong conviction, that the Portus inscription should be dated to the early third century, after 203 when M. Antius was still *pontifex Volcani* (324).

Appendix VI

FASTI

Duoviri and Praefecti

THE list of dated duovirates is taken from the Fasti, with the exception of the last two entries. Censorial years are marked with an asterisk.

B.C.   *Duoviri*
- 48 M. Acil[ius]
- 47 Q. Vitell[ius]
- 46 A. Vitelli[us]
- 45 Q. Vitelli[us II]

A.D.
- *6 A. Egrilius Rufus
  - L. Cre[pereius—]
- 14 - - - anius Gemellus II
  - - - - ranius Pollio
- 15 - - - menius Veiento
  - - - ius Rufus
- *16 - - - ius Rufus
  - [P. Paetin]ius Dexter
- 17 [A. Egrilius Rufus] maior
  - - - - us Severus
- 18 C. Volusius Flaccus II
  - P. Sabidius II
- 19 P. Lucilius G[amal]a II
  - M. Suellius M - - - s II
- 20 M. Valerius [- - -]
  - C. Avian[ius - - -]
- 30 P. Paetinius Dexter II
  - L. Iulius Carbo
  - A. Host[ili]us Gratu[s]
- *31 Q. Fabius Lo[ngus]
  - M. Naevius Opt[atus]
- 32 L. Bucius Proculu[s]
  - P. Manlius Bassus
- 33 P. Lucilius [Gamala?]
  - C. Naevius - - -
- 34 D. Otacilius Rufu[s]
  - A. Egrilius Rufus

- *36 T. Sextius African[us]
  - A. Egrilius Rufus [?]
  - *Praefecti*
  - Q. Fabius Longus [?]
  - A. Egrilius Rufus [?]
- 37 C. Caecilius Montan[us]
  - Q. Fabius Longus I[I?]
- 84 - - - Celsus ★
  - - - - uos II
- 85 - - - Ore]stes ★
  - - - - Secu]ndinus
- *91 C. Cuperiu[s - - -]
  - C. Arriu[s - - -]
- 92 L. Terentius Tertius
- 94 A. Caesilius Honorin[us]
- 95 P. Lucretius Cin[na]
  - L. Naevius Proc[ulus]
- 102 Cn. Se[ntius] Clodianus
  - P. V - - -
- 104 - - - us Verus
- 105 A. Livius Priscus
  - L. Licinius Valerianus
- *106 [M. Acilius Priscus Egriliu]s
  - Plarianus p.c.
  - - - - us p.c.
- 107 - - - us Honoratus
- 108 A. Manlius Augustalis
  - C. Iulius Proculus
- 109 M. Valerius Euphemianus
  - C. Valerius Iustus
- 110 P. Naevius Severus
  - D. Nonius Pompilianus
- *111 C. Nasennius Marcellus III p.c.

*111 C. Valerius Iustus II

112 - - - L]ongus Grattianus Cani-
        nianus

    - - - F]adius Probianus

*126 [Imp. Caesar Traianus Hadr]i-
        anus Aug(ustus) II

    - - - r p.c.

              Praefecti

    - - - pater

    - - - du - - -

127 M. Antistius Flavianus
     L. Valeriu[s - - -]

145 P. Turranius Aemilianus fil(ius)
     L. Pomponius Pri - - -]

*146 A. Egrilius Agricola p.p.c.
        D. Nonius Pompilian(us) p.p.c.

147 [L.?] Plinius Nigrinus
     P. Annius Annianus
     C. Mamilius Martia[lis]

152 M. Iulius Sever[us]

153 - - - Fortis
     L. [- - -]

*166 C. Nasennius Marcellus

(4148) M. Lollius Paulinus

*251 Q. Veturius Firmius Felix
        Socrates

(352) L. Florus Euprepes

The following, recorded in other inscriptions, can only be approximately dated:

C. Cartilius Poplicola, duovir VIII, cens. III, died early Augustus (p. 40).

Postumus Plotius M. f. V, A. Genucius A. f. II, contemporary with or earlier than Poplicola (*S* 4710).

C. Fabius, contemporary with Poplicola (4134).

C. Tuccius L. f., Voturia, ? Augustan (426).

P. Lucilius Gamala, ? Augustan (1, p. 30).

? M. Turranius, colleague of Gamala (1[30]).

— Co]rnelius [— ii]vir iter. cens., Augustan (*S* 4638).

C. Aq[uilius], ? Augustan (Bloch, 66).

— [ii]vir cens., decorated by Augustus and Tiberius (Bloch, 61).

M. Maecilius Furr[—], early Julio-Claudian, recorded on temple of Bona Dea (p. 352).

P. Lucilius Gamala IV, ? early Julio-Claudian, perhaps to be identified with duovir of A.D. 19 (p. 501 f.).

— Proculus (? Julio-Claudian, p. 323 n. 1).

C. Fabius, Voturia, Agrippa, Julio-Claudian (8).

A. Egrilius, Voturia, Rufus, ? Flavian (Bloch, 22; p. 196).

M. Acilius Priscus iivir, aedil(is) II, quinquennal(is), pr(aef)ect(us) II, Flavian (Bloch, 23; ? cutter's error in record of career, p. 197 n. 7).

Cn. Sentius, Teretina, Felix, Flavian (5, p. 200).

C. Silius, Voturia, Nerva, Flavian-Hadrian (415, p. 204).

C. Silius, Voturia, Nerva, son of above (415).

A. Livius Proculus, P. Lucilius Gamala, iivir praef. Caesaris, ? 137 (4, p. 201).

M. Aemilius Hilarianus, ? early Antonine (332, p. 204).

C. Granius, Quirina, Maturus, Antonine (364, p. 203).

P. Aufidius, Quirina, Fortis, Antonine (*S* 4620, p. 203).

P. Aufidius Fortis, son of above, Antonine (*S* 4622).

M. Junius, Palatina, Faustus, Antonine (4142, p. 209).

M. Antonius, Menenia, Severus, Antonine (298, p. 320).

M. Lollius Rufus Chrysidianus, M. Aemilius Vitalis Crepereianus, Severan (47, p. 209).

*L. Licinius, Palatina, Herodes, ? late Severan (373).

*P. Flavius, Palatina, Priscus, mid-third century (4452).

If, as is probable, the phrase *omnibus honoribus functus* implies the holding of the duovirate, the following should be added:

L. Fabricius, Palatina, Caesennius Gallus, ? early second century (354).

L. Julius Crescens (*S* 4653).

T. Antistius Favor, Severan (294).

L. Combarisius, Palatina, Vitalis, ? Severan (335).

All four are Roman knights.

The title of duovir was accepted by emperors and members of their family:

Trajan or Titus (*S* 4674–5).

Hadrian, for the second time in 126 (Fasti).

Lucius Caesar (? = L. Aelius, adopted son of Hadrian) in ? 137 (p. 201).

? Pertinax (Bloch, 54).

Decuriones

This list excludes decurions who are know to have risen to the duovirate. It is arranged alphabetically since few of the inscriptions can be securely dated.

M. Annius, Palatina, Proculus, son of president of builders (292).

T. Antistius Favor Proculeianus, knight, grandson of patron of *lenuncularii tabularii* (294).

Sex. Av[ienius L]ivianus, ? president of corn measurers (*S* 4623).

Sex. Carminius Parthenopeus, knight, president of builders (314).

P. Celerius, Palatina, Amandus, ? shipbuilder, died at eighteen (321, p. 205).

Cladius Venidius Eupalius, knight (*S* 4632).

M. Cornelius, Palatina, Valerianus, patron of *lenuncularii tabularii* in 192 (341).

M. Cornelius, Palatina, Valerianus Epagathianus, knight, patron of the *lenuncularii tabularii*, son of the above (341).

P. Cornelius Architectianus, son of president of builders (5).

C. Domitius, Palatina, Fabius Hermogenes, knight, formerly a *scriba* (**14**).

D. Junius, Palatina, Bubalus, knight (*S* 4625 = Bloch, 56).

L. Licinius M—, knight (Bloch, 57).

M. Licinii —, sons of M. Licinius Privatus, freedman (**15**).

D. Lutatius, Palatina, Charitonianus, knight (378).

P. Nonius, Palatina, Anterotianus, knight (390).

M. Orbius — (Bloch, 58).

Sex. Publicius, Collina, maior (4143).

Cn. Sergius —, son of an *Augustalis* (411).

L. Sextius Agrippinus, knight, died under twenty (414).

Q. Veturius Felix Socrates (431).

Q. Vibius Rufinus (435).

Knights, whose names are not preserved, are recorded in *S* 4680, Bloch, 60.

Ornamenta decurionatus are recorded for M. Licinius Privatus (**15**) and P. Aelius Liberalis, imperial freedman, *procurator annonae*, and formerly *praepositus mensae nummul(ariae) f(isci) f(rumentarii) Ost(iensis)* (2045).

Pontifices Volcani

? Augustan	P. Lucilius Gamala (1, p. 493).
Died in A.D. 30	P. Paetinius Dexter (Fasti).
30–36	A. Egrilius Rufus (Fasti).
From 36	M. Naevius Optatus (Fasti).
Flavian	M. Acilius Priscus (Bloch, 23).
? c. 100	? Q. Domitius — (p. 503 n. 2).
Died in 105	P. Ostiensis Macedo (Fasti).
From 105	M. Acilius Priscus Egrilius Plarianus (appointment, Fasti; still alive in 118 (Bloch, 26)).
Before 127	? C. Suetonius Tranquillus (below).
Before 128	A. Egrilius Plarianus (*S* 4445, as *praefectus aerari militaris*, not yet consul; consul in 128, Fasti).
Antonine	P. Lucilius Gamala (2, p. 493).
194–203	M. Antius Crescens Calpurnianus, recorded in these two years (325, 324); full length of office unknown.
? Early third century	C. Nasennius Marcellus (47, but possibly before Calpurnianus (p. 510)).
In 251	Iulius Faustinus (352).

That the office continued into the fourth century is shown by 132 (dated 303): *[ob redi]tum Constantin[— pontifex Volcani et] aedium sacrar—* ★

Wickert (*S* 4542) restores fragment XXXV of the Fasti (Degrassi, 210): '[in locu]m Q. Asini Marcelli *ille* pontifex Volkani creatus est.' This fragment must be dated before 115, but not much earlier (Degrassi, 239). Q. Asinius Marcellus is probably the *patronus coloniae* known from two Ostian inscriptions (p. 207), but it is very doubtful whether this entry records his death as *pontifex*: (a) the holders of the office from 105 to 118 are already known;

(*b*) the last letter of the sentence containing his name seems to be 'x', which is incompatible with the restoration proposed or any likely variant giving the same meaning. *

The inclusion in the list of C. Suetonius Tranquillus, biographer of the early emperors and imperial secretary, derives from what seems to me to be logical argument, stimulated by shrewd questions from Dr. Weinstock.

Suetonius' career was recorded on a handsome inscription set up in his honour at Hippo Regius in Africa. Sufficient fragments were found in 1950 to restore the main outline and the first editors have done their work well (E. Marec and H. G. Pflaum, *Comptes rendus . . . des inscriptions et belles lettres*, 1952, 76–85):

> C. Suetoni[o | · fil(*tribus*)] Tra[nquillo | f]lami[ni—*c.* 10—| adlecto i]nt[er selectos a di]vo Tr[a]iano Parthico p]on[t(ifici) Volca[nal]i | [—*c.* 16— a] studiis a byblio[thecis | ab e]pistulis | [imp. Caes. Trai]ani Hadrian[i Aug. | Hipponienses Re]gii d.d.p.p.

In line 5, I prefer 'pont. Volca[n]i'. The number of letters missing depends on the precise placement of the small fragment from the end of l. 4; it can, I think, be moved a little to the left.

From literary sources we have only one control for the official career of Suetonius. His biographer records that on his return from Britain Hadrian dismissed Suetonius, his secretary, together with C. Septicius Clarus, praetorian prefect, because they had been too familiar with Sabina, the emperor's wife (SHA, *Had.* 11. 3). This was presumably in 121 or 122.

The offices recorded in the inscription seem to be arranged, as one would expect, in chronological order. Suetonius was first a *flamen* (perhaps *flamen Cerialis*, cf. *ILS* 1447). He was then appointed by Trajan, perhaps to a judicial commission. The remaining offices, according to the natural interpretation of the text, fell under Hadrian. We might also infer from Pliny's letter to Trajan in 112 (*Ep.* x. 94), asking the emperor to confer the *ius trium liberorum*, that Suetonius had not yet been appointed to the emperor's service. The post of *pontifex Volcani* should have been held before or at the same time as Suetonius became *a studiis*, but it is possible that the religious post came later and was given its position in the text in order not to interrupt the impressive sequence of palace posts. These three posts are compressed within a very short period, between Trajan's death and the dismissal of Suetonius in 121 or 122. The rapid promotion is an indication of the emperor's special favour.

The post of *pontifex Volcani* is not recorded or known outside Ostia. Realizing that the priest of Vulcan at Rome was a *flamen* (Varro, *De ling. Lat.* v. 84), the editors first thought of Ostia but dismissed the possibility on the ground that all inscriptions recording the *pontifex Volcani* came from Ostia itself. They inferred that Suetonius must have been *pontifex Volcani* at Rome, and they found a parallel in the *pontifex Palatualis*, recorded in two inscriptions, though Varro (*De ling. Lat.* vii. 45) makes this priest a *flamen*. The parallel is not completely satisfying, because in the only inscription recording Vulcan's priest at Rome the title is *flamen* (*ILS* 1456), while no *flamen Palatualis* is recorded. Nor is the reason for dismissing Ostia decisive. Some sixteen letters have to be supplied at the beginning of l. 6: we could, for example, restore 'p]on[t.] Volca[n]i | [in colonia Ostiens.]'. ★

The appointment of Suetonius as *pontifex Volcani* at Ostia in one of the early years of Hadrian's reign would be intelligible. Hadrian inherited from Trajan a personal concern for the development of Ostia. Though the monumental inscription honouring him dates from 133 (95), he had accepted the title of duovir for the second time in 126 (Fasti), and one of the most important projects of the reign, involving the rebuilding of the area north of the Forum and the great new Capitolium, was carried through in his first few years of rule (p. 136). It is reasonable that he should have wished Suetonius, whom he seems to have valued highly, to acquire an Ostian association. If the *pontifex* was appointed at Rome, the formal choice lay with the emperor; if, as we think more probable the election rested with Ostia, the election of Suetonius will still reflect the wishes of Hadrian.

The Ostian evidence makes the appointment of Suetonius doubtful perhaps, but not impossible. By analogy with other such priesthoods, and by reasonable inference from the evidence (p. 179), we may assume that the *pontifex Volcani* was appointed for life. We know from the Fasti that M. Acilius Priscus Egrilius Plarianus succeeded P. Ostiensis Macedo in 105. This Plarianus was still alive in 118 (Bloch, 26); when he died we do not know. The next *pontifex* known to us is his nephew, who had been appointed to the office before he became consul in 128 (*S* 4445). Between these two dates there is room for Suetonius, though it is often assumed from the extent of his writings that he lived longer than this short interval would allow (*RE*, 'C. Suetonius Tranquillus' (Funaioli), 597).

If Suetonius had been *pontifex Volcani* at Ostia he would have been commemorated or would have commemorated himself in one or more public inscriptions. No trace of his name has yet been found. We should also expect to find some trace of his freedmen, but the family name is not recorded on surviving inscriptions. No secure inference, however, can be made from this negative evidence. Until the title of *pontifex Volcani* is found outside Ostia, Suetonius should tentatively be claimed for the Ostian priesthood.

Flamines Romae et Augusti

? Flavian	A. Egrilius, Voturia, Rufus (Bloch, 22).
Flavian	M. Acilius Priscus (Bloch, 23).
Before 141	Q. Plotius, Quirina, Romanus (400).
Antoninus Pius	P. Aufidius, Quirina, Fortis (*S* 4622).

Before 173   M. Junius, Palatina, Faustus (4142).
End of second century   — Hermias eq. Rom. (Bloch, 54).
        ?   C. Aemilius P(alatina) A—us (Bloch, 49).
Early third century   L. Licinius L. fil., Palatina, Herodes (373).
S 4674–5: — [praef.] quinq. divi T[— f]l(amini) perpetuo Ro[mae et Augusti].

Sacerdotes geni coloniae

? C. Aemilius C. f. P(alatina) A—us (Bloch, 49).
L. Licinius L. fil. Pal. Herodes (373).
P. Flavius P. fil. Pal. Priscus (*S* 4452).
M. Aurelius Hermogenes (*S* 5340).

This priesthood has also been restored (by L. R. Taylor, *The Cults of Ostia*, 35) in *S* 4671, 'eq. R. [sac(erdoti) gen(i)] col. Ost. flam. divi Ma[rci . . .]'. I agree with Bloch (ad 49) that 'eq. Rom. dec. col. Ost.' is a more probable restoration. The only other offices recorded are junior priesthoods. The *sacerdos geni coloniae* seems to have been a man who has held or is shortly to hold high office.

All four inscriptions recording the priesthood are from the third century.

Addenda

Fausto Zevi has very kindly sent me the following additions to the list of duoviri, from his paper read at the Sixth Epigraphic Congress (1972).

A.D. 53 - - - - - [? Cn.] Sergius Florus
   *66 [A. Egrilius Ru]fus II
       [- - - -]us
   69 or 72 [- - - - -]
           P. Luci[lius Ga]mala F(ilius)
   ? 93 [- - - - -]er
   140 A. Egril[ius - -

Appendix VII

THE CHRISTIAN MARTYRS OF OSTIA AND PORTUS

THE evidence of Christianity from the buildings and inscriptions of Ostia and Portus is supplemented by a substantial volume of Christian tradition and legend. In this field the basic evidence is the list of anniversaries of Christian martyrs. The first and most reliable list comes from the church calendar included in his compilation by the chronographer of 354;[1] a much fuller list is given in the so-called Martyrology of Jerome, which may date from the fifth century.[2] In the earlier list Ostia has no place, Portus martyrdoms are recorded for two dates. In the later and fuller list a substantial number of martyrs are recorded from both centres. These lists are confined to names and dates; details of some of the martyrdoms are recorded in martyrs' Acts of varying date and value.[3]

This is a notoriously treacherous field, but no historian of Ostia can afford to neglect it, for amid fantasy and exaggeration there are grains of genuine local tradition. De Rossi, the founder of modern Christian archaeology, knew Ostia and Portus well, and was able to apply his knowledge of both centres to the Christian documents. His study of Christianity at Portus[4] and his passing reflections on Ostia are still the essential foundations, but he has had no successor. Delehaye, for long the leading authority on the cult of the martyrs, has briefly and critically reviewed the list of martyrs from both centres,[5] and Lanzoni in his study of the dioceses of Italy has also examined the evidence.[6] But neither Delehaye nor Lanzoni was familiar with the topography and history of Ostia, and new evidence has accumulated since they wrote.

Ostia

The fullest of the Acts concerns a large group of martyrs, among whom Aurea has become the central figure. These Acts survive in several Latin

---

[1] Mommsen, *Chronica minora*, i. 71 f.

[2] Text and commentary, *Acta Sanctorum* Nov. ii. 2 (Delehaye and Quentin, 1931), cited as '*Comm.*'.

[3] The Latin manuscripts are catalogued in *Bibliotheca hagiographica Latina* (*BHL*). They are liberally quoted and discussed in the *Acta Sanctorum*.

[4] *Bull. arch. crist.* (1866) 37–51.

[5] H. Delehaye, *Les Origines du culte des martyrs*[2] (1933) 293–5.

[6] F. Lanzoni, *Le Origini delle diocesi antiche d'Italia* (*Studi e Testi* 35; Roma, 1923).

manuscripts which preserve two variant versions: there is also a much briefer Greek version.[1] The central body of the story is common to all versions.

Aurea, described as 'virgo sacratissima, nobili genere orta, imperatorum filia et a cunabulis Christiana', refused to renounce her faith and was sent with a retinue, whose religious views were sound, to Ostia, where she lived on her estate, 'foras muros Hostiae civitatis in loco, qui vocatur Euparisti in praedio suo'. She there got in touch with the bishop, Cyriacus, three presbyters, Maximus, Eusebius, and Concordius, and a deacon, Archelaus, who was working miracles.

Meanwhile at Rome a certain Censorinus, 'vir praepositus magisteriae potestatis', who had secretly followed the Christian faith, was exposed, refused to recant, and was sent under guard to Ostia, where he was imprisoned. He was visited by Aurea and her companions, who comforted him. On the visit of Maximus his chains were miraculously loosed and the soldiers of the guard were converted. Soon afterwards Maximus brought to life the dead son of a cobbler (or tailor), Faustinus by name. When the news came to Rome the emperor sent a *vicarius urbis Romae* to investigate. His instructions were to persuade the converts to renounce their faith and put recalcitrants to death. The soldiers remained faithful under torture. They were led to execution 'ad arcum ante theatrum'.* Cyriacus was killed in prison. Eusebius collected the bodies of the bishop and of Archelaus and Maximus by night and buried them. The bodies of the soldiers were thrown into the sea, recovered on the shore by the presbyter Concordius, hidden 'in campo Hostiae', and buried 'extra urbem in crypta Ostiensi' on 13 August. Two of them, Taurinus and Herculanus, were hidden at Portus. The tribune, Theodorus, was buried by Concordius in his own tomb. All the other bodies he eventually laid to rest by the bodies of Cyriacus and Maximus on 23 August.

On the same day Aurea was summoned and was examined. When she remained stubborn, a stone was tied to her neck and she was thrown into the sea. Her body drifted to the shore, was recovered by Nonosus, 'qui etiam Ypolytus nuncupatur', and buried by him 'in praedio eius ubi habitaverat' on 29 August. The *vicarius* then summoned Sabinianus, a servant on Aurea's estate, and demanded her possessions. He refused to obey and after a series of tortures was burnt to death and thrown into a well. His body was recovered by Concordius, who laid it beside Aurea on 28 August. Hippolytus pleaded with the *vicarius* to end the persecution and was tortured and drowned 'in foveam ante muros urbis, iuxta alveum Tyberis'. The voice of heavenly infants praising God was heard for the space of an hour. Christians secretly by night raised the body from the well and buried it in the same place 'non longe ab ipso puteo sed quasi pedes plus minus sexaginta', on 23 August.

[1] *Comm.* 264, 461; *BHL*, 808–13; *Acta SS.* Aug. iv. 755–61; S. de Magistris, *Acta martyrum ad Ostia Tiberina* (Roma, 1795); Lanzoni, 69.

In the two Latin versions there are minor variations in detail, as in the names of some of the soldiers and of the *vicarius urbis*, but the main difference is in the date. In one version Claudius Gothicus was emperor, in the other Alexander Severus. Closely related to the story of Aurea are the acts of Censorinus.[1] In this account, which closely follows the others, Trebonius Gallus and Claudius Gothicus are recorded in different manuscripts as emperor; Censorinus is described as 'vir quidam praefectoriae potestatis'. The emperor, on hearing of the raising of the dead boy, angrily exclaims 'magicam artem exercent'.

The story of Aurea has been generally rejected as historically valueless, and there are indeed many features that do not ring true. The dates of burial are not consistent. Hippolytus is martyred before he buries Aurea! The office of *vicarius urbis* had not been instituted at any of the three dates given by the traditions. The dialogue has the dramatized overtones of a late composition. The miracles are typical of the genre and therefore suspect. Until 1910 critics would not have gone beyond the evidence of the martyrology which includes Hippolytus, Cyriacus, and Archelaus and Aurea. The church of S. Aurea was clearly of early origin, and was the main centre of Christian worship in Ostia during the Middle Ages. She would have become the centre of legend and attracted other traditions to her own.

The discovery by Vaglieri of a medieval oratory at the place where tradition placed the execution of most of the martyrs, in front of the theatre, is a remarkable illustration of the value of topographical detail even in the least convincing martyr traditions.[2] In the twelfth century priests from the church of S. Aurea still celebrated mass in this 'church of S. Cyriacus'[3] and in the church was a sarcophagus, simply inscribed: 'hic Quiriacus dormit in pace.' When the church was built to commemorate the saint and his followers it would have been natural to transfer his body from its original tomb. Since the date of the relief and of the lettering are not inconsistent with the traditional date of the martyrdom it is not irresponsibly romantic to believe that this may be the bishop's sarcophagus rather than that of a roughly contemporary Christian with the same name. Delehaye dismisses even the possibility: 'ex ipsis autem verbis constat Quiriacum illum neque episcopum neque martyrum fuisse.'[4] Have we enough third-century parallels to be confident?

We conclude that there was a group of martyrs executed near the theatre, and that the leaders of the Ostian church, including the bishop, were involved

---

[1] *BHL*, 1722–3; *Acta SS.* Sept. ii. 518–24. [2] *NS* 1910, 136.

[3] In the record of the visit of Waltherus, canon of Arrouaise, to Ostia, *Acta SS.* Maii i. 485 (9): 'mane autem facto cum idem Andreas pergeret ex more cum alio ad ecclesiam S. Cyriaci extra villam ut missam dicerent.' Reference to a more detailed unpublished manuscript, *Topografia*, 163 n. 12.

[4] *Comm.* 461. Vaglieri hesitatingly suggested identification, *Nuovo bull. arch. crist.* 16 (1910) 61.

in this persecution. Of the three emperors recorded in the varying traditions all that we can say is that on general grounds Alexander Severus is the least likely and that Claudius Gothicus is the best attested. But, though there is a kernel of truth in the narrative, there has almost certainly been a conflation of different stories, apart from embellishment. In the Martyrology Aurea is recorded under 20 May, though she also appears under 22 August. It is probable that the first is the correct date and that, when she attracted to herself the story of the wider persecution, her date was correspondingly moved. The burial of Herculanus and Taurinus at Portus, when the remaining soldiers were buried at Ostia, is odd, and we shall see that they probably belong to a different martyrdom. Hippolytus also should probably be detached from the group. He is described without elaboration at a late stage in the story as *episcopus*, bishop presumably of Portus, and at Portus there was a church of S. Hippolytus. His martyrdom will be discussed later.

The story of Gallicanus is set in high places and historically he is the most important figure among the martyrs associated with Ostia. He is not recorded in the lists of martyrs, but he is connected with the stories of two other Roman martyrs, John and Paul, and also with Constantia, the daughter of Constantine.[1] According to the tradition, which is not early, he was a pagan until his mature years and, after leading a successful campaign against the Persians, asked the emperor for his daughter in marriage. Constantia declared her resolution to remain a Christian virgin but, before the situation could become embarrassing, Gallicanus was required to save the empire on the Danube front against an invasion of Scythians. It was arranged that he should take with him two of Constantia's servants, John and Paul, who, unknown to him, were devout Christians, and leave with Constantia his two daughters by a wife who had died, Artemias and Attica. The persuasion of John and Paul, powerfully reinforced by miracles in battle, converted Gallicanus. He had sacrificed to the demons on the Capitol when he left; he returned to the blessed feet of Peter. Constantine with his mother Helena, and his daughter, warmly welcomed him. He no longer pressed for Constantia's hand. He was made consul and freed 5,000 slaves.

Later he was living at Ostia, on close terms with Hilarinus, a devout man. Gallicanus provided the resources to enlarge the home of Hilarinus so that he could give shelter to foreigners, 'ad peregrinorum susceptionem'. His fame spread abroad. Men came from east and west to see a former consul and patrician washing the feet of the poor. He was the first to build a church in Ostia, 'et dedicavit officia clericorum'. This he did in response to a revelation from St. Lawrence, who exhorted him to build a church in his name 'in porta, quae nunc usque Laurentia nuncupatur'.

[1] *BHL*, 3236–44; *Acta SS*. Jun. v. 35–39.

But Julianus, when he had been made Caesar by Constantius, 'dedit legem ut Christiani nihil in hoc saeculo possiderent'. Men were sent to claim the revenue from Gallicanus' property which he had diverted to Hilarinus' house of charity, 'in Ostiensi pago quattuor casas'. The collectors were stricken with leprosy. Julian sends instructions that Gallicanus is to sacrifice to the gods or leave Italy. He goes to Alexandria, retires to the desert and becomes a hermit, is persecuted and killed. His Ostian friend Hilarinus, 'when he refused to sacrifice under pressure from the persecutors of the Christian faith', was beaten with sticks and died a martyr's death. Christians buried his body solemnly in Ostia. There is an echo of the same story in the *Acts of Constantia*,[1] and part of it was turned into elegant verse by Aldelmus, bishop of Sherborne, in the early eighth century.[2]

As in the passion of Aurea, there are serious errors in this attractive story. There are two prominent Gallicani known in the reign of Constantine, Ovinius Gallicanus, consul in 317, Flavius Gallicanus, consul in 330. The latter fits the context better, but we know nothing of his career from other sources. No war against Persia is known under Constantine until 337; the Danube war would seem to be the war of 334. Both probably fall after Gallicanus' consulship, which was, in the story, the reward for his victories. Nor was Constantine in Rome after 327, though he is made to welcome Gallicanus in his palace at Rome after the war of 334. The description of Constantine's successors is inaccurate. There is no evidence for an enactment issued by Julian confiscating the property of Christians.

And yet the story cannot be dismissed out of hand. In Anastasius' Life of Pope Silvester a Gallicanus is reported to have added very generous endowments to the basilica presented to Ostia by Constantine, and it may be significant that they included revenue from *massa Gargiliana*,[3] from which Constantine also drew part of his endowment of the Lateran Basilica in Rome.[4] The story implies a connexion between the church of S. Lawrence and the Porta Laurentina, but the Porta Laurentina derives its name from Laurentine territory. Is it possible that the gate has given the name to the church and that Gallicanus' church should be identified with Constantine's basilica, to which Gallicanus added endowments almost as substantial as those of the emperor? Nothing is heard of Constantine's basilica in medieval records; it would have been a rich prize for raiders and may have been sacked early and abandoned. Its ruins may still be found in the neighbourhood of the gate.

The nucleus of the story is probably the association of Gallicanus' two daughters, Artemias and Attica, with Constantia. They were buried with her

[1] *Acta SS.* Feb. iii. 67 f.
[2] In his poem, *De virginitate*, Mon. Germ. hist. auct. ant. xv. 302 f.
[3] *Lib. pont.* i. 184. The revenue from the properties bequeathed by Gallicanus yielded 869 *solidi*, compared with 1118 *solidi* from those bequeathed by Constantine.
[4] *Lib. pont.* i. 173.

later and had shared the latter part of her life. The main reason for the introduction of Gallicanus is that he was their father. His eagerness to marry Constantia could be invention; the embroidery around his consulship is false. But he probably did become a Christian, he may have fought in the east and north and been on familiar terms with Constantine. There is no good reason for not believing that in later life he lived at Ostia, and that he owned *casae*, probably farms, in the territory. Nor is the allusion to the attempted seizure of his rents necessarily without foundation. It may have arisen from an enactment cancelling the exemption of Christians from curial *munera*.[1]

The story of Hilarinus may also preserve sound tradition, for he is independently recorded in Jerome's Martyrology under 16 July: 'in civitate Ostia Hilarini'. There is no good evidence of an official persecution under Julian, but the pagan reaction of the emperor is likely to have met with sympathy at Ostia at least among the aristocracy;[2] and the persecutors of the faith who killed Hilarinus may have been Ostians acting on their own initiative, rather than Roman officials under direction from Rome. It would not be uncritical to watch excavation reports for the possible identification of a house enlarged to give shelter to pilgrims. The building may even have already been found. The so-called House of the Fishes is the only late house in Ostia which has what may be Christian symbolism in its decoration. The original building probably dates from the third century; at some later date, almost certainly in the fourth century, it was substantially restored and enlarged.[3] Unfortunately the house had been stripped almost bare before it was excavated, but the absence of graffiti on such of the plaster as remains might be held to weaken an attractive hypothesis.

The Martyrology of Jerome includes under 19 October 'in Hostia Asteri'.[4] That this Asterius is an historical figure is confirmed by an inscription of the late fourth or fifth century from the cemetery of Commodilla at Rome, which records that a certain Pascasus died on 11 October, eight days before the anniversary of Asterius, 'ante natale domni Asteri depositus in pace'.[5] But, though the Martyrology records only one Asterius, two martyrs of the name are associated with Ostia in tradition.[6]

Of the first we are told very little. He was a Roman priest who suffered for his persistent loyalty to Pope Callistus. When Callistus himself had been

[1] *Cod. Theod.* xii. 1. 50.

[2] Julian was commemorated at Ostia as *princeps indulgentissimus* (*S* 4408), but, since the initiative came from the *praefectus annonae*, this is not necessarily an index of local feeling.

[3] Becatti, *Case tarde*, 18. The plan (Fig. 17) shows clearly the distinction between original and later walls. The Christian reference is not certain, p. 400 n. 5.

[4] *Comm.* 562; Lanzoni, 68.

[5] Diehl, *Inscr. Lat. Christ. vet.* 2124.

[6] *Acta SS.* Oct. ix. 6–11.

martyred, Asterius was thrown from a bridge into the Tiber. His body floated down river, was discovered at Ostia by certain Christians, and buried there. It is probably this Asterius who was commemorated in the inscription referred to above.

The story of the other Asterius is more detailed and colourful. It is included in the account of the martyrdom of Marius and Martha, with their sons, Audifax and Abachuc, who had come from Persia under Clodius Gothicus to visit the holy places in Rome.[1] The part of the story which concerns Ostia opens with sympathetic remonstrances by the emperor against the Christian stubbornness of Valentinus, a priest. The emperor's better feelings are submerged by his prefect Calpurnius, who is authorized to cross-examine Valentinus: 'si sanum consilium non est quod declarat, fac in eum quod in sacrilegum leges praedixerunt; sin vero, audiatur iusta postulatio eius.' Calpurnius entrusts Valentinus to Asterius, a member of his staff. The household of Asterius was converted; his adopted daughter, who had serious eye trouble, recovered her full sight. The house attracted the curious and the faithful, including Martha and her companions. The emperor summoned Asterius, and all those in his house were arrested. Asterius was bound and, with his household, sent to Ostia 'sub poenarum examinatione iudicium sumere'.

At Ostia Asterius came before the judge Gelasius. He remained true to his faith under cross-examination and torture, and was condemned to the amphitheatre. They led him and his followers 'ad locum qui appellatur Ursariae iuxta fanum aureum, quia ibi ferae nutriebantur'.[2] The wild beasts were sent into the arena; Asterius prayed and they grovelled at his feet. Gelasius appealed to the people as witnesses of this display of magic. The wild beasts having failed, Gelasius ordered the Christians to be burnt, but fire was unavailing. They were then led outside the walls of Ostia and executed. Their bodies were buried by Christians on 18 January, and by the site a church was built, 'et ita florent beneficia Martyrum usque in praesentem diem'.

Apart from the melodramatic ending this story has the comparatively simple form of an early tradition. There is, however, no Calpurnius in the list of urban prefects of the period. Gelasius is stationed at Ostia and might be the *praefectus annonae*: that he is not otherwise known is not damaging, for there are many gaps in the list of known holders of the office. There is, however, good evidence that by the late fourth century a basilica had been built in honour of an Asterius outside the walls of Ostia. The invective against Pope Damasius, known as the *Libellus precum*, records that a certain priest Macarius, who rebelled against the Pope, was arrested with violence and sent to Ostia, where he died of his wounds.[3] The bishop of Ostia, Florentius, though supporting Damasius against the rival church faction, respected

---

[1] *Acta SS.* Jan. ii. 214–19.   [2] *Acta SS.* Jan. ii. 218 (13).

[3] *Libellus precum*, 22 (Migne, *PL* xiii. 98 f.).

Macarius and 'transferred his body to the basilica of Asterius'. In the twelfth century we hear of the bringing in of the bones of S. Asterius and twelve other martyrs to the church of S. Aurea.[1] They probably came from this basilica, then presumably in ruins.

Since the mention of a church is well founded it is not unreasonable to look for further topographical evidence in the story. If the ordeal of the arena—a set-piece in many of these stories—were described only in general terms we could ignore it; but the circumstantial detail is impressive: 'ad locum qui appellatur Ursariae . . . iuxta fanum aureum'. This seems like genuine local tradition. I accept it tentatively as evidence for an amphitheatre or at least for gladiatorial shows outside the walls.

Ostia is also the recorded burial-place of the martyrs Flora and Lucilla.[2] These virgins are said to have been captured by a barbarian king Eugegius in the second half of the second century, though no details of the nature and place of the capture are recorded. Eugegius was converted by their steadfast devotion to the faith, but after twenty years at his court they determined to go to Rome to face martyrdom. Eugegius accompanied them, and they were all put to death. In the earliest traditions of these martyrs, which defy rationalization, Ostia is not mentioned. A much later account records that their bodies were honourably buried by faithful Christians 'in suburbano civitatis Ostiae', where they remained for 700 years, until they were translated from Ostia to Arezzo by the Pope's authority in the ninth century.[3]

It would clearly be dangerous to draw historical inferences for the Roman period from such evidence as this. We can, however, infer that by the ninth century Ostia was too enfeebled and impoverished to preserve all her sacred relics. The same impression is given in what was said by the priests of S. Aurea to Waltherus, canon of Arrouaise, when he came to Ostia in the twelfth century and was allowed to take away the relics of S. Monica: 'There are so many relics of saints in that wilderness (the area outside medieval Ostia) that we could not easily decide where we should lay them to rest as was fitting. A few days ago we brought in the relics of blessed Asterius and twelve other martyrs and, not knowing where we should lay them, we dug a trench in the church (of S. Aurea) and buried them there.'[4]

Finally the Martyrology of Jerome includes under both 22 November and 22 December 'et in Ostia Demetri et Honori (or Honorati)'. Of them nothing is known or even invented.

On the basis of the story of Aurea we may believe that the Ostian community of Christians had their own bishop and priests in the third century. Constantine's basilica was probably the first church within the town; but

---

[1] Below.
[2] *BHL*, 5017–21; *Acta SS*. Jul. vii. 13–34.
[3] *Acta SS*. Jul. vii. 30 (106–8).
[4] *Acta SS*. Maii i. 485 (9).

basilicas may have been built earlier by the tombs of Asterius and Aurea. There is no evidence that Ostian magistrates or prominent laymen were concerned in the martyrdoms and the impression derived from the late houses that the aristocracy was predominantly pagan is not inconsistent with such Christian traditions as survive. Gallicanus, residing in Ostia, but probably not an Ostian, should be regarded as exceptional, though there may have been a small minority of his social peers who shared his views. The list of martyrs when analysed is also consistent with our general picture. The purge of the leaders of the community in the third century is isolated; the first scene of most of the other Ostian martyrdoms is Rome. The view that Christianity was stronger at Portus than at Ostia receives some confirmation from a study of the Martyrologies.

Portus

In the Middle Ages the church of S. Hippolytus seems to have been the main centre of Christian worship at Portus, but the problem of Hippolytus is highly controversial. Various traditions have assigned him to Rome, Portus, Antioch, Arabia. The last two identifications arise from confusions that can be easily understood; the Roman and Portus traditions require more careful disentanglement.[1]

In the time of Pope Callistus a certain Hippolytus produced a long series of learned works in Greek, many of them highly controversial in doctrine, fiercely attacking the personality and policies of the Pope. In the sixteenth century a seated statue was discovered near the Via Tiburtina; on the chair was a list of writings which clearly are those of the polemical writer. This identification is reasonably certain. The statue when found had no head. This has been restored, though the benign features are barely consistent with the fierce character of the writer. The statue is now displayed in the Lateran Museum, and the modern inscription reads 'Hippolytus, episcopus Portuensis'. Our purpose is limited to showing that this identification is wrong, that the Roman Hippolytus had no connexion with Portus, that the confused tradition which is the basis of the identification is therefore no evidence that Portus had a bishop in the early third century.

One stage in the confusion can already be seen in a colourful poem of the late fourth century by Prudentius.[2] In this poem Prudentius tells us that Hippolytus, a Roman presbyter, followed the schism of Novatus, and left Rome for Portus where he continued in heresy. He was there tortured and finally dragged by yoked horses until his body was torn in pieces. The

---

[1] For an understanding of the elements that concern this book I have relied primarily on De Rossi, *Bull. arch. crist.* (1882) 9–76; Delehaye, 'Recherches sur le légendier romain', *Analecta Bollendiana*, 51 (1933) 58–66; *Dict. d'arch. chrétienne et de liturgie*, vi. 2409–83 (H. Leclerq, 1925).   [2] Prudentius, *Peristeph.* xi.

remains were gathered together and laid to rest on the Ides of August in a tomb on the Via Tiburtina, which the poet describes in some detail. Prudentius' description of the tomb is genuine, as excavation has revealed.[1] His allusion to Hippolytus' heresy is taken from an inscription set up in the tomb on the Via Tiburtina in the fourth century by Pope Damasius. The vivid description of the martyrdom is taken, as Prudentius tells us, from a painting preserved in or near the tomb. Its value is worthless save as an example of a poet's imagination, working on a painter's imagination, working, directly or indirectly, on a tragedian's imagination. The scene is drawn ultimately from Euripides' *Hippolytus*.

There is authentic material in Prudentius. Hippolytus was a heretic, his tomb was on the Via Tiburtina. The story of the martyrdom, however, is nonsense. Can any value be attached to the introduction of Portus into the story? Almost certainly not. Eusebius, a careful and learned scholar, knew in the middle of the fourth century the writings of Hippolytus, which had not had a long currency in the west as they were written in Greek; he believed that Hippolytus was a bishop, but could not identify his seat. Later in the fourth century Jerome had the same difficulty. If the writer was bishop of Portus these two scholars would surely have known. The truth can be inferred from the chronographer of 354, who records that in 235 Pope Pontianus and Hippolytus, presbyter, were deported to Sardinia.[2] Their bodies were later translated to Rome and the chronographer's entry in his church calendar for the Ides of August reads: 'Ypoliti in Tiburtina et Pontiani in Callisti'. The natural inference is that Hippolytus remained in Rome after the death of his rival Callistus and continued his polemics and that, probably when Maximinus succeeded Alexander Severus, the leaders of the two factions were deported. Hippolytus was considered a bishop later since he had so described himself in the titles of his writings; he was in fact an anti-Pope.

This embarrassing phase in church history was best forgotten, and, as his works were in Greek, they were soon neglected. But the tomb remained on the Via Tiburtina: the existence of a cult of a Hippolytus at Portus suggested the identification. What, then, of the church of St. Hippolytus at Portus? Delehaye, whose view is accepted by Lanzoni, has suggested the most economic solution, that there is no Hippolytus of Portus, and that the date recorded in the Martyrology of Jerome, 20 or 21 August, is the date not of a martyrdom, but of the foundation at Portus of a church to commemorate the Roman Hippolytus.[3]

This extreme view carries scepticism much too far. The church of St. Hippolytus was built in what we now know to be the cemetery of Isola

---

[1] De Rossi, *Bull. arch. crist.* (1882) 9–76.
[2] Mommsen, *Chronica minora*, i. 75.
[3] Delehaye, *Les Origines du culte des martyrs*,[2] 295; Lanzoni, 79.

Sacra and this suggests association with a tomb. The site of the tomb is circumstantially described in the story of Aurea. Hippolytus was drowned 'in foveam ante muros iuxta alveum Tyberis' and his body was buried in the same place, 'non longe ab ipso puteo sed quasi pedes plus minus sexaginta'. One of the manuscripts points more specifically to the site of the church close to Trajan's canal: 'in insula, quae uno latere mare habet, a duobus divisione alvei Tyberis cingitur'.[1] Baronius, visiting the site in the sixteenth century, recorded that the famous well ('puteus ille, seu profunda fovea aquis plena, in qua sanctus Hippolytus martyri coronam accepit') could still be seen, though the church had suffered from a long series of pirate raids and was in ruins.[2]

The body of the saint was thought to rest in the church, for Pope Leo II (795–816) presented two vestments to the church, one for an altar, the other to cover the body.[3] We also hear of the translation of the body to Rome in the eleventh century.[4] It seems quite clear that the people of Portus did not believe that they were venerating a Roman saint whose tomb was on the Via Tiburtina. Nor does it seem likely on general grounds that this controversial Roman figure, whose memory was so soon obscured, would have had a church built in his honour so near Rome. We may conclude that the church of St. Hippolytus commemorates a martyr of Portus. The date of his death is unknown; the possibility that he was bishop of Portus cannot be ruled out, but we need stronger evidence than the story of Aurea to confirm the title.

In the story of Aurea and in the Martyrology of Jerome Hippolytus of Portus is also called Nonnus or Nonosus—'Yppoliti qui dicitur Nonnus', or 'Nonosus qui etiam Ypolytus nuncupatur'. The martyrs recorded by the chronographer of 354 include, for 5 September, 'Aconti, in Porto, et Nonni et Herculani et Taurini'. The date is different from that given in the Martyrology of Jerome, which is more closely associated with the Ostian persecutions. It seems likely that the martyrdoms were separate and independent and later conflated, to the greater glory of Aurea. The Martyrology of Jerome adds to the confusion by two further entries. For 25 July, 'Romae in Portu natale Aconti et Nonni': for 5 September (the date given for Nonnus by the chronographer of 354), 'in portu Romano Taurini, Herculani, et Aconti' (Nonnus is not mentioned).

This desperate tangle cannot be satisfactorily unravelled, but a few probabilities emerge. Herculanus and Taurinus in the story of Aurea were for no apparent reason buried at Portus apart from their companions. Their bodies, or what were taken to be their bodies, were translated to Rome in the eleventh century with that of Hippolytus,[4] which suggests that they were buried near him. Their martyrdom has an historical basis, because they are

[1] *Acta SS.* Aug. iv. 506 (12).   [2] Ibid. 505 (8).
[3] *Lib. pont.* ii. 12 (xlii).   [4] De Rossi, *Bull. arch. crist.* (1866) 49.

invoked in a fourth- or fifth-century Christian inscription, found either at Ostia or at Portus.[1] Acontius is also a genuine figure; a church of S. Acontius existed at Portus in the eleventh century.[2] Hippolytus was associated with these three martyrs, but probably not with Aurea. Their story belongs to Portus and not to Ostia.

Jerome's Martyrology includes among the martyrs celebrated on 15 July Eutropius, Zosima, and Bonosa at Portus, 'in porto Romano, hoc est in hiscla'.[3] We have seen that inscriptions confirm this martyrdom. The first celebrates in hexameters the reception of Zosima in heaven,[4] the second records the building by Bishop Donatus of a basilica in honour of the martyrs beside their tomb.[5] The surviving story of Bonosa may help to determine the date.

In this story the opening scenes are laid in Rome. Bonosa is a noble virgin, 'nobili quidem prosapia orta'. She was required by the emperor to recognize Jupiter, Hercules, Aesculapius, Saturnus. When she refused to abandon her faith she was imprisoned, later stripped and beaten: the angels protected her. The emperor then handed the case to a *praeses* and the scene shifts to Portus. The *praeses* at first tries persuasion, but she remains stubborn and her faith converts fifty soldiers of the guard, who are put to death. A final appeal to Bonosa to take a young husband or become a Vestal Virgin merely increases her defiance. She is condemned to a brothel, but men have no power over her. Finally she is executed outside the city walls and buried on 15 July (the day given in the Martyrology) 'non longe a portu Romano stadio uno'.

This story is unconvincing. There is no apparent motive for the shift of scene from Rome to Portus. The dialogues are set-pieces. The account has possibly been embroidered in the church of S. Bonosa in Trastevere in Rome, introducing Rome into what may have been a martyrdom which began and ended in Portus. No mention of Eutropius and Zosima is made in the story, though they are linked with Bonosa both in the Martyrology and in the inscription recording their basilica. But the distance of the burial-place

---

[1] 1942, p. 395.

[2] Delehaye, *Origines*, 295.

[3] *Comm.* 375 f.; *BHL* 1425–6; *Acta SS.* Jul. iv. 18–23; De Rossi, *Bull. arch. crist.* (1866), 45–49; Lanzoni, 80.

[4] 1938 = Thylander, B 235. De Rossi (art. cit. 48) dated this inscription immediately after the martyrdom, which he placed under Aurelian. The lettering is much more elegant than any Ostian inscription of the mid-third century that I have seen. Its style and the tone of the epitaph more probably reflect the activity of Pope Damasius (366–84) and his followers. The martyrdom itself seems to be placed by the best manuscripts under Septimius Severus.

[5] 1937 = Thylander, B 234: 'sanctis martyribus et beati[ssimis] | Eutropio Bonosae et Zosim[ae] | Donatus episc(opus) tumulum ad[ornavit] | sed et basilicam coni[un]ctam [tumulo] | a fundamentis sanctae [ple]bi d[ei construxit].'

from the walls is roughly correct. The inscriptions were found near Capo
Due Rami, where Trajan's canal and the Tiber meet.[1]

One version transfers the setting to the reign of Aurelian, but the original
tradition seems to have placed it under Septimius Severus, and the selection
of gods whom Bonosa was required to recognize may be significant. Hercules, whose cult was strong at African Lepcis from which the family of
Septimius Severus came, was regarded by the emperor as his special protector;[2] the cult of Saturn was particularly widespread in Africa.[3]

The other Portus entries in Jerome's Martyrology are mere names to us,
but their number is significant: on 24 February Primitivus (or Primitiva) and
Paulus; on 24 May Vincentius; on 18 October Agnes;[4] on 13 December
Ariston.[5] There are two further entries, on 16 April and 15 May, but their
attribution to Portus is disputed. The martyrs of 15 May assigned to Portus
seem to be from Milan, and the text can be emended to give that meaning.[6]
Martialis, however, in the record of 16 April is probably a Portus martyr,
though many of those associated with him in inferior manuscripts should be
assigned to Spain.[7]

Delehaye, followed by Lanzoni, would withdraw from this list the names
of Vincentius and Agnes, whom he identifies with the Spanish Vincentius
and the Roman Agnes to whom, he suggests, churches were built at Portus.[8]
These churches are not recorded in a list of Portus churches given in an
eleventh-century survey of the diocese;[9] but this is not a decisive argument,
since they might by then have been destroyed and deserted; the list also omits
the basilica of S. Bonosa known to have once existed. But Vincentius and
Agnes are common names, and their identification should at least remain an
open question. Both are represented with Hippolytus on a Roman glass vase

[1] There is no more precise indication of the site, but De Rossi's account (*Bull. arch.
crist.* 1866, 45) suggests that the inscriptions were found on the north side of Trajan's
canal and not on Isola Sacra. If this is so, the emendation of the obscure 'in hiscla' to 'in
insula' in the manuscripts of Jerome's Martyrology should be rejected.

[2] *RE*, 'Hercules' (Haug), 581.

[3] See index *CIL* viii.

[4] Possibly Ostian, *Comm.* 560.

[5] Possibly to be identified with a victim of Diocletian's persecution, Lanzoni, 81.

[6] *Comm.* 255 f. (18). Some of the names occur also on the previous day and are there
assigned to Milan. They include Victor, to whom a church was dedicated at Milan by
the Porta Romana. 'In portu Romae' might be a corruption of 'in porta Romana'. An
alternative possibility is a conflation of two martyrdoms, in Portus and Milan.

[7] *Comm.* 193 f. (16). The most convincing manuscript has the simple entry 'Romae in
portu, Martialis'. In the lesser manuscripts Marcialis is followed by several other names,
many of them from a Spanish martyrdom. The confusion probably represents the conflation of two separate martyrdoms.

[8] Delehaye, *Origines*, 295; Lanzoni, 80.

[9] Nibby, *Analisi della carta de' dintorni di Roma*[2] (1848) ii. 631.

decorated in gold.[1] If Hippolytus is a Portus saint, it is perhaps more probable that Vincentius and Agnes also were martyred at Portus.

Even if the benefit of the doubt is given to the critics, the Portus list of martyrs remains a much longer list than that of Ostia, and De Rossi was right in seeing in this a reflection of the greater strength of Christianity at Portus. De Rossi also thought that Portus had her own bishops in the third century, for he identified the Hippolytus who was described as 'bishop' with the Roman Hippolytus. If this identification is rejected, the question should remain open, for we have already argued that the absence of a bishop of Portus from the council of 313 in Rome is no valid evidence against a Portus bishopric at that date.[2] If Thylander's dating to *c.* 300 of the inscription recording the building of a basilica to Bonosa and her fellow martyrs by Bishop Donatus were correct, we should have an earlier *terminus ante quem*;[3] but the letters, as De Rossi argued in detail, suggest a date nearer 400.[4]

[1] H. Vopel, *Die altchrist. Goldgläser* (Freiburg, 1899), n. 401. I assume, following De Rossi and Delehaye, that 'Poltus', inscribed on the glass, represents Hippolytus.

[2] p. 88.

[3] Thylander, B 234.

[4] De Rossi, *Bull. arch. crist.* (1866) 48.

Appendix VIII

THE POPULATION OF OSTIA

WE should like to know the size of Ostia's population, particularly at the height of her prosperity in the second century. It is very doubtful whether the city magistrates, or even their clerks, could have given an accurate answer. Records of properties were kept, and the total number of adult male citizens registered in the Roman census was known, but the number of women, children, and slaves was not required to be registered for any official purpose. To think in terms of precise figures is a comparatively recent development. The size of Ostia's population is one of the first questions that a modern visitor asks; it would not have occurred to a Renaissance traveller.

The study of population in the classical world has attracted continuous attention during the past century; but, though it has sharpened our approach to historical problems, the results have been meagre. The evidence available to the ancient historian cannot match the modern historian's detailed material, and in most cases one can hope for no more than guesses of the population of ancient cities. Rome is exceptional. Figures for the public distribution of corn and for the import of corn, the sums spent on *congiaria*, the number of insulae and domus recorded in the regionary catalogues, provide the basis at least for serious discussion.[1] Ostia and Pompeii lack such controls from literary sources, but the area enclosed by their walls is known and we know also the types of houses in which their people lived. But for Ostia, even more than for Pompeii, the margin of error should not be underestimated.

Nearly all writers on Ostia have ventured a figure for the population, and their estimates range, not surprisingly, from 10,000 to 100,000. Calza alone has assembled the evidence for a rational estimate.[2] His argument may be briefly summarized.

The area enclosed by the Sullan walls is 690,000 square metres. In the area excavated the proportion of living accommodation to the rest of the city—temples, baths, *fora*, *horrea*, barracks, streets—is roughly 5 : 3 (181,405 sq. m.: 139,095 sq. m.). If it is assumed that the average area occupied per person is 26 sq. m. (including open courts, walls, gardens; 18·20 sq. m. without), and that the average height of Ostian houses above the ground floor is two stories

---

[1] A critical review of the value of the evidence, F. G. Maier, *Historia*, 2 (1953) 318–51. I accept a total of roughly a million in the early second century. The evidence for the fourth century is very much weaker.

[2] Calza, BC 69 (1941) 150–2, 156–9 (in 'La Popolazione di Roma antica', Calza, Gismondi, Lugli, 142–65).

and a half, then the total population within the walls will have been roughly 36,000.

My calculation for the area within the walls on the basis of Calza's figures gives a rather higher total, of 37,500. To this must be added some 2,000 for the built-up area outside the Sullan walls on the seaward side and for the narrow fringe of building on the right bank, giving a grand total of nearly 40,000. But the foundations on which such a total rest are weak.

Calza, in formulating his estimate, seems to discount the ground floor,[1] presumably because it was mainly occupied by shops. But, though shops lined most of the streets, the larger blocks such as the House of Diana had living quarters behind them. Nor can the shops be entirely ignored. Many had mezzanine apartments above them and even some of the shopkeepers who had no upper rooms probably lived on their premises.[2] Calza also discounts baths and *horrea*, but the smaller baths, such as the Baths of Buticosus, had apartments above them and the upper stories of *horrea* may have been partly used to house their workers. The proportion of living accommodation to the rest of the area is based on the most important quarters of the town. In the unexcavated areas, mainly near the periphery, the proportion of space occupied by public buildings is likely to have been less.

But the main margin of error lies in the two basic estimates of the average height of the houses and of the density of the population. Within the excavated area the average height of the insulae is probably nearer four than three stories, including the ground floor; but allowance has to be made for the much lower domus, which may have numbered more than thirty (twenty-two have been excavated), and for the south-eastern quarter where the level of the grass-covered ruins suggests that the buildings were much lower than in the rest of the town. Perhaps a general average of three stories should be allowed. For the density of the population, the figure most needed to re-create a realistic social background to Ostia's life, we lack evidence. Calza allows an average per person of 18·20 sq. m. of living space, excluding walls, courts, &c. On this basis a ten-roomed apartment in the House of the Painted Vaults would hold nine persons. This may allow too much space for freedmen and slaves. It is almost certainly too generous an allowance for the mezzanine rooms above shops.

These various considerations suggest that Calza's estimate is too low. My own guess, and it should be admitted that any such calculation is little more than a guess, would be a population between 50,000 and 60,000 during the

---

[1] Calza is not explicit, but his discounting of the ground floor follows from a comparison of p. 153 with p. 157. The point is emphasized by G. Girri, *La Taberna nel quadro urbanistico e sociale di Ostia* (Ist. di arch., Milano, *Tesi di laurea*, i (1956) 41).

[2] G. Girri, however, exaggerates (op. cit. 42) in assuming that all shops were lived in at night.

Antonine period; but the figure was not static.*It was considerably less before the imperial harbours were built, when houses rarely, if ever, exceeded, two stories; it shrank perceptibly in the third century, when the domus revived and many of the insulae were abandoned.

The area available for living accommodation at Portus was very considerably smaller than at Ostia, but population guesses made before the main living quarters are at least partially excavated could carry little weight. From the number of second-century tombs in the Isola Sacra cemetery and the large membership of the *fabri navales Portuenses*[1] it is clear at least that several thousand people were already living near the harbours by the Severan period.

---

[1] 354 members in their guild roll (256) in or near the Severan period.

Appendix IX

THE DATING OF OSTIAN BUILDINGS

THE chronology of republican buildings at Rome can be based in part on a series of monuments whose date is either precisely or approximately fixed by the evidence of literary sources or inscriptions. For the history of Ostian building in the Republic we have to rely exclusively on a comparative study of construction. Changes in technique can be approximately dated by reference to practice at Rome, and general historical considerations provide a measure of control, but the margin of error in dating individual buildings remains considerable.

In the imperial period we move on much firmer ground. The custom of adding consular dates to brickstamps, adopted first under Trajan, provides firm evidence for the close dating of much of the great rebuilding of the town in the first half of the second century. The material available for the comparative study of construction is considerably more plentiful than for the Republic, both in Ostia and Rome; and it now includes decorative elements as well as walls. The influence of Apollodorus' work in Trajan's Forum at Rome is apparent in the cornice of the Ostian Capitolium; the architectural decoration of the Temple of the Round Altar shows that the reconstruction of this temple cannot be far from the Flavian period.

Inscriptions also provide valuable controls. The original inscriptions from temples of Bona Dea and Bellona survive and their lettering confirms conclusions based on the study of their construction. In two cases the evidence is more explicit. A large fragment including the name of Agrippa almost certainly comes from the original inscription on the theatre (p. 42); the dating of this building to the first half of Augustus' principate provides a useful point of reference. The construction of a temple to Serapis in 127 A.D. is recorded in the Fasti; it can be identified with a temple on the Via della Trinacria (p. 139). Of more general importance are the terms in which Hadrian is honoured. Ostia is 'conservata et aucta omni indulgentia eius' (95): we are justified in looking for considerable traces of Hadrianic building.

Styles of Construction

The main succession of construction styles that can still be seen at Ostia follows the Roman pattern: *opus quadratum*; *opus incertum*; *opus quasi-reticulatum*; *opus reticulatum*; brick, accompanied at first by reticulate, later alone; block and brick; block.[1] The succession of styles provides a useful foundation

[1] English terms are retained to avoid confusion. Lugli (*La Tecnica edilizia Romana*, 40–49) has proposed a standard terminology, but *opus mixtum*, which he adopts for the

for chronology, but it is not a decisive criterion. When concrete construction has once been evolved it is normally adopted by the builder and the main change thereafter comes in the style of facing walls. But *opus quadratum* does not suddenly end with the introduction of concrete. It is still freely used for the platforms of temples, for piers supporting porticoes or strengthening walls, and even for the main walls of important buildings. It is not until after the middle of the first century A.D. that it is abandoned at Ostia. The Grandi Horrea were probably built under Claudius: though the inner walls were in brick the outer walls of the original construction were in large blocks of hard tufa, carefully cut and joined together without mortar.[1]

Similarly reticulate construction continues after the first adoption of brick, and brick with reticulate is not completely discontinued at the end of Hadrian's principate, although in the Antonine period all-brick facing dominates construction. Nor is there a neat dividing line between brick and brick-and-block; for a long time they are both in use, sometimes in the same buildings. Even *opus incertum*, which gives way naturally to *quasi-reticulatum* towards the end of the Republic, reappears in the second century A.D. A practised eye might not be deceived and it might be better to call this style *opus informe*, but some of these later walls have at first sight an archaic appearance. It is therefore necessary to control the general indication of construction style by every other criterion available. Of these the most important is the level of building. In a purely typological sequence one might place the *horrea* on the Via degli Aurighi (iii. 2[6]), which are predominantly in reticulate with a very small admixture of brick, before Julio-Claudian buildings in which brick and reticulate are evenly divided; its level, however, makes such a dating impossible and a brickstamp confirms that it is not earlier than Trajan.

When the level offers no secure clue, the relation of a building to its neighbours will often help to establish its date. A study of foundations (as well as other logical inferences) shows that the 'Curia' is earlier than the House of the Lararium, which adjoins it on the west side; and that building can be dated by brickstamps to the beginning of Hadrian's principate.[2] With the 'Curia' goes the Basilica opposite because the bricks that it uses are of the same quality and size. It is important to know that these public buildings, which considerably enhanced the dignity of the Forum, were constructed before the great building programmes of Hadrian's principate.

combination of brick with reticulate, could apply equally well to any type of facing in which different materials are combined, and has often been used for the combination of brick with tufa blocks. For this latter style Lugli suggests *opus vittatum*, but the term is not clearly descriptive.

[1] *NS* 1921, 360.
[2] Bloch, *Topografia*, 217 (i. 9. 3).

Opus quadratum

The wall is built with large squared blocks of tufa, carefully cut and carefully laid. At first there is no trace of clamps to hold the blocks together; they are found regularly from the time of Augustus.[1] This style was adopted for the Castrum walls in the middle of the fourth century B.C. and was still used 400 years later for the outside walls of the Grandi Horrea.

The earliest walls are distinguished from those that follow by their low level and by the type of tufa they use. The walls of the Castrum were built with blocks of Fidenae tufa which must have been sent down from Rome when the fourth-century settlement was established. If we discount the re-used remains of these walls, this tufa is not found later at Ostia. When the original consignment was exhausted the colonists had to find new supplies. In the late Republic and through the Empire Ostia could draw on the Monte Verde quarries at Rome and the whole range of tufas used by Roman builders. The river boats which carried corn upstream could economically bring down return cargoes of building material. In the fourth century, however, it is doubtful whether river traffic had assumed a sufficient volume; it is more probable that Ostia then drew its tufa from the quarries in the hills to the south of the Via Ostiensis, by Mezzo Cammino and Risaro.[2]

In this district there are three main types of tufa. The hardest of these is of a dark-brown, sometimes reddish, colour; it has a close texture and wears well, but it is not found at the lowest levels in Ostia. The second type resembles Roman *peperino* in colour and texture and is fairly hard. It is found at the lowest levels but not in large blocks. The third type is probably the earliest to be generally used in *opus quadratum*. It resembles Roman *cappellaccio*, which is found on the Palatine and Capitol and is widely used in very early Roman buildings. Ostian *cappellacio*, like its Roman equivalent, is normally mud-yellow in colour but occasionally reddish. It is a weak tufa, flakes easily, and wears badly; it lies near the surface, and the ease of extraction combined with its softness for cutting probably explain its early popularity. In the later Republic it was superseded in *opus quadratum* by harder tufas, though it is occasionally found, as in a pier in the House of Jupiter the Thunderer, which is not earlier than Augustus. Even for the square blocks used in quasi-reticulate and reticulate it is rarely used; an exception is the temple of Hercules.

Two good examples of this early *opus quadratum* survive:

Wall in the north-west corner of the block on the north side of the Decumanus, west of the Forum (i. 9²).

Walls abutting on the east wall of the Castrum on Via dei Molini (i. 1⁴).

It might be possible to establish a chronological sequence in the use of

[1] Gismondi, *Topografia*, 191.
[2] These quarries are briefly noted by Tenney Frank, *Roman Buildings of the Republic*, 31.

harder tufas; but a specialist is first needed to identify securely the provenance of the various tufas used.

Opus incertum

The wall has a solid core of concrete. Lime, which has to come from Rome or beyond, is mixed with volcanic earth (*pozzolana*), which could be obtained either from Rome or from the quarries on the Via Ostiensis. The aggregate is composed of pieces of tufa of varying shape and size, normally small. Tufa blocks of irregular shape form the face, large and polygonal at first, but gradually decreasing to the size and shape of a man's fist. For wall angles and the frames of doorways tufa 'bricks' are used. Foundations are little wider than the walls they support, and they are laid without timber shuttering. The earliest mortar is dark and considerably less strong than later.

It is probable that concrete construction, and, with it, *opus incertum*, was introduced to Ostia early in the second century (p. 119). The style melts into *quasi-reticulatum* before the building of the new town walls, for which a Sullan date has been accepted (pp. 35 f.).

Early examples of the style, using large polygonal blocks, probably earlier than 150 B.C., can be seen:

Wall on the east side of the western Decumanus under the Portico della Fontana a Lucerna (iv. 7[1]).

Shop walls on the south side of the eastern Decumanus in front of the Horrea of Hortensius (v. 12[1]).

Wall of early house under Vicolo di Dionisio (iv. 5[9]).

Late examples of the style, with smaller facing blocks, may be dated towards the end of the second century B.C.:

Early building incorporated in the Mithraeum of the Painted Walls (iii. 1[6]).
House of Jupiter the Thunderer (iv. 4[3]).
Three small republican houses (i. 9[1]).
House of the Peristyle (v. 7[4]).

Opus quasi-reticulatum

The size and shape of the tufa blocks of the wall's face become more regular. Foundations are normally wider and deeper than in *opus incertum*, and timber shuttering is used. Some walls are strengthened by tufa piers inserted at regular intervals.

If the quasi-reticulate town walls are rightly dated to the Sullan period, this style will roughly cover the period from the beginning of the first century to the end of the Republic and a little beyond. The following buildings, listed in roughly chronological order, are included, though there can be no clear demarcation between *opus incertum* and *opus quasi-reticulatum*:

Temple of Hercules (i. 15⁵).
Tetrastyle temple (i. 15²).
Town walls.
Four temples, west of the theatre (ii. 8²).
Temple outside east gate of Castrum (ii. 9⁴).
Shops and industrial premises near Porta Romana (ii. 2¹⁻³).

Opus reticulatum

A reasonably secure *terminus ante quem* for a mature reticulate style is provided by two buildings that can be dated to the Augustan period. The theatre is earlier than the death of Agrippa in 12 B.C. (p. 42); the tomb of a praetorian soldier of the sixth cohort is almost certainly earlier than the concentration of the guard in Rome on the accession of Tiberius.[1] In both buildings the reticulate pattern is regular. At Rome mature reticulate is found for the first time in Pompey's theatre;[2] it probably developed at Ostia between 50 and 25 B.C. It continues into the Julio-Claudian period, but meets increasing competition from brick. The strengthening of the reticulate face by tufa piers at regular intervals in the wall is more widespread than in the previous period. The following reticulate buildings can be dated to the early Principate:

Shops on south side of Decumanus by western gate of Castrum (i. 10¹).
Shops on west side of Semita dei Cippi, north of eastern entrance to Forum Baths (i. 12⁵. Pl. xl *a*).
Temple of Bona Dea at south end of Via degli Augustales (v. 10²).
House of the Mosaic Niche on Cardo Maximus (iv. 4²).
Market, south side of Via della Foce (iii. 1⁷).
Shrine of Jupiter in area of four republican temples (ii. 8⁴).
Temple of Rome and Augustus.
Temple of Bona Dea outside Porta Marina (iv. 8³).
Partly excavated public baths (v. 10³).

Brickwork

The introduction of brick facing was the decisive innovation of the Empire. At first the number of all-brick walls is small; more commonly brick and reticulate are used together. This style of construction is particularly widespread in the early building of Hadrian's principate, but from about A.D. 130 it becomes increasingly rare. The great replanning of the area which includes the Baths of Neptune and is dated to Hadrian's last years is exclusively in brick, and most of the dated buildings of Antoninus Pius follow this fashion. I know of no example of the combination of brick with reticulate

[1] *NS* 1912, 23; *Topografia*, tav. xlviii. 4.
[2] M. E. Blake, *Ancient Roman Construction in Italy*, 254.

after the middle of the second century. By the fourth century at the latest
block-and-brick construction rivals brick in quantity at Ostia, but it cannot
be chronologically separated from brick and its beginnings are to be found
as early as the second century.

Brick with reticulate

In most early examples of this style brick is introduced sparingly to surfaces that are still predominantly reticulate. The function of the brick is to
strengthen the wall as an alternative to the combination of tufa piers with reticulate; it is normally used at the main points of stress. In the so-called 'navale'
by the river west of the excavated area, which may be Augustan (p. 126), the
brickwork is confined to six courses at the top of the walls, from which the
barrel vaults spring. In the Julio-Claudian Horrea of Hortensius vertical
panels of brick are inserted in the side walls of all the rooms (Pl. XL c). Elsewhere brick frames are provided at the sides and at the top and bottom of
walls, sometimes with intermediate horizontal bands of brick. But by
the time of Trajan and Hadrian reticulate and brick are almost evenly mixed,
and reticulate panels are neatly bonded into frames of brick in a manner
that seems more decorative than functional. There is a tendency for the tufa
squares of the reticulate to become larger, from an average of 6·5 cm. under
Augustus to 7·5 cm. under Trajan and Hadrian, but the bricks normally
provide a more reliable indication of date.

Before resuming the sequence of styles it is necessary to examine the
criteria for dating brickwork.

The dating of brickwork

The history of Ostia during the Empire depends largely on the dating of
brickwork, and for the most important phase in the town's development
brickstamps provide a firm chronological framework.

Confidence in the validity of brickstamp evidence has run an uneven
course. The nineteenth-century pioneers had no qualms. Scepticism, however, grew strong in this century, especially as a result of the increasing pre-
ponderance of stamps of the year A.D. 123. Cozzo persuaded many when he
urged that the consular date on a brickstamp indicated the date not of production but of the opening of a new brickworks.[1] Cozzo's arguments, however,
have been fully answered by Bloch, who, by a detailed study of the various
sources of manufacture and of a wide range of buildings in Rome and Ostia,
has shown that the stamp gives the production date and that normally bricks
were used soon after they had been produced.[2] When they are found in the

---

[1] G. Cozzo, 'Una industria nella Roma imperiale: la corporazione dei figuli ed i bolli
doliari', *Mem. acc. Lincei*, 1936.

[2] Bloch, *I bolli laterizi e la storia edilizia* (Roma, 1938). See Addenda.

construction and not simply among the ruins, they provide valid evidence for the date of the building; when stamps of widely different dates are found in significant numbers, we must look for more than one building period. No one who has studied the material at Ostia intimately can doubt the validity of Bloch's main conclusions.

Caution, however, is needed. Dated stamps are not decisive if their number is very small. Presumably the Ostian builders ordered considerable quantities of bricks at a time. When a particular building was finished, the stock of bricks in hand may not have been used at once, and brick producers who did not sell all their current output may have sold old stock considerably after its production.

The stamping of consular dates on brickstamps begins towards the end of Trajan's principate and the proportion of stamped to unstamped is highest under Hadrian; from Antoninus Pius onwards the practice becomes less common and other criteria become more important. Similarly for the period before the last years of Trajan stamps are comparatively rare and undated: for their approximate date we depend on a study of their distribution in dated buildings.

Where brickstamps are not found, a study of the bricks themselves and the way in which they are used, together with the technique of the concrete construction, can provide important clues for dating. The pioneer in this field was Miss Van Deman, who elaborated a series of canons in 1912.[1] Her work is still important for the imperial period to the death of Hadrian; but her treatment of the later period provided only a summary outline and was based on a very limited range of material.

Miss Van Deman examined the type of brick used, the quality and measurements of the brick, the nature of the mortar and of the concrete, and other distinctive features of the construction. She showed that canons could be framed which, used with discretion, afforded valuable indications of date. Such discretion has not always been shown and Miss Van Deman has sometimes been criticized for the misuse of her methods by lesser scholars. The measurement of the width of the brick is the easiest test to apply, but used alone it can be very misleading. A false average can easily result if the number of bricks measured is inadequate, or if an untypical piece of walling is measured. Miss Van Deman herself emphasized the importance of applying every test available.

(i) *Type of brick.* Three types of brick are found in Ostian walls, derived from roof tiles, *bessales* (small square bricks), and from large bricks such as are used to line pavements, *bipedales* and *sesquipedales*.

Fired roof tiles were already being produced in large quantities during the Republic, and it is for that reason presumably that they were first used for the

[1] E. B. Van Deman, *AJA* 16 (1912) 230–57, 387–432.

N n

facing of walls. The face of the brick, broken by the hammer from roof tiles, was carefully dressed, but the shape of the brick penetrating the concrete was very irregular at first, though there was a growing tendency towards a roughly triangular form. Bricks from *bipedales* and *sesquipedales* followed the same principles, and it is not easy to distinguish the two types.

Bricks from *bessales* approach much closer to the modern brick. The square (20–22 cm.) was broken with the hammer across the diagonal and regular triangular bricks were thus formed, the largest side being used for the face. Walls built with triangular bricks can be distinguished by the uniformity of their brick lengths, as in the Basilica and the 'Curia'.

So far as our present evidence goes, only roof tiles were used under Augustus and Tiberius. Triangular bricks are found first under Gaius or Claudius;[1] they predominate in later Julio-Claudian buildings and through the Flavian period. They are still used under Trajan and Hadrian, but on a decreasing scale. In the great rebuilding of the first half of the second century there is a marked preference for using roof tiles, and *bipedales* and *sesquipedales*. There is a revival in the popularity of the triangular brick towards the end of the second century, but they are rarely found in the Severan period or later. When triangular bricks are used they are normally used throughout the construction or at least throughout certain parts of it; but occasionally all three types are found in the same wall.

The production of Roman bricks was not mechanical. The side of the brick which provided the facing of the wall was always hammer-dressed or cut with the saw.[2] Even *bessales* were not divided before firing, nor is there any trace at Ostia of surface cuts having been made in the clay. The brick was normally broken across the diagonal by the hammer after firing. This procedure, which seems strangely uneconomic to us, helps to account for the liveliness of brick surfaces in Ostian buildings.

(ii) *Brick measurements.* There is a clearly marked tendency for the width of bricks gradually to decrease, from an average of 4·0 cm. in the early Empire, to 3·8 cm. in the Flavian and early Trajanic period. By the end of Hadrian's reign the average has fallen to 3·4 cm. and in the Severan period the average falls below 3 cm. But in all periods there is a wide range in the width of contemporary bricks, and averages are misleading unless based on a wide sample. Triangular bricks also tend to be a little thicker than the two other types.

In triangular bricks formed from *bessales* the length is consistent at 26–

---

[1] In the baths under the Via dei Vigiles. Triangular bricks are very uncommon in Rome before Gaius.

[2] Illustration of the use of saw and hammer on bricks, Lugli, *La Tecnica edilizia*, 546, fig. 113. Gismondi, *Topografia*, 195, would exclude the use of the saw at Ostia. Some traces can, I think, be seen, but they are rare.

28 cm. In the other two types the length varies much more, though in the best work of the second-century rebuilding there seems to have been a deliberate attempt to secure regularity in length (20–22 cm.). Short lengths are normally a sign of later work.

(iii) *Colour* is a weak criterion. Though the tiles used under Augustus and Tiberius seem to be of a constant deep red, in later brickwork red and yellow can almost always be found together. The colour depends partly on the quality of the firing, partly on the nature of the clay and its ferric oxide content. The decisive factor may therefore be the brickfield and not the date. Only by detailed work in correlating brickstamps with the quality and colour of the bricks can useful progress be made here. In the two main Hadrianic areas at Ostia the colour is uniformly red and the bricks were probably deliberately selected; but in the Hadrianic House of the Triclinia, in the House of the Lararium, in the podium of the Capitolium, and in other Hadrianic buildings, there is an ample admixture of yellow.

It is true that by the middle of Antoninus Pius' reign the 'Hadrianic' red seems to become much rarer and mixed walls with yellow predominating become typical by the middle of the century. Therein lies evidence probably of the exhaustion of certain clay fields and of the opening of new.

(iv) *Width of joints*. There is a general tendency for the layer of mortar between bricks to become wider. The horizontal joints under Augustus and Tiberius are rarely more than 1·2 cm. wide; by the second half of the third century they are very rarely under 2·5 cm. and in the fourth they are more often over 3·0 cm. But this is only a general tendency and there are important exceptions. Thus the joints in the early Hadrianic House of the Triclinia are extremely narrow, often less than 1 cm., while the joints in the Basilica, a more important building, which is certainly not later than Trajan, average about 2 cm. Similarly in the temple of Bellona some of the joints are as wide as 3·5 cm., but the construction is certainly earlier than the Severan period.

(v) *Mortar*. Ostian mortar is formed by a mixture of lime and volcanic earth (*pozzolana*). There are considerable differences in colour, but these afford no clue to chronology during the Empire. They depend on the particular deposit used and red, light-grey, and dark-grey earths are found quite close together.[1] Sometimes the earth is not well fired and large lumps remain in the mortar, but this carelessness can be found at all periods. Nor does there seem to be any chronological clue in the proportion of lime used.

(vi) *Concrete*. Broken brick, tufa, even marble, are all found in Ostian concrete; the nature of the aggregate depends primarily on the material available from the destruction of earlier buildings. Since pre-Domitianic building at Ostia is mainly in tufa, the aggregate in the period of active

[1] Red *pozzolana*, the strongest, is not found before Augustus. The earliest to be used, in *opus incertum*, is the dark-grey, which normally lies near the surface and is the weakest.

rebuilding from Domitian to Antoninus Pius is composed almost entirely of tufa. A large admixture of brick is normally found not earlier than the late second century.

(vii) *Bonding courses.* Courses of *bipedales* running through the wall are a marked feature of Hadrianic work at Ostia, and often yellow bricks are deliberately chosen for these bonding courses to contrast with a dominantly red brick surface. Under Antoninus Pius bonding courses are not always used and, when they are used, they are less conspicuous. They receive revived emphasis under Commodus, when it becomes fashionable either to select red *bipedales* for the purpose, or to paint red courses on the wall, even when no true bonding courses are present. The fashion lasts for barely a generation and bonding courses are not found after the early years of the third century.

(viii) *Relieving arches* are first found under Trajan. They are widely used under Hadrian, but only found occasionally later. Their function should be to relieve pressure; they have a natural place over doorways or at the base of walls where the foundations are not continuous. It is difficult to understand their short-lived popularity under Hadrian; in many cases their purpose seems to be purely decorative.

Block and brick

Block and brick are combined in a wide variety of ways. Some walls are mainly of brick, with a few courses of tufa blocks interspersed; in others this relation is reversed. The most common and attractive combination is to alternate courses of block and of brick; sometimes there is a regular alternation of two courses of each. The tufa blocks are normally oblong; sometimes they are cut carefully to a rectangular shape, sometimes they are most irregular in shape and size. Less commonly the blocks are small and square and are similar to the blocks of reticulate walls, from which many of them may have come; but they are laid square rather than diagonally.

In Rome this style of construction is first used for an important building by Maxentius in his circus on the Via Appia, but it is found earlier in private building. It is common under Constantine and afterwards. Examples of its use in a subordinate role in the second century can be seen at Ostia. The first dated example is in a wall closing the entrance to the House of Jupiter and Ganymede on the Via di Diana, which is earlier than the death of Commodus.[1] From the middle of the century probably come the nymphaeum in the area of the four republican temples (ii. 8³) and a wall in the west wing of the House of Apuleius (ii. 8⁵); in both of these it is tentatively used in combination with reticulate.

A somewhat similar style is seen in the northern nucleus of the 'Imperial

[1] *MA* 26 (1920) 369.

Palace', where it is used in the peristyle court and in the baths at the east end. The bricks used in these walls are regular and well coursed, suggesting a date before the middle of the second century; they are contemporary with neighbouring brick walls, and the bulk of the brickstamps found in this part of the building are from the early years of Antoninus Pius.[1] The pattern seems experimental, varying between a mixture of reticulate with block-and-brick, and block-and-brick in alternating bands of two courses. Many of the blocks are carefully cut and regular in size. Block-and-brick is also used for some beautifully finished applied columns.

Rather later a row of shops on the eastern Decumanus (v. 11[5]) uses brick alone for its front on the street, but·block-and-brick for the dividing walls of the shops. In the easternmost of two dividing walls the lowest courses, however, are in brick. Brick-and-block is also commonly used in modifications of second-century buildings, and it is the dominant style employed in building or adapting private houses to the taste of the late Empire. No public buildings yet excavated are originally constructed in this style; it will be interesting to see whether it was used for public building on the line of the coast, where building seems to have remained active in the late period.

It is clearly very difficult to date this style of wall-facing. A possible clue to an early date may be the even quality of the bricks, suggesting that they are not reused material. More important perhaps is the shape of the blocks. In all the second-century examples that I have noted a large proportion of the blocks are carefully cut to rectangular shape; in fourth-century walls the shapes seem to become increasingly irregular. That this does not merely indicate a difference between good and bad, but also between early and late, is seen by comparing the regular blocks used in the second century for such comparatively unimportant buildings as the guild house of the *hastiferi* (iv. 1[5]) and buildings on the west side of the Via del Pozzo (v. 2[12-14]) with the extreme irregularity of the blocks in the walls framing the vestibule of a new entry to the Forum Baths in the late fourth century.

The predominance of brick over blocks also seems in general to be early, but the use of small square blocks instead of the more general larger oblong shapes recurs throughout the period, especially in small niches and apses where its convenience is manifest. Signs of lateness apart from the irregular shape of tufa blocks may be the high proportion of mortar to tufa in the face and the lack of regularity in the pattern. When, in a wall that is not unimportant to the construction, a course of tufa blocks is continued in brick, we may suspect a late date. Such signs, however, are only valid evidence when seen in important walls. In walls of only secondary importance, such as in the closing of a shop or house door, the workmanship is always likely to be rough.

---

[1] Bloch, *Topografia*, 225.

Block facing

In the Middle Ages walls were often faced with courses of tufa blocks alone without admixture of brick. Such facing is already found in the podium of the Round Temple (i. 11¹), in walls later than the original construction in the 'Imperial Palace', and in substantial repairs to an Augustan *crypta* (south of i. 4⁹). We cannot date its use within narrow limits, but it seems to be rare before the fifth century.

Early and Middle Empire

Augustus and the Julio-Claudian period

Reticulate, brick with reticulate, and brick are all found.

The earliest brick walls use broken tiles, and are probably earlier than the death of Tiberius:

Wall immediately surrounding the podium of the four republican temples (ii. 8²).
Cistern below the *palaestra* of the Baths of Neptune (ii. 1).

Triangular bricks are found towards the middle of the century:

Central rooms of the Grandi Horrea (ii. 9⁷).
Baths under the Via dei Vigiles.
Shops added to the east side of the Grandi Horrea (ii. 9⁷).

Brick is also used in association with reticulate:

The Horrea of Hortensius, the walls of which are mainly in reticulate, but have reinforcing brick panels in the side walls (v. 12¹).
External brick pilasters on reticulate walls of the Bona Dea area (iv. 8³).

The Flavian period

There is an increasing tendency towards all-brick facing, and triangular bricks are much more freely used than under Trajan and Hadrian.

The only building securely dated by brickstamps to the Flavian period is the House of the Thunderbolt, outside Porta Marina (iii. 7⁴).

The following may, by comparison, be attributed to the late Flavian period, or the early years of Trajan:

Curia (i. 9⁴) and Basilica (i. 11⁵).
Temple in Piazzale delle Corporazioni (ii. 7⁵), and rooms on the east side of the Piazzale.
First phase of fountains on eastern Decumanus (ii. 7⁶,⁷, 9¹).
Shops on eastern Decumanus (i. 1³ and ii. 9²).
Baths by Christian Basilica on western Decumanus (iii. 1³).
Temple east of Hall of Measurers (i. 19²).

Trajan

The following buildings are dated by brickstamps:

Shops backing on Castrum wall (i. 8⁵).
Baths of Buticosus (i. 14⁸).
Public building between temple of Hercules and tetrastyle temple (i. 15¹).
Horrea of Measurers (i. 19⁴).
Market on north side of Via degli Aurighi (iii. 2⁶).
Casette-tipo (iii. 12 and 13).
House of Bacchus and Ariadne (iii. 17⁵).
Baths of Six Columns (iv. 5¹¹).

The following may, by comparison, be dated to roughly the same period:

Horrea on west side of Semita dei Cippi (i. 13¹).
Shops, &c., on Via della Foce in front of Casette-tipo (iii. 15).
House at north end of Via della Casa del Pozzo (v. 3¹).
Horrea of Artemis (v. 11⁸).

Hadrian

Buildings dated by brickstamps fall into three periods.

Early

Capitolium and area to the north, *horrea*, shops, &c. (i. 5, 6, 7, 8¹, 8², 8¹⁰).
Block west of Forum, north side of Decumanus, except 'Curia' (i. 9¹⁻³).
House of the Triclinia, builders' headquarters (i. 12¹).
Portico on western Decumanus by Lamp Fountain, with adjacent building (iv. 7¹).

Middle

Bakery on Via dei Molini (i. 3¹).
House of Lucretius Menander (i. 3²).
House of the Paintings and two neighbours (i. 4²⁻⁴).
Baths of Mithras (i. 17²).
Market west of Horrea of Measurers (i. 20¹).
Shops on south side of Via della Foce (iii. 1⁸).
House of Mars (iii. 2³).
House of Painted Vaults and block to the north (iii. 4, 5).
Insula of Serapis (iii. 10³).
Insula of Annius and store with sunken *dolia* (iii. 14³⁻⁴).
Baths of Trinacria (iii. 16⁷).
Temple of Serapis (iii. 17⁴).
Loggia by monument of Cartilius Poplicola (iv. 9¹).

Late

Area north of eastern Decumanus, including Baths of Neptune (ii. 3^1, 3$^{3-4}$, 4, 5, 6^1, 6$^{3-7}$).

Among Hadrianic buildings, not dated by brickstamps, I would include:

Bakery on Semita dei Cippi (i. 13^4). See p. 134, n. 3.

Area of the Garden Houses (Hadrianic stamps, not yet recorded, can be seen in the construction) (iii. 9).

Temple of Cybele and portico (iv. 1$^{1-2}$), p. 364.

Temple of Bellona (iv. 1^4), p. 365.

Forum of Porta Marina (iv. 8^1).

Antoninus Pius

The following buildings are dated by brickstamps:

First phase of the 'Imperial Palace' (*Topografia*, 225).

House of Diana (i. 3^3).

Horrea Epagathiana (i. 8^3).

Chapel east of Insula of Serapis (iii. 2^{12}).

Schola del Traiano (iv. 5^{15}).

Building east of tomb of Poplicola (iv. 9^4).

Portico, south side of eastern Decumanus, west of Piazzale della Vittoria (v. 14, 15).

Forum Baths (i. 12^6).

By comparison I would include among the buildings of this reign:

Shrine on Decumanus near Porta Romana (ii. 2^4).

Building, east side of Via di Iside (iv. 4^7).

'Fullonica' on Via di Iside (iv. 5^3).

Insula with chapel of Isis (iv. 5^4).

House of Fortuna Annonaria (v. 2^8).

Buildings east of House of Fortuna Annonaria (v. 2$^{9-10}$).

Building at corner of Via della Fortuna Annonaria and Semita dei Cippi (v. 4^1).

House of the Sun (v. 6^1).

Marcus Aurelius to Alexander Severus

After the death of Antoninus Pius the proportion of stamped bricks, already considerably smaller than under Hadrian, continued to decrease and building chronology becomes more hazardous.

A large block on the west side of the western Decumanus, the Caseggiato dell' Ercole (iv. 2^3), has sufficient stamps to be assigned confidently to the reign of Marcus Aurelius. Two other buildings can be assigned with some probability to his reign. In the social headquarters of the Augustales (v. 7²) the brickwork seems less good than under Antoninus Pius, and the bricks less wide, often falling below 3 cm.[1] Bricks of short length, which are not often found in the first half of the second century, are common, but they do not, as later, indicate the reuse of old material. Bonding courses, which are rare after the second century, are used. The same characteristics are found in a temple on the eastern Decumanus (v. 11¹), and a fragment of entablature, probably from this temple, is consistent with this dating.[2]

For the period of Commodus the evidence is rather better. The reconstructed theatre was dedicated in the first year of Septimius Severus. Several Commodan brickstamps were found in the walls, and it is probable that the building was begun and perhaps nearly completed under Commodus (p. 80). The main rebuilding of the Grandi Horrea is also dated to this reign by brickstamps of M. Aurelius and Commodus.[3]

These two buildings have the distinctive red bonding courses which come into fashion under Commodus. The same feature is seen in the large *horrea* for the storage of corn near the Porta Romana (ii. 2⁷), and the same type of yellow triangular bricks from *bessales* are used here as in the Grandi Horrea. Other buildings may be dated to Commodus or a little later by their red bonding courses:

Building south of bakery on Cardo (i. 13⁵).
Reconstruction of north wing of Macellum (iv. 5²).
Block west of nymphaeum at south end of Forum (iv. 4⁶).
Block on Decumanus, east of 'guild temple' (v. 11³).
Walls enclosing republican monument on Decumanus (v. 11⁶).
Building by the triumphal arches opposite theatre (v. 11⁷).

For the reign of Septimius Severus there are no firm controls. The closing of the portico in the Grandi Horrea, however, has a brickstamp of the period, and there are good grounds for believing that the northern part of this building was rebuilt in the Severan period.[4]

In the walls of this section of the building ample use is made of a thin red brick (from 2·5 to 3 cm. wide) which is not found in the Commodan walls. The same brickwork is found also in a large-scale restoration of the eastern wall of the Piccolo Mercato, which therefore probably also dates from Septimius Severus. In these walls bonding courses are not used.

---

[1] The only three brickstamps recorded are from the reign of Antoninus Pius, but they come from a large apse which is a later addition; they probably were taken from an earlier building.

[2] D. E. Strong, 'Late Hadrianic architectural ornament in Rome', *BSR* 21 (1953) 140.

[3] *NS* 1921, 381.

[4] The brickwork is very similar to Severan work at Rome.

The baths on the line of the Sullan wall west of the Porta Marina (iii. 8²) are Severan. Hypocausts in this building have stamps of 210, and the brick-work has its natural context at approximately this date. It can be paralleled in the temple of 'Portumnus' at Porto, which on architectural grounds may be dated roughly to the first half of the third century (p. 167).

A date in the early third century should probably be assigned to the line of tombs on the south side of the Via dei Sepolcri outside the Porta Romana. They are designed for inhumation alone, showing that they are later than the first half of the second century, and they are homogeneous. The façades are in brick but a subordinate use of block-and-brick is made in the interior. The bricks are thin (averaging about 2·8 cm.) and the coursing is less good than in the work that has been assigned to the reign of Septimius Severus. The lettering of the inscriptions found in the tombs strengthens the dating in the first half of the third century.

The late Empire

The last Roman period at Ostia is the most difficult to unravel. Block-and-brick becomes common as an alternative to brick. The growing tendency to reuse bricks from older buildings complicates the dating of brickwork, but the width of horizontal joints helps to distinguish late walls from early. Before the fourth century the joints are rarely more than 2·5 cm. wide; in the fourth century they are rarely less.

Within this difficult period there are some possible points of departure. The approximate dating of the Round Temple (i. 11¹) is of importance because it is the last large public building known to us. Its date would also provide a standard of reference for other brick buildings. It is earlier than the House of the Round Temple (i. 11²), because the brick cornice above the podium projects into the west wall of the house.[1] The brickwork of this house is of fairly good quality. Though short lengths suggesting the possible reuse of old material are found, most of the bricks seem to be homogeneous. They are fairly well coursed, and the width of the horizontal joints is not more than 2·5 cm.

The temple itself, however, is without parallel in Ostia. The podium face is mainly in brick but has also substantial stretches in tufa blocks which are contemporary. In the cella two very different types of brick are used. The façade towards its western end has very thin long red bricks averaging under 2·5 cm., such as are found in Severan work at Rome and Ostia. The remainder of the facing bricks form a mixture of red and yellow averaging 3·4 cm. in width, but they do not seem to be old material.

The general indications of the brickwork suggest that the temple was built towards the middle of the third century.[2] Similar brickwork is seen in a small

---

[1] Wilson, *BSR* 14 (1938) 159 n. 30.   [2] See also pp. 81 f.

area west of the temple (i. 10⁴) including a guild temple, which was probably planned at the same time. The House of the Round Temple will have been built later in the century and may reflect the brick revival under Diocletian. Roughly contemporary is the House of the Columns (iv. 3¹), which is shown to be late by its level; its brickwork would fit the context.

An analysis of late work in the Forum Baths (i. 12⁶) should also provide useful clues. There were probably two main phases of restoration in the fourth century. The earlier, perhaps Constantinian, is reflected in two brick-stamps found in the apse that replaced the rectangular end of the Frigidarium. Contemporary brickwork can be seen in several of the walls of the heated rooms in the south wing, including the apse of the Caldarium. It may have been at this time that large windows framed by columns were introduced into the southern walls. Similar brickwork reflecting large-scale reconstruction in the heated rooms of the Baths of Neptune has been dated by stamps to the reign of Constantine.[1]

The other conspicuous late change in the Forum Baths is the provision of a monumental entrance on the north side towards the east end. Four tall brick piers served to emphasize the entrance and to buttress the north wall of the baths, weakened by the new opening. Inside the door two new framing walls formed a vestibule. The arches are in brick of a different character from the Constantinian work; the new walls of the vestibule are in block-and-brick. The shapes of the tufa blocks are very irregular and the proportion of mortar to tufa very high. This new entrance should probably be associated with the inscriptions recording the restoration of the baths by Vincentius Ragonius Celsus in the late fourth century;[2] the brickwork of the arches and the brick-and-block of the vestibule walls can be used as standards of reference.

On the east side of these Forum Baths outside the entrance that leads in from the Semita dei Cippi are two two-storied arches in brick, whose function is most obscure. Though the brickwork is not noticeably different from that of the entrance arches on the north-west side, large blocks of marble and travertine are used in the face near the ground level; in fact one arch rests on a nicely decorated marble panel. Such 'plugging' of brick walls with large blocks is common at Ostia in the Middle Ages, but I have not seen examples from the fourth century in important constructions. I suggest that these two-storied arches are from the fifth century.[3] It is possible that the original intention was to balance them by a second pair on the other side of the street.

---

[1] Bloch, *Bolli laterizi*, 243.

[2] 139, *S* 4717, 4718; Bloch, 'The Name of the Baths near the Forum of Ostia', *Studies presented to D. M. Robinson*, ii (1951) 412.

[3] A fifth-century restoration may be reflected in *S* 5387, found in these baths: '— l]abebatur ut lava[? — splen]dore excultum ad usum pop[uli — | —] annonae praefec—.' On the back is an earlier funerary inscription.

Considerably better than the brick-and-block of the new vestibule of the Forum Baths is the adaptation of the west wing of the Baths of Mithras to Christian use. Such adaptation must be later than Constantine's conversion to Christianity; a date towards the middle of the fourth century is suggested. To approximately the same date I would assign the construction of the new walls that formed the House of the Dioscuri from a Hadrianic insula.[1] Some of these walls are in brick; most are in block-and-brick. In some walls small squares are used, in others the more normal oblong blocks; in both styles the blocks are very irregular, but less so than in the vestibule of the Forum Baths. Perhaps a more detailed study of the mosaics and of the lettering of the proverb in the Venus mosaic would confirm a date near the middle of the fourth century.

Brick-and-block was not invariably used after Constantine's death. A small set of baths on the north side of the Via della Foce (i. 19[5]) is built in brick alone. The bricks are from earlier buildings and the coursing is very irregular. Since these baths interrupt a line of shops in brick-and-block which have a Diocletianic stamp, it is inferred that the baths are considerably later, and probably post-Constantinian. Another set of baths (iv. 4[8]) south of the Round Temple uses a small number of much earlier walls; the main construction is in brick, with a very subordinate use of brick-and-block. The brickwork is very rough and reused material; it is probably not far in date from the Baths on Via della Foce. Such a dating receives a little confirmation from the predominance of circular and apsidal rooms in both buildings.

I would also provisionally assign a late-fourth-century date to the House of Cupid and Psyche (i. 14[5]), one of the most attractive of the late houses.[2] The tufa blocks are very irregular, but more important for dating purposes is the *opus sectile* pavement of the main room of the house. The intricate elaboration of the design, the liberal use of such hard stones as serpentine and porphyry which are seldom found in early pavements, and the reproduction of minor motifs whose natural place is in cornices suggest a later date. For similar reasons the House of the Nymphaeum (iii. 6[1])[3] may be dated in the second half of the fourth century. Almost all the wall-facings in this house have been recently restored, but what little remains of the original work is irregular. It may also be significant that this house is very similar in plan to the House of Cupid and Psyche.

The most important general conclusion provisionally drawn from a comparative study of late work in Ostia is that almost all the late houses in their present form belong to the fourth century, and that some at least of them were formed nearer the end than the beginning of the century.

It may also be possible to distinguish some work of the fifth century. The core of large blocks of marble or travertine in a brick face has been suggested

---

[1] Becatti, *Case tarde*, 14.   [2] Ibid. 6.   [3] Ibid. 10.

as a reason for dating the two-storied arches on the east side of the Forum Baths to the fifth century.[1] Similar work on a grosser scale is seen in the walls built to complete the south wall of the Christian Basilica on the western Decumanus (iii. 1⁴). Huge blocks of selce, travertine, and marble are used on a scale that I have not seen in any wall of the fourth century or earlier. It is noticeable also that in the apse courses of tufa blocks are continued in brick. There is, I think, no difficulty in dating to the fifth century the inscription over the entrance to the 'baptistery'.

A fifth-century phase can perhaps also be seen in the House of the Porch (v. 2⁵). Brick is used for the main weight-carrying walls, block-and-brick for the less important walls. Since the brickwork is homogeneous and the block-and-brick fair, the original building should not be dated later than the early fourth century. The name on the pediment over the entrance doorway, however, is inscribed in lettering considerably worse than that found in Ostian fourth-century inscriptions. It is inscribed on an erasure and may represent a change of ownership, probably in the early fifth century. To this late phase should perhaps be attributed the building of the nymphaeum in the court, the closing of the underground chapel, and the paving of the vestibule with extremely large tesserae of different colours in a pattern of interlocking semicircles.

[1] Ibid. 21.

Appendix X

THE DATING OF OSTIAN INSCRIPTIONS

IN the course of my study of Ostia I have tried to see as many as possible of the Ostian inscriptions surviving in Italy. The task has been made considerably easier by the building up of a Lapidarium at Ostia, and the transfer to Ostia of the large collection of Ostian inscriptions from the National Museum at Rome. A considerable proportion of Ostian inscriptions, recovered in excavations carried out under Papal authority, remain in the great Papal Collections. Those in the Vatican are mainly concentrated in the Galleria Lapidaria and are comparatively easy to find from the indications in the Corpus; inscriptions on statue bases and reliefs are scattered through the other galleries. The Lateran Museum includes in its Christian wing the majority of the Christian inscriptions from Ostia and Portus. Pagan inscriptions are fixed to the walls round the central courtyard, and these now include fragments which were still in store-rooms when the Corpus was published. Another important collection is to be found in the Capitoline Museum.

Several Ostian inscriptions came to St. Paul's basilica, which owned property on the Via Ostiensis. The monumental inscription honouring Hadrian (95) was used for centuries in the pavement of the nave, with its face upwards. As a result the inscription now looks as if it was never completed; the weaker strokes have been completely worn away. A few of these inscriptions can now be seen in the cloisters; the remainder are in the Lapidarium of the adjoining monastery. Most of the inscriptions found at Portus since the middle of the nineteenth century remain in the possession of the Torlonia family, on the site, in the Torlonia Museum, or in the Villa Albani. They are considerably less accessible.

The history of the site after the Roman period explains the wide dispersal of other Ostian inscriptions. The most important pockets are in the museums of Naples and Florence, but individual stones, some of them important, are scattered over more than a dozen centres in Italy, in museums, churches, and private houses. The study of Ostia would gain considerably if these scattered stones could be sent back to Ostia.

My general picture of Ostia's history is in part based on the approximate dating of more than half these inscriptions. It is not practicable to give detailed reasons for each individual case, but a brief summary is needed of the criteria used. A few inscriptions are explicitly dated by consular years or imperial titles. Normally less precise indications have to be used.

1. The imperial cult was first administered by *Augustales*, later by *seviri*

Augustales. The date of the change falls between the middle of the first century and Trajan, probably under Domitian (pp. 219 f.). The names of *Augustales* help to identify families established in Ostia before the great expansion of the second century.

2. A large number of inscriptions were set up by the *fabri tignuarii*, and many of them refer to the numbered *lustrum* of the presidents. These can be approximately dated, since we know that the guild was formally incorporated near the middle of the first century A.D. (p. 331).

3. The offices of *pontifex Volcani* and *flamen Romae et Augusti* were held for life. Sufficient names, in the two series, survive to provide valuable controls.

4. Some inscriptions are associated with buildings which can be approximately dated by their style of construction, as the temples of Bona Dea (p. 353) and of Bellona (p. 365). In assembling the list of families known at Ostia by the early Principate the large group of tombs from the Via Laurentina provides particularly valuable evidence.[1] These tombs can be arranged by the style of their walls and the form of the tomb in a chronological series, and the latest tombs in the first phase of the cemetery include one that can be confidently dated to the early Julio-Claudian period. By the same means Thylander has been able to date approximately a large proportion of the inscriptions from the Isola Sacra cemetery.[2]

5. For inscriptions on decorated urns, funerary altars, sarcophagi, and reliefs the style of decoration provides important clues. The long inscription recording the career of Cn. Sentius Felix would never have been dated to the late second century if the decoration of his funerary altar had been studied (p. 200). The style belongs unmistakably to the late first or early second century.

6. There remains the examination of letter forms and style. Confidence in this criterion has fluctuated violently and it may be fair to say that more harm has been done by faith than by scepticism. A glance at the photographs of Isola Sacra inscriptions published by Thylander[3] shows how uneven in style contemporary inscriptions can be; bad workmanship may indicate a cheap job rather than a late date. Thylander has also shown that it can be dangerously misleading to follow any individual criterion such as the form of the stop, accents, or individual letter forms.[4] Caution is certainly needed, but not capitulation.

Two examples may illustrate the danger of neglecting script in dating inscriptions. Groag's authority has virtually imposed the identification of Glabrio *patronus*, who dedicated a statue to *salus Caesaris Augusti*, with the proconsular governor of Africa in 25 B.C.[5] The letters seem too mature for

---

[1] NS 1938, 26–74.　　　　[2] Thylander, *Étude sur l'épigraphie latine*, 15–40.
[3] Thylander, *Inscriptions du port d'Ostie*, Planches (Lund, 1951).
[4] Thylander, *Étude*, 40–52.　　　　[5] *PIR*², A 71.

such an early date. Q. Asinius Marcellus, consul and patron of Ostia, recorded in two inscriptions, is dated by Groag to the Julio-Claudian period, on the ground that the office of *iiivir monetalis* was the only post in the vigintivirate held by patricians from the Flavian period onward; Marcellus, a patrician, was *xvir stlitibus iudicandis*.[1] The inscriptions, however, are typical of late first- and early second-century work at Ostia, and suggest identification with a Q. Asinius Marcellus known to be consul shortly after 96 (p. 207). The number of Flavian careers recorded in full is insufficient to establish a firm law concerning the junior offices.

For purposes of dating it is important that like should be compared with like. We should not expect to find the same style in a public tribute to an emperor as in the funerary inscription of a building labourer. Inscriptions of the latter class present wide variations in all periods; the higher-class work of public inscriptions and rich men's dedications and tombstones is much more homogeneous. There are sufficient dated inscriptions in this class to provide a foundation for study. Exceptions to all rules can be found, but the following criteria, reviewed together, normally help to give an approximate date:

(*a*) *Form.* Down to the end of the principate of Augustus Ostian craftsmen show little sense of design in setting out long inscriptions. Lines are of uneven length and the general form of the text does not seem to be seriously considered. The arrangement improves in the Julio-Claudian period and reaches its best in the early second century. In the best inscriptions of the reigns of Trajan and Hadrian the general composition is particularly striking. Size of letters and length of line vary in a deliberate pattern; there is no sense of crowding. This mastery declines towards the end of the second century and is not recovered.

(*b*) *Stops.* In the Republic squared stops and circles are often used to separate words; it is doubtful whether either form persists beyond Augustus. From Augustus onwards the triangular stop is the normal form, and it is found as late as the fourth century. But within that long period a stop which resembles a comma is not uncommon. Its highest frequency is in the late Julio-Claudian and Flavian periods, though isolated cases appear earlier and later. Stops are rarely elaborate before the end of the third century. In the fourth century elaborate forms become increasingly common.

(*c*) *Accents.* In the Fasti accents are used first in the entries from A.D. 2 to 20. They drop out between 29 and 38, reappear from 82 to 112, and are not found after 112. In other inscriptions they are found spasmodically in the Julio-Claudian period, but their maximum frequency is in the Flavian period and early second century. They are very rare after the middle of the second century.

(*d*) *Letter forms.* Though there are significant changes in letter forms

---

[1] *PIR²*, A 1234.

during the Empire no tables adequately cover all cases. There is, for instance, a tendency for the tail of G to be a vertical stroke in the first century and a half; G with a curling tail is normally late: but there are too many exceptions both ways for this difference to have value. Similarly P in the early Republic resembles the Greek Γ. It remains very open until the end of the Republic and only gradually assumes its modern closed form. The closed form is normal by the third century, but it appears as early as the Julio-Claudian period, and the open form still survives in the fourth century. The most useful single letter is perhaps Q. The tail of Q gradually lengthens through the first century until in the early second century it often extends in a graceful curve below two letters. This exaggerated emphasis, which has a clearly decorative purpose, is a distinctive feature of Trajanic and Hadrianic inscriptions. After the middle of the century the length of the tail again contracts.

Apart from differences in individual letter forms there is a tendency for the general shape of letters to change from a roughly squared form to a more vertical form, common in the third century and more pronounced in the fourth. The elaboration of letter forms by the extensive use of finials is normally a sign of lateness, but from this generalization an important category has to be excepted. Many inscriptions of the first and second centuries have such elaboration, but their letters might be described as rustic capitals.[1] They are good of their kind, but it is a different kind, more suited to and probably derived from painted notices.[2]

---

[1] e.g. Thylander, Planches xxvi. 3; xliii. 3; lxxxi. 1.

[2] For the difficulties of dating inscriptions by palaeographic criteria see *Contributions to the Palaeography of Latin Inscriptions*, by J. S. and A. E. Gordon (Univ. of California Publications in Class. Arch., vol. 3, n. 3, 1957). Their inquiry, however, is concentrated on Rome and not all inferences from Roman inscriptions are valid for Ostia.

Appendix XI

SELECTED INSCRIPTIONS

1. P. Lucilio | P.f. P.n. P. pro|nep. Gamalae | aed(ium) sacr(arum) Volk(ani) |
5 aedili d(ecurionum) d(ecreto) allecto ‖ gratis decurioni | pontifici ii-
vir(o) censo|riae pot(estatis) quinquennal(i) | in comitis facto cura|tori
10 pecuniae publicae exigen‖dae et adtribuendae | in ludos cum accepisset
public(um) | lucar remisit et de suo erogati|onem fecit | idem sua
15 pecunia viam silice stravit ‖ quae est iuncta foro ab arcu ad arcum | idem
epulum trichilinis CCXVII | colonis dedit | idem prandium sua pecunia
20 colonis | Ostiesibus bis dedit ‖ idem aedem Volcani sua pecu|nia restituit |
idem aedem Veneris sua pecu|nia constituit | idem aed(em) Fortunae sua
25 pecu‖nia constituit | idem aed(em) Cereris sua pecunia | constituit |
30 idem pondera ad macellum | cum M. Turranio sua pecu‖nia fecit | idem
aedem Spei sua pecunia | constituit | idem tribunal in foro mar|moreum
35 fecit ‖ huic statua inaurata d(ecurionum) d(ecreto) | p(ecunia) (publica)
posita est | item ahenea d(ecurionum) d(ecreto) p(ecunia) p(ublica)
posita | proxume tribunal quaes(toris) | propterea quod cum res pu-
40 blica ‖ praedia sua venderet ob pol‖licitationem belli navalis | HS $\overline{XV}$ CC
rei publicae donavit | hunc decuriones funere pu|blico efferendum
censuerunt

CIL xiv. 375.

2. P. Lucilio P.f. | P.n. P.pron. Gamalae | aed(ili) sacr(is) Volcáni | eiusdem
5 pr(aetori) tert(io) dec(urioni) | adléctó d(ecurionum) d(ecreto) infanti ‖
iivir(o) praéfectó L(uci) Caesar(is) | Aug(usti) .f(ilii) cens(orio?) q(uae-
stori) a(erarii) pontif(ici) | tabulár(um) et librorum | curátori primo
10 constitut(o) | hic ludós omnes quós fécit ‖ amplificávit impensá sua | idem
munus gladiatorium ded(it) | idem áedem Castoris et Pollucis rest(ituit) |
15 idem curator pecuniae publicae exi|gendae et attribuendae in comi- ‖
tiis factus cellam patri Tiberino | restituit | idem thermas quas Divus Pius
20 aedifi|caverat vi ignis consumptas refecit | porticum reparavit ‖ idem
aedem Veneris impensa sua | restituit | idem pondera ad macellum et
men|suras ad forum vinar(ium) s(ua) p(ecunia) fecit | idem navale a
25 L. Coilio aedificatum ‖ extru[e]ntibus fere collapsum | restituit | huic
statua aenea peq(unia) pub(lica) d(ecurionum) d(ecreto) posit(a) | est—?

CIL xiv. 376. Pl. xxxviii *d.*

3. P. Lucilio P.f. P.nep. P.pro|n. P.abnep. Gamalae | aedilii trib(uno)
milit(um) dec(urioni) adlec(to) | ex d(ecreto) d(ecurionum) grateis

iiviro IIII | dec(urionum) decr(eto) publice | quod is causam coloniae | publicam egit in senatu | —

See p. 501 n. 1.

4. A. Livius Proculus P. Lucilius | Gamala f(ilius) iivir(i) praef(ect(i)) Caesar(is) | locum quo aedes Bellonae fieret | impensa lictorum et servorum publicorum | qui in corpore sunt adsignaverunt d(ecurionum) d(ecreto) | cur(antibus) | M. Naevio Fructo et — (erasure)

Mem. Pont. 6 (1943) 198 n. 1a. Pl. xxxviii *a*.

5. Cn. Sentio Cn. fil. | Cn.n. Ter(etina) Felici | dec(urionum) decr(eto) aedilició adl(ecto) d(ecurionum) d(ecreto) d(ecurioni) adl(ecto) | q(uaestori) a(erarii) Ostiens(ium) iivir(o) q(uaestori) iuvenum | hic primus
5 omnium quo annó dec(urio) adl(ectus) est et || q(uaestor) a(erarii) fact(us) est et in proxim(um) annum iivir designat(us) est | quinq(uennalis) curatórum navium marinar(um) grátis adléct(us) | inter navicular(ios) maris Hadriatici et ad quadrígam | fori vinari patrónó decuriae scribár(um) cérariór(um) | et librariór(um) et lictór(um) et viatór(um) item praeconum
10 et || et argentariór(um) et negotiatór(um) vinariór(um) ab urbe | item mensor(um) frumentariór(um) Cereris Aug(ustae) item corpor(is) | scapharior(um) et lenunculariór(um) traiect(us) Luculli et | dendróphorúm et tógátór(um) á foro et dé sacomár(io) | et libertór(um) et
15 servór(um) publicór(um) et oleáriór(um) et iuven(um) || cisianor(um) et veteranor(um) Aug(usti) item beneficiariór(um) | próc(uratoris) | Aug(usti) et piscator(um) própolar(um) cúratóri lusús iuvenalis | Cn. Sentius Lucilius | Gamala Clodianus f(ilius) | patri indulgentissimo

CIL xiv. 409

6. [A. Egri]lio A.f. A.n. A. [pr]o[n.] | Vot(uria) Rufo | [dec(urionum) d]ecr(eto) decurioni ad[l(ecto)] | [aedi]li quaesto[r]i iivir[o] | [flam]ini Rom[ae et] Augu[s(ti)] | —que? —ibu— | —u—

NS 1953, 255.

7. M. Acilius [M.f. P]riscus | d(ecurionum) d(ecreto) d(ecurio) adle[ctus] quaest(or) | aer(ari) suffra[gio de]curion(um) | iivir aedil(is) II [quinq]uennal(is) | pr[aef]ect(us) II [praef(ectus)] colleg(i) fabr(um) || Ostiens(ium) cont[inuo t]riennio | praef(ectus) cohort[is — Baracara | Augustanor[um tr]ib(unus) coh(ortis) ÌÌX | voluntariorum t[ribun(us) militum | leg(ionis) XI Claudia[e piae] fidelis || flamen Roma[e et Aug]usti | pontifex [Vol]cani | testamento f[ieri ius]sit per | A. Egrilium [Primi]genium

NS 1953, 256.

8. C. Fabió Longí p(rimi) p(ilaris) f. | Longí p(rimi) p(ilaris) n. Fabí Rufí | prón(epoti) C. Gratti abn(epoti) | Vot(uria) Agrippáe | práetori sacrís Volka[ni fac(iundis)] | dec(urionum) decr(eto) decurió[ni adlecto] | aedili ii[viro —

CIL xiv. 349.

9. C. Nasennio C.f. Marcello seniori | praef(ecto) coh(ortis) I Apamenae trib(uno) coh(ortis) I Italicae civium Romanorum volun|tariorum praef(ecto) alae Phrygum praef(ecto) fabrum aedili quaestori duumvi|ro quinquennali III curatori operum publicorum et aquarum | perpetuo praetori et pontifici Laurentium Lavinatium p(atrono) c(oloniae) Ostensium ‖ Nasennia Helpis fecit patrono indulgentissimo et C. Nasennio Sa|turnino coniugi carissimo sibi liberis libertis libertabus posteris|que eorum

CIL xiv. 171.

10. P. Aufidio P.f. Quirina | Forti | [d(ecurionum) d(ecreto) decu]rioni adlecto iiviro | [quaesto]ri aerari Ostiensium IIII | [praefe]cto fabrum ‖ [tignuariorum] Ostis patron[o] | corporum mensorum | frumentariorum | et urinatorum decurioni adlecto | Africae Hippone Regio | corpus mercatorum | frumentariorum | q(uin)q(uennali) perpetuo

CIL xiv, S.4620.

11. L. Licinio L. fil. Pal(atina) | Herodi | equit(i) Rom(ano) decuriali |
5 decuriae viatoriae | equestris co(n)s(ularis) decurioni ‖ quinquennali duumviro | sacerdoti geni col(oniae) flam(ini) | Rom(ae) et Aug(usti) curat(ori) oper(um) publ(icorum) | quaestori aer(ari) aedili flam(ini) |
10 divi Severi sodali Arulensi ‖ praet(ori) prim(o) sac(ris) Volk(ani) faciu(ndis) | ordo Augustal(ium) | optimo civi ob merita

CIL xiv. 373.

12. P. Flavio P. fil. Pal(atina) | Prisco e(gregio) v(iro) | equestris ordinis |
5 religiosa disciplina | ad centena provecto ‖ pontifici et dictatori | Albano primo annos | viginti octo agenti | q(uin)q(uennali) c(ensoria) p(ote-
10 state) patr(ono) colon(iae) Ost(iensium) | sacerd(oti) geni colon(iae) ‖ patr(ono) corp(oris) pistorum | corp(oris) mesorum | frum(entariorum) Ost(iensium) patron(o)
in latere dextro: dedicata kale|ndis Martis | Aemiliano ite|rum et Aquilin|o cos. (249)

CIL xiv, S 4452.

13. fide exercitationem | bonitati pollenti Lucio | Crepereio Madaliano
v(iro) c(larissimo) | praef(ecto) ann(onae) cum iure gladii | comiti Flavi-
5 ali corr(ectori) Flam(iniae) || et Piceni leg(ato) pro praetore prov(inciae) |
Asiae leg(ato) prov(inciae) Africae consula(ri) | aed(ium) sacrar(um)
consul(ari) molium fari | at purgaturae quaest(ori) candid(ato) | prae-
10 t(ori) consuli ob multa in se eius || testimonia ordo et populus | Fl(aviae)
Constantinianae Portuenses | statuam publicae ponendam | censuerunt

CIL xiv, *S* 4449.

14. C. Domitio L. fil. Pal(atina) F[abio] | Hermogeni | e[quiti] Romano
scribae aedil(ium) curul(ium) dec(urioni) adle[ct(o)] | fl[am(ini) divi
H]ad[ria]ni in cuius sacerdotio solus ac primus lud[os | scaenic]os sua
5 p[e]cunia fecit aedili hunc splendidissimus ordo decur[ion(um) || fun(ere)
publ]ico hon[o]ravit eique statuam equestrem subscriptione ob amor[em |
et industr]iam o[mne]m in foro ponendam pecunia publica decre[v]i[t |
inque l]oc[um e]ius [ae]dil(em) substituendum non putavit in solacium
Fab[i pat]ris | [qu]i ob honores [ei h]a[bi]tos H̅S̅ L̅ M̅ N̅ rei publicae
dedit ex quorum usuris quincun[ci]bus | [q]uod annis XIII k[al(endas)]
Aug(ustas) die natali eius decurionib(us) ✱ DL praesentib(us) | in foro ant[e
10 stat(uam) s(upra)] s(criptam) || [divi]dantur et decurialibus scribis ceraris
✱ XXXVIIS libraris ✱ XIIS item lictoribus [✱ XXV] | L. Fabius Sp.f.
Eutychus lictor curiatius scrib[a] cer[arius] | et librarius q(uin)q(uen-
nalis) collegi fabr(um) [tig]nuar(iorum) Ostiens(ium) et Artoria eius
par[entes]

CIL xiv, *S* 4642.

15. Marco Licinio | Privato | *decurionatus ornamentis honorato et* | bisellario in
5 primis constituto | inlatis rei publicae sestertis || quinquaginta milibus N̅ |
quaestori et q(uin)q(uennali) corporis pistorum Ostiens(ium) et Port(ensium) |
magistro quinquennal(i) collegi | fabrum tignuariorum lustri | XXVIIII
10 et decurioni eiusdem || numeri decur(iae) XVI decurial(i) scrib(ae) | *patri
et avo decurionum* | librario tribuli tribus Claudiae | *patri equitum Romano-*
15 *rum* | patruum et liberorum clientium || universus numerus | caligato-
rum | collegi fabrum tignuarior(um) Ostiens(ium) | magistro optimo ob
amorem et merita eius | locus d(atus) d(ecurionum) d(ecreto) p(ublice)

CIL xiv. 374. The lines italicized were added in smaller letters between lines after the
statue had been set up.

16. dis manibus | L. Calpurnius Chius sevir Aug(ustalis) | et quinquennalis |
idem quinq(uennalis) corporis mensor(um) | frumentarior(um) Ostien-
5 s(ium) et curat(or) || bis | idem codicar(iorum) curat(or) Ostis et III
honor(atus) | idem quinquennal(is) collegi Silvani | Aug(usti) maioris

10 quod est Hilarionis | iunctus[1] sacomari idem magistro ad Marte(m) ||
Ficanum Aug(ustum) | idem in collegio dendrofor(um) | fecit sibi et |
Corneliae Ampliatae coniugi suae | carissimae cum qua vixit annis XXXI |
15 Calpurniae L. lib(ertae) Pthengidi libertae || carissimae L. Calpurnio
Forti vern(ae) lib(erto) | L. Calpurnio Felici lib(erto) L. Calpurnio
Adaucto vern(ae) lib(erto) | Calpurniae L.f. Chiae vern(ae) Calpurniae
L.f. | Ampliatae vern(ae) L. Calpurnio L.f. Felici vern(ae) | L. Calpurnio
20 L.f. Pal(atina) Chio Felicissimo || libertis libertab(us) posterisq(ue) eorum
b(ene) m(erentibus)

CIL xiv. 309.

[1] 'functus' (*CIL*) is a less probable reading.

P. 56 n. 1. D. W. MacDowall, 'The Numismatic Evidence for the Neronia', *CQ* 8 (1958) 192–4, emphasizes that Nero's bronze coinage, which was not begun until 64, includes commemorations of his first *congiarium*, from the beginning of his reign, and of the Macellum, dedicated in 59 (Dio lxi. 18. 3). The harbour might also have been completed before 60; but the beginning of Nero's canal in 64 still makes 63 or 64 an attractive date for the end of the work (p. 57).

Pp. 169, 388. P.-A. Février, 'Ostie et Porto à la fin de l'antiquité', *Mélanges*, 70 (1958) 295–330, has made an important contribution to the study of Christianity at Ostia and Portus in the fourth and fifth centuries. He accepts the tradition of Constantine's basilica at Ostia, siting it outside the Porta Laurentina, and suggests approximate sites for other Christian buildings on evidence that is considerably less strong.

In discussing the Christian oratory by the theatre (302 f.) he infers that the Quiriacus whose name is inscribed on a sarcophagus lid found in the ruins is a fourth- or fifth-century Christian who had himself buried near the oratory, and that the legend of the martyrdom by the theatre may be a false deduction from the name. It is not naïve to reject such scepticism. The sarcophagus cannot be later than the late third century; the dating of the inscription on the lid is more precarious, but it must surely be earlier than the fifth century, and it is very doubtful whether burials would be tolerated within the walls during the fourth century. Février reconsiders the 'Christian basilica' on the western Decumanus (304–11). He associates the inscription over the entry to the 'baptistery' with a martyr-cult and compares the plan of the building to early double churches. His study may provoke a detailed re-examination of the history of the construction, which is badly needed.

The general assumption that the Xenodochium of Pammachius has been identified is challenged, with good reason (316 f.). De Rossi's identification rested on a hexameter incorporated in an inscription round the fountain in the centre of the atrium or court: '[qu]isq[ue] sitit veniat cupiens aurire flue[nta]'. This line occurs in verses attributed alternatively to Pope Damasius and to Jerome. Since Jerome was a friend of Pammachius, and since the inscription (Thylander, B 361, pl. cxxv. 2) shows the influence of Filocalus and is therefore probably of the late fourth century, De Rossi's identification was unquestioned. Ferrua, however (*Epigrammata Damasiana* (Rome, 1942), 219–28), gives good reasons for dating the verses attributed to Jerome to the sixth century and suggests that the hexameter in question is common stock. Février believes that the building complex is more probably the church of St. Peter and St. Paul. The question should be left open until the area can be more carefully examined.

Pp. 234, 468. P. Hommel, 'Euripides in Ostia', *Epigraphica*, 19 (1957) 109–64, reconsiders tomb 106 on Isola Sacra and its inscriptions. If his conclusions are sound he has recovered an interesting paragraph in Ostia's social history.

This tomb was built within a large enclosed area at some distance from the tombs that can now be seen and in no planned relation to them. It was one of several discovered in 1938 after the main excavation of the area and had to be covered up again; but Calza was able to give a brief account in his basic publication (*Necropoli*, 373–6). The inscription over the entry recorded that C. Marcius De[metrius], *archiatros*, and Munatia Helpis built the tomb. Within were found the record of five deaths and a portrait statue of a young woman, with the attributes of Hygia, and the name 'Julia Procula' inscribed below. According to Bloch's persuasive establishment of the relationships (*AJA* 1944, 217), Demetrius married Munatia Helpis, who had a family by a first husband, Julius Proculus. The tomb was thought to be Trajanic from Calza's judgement of the construction and the distinctive hair-style of the statue.

Hommel suggests that C. Marcius Demetrius is the Demetrius mentioned by Galen, M. Aurelius' court physician, who died *c.* 170. He derived his *nomen* Marcius from the emperor's *praenomen* Marcus, when he was freed or adopted. The quick succession of deaths, combined with the court physician's date, indicates that the tomb was built in one of two violent attacks of the plague, in 165/6 or 168/9. Hommel further suggests that Marcia Aurelia Ceionia Demetrias, known from an inscription found at Anagnia (*CIL* x. 5918), and identified by Mommsen with Commodus' mistress Marcia (Victor, *Epit.* 17. 5; Dio lxxii (lxxiii). 4. 6), may be the daughter of the court physician who married an Ostian wife.

Much of the argument is vulnerable: (1) Unless roughly contemporary parallels are cited, the derivation of Marcius from Marcus should not be accepted. (2) To reconcile his date for the tomb (160–70) with a Trajanic portrait statue Hommel has to believe that the portrait is not of Julia Procula. This is formally possible, but improbable. (3) Calza's account of the excavation lacks precision at crucial points, but his description favours, though not decisively, a date before the middle of the century. (4) There is no evidence for a quick succession of deaths. T. Munatius Proclus died when he was 6 years 14 days old; his mother was still alive then but she must have died soon afterwards, since she died just before she was 29. There is no evidence that the other deaths occurred at or very near the same time. The number of inscriptions in this family tomb is not extraordinary; the plague is an unnecessary hypothesis. (5) It is difficult to place the lettering of the earliest of the inscriptions (Thylander, pls. xlv. 4; liii. 1, 2; lvi. 1, 2) as late as Marcus Aurelius' reign.

I therefore remain sceptical. The name C. Marcius is more probably to be associated with other C. Marcii from Portus, some of whose inscriptions are earlier than M. Aurelius (e.g. Thylander, A 176, pl. l. 4; 174, pl. l. 1; B 107, C. L. Visconti, *I monumenti del Museo Torlonia* (Rome, 1885), n. 413, tav. civ). A doctor brought up at Ostia could have become a court physician, but it is very difficult to fit the date of the tomb to Hommel's identification. The possibility that Marcia Demetrias is descended from the Ostian doctor cannot yet be ruled out; I should like to believe that Commodus, who left such a prominent mark on Ostia (p. 79), had an Ostian mistress.

P. 286. A possible exception to the rule must be admitted. While I was working at Ostia I was very intrigued by the tantalizing sight of a few letters on a statue base which had been incorporated in a late, possibly medieval, wall closing the space between the piers of the portico in front of the theatre. In 1957 this base was extracted and I have to thank Professor Barbieri for confirming the text on the side of the base (the text on the face has been erased): 'quarto idus Maias | *imperatore Commodo* iterum | P. Martio Vero iterum | locus acceptus ex auctoritate | Flavi Pisonis pr(aefecti) ann(onae) adsignante | Valerio Fusco proc(uratore) Augg.'

Before this base was recovered I had assumed that, like the bases recovered from the theatre itself, it came from the gardens behind the theatre. The text, however, implies that the site where the statue was erected was controlled by the *praefectus annonae*. It can, however, be maintained that the formula on this base should have been used on all bases set up in the same place. Since all the other bases from the gardens which preserve a formula of allocation record the authority of the local council, the logical conclusion must be that this recently recovered base was set up elsewhere in the neighbourhood.

P. *428 n. 5.* There may have survived part of a more interesting Ostian tribute to Plautianus. G. Barbieri, 'Un nuovo cursus equestre', *Epigraphica*, 19 (1957) 93–108, shows that three new Ostian fragments of a base go with a fragment already published (*S* 4468/70), and that the same career is recorded in an inscription found in Rome (*AE* 1946, 95). Neither Roman nor Ostian fragments preserve the name of the man honoured, but Barbieri makes a good case for identifying him with C. Fulvius Plautianus, whose career before he became praetorian prefect was not previously known. If he is right, Plautianus was *praefectus annonae* before being put in charge of the guard not later than 197. He was already specially trusted by Septimius Severus in 193 when he was sent to seize the children of Cassius Niger (SHA, *Severus*, 6. 10). His appointment to the key position of controller of the corn supply would be interesting and intelligible. But the positive grounds for the identification are less compelling than they seem at first.

Barbieri gives four main converging clues: (1) The letters of the Ostian and Roman inscriptions seem to fit the late second and early third century. (2) To be honoured so handsomely in both Rome and Ostia the man must be an important figure. (3) The base is a particularly large base. (4) It seems clear that the base was deliberately broken. It would be dangerous to claim more than speculation from these premises. The lettering will suit any *praefectus annonae* of the late Antonine or early Severan periods; and any *praefectus annonae* might be honoured at Ostia and Rome, the two main centres of his responsibility. His status would entitle him to a specially large base at Ostia. If we could be certain that the base was violently broken the case for Plautianus would become very much stronger, but so many fragments of bases and tablets have been found in the ruins (e.g. *S* 4620, 4664, Bloch, 21) that the discovery of dispersed fragments cannot be regarded as evidence for deliberate destruction in the Roman period. Before scholars less careful than Barbieri build further on the hypothesis, two points should be considered. The promotion to the post of *praefectus annonae* is not abnormal, but by the most favoured route through posts in the palace secretariat (Pflaum, *Les Procurateurs équestres*, 257). Finally Herodian (iii. 10. 6) says that Septimius Severus raised Plautianus to power from humble status: 'πλὴν ἀλλ' ὁ Σεουῆρος ἐκ μικρᾶς καὶ εὐτελοῦς τύχης ἐς μεγάλην προήγαγεν ἐξουσίαν.' This *praefectus annonae* was nearing the climax of a distinguished equestrian career. Herodian, though a contemporary, is not a reliable source (cf. E. Hohl, 'Kaiser Commodus und Herodian', *Sitz. der deutsch. Ak. Wiss. Berlin*, 1954, 1). His language in such a context cannot be pressed too closely, but it slightly weakens the case.

P. *437 n. 1.* Ostian painting is liberally illustrated by M. Borda in *La Pittura romana* (Milan, 1958). The photographs are excellent, but the chronology is established almost exclusively on grounds of style, without reference to the walls concerned.

P. *464 n. 4.* A. W. Byvanck, 'Le Problème des sarcophages romains', *BVAB* 31 (1956)

31–38, examines early second-century sarcophagi, the decoration of which derives directly or indirectly from Greek sources, and attributes the change from cremation to burial to the influence of oriental freedmen. A wider explanation is needed of such a general change in custom.

P. 473. E. J. H. Oliver, 'Gerusiae and Augustales', *Historia,* 7 (1958) 472–96, interprets differently the registers and other inscriptions of *seviri Augustales* (316, 360, 461, *S* 4559). Though he has clarified some points of detail, some of his main inferences are unconvincing. In particular he makes no allowance for what seems to be a major change in organization in or soon after the Flavian period (p. 217).

P. 481. An important passage had escaped me (and others). In his terse account of 428 B.C. Livy (iv. 30. 5–6) mentions Ostia: 'Men of Veii raided Roman territory. It was widely held that men of military age from Fidenae had joined in the raid. L. Sergius, Q. Servilius, and Mam. Aemilius were appointed to conduct an inquiry. Some men were banished to Ostia, since there was no satisfactory explanation why they had been absent from Fidenae at the time. A number of colonists was added [? at Fidenae]. The land of those who had been killed in the war was assigned to them.'

This uncoloured passage seems to derive from an annalistic record. A motive can be found for the invention of a regal Ostia; the introduction of Ostia into any story focused on the corn supply could be a reflection of later conditions; but the mention of Ostia in a context where it has no natural place is more likely to derive from historical fact.

P. 487 n. 5. Miss Tilly, 'The Topography of *Aeneid* IX with reference to the way taken by Nisus and Euryalus', *Arch. Class.* 8 (1956) 164–72, has argued that in this passage Virgil had the detailed topography of Ostian territory in mind. Nisus, leading the attempt to break through the enemy's lines round the Trojan camp at Ostia, reaches a place called 'Loci Albani' (*Aen.* ix. 386–8): 'iamque imprudens evaserat hostes | atque locos, qui post Albae de nomine dicti | Albani (tum rex stabula alta Latinus habebat)'. Miss Tilly suggests that this was the contemporary name for the Ostian salt marshes. Though there is no other evidence for the name, there is no good reason for rejecting it; but it is more likely to have been attached to grazing land to the east of the marshes.

Her second identification is more important. Nisus and Euryalus propose to break out of camp on the seaward side (*Aen.* ix. 237 f.): 'locum insidiis conspeximus ipsi | qui patet in bivio portae quae proxima ponto.' Miss Tilly suggests that the *bivium* is the historic cross-roads outside the western gate of the Castrum, which, according to Becatti (above, p. 14), preserves the meeting-place of two early tracks from Laurentine territory and from Rome. I am doubtful whether *bivium portae* could be Virgilian Latin for 'the cross-roads outside the gate'; it should rather refer to the gate itself. (*Thes. L. L.* ii, col. 2024, compares Statius, *Thebaid,* i. 609: 'illa novos ibat populata penates | portarum in bivio.' Virgil does not elaborate the phrase; from the moment that the two heroes leave the Trojan camp the description of their route remains extremely vague.

P. 500. L. Vidman, 'De familia Gamaliana Ostiensi', *Eunomia (Ephemeridis Listz filologické suppl.)*, 2 (Prague, 1958) 1, reconsiders the career of the Lucilius Gamala whose inscription is lost. He uses some of the arguments that I also have used in favour of an early date, but assumes from the discovery of the stone at Portus that this Gamala must have died after the harbour was begun. From the *Fasti* Vidman infers that he became *pontifex Volcani* after 42 and died before 80. I still see too many pointers to the Augustan period to change my mind.

P. *540*. H. Bloch, 'The Serapeum of Ostia and the Brick-Stamps of 123 A.D.', *AJA* 63 (1959) 225–40, has considerably strengthened his conclusions by a detailed analysis of the stamps found in the Serapeum and adjoining buildings. The temple was dedicated on 24 January 127 (*Fasti*); the great majority of stamps found in the construction are dated between 123 and 126.

Pp. *522 f.* Had I been more familiar with the literature I should have been even more conscious of the difficulties of unravelling the true stories of Gallicanus and Hilarinus. To my references should be added the articles listed in the Bibliography (Religion) under the names of H. Grégoire and P. Orgels, and of B. Le Gaiffier.

BIBLIOGRAPHY

GENERAL studies of Ostia and Portus are separately listed first in chronological order. The short section on Inscriptions which follows is confined to the main collections of Ostian inscriptions and excludes individual inscriptions separately published recently. These, together with a very large number of unpublished inscriptions, are to be edited by G. Barbieri. Housing, trade, religion, and the arts are also separately classified; further subdivision would not, I think, serve a useful purpose and in many cases would be arbitrary. The unattractive heading Miscellaneous should not be interpreted as a mark of disrespect.

The books and articles listed are, with few exceptions, specifically concerned with Ostia. No attempt has been made to list the general histories, works of reference, and more specialized studies that have been useful in this inquiry.

GENERAL STUDIES OF OSTIA

C. FEA, *Relazione di un viaggio ad Ostia e alla villa di Plinio detta Laurentino*, Rome, 1802.

A. NIBBY, *Viaggio antiquario ad Ostia*, Rome, 1829.

L. CANINA, *Sulla stazione delle navi ad Ostia*, Rome, 1837.

G. TOMASSETTI, 'Vie Ostiense e Laurentina', *Archivio della Reale Società Romana di Storia Patria*, xvii–xx, 1897.

R. FISCH, *Eine Wanderung nach den Trümmern von Ostia*, Berlin, 1898.

L. PASCHETTO, *Ostia colonia romana, storia e monumenti*, Rome, 1912. (Review: J. Carcopino, *Rev. arch.* 21 (1913) 389.)

D. VAGLIERI, *Ostia, cenni storici e guida*, Rome, 1914.

J. CARCOPINO, *Virgile et les origines d'Ostie*, Paris, 1919.

—— *Ostie* (coll. 'Les visites d'art'), Paris, 1929.

F. H. WILSON, 'Studies in the Social and Economic History of Ostia', *BSR* 13 (1935) 41; 14 (1938) 152.

G. CALZA, 'Ostia', *RE* xviii. 1654 (1942).

A. BOETHIUS, *Stadsbebyggelsen i Roms hamnstad Ostia*, Göteborg, 1951.

G. CALZA, G. BECATTI, *Ostia*³ (Itinerari dei musei e monumenti d'Italia), Rome, 1954.

G. CALZA, G. BECATTI, I. GISMONDI, G. DE ANGELIS D'OSSAT, H. BLOCH, *Scavi di Ostia, I, Topografia Generale*, Rome, 1954. (Reviews: H. Schaal, *Gnomon*, 26 (1954) 551; R. Meiggs, *JRS* 46 (1956) 190; J. Le Gall, *Rev. arch.* 49 (1957) 60.)

H. SCHAAL, *Ostia, der Welthafen Roms*, Bremen, 1957.

GENERAL STUDIES OF PORTUS

C. FEA, *Alcune osservazioni sopra gli antichi porti d'Ostia, ora di Fiumicino*, Rome, 1824.

A. NIBBY, *Della Via Portuense e dell' antica città di Porto*, Rome, 1829.

G. RASI, *Sui due rami Tiberini di Fiumicino e di Ostia e sui porti di Claudio e di Trajano*, Rome, 1830.

C. Texier, *Mémoire sur les ports antiques situés à l'embouchure du Tibre*, Paris, 1858 (= vol. xv, *Revue générale de l'architecture et des travaux publics*).

R. Lanciani, 'Ricerche topographiche sulla città di Porto', *Ann. Inst.* 40 (1868) 144, with *Mon. Inst.* 8, tav. 49 (plan).

G. Tomassetti, 'Via Portuense', *Archivio della Reale Società Romana di Storia Patria*, xxii–xxiii, 1900.

J. Carcopino, 'Il Porto Claudio Ostiense secondo recenti tasti', *NS* 1907, 734.

K. Lehmann-Hartleben, *Die antiken Hafenanlagen des Mittelmeeres* (*Klio*, Beiheft xiv), 1923.

G. Calza, 'Ricognizioni topographiche nel Porto di Traiano', *NS* 1925, 45.

G. Lugli and G. Filibeck, *Il Porto di Roma imperiale e l'Agro Portuense*, Rome, 1935.

G. Calza, *La Necropoli del Porto di Roma nell' Isola Sacra*, Rome, 1940. (Review: H. Bloch, *AJA* 48 (1944) 213.)

M. Fasciato, 'Ad quadrigam Fori Vinarii', *Mélanges*, 59 (1947) 65.

G. Lugli, 'L'iconografia della città di Porto nel secolo xvi', *Rend. Pont.* 23–24 (1947–9) 187.

INSCRIPTIONS

H. Dessau, *CIL* xiv (1887).

L. Wickert, *CIL* xiv Supplement (1930).

G. Calza, *NS* 1938, 47–74 (inscriptions from tombs outside Porta Laurentina).

A. Degrassi, *Inscriptiones Italiae*, xiii. 173–241 (*Fasti*).

H. Thylander, *Inscriptions du port d'Ostie*, 2 vols. (Lund, 1952). (Reviews: A. Degrassi, *Gnomon*, 26 (1954) 102; R. Meiggs, *CR* 4 (1954) 157; *JRS* 44 (1954) 151.)

H. Bloch, *NS* 1953, 239–306 (selected inscriptions, found 1930–9).

G. Barbieri, *Scavi di Ostia*, iii. 1 (1958) 131–65 (Republican and Augustan sepulchral inscriptions revised).

HOUSING

A. A. Van Aken, 'Late Roman Domus Architecture', *Mnemosyne*, 2 (1949) 242.

—— 'The Cortile in the Roman Imperial Insula-architecture', *Opuscula Archeologica*, 6 (1950) 112.

—— 'Some aspects of Nymphaea in Pompeii, Herculaneum and Ostia', *Mnemosyne*, 4 (1951) 272.

G. Becatti, *Case Ostiensi del tardo impero*, Rome, 1949.

A. Boethius, 'Remarks on the Development of Domestic Architecture in Rome', *AJA* 38 (1934) 158.

—— 'Appunti sul carattere razionale e sull' importanza dell' architettura domestica in Roma imperiale', in *Scritti in onore di B. Nogara*, Rome, 1937.

—— 'Notes from Ostia (strip-insulae)', in *Studies presented to D. M. Robinson*, ii (1953) 195.

G. Calza, 'La Preeminenza dell' "insula" nella edilizia romana', *MA* 23 (1915) 541.

—— 'Gli scavi recenti nell' abitato di Ostia', *MA* 26 (1920) 321.

G. Calza, 'Le origini latine dell' abitazione moderna', *Architettura e arti decorative*, 3 (1923–4) 3, 49.

—— 'Esplorazione dell' isolato a ovest del Campidoglio di Ostia', *NS* 1923, 177.

—— 'Contributi alla storia dell' edilizia imperiale romana', *Palladio*, 5 (1941) 1.

P. Harsh, 'Origins of the Insulae at Ostia', *MAAR* 12 (1935) 9.

G. Hejzlar, *Obytný a Obchodní Dům v Ostii* (with résumé in French), Prague, 1933.

L. Homo, *Rome impériale et l'urbanisme dans l'antiquité*, Paris, 1951.

A. Müfid, *Stockwerkbauten der Griechen und Römer*, Leipzig, 1932.

TRADE

D. Van Berchem, *Les Distributions du blé et d'argent à la plèbe romaine sous l'Empire*, Geneva, 1936.

G. Calza, 'Il Piazzale delle Corporazioni e la funzione commerciale di Ostia', *BC* 43 (1915) 178.

—— 'Gli horrea tra il Tevere e il decumano, nel centro di Ostia antica', *NS* 1921, 360.

L. Casson, 'The Grain Trade of the Hellenistic World', *TAPA* 85 (1954) 168.

A. Cialdi, *La Navigazione del Tevere*, Rome, 1845.

P.-M. Duval, 'La forme des navires romains d'après la Mosaïque d'Althiburus', *Mélanges*, 61 (1949) 119.

R. Étienne, 'Les amphores du Testaccio au IIIᵉ siècle', *Mélanges* 61 (1949) 151.

M. Fasciato, 'Ad quadrigam Fori Vinarii', *Mélanges*, 59 (1947) 65.

C. Fea, *Storia delle saline d'Ostia*, Rome, 1831.

T. Frank, 'The People of Ostia', *Class. Journ.* 29 (1934) 481.

G. Girri, *La taberna nel quadro urbanistico e sociale di Ostia* (Ist. arch. Milan; tesi di laurea, I) Rome, 1956.

A. Héron de Villefosse, 'Deux armateurs narbonnais', *Mém. soc. Ant. de France*, 74 (1914) 153.

—— 'La Mosaïque des Narbonnais à Ostie', *Bull. arch.* 1918, 245.

L. A. and L. B. Holland, 'Down the Tiber on a raft', *Archaeology*, 1950, 87.

—— 'The Tiber in Primitive Commerce', *AJA* 54 (1950) 261.

J. Le Gall, 'Les Bas-reliefs de la statue du Tibre au Musée du Louvre', *Rev. arch.* 21 (1944) 115; 22 (1944) 39.

—— *Le Tibre fleuve de Rome, dans l'antiquité*, Paris, 1953.

A. Meyer, *L'Arte di restituire a Roma la tralasciata navigazione del Tevere*, Rome, 1685.

L. Pascoli, *Il Tevere è navigabile da Perugia a Roma*, Rome, 1740.

H. Pigeonneau, *De convectione urbanae annonae et de publicis corporibus apud Romanos*, Paris, 1876.

L. Preller, *Rom und Tiber*, Leipzig, 1849.

G. B. Rasi, *Sul Tevere e sua navigazione da Fiumicino a Roma*, Rome, 1827.

S. A. Smith, *The Tiber and its Tributaries*, London, 1877.

M. F. Squarciapino, 'Tesoretto di monete d'argento', *NS* 1948, 326.

—— 'Frammenti Ostiensi della cosi-detta ceramica tarda', *Rend. class. scienze mor. stor. fil.*, ser. viii, 6 (1951) 136.

D. Vaglieri, 'Le corporazioni professionali in un grande porto commerciale dell' antichità', *Misc. in onore di Attilio Hortis*, Trieste, 1910.

RELIGION

G. Barbieri, 'Settimio Nestore', *Athenaeum*, 31 (1953) 158.

A. Barigazzi, 'Sopra alcune epigrafi metriche di Ostia', Κρητικὰ Χρονικά, 7 (1953) 97.

G. Becatti, 'Il culto di Ercole ad Ostia', *BC* 67 (1939) 37.

—— 'Nuovo documento del culto di Ercole ad Ostia', ibid. 70 (1942) 115.

—— 'Rilievo con la nascita di Dioniso e aspetti mistici di Ostia pagana', *Boll. d'arte*, 36 (1951) 1.

—— *Scavi di Ostia, II, i Mitrei*, Rome, 1954. (Reviews: M. Bieber, *AJA* 60 (1956) 310; J. Bayet, *Gnomon*, 27 (1955) 349.)

—— 'Una copia Giustiniani del Mitra di Kriton', *Boll. d'arte*, 42 (1957) 1.

H. Bloch, 'A New Document of the Last Pagan Revival in the West', *Harv. Theol. Rev.* 38 (1945) 199.

C. R. Briggs, 'The Pantheon of Ostia', *MAAR* 8 (1930) 161.

G. Calza, 'Una basilica di età costantiniana scoperta a Ostia', *Rend. Pont.* 16 (1940) 63.

—— 'Ancora sulla basilica cristiana di Ostia', ibid. 18 (1941–2) 135.

—— 'Il tempio della Bona Dea', *NS* 1942, 152.

—— 'Il santuario della Magna Mater a Ostia', *Mem. Pont.* 6 (1946) 183.

—— 'Nuove testimonianze del cristianesimo a Ostia', *Rend. Pont.* 25–26 (1949–51) 123.

R. Calza, 'Le sculture rinvenute nel santuario della Magna Mater', *Mem. Pont.* 6 (1946) 207.

—— 'Sui ritratti ostiensi del supposto Plotino', *Boll. d'arte*, 38 (1953) 203.

L. Cantarelli, 'Un frammento epigrafico cristiano dall' isola Portuense', *BC* 24 (1896) 67.

A. Casamassa, 'Ritrovamento di parte dell' elogio di S. Monica', *Rend. Pont.* 27 (1952–4) 271.

A. C. Deliperi, 'L'Albergo di S. Agostino a Ostia', *Pantheon*, 5 (1951) 372.

P.-A. Février, 'Ostie et Porto à la fin de l'antiquité', *Mélanges*, 70 (1958) 295.

H. Fuhrmann, 'C. Caeionius Rufus Volusianus Lampadius', *Epigraphica*, 3 (1941) 103.

A. von Gerkan, 'Die christliche Anlage in Ostia', *Römische Quartalschrift*, 47 (1939) 15.

H. Grégoire and P. Orgels, 'S. Gallicanus, consul et martyr dans la passion des SS. Jean et Paul, et sa vision constantinienne du Crucifié', *Byzantion*, 24 (1954) 579.

M. Guarducci, 'Nuovi documenti del culto di Caelestis a Roma', *BC* 72 (1946–8) 11.

—— 'Traccie di Pitagoreismo nelle iscrizioni Ostiensi', *Rend. Pont.* 23–24 (1947–9) 209.

T. Klauser, 'Die Inschrift der neugefundenen altchristlichen Bauanlage in Ostia', *Römische Quartalschrift*, 47 (1939) 25.

B. Le Gaiffier, 'Les Avatars de S. Hilarinus', *Analecta Boll.* 66 (1948) 276. ' "Sub Iuliano Apostata" dans le martyrologe romain', ibid. 74 (1956) 5.

J. Le Gall, *Recherches sur le culte du Tibre*, Paris, 1953.

H. J. Leon, 'The Jewish Community of Ancient Porto', *Harv. Theol. Rev.* 45 (1952) 165.

H. P. L'Orange, 'The Portrait of Plotinus', *Les Cahiers archéologiques*, 5 (1951) 15.

J. H. Oliver, 'Gerusiae and Augustales', *Historia*, 7 (1958) 481.

R. Paribeni, 'I quattro tempietti di Ostia', *MA* 23 (1914) 441.

G. B. De Rossi, 'I monumenti cristiani di Porto', *Bull. arch. crist.* 4 (1866) 37.

M. F. Squarciapino, 'Una statua fittile Ostiense', *Arti figurative*, 3 (1947) 3.

—— 'Coppa cristiana da Ostia', *Boll. d'arte*, 37 (1952) 204.

—— 'Vetri incisi portuensi del museo sacro del Vaticano', *Rend. Pont.* 27 (1952–4) 255.

—— 'L'ara dei Lari di Ostia', *Arch. class.* 4 (1952) 204.

—— 'Placchete con simboli della Zodiaca', ibid. 5 (1953) 263.

L. R. Taylor, *The Cults of Ostia* (Bryn Mawr Monographs, XI) 1912.

D. Vaglieri, 'Scoperte di antichità cristiane in Ostia', *Nuovo bull. di arch. crist.* 16 (1910) 57.

C. L. Visconti, 'I monumenti del Metroon Ostiense', *Ann. Inst.* 40 (1868) 362; 41 (1869) 208.

THE ARTS

M. E. Blake, 'The Pavements of the Roman Buildings of the Republic and Early Empire', *MAAR* 8 (1930) 1.

—— 'Roman Mosaics of the Second Century in Italy', *MAAR* 13 (1936) 67.

M. Borda, *La Pittura romana*, Milan, 1958.

G. Calza, 'Il mosaico di Nettuno delle terme Ostiensi', *Boll. d'arte*, 6 (1912) 199.

—— 'Rappresentanze di provincie e di venti in un mosaico di Ostia', *BC* 40 (1912) 103.

—— 'Expressions of Art in a Roman Commercial City: Ostia', *JRS* (1915) 165.

R. Calza, *Museo Ostiense* (Itinerari dei musei e monumenti d'Italia), Rome, 1947.

J. Carcopino, 'La mosaïque de la caserne des vigiles à Ostie', *Mélanges*, 27 (1907) 227.

C. C. Van Essen, 'Chronologie der romeinse schilderkunst', *Meed. Ned. hist. ist. te Roms*, 8 (1954) 33.

—— 'Chronologie der romeinse mozaïeken', ibid. 64.

F. Fornari, 'La pittura decorativa in Ostia', *Studi Romani*, 1 (1913) 305.

B. Nogara, *Le Nozze Aldobrandini . . . e le altre pitture murali antiche conservate nella biblioteca vaticana e nei musei pontifici*, Milan, 1907.

M. F. Squarciapino, 'Forme Ostiensi', *Arch. class.* 6 (1954) 83.

C. L. Visconti, 'Sulle pitture murali di tre sepolcri Ostiensi discoperte nel 1865', *Ann. Inst.* 38 (1866) 292.

F. Wirth, *Römische Wandmalerei vom Untergang Pompejis bis am Ende des 3. Jhdts.*, Berlin, 1934.

MISCELLANEOUS

T. Ashby, 'Recent Discoveries at Ostia', *JRS* 2 (1912) 153.

R. Bianchi Bandinelli, 'Sarcophago da Acilia con la designazione di Gordiano III', *Boll. d'arte*, 39 (1954) 200.

G. Barbieri, 'Fistole inedite', *NS* 1953, 151.

—— 'Un nuovo cursus equestre', *Epigraphica*, 19 (1957) 93.

G. Becatti, 'Il ritratto di Ippocrate', *Rend. Pont.* 21 (1945–6) 123.

G. Bendz, 'Sur la question de la ville de Laurentum', *Opuscula Archaeologica*, 1 (1934) 47.

M. E. Blake, *Ancient Roman Construction in Italy from the Prehistoric Period to Augustus*, Washington, 1947.

—— *Roman Construction in Italy from Tiberius through the Flavians*, Washington, 1959.

H. Bloch, *I bolli laterizi e la storia edilizia*, Rome, 1938.

—— 'The Name of the Baths near the Forum of Ostia', in *Studies presented to D. M. Robinson*, ii (1953) 412.

—— 'The Serapeum of Ostia and the Brick-Stamps of A.D. 123', *AJA* 63 (1959) 225.

J. Bradford, *Ancient Landscapes*, London, 1957.

G. Calza, 'Die Taverne der sieben Weisen in Ostia', *Die Antike*, 15 (1939) 99.

P. Campana, 'Scavi di Ostia', *Bull. Inst.* 6 (1834) 129.

J. Carcopino, 'Glanures épigraphiques', *Mélanges*, 29 (1909) 341.

—— 'Le Quartier des docks', ibid. 30 (1910) 397.

—— 'Les Inscriptions Gamaliennes', ibid. 31 (1911) 143.

—— 'Notes complémentaires', ibid. 365.

—— 'Les Récentes Fouilles d'Ostie (1909–11)', *Journal des Savants*, 1911, 448.

L. Casson, *The Ancient Mariners*, London, 1959.

L. Constans, 'Les fouilles d'Ostie (1914–17)', *Journal des Savants* 1917, 465.

—— 'Ostie primitive', ibid. 1926, 436.

N. Eaton, 'A Roman Construction (Forum Baths)', *The South African Architectural Review*, Jan. 1933.

C. C. Van Essen, 'A propos du plan de la ville d'Ostie', *Hommages à Waldemar Deonna* (Coll. Latomus, Brussels, 1957), 509.

T. Frank, 'Aeneas' City at the mouth of the Tiber', *AJP* 45 (1924) 64.

—— 'The People of Ostia', *Class. Journal*, 29 (1934) 481.

I. Gismondi, 'La Colimbetra del teatro di Ostia', *Anthemon* (Scritti in onore di Carlo Anti, Venice, 1954), 1.

F. Grosso, 'Nuovo epigrafe Ostiense dei Gamala', *Atti del III° Congresso internazionale di Epigrafia greca e latina*, 1959, 133.

H. Hommel, 'Euripides in Ostia', *Epigraphica*, 19 (1957) 109.

Th. Homolle, 'Sur quelques inscriptions d'Ostie', *Rev. arch.* 34 (1877) 234, 301.

L. Laffranchi, 'La Translation de la monnaie d'Ostie à Arles', *Rev. belge de Numismatique*, 1922.

R. Lanciani, 'Le antichità del territorio Laurentino', *MA* 13 (1903) 133.

G. Lugli, *La tecnica edilizia Romana*, Rome, 1957.

H. Mattingly, 'The First Age of Roman Coinage', *JRS* 25 (1945) 65.

P. Mingazzini, 'Esisteva un abitato ostiense anteriore alla colonia romana?', *Rend. Pont.* 23–24 (1947–9) 75.

—— 'Ippocrate o Pindaro?', ibid. 25–26 (1949–51) 33.

A. Pellegrini, *Le Scienze e le arti sotto il Pontificato di Pio IX*, Rome, 1860.

A. von Premerstein, 'Untersuchungen zur Geschichte des Kaisers Marcus', *Klio*, 12 (1912) 139.

L. Rossi, *La bonifica degli stagni e delle paludi di Ostia*, Rome, 1894.

G. Stuhlfauth, 'Der Leuchtturm von Ostia', *RM* 53 (1938) 139.

L. R. Taylor, 'The Publii Lucilii Gamalae of Ostia', *AJP* 57 (1936) 183.

P p

E. A. Thatcher, 'The Open Rooms of the Terme del Foro at Ostia', *MAAR* 24 (1956) 169.

H. Thylander, *Étude sur l'épigraphie latine*, Lund, 1952.

B. Tilly, *Vergil's Latium*, Oxford, 1947.

—— 'The Topography of *Aeneid* IX with reference to the way taken by Nisus and Euryalus', *Arch. class.* 8 (1958) 164.

D. Vaglieri, 'Monumenti repubblicani di Ostia', *BC* 39 (1911) 225.

L. Vidman, 'De familia Gamaliana Ostiensi', *Eunomia* (*Ephemeridis Listz filologické suppl.*), 2 (Prague, 1958) 1.

P. E. Visconti, *Catalogo del Museo Torlonia di sculture antiche*, Rome, 1880.

L. Wickert, 'Vorbemerkungen zu einem Supplementum Ostiense des *CIL*', *Sitz. der Preuss. Ak. Wiss.* 1928, 36.

F. H. Wilson, 'The so-called Magazzini Repubblicane near the Porta Romana at Ostia', *BSR* 13 (1937) 77.

The following articles were seen too late even to be recorded in the Addenda:

C. C. Van Essen, 'Studio cronologico sulle pitture parietali di Ostia', *BC* 76 (1956–8) 155.

F. Grosso, 'L'epigrafe di Ippona e la vita di Suetonio con i fasti dei pontefici di Vulcano a Ostia', *Rend. Acc. naz. dei Lincei*, 14 (1959) 263.

M. F. Squarciapino, 'Piccolo corpus dei mattoni scolpiti Ostiensi', *BC* 76 (1956–8) 183.

OSTIA, 1960–1972

BIBLIOGRAPHY

A. ALFÖLDI, 'Die alexandrischen Götter und die vota publica am Jahres Beginn', *Jahrbuch für Antike Christentum*, 8–9 (1956–7) 53 (Ostia, 59–68).

A. AUDIN, 'Inhumation et incinération', *Latomus*, 19 (1960) 312.

S. BALBI DE CARO, 'Un nuovo pontefice di Vulcano ad Ostia', *Epigraphica* 30 (1968) 75.

G. BARBIERI (1), 'Revisioni di epigrafi', *Rend. Pont.* 42 (1969–70) 73 (Ostia, 76).

—— (2), 'Pompeio Macrino, Asinio Marcello, Bebio Macro e i Fasti Ostiensi del 115', *Mélanges* 82 (1970) 263.

G. BECATTI (1), Review of *Roman Ostia, JRS* 51 (1961) 199.

—— (2), *Mosaici e pavimenti marmorei (Scavi di Ostia*, iv), 1961.

—— (3), 'L'edificio Ostiense con opus sectile', *Rend. Pont.* 41 (1968–9) 205.

—— (4), *Edificio con opus sectile fuori Porta Marina (Scavi di Ostia*, vi), 1969.

—— (5), *AC* 19 (1967) 170, 20 (1968) 157.

—— (6), 'Scavi di un edificio termale in Ostia Antica' (Terme del nuotatore), *AC* 19 (1967) 170.

J. P. BECKER, 'The actual value of the Horrea of Hortensius at Ostia', *Rend. Ist. Lombardo di sci. e lett.* 47 (1963) 605.

L. BERTACCHI, 'Elementi per una revisione della topografia Ostiense', *Rend. Linc.* 15 (1960) 8.

H. BLOCH (1), Review of *Roman Ostia, Gnomon* 37 (1965) 192.

—— (2), 'A Monument of the Lares Augusti in the Forum of Ostia', *Harv. Theol. Stud.* 4 (1961) 211.

A. A. BOYCE, 'Nero's Harbour Sestertii', *AJA* 70 (1966) 65.

M. BURZACHECHI, 'Nuove osservazioni sull'epigrafe cristiana della basilica di Ostia', *Röm. Quartalschrift* 1964, 103.

C. BUTTAFAVA, *Elementi architettonici Ostiensi*, Milan, 1963.

R. CALZA (1), and E. NASH, *Ostia*, 1959 .

—— (2), *I Ritratti I (Scavi di Ostia*, v), 1964.

—— (3), 'Le sculture e la probabile zona cristiana di Ostia e di Porto', *Rend. Pont.* 37 (1964–5) 155.

—— (4), *Ostia* (Archaeological Guide), Rome, 1965.

—— (5), and M. F. SQUARCIAPINO, *Museo Ostiense*, Rome, 1972.

A. CARANDINI and others, *Le Terme del Nuotatore*, Ostia I and II, *Stud. Misc.* 13 (1968), 16 (1970).

L. CASSON (1), 'Harbour and River Boats of Ancient Rome', *JRS* 55 (1965) 31.

—— (2), *Ships and Seamanship in the Ancient World*, Princeton, 1971.

M. CÉBEILLAC, 'Quelques inscriptions inédites d'Ostie', *Mélanges* 83 (1971) 39.

M. A. CHASTAGNOL, 'La restauration du temple d'Isis au Portus Romae sous le règne de Gratien', *Hommages à Marcel Renard*, vol. ii, *Coll. Latomus*, 102 (1969) 135.

576   *Bibliography*

EUGENIA EQUINI, 'Un frammento dei fasti Ostiensi', *Epigraphica*, 29 (1967) 11.

B. M. FELLETTI Maj. (1), 'La casa delle Volte Dipinte', *Boll. d'arte*, 29 (1963) 69.

—— (2), *Le pitture della casa delle Volte Dipinte e delle Pareti Gialle*, Monumenti della pittura antica scoperti in Italia III, fasc. 1–2.

—— (3), *Le pitture della casa delle Muse*, Mon. Pitt. Ant. III, fasc. 3.

D. FISHWICK, '*Hastiferi*', *JRS* 57 (1967) 142.

C. GASPARI, *Le Pitture della caupona del pavone*, Mon. Pitt. Ant. III, fasc. 4.

S. GIANNINI, *Ostia* (mainly architectural), Genoa, 1970.

R. GNOLLE, *Marmora Romana*, Rome, 1971.

M. GUARDUCCI, 'Il misterioso quadrato magico', *AC* 17 (1965) 219 (Ostia, 254 f.).

T. HACKENS and NICOLE DACOS, 'Ostie: découvertes et recherches récentes (1957–1962),' *Ant. Class.* 31 (1962) 303.

M. HAMMOND, 'Three Latin Inscriptions', *Harv. Stud. Class. Phil.* 68 (1966) 78.

A. LICORDARI, 'Il rilievo funerario di Caltilia Moschis', *Stud. Misc.* 20 (1971–2) 61.

H. B. MATTINGLY, 'Suetonius, *Claud.* 24.2 and the "Italian Quaestors".' *Hommages à Marcel Renard*, vol. ii (1969) 505.

L. MORETTI, 'Sulle iscrizioni greche di Porto', *Rend. Linc.* 19 (1964) 193.

J. E. PACKER (1), 'The Domus of Cupid and Psyche in Ancient Ostia', *AJA* 71 (1967) 123.

—— (2), 'Housing and Population in Imperial Ostia and Rome', *JRS* 57 (1967) 80.

—— (3), 'Structure and Design in Ancient Ostia', *Technology and Culture* 9 (1968) 357.

—— (4), *The Insulae of Imperial Ostia*, American Academy in Rome, 1971.

F. PALLARES, 'Terra sigillata ispanica ad Ostia', *Riv. di Stud. Liguri* 29 (1963) 69.

C. PANCIERA, 'Il sepolcro Ostiense di C. Cartilio Poplicola ed una scheda epigrafica di Gaetano Marini', *AC* 18 (1966) 54.

G. RICKMAN, *Roman Granaries and Store Buildings*, Cambridge, 1971.

V. SCRINARI (1), 'Il Porto di Claudio ed osservazioni sulla tecnica del conglomerato cementizio presso i Romani', *L'industria italiana del cemento* 33 (1963) 527.

—— (2) 'Il "Portus Claudii" e i più recenti ritrovamenti nella zona di Fiumicino', *Atti del III Congresso Internazionale di Arch. Sottomarina*, Barcelona, 1961.

H. SOLIN (1), 'Eine neue Fluchtafel aus Ostia', *Comm. Humanarum Litterarum* (Soc. Scient. Fennicarum) 42 (1968) 3.

—— (2), 'Republikanisches aus Ostie (Analecta Epigraphica)', *Arctos, Acta phil. Fennica*, NS 6 (1970) 106.

—— (3), 'Griechische Graffiti aus Ostia', *Arctos* 7 (1972) 190.

M. F. SQUARCIAPINO (1), Review of *Roman Ostia*, *AC* 12 (1960) 251.

—— (2), 'Un nuovo santuario della Bona Dea ad Ostia', *Rend. Pont.* 32 (1959–60) 93.

—— (3), 'Piccolo corpus dei mattoni scolpiti Ostiensi', *BC* 78 (1961–2) 112.

—— (4) 'La sinagoga di Ostia', *Boll. d'arte* (1961) 326.

—— (5), 'La sinagoga recentemente scoperta ad Ostia', *Rend. Pont.* 34 (1961–2) 119.

—— (6), 'La sinagoga di Ostia: seconda campagna di scavo', *Atti del VI Congresso intern. di arch. crist.* (1962) 299.

—— (7), 'The Synagogue at Ostia', *Archaeology* 16 (1963) 195.

—— (8), 'Scoperte in occasione di lavori stradali tra la via Guido Calza e la via dei Romagnoli', *NS* 15 (1961) 145.

—— (9), *I culti orientali ad Ostia*, Leiden, 1962.

M. F. Squarciapino (10), 'Ebrei a Roma e ad Ostia', *Studi Romani*, 11 (1963) 129.

—— (11), 'Ostia, porto di Roma', *Economia e storia* (1964), 299.

—— (12), 'La rocca di Giulio II di Ostia', *Boll. dell'ist. storico e di cultura dell'arma del genio*, 89 (1965) 5.

—— (13), 'Plotius Fortunatus archisynagogus', *Israel* 36 (1970) 183.

R. A. Staccioli, 'Le taverne a Roma attraverso la Forma Urbis', *Rend. Linc.* 14 (1959) 56.

O. Testaguzza (1), 'The Port of Rome', *Archaeology*, 17 (1964) 172.

—— (2), *Portus*, Rome, 1970.

P. Testini, 'Sondaggio dell'area di S. Ippolito all'Isola Sacra', *Rend. Pont.* 43 (1970) 223.

M. L. Veloccia Rinaldi, 'Nuove pitture Ostiensi: la casa della Ierodule', *Rend. Pont.* 43 (1970–71) 165.

L. Vidman, *Fasti Ostienses*, Prague, 1957.

T. P. Wiseman, 'Pulcher Claudius', *Harv. Stud. Class. Phil.* 74 (1968) 207 (Ostia, 217).

F. Zevi (1), 'La sistemazione della collezione epigrafica Ostiense e la carriera di Q. Baieno Blassiano', *Acta, Fifth Epigraph. Congress*, London, 1967, 193.

—— (2), 'Quinto Baieno Blassiano, cavaliere Triestino', *Atti e Mem. della Soc. Istriana di Arch. e Storia Patria* 16 (1968) 5.

—— (3), 'Anfore Istriane ad Ostia', *Atti e Mem. della Soc. Istriana.* 15 (1967) 208.

—— (4), 'Brevi note Ostiensi', *Epigraphica* 30 (1968) 83.

—— (5), and A. Tchernia, 'Amphores de Byzacène au bas-empire', *Antiquités africaines* 3 (1969) 173.

—— (6), 'Nuovi documenti epigrafici sugli Egrilii Ostiensi', *Mélanges* 82 (1970) 279.

—— (7), 'Caserma dei Vigili. Scavo sotto il mosaico del vano antistante il "Cesareo"', *NS* 24 (1970) 7.

—— (8), 'Tre iscrizioni con firme di artisti greci', *Rend. Pont.* 42 (1969–70) 95.

—— (9), *Atti, III Congresso Internaz. sul Dramma Antico a Siracusa*, 'Iscrizione . . . apposta alla statua di Platone commediografo'.

—— (10), and I. Pohl, 'Casa delle Pareti Gialle, salone centrale. Scavo sotto il pavimento a mosaico', *NS* 24 (1970) 43.

—— (11), 'Una statua dall'Isola sacra e l'Iseo di Porto,' *Rend. Pont.* 43 (1970–71) xxiv, *Nuove Immissioni* (1971) 7.

—— (12), 'Miscellanea Ostiense', *Rend. Linc.* 26 (1971) 449.

—— (13) and P. Pensabene, 'Un arco in onore di Caracalla ad Ostia', *Rend. Linc.* 26 (1971) 481.

—— (14), and A. Tchernia, 'Amphores vinaires de Campanie et de Tarraconaise à Ostie', *Recherches sur les amphores romaines*, École française de Rome, 1972, p. 35.

References in the following sections to articles and books are given by author's name only. Numbers are added where needed from the Bibliography. The following abbreviations are used:

FA	Fasti Archeologi.
Immissioni 1971	*Museo Ostiense, Nuove Immissioni*, Ostia, 1971.
Mostra 1967	*Mostra di Rinvenimenti e Restauri del 1967*, Ostia, 1968.
Mostra 1972	*Mostra di Rinvenimenti da Scavi in corso*, Ostia, 1972.
Stud. Misc.	*Studi miscellanei del Seminario di Archeologia e Storia dell'Arte greca e romana*, Rome.

THE NEW EVIDENCE

To the casual visitor returning to the site Ostia 1972 may not seem significantly changed from Ostia 1960. There are more visitors, the trees are taller, and the landscaping of the ruins is even more attractive. But those who have followed Ostian studies more closely will soon realize that there has been a quiet revolution. In 1960 Barbieri had already laid the foundation for the more systematic study of Ostian inscriptions by bringing together all the inscriptions on the site, including even the most unpromising fragments. Since it was common practice in the late Empire to break up inscribed stones even from cemeteries and public buildings for reuse in pavements or building repairs it is not unusual to find fragments of the same inscription in widely separated parts of the town: the dispersal of the town's official record, the *Fasti*, is a conspicuous example. When the fragments are systematically arranged they have a much better chance of finding their partners. The continuation of Barbieri's work under his general supervision has led to increasingly important results (see below, p. 583). Following the same principle specimens of all brick stamps found at Ostia have been put on display in chronological order, providing an admirable illustration of Bloch's basic work, and a most useful point of reference in further excavations. Even more important has been the detailed work on the classification and dating of pottery. The tools for the study of Ostia's history have been considerably sharpened.

By 1960 the dramatic excavations of 1938–42 had been largely absorbed and it must have been very tempting to resume digging, especially along the line of the sea-shore where the height of the grass mounds suggests rich rewards, or along the line of the Tiber towards the mouth of the river, which must always have been one of the most important areas for traders. Future generations will be grateful to Anton Pietrogrande and Maria Squarciapino, his successor as director, for resisting the temptation. Working to a lean budget with a small staff they have made the conservation of what had already been excavated their first priority. The preservation of wall paintings, threatened by damp and frost, has been significantly improved by the elaboration of new techniques, and the disintegration of mosaics has been averted by raising and resetting them on concrete foundations. Apart from emergency operations to take advantage of opportunities provided by work on roads new digging has been restricted to completing the excavation of buildings only partly uncovered and investigating the lower levels at selected points within the excavated area to fill out the very fragmentary history of republican Ostia. New ground won in these ways and by the general progress of Ostian studies as the importance of the site becomes more widely appreciated requires the modification of several assumptions, and opens up new questions.

The Ostia of Ancus Marcius still remains no more than a hypothesis but scepticism is becoming less emphatic, and the rediscovery of a large cemetery half-way between Rome and Lavinium with tomb furnishings that, on present evidence, begin in the late eighth and do not yet extend beyond the end of the seventh century adds a little strength to the tradition (Zevi, *Mostra*, 1972). For Nibby had already suggested that this was the site of Politorium said by Livy (i. 33. 3) to have been destroyed by Ancus Marcius. That there were settlers in the area before the foundation of the Castrum in the fourth century is also suggested by pottery, attributed to the fifth century and possibly earlier, that was found near but not associated with some tombs exposed by road-work south-east of the 'Sullan' walls (Squarciapino 8, p. 174).

The few examples of polychrome architectural terracottas from the early years of the Castrum (*Scavi di Ostia*, i. Tav. xxii) have been supplemented by a lively fourth-century head of a Silenus found in a fill under the earliest pavement of the temple of the Round Altar. Three further fragments have been recovered from the Castle of Julius II, but there is no record of when or where they were found. The most interesting of the three comes from a group in the round, designed for a pediment or akroterion of a temple or other public building, and has been dated *c.* 350 B.C. The other two reproduce familiar decorative patterns (Zevi, *Immissioni*, 1971, 29–31).

The development of the Castrum in the middle Republic remains very obscure, but the main questions that have to be answered have been more clearly defined. The most important and embarrassing result of the widespread examination of the lower levels is that there is still no evidence of any pre-Sullan building east of the Castrum except perhaps some light structures under the four Republican temples west of the theatre (*MA* 23 (1914) 443, with p. 127 above) and a series of tufa walls running out from the east wall of the Castrum at a very low level, presumably to form shops (p. 120). Under the Baths of Neptune nothing has been found earlier than the emperor Claudius (Zevi, *FA* 18–19 (1963–4) 7429); in a limited excavation on the west side of the Piazzale delle Corporazioni nothing was found earlier than the Augustan reticulate wall enclosing the square; under the Baths of the Swimmer (*Terme del Nuotatore*) there seems to have been no building before the Flavian baths. Under the Baths of the Drivers, north of the Decumanus and just inside the Porta Romana, nothing was found earlier than the reticulate construction of the Augustan period or slightly earlier. The natural inference from this evidence is that there were no living quarters east of the Castrum, for even if all building was in perishable materials—timber, wattle and daub, or unbaked brick—floor levels should have survived and far more kitchen pottery than has been found. It has been suggested that the large area between the Decumanus and the river east of the Castrum was kept free of buildings because this was the main dock area of Rome's river harbour, where merchantmen tied up and unloaded their cargoes. This would be why a Roman praetor had a series of *cippi* set up along the line of the Decumanus declaring that on the authority of the Roman senate this land was public land belonging to the state (p. 32). If, however, this is the right explanation one would have expected, by the end of the second century B.C. at the latest, some buildings for storage and general harbour services. These may perhaps be found when it is eventually possible to extend excavation to the ancient river bank. But, even so, one would expect more evidence of trade in the form of broken amphorae if the area was reserved for shipping interests. Another possibility perhaps is that this area was reserved for the fleet. Even if the Ostian station had normally no more than thirty ships, these would have required up to 6,000 men, and they would presumably have lived in timber barracks when not required for active service. This might explain why building in the area on a substantial scale seems to have begun under Augustus (p. 539, the theatre with the Piazzale delle Corporazioni; and the large area on the north side of the Decumanus near the Porta Romana, REG. II. II. 1–3, though the dating of this area is more uncertain). The reason could be the transference of the headquarters of the Roman fleet by Augustus from Ostia to Misenum. But unless and until some secure evidence is found this will be no more than a frail hypothesis. Neither of the two explanations, however, would explain the absence of pre-Flavian buildings under the Baths of the Swimmer. If further probes on this south side of the Decumanus produce similar results we can admire the foresight which allowed so much room for expansion when the line of the 'Sullan' walls was drawn.

The most unexpected addition to our evidence for republican Ostia comes from a limited but fruitful excavation in the temple area west of the Castrum off the Via della Foce. In this triangular area dominated by the large temple of Hercules there were two other temples, the smaller of which stands beside the Via della Foce. The investigation of a small undisturbed area of the pronaos of this temple has clarified the history of the temple and strengthened the case for a pre-Sullan date, not necessarily later than the temple of Hercules (Zevi 8). A more surprising result was the discovery of three inscribed travertine blocks, carefully placed around the remains of a round peperino altar to serve as foundation for a new rectangular altar which was to replace it. The three blocks are of the same size and inscribed in Greek by the same hand. They record the titles of portrait statues and of their sculptors: 'Plato, poet of the old comedy, Lysicles was the sculptor; Antisthenes the philosopher, Phyromachus was the sculptor; Charite, priestess at Delphi, Phradmon of Argos was the sculptor.' Zevi gives good, if not decisive, arguments for dating the lettering of the inscriptions between Sulla and the end of the first quarter of the first century, A.D.: the archaeological context, he thinks, for their use as foundation blocks is probably Augustan.

There is no natural link between the three portraits nor between the three sculptors. Phradmon is the well-known contemporary of Phidias and Polyclitus; Phyromachus was an Athenian who was remembered for his work at the Court of Attalus I of Pergamum in the late third century B.C. Lysicles is not even a known name but Athens would be the most likely place for a statue of a poet of the old comedy: Lysicles was probably an Athenian. These statues must have been presented to the temple (or, possibly, to the neighbouring temple of Hercules) as artistic treasures and not for their association with the temple's cult. But were the statues Greek originals, and why were the bases buried? Zevi's conclusion is that they were in fact Greek originals brought back by Sulla or some other Roman noble from Greece and that the inscriptions are copies from the original bases. They were used as foundation for a new altar because they had been replaced by marble bases which the standards of the Augustan age demanded. These bold inferences may at first reading seem highly improbable, but they are a coherent explanation of the evidence. If the statues were forgeries this was not known to the donor. They are good evidence for the impressive patronage that Ostian temples could attract in the late Republic, and they show that the increasing influence of Hellenism in art and architecture was felt at Ostia as well as Rome. The tetrastyle temple to the north of the area may supply further evidence of this Hellenic current if Zevi and P. Zanker are right in seeing in the fine head of Asclepius, which was found at the foot of the stairs leading up to the temple, a Greek work of *c.* 100 B.C., probably the temple's cult statue (Zevi 8, p. 96).

But the wealthiest of the three temples was the temple of Hercules, and to the many fine dedications already known can now be added another statue, the base of which has been recently published (M. Cébeillac). The lettering of the inscription on the base is certainly earlier than 50 B.C. and probably earlier than Sulla, and it is made of Greek marble, a considerable luxury at such an early date: no earlier inscription on marble has yet been found at Ostia. It is particularly interesting therefore that the man who dedicated the statue was a freedman, P. Livius. To make such a dedication he must have been wealthy and it is partly for this reason that M. Cébeillac, in a discussion of the various inscriptions associated with the temple, suggests that P. Livius was celebrating his success in trade and that the Ostian Hercules may be primarily associated with trade.

The history of imperial Ostia has gained considerably more from recent excavation. Belief in the importance of Domitian's years in the rebuilding of Ostia has been strengthened. The Hadrianic plan of the Baths of Neptune is now securely known to repeat almost exactly the plan of baths built under Domitian (a provisional note by Zevi in *FA* 18–19 (1963–4) 7429). More evidence has been recovered of a Domitianic phase under the barracks of the Vigiles. Zevi (7), who was able to make a restricted investigation when the mosaic in the chapel was temporarily raised, found fragments of two inscriptions honouring emperors. The first almost certainly concerned Trajan, and, according to a convincing restoration, it was set up by the seven cohorts of the Vigiles: the emperor of the second inscription may have been Hadrian in the first half of his reign. It seems that here too Hadrian was following where Domitian had led, and such little evidence as is available is at least compatible with the adoption of the Domitianic plan by Hadrian's builders.

To the buildings of Domitian's reign can now also be added the Baths of the Swimmer (*Terme del Nuotatore*), so called from the mosaic figure of a swimming man on one of the pavements. These baths were built on the south side of the Decumanus, not far from the Baths of Neptune, and they can be firmly dated to the last years of Domitian (Becatti 5). They do not match the imperial baths in size or in the quality of their decoration, but in addition to the normal sequence of rooms they had a large palaestra.

To the new buildings already assigned to the Severan period can now be added a richly decorated arch in honour of Caracalla, one of two arches over the Decumanus in front of the theatre, to be identified with the arch by which Christian soldiers were executed at the time of the martyrdom of S. Aurea (p. 390. For the identification and reconstruction see Zevi (14) and Pensabene). The end of the Severan dynasty is followed by a bleak period at Ostia, and the decline is strikingly illustrated by the Baths of the Swimmer in the south-east quarter of the town. These baths, built under Domitian, were considerably modified under Hadrian, and remained in use into the third century. But the evidence of coins and pottery makes it certain that they were abandoned towards the middle of the third century (Becatti 5). What is even more surprising, all usable material was taken away, and there was no further building on the site, which became a rubbish dump. Zevi has brought together evidence, including a new inscription which was probably a handsome dedication to Diocletian, for a building revival under the first Tetrarchy (Zevi 13, pp. 468–72), but it is still too early to attempt more than a broad outline from the fourth to the ninth centuries.

The continuing study of all the unpublished inscriptions will eventually provide enough new material to encourage a deeper and more detailed social analysis of the population of Ostia; meanwhile important new light has been thrown on some of the town's most distinguished families. Perhaps the most interesting revision now needed concerns Marcus Acilius Egrilius A. f(ilius) Plarianus, adopted from the Egrilii into another leading Ostian family, by M. Acilius Priscus. Raised to the senatorial order by the Flavians with his elder brother A. Egrilius Plarianus, he remained a loyal benefactor of his native town, accepting the high office of *pontifex Volcani* and honoured as a patron. From the *Fasti* it was known that he had already been appointed to the military treasury, *praefectus aerarii militaris*, when he was made *pontifex Volcani* in 105. An inscription was set up by him when he was *praefectus aerarii Saturni* in honour of an emperor in the tenth year of his tribunician power. Bloch's restoration of Trajan's name seemed inevitable, requiring the date 106, and quick promotion from the junior to the senior treasury. Zevi's discovery of a new fragment of the inscription shows that the emperor was Hadrian not Trajan, and the year 126, implying a very long gap indeed between the two treasury posts. We can accept the inference that Zevi draws. The Egrilii were typical of Flavian appointments; Trajan preferred military men to businessmen, but the civil virtues of the Egrilii could be appreciated by Hadrian (Zevi 6). With the knowledge that M. Acilius Plarianus was alive in 126 the tentative suggestion that Suetonius may have been *pontifex Volcani* at Ostia before his fall in 122 must be abandoned. That the Egrilii drew their wealth from trade and commerce rather than land receives support from the addition in unpublished inscriptions of two bankers, *coactores argentarii*, among the freedmen of the family in addition to the one already known.

The very different family of the Lucilii Gamalae also have new inscriptions to add to their total. A P. Lucilius Gamala f(ilius) is one of the duoviri for A.D. 69 or 72, in a new fragment of the *Fasti* (p. 517) and, more important, a Gamala of the late Republic was married to a senatorial Octavia, who was associated with the cult of Bona Dea in Ostia. My inference that the P. Lucilius Gamala of the lost inscription lived into the time of Augustus and that the family's fortunes were based on land (p. 493) may have to be reconsidered in the light of discussion with Zevi who has attractive arguments for a rather earlier dating, an eastern origin, and trading interests. I suspend judgement until I have seen the full development of his view.

In 1960 it was not possible to trace any descendant in high office of C. Cartilius Poplicola, eight times duovir, whose monumental tomb stands outside the Porta Marina. The combination by Zevi of thirty-one fragments found at different times, some near the theatre, but others as far away as the Casette-tipo may fill the gap. The result is a monumental inscription in large letters (15.7–16.1 cm. high) recording the setting up at his own expense of a public building, probably a portico, by C. Cartilius C. f(ilius) Pal(atina) S[a]binus p(atronus) c(oloniae) omnibus hono[ribu]s fu[nct]us. The lettering suggests a date in the first or early second century A.D. (Zevi 4, p. 88). It would be interesting to know whether Poplicola whose tribe is not recorded on his tomb inscription, also belonged to Palatina. We also now know more of the Terentii, another distinguished Ostian family. The *Fasti* mention the restoration of a *crypta Terentiana* in A.D. 94. A new inscription records the gift of a *cryptam et chalcidicum* by Terentia A. f(ilia) in A.D. 6 (Zevi, 'Il calcidico della Curia Iulia', *Rend. Linc.* 26 (1971) 2). This will be the Terentia who also dedicated a well-head in the sanctuary of the Augustan temple of Bona Dea (p. 194).

For the study of Ostian housing Calza's basic articles are still fundamental, but there remains much to be done. With few exceptions, such as the Insula del Serapide and its partner the Insula degli Aurighi, and the excellent analysis of the *domus* of the late Empire by Becatti, the description of the blocks uncovered in the grand campaign of 1938–42 has remained somewhat summary. A detailed description has now been added of the interesting House of the Painted Vaults (B. M. Felletti Maj (1)), and J. E. Packer (1) has reconstructed in detail the building that was later transformed into the House of Amor and Psyche. More recently the continuation of the excavation of the Garden Houses has revealed an apartment which increases our respect for the architect who was responsible for the development of that large area (p. 139). In an apartment which basically follows his standard apartment plan he has introduced an individual touch. By prefacing the *tablinum* with two columns he has given emphasis and elegance to the main room in a way that recalls the arcaded entrance to the *tablinum* in his House of the Muses. In this he is anticipating the style of the House of the Round Temple and other houses of the late Empire (M. L. Veloccia Rinaldi).

More general questions are raised in a detailed survey of housing conditions by J. E. Packer (4 and 2). Drawing a sharp distinction between apartment blocks and blocks whose ground floor is occupied by shops he assumes that the great majority of the upper storeys of the second category were confined to single rooms or two-room apartments. From this it would follow that only a small minority of Ostian households had more than two rooms. This is probably an oversimplification, for where the shops were long there is no architectural difficulty in providing apartments of five or more rooms above them. The five ground-floor rooms of the House of the Painted Ceiling could for instance be fitted comfortably over the row of shops behind them (p. 145, fig. 13). But though Packer's survey may be too schematic it is an excellent base for further discussion and one of the most elusive problems that emerges concerns the accommodation for slaves. The very common formula in tomb inscriptions providing not only for the family but also for the freedmen and freedwomen of the family, *libertis libertabusque posterisque eorum*, suggests a large slave population widely spread, especially as it is found in small and presumably inexpensive tombs (e.g. *CIL* XIV S. 4821, 4865) as well as in large tombs. We can be certain that families who lived in apartments with rooms on two floors, and this applies to the majority of those who had ground-floor apartments, possessed several slaves: where did they sleep? In his calculation of the population total Packer allows one person for each *cubiculum* in large apartments and assumes that when the apartment is divided between two floors the upper floor will repeat the plan of the lower. This gives a total of eight persons for each of the two-floor apartments in the Garden Houses, with the further assumption that the third and fourth floors will repeat the two-floor plan of the first and second floors. But is it not more probable that the slaves would be crowded together on the upper floor? Packer's text also reminds me that I paid too little attention to domestic sanitation. The number of buildings that have toilets connected with the public drainage system is very limited indeed and this helps to explain the very generous supply of public accommodation. A detailed study of the types, location, and distribution of private toilets would be a useful contribution to a social analysis. Another and very different inquiry would, I think, repay more detailed study. How far did architects build to meet known demands? Did the architect who planned the block between the Via dei Vigili and the Via delle Corporazioni have a specific client in mind when he provided for such large industrial premises at the north end of his block and why were changes made elsewhere in the block in the course of building?

There is more also to be added to the account of Ostian trade. The more detailed and exacting study of pottery is providing a more realistic picture of important aspects of the overseas trade of Ostia, and therefore also of Rome. The excavation of the Baths of the Swimmer by members of the Archaeological Seminar of Rome University under the general guidance of Professor Becatti and the direction of Dr. A. Carandini has provided an admirable opportunity for classifying what is misleadingly called *terra sigillata* (and sometimes, even more misleadingly, Samian) and what can for convenience be called table as opposed to kitchen ware. Firmly stratified levels provide a guide to typological sequences and coins add a chronological framework. In the late Republic the highly skilled potters of Arretium had dominated the market inside Italy and outside, but for some reason that has never been satisfactorily explained this production centre flourished for little more than two generations. The tradition was carried on at Puteoli and elsewhere in Italy, but by the time of the eruption of Vesuvius in A.D. 79 Italian decorated ware was no longer being used at Pompeii. When the Baths of the Swimmer were built under Domitian Gallic decorated pottery had replaced Italian but undecorated ware still came mainly from Italy. In the Republic a significant proportion of Ostian table ware came from the East; by Domitian's reign there is only a thin trickle, from Asia Minor. From the first phase of the baths there were a few fragments of African ware; in the Hadrianic level there were more, and by the end of the second century Africa had virtually driven Italy, Spain, and Gaul from the Roman market and was the largest supplier throughout the Mediterranean coast-lands.

Considerable progress has also been made in distinguishing the various types of amphorae, and especially in the identification of African shapes (Zevi (5 and 15) and Tchernia; see also Zevi 3). It seems that in the Flavian period Ostia got most of her wine and oil from Italy, and mainly, one can assume, from Latium and Campania. Spain, which was to dominate Rome's oil supply in the first half of the second century, has only a small share of the market, and the majority of Spanish amphorae imported in the Flavian period carried *garum* or salted fish. By the end of the second century Africa dominated the market for oil as well as table ware (see Carandini, and especially *Stud. Misc.* 16, pp. 122–7).

In the field of religion also much new ground has been won. In 1960 it was reasonable, in the absence of firm evidence, to be sceptical about a Jewish community in Ostia (p. 389), but in 1959 the widening of the road leading to the international airport at Fiumicino uncovered a finely carved column base, a large Corinthian capital, and part of a column, which were found to belong to a synagogue. The building, on a valuable site near the sea-shore, goes back to the first century A.D.; it was made more handsome in the second century, and further modified in the late Empire. The function of the building was made explicit by the seven-branched candelabrum with other Jewish symbols carved on the heads of two consoles, and by an inscription in Greek recording the gift of an ark for the scriptures, prefaced by an invocation in Latin for the emperor's well-being, *pro salute Augusti* (Squarciapino 4–7). We can now be reasonably certain that the inscription from Castel Porziano (p. 389 n. 4) with its reference to a president of the elders, refers to the Ostian community. By a nice coincidence agricultural operations brought to light a few years later the funerary inscription of an archisynagogus, Plotius Fortunatus (Squarciapino 13). The name helps to explain why the Jews of Ostia were so elusive: I overlooked the fact that it was common Jewish practice to adopt Roman names.

Even more spectacular was the discovery of a hall with Christian associations in the course of following-up operations begun in the campaign of 1938–42 in the area where the Decumanus reaches the sea. The building complex which includes this hall has a monumental entrance and forms two wings, one running south and the other westwards. The original construction was in Hadrianic brick but the westward wing was completely rebuilt in the fourth century in block and brick. It was sited immediately behind a massive sea-wall, 6 m. thick, which had probably been built in the first century A.D. When the hall collapsed the elaborate *opus sectile* decoration of the walls was buried in countless dismembered fragments under a confused mass of roof tiles, bricks, and tufa blocks. Only those who study the photographic records in Becatti's monumental publication (Becatti 4; a summary in 3) can appreciate the triumph of M. A. Ricciardi, who with Becatti recovered the design, and Luigi Bracali, Ostia's senior mosaicist, who, after more than six years of patient struggle, succeeded in finding the right place for all but a negligible number of the pieces in such a gigantic jigsaw puzzle.

The hall was entered through two columns and ended in a rectangular exedra. The two side walls (7 m. long and 8 m. high) had the same scheme of decoration with only minor variations. There were three main registers, of which the second was the most striking, including two large panels showing on the left wall a tiger and on the right wall a lion devouring a deer. The representation of lion or tiger devouring a deer has a long history in both pagan and Christian symbolism, but the Christian reference is explicit in the bust of a bearded Christ with halo in the centre of the top band of the lowest register of the right wall. In the same register lower down and to the right is the bust of a youth in whose name perhaps the hall was dedicated. In the elaborate design of these walls, a wide range of marble was used with considerable skill and taste, among them *giallo antico*, *serpentino*, *pavonazetto*, *porta santa*, *rosso antico*. The decoration of the exedra (4 m. wide, 7·2 m. high) provided a sharp contrast. Here marble blocks (2·5 cm. square), in rows of yellow, green, red, white, were set in a simple design based on walls of *opus reticulatum* within a brick framework, a standard technique in the early Empire, and including four arched windows in the back wall and two in each of the side walls. Below this design was a pattern of coloured paste-glass tesserae, and the ceiling of the exedra was lined·with blue tesserae, thinly threaded with gold. Nothing survives from the main ceiling of the hall; it was probably of timber, perhaps painted.

The history of the building has been most ingeniously reconstructed by Becatti. No decoration survives from 2·50 m. at the bottom of the walls. The work had begun at the top and had not been completed, and the laying of the *opus sectile* pavement with a pattern reminiscent of the pavement of the main room in the House of Amor and Psyche had barely begun. The floor was still being used as a workshop, with miscellaneous material waiting to be sawn to shape, including several small fourth-century columns and two large blocks of *giallo antico* from the imperial quarry at Simitthus in Numidia, cut out much earlier, in the reign of Domitian. There was also a finely decorated architrave which must have once belonged to a building of the first century A.D.; it may have been intended for reuse. The series of coins ends with two of Honorius from the mint of Aquilea (after 393) and a single coin of Eugenius (between 392 and·394). It can hardly be coincidence that the coin evidence points to the time when paganism made its last bid to reverse the dominance of Christianity. It was in the brief period that was ended by the defeat of the pagan forces at the battle of the Frigidus in August 394 that the temple of Hercules at Ostia was restored by the *praefectus annonae* (p. 402). Becatti is surely right in seeing this as the context of the destruction of the Christian hall, a further sign of the surviving strength of pagan elements in Ostia.

Two more general studies have added substance to the pattern of Ostia's religions. The evidence for Christianity is still very fragmentary, and no account hitherto had made use of all the archaeological evidence. R. Calza (3) in a comprehensive review has brought together all the sculpture with Christian reference that has survived, including many neglected fragments, and has discussed the sites of Christian cemeteries and buildings: M. F. Squarciapino (9) has provided a comprehensive up-to-date account of the oriental cults in Ostia, which will provide a most useful base for further study.

In 1960 the number and quality of Ostia's public baths was already one of the most striking features of Ostian life. Four sets had by then been only partially excavated and the work is now being completed: all four have produced surprises. The so-called Baths of Marciana south-east of the Porta Marina (p. 407) prove to be even larger than was thought and an interesting series of mosaics with marine and athletic scenes have been found, most of them in good condition. Later a small but elegant set of baths very close to the south side of the Baths of Marciana, but independent, was added. The Severan baths excavated by Visconti on the line of the Sullan walls west of Porta Marina and misnamed Thermae Maritimae (p. 417) have now been found to be only half the establishment, the first half of which was built under Hadrian, perhaps in association with or in response to the development centred on the Garden Houses (p. 139). The late Empire baths south of the Forum (p. 420) of which only a few comparatively small rooms could be seen in 1960 cover in fact a large area and include a substantial palaestra. It was also surprising to find that the Baths of the Swimmer, south of the western Decumanus (V. 10³), of which only two walls could be seen, also had a well-equipped series of rooms and a large palaestra. But while restorations can be seen in most of the other baths, the Baths of the Swimmer, as we have seen, were abandoned in the middle of the third century.

The appreciation of Ostia's craftsmen has been made much easier by two major publications in the series of *Scavi di Ostia*. Becatti (2) has described, dated, and critically analysed, with full photographic documentation, all the mosaics and marble pavements of Ostia, and R. Calza (2) has provided an excellent descriptive and critical catalogue of the portraits of the Republic and early Empire. Among several important additions to the collection of sculptures found at Ostia two new discoveries, each accidental, may be singled out. The first, a sarcophagus from Pianabella has one of the finest and best preserved centauromachies known to us (*Immissioni 1971*, 21). The second is a splendid statue, slightly larger than life size, of a female figure with windswept dress, originally perhaps poised on the prow of a ship like the Winged Victory from Samothrace, now in the Louvre. The statue is made of grey marble with streaks of white, *bigio dorato*. Head, arms, and feet are missing: they were probably made of white marble. This dramatic figure, with strong Hellenistic echoes, is probably from the second century A.D., and it was found on the left bank of Trajan's canal, near the point where it flowed into the sea. This was probably Isis, protectress of seafarers, sometimes called *Pelagia* or *Pharia* (Zevi 11).

Of the new paintings discovered since 1960 the most interesting and the finest are those of a newly excavated apartment in the Garden Houses, and particularly the ceiling of the main room. When the ceiling collapsed the fragments were buried, no attempt was made to clear away the rubble, and it is hoped that eventually the painting can be almost completely re-formed (M. Veloccia). Even more recently tantalizingly small fragments of Augustan painting have come to light in a mixed fill south of the Forum which was deposited to raise the level when Ostia was being extensively rebuilt in the second century. The colours—red, blue, green, and black—remain remarkably vivid and there is a precision and draftsmanship in the painting which suggests ample means and good taste. Meanwhile much useful work has been done to conserve existing paintings, and a firmer framework is provided for the history of Ostian painting by the detailed analysis of the paintings in the Houses of the Painted Vaults, the Muses, the Yellow Walls, and in the Peacock Inn (*Caupona del pavone*) in *Monumenti della pittura antica scoperti in Italia* iii (B.M. Felleti Maj 2, 3; C. Gaspari).

The study of Portus also has received new encouragement in these years, and especially from excavations in the Claudian harbour. Draining operations deriving from the construction of the new airport at Fiumicino provided the opportunity for limited investigations which have resolved the main topographical problems. An excavation report is being prepared by V. Scrinari of the Rome Soprintendenza; meanwhile O. Testaguzza, an engineer who took part in the work connected with the layout of the general area of the airport and has carefully studied what remains of the Roman constructions, has published a detailed and lavishly illustrated account of the form and history of the Claudian harbour. It is now at last clear that the famous lighthouse was not on an island, nor even at the end of the left mole, but at a point roughly two thirds along it. It is scarcely less surprising to find that the harbour took advantage of a natural bay, and that what had been usually taken to be the beginning of the left mole was really a promontory largely composed of sand. The left mole started from the end of this promontory and can be divided into three sections. The first is made of enormous travertine blocks, those of the lowest two courses weighing 6–7 tons, and is 330 m. long. The second, separated from the first by a gap of 22 m. which was subsequently closed, had a massive core of concrete, in part formed by small ships loaded with concrete and scuttled for the purpose. This stretch was 9–10 m. wide for some 220 m. and then widened to 25 m. where the giant merchantman was sunk to provide the foundation for the light-house. If Testaguzza has rightly identified the position of the stern the ship will have been 104 m. long, one of the largest wooden ships ever built. The Monte dell'Arena which had always seemed the natural site for the lighthouse is now found to be an accumulation of rubble and sand on the north side of the mole to protect the lighthouse and act as a breakwater against the drift of sand into the harbour entrance. From the sea-side there is an inlet in the mole where small ships waiting to pilot merchantmen into harbour would be sheltered. After passing the lighthouse the mole curves slightly inward and continues with a reduced width of 5–5·30 m. for some 200 m.

The nature of the right mole is also unexpected. Monte Giulio which had been generally thought to lie over the right mole covers in fact an embankment with buildings which have yet to be excavated. The right mole extends from near the end of Monte Giulo for some 50 m. and ends a little to the north of the left mole leaving an entrance of *c.* 200 m. At its end there is a substantial building connected pre-sumably with the harbour service. Near the entrance to the harbour, by the left mole, seven boats used in the harbour were found buried in the sand. They range from a cargo-carrying barge 17 m. long to a small fishing boat 6·10 m. long and they seem to have sunk, perhaps in a storm, in the late Empire (O. Testaguzza 2, pp. 129–47; V. Scrinari 2, pp. 10–12).

No such exploration has yet been possible in the area round Trajan's harbour but the digging of a drainage canal from the airport to the Tiber has revealed a substantial length of the aqueduct which took water to the harbour settlement. It is an impressively solid construc-tion faced with large triangular bricks such as were used at Ostia under Domitian and Trajan. It was probably an integral part of Trajan's plans for improving Rome's main harbour. Trajan may also have been responsible for paving the road linking Ostia with the harbours, for we now know from a new inscription that the bridge which carried the road over Trajan's canal was named after his niece Matidia or her daughter. The bridgehead at the end of the road leading to it has been uncovered and during dredging operations a pier was found in the middle of the canal. The bridge was probably of timber. A line of arches projecting from the right bank and acting as a substructure for an embankment shows that the canal was used as a secondary harbour (Testaguzza 2, p. 183).

Dredging operations also recovered an inscription from the late Empire of considerable interest. It records the restoration of the temple of Isis by the *praefectus annonae*, acting on the emperor's instructions (*AE* 1968, 86; M. A. Chastagnol). The date lies between 17 November 375 and 3 August 378. In 382 a decree was issued banning the use of public funds on pagan temples: the temple of Isis at Portus is the last known to have been accepted as the state's responsibility. It seems probable that Christianity in the late fourth century was no more dominant than in Ostia. There was already record of a temple of Isis at Portus, but its whereabouts is unknown. It is tempting to think that it may be close to the site where the statue attributed to Isis was found (pp. 590 f.), but it would be more natural to find it on the right bank of the canal. The evidence for the Egyptian cults has been a little strengthened by the convincing attribution of three inscriptions, previously assumed to come from Rome to Portus (L. Moretti). The finding of a synagogue at Ostia has naturally raised the question whether H. J. Leon was right in attributing to Rome a number of Jewish inscriptions, until recently in the Bishop's Castle at Portus. His arguments that they were brought to Portus from Rome by Cardinal Pacca still seem convincing (p. 390 n. 1).

P. 115. There is a brief report of what was uncovered in 1950 by G. Ricci in *FA* 12, 5339. In addition to the remains of buildings a further boundary stone was found, set up by the river commissioners, similar to those already known, but by a different board. The easiest interpretation of its position is that at this point the river turned south, implying that the Tiber already followed the line of the *fiume morto*. From her interpretation of the ruins found in 1957, and following ideas first published privately by G. Pascolini, L. Bertacchi has advanced the view that the Tiber did not follow the course generally assumed until the imperial period, and that the republican river harbour was in the lagoon south-east of the modern village which from medieval times to the nineteenth century was known as the 'Stagno di Ostia'. From the latest geological survey there is no doubt that at some time the Tiber, or a branch of the Tiber, or a canal from the Tiber, flowed into this lagoon and may have found its way to the sea near Tor Paterno. On the other hand the siting of the Castrum, and the boundary stones set up along the Decumanus by the Roman praetor C. Caninius, together with the stone marked 'privatum ad Tiberim usque ad aquam' (p. 32), do seem to imply that during the middle and late Republic the Tiber's course was roughly parallel to the Decumanus (see also Becatti 1, p. 200). The area that most concerns Ostia and Portus is covered by Sheet 149 (Cerveteri) of the *Carta Geologica d'Italia* (1963). Explanatory notes (*Note illustrative della Carta Geologica*) are published separately, Rome, 1967.

P. 156. Canina's barely perceptible ridge has been vindicated, but it covered a bank of sand to protect the extended channel that had to be kept open when the sea had receded.

Pp. 156–8. The establishment of an international airport at Fiumicino provided the opportunity for a limited excavation which resolved the main problems of the Claudian harbour (see p. 591).

P. 186. It is now known that Hostilius Antipater was also responsible for the setting up of a monumental inscription, probably in honour of Diocletian (Zevi 12, p. 468).

Pp. 197–8. For new evidence on the Egrilii see the note on pp. 503–4.

P. 202. The identification of new fragments of what are found to be four copies of the inscription set up in various parts of the building shows that the first letter of the cognomen is F and not T: M. Maecilius Furr [? (Zevi (4) 83).

P. 202. Zevi (4, p. 89) has assembled several fragments of a fine inscription of the late first or early second century on an epistyle, probably recording the gift of a public portico by a C. Cartilius Sabinus. He was clearly a distinguished man, probably a Roman knight.

P. 208 T. P. Wiseman rightly reads Cl[audius], as the space requires, rather than Clodius. He identifies him with the Augustan moneyer Pulcher who served with Taurus (cos. A.D. 11) and Regulus (cos. A.D. 18) and suggests that he was the grandson of the notorious tribune of 58 B.C., and probably consul in A.D. 21 or 22. Zevi has kindly shown me a new fragment in which the name is followed not by co]ns[ul but by tr[ibun. . .

P. 220. My case for the identification of the so-called *Curia* with the cult centre as opposed to the social headquarters of the *Seviri Augustales* has won no converts, but the arguments still seem strong. I should have added that the previous building on the site was still less suited to be a *Curia* (*FA* 17 (1962) 4875).

P. 231 n. 3. H. Solin, who is preparing a corpus of Ostian *graffiti*, has now published a better text: Ἑρμῆ δίκαιε, κέρδος Ἑκτίκῳ [δί]δου, *Arctos* 7 (1972) 194.

P. 280. G. Rickman rightly points out that no evidence of raised floors was found in the Horrea Hortensia. My statement was a careless inference from the height of the thresholds which need be no more than a normal defence against the weather. The plan, however, strongly suggests the storage of corn.

P. 293. I carelessly misunderstood Pliny. As Casson points out (1, p. 32 n. 10), Pliny (xxxvi. 70) draws a distinction between the merchantmen that brought the obelisks from Egypt and the specially built boats that carried them up the Tiber. The ship that brought the fourth-century obelisk was designed to depend on oar power and was manned by 300 oarsmen, but the obelisk was unloaded outside Rome.

P. 312. While my manuscript was going through the press a substantial fullers' establishment built under Hadrian on the Via degli Augustali was being excavated. It has four large rinsing tanks in the centre of an arcaded courtyard, large sunken jars for treading or dyeing round the sides, and fixtures in brick piers for hanging cloth. The same basic plan on a smaller scale, with three rinsing tanks, was found when the partly excavated establishment to the north-west of the barracks of the Vigiles was completely uncovered. A. Pietrogrande describes all premises used by fullers in Ostia in *Scavi di Ostia*, viii.

P. 320. The suggestion that the *fabri tignuarii* had no patrons becomes less probable in the light of a new fragment of the decree honouring Quintus Baienus Blassianus (*CIL* xxiv S. 5341). The inscription was set up by the builders but his relationship with their guild depends on restoration: *patrono*, restored by Zevi (2), is the most probable, but *praefecto*, which fits the space less well, is possible. Blassianus was probably honoured by the builders when he was promoted from the post of *praefectus annonae* to become *praefectus Aegypti* in 133. In view of the intensive building expansion encouraged by the emperor there may have been a special relationship between the *praefectus annonae* and the Ostian builders under Hadrian.

P. 328. Zevi (12, p. 472), by bringing the two stones together, found that they in fact join: Divo Pio [P]ertinaci Au[g](usto) colleg(ium) fabr(um) [tigni]ar(iorum) O[st]-(iensium). The inscription almost certainly comes from the epistyle of the temple on the corner of the Decumanus and the Via degli Augustali. The builders dedicated a temple to the deified Pertinax in the early years of Septimius Severus, when he found it politic to pose as the avenger of the murdered Pertinax. The mistakes in my inferences from the two parts of this inscription are humiliating, but they repay analysis.

P. 349 n. 3. Degrassi and Barbierii confirm that there is no letter trace on the stone following *EX*, but this does not rule out the restoration ex [s.c. (see M. Cébeillac, p. 72).

P. 350. Barbieri has shown that the inscription on Poplicola's statue has been misunderstood (see Degrassi *ILLRP*, 634a.; facsimile, M. Cébeillac, p. 80. The original text was *duoviru* (an archaic form) *iterum*, changed later to *duoviru tertio*.

P. 354. The chapel with its inscriptions has now been more fully described by Bloch (2).

Pp. 389 f. The discovery of a large synagogue outside the walls near the sea-coast demands a radical change of view regarding the Jewish community in Ostia (see p. 587).

P. 397. M. Burzachechi reads Tigri[n]ianorum. This would make better sense epigraphically but the meaning is obscure.

P. 415. Zevi tentatively assigns two fragments, separately published (*CIL* xiv. 191, S. 4471), which, though not joining, clearly belong together, to the base of a statue in honour of Gavius Maximus. It would be interesting to know the reason for his special concern for Ostia.

P. 418 plan, 17 has now been almost completely excavated and is known as the *Terme del Nuotatore,* from the mosaic figure of a swimming man on one of the pavements (see p. 587).

P. 419 n. 5. A limited excavation has now shown that though many of the walls of the baths are not earlier than the late second century the mosaic of mules and drivers which gives the baths their name is Hadrianic.

P. 419 n. 6. A current excavation has shown that the Severan rooms excavated by Visconti are only half the establishment. The Severan work represents a doubling of baths built originally under Hadrian.

P. 420. These baths (n. 13 on p. 418 plan) have now been completely excavated and are seen to include a substantial palaestra. Most of the walls are in block and brick.

P. 435. A third head from this relief, of Caltilia Moschis, has been identified in the Mattei palace (A. Licordari).

P. 475. The fourth-century inscriptions in the Forum Baths are discussed with more precision by Zevi (13, p. 464).

Pp. 475–6. The correct reading of the inscription on Poplicola's statue is *duoviru iterum,* changed later to *duoviru tertio* (see note above on p. 350). New light has also been thrown on the inscription on his funerary monument. S. Panciera has recognized a copy of a new fragment, giving the ends of three lines, in the epigraphic notes of Gaetano Marini who found it in a mason's yard in the Forum Boarium in 1776 (published in *CIL* vi. 25754): *duoviro VIII terisque eius sensu.* This rules out the possibility of restoring a military tribunate. The text was confined to the local career of Poplicola: Panciera suggests for the beginning of l. 3 [censori III, et uxori (or uxsori) et] libereis. My hesitation in accepting the standard interpretation of the cognomen as a title conferred for distinguished service to his city should be abandoned in the face of the general consensus of reviewers. It remains, however, odd that only one parallel example, who is not known to be connected directly or indirectly with the Valerii, has been quoted. He is M. Antonius L. f. Quir. Publicola from Africa, who was only 25 when he died and had an undistinguished tombstone (*CIL* viii. 15929). But it must be admitted that a record of the conferment of the title would be a very suitable complement of *ob eius amorem in universos ab universieis.* The simplest explanation of the erasure that follows is the cutter's error. Panciera suggests that the correction was inscribed on a plastered surface.

P. 487. See note on p. 293.

P. 503. Zevi (6) in a masterly article adds new evidence and argument to the history of the Egrilii. His discovery of a new fragment shows that Bloch 25 must be dated in 126 (and not 106), implying that M. Acilius Plarianus, after a promising start in his senatorial career, had to wait at least twenty years between his two treasury posts. We still do not know whether he reached the consulship, but the A. Egrilius Plarianus who was consul in 128 is now much more likely to have been his brother than his nephew. Zevi adds six new fragments to Bloch 22, introduces a hitherto unrecorded daughter of M. Acilius Plarianus, and throws new light on the family's connection with the Larcii Lepidi.

P. 511. I overlooked R. Syme's convincing argument that in the entry of A.D. 84 both duoviri probably occupied a single line and that the end of the line below gave Domitian's colleague as consul in 85 [T. Aurelius Ful]vos II (*JRS* 43 (1953) 155). Zevi in a forthcoming article will suggest that the entry for 85 should be restored on the same principle, ? Ore]stes being the second consul of the last pair in 85 and both duoviri being inscribed in the following line.

P. 514. The identification of a new fragment of *CIL* xiv. 132 requires new restorations (S. Balbi de Caro): Q. Vettio Pos[tum(io) Constanti[o]. The date is probably 287.

Pp. 514–15. Barbieri (2) has shown that fr. XXXV joins and precedes XXIII, and belongs to 115 and that the last letter is more probably R than X. The position of the entry implies that the office which Q. Asinius Marcellus held when he died was Roman and not Ostian. Barbieri suggests: in locu]m Q. Asini Ma[rcelli praef. urb. f(actus) Q. Baebius Mace]r.

Pp. 515–16. The hypothesis that Suetonius the biographer was *pontifex Volcani* has become untenable as the result of the identification of a new fragment of a crucial inscription (see p. 584).

P. 519. The arch by which the soldiers were executed has now been identified as an arch in honour of Caracalla spanning the Decumanus in front of the theatre (Zevi 13).

P. 534. J. E. Packer (2, 4) has used a different method to calculate the total population. Calza based his figure on an estimate of the total living space available and an average living space of 18·20 sq. m. per person. Packer rightly points out that this average is arbitrary and instead he attempts a block by block census. He divides the buildings into two main categories, those that have shops (126) and those that have apartments (58) on the ground floor. For shops, all of which, he thinks, served as living quarters, he allows a household of four persons, whether the shop had a back room or mezzanine floor, or both or neither. For apartments he allows one person for each *cubiculum*. His conclusion is to lower the total to not more than 27,000. This method which at first seems promising is no less vulnerable than Calza's. A large shop with a mezzanine floor will almost certainly have significantly more inhabitants than a small shop without mezzanine or back room. Nor is it safe to infer that nearly all the buildings with shops on the ground floor will have their upper floors confined to single rooms or two-room apartments. Where there is sufficient depth there could be apartments with five or even more rooms. In apartment blocks also distinctions need to be made. Packer's method makes no difference in the basis of calculation between such apartments as the Garden Houses (Reg. III. Ins. IX. 13–20) and the Casette-tipo (Reg. III. Ins. XII, XIII). The Garden Houses are well built in a garden setting; the Casette-tipo are very roughly built and have wooden rather than brick or stone stairs to the upper floor(s). To assume the same density in both is surely very misleading; the size of the latrines in the Casette-tipo is good evidence that these apartments were crowded. In both systems of calculation the margin of error is too considerable to encourage confidence in the result. In both systems we have to assume answers to the questions that most interest us. What was the average size of a family? How widespread was the possession of slaves and what accommodation were they given? Were the upper floors of apartment blocks similar in plan and in social status to the lower floors? Was there any part of Ostia as overcrowded as the Subura at Rome? (see also pp. 585 f.).

INDEX OF INSCRIPTIONS

INDEX OF CLASSICAL AUTHORS

GENERAL INDEX

Numbers in heavy type refer to the inscriptions of Appendix XI

PLATES

PLATE I

A, Ostia. B, Claudian harbour. C, Trajan's harbour. D, Tombs on Isola Sacra. E, Roman salt-beds. F, Ostian salt-beds.

The Roman road that passed through the Isola Sacra cemetery (D) and linked Portus with Ostia ran near the coastline. The advance of land since the Roman period is marked by parallel lines of successive sand dunes. The Via Ostiensis from Ostia (A) to Rome followed the line of the modern road. The land to the south (l.) of this road sinks below sea-level and is here flooded, because the pumps that normally drain it had been destroyed by the German army for defensive purposes. In the Roman period this was a marshy lagoon, and the salt-beds lay at the northern edge (F), where soil and crops are still affected. Between the road and the river the level is raised by the alluvium of Tiber floods; the earliest Roman settlement may have been on this higher ground between salt-beds and river (p. 479). The higher ground extends to the north of the river; the level then sinks, where further flooding can be seen. E marks the approximate site where what became the main Roman salt-beds were developed.

PLATE I

TIBER DELTA (1943)

PLATE II

A, Porta Romana. B, Porta Laurentina. C, Porta Marina. D, Forum.
E, Garden houses. F, 'Imperial Palace'. G, Probable course of Tiber.

The fourth-century Castrum, from which imperial Ostia developed, remains a recognizable rectangle round the Forum (D). The Decumanus Maximus represents the continuation of the road from Rome. The land between this street and the river was declared public land in the second century B.C. (p. 32); its regular plan contrasts with the irregularities of the area south of the street (p. 122). The main problem is to determine the reason for the departures from the standard Roman rectangular plan. It has been suggested that the southern Cardo (B–D) and the Via della Foce, proceeding to the river mouth, represent an original track from Laurentine territory. The view that the plan is artificial is preferred above (p. 122).

The setting of Ostia is better seen in the Frontispiece. Tor Boacciana (H) marks the Roman river mouth. The modern road southwards follows approximately the Roman coastline. The present course of the river is the result of a sixteenth-century flood; G–G marks the Roman course, but the precise line of the river bend is uncertain (p. 115). To the south of the Porta Romana (A) a white triangle represents an area cleared for huts. At its west end is a large Roman rubbish dump. On its south side a series of brick piers remain from the aqueduct, and meet the 'Sullan' wall, which can be traced from this point to the Porta Laurentina (B).

PLATE II

STREET PLAN (1943)

PLATE III

A–A, Probable course of Tiber. B, Baths of Neptune. C, Barracks of Vigiles. D, Theatre, with Piazzale delle Corporazioni. E, Four republican temples. F, Grandi Horrea. G, Forum. H, Forum Baths.

When this photograph was taken the south side of the Decumanus had not been excavated (cf. Pl. II), but the Forum Baths (H) had been partially explored by Petrini. The Via dei Molini, on the west side of the Grandi Horrea (F), roughly marks the eastern limit of the Castrum. The block on the Decumanus between the Via dei Molini and the Forum consists mainly of shops and housing. Parallel to the Decumanus, the Via di Diana. On its north side, from east to west, bakery, House of Diana, shops, House of Jupiter and Ganymede. At the north end of the Forum, the Capitolium. Behind it, leading to the river, the Cardo Maximus, flanked by porticoes. The modern building (r.) was formerly the Casone del Sale, where salt was stored before dispatch to Rome by river; now, museum, with library and administrative offices above.

PLATE III

EASTERN DECUMANUS MAXIMUS (1929)

PLATE IV

A, Monte Giulio, covering an embankment with buildings. A short right mole runs out from the end of the embankment. B, Monte dell'Arena composed of rubble and sand on the seaward side of the lighthouse. The left mole runs from the end of a sandy promontory in a straight line through C to the lighthouse near B, and then, with width reduced, curves gently inward for *c.* 200 m. The first section, *c.* 330 m., was built with large travertine blocks. At C there was originally a gap of 22 m., subsequently closed, and from C to B the mole was concrete faced on the seaward side with squared tufa blocks (pl. xix). D is a mole to protect the entrance to Trajan's harbour, probably built in the late Empire.

PLATE IV

THE IMPERIAL HARBOURS (1943)

PLATE V

A, Late imperial mole. B, Basin for small boats ('darsena'). C, Temple of 'Portumnus'. DD, Via Portuensis. E, Isola Sacra tombs. F, Bishop's palace.

Trajan's harbour has been restored to its original form. The basin was surrounded by warehouses, except on the north-west side, where was the 'Imperial Palace' (pp. 163 f.). The main living quarters were to the east and to the south of the basin. The temple of 'Portumnus' (C) was just inside the eastern gate. The road to Rome (D–D) ran in a straight line from this gate to the river, with tombs on either side, and then curved northwards to follow the river.

On the south side of the canal there was a narrow fringe of buildings and, behind it, a large cemetery partly excavated (E). The road from Portus to Ostia passes through this cemetery. Its line suggests that the road preceded the building of Trajan's harbour.

PLATE V

PORTUS (1943)

PLATE VI

a. The larger of two arches in a bridge near Magliana. M. E. Blake, *Ancient Roman Construction in Italy*, 212 with pl. 21. 2. Tufa construction with travertine keystone. ? Late republican or early Empire.

b. Small bridge, near Acilia, west of Ponte della Refolta. By 1957 this bridge had been converted into a cellar.

c. Modern bridge, over Roman road on two-arched Roman bridge, near Vitinia (formerly Risaro). Phot. 1925. In 1943 the bridge was destroyed.

d. The river embankment opposite Tor Boacciana. Only the concrete core is visible. The timbers that originally laced the concrete have left grooves.

PLATE VI

a–c. BRIDGES ON VIA OSTIENSIS. *d.* TIBER EMBANKMENT

PLATE VII

a. Castrum wall, east side, on Via dei Molini. Height preserved, m. 6·06. There are two periods in the rooms, probably shops, built out from this wall. The first construction, in large blocks of soft granular tufa, may be early second century B.C. (p. 120). The rooms were rebuilt at a higher level in brick and reticulate in the second century A.D.

b. Porta Laurentina in 'Sullan' wall. The level has been considerably raised in the Empire, but the original wall is well preserved on the west (l.) side. The gate was flanked by two squared towers (not shown) at a distance on either side of m. 6·30. Plan of gate, *Topografia*, 85, fig. 26.

PLATE VII

a. CASTRUM WALL

b. PORTA LAURENTINA

PLATE VIII

a. Cardo Maximus, south of Forum, showing continuous portico (Antonine) and fountain at the street side.

b. The west side of the House of Diana (Antonine). The ground floor is used for shops. Small windows over the doors light the mezzanine floor, which is reached by an inner staircase at the back of the shop. The narrower central doorway is the side entrance to the main apartment block. The 'balcony' does not correspond with a floor level and is decorative rather than functional.

PLATE VIII

a. SOUTHERN CARDO MAXIMUS

b. VIA DEI BALCONI

PLATE IX

a. Via della Fontana. Part of an area rebuilt at the end of Hadrian's reign (p. 136). Of the two entrances in the foreground the left joins two streets, the other leads to a side entrance to the large apartment which extends for nine windows along the street. The main entrance can still be seen in the centre of the street front. It was subsequently blocked up when the apartment was divided at this point (plan, p. 245, Fig. 13). On the right, concealed by greenery, a cistern from which the tenants of these houses drew their water.

b. Public latrine. Originally two shops built under Hadrian on the south side of the block which contains the House of the Triclinia (builders' guild house). The dividing wall between the two shops was pulled down and the combined room converted to a lavatory, probably in association with a large-scale restoration of the Forum Baths on the opposite side of the street in the fourth century (p. 551). The threshold suggests that the latrine was entered through a swing-door.

PLATE IX

a. VIA DELLA FONTANA

b. PUBLIC LATRINE

PLATE X

a. House of the Painted Vaults (Hadrianic), doors modern. The house is lighted from all four sides. The rooms are disposed on either side of a central corridor, entered through door on right. Plan, p. 248, Fig. 16.

b. The House of the Muses, built under Hadrian on the north-east side of the Garden Houses. Pl. II E; plan, p. 243, Fig. 10. Timber ceilings and door restored. The house is built round an open courtyard. Court and portico are paved with simple-patterned black and white mosaic. The brick piers were plastered and painted. The house had at least two stories, probably three or four.

PLATE X

a. HOUSE OF THE PAINTED VAULTS

b. HOUSE OF THE MUSES

PLATE XI

During the second-century building boom architects (or builders) were very successful in varying their treatment of entrances. *a*. 'Horrea Epagathiana et Epaphroditiana' (inscribed over the doorway), built under Antoninus Pius (p. 277). *b*. A group of store-rooms on the Via degli Aurighi, built under Trajan, mainly in reticulate, but with a small admixture of brick (p. 134). *c*. The House of the Well, Hadrianic (p. 257). *d*. The House of the Painted Vaults, Hadrianic. Plan, p. 248, Fig. 16.

PLATE XI

a

b

c

d

SECOND-CENTURY ENTRANCES

PLATE XII

a. Peristyle of late republican house (*c.* 100–80 B.C.) on Via della Fortuna Annonaria. The framing wall (at the right edge of plate) is in *opus incertum*. The original columns, with plastered fluting, survive on the south side; the remainder have been replaced by brick piers. In the background a brick apse has been added to the social headquarters of the *seviri Augustales*. The pavement in the foreground is typical of the period preceding the regular use of black and white mosaic (M. E. Blake, *MAAR* 8 (1930) 23–34). This peristyle was originally approached through an atrium, which was destroyed in the general rebuilding of the second century. The peristyle was incorporated in what were probably industrial premises.

b. The House of the Thunderbolt (Flavian), outside Porta Marina. In the background, a *biclinium* and altar. In the centre of the garden, a basin filled with water. The rooms of the house open off the portico surrounding the garden. Such 'peristyle houses' were the successors of the atrium-cum-peristyle houses of the late Republic. They were elegant, but much more economic in space. Normally they had at least two stories.

PLATE XII

a. REPUBLICAN PERISTYLE

b. FLAVIAN PERISTYLE HOUSE

PLATE XIII

a. House of the Round Temple, late third century (pp. 255 f.), repeating the basic 'peristyle' plan of the House of the Thunderbolt (Pl. XII *b*). The main room faces the entrance; the secondary rooms open off a portico. Furnaces heat the west side (l.). In the background, r., the Capitolium.

b. Nymphaeum of the late fourth or fifth century, on the Cardo Maximus south of the Forum. Opposite the entrance, a niche for sculpture, framed by spiral columns. Similar niches in the other two sides. The lavish use of marble on the walls as well as in the pavement is typical of the late Empire.

PLATE XIII

a. HOUSE OF THE ROUND TEMPLE

b. LATE IMPERIAL NYMPHAEUM

PLATE XIV

a. House of Fortuna Annonaria. The house was originally built under Antoninus Pius (p. 254). This main living-room, at the west end of the garden, was remodelled in the fourth century to introduce a more imposing entrance, an apsidal end, and a large nymphaeum (l.).

b. The House of Amor and Psyche, late Empire (p. 260). Looking from the central corridor across a small ? garden to the nymphaeum. The niches, curved and rectangular alternating, were probably lined with glass mosaic. The water pipe was carried round the base of the niches. Plan, p. 259, Fig. 19. A few earlier walls in brick are incorporated, but the main construction is in block and brick of fair quality.

PLATE XIV

a. HOUSE OF FORTUNA ANNONARIA

b. HOUSE OF AMOR AND PSYCHE

PLATE XV

a. Horrea Epagathiana et Epaphroditiana, Antonine. Store-rooms built round an open courtyard, the plan repeated on the first floor (p. 277). At the entrance, in mosaic, a panther; opposite, a tiger. The decorative niches in terra-cotta carried statuettes.

b. The 'House of the Lararium'. Shops grouped round an open court, Hadrianic. Plan, p. 273, Fig. 21. Internal stairs in each shop lead to the shopkeepers' living quarters. More substantial stairs at the angles of the court serve apartments on the floors above.

PLATE XV

a. WAREHOUSE COURT

b. SHOPPING MARKET

PLATE XVI

a. Hunter and stag, in brown and green, with a little blue; small scene on a white wall. Height of horse and rider, 17 cm. In the same room an effective painting of a panther, Maurizio Borda, *La Pittura Romana* (1958) 304 f. In the west wing of the Insula of the Charioteers. According to Borda (loc. cit.), Severan; more probably Antonine (p. 442).

b. A typical corridor painting (p. 441), from the House of Jupiter and Ganymede (Hadrianic). The original design was in white with yellow and green, still visible at the far end. The main section has been repainted with a red background, late Antonine. The stands are painted in a buff wash, with some parts picked out in white, grey-blue, ochre, and dark grey. The garlands consist of green and light ochre leaves on ochre stems.

c. A typical Severan foliage design, on a pier in the Insula of Serapis. Olive-green and deep purple leaves on a red background.

PLATE XVI

a

b

c

HOUSE PAINTINGS

PLATE XVII

a. Museo, 63. O. Vessberg, *Studien zur Kunstgeschichte der röm. Republik* (1941) 251; R. Calza, *I Ritratti*, no. 20.

b. Museo, 50; R. Calza, *op. cit.*, no. 78.

c. Museo, 38. C. Volcacius Myropnous (name inscribed on base). Greek marble, *c.* A.D. 160. G. Calza, *Necropoli*, 225 ff. O. Vessberg, *Romersk Porträtt Konst* (1950) 76.

d. Museo, 46. R. Calza, *Arch. Anz.* (1938) 660, fig. 21. Cf. *Museo*, 42, possibly the same man; L'Orange, *Studien zur Geschichte des spätantiken Porträts* (1933) 86 f., figs. 221, 223. Cf. B. M. Felletti Maj, *Museo Nazionale Romano, i ritratti* (1953) n. 325.

PLATE XVII

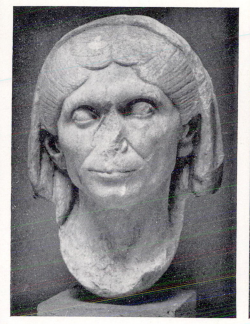

a. LATE REPUBLICAN

b. FLAVIO-TRAJANIC

c. ANTONINE

d. FIFTH CENTURY

OSTIAN PORTRAITS

PLATE XVIII

a. Sesterce, Nero. Probably issued in 64 (p. 55). Münzhandlung, Basel, Sale cat. 7, no. 182 (Nero). T. L. Donaldson, *Architectura Numismatica* (1859) 332–8; Cohen, *Méd. imp.*[2] Nero, 33–34, 250–4; BMC Emp. I, Nero, 130.

In arc above, AUGUSTI; in arc below; S PORT OST C (portus Ostiensis Augusti, senatus consulto). A bird's-eye view of the Claudian harbour. The right mole appears to be carried on arches, to allow the sand drifting into the harbour to be swept out (but this interpretation is disputed, p. 158). At the seaward end of this mole, the figure of a ? Triton. At the seaward end of the left mole, a temple; in front, a figure sacrificing at an altar. The rest of the mole is occupied by two long buildings, porticoes or perhaps warehouses. Between the moles, a colossal statue, probably of an emperor (? Claudius or Nero), standing on what seems to be a two-storied base. It may, however, represent a statue standing on the lighthouse, as in the Torlonia relief (Pl. XX). To l. of statue, a merchantman enters harbour in full sail; to r., an oared war galley, probably a trireme, leaves harbour, with auxiliary sail (*artemo*) just raised: it reflects the fleet's responsibility for policing the harbours and the sea routes.

Within the harbour, four merchantmen with sails furled. The small boat with two oarsmen may represent the tugboats used for auxiliary services in the harbour. In different dies there are minor variations in the number and disposition of the boats within the harbour. The reclining figure in the foreground, with dolphin in l. and rudder in r., may be a harbour god, cf. A. A. Boyce, 'The Harbour of Pompeiopolis', *AJA* 62 (1958) 718. Neptune would more probably carry a trident; the dolphin, symbolizing the sea, would be inappropriate to Tiber.

b. Sesterce, Trajan. Probably issued in or after 113 (p. 489). Hirsch Sale cat. xviii, no. 770 (Trajan). T. L. Donaldson, *Architectura Numismatica* (1859) 339; Cohen, *Méd. imp.*[2] Trajan, 305; Strack, *Reichsprägung des zweiten Jahrhunderts* (1931) i. 212.

POR[TUM TRAI]ANI S C. Within the harbour, three merchantmen. The buildings round the harbour are not clearly recognizable. Those that repeat a common form are probably warehouses. The buildings on the l. side are more individual and may represent the 'Imperial Palace' (pp. 163 f.). On each side of the entrance and at least two other angles of the harbour, columns surmounted by statues (p. 165).

c. Sesterce, Antoninus Pius, 145–161. BMC Emp. IV, pl. 40. 1; Cohen, *Méd. imp.*[2], Ant. Pius, 54.

ANNONA AUG FELIX S C. Annona, draped, holding rudder in l., and ? papyrus roll in right (which might reflect the administrative side of the corn supply). To l., modius (with corn ears and poppy, the normal attributes of Ceres) resting on horizontal top of ? ship floating on water; beyond and to l., stern of ship terminating in a typical plumed ornament, *aplustre* (Torr, *Ancient Ships*, 68). For a clearer definition of the lines in this part of the design see the line-drawing in Cohen and the photo in BMC catalogue (ref. above).

In the background the Claudian lighthouse, with beacon. Four stories, rather than three (BMC), are intended, the fourth being concealed by the rudder. This issue may be associated with a restoration of the lighthouse by Antoninus Pius. The public works listed by his biographer (SHA *Pius*, 8. 2–3) are divided into three sections: (*a*) buildings in Rome, (*b*) harbour works, (*c*) buildings at Ostia, Antium, Lanuvium. The harbour works comprise 'Phari restitutio, Caietae portus, Tarracinensis portus restitutio'. Since all the other buildings are in Italy Pharus may refer to the Ostian rather than the more famous Alexandrian lighthouse. Further evidence of Antoninus Pius' concern for the corn supply may be seen in Alexandrian coins of his reign showing Nile and Tiber clasping hands (G. Dattari, *Numi Augg. Alexandrini* (1901) 2782, pl. xx).

d. Bronze medallion, Commodus, 191. Gnecchi, *Medaglioni Romani*, pl. 89. 7; Cohen, *Méd. imp.*[2], Commodus, 993–8; BMC Emp. IV, pl. 40. 1.

VOTIS FELICIBUS. To r., Claudian lighthouse. To l. of lighthouse, the emperor, in pontifical robes, sacrificing on a tripod altar; with him another figure, unidentified. In the field, a large merchantman in full sail; Jupiter Serapis seated in the stern (cf. *Aelius Aristides*, i, p. 92 (Dindorff): καὶ ἐν θαλάττῃ μέγας οὗτος ὁ θεὸς καὶ ὁλκάδες καὶ τριήρεις ὑπὸ τούτῳ κυβερνῶνται; *IG* xiv. 917, a prayer for the safe return of Septimius Severus

PLATE XVIII

a. NERO   b. TRAJAN

c. ANTONINUS PIUS   d. COMMODUS

COINS AND MEDALLION ILLUSTRATING THE IMPERIAL HARBOURS

and for the safe journey of the Alexandrian corn fleet, set up by the temple warden of the temple of Serapis at Portus). Above, a similar merchantman, also in full sail. The two small boats beside the merchantmen may be ship's boats. Below, r., a war galley, probably a trireme, reflecting, as in Nero's coins, the fleet's protection of the corn ships. In the foreground, on land, a dead bull; above (l.) a ?patera, associated with the sacrifice. Perhaps representing a sacrifice to Serapis; but possibly reflecting a *taurobolium* to Cybele: 'is qui in portu pro salute imperatoris sacrum facit ex vaticinatione archigalli a tutelis excusatur' (p. 387).

After a severe corn crisis in 189, Commodus instituted an African corn fleet on the model of the Egyptian (SHA, *Commodus*, 17. 7). In this medallion, of which many copies survive, with minor variations in the design, the ship with Serapis may represent the Egyptian, the ship above, the African fleet. Another medallion, of 190, shows a reclining Africa, holding ears of corn (BMC, Med. Commodus, 29); cf. Cohen, *Méd. imp.*² 992: VOTA FELICIA, Commodus sacrificing before Neptune (190); cf. *IG* xiv. 918, an inscription in honour of Commodus, set up by the shipmasters of the Alexandrian corn fleet.

PLATE XIX

Operations associated with the construction of a new airport have exposed (1957) part of the left mole near Monte dell' Arena.

a. Timber planking, found in good condition, from the inner face.

b. Seaward face in *opus quadratum*.

c. A channel has been cut through the mole exposing the concrete core. At this point the width increases from *c.* 50 ft. to *c.* 75 ft. This is where the giant merchantman was sunk to provide the foundation for the lighthouse.

PLATE XIX

a. TIMBERED INNER FACE

b. SEAWARD FACE   *c*. CROSS-SECTION

LEFT MOLE OF THE CLAUDIAN HARBOUR

PLATE XX

The Torlonia harbour relief. P. E. Visconti, *Catalogo del Museo Torlonia* (1880) n. 338; G. Henzen, *Bull. Inst.* 36 (1864) 12–20; G. Cavedoni, ibid. 219–23; Guglielmotti, *Delle due navi romani scolpite sul bassorilievo portuense del Principe Torlonia* (1874); K. Lehmann-Hartleben, *Die antiken Hafenanlagen des Mittelmeeres, Klio*, Beiheft 14 (1923) 235 f.; M. Fasciato, *Mélanges*, 59 (1947) 65–81; L. Casson, *The Ancient Mariners*, 218 f.

Relief in Greek marble, m. 1·22 × 0·75, found in 1863 or 1864 near the Torlonia villa on the north-east side of Trajan's harbour. Probably a dedication from the temple of the wine god, which was found near by (p. 165). The letters on the sail are usually supplemented 'V(OTUM) L(IBERO)', unparalleled and difficult; 'V(OTUM) L(IBENS) (S(OLVIT))' is perhaps easier. The hair style of the woman in the stern of the ship in sail implies a Severan date.

The ship r., with furled sails, is tied by rope to a mooring block (similar to examples found in Trajan's harbour, phot. *NS* 1925, 56). A man carries an amphora of wine from the ship over the landing plank. The dedicator was probably a wine merchant. The large eye is to avert ill fortune. The second ship has just entered harbour. The topsail is furled, the *artemon* is down, only the mainsail is still up. In the stern the ship's master and ? his family are sacrificing to celebrate their safe arrival. The ship's boat is about to be tied up alongside. In the bows a man is manipulating from the *artemon* mast what is probably a buffer to protect the bows when the ship comes to the quayside; the same contraption can be seen on the other ship and in Pl. XXIV *b* (see J. Le Gall, 'Graffites navals du Palatin et de Pompéi', *Mem. Soc. Nat. Ant.* 83 (1954) 48 f.). The two representations of the wolf suckling twins suggest embroidery rather than painting. Between the two ships, Neptune with trident, symbolizing the sea.

In the background a four-storied lighthouse with beacon. Since this is a realistic reproduction of the Claudian lighthouse it is reasonable to believe that the other monuments in the relief could also be seen at Portus. The colossal statue on the penultimate stage of the lighthouse may be an emperor (?Claudius or Nero). The two figures on either side of the lighthouse, each with wreath and cornucopia, seem to be associated. Since they stand on bases, unlike Neptune, they may reproduce statues. The female figure (l.) has a lighthouse on her head, a variant of the turreted crown associated with personifications of towns or their Tyche. This figure probably personifies the Ostian harbour settlement (not Alexandria, as has been suggested, since the lighthouse is radically different from the Alexandrian pharos). The male figure r. may be the *genius* of the harbour. There are two very similar male figures, framing an inscription in the Vatican. Each is crowned with a lighthouse and they probably represent the *genii* of the harbours of Alexandria and Portus (Thiersch, *Pharos*, 18 f.).

It has been suggested above (p. 158) that the arch surmounted by an elephant quadriga may have stood on the right mole, and that the rider may be Domitian. In his l. he carries a sceptre terminating in a human head, as in coins of Domitian's second consulship in 73 (BMC II, pl. 12. 2). To r. the god of wine, with thyrsus in l., and panther at his right side. This figure, not standing on a formal base, may represent the temple in which the relief was dedicated.

Mlle Micheline Fasciato has given more precision to the scene by associating with it certain Ostian inscriptions. These record a Forum Vinarium (430), a 'quadriga fori vinarii', and a 'templum fori vinarii' (Bloch, *Epigraphica*, 1 (1939) 37). She suggests that the quadriga is the elephant chariot and that the temple of the inscription is the temple discovered on the north-east side of Trajan's harbour. The scene, therefore, she thinks, depicts Trajan's harbour, and the lighthouse is at the entrance to this harbour. This last identification cannot be accepted. The sculptor has given a faithful reproduction of the famous lighthouse at the entrance to the Claudian harbour; the lighthouse at the entrance to Trajan's harbour must have been a much more modest building. The Forum Vinarium is better placed in Ostia (p. 288). I should hesitate to draw topographical inferences from this rough work, or to estimate the capacity of the merchantmen.

Another realistic harbour scene, on a sarcophagus now in Copenhagen, has been attributed convincingly to Portus. It shows an attempted rescue of a drowning man and incidentally provides valuable evidence of Roman sailing techniques (L. Casson, *The Ancient Mariners*, 220–2).

PLATE XX

HARBOUR SCENE IN SEVERAN RELIEF

PLATE XXI

a. Detail from Pl. XX.

b. Roman tower, in the wall surrounding the bishop's palace at Porto (Pl. V F). The main construction is medieval, but at the south-east corner this tower is incorporated. The rows of block and brick are regular and well laid, suggesting a comparatively early date, not later than the early fourth century. The relation of this tower (to which I have seen no earlier reference) to the defences of Portus needs investigation.

PLATE XXI

a. HARBOUR SCENE, DETAIL

b. ROMAN TOWER WITH MEDIEVAL WALL

PLATE XXII

a. Theatre, before reconstruction. The inscription above the entrance records the rebuilding at the end of the second century. The columns of the portico behind the stage replaced tufa piers of the original Augustan construction.

b. Looking north. The Piazzale delle Corporazioni, from the reconstructed theatre. In the centre, a small temple (p. 329). In the surrounding garden, statues of distinguished Ostians, and imperial procurators. The mosaics of Pl. XXIII come from the pavement of the surrounding colonnade. The Tiber flowed less than 50 yards to the north.

PLATE XXII

a. THEATRE BEFORE RECONSTRUCTION

b. PIAZZALE DELLE CORPORAZIONI FROM THE RECONSTRUCTED THEATRE

PLATE XXIII

These mosaics, paving the colonnade, illustrate the business of the occupants of the small rooms associated with them (as in *d*). The size of the mosaics varies slightly, but m. 3·40 × 3·10 (*c*) is typical.

a. Stat(io) Sabratensium. *NS* 1912, 435, n. 14, east side. An elephant, reflecting the trade in ivory that came from the interior to the coast at Sabrata in Africa. The importance to Sabrata of this trade with Rome explains their setting up of a statue of Hadrian's wife Sabina in the Forum of Caesar, *AE* 1934, 146.

b. Boar, stag, and elephant (no inscription). *NS* 1914, 288, n. 28, north side. Possibly representing animals imported for the arena.

c. 'Navi(cularii) et negotiantes | Karalitani', shipowners and traders from Cagliari in Sardinia. *NS* 1914, 99, n. 21, east side. A merchantman with mainsail and *artemo*. On each side, a corn measure, showing that corn was the normal cargo.

d. 'Navi(cularii) Narbonenses', shipowners of Narbo in Gaul. *NS* 1916, 326–8, n. 32, north side. Once thought to be a ship being loaded by a crane at Narbo. The 'crane' is a sail; the 'tower' is the top of the Claudian lighthouse, the base of which can be seen below the break in the mosaic. For the shape of the ship, cf. Pl. XXIV *b*.

PLATE XXIII

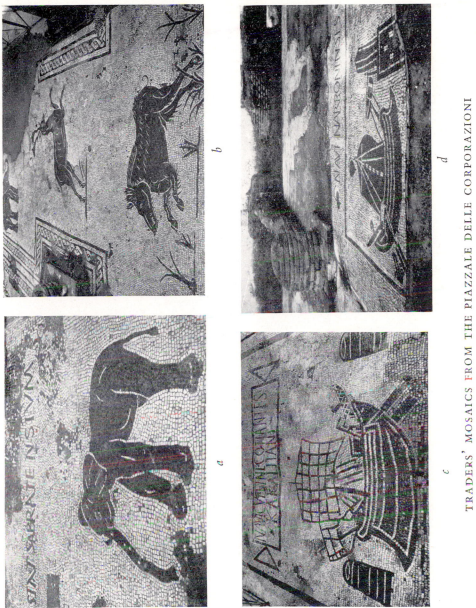

PLATE XXIV

a. Relief of a merchantman in sail. Italian marble, m. 0·64 × 0·62. Found at Porto (P. E. Visconti, *Catalogo del Museo Torlonia*, n. 341).

Above the ship, 'q(uin) q(uennalis) c(orporis) f(abrum) nav(alium)'. The inscription is cryptically brief. Perhaps a dedication by a president, or by all the presidents of the guild of Portus shipbuilders to a temple (? specially associated with the guild, cf. p. 329).

b. '(m) f | [navic]ulari Syllecti[ni]', shipowners from Syllectum in Africa (*CIL* viii, p. 13). *NS* 1914, 285, n. 23, east side. Above, the Claudian lighthouse (three instead of four stories). Two ships with mainsail and *artemo*; the topsail has been furled. One of the ships has a third mast and sail, which is rare. The two ships illustrate the main designs for merchantmen. The projecting forefoot of the ram-shaped profile is probably designed to protect the stem and keel when the ship anchors at the quay. The ship with a curving prow has a projecting beam which gives similar protection (see Pl. XX with description).

The letters in the first line were originally published as N F. The original photograph seems to confirm the reading, and these letters are reprinted in an adjacent mosaic. They were plausibly supplemented by Héron de Villefosse: 'N(AVICULARIIS) F(ELICITER)'. Below, two dolphins, devouring an octopus. Trade with Syllectum is also reflected in the tombstone of a *civis Sullecthensis*, who died in Ostia, *CIL* xiv. 477.

PLATE XXIV

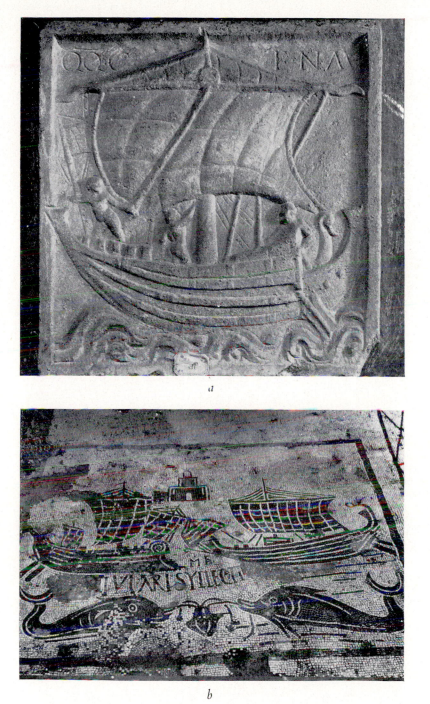

a

b

MERCHANTMEN

PLATE XXV

a. Mosaic in the Piazzale delle Corporazioni (north side). *NS* 1914, 285; Le Gall, *Le Tibre*, 230. ? Transferring wine from a merchantman to a river boat. The dolphin on the side of the ship r. suggests the open sea. The stepped mast of the other boat is irreconcilable with sails and is probably a towing mast, over which passes the tow rope.

b. Relief in the National Museum at Rome. Le Gall, op. cit. 228. River boat, *navis caudicaria*, on the side of a cippus, which has two inscriptions (*CIL* vi. 36954). The first preserves the date of the original dedication (A.D. 284); the main inscription of this date has been erased, and replaced by a dedication to the Emperor Constans by a *praefectus annonae*, Symmachus, father of the orator. The relief probably belongs to the earlier dedication. Apart from the rudder oar the boat has no oars and no sail. The mast, stepped as in *a*, is a towing mast. The cargo includes amphorae.

c. Mosaic from the Piazzale delle Corporazioni (east side). Corn measurer (*mensor frumentarius*) kneeling, with *modius* and measuring rod, with which he levels off the corn.

d. Warehouse for oil or wine (Hadrianic). *NS* 1903, 201; 1907, 357. Large amphorae sunk in the ground (*dolia defossa*); capacities are marked, averaging 40 amphorae. Traces survive of repairs in lead.

PLATE XXV

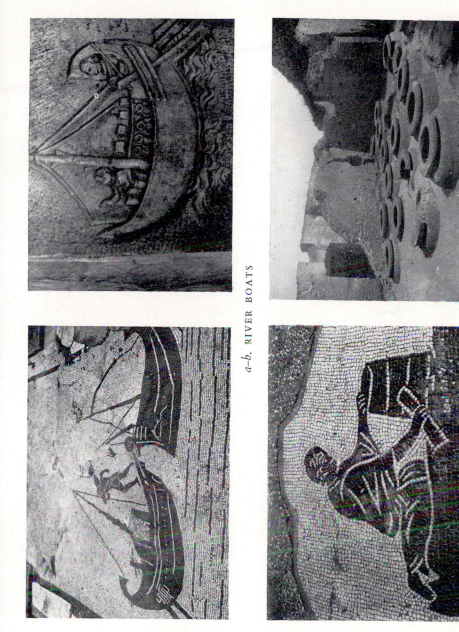

a–b. RIVER BOATS

c. CORN MEASURER

d. STORAGE FOR OIL OR WINE

PLATE XXVI

a. Relief in Greek marble (m. 0·43 × 0·33), found at Porto, now in the Torlonia Museum. Visconti, *Catalogo*, n. 338. Wine is being unloaded from a merchantman. The three seated figures may be a *tabularius* with two *adiutores*, recording the cargo on wax tablets in the form of a book. The leading porter receives a ? tally as he passes. Perhaps a customs scene.

b. Funerary relief in Italian marble (m. 1·40 × 0·62 × 0·33) closing a burial recess in tomb 90 on Isola Sacra. Calza, *Necropoli*, 203. The tomb probably dates from Hadrian, Thylander, *Étude sur l'épigraphie latine*, 19. Two associated scenes. Left, a ship, with furled sails, is approaching the Claudian lighthouse. It is perhaps being towed into harbour by its ship's boat (*scapha*). Right, refreshment at a harbour inn after safe arrival. The dolphin (? on the inn door) is a very appropriate decorative feature; the dog adds a genial touch of realism. Calza (loc. cit.) suggests that the scenes may be symbolic, representing the end of life's journey, and the funeral banquet (? or, rather, the happy feasting of the after-life); but see above, p. 470.

PLATE XXVI

a. UNLOADING AND CHECKING WINE

b. ARRIVAL AT PORT

PLATE XXVII

a. One of two terra-cotta reliefs (m. 0·47 × 0·48) from the face of tomb 29 on Isola Sacra. Calza, *Necropoli*, 251, 303. The tomb was built under Hadrian or Antoninus Pius, Thylander, *Etude*, 24. The standing figure is perhaps sharpening or cleaning tools on a portable table; the dog's head is ? decorative. The seated figure below is probably the same man, ? making tools. He probably makes, sells, and reconditions the iron tools that fill out the relief. Among them may be: top row (from l. to r.), (1) shears, (3) punch or mason's chisel, (4) surgical instruments in case; second row, (1) awl, (2) ? adze, (3) and (4) knives; third row, (1) hammer, (2) leather cutter (Blümner, *Technologie*, i. 280, fig. 26c); fourth row, (1) forceps, (2) anvil (above), (3) two saws. For iron tools, Liger, *La ferronerie ancienne et moderne* (Paris, 1873); John Ward, *The Roman Era in Britain* (London, 1911) 194–207.

The balancing relief represents a man sharpening a tool, with a further variety of tools in the background.

b. Funerary relief of a butcher (m. 1·22 × 0·20). *Museo*, 133. *Capitolium*, 11 (1935) 421. Hanging, various cuts, with a calf's head. To r., largely lost, a boar's head. To l. scales.

PLATE XXVII

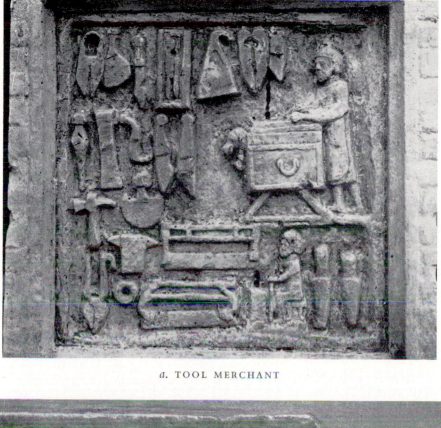

a. TOOL MERCHANT

b. BUTCHER

PLATE XXVIII

Two reliefs in terra-cotta from the face of tomb 78 on Isola Sacra. Calza, *Necropoli*, 254. The tomb described, Calza, 336; dated to Trajan, Thylander, *Étude*, 17. The two trades represented were presumably carried on by members of the same family or their freedmen. (Ti. Claudius Eutychus made provision for children and freedmen, as well as for his wife and himself, in his tomb, Thylander, A 61). The reliefs are of different size: *a*. m. 0·58×0·39, *b*. m. 0·405×0·41.

a. Three oarsmen and a standing cox, with very large steering oar. The attached rope suggests that this is a harbour tugboat, used for towing merchantmen into position (p. 298). The mast at the prow might be for an auxiliary sail. A boat of similar form is incised on a travertine stele in the face of an Augustan tomb outside the Porta Laurentina; underneath is inscribed *Embaenita* (? *rius*), the precise meaning of which is uncertain; *Scavi di Ostia,* iii (1) 66.

b. A grain-mill. The upper stone (*catillus*) is being turned round the stationary lower stone (*meta*), which rests on a concrete base. A slave with whip keeps the horse moving. The horse (less common than asses in mills) is blindfolded, cf. Apuleius, *Met.* ix. 11. The details are not precisely paralleled elsewhere. Mr. Moritz suggests to me that the triangular fitting over the centre of the *catillus* may be a hopper for feeding grain into the mill, and that the fitting on the right of the top of the *catillus* may be a bell which showed by its ringing that the mill was moving. Such bells were commonly used later with stone-mills. The vertical beam on the left of the *catillus* might then be intended to strike the (stationary) bell every time the stone revolved. To the r., ? a sieve (Calza). For the processes of milling, L. A. Moritz, *Grain-Mills and Flour in Classical Antiquity* (1958), and especially pl. 5, p. 65 and pl. 7, p. 77.

PLATE XXVIII

a. TUGBOAT

b. CORN MILL

PLATE XXIX

a. Reconstructed 'Thermopolium' on the Via di Diana, p. 428.

b. Paintings from a wine shop (p. 429). Two seated figures, Solon and Thales, from a series of the seven sages. The height of the figure of Solon is m. 0·70, of Thales, 0·70. Below, Σολων ᾽Αθηναιος, Θαλης Μειλησιος. Above Solon, 'ut bene cacaret ventrem palpavit Solon'. Above Thales, 'durum cacantes monuit ut nitant Thales'. Later this wine shop was incorporated in the baths between the Insula of Serapis and the Insula of the Charioteers, but these paintings were preserved. Dated by M. Borda, *La Pittura Romana*, 289, in the late-Antonine period, presumably on grounds of style. I have assumed from the plaster that these paintings are contemporary with the original building, Trajanic or a little later.

PLATE XXIX

a. RECONSTRUCTED INN

b. PAINTINGS FROM A WINE SHOP

PLATE XXX

a. Marble relief (m. 1·45×0·71). Late republican, found near the temple of Hercules. Becatti, *BC* 67 (1939) 39. Above, 'C. Fulvius. Salvis. haruspexs. d(edit). d(edicavit)'. Three scenes: r. archaic statue of Hercules in a fishing net; centre, Hercules gives a tablet (containing an oracle) to a boy (above, an open tablet, with '[s]ort(es) H(erculis)', difficult to read); l. a male figure, and, above, a winged Victory, with ? one other figure missing, perhaps the fulfilment of an oracle. The meaning of the relief is discussed above, p. 347.

b. Terra-cotta relief (m. 0·42×0·28) from tomb 100 on Isola Sacra. Calza, *Necropoli*, 248 f., 367. Woman seated on a maternity chair, which may have special hand-grips. Behind her, an assistant with l. hand on her shoulder holds her down, with right ?massages. The midwife, on a stool, is ready to deliver the baby. Her face is averted, not 'to face the camera', but in order not to embarrass the mother. I have to thank Mr. P. M. Fraser for drawing my attention to a nearly contemporary medical text. Soranus, an Ephesian doctor, practised at Rome in the early second century. He wrote in Greek two gynaecological works, a practical handbook, in two books, and a fuller treatise, in four books. Most of the longer work survives; the handbook is lost, but we have a sixth-century Latin translation. It omits controversy, is clear and concise, and differs in minor points of detail from the main treatise. It is closer to the Ostian relief. Soranus, *Gynaecia*, ed. Rose, 1882 (for the corresponding text of the main treatise, *MG* iv. 2. 4–5).

65 ministrae cum obstetrice quot sunt necessariae?
> tres enim necessariae sunt, ex quibus duae dextra laevaque ad latera stare debent, in quas incumbere possit, tertia vero a dorso eam teneat ut occurrentibus doloribus non se in latus inclinet, hortantes eam ut fortiter sustineat.

66 obstetrix quomodo et ubi sedere debet?
> scilicet viriliter cincta sit, et si in lecto partus effici habet, modice inferius. si vero sedens in sella paritura sit, inferius obstetrix sedeat in humiliori scilicet sella, ut possit ex superioribus partibus facile infantem adducere, et in aliquantum apertis pedibus suis, plus tamen humilioribus ut ei non impediatur [manus]. faciem suam retrorsus avertat, ne pariens verecundia se concludat.

The only significant difference between text and relief is that Soranus regards three assistants as necessary; the relief has only one. The reason is probably economic, but it is possible that the craftsman did not want to spoil his 'picture' by two further figures.

PLATE XXX

a. THE ORACLE OF HERCULES

b. CHILDBIRTH

PLATE XXXI

a. and *b*. Two Italian-marble reliefs (m. 0·62 × 0·40 × 0·90), found in the Isola Sacra cemetery, but not in their original position in a tomb. With them was found a reclining figure in relief on the lid of a sarcophagus. His costume shows him to be a high priest of Cybele (*archigallus*); he is also represented in the two reliefs. Calza, *Necropoli*, 209 ff.; *Museo*, 58–60.

a. The priest, holding a lighted torch in each hand, approaches a pine tree, from which hangs a bell. Below, on a base, the figure of Attis, with shepherd's crook.

b. The priest puts an offering (? of fruit) from the *patera*, held in his left hand, on a lighted altar. Behind, on a high base between two lighted torches, Cybele, with turreted head-dress. In front of her, a small Hermes, with *caduceus* in his left hand, purse in right.

c. Mithras and the Bull, from a Mithraeum in the service corridor of a set of public baths. Greek marble. Height, m. 1·70; length, 1·93; width (front) 0·58, (back) 0·72. Becatti, *I Mitrei*, 32. This sculpture is unique in representing Mithras in Hellenic dress and in being a free-standing group rather than the normal relief (p. 372). ? Hadrianic. Becatti has brilliantly identified a copy of the Ostian group, clumsily restored in the Renaissance as a gladiator slaying a lion, in the Giustiniani collection ('Una copia Giustiniani del Mitra di Kriton', *Boll. d'Arte* (1957) 1).

d. ? Support for table in a temple (? of Isis). Dark-red porphyry. Height, m. 0·70. Visconti, *Catalogo del Museo Torlonia*, n. 20. Found at Porto. Bust of Isis; below, Bes. This Egyptian god is often associated with childbirth, his function being to ward off evil spirits (H. Bonnet, *Reallexikon der ägyptischen Religionsgeschichte*, 105). That is perhaps why he is here linked with Isis, though I can find no parallel.

PLATE XXXI

a. ATTIS

b. CYBELE

c. MITHRAS

d. ISIS AND BES

OSTIAN CULTS

PLATE XXXII

a. Tomb 10 outside Porta Laurentina, *NS* 1938, 51; *Scavi di Ostia*, iii
(1) 74. Plan, p. 458, Fig 31. The reticulate face and incorporated tufa
monument are original; other standing walls belong to a later period.
Such tombs are common in the late Republic and under Augustus
(p. 457); the public tomb of C. Cartilius Poplicola belongs to the series.
On the tufa face: 'ex t[esta]mento [? 5] arbitratu | [T.] Manli T. l.
Niconis'. Dessau (*CIL* xiv. 1307) interprets the sum of money in the
first line, of which uncertain traces remain, as 6,000 sesterces. Embedded
in the reticulate face, two travertine cippi. One was found *in situ* in
1937; the other had been removed in the nineteenth century to the castle,
where it was seen by Dessau (1301); it has now been replaced: 'T. Man-
lius | T. l. Alexsa | Labicia M. f. | in fr(ontem) ped(es) XX | in agr(um)
p[edes] XXXV.' (Dessau read 'Laricia'). Presumably T. Manlius Alexsa
made provision for his tomb in his will, and T. Manlius Nico, perhaps a
fellow-freedman, acted as his executor.

b. Tomb 32 outside Porta Laurentina, the so-called tomb of the
Claudii. Paschetto, 472; Calza, *NS* 1938, 69; *Scavi di Ostia*, iii (1) 118.
Plan, p. 458, Fig. 32. Early Julio-Claudian, in reticulate with subsidiary
use of brick at points of stress (the use of tufa bricks as in the upper half
of the l. angle is not common). The decorative frame in terra-cotta and
pumice held the inscription recording the owner of the tomb, C. Iulius
Pothi l. Nymphodotus, and its dimensions (frontage, 30 ft.; depth, 20
ft.), 482; Bloch, *NS* 1953, 300. On either side of this inscription, a winged
phallus. At the north-east angle (r.), a low rectangular annexe (m. 2·13 ×
3·20; height, 1·56), the *ustrinum*, for private cremations (cf. *NS* 1938,
42, fig. 15). By the end of the Julio-Claudian period bodies were normally
cremated away from the tomb.

PLATE XXXIII

a. EARLY SECOND–CENTURY TOMBS ON ISOLA SACRA

b. ANTONINE TOMB INTERIOR

PLATE XXXIV

a. Block from the front face of the frieze. Italian marble. Height, m. 0·60. From the left side there survives only the figure of a horse; little of the front face has been lost. To the l. are four standing male figures, all with oval shields, two with spears also. The block shown immediately adjoins these figures. The middle of the trireme is lost, but the stern is preserved on the end block (r.) which has on its other face the prow of a second trireme. There is no clear relationship between the triremes and the standing soldiers.

The form of the trireme is typical. Above the trident ram, the *proembolion*, designed to destroy the enemy's oars, and terminating in a lion's head. The three tiers of oars are clearly marked; to the left, the ship's ? eye (a circle) and ? ear (*epotis*). The attachment below the *proembolion* may be of metal, to strengthen the ram. Above, a parapet. In relief on the prow, head of ? Roma or ? Minerva, in Corinthian helmet. The first figure, nude, with rectangular cylindrical shield, is poised to throw a spear. The second figure, in tunic, with small round shield, stretches out the right arm with open palm, perhaps having thrown a spear. The types of shield and the somewhat crude style of the relief suggest an early Augustan date. Detailed description and illustration, M. F. Squarciapino in *Scavi di Ostia*, iii (1) 195–206, with Pls. XXXIX–XLIII.

b. Probably Hadrianic (pp. 200 f.). Between the capitals, in a narrow frieze, an acanthus scroll with two lions. For this type of decoration see J. M. C. Toynbee and J. B. Ward Perkins, 'Peopled Scrolls: a Hellenistic Motif in Imperial Art', *BSR* 18 (1950) 16. Above, two Cupids supporting a laurel wreath, symbolizing the victory of the good life (Cumont, *Le Symbolisme funéraire*, 487). The inscription (**5**) is cut below the frieze.

A very similar altar, roughly contemporary, and perhaps from the same workshop, was found in tomb 97 on Isola Sacra (Calza, *Necropoli*, 365; Thylander, A 147, pl. xliii. 1). Other examples, less ornate, of the type in Altmann, *Römische Grabaltäre*, 40, fig. 26; 42, fig. 30.

PLATE XXXIV

a. FROM THE TOMB OF C. CARTILIUS POPLICOLA

b. FROM THE FUNERARY ALTAR OF CN. SENTIUS FELIX

PLATE XXXV

a. From the vault of tomb 18, outside Porta Laurentina, *Scavi di Ostia,*
iii (1) 85–91 (M. F. Squarciapino), pls. xiv, xv. These Augustan stuccoes
are the finest of those preserved in Ostia, both technically and artistically.
They have been compared, fairly, with the famous stuccoes from the
Farnesina palace, now in the National Museum. The themes of the
surviving scenes are Dionysiac.

Lower register, r., male bust, bearded, perhaps a priest. In the long
rectangle, r., wreath. r., pillar, from which hangs a garland; against the
pillar, a ribboned thyrsus; by the pillar, a ?base with ?statuette. r., a
second wreath. r., pillar or herm; against it, a pipe. Upper register. l.,
mongoloid mask. In this main panel, l., female figure, ?holding in her
r. hand an offering. In the centre, ?statuettes on a three-legged table and
a pillar. r., a ribboned thyrsus, carried by a ?male figure, largely lost.

b. Nilotic scene from a burial recess in tomb 26 on Isola Sacra, Calza,
Necropoli, 150 (reproduced in colour, 152, pl. v). This painting would be
concealed by the closing of the recess when the body had been deposited
in it.

PLATE XXXV

a. STUCCO DECORATION IN AN AUGUSTAN TOMB

b. PAINTED BURIAL RECESS IN A SEVERAN TOMB

PLATE XXXVI

a. Attic sarcophagus (m. 1·25 × 0·76), ? early second century, from Isola Sacra, but not found in a tomb, Calza, *Necropoli*, 210; *Museo*, 34. The reclining figure of a youth on the lid of the sarcophagus holds a bird in his right hand and in his left a plate of fruit. The mattress on which he rests is decorated in front with pairs of racing animals. The sarcophagus has reliefs on all four sides. On the face, shown here, cherubs dancing under the influence of wine to zither and cymbal, a Dionysiac paradise. On the back, similar cherubs in a boxing scene, the athletic life. For the symbolism, Cumont, *Le Symbolisme funéraire*, 471. On the lid of the sarcophagus is a poorly cut inscription, ill matching the quality of the decoration, Calza, 213, fig. 113. It shows that this imported sarcophagus was used for a brother and sister, probably of Egyptian origin, Thylander, A 41.

The back (Calza, fig. 115) is considerably less finished than the face (fig. 112), as in other sarcophagi in this style. J. B. Ward Perkins, 'The Hippolytus Sarcophagus from Trinquetaille', *JRS* 46 (1956) 10, suggests that normally these sarcophagi were shipped in a rough state to avoid damage to delicate detail, and finished at the receiving end by Attic craftsmen. The degree of finishing would depend on the placing of the sarcophagus.

b. Sculpture group from an Isola Sacra tomb, Calza, *Necropoli*, 233, 236; *Museo*, 33. Child on horseback followed by slave. From the horse's back hang three ducks and a large wine-skin. The group has no religious significance (p. 469).

PLATE XXXII

a. AUGUSTAN TOMB

b. EARLY JULIO-CLAUDIAN TOMB

PLATE XXXIII

a. From l. (south) to r. (north), tombs 80, 79, 78, 77. These tombs are among the earliest in the cemetery (Thylander, *Étude*, 17 f.). A late Trajanic brickstamp was found in 78; all are earlier than the death of Hadrian. They have no enclosure attached to the tomb chamber and provide for cremation alone. 79, 78, 77 have terra-cotta reliefs, illustrating trades, on each side of the framed inscription over the door. Those from 78 are shown on Pl. XXVIII.

The entrance to 80 (l.) is flanked by a biclinium, used for funeral banquets. In the foreground (r.) attached to a wall, the heads of the Muses in coloured mosaic from 80 (Calza, *Necropoli*, 173).

b. Tomb 19 from Isola Sacra, Calza, *Necropoli*, 130, 299. Built under Antoninus Pius, Thylander, *Étude*, 25. Above, niches for urns; below, recesses for burial. The paintings in the two largest niches here shown, a rider and horse (Calza, loc. cit. 130, fig. 61) and a man and wife clasping hands (*dextrarum iunctio*) are among the finest paintings in the cemetery.

PLATE XXXVI

a. IMPORTED ATTIC SARCOPHAGUS

b. SCULPTURE GROUP FROM AN ISOLA SACRA TOMB

PLATE XXXVII

a. Spiral staircase, at right side of entrance to the Round Temple, mid-third century (p. 550), giving access to the roof. A travertine column, taken from an earlier building, serves as newel.

b. Entry, seen from above, to what was probably a baptistery, associated with a late Christian basilica (but the function and the date of the building are controversial, p. 397). The architrave block above the columns had been used before (p. 398).

c. Neo-Attic well-head from the House of Fortuna Annonaria.

d. Terra-cotta sarcophagus, showing head-rest (p. 465). This undecorated form was widely used by those who could not afford marble.

PLATE XXXVII

a. SPIRAL STAIRCASE

b. FROM THE 'CHRISTIAN BASILICA'

c. ATTIC WELL-HEAD

d. TERRA-COTTA SARCOPHAGUS

PLATE XXXVIII

a. Inscription recording the assignation of the site for the temple of Bellona at the expense of the lictors and public slaves (4). Discussed, p. 201; a date at the end of Hadrian's reign is suggested.

b. Fragment of architrave block, found in Rome, but probably coming, like *c*, which it closely resembles, from the Forum Baths at Ostia, commemorating an early fourth-century restoration (p. 475).

c. A similar fragment, still preserved in the Forum Baths, probably commemorating a later restoration (p. 475): λουτρον ἀλεξιπο[νον]. Height of letters, 10 cm. The top of the block has been cut off. A second fragment gives the end of the pentameter: κυδιμος Ἀυσονιης.

d. Small cippus (m. 0·54 × 0·19) in the Galleria Lapidaria of the Vatican, recording the career of the Antonine P. Lucliius Gamala (2). See Appendix V, p. 493.

PLATE XXXVIII

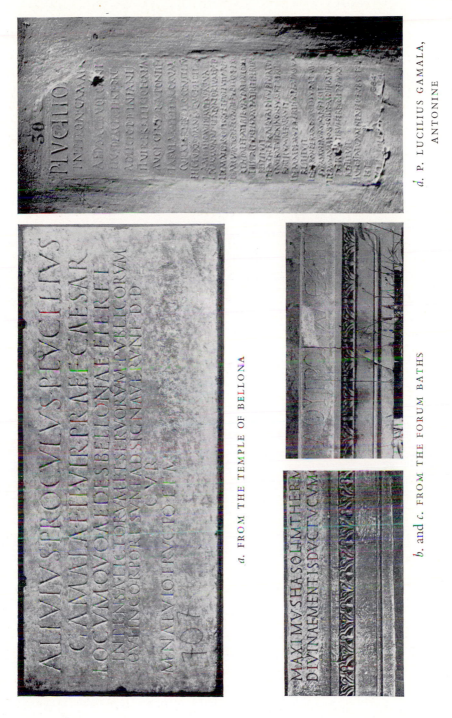

a. FROM THE TEMPLE OF BELLONA

b. and *c.* FROM THE FORUM BATHS

d. P. LUCILIUS GAMALA, ANTONINE

PLATE XXXIX

a. Temple of Rome and Augustus. *b*. Temple of the Round Altar. *c, d*. Capitolium. *e*. ? Guild temple on the Eastern Decumanus, c. 194 A.D. (pp. 328 with 595).

PLATE XXXIX

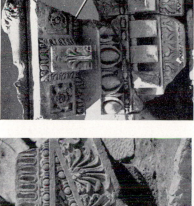

c. HADRIANIC

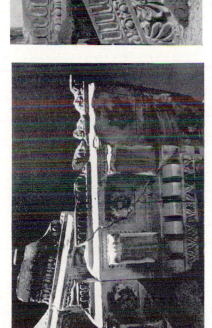

b. FLAVIO-TRAJANIC

a. JULIO-CLAUDIAN

e. ANTONINE

d. HADRIANIC

ARCHITECTURAL DECORATION FROM OSTIAN TEMPLES

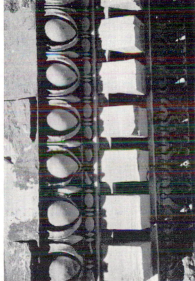

PLATE XL

Changing styles of construction are described in Appendix IX, p. 535.

a. Semita dei Cippi. Reticulate reinforced with tufa piers (Julio-Claudian, pp. 538 f.). Part of the wall (l.) has been rebuilt in block and brick. The regularity of the coursing and of the tufa blocks suggests (p. 545) a comparatively early date (? third century).

b. South of the Horrea of Hortensius. In the foreground, reticulate wall with tufa–brick buttress (Julio-Claudian). Similar piers have recently been found in early imperial *horrea* underneath the Via della Trinacria. In the background, concrete foundations showing the imprint of timber shuttering, with brick and reticulate above (Hadrianic).

c. Horrea of Hortensius. Brick panels in reticulate wall, serving the same structural function as the tufa pier in *a* above. The bricks are mainly triangular, and yellow, with an unusual variation in width (3 to 4 cm.). The construction is described by M. E. Blake in *Roman Construction in Italy from Tiberius through the Flavians*, 66.

d. Via della Calcara. A small part of a Trajanic building, l., was incorporated in the Hadrianic Insula of Serapis, r. (p. 429). At l. edge a doorway which was the original entrance to the closed wine shop of the Seven Sages (Pl. XXIX *b*).

PLATE XL

a   *b*

c   *d*

BUILDING STYLES

TOPOGRAPHICAL INDEX